*Newswriting
and
Reporting
Public Affairs*

Newswriting and Reporting Public Affairs

Chilton R. Bush STANFORD UNIVERSITY

CHILTON BOOKS

A Division of Chilton Company · Publishers · Philadelphia and New York

Copyright © 1965 by Chilton R. Bush

First Edition

All rights reserved

Published in Philadelphia by Chilton Company
and simultaneously in Toronto, Canada,
by Ambassador Books, Ltd.

TO
TURNER CATLEDGE

Preface

In 1927, the author originated the course that is generally entitled "Reporting of Public Affairs" and, in 1929, published *Newspaper Reporting of Public Affairs*. The scope of that book was limited to the subject matter which the undergraduate needed for the practice of his profession but which was not available to him in the undergraduate curriculum; for example, procedural law and the operation of the federal government at the local level.

The author has never believed that this course should be a duplication or a regurgitation of the courses in local government which are available to the undergraduate. Such instruction is best presented by the specialist because the specialist keeps up with his field and has a superior insight into the developing problems in the field. What the instructor in journalism can best do for the prospective reporter is to explain the duties of the specific officials and the actual procedures in such matters as property assessment—matters which the usual instructor in local government does not present adequately.

The early textbooks related only to newswriting and newsroom organization and procedures. Since the publication of the first edition of *Newspaper Reporting of Public Affairs,* however, many beginning textbooks have included a smattering of the content which is the second part of this book. The author believes that it is advantageous to the student, first, to learn newswriting, and, second, to study the content of the second part in depth. Hence, this volume, which is designed for a full-year course.

The book likely will be used as a handbook after the student's graduation. For that reason, the discussion of certain subject matter is fairly complete. But it does not mean that the instructor will wish to assign every chapter in the second part if he prefers to allocate time for thorough learning of the more technical subject matter.

At appropriate places within the text are exercises and questions for class discussion. The author assumes, however, that the instructor will prefer to substitute some of his own exercises. The discussion in Chapter 1 should enable the instructor to assign a newswriting exercise in the first week of the course.

The author is indebted to Professor Clifford F. Weigle, who read and criticized a considerable portion of the manuscript.

C. R. B.

Stanford, California

Contents

Preface   vii

WRITING THE NEWS

1	Writing News for the Smiths	3
2	The People Who Write and Edit the News	13
3	What Is News and Who Reads It?	26
4	The Lead	43
5	Organizing the Facts	64
6	Making the News Meaningful	84
7	Syntax	102
8	Diction	111
9	Making the Event Vivid	119
10	Speeches and Conventions	128
11	Human Interest Stories and Interviews	140
12	The Obituary	152
13	Science and Technology	159
14	Some Communication Theory	165

REPORTING PUBLIC AFFAIRS

15	The Courts	173
16	Civil Actions: Plaintiff's Pleading	201
17	Civil Actions: Responsive Pleading	225
18	Civil Actions: The Trial	238
19	Law Enforcement Agents	274
20	Criminal Actions: Crimes	304
21	Criminal Actions: Arrest	315
22	Criminal Actions: Accusation	328
23	Criminal Actions: Defendant's Pleading	342
24	Criminal Actions: The Trial	352
25	Fair Trial vs. Free Press	387
26	Probate	399
27	Bankruptcy Proceedings	408
28	Extraordinary Remedies	416
29	Appellate Procedure	429

30	Corporate Finance		441
31	The County Building		467
32	The City Hall		479
33	The Federal Building		506
34	Political Party Organizations		525
35	Labor		538

APPENDICES

A	Style Guide	553
B	Glossary of Newspaper Terms	556
C	Glossary of Legal Terms	559
D	Glossary of Business-Financial Terms	563
E	Suggested Readings	566

INDEX 569

Writing the News

CHAPTER *1*

Writing News for the Smiths

When Mrs. John Smith unfolded her afternoon newspaper, the Jonesville *Gazette,* the first thing that attracted her attention on page 1 was a four-column headline about a coal miners' strike. She read the headline quickly, was not interested enough in the event to read further, and skipped to another headline:

Jonesville Woman Attempts Suicide

Mrs. Smith read only the first two paragraphs because the woman mentioned was the wife of a laborer on the other side of town and unknown to Mrs. Smith. Mrs. Smith had been attracted by the headline, however, because the words, "Jonesville," "woman," and "suicide" were very strong cues for her reading interests.

Mrs. Smith's eyes next caught this headline:

Mother, Children Escape Injury In Runaway Car

She went on to read the entire news story:

> A young mother, clinging half in and half out of a runaway automobile containing three small children, fought vainly to stop it on a steep Protrero district hill yesterday.
> The car plunged more than 500 feet

3

down the hill, battering parked cars and buildings on the way, and wound up smashed partly inside the living room of a home at 585 Texas Street.

The crash pinned the young woman, 24-year-old Susan Martin, of 614 Missouri Street, tightly between the car door and driver's seat.

But police reported she was not severely hurt. The children also escaped injury.

Mrs. Martin told a policeman she had parked the car, a new model Mercury, on Texas Street, near 20th, at noon, to pick up her 5-year-old son, Robert, from Daniel Webster School. The hand-brake was set tightly and the wheels were curbed, she said, but the car started just as she was entering it.

Mrs. Smith completed reading this news story and turned to the other headlines. She used the headlines as indexes to her selective reading behavior. The headlines contained an average of only five words; since the main function of the headline is to synopsize the news story, five words can usually present the substance of the event. Mrs. Smith made instant decisions to read or to reject each news story. Of those she decided to read, she read all of some of them but only the first few paragraphs of the others; she was not interested in reading all of the details in some of them. She had already learned about some of the news from radio and television newscasts and skipped some of those news stories. But she read some of the news stories she had first learned about from radio and television newscasts because the newspaper presented additional details of those events. In some instances, a picture drew her attention to a news story, and she usually read all or a part of such a story. She continued to turn the pages, reading something and skipping something until she had gone through the whole newspaper.

WHY READ NEWS WHEN YOU CAN DO SOMETHING ELSE?

Mrs. Smith allocated some of her time to reading a newspaper and to attending to newscasts because she received a psychological reward. But to obtain this reward she had to expend a certain effort and a certain amount of money. She paid about two dollars a month for the newspaper; she had to walk out a certain distance in her front yard to get it; and she allocated some of her time to reading the paper at the expense of some alternative behavior that was pleasurable, such as viewing television or talking on the telephone to a friend. She also had to expend some effort to hear the radio newscast—to the extent that she had to arrange her behavior to correspond to the exact time of the newscast.

Whether one reads a particular news story or listens to a particular newscast is determined by what Wilbur Schramm has called the *fraction of selection*.[1] It is

$$\frac{\text{Expectation of reward}}{\text{Effort required}}$$

As Schramm says, "You can increase the value of that fraction either by increasing the numerator or decreasing the denominator, which is to say that an individual is more likely to select a certain communication if it promises him more reward or requires less effort than comparable communications."

News writers and editors can do certain things to increase the value of this fraction, that is, to insure that more people begin and finish reading a particular news item. For example, the writer can often enhance the reward by reporting a public affairs type of news in terms of the people involved (an example is mentioned on p. 52). Interest in a news story is also increased when the newspaper presents "sidebar" biographies, or "profiles," of persons in the news. Newspapers today publish more biographical matter than formerly about sports personalities because many of their readers have already witnessed the game on television. Newspapers also report more about the personalities of persons involved in news about government and international politics.

The editor and the news writer can also do certain things that reduce the amount of effort required from the reader. For example, newspapers can "jump" fewer stories from page 1 or can make it easier for the reader to locate a story that is "jumped" to an inside page. More important, however, is writing the story in a way that makes it easier to read and more gratifying emotionally. Some of the ways to do this are discussed in later chapters. Most editors realize that they are competing for the reader's time—against his television viewing and other kinds of individual behavior.

What we have just said about Mrs. Smith's newspaper reading behavior is approximately true of her husband's. The main reason that Mr. and Mrs. Smith expend money and effort to get news from the newspaper is that they feel compelled to make a daily surveillance of their environment. There are uncertainties—and even threats—in the environment that Mr. and Mrs. Smith feel they must know about. The news tells what certain people have done or plan to do, and these actions can affect the lives of Mr. and Mrs. Smith. The city planning commission has just rezoned some property in the Smiths' neighborhood, affecting the value of their property; some scientists have developed a big bomb; a friend has just died; etc.

[1] *The Process and Effects of Mass Communication*, p. 19.

THE NEWS STORY

The form in which an event is reported is called the *news story*. We shall defer until later chapters a discussion of news writing style, but at this point we shall discuss in a preliminary way the structure of the news story.

It has never occurred to Mrs. Smith (or to most other readers) that the news story has a particular structure. But the writers and editors of news are very much aware of the structure because it is designed to facilitate immediate comprehension. News writers and editors are aware of the conditions under which readers read news and of readers' motivations for reading news. The structure of the news story, therefore, satisfies those conditions.

A simple model of the news story is one that merely answers the questions *what, who, when,* and *where,* and sometimes *why* and *how*. This model, which fits ordinary chronicle, was adopted by the competing Jonesville newspaper, the *Times,* when it reported Mrs. Martin's automobile plunging down the hill. The *Times's* news story was as follows:

> Mrs. Susan Martin, 614 Missouri street, and her three small children escaped injury yesterday when her automobile plunged 500 feet down a hill.
>
> The car, which had been parked on Texas street, near 20th, battered other parked cars and buildings and finally stopped inside the living room of a home at 585 Texas street.

The *Times* merely told its readers the what, who, when, and where of the event. Its editor reasoned that the event was not very newsworthy since the personal injury was minor. The *Gazette,* however, had organized the same facts so as to give the reader an *image* of the happening. When you were reading the *Gazette's* story, you had some feeling that you were *witnessing* the event. The *Gazette* believed it should reward the reader emotionally for taking time to read five paragraphs rather than save the reader's time, as the *Times* did.

NEWS VALUES

Each day the newspaper has available much more news copy than it has space for. The editors, therefore, make decisions as to which events they will report and as to how much space they will allocate to each event. The basis of their selection is the degree of importance of the event and the intensity of interest they estimate their readers will have in the event. Both Jonesville newspapers decided to report the runaway automobile event—but the *Gazette* allocated almost three times more space to it than did the *Times*.

Both city editors reasoned that the event had some degree of importance, for it was a way of telling readers they should take care to set their brakes properly. Thus, those automobile owners who read their newspaper to make a surveillance of their environment perceived a threat and became aware of a problem in their lives.

The *Gazette's* city editor, however, had a keener sense of the dramatic and directed a rewrite man[2] to write the news story in a form that would convey to the reader the suspense that was inherent in the event. He wanted his readers to *see* the event. One might say, therefore, that the *Gazette* added a dimension of intensity.

> For class discussion: If you were an editor, which policy would you adopt for that particular event?

THE SUMMARY LEAD

The bulk of news stories are mere chronicle. They are written on the model of the *Times's* story about the runaway automobile: they merely tell the what, who, when, and where. When such news stories are several paragraphs in length they have two parts. These are called the *lead* and the *body*. The lead in this kind of news story is usually the first paragraph. It summarizes the what, who, when, and where. The part of the story below the lead—the body—presents details that elaborate the summary lead and supplies additional minor details.

The two parts of such a news story can be thought of as being separable; if the body of the story happened to be omitted for reasons of space, the reader still would know the main facts about the event from reading only the lead. Here is an example:

Lead
: Mrs. Henry Metcalf, 91, of 1214 Hamilton avenue, died early this morning at Mercy Convalescent hospital of cancer.

Body
: Mrs. Metcalf was born in Salem, Mass. She was a member of the old Bolt family of Salem which settled there in 1630.
  She lived in New York for many years but moved here 12 years ago to make her home with her daughter and son-in-law, Mr. and Mrs. Harvey Moss.
  Funeral services will be held . . .

---

[2] An editorial worker who writes news stories from facts telephoned by a "legman" from his "beat." See p. 20.

You will note that the lead of this story not only tells what, who, when, and where, but also *why*. Some leads also tell *how* and some tell the *effect* of the what.

Exercise: Write a news story based on the following facts. Use all of the facts. Tell what, who, when, where, and why in the form of the Jonesville *Times* story on page 6. The summary lead should not be longer than 25 words.

A blaze was discovered shortly before 3 a.m. this morning in the home of John Painter at 7341 Meadow street. Malcolm Perkins, 5015 Peggy Lane, who was on his newspaper delivery route smelled smoke as he drove past Painter's cottage and stopped to investigate. He peered through a window and saw Painter's bed afire. He was not able to enter the house. He drove three blocks to a fire station and led firemen to the scene.

Painter was partially paralyzed. Neighbors said he had had a paralytic stroke and had difficulty getting about. He lived alone.

He was 56 years old.

Besides a brother in Minnesota, Painter's only other survivor appeared to be a small black kitten which curiously probed the charred interior of the cottage today.

Assistant Fire Chief Walter Barbour said Painter probably died of carbon monoxide poisoning. He explained that smoke damage to the cottage indicated the fire had consumed almost all available oxygen. He said all windows were tightly closed.

Barbour said that Painter was known to smoke. The origin of the fire was in the mattress. Checks of wiring and gas lines as potential causes of the blaze proved negative.

Damage to the cottage was estimated at $2,000.

A neighbor said of Painter, "He seemed like a nice, quiet guy. He'd sit on the porch for hours playing with that little kitten."

TYPOGRAPHICAL STYLE

Most newspapers, including student newspapers, have a style book to standardize capitalization, abbreviations, titles, figures, and certain kinds of punctuation. The purpose of the style guide is to insure uniformity; that is, to avoid the possibility of typographical anarchy.

No specific typographical style is "correct"; the rules represent mainly the preferences of the person or persons who control the particular newspaper, although logic does determine some of the rules.

There has been some tendency for newspapers in certain geographical regions to adopt somewhat the same style. Thus, many eastern newspapers have an "up" style regarding capitalization, and many middle-western newspapers have a "down" style. "Up" style calls for more capitalization than

WRITING NEWS FOR THE SMITHS 9

SPECIMEN OF REPORTER'S COPY

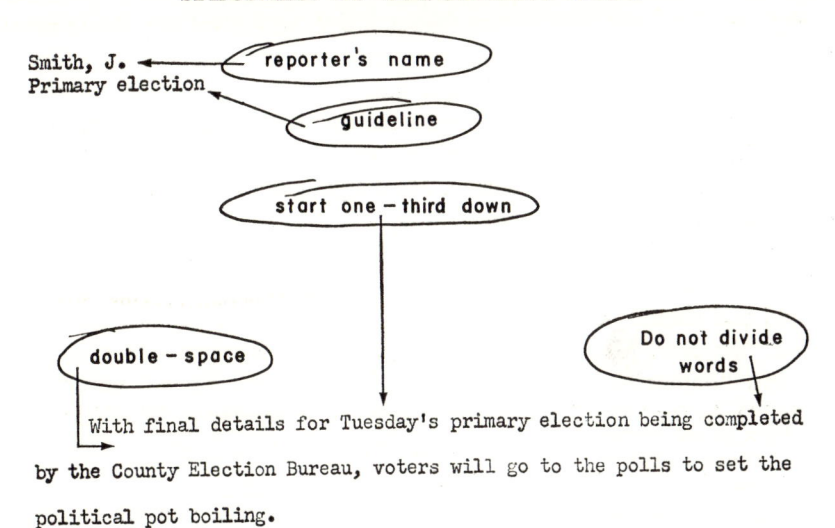

Smith, J. ← *reporter's name*
Primary election ← *guideline*

start one-third down

double-space *Do not divide words*

    With final details for Tuesday's primary election being completed by the County Election Bureau, voters will go to the polls to set the political pot boiling.

    Election Commissioner John H. Bachman said that supplies for city polling places were received yesterday, and will be delivered to polling places in the towns today.

    It will not only be the earliest date that a primary election has been held, but it will be the first time that four political parties will conduct primary elections in the county: Republican, Democrat, American Labor, and the new Liberal party.

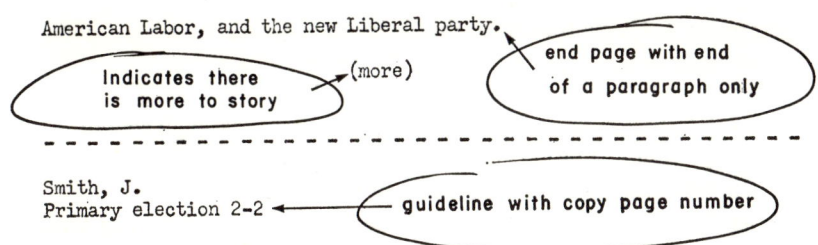

(more) ← *Indicates there is more to story*   *end page with end of a paragraph only*

Smith, J.
Primary election 2-2 ← *guideline with copy page number*

    Party leaders admitted that they do not expect a large vote and that the primaries are not exciting much interest. The fact that only delegates to the national conventions and state and county committeemen are to be elected is the reason, leaders believe, for the lagging interest on the part of voters generally.

    Polls will be open from 12 noon to 9 p.m. in the city and towns.

← *end mark*

does "down" style. An example: "East First Street" and "East First street."

Style guides also specify when figures are to be spelled out. Some newspapers, for example, spell out figures below ten, but others specify fifty or some number in between. Most style guides prohibit beginning a sentence with a numeral. Instead, they require the number to be spelled out or, if not, to be preceded by a word such as "exactly." This rule was developed by printers for an aesthetic reason. Most style guides also prohibit the use of unnecessary ciphers ($7, not $7.00).

Newspapers differ in their use of "Mr." (see p. 85). *The New York Times Style Book*[3] devotes 68 lines to instructions about when this title should and should not be used. Some style guides also require the appellation "the Rev. Mr. Kelly," not "Rev. Kelly." (Roman Catholic usage requires "Father Kelly" or "the Right Rev. Joseph Kelly," never "Mr. Kelly."[4]) As for "Mrs." and "Miss," they are, according to *The New York Times Style Book,* "to be used for all females, reputable or not, since they are needed to denote marital status."

Your instructor will decide which style guide, if any, you are to use. It would be well to develop the habit of following some specific style since probabilities are fairly high that you will have to follow certain rules of style on your first newspaper job. You might wish to obtain a copy of the style guide adopted jointly by the Associated Press and United Press International for their transmission of copy by teletypesetter. Because many small dailies receive wire copy on the TTS wires, they have the typographical style of their locally written copy conform to the style guide developed by the wire services.

Exercise: *1.* Circle the usage that is in accord with the Style Guide (Appendix A).
- *a)* M. J. Cox, Jr.   M. J. Cox Jr.   M. J. Cox, jr.   M. J. Cox jr.
- *b)* West High school   West High School   West high school
- *c)* 11 p.m.   11:00 p.m.   11:00 P.M.   11 P.M.
- *d)* Mississippi River   Mississippi river
- *e)* William McKinley was President.   William McKinley was president.
- *f)* 25%   25 per cent   25 percent
- *g)* A room 9 x 12   a room nine x 12   a room nine by twelve
- *h)* Tuesday   Tues.
- *i)* Governor Mark Garver   Gov. Mark Garver
- *j)* Professor Clarence Green   Prof. Clarence Green
- *k)* ten cents   10 cents   ten ¢   .10¢

[3] P. 63.
[4] A further discussion of the use of "Mr." is on p. 85.

COPY MARKINGS

⏎By Donald Ames ⌐ BF

⌐WASHINGTON--Army engineers have poured cold water, in reasonable quantities--on a suggestion they might turn the Missouri River around and run it in another direction⊙

The idea was Advanced yesterday at ab a Senate Appropriations Subcommittee hearing on funds for various flood control projects. ⌐Sen⏋ Thye (R.⌃Minnesota) started a discussion with brig. gen. C. J. Chorpening, chief deputy of Army engineers.

"I notice on the map," Thye said, "that the Missouri flows south about to Kansas City and then almost turns a right angle (to the east).

Would it be possible, general, perhaps to change the river *stet* and divert it ~~south or~~ south west where its waters might be more in demand?"

¶⌐	Paragraph indention	⏌	Flush right
⌒	Run in; no paragraph	⌐	Flush left
⊝the⊝	Elision	⋀	Caret ("insert")
⌐⏋	Transpose	#	Space (also "end of item")
(sixty)	Use figures	ʕʔ	Quote marks
(Minnesota)	Abbreviate	⋁	Apostrophe
(Sen.)	Spell out	⋏	Comma
brig.	Capitals	⊙ or ⊗	Period
Ądvanced	Lower case	=	Hyphen
south west	Join	⊢⊣	Dash
about/it	Separate	melba	Underline
BF	Bold face (black type)	toast	Overline
⏌⌐	Center	(stet)	Retain

l) one dollar   1 dollar $1.00 $1
m) sixty-five dollars   65 dollars $65.00 $65
n) "South Pacific" is a fine show. South Pacific is a fine show.

2. In your journalism library you will find a copy of the New York *Daily News*. Compare and contrast it with your hometown metropolitan newspaper as to: (*a*) format and typography; (*b*) use of graphic material; (*c*) general content; (*d*) newswriting style; (*e*) kinds of advertising.

3. In your journalism library you will find copies of *The Times* (London) and the *Daily Express* (London). Compare and contrast them by the criteria listed in Exercise 2 above.

CHAPTER 2

The People Who Write and Edit the News

The newspaper business is unusual in that it is one of the few businesses which manufacture a completely new product each day and deliver it to the consumer on the same day. This process has to be accomplished within a period of a few hours. On the news side of this operation, the editors can make a product only from the material that becomes available to them on the particular day, although in printed wordage the news content is the equivalent of a full length novel.

The editorial functions are (1) getting the news, (2) writing the news, (3) selecting the news, (4) processing the news copy, and (5) displaying the news.

The men who perform these tasks are reporters, rewrite men, copy editors, photographers, and a makeup editor. They are supervised by a telegraph editor, a news editor, a city editor, a picture editor, departmental editors (e.g., sports and women's pages), and a managing editor. Some of these supervisors have assistants. The titles held by such editors on one newspaper do not always correspond to the titles of editors performing the same functions on another newspaper. Thus, some newspapers have an executive editor, a feature editor, and a cable editor, or the news editor on one newspaper is the makeup editor on another. For the purposes of this discussion, we are concerned with the functions, the processes, and the decision-making—not with the titles. Your understanding of the editorial processes will be assisted if you first understand *newshole* and *copy flow*.

THE NEWSHOLE

Before the editors start their daily tasks they receive from the advertising department a dummy of each page on which advertising is to run. The aggregate space that remains on these pages, plus other pages that carry no display or classified advertising, constitute the newshole. The newshole is filled with both news and non-news content, such as comics, editorials, and feature columns.

Much of the newshole is not controllable on a particular day, for the newspaper has a standing policy which has determined in advance the space to be allocated for editorial-opinion matter, sports, women's departments, and certain features. On certain days of the week and in certain circumstances, the amount of actual news varies, but it is usually the same on most days.

The size of the newshole and the size of its components are indicated by a measurement of space in twenty selected California newspapers.[1] The measurements reported are an average for newspapers with circulations varying from 4,000 to 110,000; they do not include newspapers published in San Francisco and Los Angeles. The average size of the twenty newspapers was 48 pages, or 384 columns. The percentage of advertising was 70 per cent, leaving a newshole of 30 per cent, or 115 columns. The newshole was divided into local news, 45 per cent (85 items); wire news, 32 per cent (65 items); and non-news, 23 per cent. Pictures were 13 per cent of the newshole; sports news and sports features, 12 per cent; and women's page matter, including food features, 15 per cent.[2]

In a very large newspaper, news of the world, the nation, the state, and the community occupies a smaller proportion of the total newshole than does such news in the newspaper mentioned above. One writer reports[3] that such news is only 38 per cent of the newshole. The editor of the largest newspaper in the country, the *Los Angeles Times,* reports[4] that the *Times's* newshole on week days (except Saturday) is about 170 columns, but sometimes is as high as 220 columns. Of the 170 columns, "straight," or "real," news occupies about 47 columns. This is exclusive of business-financial news and tables (20 columns), women's features (18 columns), comics (8 columns), editorial-opinion matter (16 columns), television and radio logs (7 columns), the picture page (8 columns), and vital statistics (5 columns).

Most newspapers have a standing policy as to the proportion of wire news and locally written news. Both the city editor and the telegraph editor know that they have a certain number of columns available on an average day.

---

[1] Charles F. Massey, address to the California Editors' Conference, June 22, 1963. Mr. Massey is the executive editor of the Yakima (Wash.) *Herald* and *Republic.*

[2] Mr. Massey also measured the content of twenty-two newspapers in Washington, including the Seattle newspapers. The percentages were about the same as he reported for the selected California newspapers.

[3] Ben Bagdikian, "Why Dailies Die," *New Republic,* April 16, 1962, pp. 17–23.

[4] Nick B. Williams, "The Nation's Biggest Newshole and How It Gets Filled," *Bulletin of the American Society of Newspaper Editors,* Sept., 1961, p. 15.

When, however, on a particular day there is a "newsbreak" which deserves an unusual amount of space, a decision is made either to change the established proportion or to increase the total space available for news. This decision is made by the managing editor. Some newspapers have principal editorial executives attend a formal conference at the beginning of the day. By this time the telegraph editor has received an advance "budget" from the wire services, and the city editor knows approximately what local news will develop. The conference discusses the news that is anticipated and decides how to display the major news stories. It is at this conference that the managing editor makes the decision mentioned above. On those newspapers which have no formal editorial conference, the editorial executives confer informally about changing the allocation of space.

Some morning newspapers departmentalize news by allocating certain pages for international, national, and local news. This "anchoring" of such types of news improves the newspaper as a utility in that readers know where to find certain news and features. Departmentalization, however, is more difficult to achieve on an afternoon newspaper because less time is available for processing the copy. Most afternoon newspapers, however, "anchor" comics and other features, business-financial news, sports news, women's features, and the television and radio logs; a few newspapers have a policy of "floating" comics which is probably inadvisable. Some newspapers also carry an index on page 1 to help the reader find certain kinds of content, and some newspapers also digest the main news stories. A good part of the non-news content of afternoon newspapers must be written or processed on the previous day and is set into type overnight. For the first edition, a kind of news called "time" copy (i.e., news without the time element) or some of yesterday's wire news received after midnight is printed; in later editions this is replaced by fresh news.

> Exercise: Determine the size in inches of the newshole of one of your local newspapers. Report the percentage of the whole newspaper it represents. What percentage of the newshole, including pictures, was devoted to sports, women's pages, and business-financial news? What percentage was devoted to non-news matter exclusive of sports, women's page matter, and business-financial? Of the total amount of space devoted to news of the world, the state, the nation, and the community, what percentage was locally written and what percentage was received by wire or mail, including pictures? How many local items (exclusive of items on women's, sports, and business-financial pages) were there? How many wire-mail items?

COPY FLOW

A fairly large metropolitan newspaper receives and some of its editorial workers must read in a few hours each day a half million words of news copy; the *New York Times* receives one million words each day. The task of reading the copy input on even the small daily of 5,000–6,000 circulation has increased because of the recent step-up in the speed of wire news transmission. A typical small daily, for example, publishes 12,000 words of local copy and receives by wire more than 60,000 words of teletypesetter copy (in a 15-hour cycle) plus 15,000 words of copy received by mail. Obviously some kind of system is necessary to facilitate the selection of news and the processing of the copy that is to be printed. Numerous quick decisions are necessary.

The conventional system is to have a "universal" copy desk. Its name derives from the fact that all copy received flows to this desk—local copy, wire service copy, and mailed copy from syndicates. This large desk has the shape of a horseshoe. Around its outside rim sit several copy editors (also called copyreaders); within the horseshoe sits a "slot man"; at or near the two ends of the horseshoe are the news editor, telegraph editor, and picture editor. The news editor is the key decision-maker; he is a sort of gatekeeper of the news. He reads quickly all of the local copy that comes from the city desk and all of the wire copy that the telegraph editor (a gatekeeper of the wire news) permits to filter through. The news editor has a dummy of every page in the paper and makes a cumulative record of the amount of copy he passes. As he glances at the copy he decides where it will go in the paper, what size headline it should have, and how much of it is to be used. He passes all copy to the slot man who selects a copy editor to edit it and to write a headline for it. The slot man also supervises the headline writing and controls the flow of copy to the composing room. Each news story and each headline carries a "guideline," or "slugline," such as "Fire," "Belgium," or "Queen" so that the story and the headline can be matched in the composing room after they have been set into type on different linecasting machines. The picture editor makes decisions about all of the pictures in the way that the telegraph editor makes decisions about wire and syndicate copy.

The copy editor is an important part of this system. He checks the copy for accuracy, typographical style, libel, and taste and sometimes improves the syntax and diction. He trims a story to meet the news editor's specifications and sometimes amplifies the story by writing background information. After a copy editor has written the headline, he returns the copy to the slot man.

After the slot man has approved a story and headline he conveys them to the composing room in a pneumatic tube. There a "copy cutter" pastes the pages together and cuts the whole story into "takes." He divides the takes among the linecasting operators or tapepunchers. The type that each linecasting machine has set, including the headline, is assembled on a "bank." When an important story breaks just before an edition deadline, it can be set quickly when each operator sets only one or two paragraphs.

The makeup editor (whose function on some papers is also that of slot man) is the editorial room's liaison with the composing room. He shows the printers where to place each story in the "chase" (i.e., a metal frame for holding the type for one page). Sometimes he has to make minor changes in the dummy, change a headline to fit the column width, or write "jump" headlines.

After each page of type has been assembled, the stereotyping department, first, makes a papier-mâché matrix of it and, next, casts a semicylindrical metal plate of the matrix. This plate is fastened to the press.

The "News Control" Desk

Some large newspapers have recently discontinued use of the universal desk and have substituted a decentralization of decision-making. This is on the theory that the news editor and telegraph editor were overburdened and that there were too many restrictions on the space allocated to the city editor. How a "control desk" system operates is described by the former assistant executive editor of the Detroit *Free Press:*

> ... In place of the one-man news desk, we set up a central control desk with an executive news editor in charge. In our case, this was the former news editor in an expanded role.
> On his left, he has an assistant news editor for the presentation of telegraph news.
> On his right sits an assistant city editor in charge of the presentation of local news.
> Sharing the control desk within speaking distance of those three key editors are the picture editor, the city editor and the telegraph editor.
> The executive news editor gets comprehensive written news budgets from the telegraph desk, the city desk and the picture desk.
> On the basis of these, his own reading and a short news conference, which also includes other departmental editors, he apportions the inside page dummies.
> The assistant news editor for telegraph dummies inside pages which have newsholes designated for telegraph. The assistant city editor does the same for local, including the all-local second front page.
> Backing up these two editors and located physically adjacent to them are teams of specialists who rewrite, edit and headline news with which they are familiar.
> The telegraph editor has a full-time rewrite man to combine wire dispatches and handle news roundups. He has two assistants, one of whom

supervises the parceling out and processing of national copy and the other specializes in international stories. They have a team of copyreaders who understand the news they're handling.

The telegraph editor himself now has time to plan, organize and edit with the reader in mind. He keeps a future file just like the city editor's. He has time to review stories—and prod the wire services to fill in the gaps.

The local news team has a similar makeup.

In addition to the usual rewrite men and assistant city editors, this team now includes copyreaders who edit and write headlines on local stories. They were picked for these assignments from the old universal desk staff because of their interest in local news.

Four assistant city editors are being rotated into the control desk spot, so each gains layout and display experience.

This has developed in the city desk team an awareness from the beginning of any story how it may finally be presented most effectively for the reader.

And this thinking shows up these days as city desk editors and reporters think in terms of logically broken down sidebars instead of mile-long stories in terms of explanatory or background boxes, about good illustrations for each story.

The executive news editor, who under the old system carried the full load of dummying all news pages, now has been freed to concentrate on page 1.

Besides personally handling the showcase page, he is the strong man, the coordinator, who pulls together the efforts of the specialized desks and teams.

He now has time to think.

He reads thoroughly the important stories; he plans special groupings and displays; in short, he concentrates on making the complete paper balanced, comprehensive, attractive and giving the reader every break we can give him.[5]

A systems engineer who has experimented in automation processes for newspapers predicted in 1963 that, by 1973, news will be processed electronically by means of editing consoles connected with a central computing system for information storage and retrieval.[6]

REPORTING LOCAL NEWS

The city editor—sometimes with the help of one or more assistant city editors—supervises the work of a staff of reporters and rewrite men. Some morning newspapers have a day city editor who, in addition to his duties as a personnel manager of reporters, develops the local news report by assigning reporters to specific events. The night city editor's main duties

---

[5] A. Neuharth, "Farewell to a Horseshoe," *Bulletin of the American Society of Newspaper Editors,* Nov. 1, 1962, pp. 10–11.

[6] John Diebold, "Automation and the Editor," *Problems of Journalism* (Proceedings of the 1963 Convention, American Society of Newspaper Editors), pp. 140–50. See also illustrations in *Editor & Publisher,* June 8, 1963, p. 80.

THE PEOPLE WHO WRITE AND EDIT THE NEWS   19

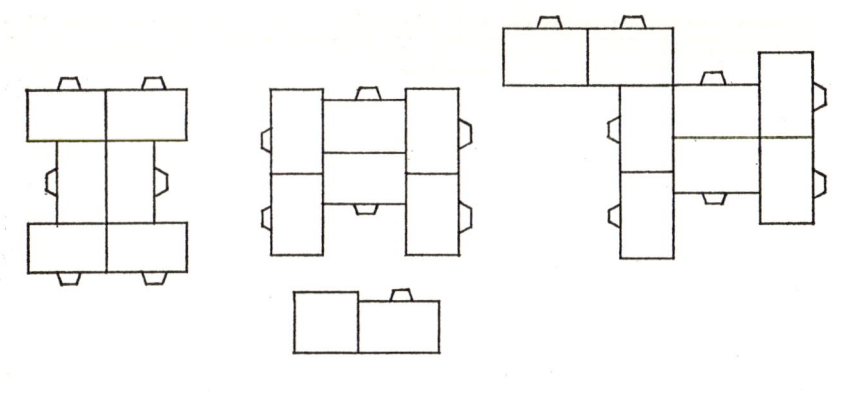

TELEGRAPH DESK
National Editor
World Editor
Telegraph Rewrite
Copyreaders

CONTROL DESK
Exec. News Editor
Ass't News Editor
Telegraph Editor
City Editor
Ass't City Editor
Picture Editor

CITY DESK
Ass't City Editors
Local Rewrite
Local Copyreaders

are to supervise the execution of the assignments previously made by the day city editor and to supervise the reporting of late newsbreaks. The city editor, often with the assistance of a secretary, keeps a "future book," which is a calendar of future events. Some city editors also have a "contact file," which lists the names, addresses, and telephone numbers of local persons who can supply information about certain matters. The city editor sometimes makes assignments of "local angles," that is, assignments to develop local stories that are related to wire stories, as when a wire service reports an epidemic of Asian flu in another part of the country and local health department officials are interviewed. Since the growth of suburbs in the nineteen-fifties and nineteen-sixties, most metropolitan newspapers station reporters in the communities who work under the supervision of the city desk. A few newspapers have changed the title "city editor" to "metropolitan editor."

Some reporters are assigned to a "beat," and others are on general assignment. The beats are those public places in which news events are recorded (e.g., a police station) or in which public affairs news develops (e.g., the city hall). Most of these beats are discussed in the later chapters of this book.

General assignment reporters are given assignments from the city desk to report events that develop elsewhere than on the beats, including feature stories and interviews. Some general assignment reporters specialize to the extent that they may be said to have the "labor beat" or the "science beat." On most newspapers, however, such specialists also do general reporting.

Rewrite men are generally capable writers who take notes from "legmen" on the beats and write the stories. They are accustomed to writing under the pressure of deadlines. Some legmen, however, dictate their stories to rewrite men who merely perform a stenographic task. The reporter who telephones to a rewrite man spells out most of the names of the principals in the story, using a phonetic alphabet such as *"A* as in Able," *"C* as in Charley," etc. The newspaper office and the pressrooms in public buildings have reverse telephone directories in which the address is the first listing and is followed by the subscriber's name and telephone number; this is of assistance, for example, when an explosion at or near a certain address is reported.

Rewrite men also rewrite stories from newspapers published in the previous news cycle and from "handouts" supplied by public relations men. Newspapers depend to a great extent on information supplied by public relations men. These include not only employees of business corporations, but also representatives of art associations, churches, and government offices. The newspaper, of course, rejects a large amount of information supplied by public relations men because it is either not newsworthy or is puffery.

Reporting a Fastbreaking Event

The following narration of how one newspaper handled a fastbreaking news story will help you to understand how a local staff is coordinated. It is by Jean Reiff, of the *Washington Post:*

> The city room of the *Washington Post* was comparatively quiet.
> The day was December 7—cold and rainy.
> Suddenly the police dispatcher's voice blared out over the radio located directly behind the city desk:
> "Scout cars 81 and 82. Holdup! It's at the Spring Valley branch of the National Metropolitan Bank!"
> Assistant City Editor James E. Hague jumped from his chair and dashed a dozen paces to the photographic department.
> "Get a man ready. We've got a bank holdup," he shouted. Then he turned to Sam Zagoria, one of several general assignment reporters at their desks, and told him to get ready to go to the scene.
> Back at the city desk, Hague took a telephone call from police reporter Alfred Lewis, who had heard the same call over the radio in the press room at police headquarters, a dozen blocks away.
> Lewis checked with Hague to make sure he was sending someone out on the story and supplied him with the bank's address, 49th street and Fordham road, which Hague gave to Zagoria and photographer Charles Del Vecchio as they left the city room on the run.
> About six minutes after the original call was broadcast, police at the scene called in to the radio dispatcher with a description of three holdup

men. Lewis heard it over the two-way radio, took it down word for word and relayed the information to Hague.

Within a half hour after the first word of the holdup, Lewis, through repeated telephone calls to the central bank, learned that approximately $40,000 had been taken in the holdup. Again he relayed the information to Hague, and kept in touch with him the entire afternoon as each small piece of information began to filter in.

Hague meanwhile went to the newspaper's library, located near the back of the city room. There he asked for the newspaper clippings telling of other bank holdups in the Washington area.

Hague also contacted by telephone Acting City Editor John Riseling, who was not scheduled to come on duty until later in the day, and discussed the coverage of the story with him.

In the meantime, Zagoria and Del Vecchio arrived at the bank to find its doors locked by police as they talked to employees inside.

Whenever a policeman came outside they cornered him and started asking questions.

After several hours they were let inside the bank, where Zagoria questioned the vice president and manager, Francis E. Hildebrand, and four employees about what had happened. Del Vecchio was busy taking pictures of the victims of the holdup men and the interior of the bank.

About 4 p.m. Hague relayed the information he had received to an assistant city editor, John Brigham, assigned to copyread the story after it was written and to write its head.

Brigham's first job was to budget the story. Giving it the name—or slug—"Rob," he wrote a terse one-sentence account:

"National Metropolitan Bank branch robbed of $38,825 in noon holdup." Tentative length of the story was set at 22 inches of type.

A copyboy typed this on a long list, known as the local news budget.

Around 5 p.m. Zagoria and Del Vecchio returned to the city room after getting whatever information they could obtain at the scene.

Zagoria immediately got in touch by telephone with Lewis, who had talked meanwhile to police officials as they returned to headquarters from the bank.

From the information they got between them, Zagoria wrote the story.

"Three bandits—two masked with silk scarves—yesterday robbed the National Metropolitan Bank's branch in fashionable Spring Valley of $38,825.

"It was the biggest holdup here since 1941. They overlooked another $10,000."

When the story was done, Zagoria handed it to Brigham for editing.

The story was then turned over to an assistant news editor, James Hagee, for another editing before it was sent by pneumatic tube to the composing room on the floor below.

Keeping a carbon copy of Zagoria's story before him, Brigham next wrote this head to appear at the top of the story in the newspaper:

"Three Masked Men Rob Spring Valley Bank of $38,825. Robbers' Haul Biggest Here in 19 Years. Four Employees, Customer Cowed; Vice President Forced to Open Vault."

This also was turned over to Hagee, who read it and sent it by tube to the composing room.

In the meantime, Acting Assistant Managing Editor James Cutlip, and Riseling decided the story, because of its importance and news interest, should go on the front page. In the first edition it appeared there with a picture.

Lewis went off duty at police headquarters in the evening. Not, however, before he had filled in night police reporter Paul Herron on the details of the robbery. From then on it was Herron's job to be on the alert for any new developments in the holdup and to keep the city desk informed of them.

Zagoria also went off duty. Additions to the story were written by a rewrite man during the night.

A new head—"Bandits Get $38,825 in Holdup at Branch Bank. Haul at National Metropolitan in Spring Valley is Biggest Since 1941"—replaced the first edition head in the later editions. The picture was transferred to an inside page and the story was moved to the first column of the front page, where it remained through the final edition.[7]

The Reporter's Skills and Attitudes

The reporter needs these skills and attitudes if he is to be successful in getting the news:

1. The reporter should develop as many sources of news as possible. This requires that he be *gregarious*—that he develop a friendliness with the stenographers and clerks in the public offices as well as with the officers themselves.

2. The reporter should have *curiosity*. Since a main function of the newspaper is to satisfy the curiosity of its readers, newspapers must have reporters who themselves have curiosity.

3. The reporter should be *enthusiastic*. Although newspaper reporting is sometimes exciting, on many days the work is dull. The reporter cannot permit himself to become blasé, for he must satisfy as far as possible every day those needs of the reader which the reader expects to have satisfied by the newspaper. This does not mean, of course, that the reporter should magnify any event out of a meaning it does not intrinsically have.

4. In narrating the event the reporter should try to answer for his readers those significant questions about the event that naturally arise in the reader's mind. While gathering information he tries to imagine what these questions are. Here is one example: In Columbus, Ohio, the governor commuted the death sentences of two deaf-mute brothers to life imprisonment. Art Parks (of the Associated Press) wasn't satisfied with the bare facts. "How was the news given to the brothers?" he asked the warden. Result: a dramatic account of a priest spelling the message with flickering fingers as the brothers' facial expressions changed from bewilderment to incredulity and, finally, to "hysterical happiness."[8]

[7] *Washington Post,* Jan. 23, 1951, p. 7C.
[8] *AP Log,* Nov. 11–13, 1958.

5. The reporter must have a *critical sense*. This means that he must develop a habit of verifying information given him by checking it against his own sense of the probabilities. The habit should not amount to skepticism, but it should amount to much less than credulity.

6. The reporter must be *resourceful*. This means that when information is denied him from the most obvious source he tries to locate another source.

7. The reporter must *respect confidences*. This matter is discussed on pages 89–90.

8. The good reporter is also a *literary craftsman*.[9]

THE WIRE SERVICES

The Associated Press and United Press International[10] have domestic bureaus in all of the major cities and state capitals plus several smaller cities. A few of these are relay points at which the daily report is edited to fit the needs of certain regions of the country. These services also maintain bureaus in the most important foreign capitals. In the London office, for example, the staff of each of the two major wire services is composed of forty-odd persons of whom about one-third are United States citizens. In the lesser foreign capitals the wire services have "stringers," employees of native newspapers who file dispatches to the wire services. The wire services get their domestic news from local newspapers and by doing their own reporting.

Speed is important to the wire services because they sell their report to newspapers throughout the world. Somewhere around the clock some client newspaper has an edition deadline every minute seven days a week as compared to a United States newspaper which has from one to a dozen editions. The wire service which is one or two minutes behind its competitor may find that a newspaper somewhere has used its competitor's report.

At the beginning of a news cycle the wire service sends newspapers a "news budget," a list of stories that will be moved on the wire. The budget assists the editors in their planning. Stories of some length are moved in takes so that the first portion of a maximum number of stories is made available to the newspaper before its edition deadline. Since the wire has

---

[9] For an explanation of different kinds of reporting, see D. Botter, *News Reporters and What They Do* (New York, 1959).

[10] These are major wire services. Some American newspapers also subscribe to Reuters, the British overseas wire service. A few newspapers with fairly large foreign staffs also deliver a service by wire or mail to subscribing newspapers. Among these are the *New York Times,* the Chicago *Daily News,* the Chicago *Tribune–New York News,* the New York *Herald-Tribune,* the *Washington Post—Los Angeles Times* service, and the Copley News Service. Certain syndicates also supply news and news features, such as the North American Newspaper Alliance, Science Service and the Newspaper Enterprise Association.

a limited capacity, the wire service has the problem not only of moving many news stories but of moving them in time to be used in the next edition of as many newspapers as possible.

The staff member of a wire service has to consider which newspapers will and which will not be interested in receiving a particular item. Many items are not transmitted to all newspapers in the country, but are eliminated at some regional relay point.

RADIO AND TV STATIONS

The major wire services deliver special reports to radio and television stations. Many of the stories are somewhat shorter than the stories sent to newspapers because few stations report many details of an event. They are also written in a somewhat different way because they are meant to be spoken rather than printed; they are meant for the ear, not the eye. Such stories are written as if the narrator were sitting in one's home talking. Since the items have no headline, the beginning of each item is a substitute for a headline. For example: "A Communist intellectual defected to the West today" and "Louisiana schools moved a step nearer integration today."

Some radio and television stations do much of their own local reporting; they rely a great deal on the telephone. Some stations insert in the newscast tape recordings of portions of speeches and announcements or film clips of an event. Some effort is made to have a slightly different "edition" of each newscast.

For class discussion: *1.* Rank in descending order of their importance and interest the eight paragraphs below. Defend your ranking.

> Mr. and Mrs. Oliver Cortesi, owners of Oliver's Restaurant, met instant death last night when their automobile was struck at the Linden Avenue crossing by a C. X. & Y. passenger train.
> Both were 56 years old.
> The accident happened at 10:20 p.m. at the same point where four other motorists had met death this year.
> There were no witnesses other than the train crew.
> The train, a southbound local, struck the Cortesi car broadside, carrying it a distance of 216 feet, Police Chief Louis Belloni said.
> The Cortesis had just left a Burlingame mortuary, where they had paid respects at the bier of a friend.
> The bodies remained in the car after the car was struck.
> Mr. Cortesi was a brother of Mayor Emilio Cortesi.

2. What kinds of news do you find in newspapers that radio and television stations seldom or never present?

3. How many sibilants can you eliminate from these sentences to make them more acceptable for radio newscasting: "Starting in the basement, the fire spread through the shafts. . . . Two firemen suffered fractured skulls and one a painful skin abrasion. . . . Fire Chief Sheehan estimated that five-sixths of the structure was destroyed"?

4. This is probably a good lead. Why did the writer emphasize the *who* instead of the *what?*

> Senator Clinton P. Anderson, who was secretary of agriculture in the Truman administration, testified yesterday in a trial in federal District Court.
> The Senator, who testified for the Government, explained the Truman administration's farm price support program.
> He was a witness in the suit in Judge George Harris' court brought against the Commodity Credit Corporation by Rosenberg Brothers and Company, Inc. The firm alleges it lost $400,000 in its raisin merchandising because the CCC forced the price of raisins up through competitive bidding.

5. Read Alan S. Donnahoe, "Space Control by Newspapers: An Analysis and a Plan," *Journalism Quarterly,* 33:279–86 (1956). Why does the newshole not increase, on the average, when the newspaper has more than sixty pages?

CHAPTER *3*

What Is News and Who Reads It?

In Chapter 1, there was no statement that Mr. and Mrs. Smith are typical newspaper readers. About the only information about the Smiths in Chapter 1 is the implication that they have an income sufficient to afford ownership of a radio and a television receiver and a subscription to a newspaper. The chapter does imply, however, that the Smiths have lived in Jonesville long enough to have acquired some interest in what happens in the community. The Smiths, moreover, are representative of the newspaper audience to the extent that they were interested in reading about the ordeal of the mother in the runaway car, for city editors believe that most of their readers want to read such an item.

But a community has some people who have not lived in it long enough to have acquired an interest in an event just because it happened in their community. And some people in nearly every community are more interested in news about the national government and in international politics than they are in news about local events.[1] Thus, *the newspaper has several audiences, not just one.* A description of some of these audiences will be presented in a later section of this chapter.

If we were to make a readership survey of a typical daily newspaper to find out what percentage of our total sample of readers had read each news item, we would find that the typical (median) reader had read from 20 to 25 per cent of all the items. The percentage who had read a particu-

---

[1] A national study reported these preferences:

I am personally *much more* interested in what is happening on the national and international scenes	23.3%
I am *slightly more interested* in what is happening on the national and international scene	19.5%
I am *slightly more interested* in what is happening in my own city or town	23.7%
I am *much more interested* in what is happening in my own city or town	28.1%
No preference stated	3.0%

(Newsprint Information Committee, *A National Study of the Newspaper Reading Public* [New York, 1961], Vol. II, p. 37.)

larly interesting news story, however, would approach 70 to 75 per cent. For several items we would find a large difference between the choices of men and women readers.

Exercise: *1.* Count the number of pages in the last daily newspaper you read. Estimate the time you spent reading the paper. Divide the time into the number of pages in the newspaper. On the average, how much time did you devote per page?
2. Look at a newspaper readership study in your journalism library and compute the average readership score for the front page news items by men and by women.

THE NATURE OF NEWS

What are the psychological processes that determine the news reading choices of the individual readers? One of the best explanations we have, that of Wilbur Schramm, is reproduced, in part, below. You should read it carefully, for you will be asked some questions based upon it.

I think it is self-evident that a person selects news in expectation of a reward.

This reward may be either of two kinds. One is related to what Freud calls the Pleasure Principle, the other to what he calls the Reality Principle. For want of better names, we shall call these two classes *immediate reward* and *delayed reward*.

In general, the kinds of news which may be expected to furnish immediate reward are news of crime and corruption, accidents and disasters, sports and recreation, social events, and human interest.

Delayed reward may be expected from news of public affairs, economic matters, social problems, science, education, and health.

News of the first kind pays its rewards at once. A reader can enjoy a vicarious experience without any of the dangers or stresses involved. He can shiver luxuriously at an axe-murder, shake his head sympathetically and safely at a tornado, identify himself with the winning team or (herself) with the society lady who wore a well-described gown at the reception for Lady Morganbilt, laugh understandingly (and from superior knowledge) at a warm little story of children or dogs. News of the second kind, however, pays its rewards later. It sometimes requires the reader to endure unpleasantness or annoyances—as, for example, when he reads of the ominous foreign situation, the mounting national debt, rising taxes, falling market, scarce housing, cancer, epidemics, farm blights. It has a kind of "threat value." It is read so that the reader may be informed and prepared. When a reader selects delayed reward news, he jerks himself into the world of surrounding reality to which he can adapt himself only by hard work. When he selects news of the other kind, he retreats usually from the world of threatening reality toward the dream world.

For any individual, of course, the boundaries of these two classes are not stable. For example, a sociologist may read news of crime as a social problem, rather than for its immediate reward. A coach may read a sports story for its threat value: he may have to play that team next week. A politician may read an account of his latest successful rally, not for its delayed reward, but very much as his wife reads an account of a party. In any given story of corruption or disaster, a thoughtful reader receives not only the immediate reward of vicarious experience, but also the delayed reward of information and preparedness. Therefore, while the division of categories holds in general, the predispositions of the individual may transfer any story from one kind of reading to another, or divide the experience between the two kinds of reward.

But what is going on psychologically beneath these two kinds of choice of news?

The kind of choice which we have called immediate reward is simple associational learning, or problem solving. A stimulus is presented; a response is made; the response is rewarded. When the stimulus is again presented, there is a tendency to make the same response. If it is again rewarded, the tendency to make that same response is progressively reinforced. If it is not rewarded, the tendency is progressively extinguished. The stimulus in this case, of course, is the news item. The response is the decision to read or listen to the item. The reward may be either a reduction of tension or discomfort (e.g., curiosity, worry) or an increase in satisfaction (e.g., from a vicarious enjoyment of the achievements of the winning team).

But what is the process which leads a reader or listener to select a news item even though he knows it may not reduce tension, but actually *increase* tension; not relieve discomfort, but actually *increase* discomfort; not bring satisfaction, but actually bring dissatisfaction and worry? We have already suggested that these two kinds of reading are related to what Freud called the two principles of mental functioning, the Pleasure Principle and the Reality Principle. That is, the immediate reward choice is learned through trial and error because it succeeds in reducing drives and tensions. The delayed reward choice, on the other hand, is made not because it is pleasant, but because it is realistic. It is not pleasant to be afraid or to anticipate danger; but it is necessary, if one is to avert harm and avoid danger.

O. H. Mowrer, in his reinterpretation of conditioning and problem solving, has advanced a concept of learning which is extremely suggestive to any student of the process of communication. He points out that there are really two aspects of learning, related respectively to the two nervous systems. The central nervous system is the one chiefly through which we affect society; the autonomic nervous system is the one chiefly through which society affects us. The central system is the one through which habits—that is, learned responses of the skeletal musculature—are formed. The autonomous system is the one through which attitudes or emotions—that is, learned responses of glands, smooth muscle, and vasomotor tissue—are formed. Habits, of course, come into being to reduce drives and solve problems. Attitudes and emotions, on the other hand, are themselves drives or problems, and call forth skeletal reactions on the basis of which the central nervous system may go into action and develop habits.

Therefore, responses to the two kinds of news corresponds to what Sherrington calls *anticipatory* and *consummatory* responses. One is made as the consummation of a drive and with the expectation of immediate reward. The other is made to set up a drive, and in expectation of danger or delayed reward. One reduces a drive and is therefore pleasant; the other sets up a drive and may be painful. The two responses are not always cleanly differentiated. For example, the dramatic quality in a foreign news story may give an immediate reward, while the content arouses only fear or anticipation of danger. But learning may take place through either method. Gordon Allport gives an example of learning through the anticipatory response: "Suppose I mispronounce a word in a public speech . . . and suffer mounting shame and discomfort. Tension has been *created*, not reduced; dissatisfaction and not satisfaction has resulted; but in this sequence of events I shall surely learn."

When a child starts to read a newspaper he usually begins with the comics and the pictures. He proceeds to the sports news, the human interest stories, and sensational stories of crime and disaster, all before he makes much use of public affairs news. It is interesting to conjecture how a child begins to read public affairs news. Perhaps he has an experience in which he is able to make not-too-long-delayed use of something he has read in the paper. Perhaps it helps him to answer a question at school, or to take his raincoat and avoid a soaking, or to avoid a street which is closed for repairs—in other words, to avoid trouble by being informed. He looks at the paper with respect. If reading the particular item was of benefit to him, would it not be well for him to read other items also? As his understanding broadens, he perceives more of the causative and repetitive relation of events in society. And thus he substitutes other stimuli for the stimulus which has had a proved reward, and as his horizon broadens comes to see more and more reason for reading news of public affairs.

Thus the time when he comes to read public affairs news is an important point in his socialization. Most of the news in the immediate reward group is important to him individually because of the individual satisfaction and drive-reduction it accomplishes. But the news in the delayed group is important to him because it arouses the tensions and anticipation that are necessary for survival and development, that help him to be more effective, better prepared, *socially*. . . .

If we accept tentatively the theory that there are two general classes of news, two patterns of reading, and two aspects of the learning process involved, then another variable becomes important. Within each kind of news, what determines the likelihood that a given item will be selected? What determines the attractiveness of a given item to the reader?

Leaving out chance, conflicting mental sets, and the qualities of presentation which call attention to one item over others or make one item easier to read than others, we can hypothesize that a person chooses the items which he thinks are likely to give him the greatest reward. The exact yardstick by which he measures this predictive value is an individual matter based on experience and personality structure, and powerfully influenced by the momentary situation. But in general there seems to be greater expectation of reward when there appears to be greater possibility of the reader identifying himself with the news.

This may be what the textbooks mean by proximity as a news value, but is not to be interpreted as mere physical proximity. For example: a fight in an American city may be physically nearer than a battle in the South Pacific, but if a mother has a son in the battle then how much more easily can she identify herself with the distant battle than with the nearer fight. On the other hand, the American scrap is likely to seem closer to the average reader than a Dutch coup in Indonesia, although one may ultimately have large repercussions for the colonial system and for international trade, whereas the other will doubtless pass out of the realm of important affairs as soon as the participants sober up. Similarly, it is a greater reward to identify oneself with the local team which is winning a championship than with a faraway team that is equally good. One of the startling accomplishments of mass communications has been to bring far corners and faraway people almost next door, so that it becomes relatively easy for a reader to identify himself with the personal affairs of movie stars in Hollywood, and for thousands of sports fans who have never been in South Bend to feel like alumni of Notre Dame. It is also easier to identify oneself with an event which is vividly described and which has a minimum of indirection. But I think it is safe to say that the individual world of the reader will for the most part determine the ease with which he can identify himself with the given item, and this in turn will powerfully affect the probability of the item being read.[2]

Exercise: *1.* In which of the following news stories (synopses) would you have a high interest? A low interest?

a) A prominent clubwoman was beaten and choked to death today by her 15-year-old son, who said she had nagged him ever since he was arrested for trying to chloroform and photograph a girl friend.

b) The Soviet Union today threatened to resume testing atomic and hydrogen bombs unless France stops nuclear tests in the Sahara.

c) An 18-year-old youth was executed today for a murder shot he did not fire—despite a dramatic appeal for his life to the governor.

d) There's a farmer near here who makes more money selling water than he makes from the eleven oil wells on his farm.

2. Below is a list of twenty reasons that people have assigned for their choosing to read a particular news story. For each of the four news stories above check as many of the reasons as *you* would apply to the choices you made of the stories you would read (if any) and of the stories you would reject (if any).

a) This might be amusing.
b) Somebody should do something about this matter.
c) This needs explaining.
d) I know someone who'll want to hear about this.

[2] "The Nature of News," *Journalism Quarterly,* 26:259–69 (1949).

e) I dislike such stories.
f) I'm tired of reading about this.
g) I know something about this that's not in the papers.
h) This makes me feel sad.
i) This will help me keep up with what's going on.
j) This may affect me personally.
k) This is disturbing.
l) I can imagine this happening.
m) This might be exciting.
n) This might give me something to talk about.
o) This is something I should be concerned about.
p) I always read stories like this, but I don't know why.
q) This information might be useful to me.
r) This looks like good news.
s) I'd like to find out how this happened.
t) I know how that person must feel.

AUDIENCE TYPES

Merrill Samuelson[3] presented sixteen synopses of news stories (of which the news stories in Exercise 1 above are representative) to a sample of readers and asked them (1) to rank the stories in an order of interest (i.e. preference) and (2) to apply to each story one or more of the reasons for reading that are listed in Exercise 2 (above). By factor analyzing these data, he was able to differentiate five different types of readers.

One type (D) had high interest scores on such stories as the Soviet Union's threat to renew bomb testing and very low interest scores on crime stories and the trivia-puzzle type of story such as the one about a farmer making more money selling water than from his eleven oil wells. Moreover, the reasons assigned for the preferences were mainly "This needs explaining," "This may affect me personally," and "This is something I should be concerned about." On the basis of the interest scores and the reasons given, he categorized this type of reader as one who reads mainly for delayed reward.

A second type (A) had high interest scores on many of the same news stories on which Type D readers had high interest scores, but they did not give as many of the same reasons as did the Type D readers. This type of reader, who was more highly educated than the other types, was less involved in the events he preferred to read about than were Type D readers.

[3] "Some Patterns of News Reading." (Paper read at Second Annual Conference of the Pacific Coast Chapter of the American Association for Public Opinion Research, January 27, 1962.)

The interest scores of a third type (B) and the reasons they assigned enabled the experimenter to categorize them as an immediate reward type of reader. This type preferred the stories that were puzzles and which supplied a complete and early solution, such as how a youth could be executed for a shot he did not fire and how a farmer could make more money from selling water than from eleven oil wells. The main reasons this type gave were "This needs explaining," "I'd like to find out how this happened," and "This gives me something to talk about." This type of reader is less concerned with the environment he lives in than are Types D and A, and is less interested in the deferred solutions to the long span problems that are inherent in international politics and social problems.[4]

Readers of a fourth type (E) selected both immediate reward and delayed reward kinds of stories, although they had a low preference for crime stories. The main reasons they gave were "This will help me keep up with what's going on," "This needs explaining," and "I'd like to find out how this happened." The main reasons given for rejecting stories (mostly about crime) were "This is disturbing" and "This is something I should be concerned about."

The preferences, rejections, and reasons of a fifth type (C) did not form a pattern that could be explained by the experimenter.

As research into news reading behavior continues we may learn more about the motivations of different types of readers. As the studies presented in this chapter suggest, the explanations are in the personality structure of the individual reader. Researchers need to develop better personality measures that would be appropriate in this area and to include in their studies more questions than have so far been asked.

> Exercise: *1.* How would you categorize each of the stories in Exercise 1 on page 30—as immediate reward or as delayed reward?
> 2. An editor to whom you have applied for a job asks you to write an explanation of not more than 150 words on why people choose to read a particular news story and reject a particular news story. Write your explanation in the terms used by Schramm (see pp. 27–30).

READING IN A ROLE

Although the news that one selects to read is determined by his basic personality needs and drives and his life history, it is also related to one

[4] Two great British newspaper enterprises were founded at the end of the nineteenth century on the enormous success of two publications whose content was exclusively of the kind which Type B readers preferred. One was George Newnes' *Tit-bits* and the other was Alfred Harmsworth's (Lord Northcliffe's) *Answers*. See H. Herd, *The March of Journalism* (London, 1952), Chap. 12.

or more of his roles in society. As a voter and a taxpayer, the reader is interested in some of the news about government, and newspapers accept an obligation to inform him in that area. As a housewife, a reader is interested in news about prices of consumers' goods. As a parent, a reader is interested in news about education and juvenile delinquency. As an investor, a reader is interested in some of the news about business; most investors are forty or more years old and most are men, although an increasing number of women read business news. As a member of some group, a reader is interested in news about that group and about the matters with which the group is concerned—for example, religion. Most readers have one or more hobbies—for example, sports and bridge—and the newspaper caters to their interests. So many people have some community of interest that specialized magazines are published about the interests; the amount of space that a newspaper can devote to each of these special interests, however, is limited.

The same news story is sometimes read by some persons in one role and by other persons in a different role. An example of such a story: "The United States Supreme Court ruled yesterday that natural gas pipeline companies may use a 'short cut' procedure to increase gas rates without consent of their customers. . . . The decision brought a surge in the price of major natural gas stocks on the New York Stock Exchange." Some readers were interested in this story as consumers of natural gas and some as investors in a natural gas pipeline or local gas distributing company. A wire service which reported this decision tied into the decision the effect on the stock market, and a local newspaper tied in an interview with the local gas distributing company which purchased its gas from a pipeline company. The competent newspaper and wire service editor analyzes every event with the view to supplying answers to questions which will come to the mind of readers who will read in different roles.

SOME DIMENSIONS OF INTEREST

There have been many definitions of news, but none is quite satisfactory. Perhaps as good a definition as any is that of Turner Catledge, executive editor of the *New York Times:* "News is anything you find out today that you didn't know before."[5]

Since, however, a newspaper's capacity for printing news compels it to be selective, an editor needs some kind of guideline or benchmark for estimating what will interest his readers. What he does, therefore, is to look for the presence in each event of certain *elements* which he believes to be interesting. Although he thinks of a story as being about some subject matter, such as crime, labor, or death, he also looks for an additional

[5] Quoted by H. Brucker, *Journalist, Eyewitness* (New York, 1962), pp. 116–17.

dimension which makes the event different from similar events of its class. Sometimes this element is odd, eccentric, or bizarre, but most often it is merely unusual. Some examples:

> A St. Paul man today shot and killed his second wife, 12 years after he killed his first wife.

> Cancer killed bandleader Jimmy Dorsey today, less than seven months after the death of his brother Tommy [also a bandleader].

The first story was a crime story about an obscure retired postal employee. The second story not only had a similar unusual element, but it concerned two persons who were well known. Thus, if we were designing some calculus of reader interest, we would say that the second story has three interest elements: (1) death, (2) well-known person, and (3) singularity.

Well-known Persons

When a participant in an event is well known, the event is more newsworthy than when the participant is not well known. Some persons are prominent because of their high status in society and others because of the frequent exposure of their name or face or voice to newspaper readers or television viewers. Personalities on the television screen, for example, become so familiar to the viewers that the viewers come to feel they know them well.[6] The following Associated Press story was well displayed in a San Francisco newspaper:

> LAKE SUCCESS, N.Y.—Television personality Arlene Francis suffered a brain concussion yesterday when her convertible went out of control on the Northern State Parkway and collided headon with another car. A woman in the second auto was killed. . . .
> Authorities at Harkness Pavilion said she was being treated for a minor concussion, a fracture of the collar bone, a cut on the scalp and bruises. . . .
> Miss Francis is a regular panelist on the TV show, "What's My Line?"

---

[6] See B. Berelson, "What Missing the Newspaper Means," in P. F. Lazarsfeld and F. M. Stanton (eds.), *Communication Research* (1948–49), pp. 120–21. The day after the suicide death of Marilyn Monroe, the circulation of the San Francisco *Examiner* increased 71,000 and of the New York *Journal-American* 160,000.

The points to be noted in the foregoing story are that injuries to the women were of two different orders but that the orders of prominence were reversed. If neither woman had been prominent, regardless of the order of the injuries, the event would have been a "constant."[7]

Proximity

Readers identify easier when events are near to them. If you will reread the last paragraph of Schramm's explanation of the nature of news on page 29, you will observe that he defines proximity as being psychological, not merely physical. An event that happens in our own community has higher news value than an event that happens a considerable distance away. But, as Schramm said, a mother whose son was in military service in the South Pacific would be more interested in a battle in that area than in a fight in an American city. Readers are also interested in events that happen in places in which they have formerly lived or have visited.

An editor whose newspaper is read by most of the people in his community always assumes that the presence of a local element in any story makes it more interesting than a story in which the local element is absent. Thus, a news story about a fatal automobile accident in another community has a higher news value when one of the persons killed was a resident of the editor's community.

Editors also are alert to "local angles" in wire service stories. An example: a wire service reported the explosion in Berlin, New York, of a propane gas tank truck which killed two persons and injured fifteen others. This dispatch generated a "could-this-happen-here?" story in a California suburban newspaper in which local fire marshals and highway patrolmen were quoted as to the California laws which regulate the transportation of propane on highways.

If you should ever work for a wire service, you would learn early in your employment about the importance of the "points" on a wire; a "point" is one of the cities in which a newspaper receives the wire report. Thus, you would include in a story a reference to any person living in any of the communities and any reference to any of the communities. Whenever a wire service correspondent in World War II wrote about some soldier or sailor involved in a military action, he included the name of his city and, when available, his street address.

Other Dimensions of News

Our knowledge of the news value of the two dimensions of interest we have just discussed—well-known persons and proximity—is soundly based in psychological theory. Perhaps psychological theory also tells us something about the interest value of certain other kinds of news, such as news

[7] See p. 38.

about cute children, animals, and money, but we have little objective evidence to support some of the dicta that have been mentioned by textbook writers. Below, however, is a list of about fifty mutually exclusive categories of news elements that were developed for a content analysis, and it might be interesting to speculate about the degrees of interest readers would have in some of them. Only a few are defined here; definitions of the others will be found in the article which reported them.[8] Keep in mind that each news story is likely to have *two or more* of these elements. Thus, a particular news story might be classified as "Our Community/Crime" or "Persons Well Known/Labor." These categories fit only the content of the particular issues of the newspapers which were studied. For an analysis of other newspapers at other times a few of these categories would be dropped and perhaps certain new categories would have to be developed.

Persons Well Known—Persons presumed to be well known to most readers of the particular newspaper because of their fame or notoriety or particular accomplishment.

Persons Not Well Known—Persons in the news because of their particular accomplishments or activities or position, but not well known to the usual reader of the particular newspaper.

People in Groups—Persons in the news because they are officers or committee members of their clubs, lodges, societies, fraternal organizations, Boy Scouts, and other nongovernmental groups; pallbearers, etc.

Hollywood—Persons not otherwise well known who are associated with the Hollywood entertainment industries. Excluded: activities of those persons classified as "Persons Well Known."

Our Community, Our Region—An element with which all members of the newspaper's community (or region) identify themselves because of the place of the community in the news item or the effect this news may have on the community.

Our Nation—An element with which almost all readers of United States newspapers might identify themselves as members of this nation. This does not imply that all events happening within the boundaries of the United States have this element; nor does this element apply only to stories taking place within these boundaries.

Our Allies—During a "cold war" period, some political and economic events in a country formally and informally allied to the United States have a peculiar meaning to an American reader because they are or seem to be related to the security or welfare of the United States. Excluded: news in which American men or equipment are directly involved or in which the United States' interest is *directly* stated (see "Our Nation").

Our Enemies—Most political and economic events in the Communist-controlled nations affect the American reader in a different way than do events in other foreign countries. Such events may be threatening or reassuring.

Other Nations—(*a*) News about happenings in foreign countries other

[8] C. R. Bush, "A System of Categories for General News Content," *Journalism Quarterly*, 37:206–10 (1960).

than those mentioned in "Our Nation," "Our Allies," and "Our Enemies." (*b*) Also those happenings in the countries included in "Our Allies" and "Our Enemies" which do not directly or indirectly affect the welfare of the United States.

Governmental Acts	Social and Safety Measures
Politics	Race Relations
Rebellion	Alcohol
War	Money
Defense	Health, Personal
Atomic Bomb-Atomic Energy	Health, Public
Diplomacy and Foreign Relations	Science and Invention
Economic Activity	Religion
Prices	Philanthropy
Taxes	Weather
Labor, Major	Natural Deaths
Labor, Minor	Transportation
Agriculture	Education
Judicial Proceedings, Civil	Children, Welfare of
Crime	Children, Cute
Communism in the U.S.A.	Animals
Sex	Marriage and Marital Relations
Accidents, Disasters:	Amusements
First order	The Arts, Culture
Second order	Human Interest
Third order	

For class discussion: *1.* Which combinations of two or more elements in a news story would you speculate would generate the highest interest? The lowest?

2. These news stories evoked tremendous reader interest at the time they were published: Lindbergh's flight across the Atlantic, Gertrude Ederle's successful swimming of the English Channel, and Floyd Collins' entrapment in a Kentucky cave. What common element did they have that evoked so much interest?

SOME KINDS OF NEWS

News may be classified in various ways as to origin, subject matter and treatment. Here are a few kinds of news that get published; this list of categories, however, is not exhaustive.

Chronicle

Much of the news is taken from records in public offices and from reports by police and other officials. It is a kind of news that is easy to get: a newspaper just assigns a reporter to the police station, courthouse, city hall, and federal building.

In small cities, nearly all of this kind of news that is available is published, but in large cities only the news that is important or interesting is selected by editors. Much of this kind of news could be called a "constant" because it relates to something the reader has often read before with only the names of the participants being different. Most accidents and crimes are constants. The reaction of readers is often "I'm tired of reading about this" or "I always read stories like this, but I don't know why." Some newspapers publish this kind of news only as a record.

Editors would like to cover a wider range of readers' interests than they do but have not developed an adequate technique for finding out about a different kind of news. It is the practice of London popular newspapers to pay informants for tips about news, but few American newspapers have done that. The Council Bluffs (Iowa) *Nonpareil,* however, developed a list of persons who often supply tips on "off-beat" news sources. Reporters contact them daily, weekly, or monthly. One example: a story that the federal building was tilting and was scheduled to be demolished; the tip came from an architect.

Sometimes it is possible for the news writer to organize the facts in a chronicle type of news story so that reading the story is emotionally rewarding. One way is to organize the facts in a climactic order (as illustrated on pp. 78–80) when the facts justify that form of news story.

Some chronicle type items are highly read. Example: obituaries (discussed in Chap. 12).

Background News

In 1922, Walter Lippmann said it was the nature of news to signalize an event; that is, to report (only) some overt act. News, he said, is "but the report of an aspect that has obtruded itself. The news does not tell you how the seed is germinating in the ground, but it may tell you when the first sprout breaks through the surface."[9] Thus, a labor dispute doesn't get reported until there is an overt act, such as a strike, and most white readers could not have been aware of the frustrations and aspirations of Negroes until the Negroes had conducted public demonstrations of protest.

Since Lippmann wrote in 1922, however, newspapers and wire services have been perceiving news as more than just "spot" news. They are reporting facts that may indicate what is going to happen. They are trying to supply more background about overt events and the people who participate in some of the events, and they try to report change in society. As students of history know, social change is brought about by new technology and new ideas. Editors are now more habituated to perceiving

[9] *Public Opinion,* Chap. 23.

change and the causes of change as something to be reported—what James B. Reston has called the reporting of "quiet revolutions." Newspapers also are reporting changes in manners and morals.

> For class discussion: *1.* What is your evaluation of this statement: "Because of the excellence of our newspapers and magazines Americans are the best informed people in the world"?
> *2.* A competent foreign correspondent who is a Latin America specialist has said that most American editors were surprised by the success of the Castro revolution in Cuba because, instead of publishing the "what's behind the news" kind of news they had been receiving from Cuba, they substituted the more dramatic "spot" stories received from Cuba and other parts of the world. If this is true, whose fault was it?

"Give a Lift" News

Since newspapers report so much news about conflict, most editors would like to report more news about people who exhibit courage, sacrifice, and compassion—news (to paraphrase William Faulkner) which suggests to readers that man's spirit will endure and prevail over the basic animal drives. Such news gives the reader a "lift" spiritually and suggests to him that we do not live in a jungle world.[10] Here are two examples of such local news stories that the Associated Press thought were worthy of being included in its daily report; the stories were widely used by newspapers.

Christians Help To Remodel Synagogue

LAWRENCE, KAN.—Somewhat to the surprise of the 35 Jewish families in Lawrence and about 80 Jewish students at the University of Kansas, a quiet campaign is going on to raise funds for remodeling the Jewish community center into a synagogue.

"We did not know about it; we did not organize it," said Herman Cohen, president of the community center.

Who did? Some Christians. One of them, O. O. Ringler, explained the project was started because the Jews are the only religious group in Law-

---

[10] Newspapers do not publish as much news about conflict as many people suspect. See E. R. Cony, "Conflict-Cooperation Content of Five American Dailies," *Journalism Quarterly,* 37:206–10 (1960).

rence with no place to worship. The closest synagogues are in Kansas City and Topeka.

"It gives a person a wonderful feeling to have something like this happen," said Cohen. "It is a fine thing to have others trying to help us."

Know Anybody Salvation Army Has Helped?

KINGSPORT, TENN.—The newsboy kept walking past the Salvation Army Christmas collection kettle. Each trip he dropped in two cents.

An Exchange Club member, helping man the kettle station, finally figured it out. The 9-year-old lad was donating his two cents profit from each paper sale.

Just to be sure, the clubman went up and purchased a paper and gave the boy a nickel tip. A few minutes later the lad was back at the kettle. This time he dropped in seven cents.

"Do you know anybody the Salvation Army has helped?" a club member asked the newsboy.

"Yes, sir. We got a Christmas basket last year," the boy replied.

Wednesday, the Exchange Club had the newsboy as its special guest at a luncheon. He left with a new bicycle, wearing a new jacket, and with a savings account book showing more than $60 on deposit for his future education.

He was introduced only as Gary. The club said it wanted to publicize the deed rather than the boy and his family.

Salvation Army records showed that Gary is one of five children, aged 2 to 13. The parents have worked irregularly this year with the top income for one month about $57.

Gary's third-grade teacher said he almost never misses a day of school and often shares what he has with some youngster less fortunate than he.

HOW, WHEN, AND WHERE THE NEWSPAPER IS READ

The newspaper, like the telephone and the automatic washer, is a utility. How, when, and where is it used? A 1961 study[11] has supplied some answers to these questions. The study revealed that readers use their newspapers in these ways:

50.4%	Proceed through most of the paper one page after another and read whatever is interesting;
14.2%	Proceed through the paper page by page, but scanning quickly;
20.0%	Turn first to some specific item (e.g., the stock market tables or a particular column) and then proceed through the paper one page after another;
12.6%	Turn first to some specific item and then proceed page by page, but scanning quickly;
2.8%	Turn to a specific item but do not look at or read anything else.

These findings indicate not only that the newspaper is read rather thoroughly but also that a large majority of readers expose themselves to a synopsis, at least, of everything in the newspaper. This fact explains why some readership studies have turned up news stories on the inside pages which have had higher readership than any story on the front page. The findings are confirmed by the "reader traffic" data obtained from several hundred readership studies: a large majority of readers go clear through the paper; whether they read or do not read something on each page depends upon what is on the pages and the interests of the individual readers. Some readers scan but do not read anything on some pages; for example, some men are not interested in the content of women's pages. The amount of newspaper content that each reader reads is determined by (1) his needs and interests and (2) the amount of time available to him.

Mental Set

The reader has a different mental set when he reads a newspaper and when he reads a book or magazine. "Reading a book," says Irving Kristol,[12] "is quite a different experience from reading a magazine. The original commitment by the reader is much more substantial. . . . Picking up a book is . . . an affirmation of more serious purpose." There is also some difference in original commitment in reading a newspaper and reading a news magazine because they are read under different conditions.

> For class discussion: Considering the fact (*a*) that the newspaper reader has a different original commitment when he reads opinion

[11] Newsprint Information Committee, *A National Study of Newspaper Reading* (1961), Vol. II, p. 17.
[12] "Confessions of a Publisher," *New Leader*, May 13, 1963, p. 17.

and when he reads news and (*b*) that most readers (see p. 41) go through the newspaper page by page selecting to read those items that interest them, what is the proper location in the newspaper for the editorial-opinion page?

Ninety per cent of readers of a weekday newspaper read it at home, 6 per cent at work, 3 per cent when visiting, and about 2 per cent on their way to or from work.[13] This is a national average; it would not apply, for example, in New York city, where fewer newspapers are home delivered.

The average weekday newspaper is read at different times of the day. It is picked up and looked at 2.4 different times by each individual reader.[14] The study which reported this finding also reported that the average reader spent 36 minutes a day reading his newspaper; this is a self-estimate and is about the same self-estimate reported in previous studies.[15]

The editor tries to produce a newspaper that will maximize the time a reader will devote to it. Nevertheless, the amount of time that a reader allocates to newspaper reading is determined, to some extent, by the reader's individual living habits, such as the time he or she gets up in the morning, the time the children leave for school, the time the housewife does her marketing, and several other reasons.

The following table[16] shows when people read a newspaper, listen to news on the radio, and watch television news:

	Read Newspaper	Listen to Radio News	Watch TV News
Early morning	16%	25%	3%
Late morning	12	8	1
Midday	1	18	1
Early afternoon	7	5	3
Late afternoon	21	9	3
Early evening	20	12	17
Late evening	8	5	17
Other, not specified	2	3	0
	87%*	85%*	45%*

* Since multiple answers were frequent, the sum of all three columns is more than 100 per cent.

The table indicates that more people listen to news on the radio before nine o'clock in the morning than read a newspaper before that time. It also indicates that fewer people get their news from television than from the newspaper or radio. When respondents in this sample were asked, "Where do you usually get the news of the day first?" their answers were: radio, 52 per cent; newspapers, 28 per cent; television, 17 per cent; "can't say," 3 per cent.

[13] Newsprint Information Committee, *op. cit.*, Vol. II, p. 19.
[14] *Ibid.*, Vol. II, p. 15.
[15] *Ibid.*, Vol. II, p. 18.
[16] American Institute of Public Opinion (Gallup), *The Public Appraises the Newspaper: 1958* (Princeton, N.J., 1958), p. 12.

CHAPTER 4

The Lead

The beginning of the news story is called the *lead* or *intro*. For many years the beginning was a formless, rambling sentence or combination of sentences that led up to the account of the event. Here is an example from the report of a national political convention:

> This, the last day of the Republican jubilee, dawned as bright as the prospects of the great party of freedom, and remained throughout one of those days of brilliant sunshine which are set at long intervals as are diadems in the early Summer. As on the previous day, the streets were crowded at an early hour with surging crowds. . . .[1]

THE SUMMARY LEAD

Some time after the Civil War a definite form developed which summarized the what, who, when, and where of the reported event.

It has been stated that the summary form of lead originated during the Civil War; that, because of the unreliability of the telegraphic services, some war reporters adopted the procedure of reporting a battle by sending a brief summary followed by a detailed elaboration. Their reasoning was that the summary would reach the newspaper speedily even though the more lengthy "body" of the story might be delayed.[2]

We find the summary lead being used in the eighteen-eighties, first by wire services and later by local reporters. This way of reporting news had a particular advantage, in the opinion of Melville E. Stone, the first general manager of the Associated Press: it virtually assured objectivity in reporting because it restricted the writer to the what-who-when-where formula. Since the Associated Press supplied news reports to newspapers supporting both political parties, Mr. Stone believed the Associated Press should estab-

---

[1] The *New York Times*, June 7, 1872. Quoted in F. L. Mott, *American Journalism* (3d ed.), p. 496.

[2] J. Tebbel, *The Compact History of the American Newspaper* (New York, 1963), pp. 121–22.

43

lish a reputation for reliable factual reporting even though some inherently interesting events had to be reported in a colorless manner. This form also permitted a newspaper to eliminate all or a part of the *body* of an Associated Press dispatch.

The advent of the spoken radio newscast influenced newspapers to abandon the practice of having a summary lead for all news stories. Summary leads are still used for most routine news stories, but news writers now often write in the way that people talk. If a person talked in the way that some summary leads are written, he would sound as if he was out of breath. The comprehension of the reader of a long lead is about the same as the comprehension of a listener to such a lead. A listener, in most circumstances, has the opportunity of interrupting a speaker with questions and of asking him to repeat all or a part of his narrative. Since a newspaper reader cannot employ this "feedback" he must regress in his reading. This is frustrating, and it sometimes causes the reader to abandon his reading of a news story just as he would turn the dial on his radio. His reward from reading under such conditions does not justify his effort.

LENGTH OF THE LEAD SENTENCE

It is important for comprehension that the first *sentence* of the news story be fairly short. An easily comprehensible sentence has the effect of drawing the reader into the story—of inducing him to continue reading. The average number of words in the first sentence of the Associated Press A-wire report is 23 words. Since the Associated Press makes a strong effort to achieve ease of reading, this score may be regarded as a suitable par for the local news writer.

The writer should summarize as much as possible in the first sentence without letting it be too long. In some instances he has to sacrifice brevity to include a key fact, but he should try for brevity. The way he achieves this goal is by *distributing* some of the *W*s in the first two or three sentences instead of including all of them in the first sentence. Here are two ways of reporting the filing of a damage suit:

> Irving Loring, 40, of 268 Brucker street, a passenger in a sports convertible that toppled off a Shoreline highway cliff last March 24, filed a $200,000 damage suit in superior court yesterday against the driver, Walter Patterson.
>
> Loring, a credit manager for a wholesale liquor company, alleges that Patterson, 22, of Piedmont, drove the car at a "wanton and reckless rate of

speed" and was under the influence of intoxicants at the time the car went off the cliff.

Loring says he suffered severe face and skull injuries that required 140 stitches.

As rewritten:

What	A passenger in a car that toppled off a Shoreline highway cliff last
When	March 24 sued the driver yesterday for $200,000 damages.
Who	Irving Loring, of 268 Brucker street, a credit manager for a wholesale
Why	liquor company, alleged his facial and skull injuries required 140 stitches.
Where	In a complaint filed in superior court, he charged that the driver,
Who	Walter Patterson, 22, of Piedmont, was under the influence of intoxicants.
Why	He also alleged that Patterson was driving at a "wanton and reckless rate of speed."

The second version of this report is more easily comprehended because (1) the number of words in the first sentence is only 19 instead of the 33 words in the first version, and (2) most of the *W*s are distributed through the first three paragraphs. Since the names of the principals are not well known, they are referred to as "passenger" and "driver" in the first sentence so that the reader understands the "what" without having to think about who they are while he is reading the first sentence. He may continue reading to find out whether or not the principals are persons he knows or has heard about. The first sentence in the second version also corresponds more closely to the way one person would tell another person about the event.

Exercise: Rewrite this lead: "An early transfer of between 200 and 300 flights daily from the traffic jam at Chicago's O'Hare International Airport to Midway Airport on the southside was recommended yesterday by John E. Egan, former alderman from the Midway ward [13th] and for 17 years chairman of the city council aviation committee. Egan now is a sanitary district trustee."

PURPOSES OF THE LEAD

The lead has three objectives. Whether a writer tries to achieve all three of them or only one or two depends upon the character of the event. The objectives are (1) to tell the gist, or substance, of the event, (2) to draw the reader into the story, and (3) to cause the reader to *see* the event.

STATING THE SUBSTANCE OF THE EVENT

Before a reporter writes or dictates a story he decides which aspect of the event to put in the lead. This decision is sometimes called "playing the feature" or "playing up the angle."

When the action reported has been completed it is often possible for the lead to be a single sentence.

> A juror in a burglary trial was himself arrested yesterday.

> A new way of producing atomic energy without either uranium or million-degree heat was announced today.

> "Go ahead and smoke—moderately" is the recommendation of Dr. William A. Reinhoff, noted Baltimore surgeon, who discounts the idea that smoking causes lung cancer.

Multiple "Whats"

In some events the news writer perceives two aspects to feature. The second of these is an aspect that adds interest to the report.

> A laborer was sentenced yesterday to pay a $150 fine for stealing three chunks of copper worth $65 from a University laboratory.

> The State of New Jersey, which spent $1,200,000 to capture and convict Bruno Richard Hauptmann, executed him tonight with a penny's worth of electricity.

Some "whats" are so routine that they are barely newsworthy, but some circumstance, when added, may enhance interest in the report. An example: a woman sued an automobile driver for injuries she received when she dashed into the street to rescue her small son from the path of the car. She lost her suit for damages.[3] One reporter wrote the lead this way:

[3] For an explanation see p. 204.

> A verdict in favor of Samuel Howell, charged with negligence when his automobile struck Mrs. Nancy Farlow, was brought in by a circuit court jury yesterday.

Another reporter's lead was:

> A mother, who was injured while trying to save her 4-year-old son from the path of an automobile, was denied damages by a circuit court jury yesterday.

Not a great many readers of the first version would continue after reading the lead sentence unless they knew one of the principals. But a very large number of readers would continue reading the second version to get an answer to the "why."

Here is an example of a news story that left out of the lead an essential part of the "what":

> A Jonesboro man today sued the Universal Oil Co. and its employee, Ira Thompson, for injuries received in an automobile accident last November 6.
> The complaint, asking $10,000 damages, was filed in circuit court by Madison Wilson. He alleges Thompson was driving the company's car.

What is the "what"? Was this an accident in which two cars collided? Since it was not that kind of accident, the writer had to write a third paragraph to tell all of the "what." A better lead would have been:

> A Jonesboro *pedestrian* sued the Universal Oil Co. and its employee, Ira Thompson, today for $10,000.
> Madison Wilson filed the complaint in circuit court alleging he was struck by a company car driven by Thompson last November 6.

The second version is seven lines shorter than the first version. Since the key word "pedestrian" was the second word in the lead sentence the reader knew at once the nature of the event.

The *effect* of an action or an event is sometimes the principal "what" in a lead.

> Hundreds of thousands of New Yorkers went thirsty and unwashed today in a large part of downtown Manhattan as the result of a break in an important water main.

> Local residents will find a 10 per cent reduction in their electric bills beginning March 1.
> The City Council last night approved the reduction, which will mean a saving of about 60 cents a month to the average householder.

Two related matters are sometimes combined in a lead, which is sometimes called a "one-two" lead.

> Hand to hand battling broke out on the waterfront today while Mayor Harvey Moss mapped action to halt further strike violence.

> WASHINGTON—House Democrats yesterday pushed through with little trouble an administration proposal to provide federal aid to medical schools. But Republican delaying tactics in debating the medical bill may have blocked a House vote this week on the administration's feed grains program. . . .
> Republicans wanted to bottle up the feed grains proposal for about a month so they would be in a better position to attack the administration's plan for tight controls on wheat marketing, which the nation's farmers will vote on in a May 21 referendum.

For class discussion: Do you approve or disapprove of this lead?

> LAS VEGAS—The biggest blast of the new atomic test series flashed forks of light visible in a dozen states today, caused an earth rumble 360 miles away and sent scientists and soldiers scurrying for safety from the Nevada test site.

The "what" plus "why" lead: The *cause* of the event reported is sometimes an element in the lead and is combined with the "what."

> PRINCETON, N.J.—A loose safety belt was the instrument of death for a New York man who died today from car crash injuries.

> A spark from a worker's spray gun touched off a $500,000 fire that destroyed the Lutz Ford sales agency yesterday.

> A Kentfield clerk's car stalled with a flat tire on the Greenbrae bridge at 7 a.m. yesterday—and as a result four other vehicles were involved in a crash that sent one car through the bridge rail and into the mudflats 30 feet below.
> Two men were hospitalized.

> A 14-year-old Mountain View boy, whose mother once told the police she "doesn't have time" to watch over him, was jailed today on suspicion of raping a 4-year-old girl and setting a spectacular residence fire 10 days ago.

The contrast lead: Some leads combine the "what" with an *antithetic* element to make the story more meaningful or more newsworthy. In this example the "what" is contrasted with an historical fact:

> DETROIT—Auto engineers, who for years have concentrated on boosting the horsepower under the hood, now are checking the stopping power under the brake pedal.

In the following example the antithetic element generates surprise and causes the reader to continue reading to learn the "why":

> A bank president was arrested for a half-million dollar manipulation today, and townspeople rushed to the bank—not to withdraw but to deposit.

Exercise: Write a news story based on the following facts. Also write a two-line headline, any count. This is mainly a test of your ability to select the most interesting aspect of the event. The critical part of your story is the lead.

Pedro Lopez, alias Peter De Lucci, age 34, entered the home of J. F. Foderer, 1548 Howard street, on January 19 (according to his own testimony) at about 5:20 p.m., and stole a radio and some jewelry. He aided the police in recovering the loot. His attorney was Percy Jackson and the assistant district attorney was L. D. Matteis. Lopez was born in Puerto Rico. He had served two terms in San Quentin reformatory.

Burglary after sunset constitutes first degree burglary. Second degree burglary is burglary during daylight. Lopez was tried yesterday in superior court presided over by Judge Aylett Cotton. If he had been convicted of first degree burglary, he would automatically, under the statutes, have been a third offender, and his sentence would have been 12 years to life. Second degree burglary carries a sentence of one to five years. Judge Cotton ruled that Lopez committed the burglary in daylight although the prosecutor conjectured that Lopez would certainly have been seen carrying away property in daylight. Sunset, it was stipulated in the evidence, was 5:42 o'clock. The defendant was convicted of second degree burglary and sentenced to San Quentin for one to five years.

In the type of news story which reports changes, innovations, and developments in society, industry, education, and other spheres of life, the best lead is often one of the *concrete* instances or examples of the matter being reported.[4] The beginning of such a news story also, as a rule, presents a scene or a person doing some act or talking.

LUBBOCK, Texas—Thousands of white-faced cattle, with round, sad eyes and unsophisticated tastes nose about in long troughs filled with a green, flaky concoction.

Nearby, workmen are finishing off a new 25,000 square-foot meat-packing plant scheduled to begin handling 400 head of cattle a day next month.

"We can do as good a cattle feeding job here as anybody in the Corn Belt—and do it cheaper," boasts sport-shirted Durward W. Lewter, part owner of Lewter, Inc.'s feed lot and packing plant here.

"We have our choice of the best cattle here. We're in the heart of the grain sorghum area with its cheap feed. And right at hand is the cotton that supplies us with the meal and hulls for feed supplements."

A Change on the Range

Mr. Lewter's words sum up some of the reasons for a quiet but signifi-

---

[4] See pp. 38–39.

cant change taking place today on the western range lands—a change that already is having an economic impact in these parts and one that's likely to have increasingly-wide repercussions on traditional patterns of raising and marketing beef cattle. . . .

Historically, cattlemen in the range lands stretching through New Mexico, west Texas, Oklahoma, western Kansas and Colorado have shipped most of their herds to other areas, principally the Midwest, for fattening on corn before they were sent to market. . . . (*Wall Street Journal*.)

DRAWING THE READER INTO THE STORY

There are several ways of writing the lead sentence that induce the reader to continue his reading. One of them was mentioned before,[5] viz., generating surprise by adding an antithetic element to cause the reader to learn the "why." A somewhat similar device is the *question* lead. It prepares the reader to make a response in somewhat the way he is prepared to respond when personally addressed in a face-to-face relationship.

Who should pay for the proposed addition to the Community Hospital—patients who would pay higher room charges or city taxpayers?

The City Council will discuss this question tonight after it has received a report from a citizens' committee.

A lead which is a *direct address* to the reader—a "you" lead—is also calculated to induce the reader to continue reading because it involves him to some degree.

If you've recently had a baby, bought a car, or moved, chances are your name is for sale.

It's worth from a penny to a dollar in the expanding market for mailing lists of people with special interests or needs.

Such lists are purchased by advertisers from firms that cull names and addresses of potential customers from public records, newspapers, subscription rolls and other sources. . . .

[5] P. 49.

The quote lead: Beginning the story with a quotation is, in most instances, disapproved. The reason is that readers are mainly interested in action, not talk. Quotation may repel the reader instead of drawing him into the story. In some circumstances, however, a quotation can draw the reader into the story when the quotation is very brief. One instance is when it is a part of the gist of the story.

> "Under no conditions."
> That was Governor Cox's answer yesterday when asked whether he might change his mind and accept the Republican nomination for Vice President.

A quote lead is sometimes a good way to introduce a personal experience story.

> "My fingers were raw. We figured that if we could hang on, by morning, someone would find us."

> "I kept hold trigger till no noise. Then saw blood."
> So Takao Phillyaw, a Japanese-born widow, explained how she killed her husband's cousin at her east side apartment last night.

When there is no other way to put people into a dull story a quote lead may draw the reader into the story. Reports of meetings of the city council, the planning commission, and the school board are often reported without a single name's being mentioned. The news story reports only the actions taken, and the actions relate only to inanimate objects and abstract matters such as proposals, plans, and taxes. The reader is not able to visualize the proceedings. Here are two versions of a report of a planning commission meeting; the main difference is that a single quotation in the body of the first story has been transposed to the lead in the second.

80-Foot Dome Shopping Center Plan Put Off

Action on a proposed hemispherical, 80-foot high, $550,000 shopping center for Alto was postponed yesterday by the County Planning Commis-

"Isn't anyone objecting to the height of the building?" asked County Planning Commissioner Felix M. Warburg yesterday.

sion pending notification of nearby residents of the height of the building.

Samuel Nelder, Tiburon Peninsula property owner, had requested a use permit and architectural supervision for the shopping center on eight acres on both sides of Belvedere drive between Reed boulevard and Highway 101.

Architect John S. Bolles has planned an 80-foot high "geodesic dome" of aluminum.

"Isn't anyone objecting to the height of the building?" asked Commissioner Felix M. Warburg.

R. D. Dobbs, principal planner, explained that the height was not mentioned in the notice to property owners.

Planning Director Mary Summers pointed out that a county ordinance limits buildings to 45 feet in height unless a variance is granted.

The commission was considering Samuel Nelder's application for a use permit and architectural supervision for construction of a 80-foot high "geodesic dome" of aluminum for his $550,000, eight-acre shopping center.

The commission decided to postpone action pending notification of nearby residents about the proposed height.

The dome was recommended by architect John S. Boles. The property is on both sides of Belvedere drive between Reed boulevard and Highway 101.

R. D. Dobbs, principal planner, explained that the height was not mentioned in the notice to property owners.

Planning Director Mary Summers pointed out that a county ordinance limits buildings to 45 feet in height unless a variance is granted.

For class discussion: Which version of the foregoing news story do you prefer, considering that the action taken by the commission was reported in the third paragraph of the second version?

There tends to be an overuse of quotation *marks* in both the lead and the body of news stories. Words and expressions carry unnecessary quotation marks.

> The Governor today characterized as "inaccurate" the legislative counsel's report on dividend tax withholding.

The main purposes of quotation marks in the lead are to indicate exact language, to set off an obvious error, a nickname, and a slang expression.

Conversion of a lengthy quotation in the lead to indirect quotation often facilitates comprehension.

This lead was written from a "handout":

> DETROIT—The United Auto Workers Union today announced a new collective bargaining program for next year, which, it said, "features a division of profits above ten per cent on net capital before taxes between the corporate executives and the stockholders; the workers and consumers."

As rewritten:

> DETROIT—The United Auto Workers Union today called for a profit-sharing plan in next year's wage contracts, and postponed demands for a shorter work week.

Some Pitfalls

A few statements may be made about what to avoid in writing the lead.

1. *Avoid the say-nothing lead.*

> Stanford University research scientists announced today they have uncovered surprising new information about the neutron, one of the small particles which make up the atom.

As rewritten:

> Stanford University scientists plucked a secret from the heart of the atom today. They found a way to measure the size of neutrons—a key that may open doors to other mysteries of the atom age.

An empty lead sometimes results from the writer's abortive effort to introduce some kind of image into his reporting of a fact.

> With aplomb despite a hair-disarranging wind, Mrs. Lyndon B. Johnson christened an 11,000 ton ship today. But because of the weather, the big cargoliner had to stay where it was.

A former editor of the London *Daily Express* wrote in his memoirs:

> I saw the MS. of a reporter's story about Mr. Churchill's meeting at Woodford last night. It opened with an amusing incident about the electric lights failing. But, of course, it was a most important speech and the introductory angle was wrong. In fact, it sacrificed the substance for the shadow. It was rather like saying "Nibbling an olive and holding a glass of vodka in his hand, Stalin declared war on Britain last night."[6]

2. *Avoid the cluttered lead.* Too many names and too many facts are sometimes crammed into the lead sentence. This can be avoided by dis-

---

[6] Arthur Christiansen, *Headlines All My Life* (London, 1961), p. 164.

tributing some of the names and some of the modifiers of the essential elements in succeeding sentences and paragraphs.[7] One idea in the lead sentence is about all the reader can comprehend easily. Nevertheless, necessary qualifications that are omitted result in an overgeneralization that can mislead the reader.

> Charles F. Noyes Co., Inc., through Herbert C. Born, vice president, in a $350,000 transaction, has leased for Emily S. Goyer to Ninth Federal Savings and Loan Assn. of New York City, one of the largest in the nation, with its main offices at Broadway and 42nd street, the property at the northwest corner of First avenue and 45th street, directly opposite the United Nations development, a plot of 4,800 square feet, fronting 40 feet on First avenue, and 100 feet on 45th street, for a long term of years with options of renewal, on which the buildings are being demolished, as a location for its first branch office.

Exercise: The foregoing news story is an unedited handout that was published in the real estate section of a New York newspaper. Rewrite it for an *average* sentence length of 21–25 words.

A second example which was not a handout:

> The Bridges trial jury was excused over the Thanksgiving week-end today as defense counsel Vincent Hallinan, supposedly chastised by a six-month's contempt sentence, nevertheless raised a dispute over prior Communist hearings that provoked a day of argument.

Overstuffing the lead sentence may often be avoided by making two sentences of the lead paragraph.

> A 21-year-old reformatory parolee, who said he wanted to "point up inequalities of the parole system," set fire to a newspaper pressroom and fired a shotgun blast in a radio station last night.

---

[7] An example is on p. 45.

As rewritten:

> A youth on parole from a reformatory set fire to a newspaper pressroom and invaded a radio station with a shotgun last night.
> He said he wanted to "point up inequalities in the parole system."

3. *The lead sentence should not present a false tone for the news story.* The lead sentence is a lens through which the reader looks at the rest of the story. A frivolous lead sentence, for example, is inappropriate to serious subject matter. The following sentence began a story for which the lead was appropriate; it signals the reader that the event is humorous.

> An optimist attempted to cram himself and a tuba he was carrying aboard one of New York's jammed subway trains today. He didn't make it. He should have taken up the piccolo.

If the man with the tuba had been killed or injured, the lead would have been inappropriate.

HELPING THE READER TO SEE THE EVENT

The reading of a news report, unlike viewing some television news shows, is often two or three degrees removed from reality. The police reporter, for example, gets most of his facts from policemen who have gotten them from eyewitnesses and participants. The reporter translates the words he has heard into written words. The written words are symbols of spoken words. The reader, in consequence, reads only the symbols.[8]

An appropriate choice of words can enhance vividness. But the news writer, with respect to some events, may also enhance vividness by reconstructing the event for the reader in one or more sentences in the lead. He adds the dimension of visualization.

> A school bus carrying an estimated 38 children struck a wrecker, sideswiped an automobile, then plunged

---

[8] See G. D. Wiebe, "A New Dimension in Journalism," *Journalism Quarterly*, 31:411–20 (1954). This article reports a study which compares the learning of newspaper readers and television viewers of an important event. See also C. W. Morris, *Signs, Language and Behavior* (New York, 1946), Chaps. 2 and 4.

into the Levisa fork of the Big Sandy river today.

A construction dredge, under tow in wind-whipped Lake Michigan, early today dipped under high waves and plunged to the bottom, taking the lives of eight of the 18 men aboard.

A driverless butane gas truck, belching flame, struck a mailbox Friday and headed straight down a sidewalk into the front door of the Hillcrest Haven rest home, killing three elderly patients.

NEW YORK—The crowded Lockheed Electra crashed into a dike, flipped on its back and plunged, blazing, 500 feet along a swamp. Seventy-six passengers and crewmen hung head downward, pinned in their upside-down seats by safety belts as flames closed in on the cabin.

But not a life was lost today when American Airlines' Electra Flight 361 crashed at the end of a runway at New York's LaGuardia airport.

In some instances, it is better to make the lead sentence longer by adding a few words than to strive merely for brevity. This is justifiable because the headline has already reported the substance of the event and that information has been stored in the mind of the reader before he started to read the lead. In the fourth lead quoted above one newspaper's headline was "AIRLINER CRASHES, BURNS; ALL 76 ABOARD SAFE" and a four-column picture showed the upside-down plane. Another example:

FORT WORTH, Texas—An angry mob yelling "get those niggers" tonight hung an effigy of a Negro from a tree in the front yard of a Negro barricaded in his home.

Here are two ways of reporting a certain kind of event. The writer of one of the stories, however, had an advantage over the second writer because he wrote the story for the succeeding news cycle and had more time for both writing and for obtaining one or two additional facts.

Police Tumble
In Trap, 1 Dies

HOLLYWOOD—A police detective was shot to death Sunday when he and his companion were kidnaped on Hollywood boulevard and forced to drive two ex-convicts 60 miles.

One suspect, Gregory Powell, 20, of Boulder City, Nev., was captured. An all-points bulletin was issued for Jimmy Lee Smith, 22, whose last known address was Bakersfield, Calif.

Detective Ian Campbell, 30, of Chatsworth, Calif., was shot to death two miles southwest of the small community of Mettler, near Bakersfield. He was married and the father of two children.

"Campbell was ordered out of the car and apparently shot on the spot," said Officer Howard Wines, of the Bakersfield sheriff's office.

"He was shot once in the face and four times in the chest," Wines said.

When Campbell was shot his companion, Detective Carl Hettinger, escaped. The suspects fired at Hettinger but missed. He ran about three miles to a farmhouse and called the sheriff's office.

Hettinger told officers he and Campbell stopped the two suspects at Hollywood boulevard and Gower street for routine questioning. When they approached the car, one of the men pulled a .32 caliber automatic and ordered the officers to get in the car and drive toward Bakersfield.

Hettinger said the men began talking about California's "Little Lindbergh law" which provides a death penalty for kidnaping. Then they stopped the car and ordered the officers out.

After the shooting, said Wines, Smith sped away in the kidnap car.

The two men split up and Powell was arrested shortly afterward in another stolen car. Campbell's briefcase, Hettinger's flashlight and an automatic were discovered in Powell's vehicle.

Smith stole still another vehicle

HOLLYWOOD—Two policemen stood in a lonely moonlit field 75 miles north of their home base with their hands in the air. Two former convicts faced them, holding guns.

One of the gunmen asked Officer Ian James Campbell, 31, married and the father of two little girls, a question. Campbell answered, "Yes"—and the ex-convict shot him in the mouth.

Suddenly a cloud passed over the moon. Officer Karl Hettinger, 28, whirled and ran in the darkness. The gunmen fired but missed him.

Hettinger crashed through a barbed-wire fence and hid in brush while the ex-convicts pumped four more shots into Campbell, killing him.

Then they came after Hettinger in their car. The fence blocked them and they fled.

Hettinger ran four miles to a farmhouse and called local authorities. He told this story:

Campbell and Hettinger, both in plain clothes, stopped a suspect's car about 10 p.m. Saturday in downtown Hollywood. Its rear license plate light was off and the car matched the description of one used in several holdups.

Two suspects, later identified as Gregory Ulas Powell, 29, and Jimmy Lee Smith, 32, jumped from the car. One pointed a .32 caliber revolver at Campbell.

"I could have shot the other suspect," said Hettinger, "but Campbell would have been shot."

The men took the officers' guns and forced them into their old car with Campbell driving and Hettinger in the back seat. The suspects made the officers take them northward on heavily traveled U.S. 99, the main inland north-south route.

Near Mettler Station, 25 miles south of Bakersfield, the plain-clothes men were ordered out into a field.

Powell asked Campbell, "Have you ever heard of the little Lindbergh from the Clifford Mettler ranch after abandoning the kidnap car near Lamont, Calif. Two .38 caliber revolvers were found in the vehicle. Sheriff's deputies said it was believed Smith stole a small sports car and fled the scene.

Bakersfield sheriff's deputies said Powell admitted his part in the kidnaping.

law?" When Campbell said "yes," Powell shot him.

The kidnapers referred to a California law which provides the death penalty for kidnaping that involves harm to the victim.

That's when Hettinger made his move.

"At the first shot the moon was shining brightly," he said. "Suddenly it was covered by a cloud, and I guess they couldn't see me very well.

"I zigzagged across the plowed ground and crashed right through a barbed-wire fence. Then I hid. I crouched down in some tumbleweeds and I could see their headlights when they came looking for me. Finally they gave up."

At 1:50 a.m. Sunday, California Highway patrol officers spotted a stolen car 16 miles south of Bakersfield on U.S. 99. They pulled it over.

Powell was alone in it.

"He didn't try to resist," said the officers. "He seemed pretty calm until we noticed a gun and a flashlight that said 'Hettinger—LAPD.' Then he started shaking all over."

Powell was arrested on suspicion of murder and jailed in Los Angeles. Police said he admitted the kidnaping but claimed—contrary to Hettinger's account—that his partner did the shooting. Powell, of Boulder City, Nev., has a stolen auto and escape record.

Smith was arrested about 10 hours later in a rooming rouse in Bakersfield. The arresting officers said he offered no resistance.

Smith has a record of burglary and narcotics convictions.

For class discussion: Which of the following leads do you prefer?

WASHINGTON—The good looking young man in the sharp pink shirt carefully picked up one end of the small wire and deftly plugged it in the proper hole of the complicated board in front of him.

Cameras clicked, big shots in the Veterans Administration beamed, reporters took notes.

WASHINGTON—Robert L. Smith, a quadruple amputee who "got tired of sitting around and doing nothing," started work today as a tabulating machine operator for the veterans administration.

Despite the fact that he has hooks where other technicians have hands, the young Korean

For Robert L. Smith, a Korean War veteran without hands or feet, was showing a news conference today how he goes about his new job as a tabulating machine operator for the Veterans Administration.

War veteran from Middleburg, Pa., was assigned to wire panel controls for the intricate electronic equipment.

He explained that he wanted to prove to himself and others that he could earn a living in spite of his handicap.

THE SYNTAX OF THE LEAD SENTENCE

The lead sentence, generally, should be in the *normal sentence order*. The normal sentence order is (1) the subject, (2) the finite verb, and (3 or 4) indirect object or direct object. Thus: (1) Stanford University scientists (2) plucked (3) a secret (4) from the heart of the atom.

Of the sixty lead sentences quoted in this chapter, all but four are written in the normal sentence order. One sentence begins with a conditional clause ("If you've recently had a baby . . . ," p. 51); one is an interrogatory sentence (p. 51); one is an ellipsis with the normal sentence order implied ("Under no conditions . . . ," p. 52); and one begins with an adverbial clause modifier ("With aplomb . . . ," p. 54).

The subject of the lead sentence is usually the "who" ("A passenger in a car . . . ," p. 45) or the "what" ("A verdict in favor of Samuel Howell . . . ," p. 47). It is nearly always easier to write a lead sentence in the normal sentence order because the modifiers tend to fall into their normal places automatically. Moreover, since the normal sentence order is *fixed* in the English language by our habits of speech, a sentence in the normal order facilitates the reader's comprehension.

The writer should deviate from the normal sentence order only when he wishes to *emphasize* a sentence element other than the subject. The beginning of the sentence and the end of the sentence are the emphatic parts. When, therefore, the writer wishes to emphasize the *time* aspect of the event—the "when"—he begins with the time.

Five minutes before the legal deadline, Mayor George Wilson today filed for reelection.

Six days before he was scheduled to retire on a pension, an Air Force officer was given a dishonorable discharge from the service today.

There is no justification, however, for this kind of lead:

Meeting at noon today, the Rotary Club heard Governor Morris defend his tax program.

You may already have noticed in the leads that have been quoted in this chapter that "today" and "yesterday" were nearly always "buried" inside the sentence. The "when" aspect of the event is seldom important or interesting. In some news stories the "when" is reported as far down in the story as the fourth or fifth paragraph, so that the reader can concentrate on the more important or more interesting aspects.

To stress immediacy, newspapers and wire services "update" the lead of a news story for the succeeding news cycle (called a *second-day lead*); for example, they change the lead in an afternoon newspaper of a news story that was first written for a morning newspaper. Believing that readers are more interested in fresh news, they rewrite the lead to give the story that appearance. Because this effort has sometimes led to absurdity, now there is less stress on the "when" in the second-day lead. Here is an approved example of "updating" in the afternoon news cycle:

> NEW YORK—Novelist Virgil Payson was in Bellevue hospital *today* for psychiatric observation.
> City Magistrate Joseph Martin ordered Payson committed after the author was arraigned *yesterday* on a charge of simple assault brought by his wife, singer Margaret Newsom.

Obituaries often are "updated" for the second-day lead in this form: "Funeral services will be held today for . . . , who died yesterday."

The "where" element of an event is sometimes worthy of emphasis:

> Within 100 yards of the road intersection at which his wife met death in an auto accident last year, a Jonesboro man was killed in the same way last night.

Also sometimes worthy of emphasis are the "why" element ("Because he was discharged, a laborer yesterday shot . . .") and the "how" element ("Caught in a collapsing slag pile, . . . was crushed to death yesterday").

To emphasize some unusual aspect of the event or to hedge a prediction, the writer begins the lead sentence with a modifier.

> Barring unforeseen developments, the local baseball club will be sold to Kansas City interests.

> Even though he killed his wife for their joint insurance, the policy of William and Henrietta Fleming is

valid, a pleading filed in circuit court today avers.

Alive but incoherent, a wrong-way turnpike driver was the only survivor of a head-on collision that killed seven persons last night.

Exercises: *1.* Below are several leads containing one or more of the following errors: (*a*) main feature buried under unimportant details; (*b*) sentences overloaded with details; (*c*) *when* or *where* put before the *who* or *what* when unjustified by relative importance; (*d*) editorial comment introduced; (*e*) style used too rambling; (*f*) wordy phrases used at start.

Rewrite each of these leads in a clearer, more effective and concise form.

a) In a survey to learn something about the effects of television on the American home conducted by the Business Administration students at Western State University, using 1,000 local television fans as "guinea pigs," it was found that the average televiewer spends three and one-half hours per day at his television set on the occasions when he stays home.

b) Disclosure that local post office officials are conducting a drive to discover the identity of the largest distributors behind the Irish Sweepstakes ticket-selling in this vicinity, plus the revelation that last May's winners have not been paid off, have already resulted in blocking the sale of at least $250,000 in tickets and the disposal of $575,000 worth may be prevented.

c) During a meeting recently of Phi Pho Nu, national social sorority, elections were held for the coming year. After counting of ballots by election officers, it was discovered that the new secretary will be Hermina Knox. Other officers include Donna Snell, first vice-president; Illene Kennedy, second vice-president; and social activities director, Gwen Scheively. Alice Niffern will serve the group as president again, having held that post last year.

d) Among the many fine firms exhibiting in this year's county fair, which continues through Sunday, March 28, in Woodland Park Auditorium with admission free to all, is the Wiere Jewelry Company, which is displaying 250 antique and unusual watches and clocks, many of which date back 200 years or more.

e) At a meeting of the Greene County election commissioners, held last Tuesday, the recent school trustee election was held null and void, due to a technicality in the manner of conducting the balloting. As a result, Ivar Petrone, Leslie Siedbe, and Frank Mulligan now find themselves no longer newly elected members to the trustee board.

2. Rewrite this cluttered lead to facilitate the reader's comprehension:

> Robert Rogers, Fremton police officer, testified in superior court today that Philip Snead, plaintiff in an assault and battery suit against Sam Vossler, bartender, was drunk and disorderly at the time of the alleged assault.
> Rogers' charges came under the direct examination of Paul Ghezzi, attorney for the defendant. Rogers asserted that Snead was . . .

For class discussion: *1.* Why was this lead written this way?

> AMES, Iowa (AP)—A rule of the college at Iowa State University requires that administrative officials retire on the July 1 after they reach 65 years of age. Dr. Charles E. Friley has bowed to the rule and quit office as president of Iowa State.
> The rule doesn't apply to teachers. Dr. Friley will, accordingly, join Iowa State's faculty as a teacher and researcher.

2. Which of these leads is better calculated to educe an image?

> Dr. Otis Barton, 48-year-old undersea explorer, went farther under the ocean today than man had ever gone before when he dived 4,500 feet into the dark Pacific in a five-foot round steel ball.

> A man in a steel ball saw weird and wondrous marine life 4500 feet down in the Pacific Ocean today, the deepest descent in history.

CHAPTER 5

Organizing the Facts

You have already learned that the conventional news story of several paragraphs in length has two parts—the lead and the body—and that they may be thought of as being separable. These two parts are not usually separable in a short news story because most of the minor facts can be told along with the statement of the *W*s; that is, the *W*s are distributed in several of the paragraphs. (See news story on p. 45.)

The body of a longer story, however, may be thought of as having the form of an inverted pyramid. This means that the writer presents the facts in a *descending* order of their importance or interest. The writer assumes that some readers will not read clear through the story. Here is an example of this form in a four-paragraph story.

Giant Elm Tree Kills 7 Persons

A giant elm tree toppled by a violent storm killed seven members of a picnicking family last night.

The tree, 70 feet high and weighing 30 tons, fell on a car being driven homeward by Ainsley Joseph Glazier, 29.

In the car with him were his wife, 26, their two sons, Allen, 4, and Donald, 16 months; Mrs. Glazier's parents, Mr. and Mrs. Fred Jones, and their son, Boyd, about 10. All live in Toronto.

The car was crushed into wreckage only a foot high. Ten men worked two hours to cut the tree in sections and drag it off the car with a tractor.

ORGANIZING THE FACTS   65

Here is an example of the inverted pyramid form in a much longer story.

Mechanic Sucked Into Jet, Killed

Who, what when, where, how

Bernard Robert McGrath, 19, died in a "one in a million" accident yesterday at 4:30 p.m. when he was sucked into a jet engine at Moffett Field.

Facts 6 and 7

The accident happened as a supersonic F11F-1 Tiger jet was being put through a pressurization check by a maintenance crew. Officers said that probably McGrath was on the ground signalling to a man in the cockpit above his head.

Facts 8 and 9

McGrath, aviation structural machinist's mate 3c, from Floral Park, N.Y., must have been about a foot from the jet intake, a squadron officer said. Another officer in the attack squadron, VA-156, called the incident a "one in a million happenstance."

Fact 10

McGrath's skull was fractured by the tremendous force and he was pronounced dead on arrival at Moffett infirmary.

Walked Too Near

Fact 11

He and two other members of the squadron were checking the aircraft just south of hangar 3 at the parking line.

Fact 12

For some reason McGrath walked close to the plane alongside the cockpit.

Fact 13 (explanatory)

The Grumman Tigers have one Wright turbojet engine fed by two relatively narrow intakes—one on either side starting about halfway down the cockpit.

Fact 14

McGrath was pulled into the intake and into the whirling blades of the engine, one spokesman said.

Fact 15

The man in the cockpit at the time was James T. Vernon, aviation machinist's mate 2c. He was treated for shock after he witnessed the accident.

Fact 16

Airman Bobby J. Bunn, standing beside the cockpit canopy, saw McGrath disappear and immediately yelled at Vernon.

66 WRITING THE NEWS

Fact 17
(explanatory)

Safety Improved
The accident, in the memory of present Moffett personnel, is the first of its kind—certainly in recent years.

Fact 18
(explanatory)

Danger from jet suction "is not nearly the problem it used to be," according to Lt. Cmdr. Paul Halstrom, the station's public information officer. Design has improved safety factors, he indicated.

Fact 19
(explanatory)

Early jet planes posed a threat, but today "it's a pretty rare thing even on an aircraft carrier when they have to get close to the intake," he added.

Fact 20
(explanatory)

VA-156 is the only squadron in the navy equipped with the wasp-waisted Tigers, whose "Marilyn Monroe" shape reduces drag as they whip through the sound barrier.

Fact 21
(explanatory)

Some aircraft have wire "muzzles" over their intake when men work around them, but Tigers at Moffett have none. One officer surmised that possibly the cages are deemed unnecessary.

Fact 22

The dead sailor was the son of Bernard McGrath, of 6 Pansy avenue, Floral Park.

Fact 23

He had been with VA-156 since June 11, and had entered the navy about two years ago.

For class discussion: *1*. Speculate as to what kinds of readers would read all of the foregoing story; there are several audiences for it.
2. Do you approve of stating the names in the sixth paragraph of the following story, or would you tell them earlier?

Three Alcatraz convicts dug their way out of a thick concrete cell block with spoons and escaped from the prison early yesterday.

Their fate is unknown.

One of three things is possible: they made it to San Francisco or Marin by swimming or on a driftwood raft; they are in hiding in a waterline cave on The Rock; or they drowned.

The men were being sought by air, sea, and land—a helicopter circling over the area, patrol boats cruising from the Golden Gate to Angel Island and roadblocks from the Tiburon peninsula.

The escaped trio were desperate bandits who had robbed banks after escaping from Florida and Louisiana state prisons.

They were identified as Frank Lee Morris, 35, a robber from Louisiana; John W. Anglin, 32, and Clarence Anglin, 31, two of three Florida brothers doing time for an Alabama bank job.

Their breakout was an incredible performance, apparently engineered by Morris, toughest of the trio and a man of superior intelligence, with an IQ of 133. . . .

HOW MUCH OF A STORY GETS READ?

From several hundred studies we have readership scores for different news stories. But these scores measure only the reading of the headline plus some significant part of the story—not always the whole story. We have only one study of how much of a story people read who began a story.[1] The main finding of this study is illustrated in the accompanying table as adapted from the article. The percentages refer only to a large daily newspaper and represent *averages* for several stories.

N paragraph equals number of paragraphs read:	Percentage of those who began a story of N paragraphs, who completed it:
2	87.9%
3	71.8
4	62.8
5	56.7
6	51.6
7	46.7
8	43.0
9	39.8
10	39.4
11	38.6
12	38.0
13	37.9
14	36.1
15	30.7

The table shows, for example, that only about four out of ten readers who begin a story of ten or more paragraphs in length get as far as the tenth paragraph. However, you know from your own newspaper reading that you often read all of a very interesting news story.

A second finding of this study (not exhibited in the table above) is that

[1] Wilbur Schramm, "Measuring Another Dimension of Readership," *Journalism Quarterly*, 24:293–306 (1947).

the longer the story, the smaller proportion of it is likely to be read and the faster it loses readers.

A third finding is that a story in a feature form seems to hold readers better than a story in the inverted pyramid form. We discuss that point later.[2]

> Exercise: Look up the Schramm article and refer to the percentages for weeklies and small dailies. How do they compare with the percentages for a large metropolitan daily, as stated above?

THE POTPOURRI TYPE OF STORY

When the city council takes several different actions at the same meeting, the reporter must decide how to allocate the emphasis. A conventional way of organizing such a story is to *select one of the actions for the lead* and to report the other actions in a series of paragraphs in the body.[3] This is a potpourri, or medley, kind of organization. The reporter of a convention at which several persons spoke must make the same decision about his story organization. Here is an example of the way a newspaper reported the several decisions of the United States Supreme Court on "decision day."

Only One Partner Liable: Decision

WASHINGTON—The Supreme Court yesterday refused to penalize an entire brokerage firm because it made a heavy profit on a short-swing stock transaction while one of its partners was a director of the company whose stock was involved.

Instead, the court, voting 6 to 2, with one justice not participating, upheld a lower court ruling that only the one partner directly involved must forfeit his proportionate share of the profit.

In other actions the court:

Agreed to review a lower court decision branding illegal under the antitrust laws the practices of six movie distributors who tried to license films to television stations in blocks that included both desirable

---

[2] P. 140.
[3] For a variation of this method, see p. 73.

and less desirable movies and who assertedly refused to license individual pictures.

Decided to review a decision that the Federal Power Commission said could blunt one of its more effective rating-making tools in natural gas cases.

Refused to review two cases dealing with so-called rate increase "pancaking" in the natural gas industry, a practice of stacking one proposed rate increase on another before the FPC has decided whether the first rise is reasonable and proper.

The stock-trading case developed from this situation: . . .

In the foregoing story, the reporter, having emphasized one decision in the lead and having summarized briefly the other cases, resumed his report of the first by writing 630 additional words about the case. Next, he wrote 400 words about the movie block booking case and 680 words about the two gas pipeline cases, all of which had been summarized earlier.

WHAT IS THE "WHAT"?

The reporter sometimes organizes a story in such a way that the reader has difficulty *at the beginning* in comprehending what the story is about. An example is the automobile accident suit discussed on pages 46–47. The "what" of some events cannot be comprehended unless the "why" is also included early in the story. If the following news story had been organized in a different way, the reader would have wondered while reading why police happened to search the woman's car. Comprehension of this event is facilitated by putting the "why" of the "what" at the beginning.

Towaway Cops Find $11,000

Before San Francisco police haul a car out of a towaway zone, regulations say they must search it thoroughly for valuables.

They found more than they'd bargained for yesterday in a sleek new Pontiac on Turk street.

Neatly tucked under some papers on the front seat was a canvas bank bag containing $11,000 in bills.

The surprised officers whisked the money to safekeeping, then towed the car to a garage to wait for the owner—a lady banker.

They said the car, parked in front of 74 Turk street, was registered to Marge Wierman, president of the Frontier Bank in Covelo, Mendocino county.

She got the currency from the Golden State National bank, they said—then apparently went shopping. . . .

Here are two stories that report the same event. The organization of the first one suggests why some stories lose readers. One can imagine the reader knitting his eyebrows as he read the first 114 words, wondering why the defendant assaulted the victim and why the victim caused the police to ticket the defendant's car. Many readers would not have read much of the story. Readers of the second story, however, knew what the story was about after they had read only 50 words.

Assault Over Ticket Draws Jail Term

A man accused of assaulting an automatic laundry owner who caused him to get a parking citation was sentenced to 60 days in jail after he was found guilty of the charge by a municipal court jury Tuesday.

Judge John Sanchez sentenced Michael Jelen, 30, to jail and fined him $200 after he was convicted of assaulting Sy Cohen, 32, of 1325 Winona court, last July 13.

According to Ted Borillo, a deputy district attorney, Jelen and two other men parked their cars in Cohen's lot at 5134 W. 29th avenue, and then went to a nearby tavern.

Cohen said his lot would hold only six cars and if it were full, customers would go to another laundry close by.

For this reason, he called police and asked them to ticket the cars for parking on private property.

Soon after the cars were ticketed, Cohen testified, Jelen, who is a 6-foot 1-inch heavy equipment operator, burst into the laundry and demanded:

A municipal court jury Tuesday convicted a 6-foot, 1-inch Yugoslavian immigrant of assault for beating up a laundromat owner who summoned police to ticket his car.

"My lot would fill up with people who weren't customers if I didn't have police ticket their cars," explained Sy Cohen, 32, of 1325 S. Winona court.

"Then people would come by with their laundry and if they had no place to park they'd go somewhere else.

"There's another laundromat up the street.

"My lot held only six cars. Other people parking there just about ruined my business."

For this reason, Cohen testified, he called police July 13 when he found his lot full and no customers in his Brite Day Self Service Laundermat at 5134 W. 29th avenue.

About an hour after police ticketed the cars, Cohen testified, Michael Jelen, 30, of 8010 W. Sixth avenue,

"What are you going to do about this ticket?"

Cohen said Jelen choked him and threatened to make him "eat the ticket." "Jelen then hit me alongside the face, breaking my glasses and knocking me 12 feet," Cohen testified.

Jelen denied that any blows were struck. He said that when he went into the shop Cohen, who is 5 feet 4 inches tall and weighs 135 pounds, shouted: "Get out of my shop or I'll throw you out."

"Not wanting any trouble," Jelen testified, "I just wheeled around and left the place. When I turned Cohen lunged at me and he must have struck my shoulder with his head. I don't know how else it could have happened."

in Lakewood, burst into his shop with two other men.

The three had been drinking in a nearby tavern, Dep. Dist. Atty. Ted Borillo said.

"What are you going to do about this?" Cohen quoted Jelen, a construction worker, as demanding.

"I'm not going to pay this ticket; you are," Cohen said Jelen shouted.

Cohen testified Jelen then choked him, tore his shirt, pushed him against a laundry machine, and hit him in the face with a fist, breaking his glasses.

Jelen, he testified, tried to ram the ticket down his throat, shouting "I'll make you eat this."

An eyewitness, Kenneth Abramowitz, of 20 Wadsworth boulevard, supported Cohen's testimony.

Jelen testified no blows were exchanged, but that he left when Cohen "lunged" at him.

Cohen testified he is 5 ft. 4 inches tall and weighs 135 pounds.

The jury deliberated 30 minutes before reaching a verdict.

Judge Sanchez sentenced Jelen to 60 days in jail and fined him $200 plus $16.50 witness fees, $15 jury costs and $5 court costs.

Cohen, now a radio engineer, said he has given up the laundry business for a safer job, "I hope."

Exercise: Here is a news story in which one of the "whys" is stated in the last paragraph. Reorganize the facts in a way that is calculated to induce the reader to read all or nearly all of the story. Rewrite only that part of the news story that is relevant to that objective.

Split Rule Upholds Drugs Conviction

A Denver man's appeal from his conviction in U.S. district court on dope-peddling charges met with a rare 3-3 split decision in the six-member U.S. 10th Circuit Court of Appeals here Thursday.

Effect of the decision was to deny

the appeal of Steve Casias, 22, of 3908 Jackson street.

When the court is evenly divided, the judgment of the lower court is affirmed.

Major Issue

Major issue in the controversial case was whether an impartial jury considered Casias' case.

"The claim of an unfair jury was without merit," declared an opinion written by Circuit Judge Jean S. Breitenstein, upholding the conviction.

An opinion to reverse, written by Chief Judge Alfred P. Murrah of Oklahoma City, questioned impartiality of the array of jurors at Casias' trial.

"We think the array should have been discharged for implied bias," Murrah asserted.

Concurring with Breitenstein were Judges John C. Pickett, of Cheyenne, and David T. Lewis of Salt Lake City.

With Murrah

Agreeing with Murrah were Judges Oliver Seth of Santa Fe, and Delmas C. Hill of Wichita.

Casias was previously sentenced in the lower court to 14 years in federal prison.

He was one of more than two dozen suspects arrested here by federal narcotics agents last year. Later, 24 were convicted, 12 of whom pleaded guilty to dope peddling.

At successive narcotics trials within a two-month period, the other 12 were convicted by federal juries.

Casias, through his attorney, James Heyer, contended prior service by members of the jury panel on other narcotics cases—in which the government witnesses in his own case had also testified—raised a presumption of law that the entire panel was partial.

READERS' COMPREHENSION OF ISSUES

Not all news stories are about a happening; many are about political, social, and economic issues. The statement of the controversial issues is often hung on a "newspeg" such as a debate. What is the best way to organize the facts to facilitate the readers' comprehension of the issues? Richard F. Carter tested experimental groups on three types of story organization.[4] The issues related to proposals in Congress for guaranteeing the farmer an adequate price for his products, viz., high, rigid price supports versus lowered, flexible price supports. This is the version that Carter approved after testing three different ways of organizing the facts:

> One of the big political questions of 1954—how much should the farmer be guaranteed for his products—came up in Washington again today.
> There are two suggestions: flexible, lowered price guarantees or fixed, high guarantees of 90 per cent or more.
> Agriculture Secretary Ezra Taft Benson gave two reasons for a plan of flexible, lowered price supports:
> 1. They would bolster farmers' income through increased consumption.
> 2. Prices would rise because of the administration's plan to take 2½ billion dollars of surpluses off the market.
> Republican Senator Alexander Wiley, Wis., argued against flexible supports, because, he said:
> 1. They do not take into consideration rising costs of farm labor, seed, and machinery.
> 2. They would bring on economic disaster. [Etc., etc.]

Note that this organization presents (1) the controversy, (2) the name of the advocate of one proposal with two supporting reasons, and (3) the name of the advocate of the second proposal with two supporting reasons. This parallel presentation of the advocates and their reasons, preceded by a statement of the issues, is calculated to facilitate not only comprehension of the issues but of the related arguments for each of the issues.

> Exercise: Unscramble the facts given below and organize them. Then write a news story in inverted pyramid form.
>
> *Who* (Killed)   1. William E. Schultz, 28, of Winger, Minnesota, driver of the car, containing seven passengers, that struck and sheared off a pole of a high tension electric line.
> 2. Donald Haugen, 21, of Winger, Minnesota, a passenger in the Schultz car.
> 3. Marvin Duncan, Jr., 18, of Fosston, Minnesota, who leaped from the first car passing by the scene of the accident and attempted a rescue.
> 4. Orville Rolf, 18, of Fosston, Minnesota, who also

[4] "Writing Controversial Stories for Comprehension," *Journalism Quarterly,* 32:319–28 (1955).

	leaped from the first passing car and attempted a rescue. 5. Clark Hoidal, 21, of Winger, Minnesota, driver of a third car.
(Survivors)	Seven persons whose names were not obtained. Five were taken to the Crookston, Minnesota, hospital and given sedatives for shock and minor injuries.
Where	On Highway 59 one mile north of Mahnomen, Minnesota.
When	Early today.
How	The Schultz car sheared off a power pole and plunged into a water-filled ditch into which a high tension wire had fallen. Schultz apparently was killed by the crash. Haugen was killed when he stepped out of the car into the water. "I'm being shocked; somebody help me," a survivor quoted Haugen as saying. The other six passengers in the Schultz car stayed inside the car.

The car containing Duncan and Rolf drew up. The two youths, apparently unaware of the lethal current in the pool of water, raced into it to help. Both fell dead.

Highway patrolmen said that two passengers in the back seat of the Duncan-Rolf car apparently owed their lives to the fact they couldn't get out of the car as fast.

Then Koidal drew up in a third car, raced to the wrecked car before the others could stop him, and met the same fate.

The five youngsters trapped in the wrecked car then climbed to the top of it and leaped to dry ground and safety.

THE NEWSPAPER PARAGRAPH

The standard newspaper column is slightly less than two inches wide. This means that the newspaper paragraph is not a unit of thought, as it usually is in books and magazines, but a *unit of type*. To facilitate comprehension, the newswriter indents—on the average—about every thirty-five words. Thus, the paragraph consists of only one or two sentences. The writer strives for an approach to unity, not in the paragraph, but in a succession of paragraphs. This *block* of newspaper paragraphs is somewhat the equivalent of the literary paragraph. Since most news stories are narration, paragraph unity is less important than in other forms of discourse. This is also true of a speech report (see Chap. 10).

Some newspaper paragraphs are made very brief for emphasis. The second paragraph in the prison escape story on page 66 is an example.

TRANSITION

There are several stopping places in the news story of average length because many news stories are like a string of beads. Nevertheless, the writer can give some stories a momentum that links the separate thoughts, carries narrative forward, and stimulates the reader to continue his reading. This is known as *transition*. It is achieved by the use of (1) linking words or phrases, called connectives, and (2) by reference to what has gone before.

The most frequently used linking conjunctions and adverbs are *and, or,* and *but*. Less frequently used are *hence, so,* and *therefore*. The *and* relationship of two thoughts can also be implied by a 1-2-3 arrangement: the reader perceives the pattern and anticipates its continuation as he reads. An example:

> . . . Meanwhile, three Haynes county communities planned studies of their flood control problems.
> 1. The Jonesboro city council last week authorized a $10,000 study to control street and house floods.
> 2. The Williamsburg city council assigned the city engineer to survey trash-clogged basins in areas in which new building has outstripped drainage capacity.
> 3. The Westown city council discussed a proposal for joining with Jonesboro to form a flood control district.

Some linking words and phrases that express time are *at the same time, meanwhile, more recently, just before, next, earlier,* and *later*.

Radio, which has no headlines to synopsize its separate news stories, uses transitional phrases relating to time and place to achieve transition within the whole newscast. Two examples: "In another part of Europe today . . ." and "While the auto workers in Detroit were settling their strike. . . ."

Reference to a preceding unit of thought achieves transition by repeating or rephrasing the unit of thought. A simple example of such a device is the use of a specific noun and then its generic equivalent: "He said he sold the *cow* for $90. The *animal* had cost him only $40." Here are other devices, all of which were used in reporting a meeting of a city council:

Similarity: By an identical vote the city council turned down another proposal . . . .
Somewhat the same arguments were advanced when the council debated the . . . .
In another action, the council . . . .

Contrast: The heated discussion about apartment house zones was absent when the council took up the recommendations of . . . .
A project calling for a greater expenditure . . . .

Role change: Councilman Marshall, who led the minority seeking abandonment of S zone, joined the majority in another zoning vote.

Mere arrangement to achieve a certain kind of emphasis may also assist transition. Here is a bad example on the left-hand side below and a rearrangement on the right-hand side.

Complaints flooded the city council last night as property owners from the undeveloped area of East Belmont demanded to know why the city is assessing them for additional storm drainage and street repairs.

Forty taxpayers attended the hearing on the complete improvement of N. Woodland avenue and adjacent streets.

The council passed the resolution of intent to make acquisitions and improvements *despite the protests from the floor.*

Complaints flooded the city council last night as property owners from the undeveloped area of East Belmont demanded to know why the city is assessing them for additional storm drainage and street repairs.

Forty taxpayers attended the hearing on the complete improvement of N. Woodland avenue and adjacent streets.

Despite the protests from the floor, the council passed the resolution of intent to make acquisitions and improvements.

Exercise: Rewrite the following news story for a broadcast:

A driverless sedan leaped a curbing and crashed through the plate glass front of a Southeast Denver dry cleaners Monday night, dragging its owner —a 50-year-old schoolteacher—the length of the store.

Critically hurt in the freak accident was Miss Katherine Abel of 2301 S. Franklin street, a teacher at Pleasant View School in Golden District. She is in Denver General Hospital with head, chest, leg, hip and internal injuries suffered when she was pinned under her car, Traffic Investigator Al Preble said.

2 Others Hurt

Also hurt were two clerks, knocked aside as the auto careened into the Silver State Cleaners and Laundry, 2439 S. University boulevard.

They are Mrs. Barbara Lucero, 22, of 1453 Tennyson street, in fair condition in the hospital with a leg injury, and Miss Betty Dykstra, 16, of 2420 S. Josephine street, treated for a knee injury by a private doctor.

Preble and Patrolman William Swope said Miss Abel left her car in front of the cleaners with her parents, Jess and Georgia Abel, 80 and 75, in **the car.**

The teacher told her mother to keep the engine running, but apparently left the automatic transmission in drive gear, Preble said.

Mrs. Abel depressed the accelerator to keep the motor running. The auto leaped the curb and slammed through the front of the store.

Knocked Aside

The Abel auto knocked two clerks aside and pushed the counter and several clothes racks to the rear of the store.

The manager, Norman Hansen, 34, said he was sitting at his desk at the back of the establishment when he heard a "tremendous crash. I looked up and saw all these clothes on racks coming at me."

Hansen suffered a few bruises. The Abels were unhurt, but were reported suffering from shock.

THE UNITY OF A NEWS STORY

Very few news stories can have the unity of a fiction short story to the extent that they relate to a single situation or create a single impression. For that reason, few news stories require an ending that contributes to the impression of unity. Most news stories have no ending; they just taper. There are two kinds of events, however, that permit of an ending that contributes to unity. One is an event which has suspense; it is discussed in the next section. Another is an event that does not involve suspense but is one that can be treated by the writer in such a way that the story makes a single impression.

Hot Pursuit in San Mateo County

It is not often in the course of his daily assignment that Deputy Sheriff Frank Bastasini of San Mateo county is asked to chase a naked girl through the woods.

But it was awfully warm in San Mateo county yesterday.

And the girl, an "attractive, mature, well-developed brunette" of 16 summers, was fully clothed when she escaped from County Probation Officer Estelle Woodside, who was taking her to the Hillcrest Juvenile Hall near Belmont.

The girl, Mrs. Woodside reported frantically, took off at a gallop into the hills beyond the Crystal Springs Shopping Center—where Deputy Bastasini was spending another routine day.

Spotted Her

Bastasini got the message and roared off into the hills.

In no time at all, he spotted his quarry. But she ambled out of range into some bushes, apparently—no, obviously—unaware of Deputy Bastasini's presence.

Bastasini abandoned his patrol car and followed on foot. In a twinkling, he spotted the fugitive . . . lying bare as an onion in a little clearing in the woods.

Bastasini's own report covers the rest of the distance:

The girl, forgetting her clothing, scampered away and, "after a struggle," Bastasini "got hold of her" and . . . "subdued her."

Once "subdued," the girl was contrite. And, as Deputy Bastasini put it, he "turned his head" while she assembled herself for the trip back to Juvenile Hall.

Much of his job, of course, is routine. (*San Francisco Chronicle*.)

THE SUSPENSE STORY

A newswriter who has a sense of the dramatic sometimes perceives in an event those characteristics that will permit him to organize the facts in a climactic structure. He writes so that the story unwinds—sometimes with the suspense building up.

Some stories are climactic in form in that they merely defer the "why" until the end.

Boy Electrocuted By Television Set

A 4-year-old boy was electrocuted yesterday by a television set.

Gary Putnam was viewing a program with his mother, Mrs. Arnold Putnam, and his half-sister.

"One minute he was sitting there and when I looked again he was lying on the floor," the weeping mother related.

Authorities said the boy simultaneously touched the metal chassis of the television set and a nearby radiator. A short circuit in the set sent current through his body.

The deferred "why" in some stories amounts to surprise.

Hi-Fi Rendition of Decibels in the Night

Conrad Wisniewski's neighbors complained to police last night about the noise emanating from his home.

Police found Wisniewski's hi-fi machine going full blast, making an awful racket.

When told to shut it off, Wisniewski said he would if the cops would see to it that neighbor Joseph Stanulis muted the noises coming from his general welding shop in the same block.

They said they'd talk to Stanulis, so Wisniewski pulled down the windows and flipped the switch—for the night.

What Wisniewski plays at night is what he tape records during the day coming from Stanulis' welding shop.

Some events are more interesting to the reader when they are reported in a climactic form although they have no element of surprise or mystery.

A Drama of Death In an Oakland Bar

William Francis Swensen was in the habit of going to the bar of the I Know You steak house in Oakland, ordering a screwdriver, and talking about his problems.

"Does a guy good to think out loud," he often told bartender Ed Nobriga.

The 33-year-old Swensen had a litany of worries: He lost his job as a shipping clerk, he had "home troubles," Christmas was coming and money was scarce.

Yesterday about 5 p.m. Swensen climbed onto one of the red leatherette stools at the end of the bar and ordered his usual screwdriver.

Police Come

He nursed the drink until 7:30.

Then he put a .38-calibre revolver to his ear and cocked the trigger.

Four shuffleboard players ran out of the bar at 100 Seventh street.

Swensen wouldn't talk to policemen who arrived minutes later.

"Call a priest," Nobriga suggested.

The Rev. Fred Caldwell, of Old Saint Mary's Catholic church, was summoned.

He sat on a faded red stool near Swensen.

The unemployed shipping clerk kept the gun at his ear. But he chatted animatedly with the priest.

After 45 minutes, Swensen seemed happier. He took a sip from his screwdriver.

Fr. Caldwell, two stools away, opened his hand to accept the pistol.

Three policemen moved slowly in from the doorway where they had stood for a tense quarter-hour.

Swensen slowly moved the gun away from his head.

Then, abruptly, he shoved it inside his mouth and pulled the trigger.

He fell dead on the floor at the feet of the stunned priest and policemen. (*San Francisco Chronicle*.)

THE SECOND-DAY STORY: TIEBACK

The newspaper publishing in the second news cycle either omits or rewrites a story that was published in the previous cycle. When there are new developments the newspaper emphasizes them in the lead of the rewritten story. The newspaper in the second cycle should assume that its readers have not read the earlier story in another newspaper.[5] This necessi-

---

[5] This is not an unreliable assumption since the average daily newspaper adult reader reads only 1.4 newspapers each week day. See Newsprint Information Committee, *A National Study of Newspaper Reading* (New York, 1961), Vol. II, p. 18.

tates writing a "tieback" to supply enough information to facilitate the readers' comprehension of the event. Sometimes this is not done, and the reader is as uninformed and as unoriented as is the person who enters the theater at the beginning of Act II or Act III.

When trials and legislative hearings extend over two or more days, the newspaper should also assume that the reader has missed the previous stories. Inadvertently in some instances, the newspaper omits from the later stories such facts as the nature of the accusation in a criminal trial or the name of the committee or subcommittee holding the legislative hearing.

Exercise: From the facts listed in II and III below, write two follow stories, one dated July 18 and the second dated July 19, which refer to the news story below, which is dated July 15 and designated I. Use as many of the facts in I as you think are necessary for the reader's comprehension.

I

BAR HARBOR, Me.—Alice Lundborg, 25-year-old bride of a year and an expert swimmer, became the object of a police search today when she failed to return from a swim.

The search was begun after her clothing was discovered under circumstances not immediately explained and tending to throw certain elements of mystery into the disappearance.

Mrs. Lundborg, wife of Lieut. Walter F. Lundborg, now in Germany, left the home of her husband's parents, Mr. and Mrs. Henry Lundborg, 6500 Warren street, at 8 a.m. She carried her swimming suit, boarded a bus and started for the beach.

Her mother-in-law reminded her the ocean had powerful currents and suggested she swim in the Wayside pool. The suggestion was prompted by the fact that the bride had been under observation for appendicitis symptoms two weeks ago.

The younger Mrs. Lundborg laughed, reminding her mother-in-law that she held several medals for life saving.

When she failed to return this afternoon, police and Coast Guard were notified and hospitals checked.

James Lundborg, 19, her brother-in-law, found her street clothing at 3 o'clock at a point known as Fisherman's Cove, below Lookout Point. It appeared as if she had changed her clothes on the beach, but police discovered it is an exposed spot and doubted that she would disrobe there, in sight of thousands of people.

They also discovered that a small amount of money and a house key she had in her possession when she started were not in the clothing when found.

The missing girl came to Bar Harbor a year ago from the home of her parents in Lawrence, Kansas, to await her husband's return from overseas. She had been a skiing instructor during the season at Sun Valley.

Lieut. Lundborg has been stationed in Germany and is expected here on or about August 30. He married his bride at Camp Patrick Henry last August.

II

BAR HARBOR—July 18

Mr. and Mrs. William Reuter, parents of Alice Reuter Lundborg, arrived in Bar Harbor yesterday.

They rushed here from Kansas after receiving news of their daughter's disappearance. A former mayor of Lawrence, Kansas, Reuter is a professor at the University of Kansas.

The Reuter family has spent several vacations in Canada in past years.

Mr. Reuter knew his daughter liked Canada.

He sent telegrams to resorts and hotels in Canada where they had stayed on their earlier trips, asking for the information concerning Alice.

Yesterday afternoon a telephone call came from a hotel manager in Quebec. The message stated that a girl of Alice Lundborg's description was believed to have boarded a plane at Quebec for Montreal.

Upon receipt of the telephone call, Reuter immediately left by train for Portland. From Portland he will fly to Montreal.

The day before Mrs. Lundborg disappeared she cashed an $1100 draft her father had sent her to buy an automobile.

She showed members of the Lundborg family a $1000 bill and a $100 bill that day.

Search of her purse following her disappearance disclosed the $100 bill, two tens and three ones, but no trace of the $1000 note.

It was learned that some of her newer clothes were missing from her closets at the Warren street home.

Her brother was in training at Camp Patrick Henry at the same time as her husband.

Lundborg brought his bride to the Bar Harbor home of his parents last August and soon afterwards left for overseas.

Police and Coast Guard have carried on an intensive search for her body.

Relatives said she seemed in good spirits usually, although she was rather emotional and subject occasionally to periods of depression.

She was away from the Warren street residence much of the time.

She spent three months in Canada last fall and following that was in Sun Valley during the winter season.

III

BAR HARBOR—July 19

Mrs. Reuter received a telegram from her missing daughter, Mrs. Alice Lundborg, last night.

The wire came from Montreal and stated that the younger Mrs. Lundborg is well.

The telegram came after wire services had distributed the *Transcript's* story of yesterday that Mrs. Lundborg had not drowned.

Her disappearance was evidently a planned one.

Mr. Reuter, who is in Portland awaiting plane space, revealed the contents of the telegram after a telephone conversation with his wife.

He declined comment on the telegram.

The telegram read: "Sorry I had to do it this way. Just had to get away for a while and be myself. Don't worry. You'll hear from me soon."

Mrs. Reuter said she thought her daughter "was in a highly nervous state because of the separation from her husband."

Mr. Reuter has booked passage for Montreal, but Mrs. Reuter said, "We don't want my daughter to know that anyone is going after her."

For class discussion: *1.* This story could have been written in an inverted pyramid form with the lead, "A 27-year-old girl was kidnaped by four youths from the steps of a church early this morning and raped in Milby Park." Instead, Lee Pitt, of the *Houston Press,* wrote it this way:

> A 27-year-old girl, her black-and-gold prayer book in her hand, stopped for an instant on the steps of Immaculate Conception Church.
>
> It was 5:50 a.m.
>
> She was there especially early for Lenten Mass this morning, for her mother was sick and she wanted to attend Mass, get home quickly, cook breakfast and go to her job at an insurance company.
>
> Suddenly two young men came from behind her, pinned her elbows. A car pulled up. The girl was thrust violently into the car, screaming for help that didn't come.
>
> Thus began what Homicide Lt. Frank Murray calls "one of the most vicious crimes ever committed in Houston."

In which form would you write the story?

2. Which is the more accurate term for a female of her age—"girl" or "woman"—in the foregoing news story?

CHAPTER 6

Making the News Meaningful

The main characteristics of news story style are conciseness and objectiveness. The writer of the conventional news story has the point of view of the detached observer—not the point of view of a participant in an event or of a critic. The omission from the news story of surplus words and the organization of the facts in the summary-lead-inverted-pyramid form are restrictions that contribute to the quality of objectivity.

When, however, the writer does a feature story or a descriptive story he writes from a different point of view. This is because he is trying to do more than merely inform the reader: he is trying to entertain or to convey his own sense impressions to the reader. Such stories are discussed in Chapters 9 and 11.

In addition to achieving conciseness and objectiveness, the news writer also strives to do certain things that are calculated to make the facts meaningful to the reader.

IDENTIFICATION

Newswriters take great pains to include certain facts about some of the *W*s in the story so that the story will not be ambiguous in any respect.

Where

Although news stories always state the place of the event, the information they supply is sometimes inadequate for some readers. Thus, the address "4281 Hudson street," in a large city, could be made more specific by adding "on the east side." When the event is at or near a small town, the place may be designated as "near Kansas City" or "40 miles south of Oklahoma City" or, in a wire service story, "an industrial city of 32,500 in the Mohawk Valley about 35 miles west of Albany."

Who

The full name of every person mentioned in a news story is given the first time the name is used; thereafter only the last name is used. As was explained earlier,[1] most newspapers have a "style guide" which specifies whether or not "Mr." should be used with the last name. When a title is used with the full name the first time it is also used with the last name in most newspapers. An exception on some newspapers is when the person is so well known that the full name is not used the first time, as in "Governor Black" instead of "Governor Henry Black." Most newspapers disapprove of the use of long titles or appellations preceding the name, such as "glass jar manufacturing heir John A. Kern."

An identifying phrase in apposition to the name of a person can sometimes make the story more newsworthy or cause the reader to recall a previous news story about the person. Some examples: "James Duncan, former chief of police"; "Homer Murphy, who turned down a Pulitzer prize"; or "Henry Fowler, brother of Mayor Martin Fowler." Persons in the news are usually identified as to occupation because occupation indicates social status and answers the reader's question, "Who is he?"

Since the advent of television, newspapers and wire services have carried more background information about personalities in the news than they formerly did. Viewers who see news personalities on television want to know more about them. The newspaper, by supplying this information, supplements television. Much of the news in *Time* magazine is interesting because it tells the news in terms of the people who make the news.

Readers like to see their own names in the newspaper when their action is a socially-approved action. Even some metropolitan newspapers try to get as many local names as possible in the newspaper. This is accomplished sometimes in the "Vital Statistics" columns.[2]

> For class discussion: *1.* An identification in some circumstances is evaluative. For example, is the identification in this sentence justified or not justified: "Police Judge Claude A. Downs, a former official of the AFL Painters Union, dismissed the dynamiting charges against the strikers"?
> 2. When is a newspaper justified in identifying a person in the news by his race or national extraction?
> 3. When may the initials of an organization (e.g., A.F.L. for American Federation of Labor) be used in a news story?

[1] See p. 10.
[2] See C. R. Bush and R. K. Bullock, "Names in the News," *Journalism Quarterly*, 29:148–57 (1952).

Adjectives and adverbs: In general, newspapers refrain from using adjectives and adverbs whenever possible because they prefer that writers use nouns and verbs that suggest an image. But in some instances it is desirable that the reader see the persons in the news, and only adjectives and adverbs will suffice.

> Prather is a slight, gray man, ruggedly handsome. His near-blind eyes show pale through lenses the thickness of bottle glass.

> A curly-haired young man with a small goatee capped a night of beer drinking by invading a neighbor's home today, terrorizing the family and beating a 13-year-old daughter to death with a claw hammer.

> A jovial "lonely hearts" widow confessed tonight she killed four of her five known husbands by giving them rat poison.
> Mrs. Stanford Marquis, plump and rosy-cheeked, told officers . . .

For class discussion: Are the adjectives and adverbs in this lead justified or not? "Patricia Ann Murphy, 17 years old and very pretty, applied her lipstick for the last time yesterday and then stepped off the roof of a downtown hotel to join the man she loved."

Age: The age—exact or approximate—of persons in the news is stated in those stories in which age is an important or essential characteristic of the person. You have probably noted this in several examples in earlier chapters. In some instances, these terms are used: *child, youth, youngster, middle-aged,* and *elderly.* Some persons in the news have objected to being described by some of these terms because, in their own minds, the term did not fit. One editor has arbitrarily defined some of these terms in his style guide as follows:

> *Child:* person up to 13 years of age
> *Youth:* person from 13 to 21, unless married
> *Young people:* those from 15 to 25
> *Middle-aged:* persons from 45 to 65
> *Elderly:* persons over 70

But another editor disagrees with these definitions of "middle-aged" and "elderly." Webster's dictionary defines "middle-aged" as "being about the middle of the ordinary age of man, between youth and age." The Century dictionary's definition is: "intermediate in age between youth . . . and old age; commonly from, about 40 to about 50 years old."

Names, when and where: In a news story of several paragraphs in which the names of several persons who are not well known are used, the reader forgets which are which. The reader's memory is aided, therefore, when the persons in the latter part of the story are referred to as "the taxi driver" or "the defense attorney" or are identified in a similar way instead of by name. A somewhat different type of advice is suggested for reporting pleadings in court trials.[3]

In a potpourri kind of story or when two or more persons are quoted directly and successively in a fairly long story, the writer should signal the reader when he reports a different action or quotes a different person. Here is an example of failure to follow this procedure when quoting two persons:

> Mr. Ratliff said Congress would do more to aid the coal industry by restricting imports of residual oil and voting more money for coal research.
> "This bill would benefit only a few 'Goliaths' in the coal industry," Mr. Chandler said.

In this form, the reader's thought carries over to the second paragraph and for a while he thinks that Mr. Ratliff is still testifying. This could not happen, however, if the next paragraph had begun: "Mr. Chandler said 'this bill will benefit only a few "Goliaths" in the coal industry.' "

Accuracy in Use of Names

One of the first rules in journalism is to spell a person's name correctly; that is, as the person himself spells his name. For example, some persons spell their name as "Paine" and others as "Payne." The writer should look up in a directory every name he uses when there is a possibility of making a mistake. The federal Social Security files contain 1,100,000 different surnames. Some editor has said: "Names make news, but errors make enemies."

ATTRIBUTION

The events that reporters witness and the events they learn about from police are reported as if the reporter were an omniscient observer. But some details of these events and the facts of many other kinds of events are attributed to a source, such as a public official or an eyewitness. What

---

[3] See p. 233.

is said by speakers and persons interviewed is also attributed to them so the reader may know who is speaking.

In many instances in which information is supplied by a source the reporter states the source of his information for the purpose of fixing responsibility for the report. When the source supplies misinformation and the reporter fails to attribute the information to that source, the prestige of the newspaper is impaired. Two examples: (1) In the Chicago race riots of 1919, the number of casualties and participants and the amount of property damage was highly exaggerated in the newspaper reports; but the newspapers had relied on police. (2) When Roy W. Howard prematurely reported the end of the first World War he did not cite the (unreliable) source of his information, and thousands of persons celebrated the false armistice a few days before the German surrender.

The literature of social psychology reports numerous experiments which show that the receiver of a message interprets its content to fit his evaluation of the source.[4] It is for this reason that the Associated Press recommends to its writers that, when it seems important to establish the source in the reader's mind, the writer begin the lead sentence with the source. Thus:

> CAMBRIDGE, MASS.—The Harvard *Crimson,* student newspaper, said yesterday that Professor Henry Smith, of the department of psychology, had been dismissed.

This procedure is often followed deliberately by the Associated Press even though the effect is weakened.

When the source of a statement is a person or an organization with a self-interest and the name does not identify that interest, the newspaper sometimes supplies that identification.

> NEW YORK—George Champion, chairman of Chase Manhattan Bank, the country's largest *state-chartered* bank, today criticized moves that, he said, would give federally-chartered national banks more powers than are allowed state-supervised banks.

> WASHINGTON—A *business-financed* research group said today the government could solve most of the nation's farm problems in five years

---

[4] See C. E. Osgood, P. H. Tannenbaum, and G. J. Susci, *The Measurement of Meaning* (Urbana, Ill., 1957), Chap. 5, and S. E. Asch, *Social Psychology* (New York, 1952), pp. 420–26.

> with a shock treatment of sharply lower commodity prices.
>
> The research and policy committee of the Committee for Economic Development described its proposals as "a program to improve the profits of agriculture without government controls." CED is a non-profit organization supported by contributions from business concerns.

"According to"

What is the effect of the use of "according to"? This expression may be used at the beginning of the story to emphasize the source whether the source be of low or high credibility. An example:

> According to information from both major and minor league sources, organized baseball is due for a startling and important reorganization within the next year.

Often, however, "according to" is merely a long expression for "said." An example from a corporation's press release:

> The Rexall Drug Co. has purchased Carnegies of Welwyn, Ltd., of England, a manufacturer of fine chemicals, according to an announcement today by Justin Dart, Rexall president.

Why not "Justin Dart, president, announced today"?

Excess Attribution

Newspapers are sometimes guilty of overattribution in that they quote the source so often that the continuity of the story is interrupted. An example: ". . . The sheriff said that Smith entered the victim's home through the back door, which, he said, was not locked." An attribution may often be omitted in the body of the story when the fact stated is not in dispute; that is, when the statement is a mere recital, not an averment.

Stories "Not for Attribution"

Some officials and employees of a government wish to have something published but are unwilling to be quoted. And some persons wish to say certain things in a large gathering of people but not for publication. Newspapers almost universally refuse to publish any statement without some kind of attribution. Yet there are several situations in which the newspaper must make a decision either about publishing or about the kind of attribution it will use.

Suppose a reporter attends a meeting of as many as twenty-five persons to which the public has been invited and a speaker states that what he is going to say is "off the record." The reporter should feel free to report what the speaker said, for it is a public meeting and the newspaper has no obligation to protect a timid speaker.[5]

Suppose again that the reporter is invited as a member of the press to attend a gathering of as many as twenty-five persons who are members of an organization and a speaker announces that his remarks will be "off the record." Since the reporter is a guest he should not ignore that circumstance. But he should point out to the speaker that the meeting was announced as being open to the public, that a good many people are present, and that he would not have attended if he had known of this restriction. If the speaker persists in his intention, the reporter should leave the meeting and report the circumstances to his editor. He should also learn from members of the audience—checking one against another—what was said by the speaker.

In a conversation or interview with a person who wishes to state something "off the record," the reporter is bound not to publish the statement, with or without attribution, if he listens to it. In circumstances in which the reporter is seeking information, he should tell the person not to make the statement. Then he should seek the information from another source and be free to report it.

There are two "don't quote me" situations in which a reporter is sometimes involved. In one situation the informant's motive is to injure another person or to embarrass a political rival or party. The reporter, as a rule, cannot use such a statement, for the newspaper should not accept responsibility. There is a second situation in which the newspaper may publish a statement with an anonymous attribution (e.g., "a reliable source"). In this situation the reporter or his editor knows that the source is reliable and the statement has been made for an honorable purpose.

"Backgrounding"

In addition to all of the situations mentioned above, there is the "backgrounding" situation. A high official talks to one or more reporters on the understanding that his statements are to be attributed anonymously. This situation usually arises only in Washington or a foreign capital or at an international conference, where the "ground rules" of diplomacy often inhibit attribution. From a backgrounding situation, however, a reporter

---

[5] For a discussion of the reporting of "executive sessions" of public bodies at which action is taken, see p. 486.

obtains information that contributes to his understanding of issues and policies. In these instances the high official has honorable as well as practical reasons for not being quoted. The wire services use several forms of attribution for news about diplomacy, such as "an informed source" or "a Western diplomat." When the informant objects to any attribution the reporter uses the expression "it was learned"—provided that the source is reliable. The "management of news" by officialdom deserves a much more elaborate discussion than has been presented here; such a discussion, however, is beyond the scope of this textbook.

Similar to the background situation is the "embargo," or "release date," on certain governmental information. The purpose of the agency which imposes the embargo is to make the information available to all reporters at the same time, especially when the reporters need a considerable time for reading and analyzing the release. An example is the annual budget message of the President or the Governor. The agency which releases the information specifies the exact time for release. Some embargoes are unreasonable and problems arise in connection with stipulations regarding advance interviews based on the information and the disregard of a stipulation by a rival reporter or editor. The usual practice is to disregard the release date after a rival has disregarded it.

EXPLANATION

The reader of news is not rewarded for his effort when he does not understand what he has read. The news writer, therefore, should assume that the reader lacks knowledge of many things and is entitled to an explanation.

There are, for example, certain *magnitudes* that many readers do not comprehend, and they should be translated into magnitudes that the usual reader can comprehend. When a wire service reported that the United States had allocated two hundred pounds of atomic material to other nations for peaceful purposes, the writer added that this amount was sufficient to supply thirty to forty reactors. Large sums cannot be comprehended unless they are translated: rather than merely stating that Marshall Plan aid to Europe aggregated 20 billion dollars, a news writer added that the sum was equivalent to 112 dollars a year to every person in the recipient European countries.

An *analogy* is sometimes helpful to the reader. For example, in reporting popular reaction to the French government's dismissal of Marshal Juin, the Associated Press writer added: "The firing touched off a furor in France *comparable* to that in America following President Truman's dismissal of General Douglas MacArthur." In describing a new locking device on nuclear warheads that is controlled by a radio signal, the news writer included this statement: "The device itself would not do the firing, but it could control the arming of the warhead. This is *comparable to* cocking a rifle in advance of firing it by pulling the trigger."

Terminology: Newspapers report so much about technology, science, finance, and social studies that the use of technical terms is unavoidable. The news writer, therefore, must define them. In some instances, the context of the article supplies an adequate definition, but usually the writer has to interrupt the continuity by inserting a definition parenthetically. This does not mean necessarily inserting the definition in parentheses but adding one or two additional sentences.

> "The area has had an inadequate water supply dependent on deep wells —a most insecure supply," Warne said. "The farmers have been overdrawing 800,000 acre-feet of water a year."
> An acre-foot is the amount of water it takes to cover one acre with a foot of water, or 325,850 gallons. A figure of 800,000 acre-feet is the equivalent of a two-inch sheet of water covering the entire state of New Jersey.

> Dr. Fister said that the survey showed that the median value of assets owned by families with the head of the family over age 65 was $8,349.
> Median is a point chosen in a series of figures so that half are on one side and half on the other.

> . . . The investigators found that some of the concrete blocks which contain reinforcing steel at the front of the building were not grouted properly.
> Grout is the special concrete mixture used to fill up the holes in concrete blocks which contain reinforcing steel.

Increasingly, newspapers and wire services are explaining that an accusation of a person or a corporation by a government agency is not equivalent to a finding of guilty. The law relating to unfair trade practices and monopoly is ambiguous, and many accusations are not upheld by the courts. Yet the mere accusation made public by the government is harmful to the innocent accused.

> WASHINGTON—The Federal Trade Commission today charged the New York Coffee and Sugar Exchange has unlawfully restrained international trade in coffee and thereby "promoted substantial increases" in price. . . .
> A complaint issued by the FTC is answerable before the commission itself. In the normal course, a hearing is held and the commission then makes a decision as to whether the charges have been substantiated.

Most news stories about scientific discoveries and inventions are explanation. Such stories are discussed in Chapter 13.

INTERPRETIVE REPORTING

Some events cannot be comprehended by the reader unless the reporter supplies, from his own knowledge or from his investigation, certain facts that make his report meaningful. This type of reporting has come to be called "interpretive reporting," as distinguished from the reporting of only objective facts. Interpretive reporting is not just a way of presenting the news, but often is the reporting of additional facts which the reporter has had to dig for. In the so-called McCarthy investigation in 1954 of the Army's security safeguards, one of the controversial issues was the taking of a picture of the Secretary of the Department of the Army and a private by an army photographer at Fort Monmouth, New Jersey. The private (later an investigator for Senator McCarthy) testified before the Senate committee that the Secretary had asked to have the picture taken. The committee did not ask the photographer why he took the picture. But a *New York Times* reporter did ask him, and he said that it was his own idea. Thus the reader of the *Times* was able to make a different evaluation of the testimony and of the principals involved than were nonreaders of the *Times*. This is sometimes called reporting "in depth."

Here is an example from the *New York Times* of how a reporter, by asking questions, was able to explain the meaning of an important decision taken by the United Nations.

> UNITED NATIONS—The Soviet Union agreed today to the reelection of U Thant to a full term as Secretary General despite previous Soviet insistence that the Cuban crisis be settled first.
> *Reliable sources said* that Soviet representatives had accepted the

United States view that the question should be settled soon. . . .

The decision *evidently meant* the postponement, not the abandonment, of the Soviet demand for a triumvirate to replace the Secretary General. No comment on this was available tonight. . . .

The 11 members of the Security Council are to have their regular monthly luncheon meeting tomorrow. *It was believed* they might use that occasion to agree on a date for a meeting. . . .

The election of a Secretary General is carried out by the General Assembly on the recommendation of the Security Council.

The election question *apparently* was the only point settled in talks that went on from 10:30 a.m. to 1:10 p.m. . . .

Mr. [Adlai] Stevenson, United States ambassador to the UN, said as he left the meeting that the Soviet group had again brought up Premier Fidel Castro's five conditions for settlement of the Cuban crisis, made public October 28.

United States sources have said repeatedly that those points could not be a basis for discussion.

Merely digging for additional facts does not enable a reporter to interpret some events: he must have acquired a specialized knowledge of the field in which he is reporting. Here is an example from a dispatch by Theodore Shabad to the *New York Times*:

MOSCOW—A revolutionary overhaul of economy-planning procedures appears to be in the making in the Soviet Union. . . .

These reforms are expected to be enacted at a plenary meeting of the Communist party's Central Committee next month.

As usual in major Soviet reforms, intensive public discussion in the press indicates that the basic decision has already been taken and that details are being worked out.

Reporting audience reaction to a political speech is hazardous. A reporter usually cannot make an adequate evaluation of applause or booing when the audience is large. United Press International's policy has been stated as follows: "Our practice is to avoid appraising audience reaction on our own responsibility, although we often quote individuals in an attempt to give a cross-section of opinion."[6]

The Q and A Device

Probably the most effective way to explain complex new legislation, economic problems, and international issues is the question-and-answer method. This method facilitates the reader's comprehension because the writer breaks down the components of the problem or issue by stating them in question form and then supplies the answer for each component. It is especially helpful for informing different audiences, some of whom are concerned with one or more aspects of a problem or issue but not with all. The writer, therefore, tries to think of all of the audiences and to inform each of them. Here, in part, is an example from the *Wall Street Journal* about a business tax credit bill before Congress:

> WASHINGTON—The dairy that buys a new milk truck, the steel company that acquires a new blast furnace, and the railroad company that lays down new track—all can expect some tax relief beginning this year. . . .
>
> Here are answers to some of the questions most often asked about the Ways and Means Committee's latest version of the plan first submitted by the President last year.
>
> *Q. Just what is the tax credit?*
> A. It is an amount subtracted from a concern's tax liability; that is, from the amount of federal taxes owed by the concern; it is not a deduction from taxable income. Thus, a company that owes $300,000 in federal taxes and claims a $10,000 credit for investment would pay a $290,000 tax.
>
> *Q. What property is eligible for the credit?*
> A. Tangible personal property as defined by the government, or other property—except buildings—used directly in manufacturing, production, extraction, transportation or communications and purchased after December 31, 1961. . . .
>
> *Q. Is no real property eligible for the credit?*
> A. Exclusions include, besides buildings, land purchased for the con-

[6] *UP Reporter,* May 22, 1958.

struction of business facilities. But railroad tracks would be eligible. Moreover, items classified as real property in many states are regarded as tangible personal property by the federal government and hence are eligible for the credit. . . . Thus, refrigerators installed in a grocery store—classed as real property in many states—would be eligible for the credit.

Q. Does the credit apply to investment in both new and used property?

A. Yes. But in the case of used property a businessman can claim the credit on only $50,000 worth of purchases in any one year.

Q. How is the tax credit calculated?

A. That depends on the useful life of the item acquired.

If it has a useful life of eight years or more, the credit would be 8% of the cost of the equipment; if such an item cost $10,000, the credit would be $800.

If the item has a useful life of six years or seven years, the credit would be 8% of two-thirds of the cost. For a $10,000 item, the credit then would be $533. . . .

Q. Who determines the useful life of an item?

A. Useful lives are listed in the Treasury's Bulletin F. A business man can challenge any such listing, but the Treasury makes the final decision.

Q. Does the credit apply to equipment purchased by public utilities?

A. Partly. The credit is only half as much, or 4%, for public utilities. . . .

Q. When would the plan go into effect?

A. During the current taxable year, that is, the year beginning December 31. . . .

Exercise: Here is (1) a wire service dispatch from Washington which reports a revision by the government of its restrictions on the import of oil, and (2) additional facts. Rewrite the story in 500 words to include the additional facts. Try to organize the facts in a way that will facilitate the reader's comprehension. Before you begin your organization of facts, however, consider who are your audiences for this story. You need not include all of the facts. First the news story:

WASHINGTON—The President yesterday revised oil import rules to guarantee domestic producers what White House sources called a "fair share" of United States petroleum sales.

Officials said the new order would not cause immediate or direct hardship to nations which sell oil in the U.S. It appeared clear, however, that the eventual effect would be to put something of a squeeze on imports.

An important aspect of the order would limit imports of liquid petroleum east of the Rocky Mountains on the basis of production rather than demand.

Percentages

Imports are now limited to 9 per cent of probable demand. The new formula would set the import limit at 12.2 per cent of all crude oil and natural gas liquids produced over the preceding six months.

Under the order, effective January 1, imports from Mexico and Canada —which previously have not counted against the import limits—would hereafter be included in the overall import ceiling.

Canada's imports would not be restricted. However, Canadian oil or oil products Canada sold in this country would hereafter be charged against the total allowable imports, with the result that less would be left for other importing nations such as Venezuela.

Security

The President said he issued the order to "enhance the ability of the petroleum industry to meet possible national security demands."

Interior Secretary Udall said the most important of the changes ordered by the President was designed to insure that domestic oil production and oil imports will share proportionately in future increases in demand in the area east of the Rockies.

The new order affects only that area.

Here are some additional facts:

a) The oil import issue first reached the crisis stage eight years ago. It was a year when Congress was enacting basic United States trade legislation. Domestic oil and coal interests threatened to amend the law with specific curbs on oil from abroad.

These curbs were forestalled by another amendment embodying a so-called "national security clause." The clause, which is still in the law, permits the President to impose curbs on a product if imports of it are found to be a threat to national security.

The clause has been invoked for only one product—oil. The ground was that imports of less expensive foreign oil were a deterrent to development of new oil resources in this country. In event of war, it was argued, the United States would be cut off from foreign oil and would need more domestic production.

At first, after passage of the legislation, so-called "voluntary controls" were tried. But later the controls were made mandatory on importers.

b) The effect of oil-import curbs is to make oil and its derivatives, including gasoline, more expensive in this country. Foreign oil costs less to produce and deliver to the United States than domestic oil costs.

c) Defense planners figure that the United States would be cut off from most foreign sources of oil should a shooting war break out and that the government should encourage domestic producers to stay in business by maintaining oil import curbs.

d) Oil producers, mostly small independent operators, have been pressuring the government to reduce imports to bolster their sagging sales. Although demand for oil is rising, domestic output has leveled off chiefly because of the steady increase in imports and because of fast-rising unrestricted shipments from Canada.

e) Administration spokesmen emphasized that the new control formula would not reduce total imports, but will hold down increases that might have occurred had the demand-based formula been maintained. The long-term uptrend in demand probably will continue.

f) It is understood that imports authorized for the first half of next year will total about 783,000 barrels, about 2,250 barrels more than in the first six months of this year.

g) Allocations for individual companies probably will be announced this week by the Department of the Interior.

h) Mexico has for the past 18 months voluntarily restricted its shipments into the United States to 30,000 barrels daily. Canada has made no similar pledge, but officials say oil talks with the Canadians will begin probably early next year. Oil imports from Canada to areas east of the Rockies have risen from around 60,000 barrels daily in 1959 to more than 100,000 barrels a day.

i) The change is aimed at reserving for domestic producers a greater portion of the annual 2% to 2.5% growth in this area's demand for petroleum products.

OBJECTIVENESS

Where does explanation end and evaluation begin? This question has perplexed newspaper men in recent years after it had become apparent that certain politicians were taking an illegitimate advantage of newspapers' efforts to be objective. The question has never bothered the French because every reader of a French newspaper is aware of the particular bias of each newspaper and reads a newspaper with a certain amount of skepticism. Most American newspapers, however, have taken pride in the fact that they reserve evaluation of persons, policies, and events for the editorial page.

One way in which propagandists for business and labor groups have taken advantage of the objectiveness of newspapers has been their use of certain evaluative terms which the newspapers have accepted uncritically. Some examples: "right to work law," "full crew law," and "fair trade law."

A newspaper that is entirely objective may also assist a propagandist who makes a false derogatory statement about another person. When a United States senator makes an accusation, it is newsworthy because of the importance of the source. The report that Senator A *says* that Mr. B is a "fellow traveler" is an objective fact. But it may not be a fact that Mr. B *is* a "fellow traveler." In most circumstances, a reporter is not able to controvert the assertion; about all he can do is to give Mr. B an opportunity to deny the accusation—a practice that is standard in newspaper journalism. The *New York World-Telegram and Sun* reported a senator's charge that the Democrats deliberately sent American forces to defeat in Korea, but it carried the following "precede" to the story that quoted the senator: "The *World-Telegram and Sun* prints the following dispatch because it is a statement by a United States senator. It should be pointed out, however, that Sen. William E. Jenner offered no facts to substantiate his irresponsible charge."

Newspapers in recent years have corrected statements made by politicians and officials. In the 1954 Republican senatorial primary in Maine, Senator Smith defeated an opponent who, she had said, was "planted" in the race by Senator McCarthy. The public was entitled to know to what extent this result was a true measure of Senator McCarthy's influence. One wire service reported the result in this way: "Senator Margaret Chase Smith, a longtime foe of Senator Joseph R. McCarthy, today scored a landslide victory over Robert L. Jones, a candidate she charged was planted in Maine's senatorial primary by the Wisconsin Republican." Another wire service, however, included these paragraphs in its report:

> . . . While the balloting bestowed a heavy vote of confidence on the silver-haired, 56-year-old Mrs. Smith and the record on which she ran, the Jones defeat scarcely could be translated into one for McCarthy too.
> The Wisconsin senator never was a

> solid issue during the campaign and neither contestant contended he was.
>
> Furthermore, it wasn't until the eve of the primary that Senator Smith came out and said that it appeared McCarthy deliberately planted Jones in the race against her. That was at a time when she herself said the people already had made up their minds how to vote and "last-minute appeals and charges" could have little effect on them.

In 1962, the United States delegation to a conference of American states at Punte del Este, Uruguay, obtained very few of its objectives and the prestige of the United States was considerably lowered. These facts were reported by the American wire service reporters who attended the conference. When the Secretary of State returned from the conference he received a hero's welcome from President Kennedy in an elaborate White House reception to which leading members of Congress were invited. The President spoke of the great success of the diplomatic mission. The *New York Times,* in reporting the reception, included this paragraph: "Some observers thought the intensive administration publicity was aimed at Congress, whose support is needed for the expensive Alliance for Progress hemispheric aid program."

When is a reporter justified in abandoning objectiveness by making evaluations on his own responsibility? There appear to be two answers to this question: (1) Only the most competent reporter should be entrusted by his editor with this freedom; a reporter of mediocre ability should not attempt this kind of reporting. (2) The competent reporter should always remind himself of his own fallibility.

> For class discussion: *1.* Is this lead objective: "Patrolman Wade Powell resigned today from the police force. This was the fourth resignation within the last three weeks"? *Note:* the size of the police force is seven patrolmen and sergeants plus the chief of police.
>
> 2. Do you think a reporter can pretend to objectivity by asking embarrassing questions to which the reporter already knows the answers?
>
> *3. Time* says: "Is *Time* objective? The answer: *Time* has certain basic convictions as well as a sense of obligation to evaluate the news in the light of these convictions."
>
> *Newsweek* says: *"Newsweek's* coverage is complemented with signed-opinion articles, which are set apart from the main body of the magazine . . . *Newsweek* believes that no one wants to read

an editor's or publisher's opinions, skillfully inserted and disguised as news. That is why opinion articles are always signed, and even interpretive paragraphs are labeled as such and set apart from the straight news reporting in a story. *Newsweek* believes . . . that the adult reader, once he understands an issue, is fully equipped to make up his own mind."

Which philosophy do you prefer, and why?

CHAPTER 7

Syntax

In the last chapter we discussed the organization of facts in the news story form. This chapter will discuss the proper and improper arrangement of words and word forms within the sentence. Chapter 8 will discuss the news writer's choice of words and other expressions. The discussion in this chapter is limited to those aspects of syntax with which the beginning news writer seems to have the most difficulty.

SENTENCE LENGTH

It is often easier to write a long sentence than a short one. The writer who is narrating several facts finds it easier to string the facts (or thoughts) together with conjunctions and relative pronouns than to use periods. One reason for long sentences—paradoxically—is the writer's desire to reduce redundancy and to achieve rhythm. G. A. Miller[1] has illustrated the purpose of abbreviation. When the writer says, "Joe, who lives in Boston and writes books, has a brown hat," he is abbreviating a series of four sentences: "Joe lives in Boston." "Joe writes books." "Joe has a hat." "Joe's hat is brown." By using a conjunction and a personal pronoun, the writer avoids both the repetition of the word "Joe" and a breathless, staccato style.

A second reason for overlong sentences is the need to qualify the main thought in the sentence. In legal and scientific writing, qualification is necessary to achieve precision. But in news writing the qualifying phrases and clauses usually serve only the purpose of particularizing. It is not necessary, therefore, to put all of the qualifying elements in one sentence. Here are two bad examples:

French officials expressed concern that fighting in this neighborhood might interfere with traffic on colonial route No. 1, the great highway crossing North Africa from Tunis to Casa-

[1] *Language and Communication* (New York, 1951), pp. 125–26.

> blanca which passes through the village of Culmes, 12 miles northeast of Tiliouine, a resort popular for its mineral springs.

> On the heels of its weakness, marketwise, following the publication of its earnings statement for the fiscal year ended March 31, showing $2.59 a common share, compared with previous estimates holding close to the $3.03 a common share realized in the previous fiscal period, Beaunit Mills, Inc. common stock has recouped most of its previous loss, as followers of this situation apparently gained encouragement from management's comments regarding the extremely satisfactory state of current operations.

Exercise: Without omitting any fact, recast the following sentence by breaking it into two or three sentences, beginning as follows: "Authorities believe they have found a connection between gambler Frank Costello and a Las Vegas hotel."

> NEW YORK—The mysterious $651,284 notation on a slip of paper found in racketeer Frank Costello's pocket the night he was shot tallies exactly with the total gambling winnings for a 24-day period at the Tropicana Hotel in Las Vegas, a spokesman for Manhattan District Attorney Frank S. Hogan said today.

Statistical studies of those language elements thought to be related to ease of understanding (often called "readability") show that sentence length and sentence complexity are among the most important explanatory factors.[2] Sentence complexity is related to ease of understanding—independent of sentence length.

Several "readability" formulas have been developed so that a writer can test his success in facilitating ease of understanding. Most of them include average sentence length as a factor. They will be discussed on pages 111–112.

An average sentence length of about twenty words is desirable. The average lead sentence, however, is necessarily a little longer; a desirable length is less than twenty-five words.

When we say an "average" sentence length, we assume there will be

[2] J. E. Brinton and W. A. Danielson, "A Factor Analysis of Language Elements Affecting Readability," *Journalism Quarterly*, 35:420–26 (1953).

considerable variation in the length of all of the sentences in a news story. Sentences of uniform length result in a monotony of rhythm.[3] An example of variation in length is a news story in the *Wall Street Journal* which had fifteen sentences with an average length of twenty-four words; the length in words of each sentence was 27, 46, 15, 29, 33, 36, 16, 18, 7, 7, 22, 23, 15, 37, and 29.

A skillful writer, however, can sometimes construct a long sentence which yields a more pleasing style than would have resulted from writing the thoughts in two or three sentences. Here is an example from E. B. White: "The liquor store in the county seat was held up by a masked gunman recently of $2,672.45, which turned out to be the day's receipts and, of course, gave a much clearer picture of the amount of drinking done around here than any previous event."

POSITION OF ELEMENTS WITHIN THE SENTENCE

The normal sentence order, as was mentioned on page 60, is (1) the subject, (2) the finite verb, and (3, 4) the indirect and direct objects. But these elements often have modifiers. The position of a modifier within a sentence can (*a*) determine emphasis within the sentence and (*b*) violate logic so as to confuse the reader.

Emphasis

The emphatic parts of a sentence are the beginning and the end; in a long sentence the end is more emphatic than the beginning because the thought builds up to a climax. This means that *however, therefore,* and similar adverbs should be buried within the sentence—unless there is a particular reason for stressing them. Since the time element in a news story is seldom of much importance, *today* and similar adverbs should usually be buried within the lead sentence, as was explained on page 60.

Use of the passive voice is also a device for emphasizing a particular element in the sentence because it reverses the positions of the object and the subject of the verb. When, for example, the writer wishes to emphasize the object, he writes "The proposal was referred to the Committee on Public Works" instead of "The Council referred the proposal to the Committee on Public Works."

Punctuation can also determine emphasis when it is used in connection with the interpolation of a word or phrase between the subject and the verb. Because commas and dashes interrupt the flow of the sentence, they focus attention on the interpolation. An example: "Prospective employers—and the government—ask such searching questions nowadays about

---

[3] Sentence rhythm is discussed on pp. 125–126.

what college students say in the classroom that University of California teachers decided yesterday not to give any voluntary answers."

Iteration of a word or a phrase is obviously a way to obtain emphasis of the writer's main thought. An example in a news story about the absence in Texas of laws to regulate the sale of certain firearms: "All you need to buy a $29.50 pistol in Houston is $29.50."

Parallelism

When a writer puts logically parallel thoughts in constructions that are not grammatically parallel he confuses the reader: like meanings should be put in like constructions. The most common violation of parallelism is to use an infinitive and a gerund in a parallel construction. Thus: "To swim and skating are his favorite sports" instead of "Swimming and skating are his favorite sports."

A second kind of violation of parallelism is to change the subject in the middle of the sentence whereas logic calls for coordinate clauses joined by *and* and *but*. An example: "One of the amendments was approved but rejections were voted on the others." This should be: "One of the amendments was approved but the others were rejected."

> For class discussion: Here are three ways to write the same thought. Which of these sentences best meets the requirements for parallel construction and sentence emphasis?
>
> *a*) Councilman Mitchell pointed out that the city is growing rapidly and that an improved system for distribution of electricity is needed.
>
> *b*) Councilman Mitchell pointed out that since the city is growing rapidly an improved system for distribution of electricity is needed.
>
> *c*) Councilman Mitchell pointed out that, since the city is growing rapidly, it needs an improved distribution of electricity.

The Position of Modifiers

A modifier is a sentence element which describes, defines, or restricts some other sentence element. The modifier may be a word, a phrase, or a clause. *The writer facilitates comprehension when he places the modifier as close to the element it modifies as logic requires.* This rule is sometimes violated in these ways:

1. *When the modifier (or modifiers) is interposed between the subject and the verb in a long sentence.* Here are two examples from wire service reports:

LOS ANGELES—Bos Burns, whose tall tales of Arkansas country folks and serenades on a gaspipe and whiskey funnel contraption called a bazooka that made him one of the nation's favorite comics, died today.

LONDON—Edgar James Sullivan, in his 60s, known professionally as James Bonar Colleano, who with his wife and son were part of the famous Colleano family acrobatic team that toured the United States with the Ringling Bros. circus, died yesterday.

2. *When a modifier is out of place.* This creates ambiguity. There are several varieties of this violation of the rule about keeping modifiers close to the elements they refer to. Here are some examples:

. . . Pressing too hard to make double plays, three errors resulted.

. . . If convicted on the assault charge, a judge may impose any sentence he sees fit on the defendant.

. . . Henry Miller was sentenced to five years in the reformatory for robbery in superior court today.

Exercise: Recast the foregoing sentences.

3. *When a nonrestrictive (i.e., nonlimiting) relative phrase or clause is* not *set off by commas or when a restrictive relative phrase or clause* is *set off by commas.*

An example of a nonrestrictive clause: "He arrived from Kabul, which is in Afghanistan."

An example of a restrictive clause: "A shortstop who can hit .300 deserves more salary."

Because the following sentence is correctly punctuated it is not ambiguous: "He was a former lover of Christine Keeler who was sentenced to three years in prison for beating her up."

When the modifying phrase or clause can be omitted without changing the meaning of the main clause, the modifying clause is nonrestrictive. When omission of the modifying clause changes the meaning of the main clause the modifying clause is restrictive.

For class discussion: Is this sentence properly punctuated? "Cohn was called into Harry Weinberg's takeover of the Fifth Avenue Coach Co. through Jerry Finkelstein, owner of Gray Line Motor Tours, Inc., a subsidiary of Fifth Avenue, whose sole asset is 204,403 shares of Fifth Avenue."

TENSE

For reasons mentioned below, news writers need to make more decisions about the sequence of tenses than do other writers. The following discussion of time relationships of verbs is by Theodore M. Bernstein, an assistant managing editor of the *New York Times:*

> The conventional books on grammar and syntax lead you a little way into the forest, point out a few trails that you probably would have no difficulty in discerning for yourself, then abandon you. For most users of English this is sufficient. For the newspaper writer, however, it is not enough because journalism is, for the most part, recording the past—and not exclusively the immediate past, but successive layers or planes of past time. Hence, the proper alignment of tenses is a continuing problem and a constant challenge.
>
> *Brass tacks.*
> 1. In the present tense the sequence presents no problem: "He says he is hungry." Turning it into the past tense, you get, as the *normal sequence:* "He said he was hungry."
> 2. To this normal past-tense sequence there are exceptions. When the subject matter of the dependent clause concerns something that is habitual or permanently true the present tense is retained. The *exceptional sequence* (or, as Fowler terms it, the vivid sequence) is used in such sentences as these: "The child did not know that dogs bite." "The teacher told the class that the earth revolves around the sun."
> 3. A simple past event is recorded in the past tense: "The police *reported* the accident." An event prior to a simple past event is recorded in the past perfect tense: "The police reported a car *had swerved* off the road." Still earlier events are also recorded in the past perfect tense: "The police reported a car had swerved off the road after its steering gear *had broken.*"
>
> That is about as far as most syntax books take you. But let us unclasp our Boy Scout knives and proceed.
> 4. The purpose of using the past perfect tense, of course, is to indicate the priority of events. If the subordinate clause includes a time element that itself indicates the priority, the past perfect becomes unnecessary, even redundant. Proper usage would be: "A close friend reported Jones *said* (not had said) *last week* that he would be elected."
> 5. When the "he said" phrase appears anywhere in the sentence but at the beginning the verbs in the other clauses are not affected by it; they remain in the same tense as in the original direct quotation. In such cases the "he said" phrase does not govern the sentence; it is a mere parenthetical

interpolation. . . . Hence this sentence is proper: "Jones is sure, he said, that he will be elected."

6. To the foregoing paragraph there is one exception: When a statement is unequivocally associated with a particular time in the past, the tense used must indicate this. Although it is correct to use the present tense— that is, the tense of the original direct quotation—in such a sentence as, "He is sick and tired, he said, of graft in the police force," it is necessary to use the past tense in one like this: "He was sick and tired, he said, and asked to be excused from testifying." Another example of a statement associated with a particular time in the past: "He was glad, the speaker said, to see so many friendly faces." These past-tense usages, it should be emphasized, are exceptional.

7. Phrases like "according to" and "in the opinion of" are equivalent to "he said." When they appear at the beginnings of sentences they govern the subsequent verbs; when they appear anywhere else they are considered to be mere parenthetical interpolations and do not govern the verbs.

8. The tense of the dominant verb in a sentence does not necessarily and indiscriminately govern every other verb in the sentence. Sometimes clauses are interpolated or added almost as if the writer were taking you aside and giving you some information quite outside the context of the rest of the sentence. In such cases the verbs of these clauses go their own way. Example: "Congress *was prepared* to fight it out no matter how long it *took*, and it obviously *will* (not would) take many days." Another example: "George M. Haskew, water engineer, *said* the main reservoir of the Plainfield Union Water Company, which *supplies* (not supplied) many communities in that area, *was* full for the first time since early June."

In the foregoing eight items the forest undoubtedly has not been fully explored. But the items should be of some help in permitting you to pick your way through it.[4]

For class discussion: In which of these sentences has the writer used the appropriate sequence of tenses?

a) He said last night that he had been labor secretary of the Communist party in New York from 1959 until he was expelled last year.

b) A group of Air Force officers staged a sudden counter-coup and arrested Rodriguez Echevarria, who seized power and ousted the Council of State Tuesday.

c) Among those subpoenaed has been Harley Rothschild, 37-year-old chairman of the Progressive Labor Movement.

d) Eisenhower said emphatically that he is pledged not to destroy TVA.

e) Two small children were burned to death in their Oakland bedroom early yesterday, and a few hours later police said their father had confessed setting the fire.

[4] "Winners & Sinners," Oct. 1, 1954.

f) He said that oak is the best wood for floors.

g) Communist diplomatic sources said today that Soviet Premier Nikita Khrushchev was planning to visit Africa next autumn.

h) The Red Cross opens its annual drive at a luncheon today.

WORDINESS

Beginning news writers frequently are guilty of wordiness (verbosity, verbiage) in sentences. Examples:

1. "The carpenters' union claims *it holds* jurisdiction over the installation of steel platforms in the warehouse."

2. "The company is *engaged in construction of* several motels (instead of *building*)."

3. "He was indicted *on a charge of* robbery" (instead of *for robbery*).

4. "*Both* sides are deadlocked in the negotiations. . . ."

This fault is often the result of the writer's failure to reread his story to test for sentence logic.

Redundancy also results from using formal phrases which have unnecessary words. Some examples: *on the occasion of* ("when," "on"), *in the event that* ("if"), *with the exception of* ("except"), and *at the present time* ("now").

A writer is also sometimes guilty of this kind of tautology: *prior preparation, young debutante, a goatee on his chin, totally destroy, Jewish rabbi, mesh together, still persist, new innovation, plummet downward, continue on, throng of persons, young children, the same equality, flaming inferno, strangle to death, over exaggerate, elaborate further,* and *surprising upset.*

PUNCTUATION

A good many beginning news writers do not punctuate correctly (and, therefore, retard the reader's comprehension). The failure occurs in these instances:

1. Use of commas and dashes with appositional words, phrases, and clauses.

2. Use of the comma with a dependent conditional clause preceding the principal clause.

3. Use of commas with nonrestrictive relative clauses.

4. Use of the semicolon in a series of names with addresses.

5. Use of quotation marks when a quotation is within a quotation.

6. Use of the apostrophe in the possessive pronoun *its*.

Exercise: *1.* Referring to the section on punctuation in *Webster's New Collegiate Dictionary* (1960 ed.), beginning at page 1149, write the rules for correct punctuation in the six instances mentioned above.

2. Copy and punctuate these paragraphs:

a) Wilson alleges that since Thompson was an employee of the Universal Oil Company and was acting as its agent at the time of the accident the company is also responsible.

b) Well I was looking down toward the sidewalk when I heard a woman shout Richie get out of the street Then I saw this woman run across the street into the path of Mr. Clark's automobile.

CHAPTER 8

Diction

This chapter has to do with two matters: (1) what kinds of words and expressions facilitate comprehension and (2) what kinds of words are proper, or correct.

WORDS THAT FACILITATE COMPREHENSION

We referred in Chapter 7 to formulas which had been developed so that a writer could test the ease of understanding of his composition. These are called "readability" formulas.[1] The formula most often used by news writers is the revised Flesch formula. It is in two parts: the first is called "reading ease" and the second is called "human interest."

The Flesch Readability Formula

The reading ease formula uses two elements: (1) average sentence length in words; and (2) average word length in syllables. The human interest formula also uses two elements: (1) average percentage of "personal words" (i.e., all nouns with natural gender, all pronouns except neuter pronouns, and the words *people* when used with the plural verbs and *folks*); and (2) average percentage of "personal sentences" (i.e., "spoken sentences," marked by quotation marks or otherwise; questions, commands, requests, and other sentences directly addressed to the reader; exclamations; and grammatically incomplete sentences whose meaning has to be inferred from the context").

Both formulas yield a score of from 100 to 0. The numerical scores correspond to such verbal descriptions of style as "easy," "fairly easy," and "very difficult" for reading ease; and "dull," "interesting," and "dramatic" for human interest. These are exhibited in the following table:

[1] Most of these are described and evaluated in J. S. Chall, *Readability: An Appraisal of Research Application* (Columbus, Ohio, 1958). See also G. R. Klare and B. Buck, *Know Your Reader: A Scientific Approach to Readability* (Ames, Iowa, 1963).

Reading Ease Scores	Description of Style	Human Interest Scores	Description of Style
0 to 30	Very difficult	0 to 10	Dull
30 to 50	Difficult	10 to 20	Mildly interesting
50 to 60	Fairly difficult	20 to 40	Interesting
60 to 70	Standard	40 to 60	Highly interesting
70 to 80	Fairly easy	60 to 100	Dramatic
80 to 90	Easy		
90 to 100	Very easy		

The reading ease formula is not a recipe for writing, but a way to tell whether or not one has been writing in a way that decreases the efficiency of his communication. Its main value is that it provides a definite measure that the writer, from time to time, can use as a check. Editors have always directed writers to use average short sentences and short words but the writers, after an initial conscious effort to comply, drift back to the easier method of long sentences and long words. Now, with this formula, editors have a way of keeping the writers in line.

We repeat that the formula measures only an *average*. It does not require every sentence and every word to be short. It does require that there not be a long succession of long sentences and that short words are to be preferred to long words.

The reading ease formula is as follows:
1. Multiply the average sentence length in words by 1.015.
2. Multiply the number of syllables per 100 words by .846.
3. Add these figures together.
4. Subtract this sum from 206.835, to give you your readability score.

For more complete directions for computing the reading ease and the human interest formulas, refer to R. Flesch, *How to Test Readability*.[2]

Short vs. Long Words

It is not intended that you follow a readability formula out of the window. As G. A. Miller has said: "The use of short sentences, simple words and personal references does not mathematically make the writing good. It merely avoids one common way in which writing is bad."[3]

Generally, it is preferable to use a short word (usually of Anglo-Saxon origin) instead of a long word derived from the Latin or Greek. Examples: *audacious* ("bold"), *encumbrance* ("burden"), and *remonstrate* ("protest," "object"). One should keep in mind, however, that Latin derivatives,

---

[2] (New York), 1951. These formulas are also in R. Flesch, "A New Readability Yardstick," *Journal of Applied Psychology*, 32:221–33 (1948).

[3] *Language and Communication* (New York, 1951), p. 139.

with their affixes and suffixes, can often convey a more precise meaning; for example, *pay* is not synonymous with *compensation* in all circumstances.

Familiar words (i.e., words most frequently used) are usually short words. But there are some exceptions: *fundamental* is somewhat more familiar than *basic*.[4] The writer should choose a familiar word when possible, although he must make a guess as to how frequently the word has been used since he cannot conveniently consult a word list.

Concrete vs. Abstract Words

Long words are more likely to be abstract words, but the writer should prefer a concrete word regardless of its length. Here are some paragraphs that have too many abstract words:

> Members of the Oregon state liquor commission have completed a compilation of recommendations on administration of the liquor-by-the-drink law.

> The pamphlet held that the Port Authority had the financial ability and know-how to assume the rail problem and integrate it with overall developments and administration of transportation policy.

Abstract words and expressions must be chosen sometimes to avoid an insufferable redundancy. Thus "transportation facilities" is an abbreviation of the sum of such concrete words as "railroads," "steamships," "airplanes," "buses," and "automobiles." In some instances it is an appropriate expression because an abbreviation is required. But in other instances it is, at first reading, ambiguous and its use compels the reader to translate it into some of its components so that he has an image of one or more of them. This process of translation, of course, retards comprehension. The two quotations above are illustrative of what has just been said.

Abstruse and Technical Words

When the writer uses a word or a term that is abstruse or recondite or obviously unfamiliar to most readers he should either define the expression or put it in a context which defines it.

The following is an example:

> WASHINGTON—Attorney General Brownell will study the "wet-

[4] See E. L. Thorndike and I. Lorge, *Teachers' Word Book of 30,000 Words* (New York, 1949).

back" problem on the spot—the California-Mexico border.

The Justice Department said yesterday he was leaving soon to look into the situation created by Mexican migratory laborers, some of whom enter the country illegally by swimming streams.

A technical term, however, can seldom be defined by context: it must be defined parenthetically. The use of scientific and legal terms is discussed at various places in later sections of this textbook.

For class discussion: Why did the writer of the following news story translate "establish criteria" into "pin down" in the first paragraph and then use "establish criteria" in the second paragraph?

E. William Henry, in his first speech to a broadcasters' group since he became Federal Communications Commission chairman, said it is time the FCC pinned down its own idea of how much radio and TV commercialization is too much.

"Whether by rule or by policy statement," he told the International Radio and Television Society, "we need to establish criteria which will tell the public and the industry what we mean."

Words That Bring Out an Image

Comprehension is facilitated by the choice of words which educe an image. Thus: "The riot was *precipitated* by the. . . ." "Precipitate" is of Latin derivation and originally meant "to hurl down," as from a precipice; it does not bring out an image. The meaning of "precipitate" has been learned by most newspaper readers, but the meaning of "touched off" is supplied instantly by the context.

Figurative expressions that are appropriate to the event being reported supply an additional dimension of meaning. An example: "A gas turbine engine developed by General Electric Company to drive boats and oil rigs has *sputtered out and died*. GM's flight propulsion division yesterday announced that it had dropped plans to produce the LM50, a 500-horsepower turboshaft engine for marine and industrial use."

When the United States Senate finally passed a bill for the establishment of an agency to control and manage communication by satellites (e.g.,

"Telstar") after a filibuster against it had failed, the Associated Press reported that the bill "finally broke through the Senate sound barrier." In reporting abandonment of a flood control plan, a newspaper said the plan was "washed out because. . . ." This is the way the *New York Times* reported a schism in an Argentine political party: "Every time Argentine politicians try on the tattered coat of political cooperation there is a ripping sound and the elbow of dissension pops through. This has just happened in the big Intransigent Radical party. . . ."

The news writer, however, must beware of false analogies that do not educe an image. For example, in reporting the collision between two ships a writer said that one vessel was hit with "a fatal force that ripped open staterooms and crumpled one vessel like a smashed banana." Another example: "Dan Molina ran screaming from the building looking as if he had been hit by a flame thrower." How many readers had seen such an incident or a picture of the victim of a flame thrower?

> Exercise: The title of the foregoing section is "Words that *bring out* an image." The writer might have said *"educe* an image." Would *educe* be appropriate for a textbook but not for a news story? Would it be correct to say in a textbook *"evoke* an image"? From what Latin words are *educe* and *evoke* derived?

The Meaning of a Word Is Its Use

The lexicographers who make our dictionaries merely *record* the usage of words. They and others whom they employ make "citation slips" of individual words and the context in which the words were used. For each word there is a citation slip on which is written the exact quotation from the writer who used the word. These citations prepared by the "word watchers" are collected over a quarter century. Then the lexicographers construct definitions of the words as determined by the context of the quotations. That is, they state what the word meant to the particular writer who used it. The lexicographers themselves do not determine what the word means nor do they decree what the usage ought to be. It is in this way that new words acquire general usage and are admitted into our dictionaries.

Some words have been used by writers in different "senses" and all of the senses are stated by the lexicographers. The word "key," for example, has about twenty different meanings, each one being related to a specific operational referent (e.g., music, lock, fraternity).

Over a long period the meaning of some words changes. That is because writers have ceased to attribute the previous meaning to them. Such words are designated in a dictionary as "archaic." An example is *prevent*, which formerly meant "to anticipate" and "to precede," but now means "to forestall" and "to hinder."

LEVELS OF LANGUAGE: USAGE

Dictionaries report words on three levels—formal, informal, and what might be called vulgate—and they distinguish these levels. Formal language is that used in official documents, in scientific and academic writings, and in dignified public addresses. Informal language is that used by educated people in conversation and in popular literature and broadcasting. The third level is slang and other neologisms; when a dictionary reports words on the third level, it specifies that level.

Although scholars today (unlike in an earlier day) agree that there is no "transcendental standard of correctness,"[5] some persons resist neologisms. When, for example, *Webster's Third New International Dictionary* was published in 1961, the *New York Times* decided to continue to use the second edition for spelling and usage and to use the third edition only for the definitions of new words, especially scientific words. This newspaper believes that much of the usage reported in the third edition does not conform with educated conventions. Since the *Times* is published for a serious and educated audience, it believes that its decision was correct. For a newspaper with a more general audience, perhaps the best practice is to fit the language to the subject matter of each news story, using a more formal language for serious reports and informal language for stories of a lighter tone. It should be kept in mind, however, that our language changes because society changes and that much of the language of daily conversation irresistibly forces its way into general usage.

CANT, JARGON, ARGOT, AND SLANG

Cant, in the sense used here, is the vocabulary and idiom of a profession or trade. Numerous words have come into our formal language from the stage, from aviation, and from sports (e.g., *stooge, takeoff, kickoff*). H. L. Mencken, in his *American Language, Supplement II,* lists forty-six pages of cant terms classified by occupation.[6]

The special vocabulary of the world of criminals, prostitutes, and gamblers is a form of cant called *argot*. Some of this argot has been admitted into our standard language (e.g., *racket, kickback*).

---

[5] See Jeremy Warburg, "Notions of Correctness," Supplement 2 to R. Quirk, *The Use of English* (London, 1962), p. 315.

[6] (New York, 1948), pp. 731–77.

The term *jargon* is also sometimes synonymous with cant, although the term is also applied to language that is "pretentious and unnecessarily obscure," such as is often used by bureaucrats; another term for it is *gobbledygook.*

Slang, as now defined by Webster, is "a nonstandard vocabulary composed of words and senses characterized primarily by connotations of extreme informality and usually a currency not limited to a particular region and composed typically of coinages or arbitrarily changed words, clipped or shortened forms, extravagant, forced, or facetious figures of speech, or verbal novelties usually experiencing quick popularity and relatively rapid decline into disuse."

A large part of slang, according to H. L. Mencken, is invented by "gag-writers, newspaper columnists, and press agents and the rest borrowed from the vocabulary of criminals, prostitutes and the lower orders of showfolk."[7]

Some of our standard words once were slang (e.g., *mob,* from *mobile vulgus,* and *bus* from *omnibus*). But most slang has a brief currency. It sometimes becomes acceptable because it is a shortened form and because the word for which it is a substitute is not frequently used and is, therefore, unfamiliar (e.g., *yesman* for *sycophant*) or metaphorical.

> Exercise: *1.* Look up in *Webster's Third New International Dictionary* and decide whether or not *know-how* is a better term than *skill.* Is *boo-boo* to be preferred to *mistake?* Also evaluate *hokum, phony, rubberneck,* and *blah.*
> 2. Improve this sentence: "Although he lost the *mayoralty* election, Hansen said he intends to enter the *gubernatorial* contest."
> 3. What is the meaning of these words: *co-ed, shambles, flaunt, flout,* and *media?*

SIBILANTS IN NEWS BROADCASTS

A problem that is more serious for radio and television news writers than for newspaper writers is the overuse of sibilants, as in this sentence: "The explosion sent scientists and soldiers scurrying for safety from the test site."

> Exercise: *1.* Referring to R. Flesch, *How to Test Readability,* for precise instructions, compute the reading ease score for the last newswriting exercise you did. Then analyze your story to ascertain whether you can improve its readability without any sacrifice of good style.
> 2. Here is a sentence which contains an excess of abstract words:

[7] *Ibid.,* p. 644.

"The cessation of home construction, which operated throughout the war period, developed an accretion of demand." How can you rewrite it to make it more concrete?

3. Are the following pairs of words synonymous?

revolver/pistol   sewage/sewerage
anxious/eager   another/additional
less/fewer   substitute/substitution
amateur/novice   realtor/real estate broker

CHAPTER 9

Making the Event Vivid

The news writer sometimes describes an event to which he has been an eyewitness. Among such events are parades, ceremonies, funerals of distinguished soldiers and statesmen, the dedication of bridges and buildings, missile shots, sports contests, and the execution of criminals. Because most events of this kind are spectacles, the writer's objective is to achieve vividness.

THE IMPORTANCE OF DETAIL

Vividness is achieved mainly by observing and presenting the details of the event. Presentation of the details and their order in time or space can cause the images to be sharp, clear, and salient. This means that the writer must be observant, as was the Associated Press reporter who wrote about a murder: "The *seersucker* night gown, with *white and red polka dots*, lay *eight* feet from the body. . . . Police were called *at 10 a.m.* The car was found *four hours and ten minutes* later."

When he reports certain ceremonies, parades, and criminal executions, the writer can usually obtain certain facts in advance of the event; for example, the order of personages and groups in the procession, or the number of steps on the scaffold. Here, in part, is a description of a criminal execution written by Art Hoppe of the *San Francisco Chronicle:*

> Barbara Graham, Jack Santo, and Emmett Perkins died yesterday in the San Quentin gas chamber, but only after the last frantic maneuvers of their attorneys had forced two delays.
> Mrs. Graham died as she had lived —in a tangle of emotional confusion. She was executed at 11:42 a.m., after two 45-minute delays.

One came at 10:43:30 a.m., just as she was leaving the death cell to make the 15-foot walk to the gas chamber.

"Why do they torture me so?" she asked Warden Harley O. Teets when he informed her of the latest delay. "I was ready to go at 10 o'clock."

Everyone agreed that, in the circumstances, she died well. She died with a black band across her eyes and a prayer on her lips. She died with her small pendant earrings quivering nervously.

'I Don't Want to Look'

She had asked for the mask yesterday morning. "I don't have to look at people," she said.

The mask hid her tired eyes and she looked pretty in her beige suit. Her lipstick was fresh, her short brown hair neatly done. The mask was placed over her eyes in the death cell and she made the last walk guided by two Catholic priests.

Her hands were trembling as three guards strapped her into the iron chair and the gold wedding band on her finger flashed in the bluish light.

She entered the chamber at 11:31 a.m.

At 11:33 a.m. the guards left the little window-lined steel tank, one pausing to pat her on the shoulder. The heavy steel door slammed shut.

'Hail Marys'

She sat there, swallowing nervously, her lips moving silently in what appeared to be "Hail Marys." At 11:34 a.m. Warden Teets gave the signal and the little cloth bag filled with cyanide tablets descended into the tank full of sulphuric acid beneath her chair.

She breathed deeply and her head slumped forward on her chest. Eight minutes later Dr. M. D. Wilcutts, chief medical officer of San Quentin, pronounced her dead. . . .

Here is a description of a person written more than one hundred years ago. It is a word portrait of Abraham Lincoln by William Howard Russell, war correspondent of *The Times* (of London), written for his diary:

. . . Soon afterward, there entered, with a shambling, loose, irregular, almost unsteady gait, a tall, lank, lean man, considerably over six feet in height, with stooping shoulders, long pendulous arms, terminating in hands of extra-ordinary dimensions, which, however, were far exceeded in proportion by his feet.

He was dressed in an ill-fitting, wrinkled suit of black which put one in mind of an undertaker's uniform at a funeral; round his neck a rope of black silk was knotted in a large bulb, with flying ends projecting beyond the collar of his coat; his turned down shirtcollar disclosed a sinewy muscular yellow neck, and above that, nestling in a great black mass of hair, bristling and compact like a riff of mourning pins, rose the strange quaint face and head, covered with its thatch of wild republican hair, of President Lincoln.

The impression produced by the size of his extremities, and by his flapping and wide projecting ears, may be removed by the appearance of kindliness, sagacity, and the awkward bonhommie of his face; the mouth is absolutely prodigious; the lips, straggling and extending almost from one line of black beard to the other, are kept in order by two deep furrows from the nostril to the chin; the nose itself—a prominent organ—stands out from the face with an inquiring, anxious air, as though it were sniffing for some good thing in the wind; the eyes dark full and deeply set, are penetrating, but full of an expression which almost amounts to tenderness; and above them projects the shaggy brow, running into the small hard frontal space, the development of which can scarcely be estimated accurately, owing to the irregular flocks of thick hair carelessly brushed across it. . . .

Time describes a surgical operation on a President:

. . . Only the President's lower-right belly peeped from beneath his green surgical sheets. Surgeon Heaton swabbed the area with an antiseptic, then raised his scalpel and made a six-inch incision to the right of the midline (between the navel and Ike's old appendectomy scar), extending upward to the rib margin. A trickle of blood was swabbed. Then Heaton cut through the relatively bloodless muscle wall into the abdominal cavity. Retractors held the gaping wound open as Heaton and Ravdin explored deeper. Under the brilliant lights, the surgeons worked without seeming hurry but with a tremendous sense of urgency. Every two or three minutes the anesthesiologists reported: "Your patient is doing well."[1]

A classic descriptive news story is that of the arrival of the body of "The Unknown Soldier" at Washington on November 9, 1921, written by Kirke L. Simpson of the Associated Press. This story was written at a time when newswriting generally was stodgy and good writing was not highly valued by many newspaper editors. Simpson's story caused several editors to reappraise newswriting with a resultant improvement in writing.

A plain soldier, unknown but weighted with honors as perhaps no American before him because he died for the flag in France, lay tonight in a place where only martyred Presidents Lincoln, Garfield and McKinley have slept in death.

He kept lonely vigil in state under the vast, shadowy dome of the Capitol. Only the motionless figures of the five armed comrades, one at the head and one facing inward at each corner of the bier, kept watch with him.

But far above, towering from the great bulk of the dome, the brooding figure of Freedom watched too, as though it said "well done" to the servant faithful unto death, asleep there in the vast, dim chamber below.

America's unknown dead is home from France at last, and the nation has no honor too great for him. In him, it pays its unstinted tribute of pride and glory to all those sleeping in the far soil of France. It was their home-coming today; their day of days in the heart of the nation, and they must have known it, for the heart beat of a nation defies the laws of space, even of eternity.

Sodden skies and a gray, creeping,

[1] June 18, 1956, p. 51.

chilling rain all through the day seemed to mark the mourning of this American soil and air at the bier of this unknown hero. But no jot of the full meed of honor was denied the dead on that account. From the highest officials of this democratic government to the last soldier or marine or bluejacket, rain and cold meant nothing beside the desire to do honor to the dead.

The ceremonies were brief today. They began when the far boom of saluting cannon down the river signalled the coming of the great gray cruiser Olympia. The fog of rain hid her slow approach up the Potomac, but fort by fort, post by post, the guns took up the tale of honors for the dead as she passed.

Slowly the ship swung into her dock. Along her rails stood her crew in long lines of dark blue, rigid at attention and with a solemn expression uncommon to the young faces beneath the jaunty sailor hats. Astern, under the long, gray muzzle of a gun that once echoed its way into history more than twenty years ago in Manila Bay, lay the flag-draped casket. Above a tented awning held off the dripping rain, the inner side of the canvas lined with great American flags to make a canopy for the sleeper below. At attention stood five sailors and marines as guards of honor for the dead at each corner and the head of his bier.

Below on the cobbled stretch of the old dock at Washington Navy Yard, a regiment of cavalry waited, sabers at "present," and the black-draped gun caisson with its six black horses to carry the casket to the Capitol. The troopers formed in line facing toward the ship as she swung broadside to her place and the gangway was lifted to her quarterdeck. To their right a mounted band stilled its restless horses.

On the ship, the trim files of her marine guard stood at attention. Rear-Admiral Lloyd H. Chandler, to whom had fallen the duty of escorting this dead private soldier over the Atlantic from France, was garbed in the full, formal naval dress as were officers of his staff.

Just as the ship's bell clanged out the quick, double strokes of "eight bells," the sailors' four o'clock and the hour set for arrival, the bugles rang again and the crew again lined the rails far above the dock. The marine guard filed down the gangway to face the troopers across the dock, the ship's band came down and formed beyond the marines. On deck at the gangway head, four sides-boys took their place on each side facing toward each other, the boatswains waiting behind them to pipe a dead comrade over the side with the honors accorded only to full Admirals of the fleet.

Cars bearing Secretaries Weeks and Denby, Assistant Secretary Wainwright, General Pershing, Major General Harbord, Admiral Coontz and Major General Lejeune, the Marine commandant, and their aides rolled up, with Secretary Weeks on the right next to the gangway and Secretary Denby next, then General Pershing and Admiral Coontz; these highest officers of the army and navy formed in line facing down the open space between the troops and marines.

On deck the bugles called attention. A group of petty officers stepped forward to raise the casket. A forward gun crashed to the first drumming roll of the minute guns of sorrow. The Olympia's band sounded the opening chords of Chopin's "Funeral March" and to the slow half-step and carried high on the shoulders of his navy and marine corps comrades, the unknown was tenderly lifted down the steep pitch to the dock.

Admiral Chandler and his aides came behind, cocked hats off in the cold rain and held across their breasts. Below the cabinet members also stood bareheaded in the rain, the army and navy officers at salute.

Just as the casket passed out through the rails, overside to the plank, the wail of the bo'sun's pipe sounded shrilling the last salute of the sea to the dead. It sounded oddly against the background of the dirge and as the sound of the pipe died away, the gun forward barked again the passing of another minute.

Step by step the bearers labored down the plank, sanded against the slippery murk of the rain, to the cobbled dock floor below. Again the pipe above wailed as they stepped ashore at last and the unknown was again on American soil.

Slowly the flag-draped casket moved down between the line of troops and marines and under the eyes of the bluejackets standing rigidly at the ship's rails high above. As they came abreast of the ship's band, the dirge was stilled, a marine bugler sounded four flourishes of salute to a general officer. Then the stirring, lifting strains of "The Star Spangled Banner" rang out to the gray sky, the nation's own hymn of freedom.

Again the slow march to the waiting gun carriage was taken up; again the wail of the funeral march, cut through with the crash of the gun above, sounded. The caisson waited in a space between the second and third squadrons of the full strength of the Third Cavalry from Fort Myer and beside it stood the eight body bearers of the army headed by Sergeant Woodfill, hero of heroes among Americans who fought in France. . . .

Exercise: If you had been assigned to report the event described above, what preparation would have been necessary? Would you have known all of the technical terms that were used? Select at least two verbs that are appropriate for the sound or movement that the reporter heard or saw.

SENTENCE RHYTHM

When the writer is describing an object in motion, he can sometimes use sentence rhythm to cause the reader to sense the motion. When there is a rise and fall and a pause in a series of sentences there is sentence rhythm. The lengths of the individual sentences match the rise, fall, or pause or acceleration of the object. The following description by Russell Owen in the *New York Times* of Colonel Charles Lindbergh's take-off on his transAtlantic flight is an example:

. . . A sluggish gray monoplane lurched its way down Roosevelt Field this morning at 7:52 o'clock, slowly gathering momentum. Inside sat a tall youngster, eyes glued to an instrument board or darting ahead for swift glances at the runway, his face drawn with the intensity of his purpose.

Death lay but a few seconds ahead of him if his skill or his courage faltered. For moments as the heavy plane rose from the ground, dropped down, staggered again into the air and fell, he gambled for his life against a hazard which had already killed four men.

And then slowly, so slowly that those watching it stood fascinated, as if by his indomitable will alone, the young pilot lifted his plane into the air. It dipped and then rose with renewed speed, climbing heavily but steadily toward the distant trees. . . .

And then, very gradually but surely, the wide silver wings lifted toward the skyline. A pale sky showed between them and the green beneath.

A soft glow came above the clouds, the first of the sun breaking through. Far off above the trees the silver wing dipped and was gone.

Lindbergh was on his way to Paris.
. . .

Here is another example:

. . . Now Wolcott was in full flight, and the crowd was booing him. He ducked and danced and ran. He was caught and hit; he clinched and held; he ran again.

The writer can test for sentence rhythm by reading his composition aloud. Do the sentences sound well? Do they swing?

ADJECTIVES, ADVERBS, AND VERBS

In descriptive writing the aim of the writer is to create a single dominant impression. He achieves this by organizing the details with that aim in view. He cannot succeed by relying on the use of adjectives and adverbs. He is privileged to use more adjectives and adverbs than he should use in a straight news story, for he is not concerned about his objectivity; in fact, he is writing to convey his own sense impressions to his readers. But he will fail when he relies too much on adjectives and adverbs.

MAKING THE EVENT VIVID

Verbs that connote movement and sound are among his principal tools. He should search his mind for the most appropriate verb instead of using the first one that comes to mind. Thus, instead of "He *walked wearily* to his post," "He *trudged* to his post."

For class discussion: Are the adjectives and verbs in this sentence well chosen: "The slashing blades of a giant cement mixer ripped Harley Ashburn to death today after he had gone inside it to make repairs"?

CHAPTER *10*

Speeches and Conventions

At any moment between 9:30 a.m. and 9:30 p.m. somebody is probably talking to an audience in your town. The people in the audience are usually members of a local official body or a voluntary organization. The group may be a national convention or merely a local Parent-Teacher Association. The city editor assigns a reporter to report the meeting and instructs him as to the number of words he should write. The reporter finds some of the speeches more newsworthy than others.

When an advance copy of a speech is available, the reporter's task consists mainly of selecting the most important and most interesting parts. When no advance copy is available, the reporter needs to take copious notes, for he cannot know whether the most newsworthy parts of the speech are to come early or late in the talk. He will find it helpful while taking notes to circle or otherwise indicate those expressions which are the exact words of the speaker so that he may quote the speaker directly instead of paraphrasing his remarks.

THE FORM OF THE SPEECH REPORT

The *W*s of the speech report are the *what, who, when* and *where*. The *what,* of course, is what the speaker says. Mention of the title of the speech is often not essential. The *where* and *when* are essential but are not usually important elements. They should, however, be mentioned in an early paragraph, although not necessarily the first paragraph.

The *who* may be a very important part of the speech report. Beyond mere identification of the speaker the reporter should sometimes obtain biographical data from *Who's Who in America* or from other sources, such as an officer of the sponsoring organization. The reporter in some circumstances should interview the speaker in advance of the talk. Some of the biographical information should be included in the news story as when the speaker, a missionary in a primitive area, has had hazardous adventures.

The lead of the news story is nearly always a concrete statement of the speaker. Most desirable is a statement which epitomizes the talk. An example:

> The shortage of scientific manpower can be overcome, a leading scientist said yesterday.

The lead statement should usually be in indirect discourse rather than direct quotation. The reporter should resist the temptation to select for the lead an unimportant or irrelevant statement just because it is witty. Sometimes, however, a witty remark epitomizes the speech. An example: Two wire services reported a speech by Ted Williams, the former Boston Red Sox baseball player, to inmates of a prison. One lead was vague and general:

> Ted Williams gained new friends last night—at Massachusetts State Prison.

A second wire service used this lead:

> Ted Williams told State Prison inmates last night "all of us make mistakes; that's why we have the errors column in the box score."

The reporter should not select a statement for the lead which, although interesting, is out of context. Some speakers have been treated unfairly when a reporter has made a lead out of some answer to a question from the audience: the speaker is entitled to have his views reported as he presented them in a prepared talk. Since the headline on the news story is usually based on the lead there is a high probability that the reader will misinterpret the primary message the speaker presented. There are circumstances, of course, in which an answer to a question can be justified in the lead.

After writing the lead, the reporter should alternate direct and indirect discourse. A long column of direct quotation is not only monotonous for the reader, but requires more space because the indirect discourse is usually a paraphrase of the speaker's exact words. One paragraph of indirect quotation separating two or three paragraphs of direct quotation makes the story more readable and enables the writer to preserve the unity of certain of the speaker's remarks.

Every statement or nearly every statement of the speaker should be attributed to the speaker. This requires that the reporter use such synonyms for *said* as *asserted, declared, stated, explained, added, continued, went on,* and *pointed out.* Use of *pointed out,* however, sometimes implies that the reporter has endorsed the speaker's assertion.

Here is an example of a well-written speech report, although it includes fewer direct quotations than does the usual report:

Adler Differentiates Opinion, Knowledge

You can say, "I believe gentlemen prefer blondes." But you can't say, "I believe two plus two equals four."

That, Mortimer J. Adler told a packed house at Marina Junior High School auditorium last night, is the difference between opinion and knowledge.

In the third of a series of lectures sponsored by the Great Books Council, Adler, director of the Institute for Philosophical Research, told an interested audience that, "Between sovereign nations there is always a state of war—actual or potential."

That statement, too, is knowledge, he said.

Definition Given

He threw out a few definitions to support his claim, namely, "The objects of knowledge consist of all those things about which you cannot think otherwise."

Thus, you can't think otherwise about two plus two equaling four. That's knowledge.

But you can think otherwise about gentlemen and blondes. Some prefer brunettes. Some, even redheads. So that's opinion.

Adler, the one-time stormy petrel of the educational and philosophical world, said there can be no disagreement about knowledge—only about opinions.

War Defined

And he defined war as "the forceful resolution of differences of opinion."

He said the difference between knowledge and opinion explains government.

"We wouldn't need government if all men had only knowledge and not opinion," he said, "because with only knowledge it is impossible to have differences of opinion."

Authority-Government

But, he said, reasonable men can disagree on their opinions and have these disagreements resolved by authority. This authority is government.

The second consequence, he declared, is that human freedom is not separable from a mixture of knowledge and opinion.

There is no freedom with knowledge alone, he stated, "because knowledge is necessitated by its objects," which means you can't deviate from a necessary action.

He concluded, "It is an indisputable fact of our freedom that we don't know everything."

Presumably, that goes for blondes, too.

Exercise: Write a 700-word news story based on the following address by author Bruce Bliven to a convention of the American Association of University Presses at Palo Alto, California. Mr. Bliven is a former editor of *The New Republic*. The title of his address was "Mass Communication and American Taste." Use a little more direct quotation than was used in the report of the Adler speech, but try to include as many of the speaker's points as possible; that is, do not devote all of your space to a few points.

I am delighted to be here this evening for several reasons, one of which is that for thirty years I was editor of a magazine that had a small circulation and usually lost money. I have heard rumors that once in awhile this has been true of a university press, here and there. We didn't set out to achieve these goals; we should have been delighted to have a big circulation and fat profits, but there were other things that we thought were more important. Perhaps you are now all heavily in the black, and my retroactive empathy is misplaced, and in that case I both congratulate and commiserate with you. It's fun to be rich (I am told); but poverty has its compensations, too—especially in the field of communication, where the rich so often give hostages to fortune.

It is fashionable nowadays to wring hands over what mass communication is doing to American society. Whenever I find hands being wrung I have an almost irresistible temptation to join in, but in a matter so important it is worth while to stop a moment and see whether the hand-wringers know what they are doing.

What is the indictment of mass communication? That the product is superficial, shallow, not a true picture of life, that it makes the communicatee feel cultured when he is not. Prof. Daniel J. Boorstin of the University of Chicago says that it creates fictitious events to report, and *Time* magazine speaks in particular of "non-books," put together by means other than Mary Heaton Vorse's famous recipe of somebody's applying the seat of the pants to the seat of the chair until a book is written.

The purpose of most of the mass media, we are told, is just to sell goods; to paraphrase a common complaint, they are used by greedy crooks who hypnotise fools to sell shoddy and unneeded merchandise. If what is said about the printed word is true, it may be a good thing that Johnny can't read—if in fact he can't.

Television, the handiest whipping boy just now, is supposed to debauch our children with crime and violence. The five hours a day and more that the average TV set is turned on are making our muscles as well as our minds to become flabby.

Some of this indictment is true, and some is false. The part that is true needs to be seen in a context of historical facts which to some degree may mitigate the sting of the charges.

Much of this indictment comes from the intellectuals, and it varies in inverse ratio to the amount of actual experience they have had in the production of the mass media. Newspapers, for instance, are criticised furiously by those who have never worked on one, who are outraged because the papers deliberately try to appeal to more than the 4.4 per cent of the population who have I.Q.'s above 130 and may properly be classified as eggheads. It is true that I have never yet met one of these critics who had, that very morning, read all of the solid world news that the paper *did* have; he was too busy being angry to stop to examine the loathsome object of his disapprobation.

I know that at this point I ought to define "the intellectual," but it is hard to do. The only safe rule is that if you claim to be one, you aren't. The intellectual is a member of the group who wouldn't dream of listening to a phonograph until it was renamed a hi-fi; who despise AM radios but adore FM; who never looked at a movie until the Scandinavians and the French began producing films that are happily unintelligible; who repudiate their own egghead friends if by chance they write a book that sells widely; who won't have a TV set, but go next door to look whenever a good documentary is scheduled.

To be sure, there is conformity everywhere today, even among the nonconformists. There is truth in the old joke about one intellectual who says to another, "Why can't you be an offbeat, bourgeois-baiting, society-repudiating individualist, like everybody else?"

These "intellectuals," of course, form only a part of the high-I.Q. population. Dr. Lewis Terman, whose brilliant studies of intelligence were conducted here at Stanford, proved that many, perhaps most, of the especially gifted people are also gregarious, outgoing, willing to accept life on its own terms. The nay-sayers described above have, however, an importance beyond their numbers because they are so articulate. They are also sure they are right; anybody of whom this is true is in time bound to develop a following.

These and other critics tend to look back nostalgically to a utopian past which, like all the pasts remembered nostalgically—including Barry Goldwater's—never existed. They recall the founding fathers two hundred years ago, or the giants of Concord just before the Civil War, who had the classics at their fingertips, wrote (most of them) beautiful English and were full partners in the society of educated men. The critics tend to assume that in those days everybody was like that; but in fact, the proportion of highly civilized men a hundred or two hundred years ago was probably no larger than it is today. The great majority of the people had few recreations any more ennobling than those of the present.

American taste in houses and furniture in the seventeenth and eighteenth centuries was good, because things were made by hand by skilled craftsmen, whose products were beautiful since they were simple and functional. People had so little that there was less chance to go wrong. In the nineteenth century we got machine production with no controls, and most of what was produced was ugly. American taste in general in the nineteenth century was far worse than it is today; in fact, it was the editor of a popular magazine, Edward Bok of the *Ladies' Home Journal,* who worked for years at the end of the century to persuade the nation's housewives to abandon the whatnot in the corner, filled with bad China figurines marked "Souvenir of Atlantic City," and the sheaves of pampas grass stacked in an umbrella stand that might have been an elephant's leg, and sometimes was.

For many years before the First World War, American popular cultural standards were those of the European peasantry who came here in such floods until they were cut off by the new immigration laws. Mary McCarthy blames the sterility and vacuousness of so much of our life today on the sterility and vacuousness of the European mold in which it was cast, but this seems to me quite wrong. The European peasant on his native ground, at least until lately, had a rich and colorful culture of his own, expressed in his costume, his art, his music. The sad thing is that when he came to America, he was forcibly divorced from all this background. Clinging to the past became a sign of the "greenhorn"; the peasant's own children repudiated his language, his folkways, his whole culture, and turned eagerly to the new American things—automobiles, baseball, hot dogs, the funnies.

When it began, America's attempt to make literate a whole population based essentially on peasant stock was the boldest, most dramatic such effort in all history. It would be a miracle if we could accomplish it fully in two hundred years, to say nothing of fifty or seventy-five. That there would be more fumbles and failures was inevitable. Cultivated Europeans are scornful, for example, of some of the eccentricities of American college life, forgetting that we have by far the largest proportion of our young people in college that has ever been seen in any large Western country. Give us another hundred years—a mere eyeblink in the annals of history—and these eccentricities will have been ironed out.

It is a firm tenet of the intellectual that American society as a whole is hostile to him, and that this is especially true of the mass media. In the past, there was some merit in this charge. The United States was dominated by a pioneer psychology long after 1894, the date set by

Frederick Turner as the end of the frontier, and among pioneers the man of action is always preferred over the man of ideas, who is so often beset by Hamlet-like doubts and fears. For the past forty years the intellectual has also been suspected of extreme Leftist leanings, an accusation he was too proud to repudiate even when it was false, as it often was.

But this situation is rapidly passing, spurred on by the atom bomb and other things that have suddenly put the egghead scientist at a premium in our society. We seem to be moving toward the European condition, where the college professor, the writer, anyone who deals in ideas, has always enjoyed high esteem. President Kennedy has helped this process by bringing poets, playwrights, Nobel Laureates, into the White House, people with whom some recent Presidents had no possible means of communication. . . .

How much of the indictment of the mass media is true? We might begin with television, the most powerful device for rapid social change that has ever been invented, with the possible exception of the automobile. While no one has yet proved that violence in television shows breeds delinquent children—any more than Jack the Giant Killer caused an earlier generation to become infant decapitaters—there seems little doubt that some children look at too much of it. . . .

We know that the fear television would drive out books and magazines has not been realized. Sales of books, including children's books, are at an all-time high. So are magazine and newspaper circulations. The magazines that television has hurt have been those of the lowest intellectual content; the best ones have been increasing their circulations at a higher percentage rate than the rest. The real harm that has been done lately to most magazines has come from the fierce competition for the advertising dollar. Professor Boorstin complains that people look at reproductions of Old Masters in *Life* instead of the originals; but that is not the choice by which we are confronted. For 95 per cent of the twenty-five or thirty million people who see each issue of *Life* the choice is between these excellent reproductions and nothing at all. The eggheads can't bear to admit it, but that magazine's articles on anthropology, geology and natural history have had a valuable educational effect on millions of people—including a lot of college graduates who never knew, or have forgotten, these things. So has the *Saturday Evening Post* series, Adventures of the Mind, as well as many other things in a wide spectrum of periodicals.

The sale of soft-cover books is one of the wonders of the world, more than a million a day. While many of them are meretricious, many others are not; the last time I looked, Shakespeare was selling about 1,400,000 a year. Very difficult books of philosophy and science, that used to sell three or four thousand a year, are today put out in soft-cover editions where the break-even point may be up in the hundreds of thousands. Never have so many books that are so good been read by so many.

School teachers are beginning to testify that television has awakened intellectual curiosity among students that leads them to read books about things of which they first learned through TV viewing. A few years ago I went back to my little home town in Iowa and they persuaded me to give a talk to the high-school students on the current situation in Europe. When I was a boy in this town, we hardly knew that Europe existed; but these youngsters were well informed. They asked me questions for two hours, and I perspired trying to keep up with them. Most of their information, I was told, they had obtained from the radio and from television news and documentaries.

The provable sins of television lie in the field of omission, not commission. When Newton Minow called it "one vast wasteland," he might have added the words, "of mediocrity." As someone has said, it is a case of the bland leading the bland. The advertisers are so fearful of offending somebody that they interest and excite nobody. It is when I think of what television might do, of the wonderful opportunities missed, that I start a handwringing movement of my own. . . .

I don't want to appear to pick on the intellectuals; some of my best friends are eggheads. It seems to me clear however that in regard to mass communication they are nursing to their bosoms at least five myths:

1. The myth that there is a mysterious "they," who are conspiring to debauch our culture for their own fell purposes. "They" are only business men, trying to make an honest though speedy buck, and any destruction of our culture is incidental and accidental.

2. That things were better in some halcyon past, and have lately been degenerating at an ever-increasing pace.

3. That if you just denounce television long and loudly enough, maybe it will go away.

4. That most people are poor little whiffenpoof sheep, easily led astray, and greatly harried by things that do the intellectual no harm at all.

5. That their own tastes are automatically and forever the best, and anyone who disagrees is tainted at least slightly with moral leprosy.

Professor Boorstin complains that our life today contains too many "non-events"—fictitious happenings dreamed up in advance by press agents. But I feel he misses the real point. We get too many of both non-events and events. The machinery of communication is overbuilt; we are inundated by a Niagara of too much information. I don't really want to know as much about anything as I am told nowadays about practically everything. After awhile, a merciful shield of inattention is created—but this has its bad side too.

I hold no special brief for American culture today. Some things about it are bad, and may even be getting worse. But many things are good, and are getting better. It is going in all directions at once, like so many other aspects of life. No other country in the world to my knowledge has more intellectual curiosity, or so many easy ways of gratifying it. In no other country are the people so humbly eager for self-improvement, or willing to spend so much time and money on the effort.

And finally, despite the efforts of the John Birchers to smear the word, we are politically a democracy. We can't practice our democratic faith successfully unless we are willing to accept cultural democracy as well. There are a lot of discouraging features about democracy; the only thing you can say for it is that it is better than any other system ever invented. There are discouraging things about cultural democracy; but they are curable and some of them are being cured. Our way of life is being challenged in the Cold War as never in the past; we can't afford to have our intellectuals acting like passengers on a ship in a bad storm, standing on the top deck and sneering at the efforts of the crew. I would appeal to them to "rejoin the human race," and instead of spending their time in the deploring that is so much fun, to join in the common effort.

CONVENTIONS AND SYMPOSIA

A symposium is a conference, usually of experts, in which several speakers discuss the same subject. The speakers usually have different, as well as common, points of view. The reporter, therefore, writes a news story in which he reports some or all of the speakers. When he quotes a speaker who has followed a previous speaker, he should begin that paragraph with the next speaker's name to avoid confusing the reader as to which speaker he is quoting.

Conventions often last two or more days and there are more speakers than the newspaper has space to report. The reporter, therefore, tries to learn in advance which talks are calculated to be most newsworthy. He can determine this when advance copies of all or almost all speeches are available, as at scientific meetings. In some instances, after reading the advance copy, the reporter interviews the speaker about his talk. When the subject matter is technical the interview supplies the reporter with an opportunity to request an explanation of some points. The reporter can also ask questions for the purpose of making the speech more comprehensible to the reader.

The reporter leads his story with the most interesting talk of the day and reports other speakers to the extent that his space permits. In some instances, separate stories are written about two or more talks because all are interesting.

Here is an example of the way a reporter covered a convention of candy manufacturers by visiting the exhibits and interviewing some of the participants in addition to reporting some of the speeches. It is by Art Hoppe of the *San Francisco Chronicle*:

Candy Game Isn't All Sugar and Spice

The candy industry is bitter.
The Chronicle found this out by joining some 600 bitter candy men—

or, rather candy men who felt bitter —at the closing sessions of the Western Candy Conference yesterday at the Sheraton-Palace Hotel.

What makes the candy men bitter is all this talk about candy wrecking your teeth, ruining your figure and sneakily undermining your health.

This "rising tide of anti-candy propaganda"—as one speaker put it—is not only mostly hogwash, but it's driving candy out of its "rightful place in American life."

The speaker happened to be Kalman Druck of the New York publicity firm of Carl Byoir Associates, which has prepared a $250,000 nationwide publicity campaign for the candy industry.

Colored Slides

Druck used handsome colored slides to show how the campaign would stress such nice things about candy as "candy nutrition," "candy sociability," "quick energy" and nine other favorable points.

Another good idea along this line, Druck said, would be to promote a "daily candy break" for the nation's workers—"similar to the coffee break or the milk break the milk industry has started."

A slide popped on the screen with envisioned newspaper headlines—such as "7th Inning Candy Break Gives Ace Pitcher a Lift."

These are just the kind of things the industry needs to combat a "hostile press," Druck said firmly.

The Exhibits

The meeting adjourned briefly for a five-minute orange juice break—courtesy of Sunkist Growers, Inc.—and the Chronicle decided to sneak out and mingle in definitely friendly fashion with the candy men in the exhibit room next door.

The most fascinating of the exhibits, in our opinion, was the Carlson Cherry Dipper, $350 F.O.B. Pasadena.

Fred Carlson was kind enough to show us how it worked, although he could tell we weren't ready to buy.

"You put the cherries on here," he said, pointing to a row of metal toothpicks on a moving belt. "They go around here and down there and dip into the pot of fondant—that's the goo—and then come up here where you take them off.

"One girl, working with this machine, can turn out 400 to 500 pounds of cherry cordials a day," he said proudly.

Free Samples

We munched our way through free samples of bon bons, mints and Boldemann's Candy-Coated Milk Chocolate Pokies and came at last to the end of the room where a big red and gold parrot was sitting on a perch under a picture of a big red and gold parrot labeled "Say Gear-Ar-Delly!"

"Her name's Rosie and she's not a parrot; she's a scarlet macaw," said Sid Lawrence, representing Ghirardelli's chocolate. "Just like our symbol."

"Say Gear-Ar-Delly, Rosie," said Lawrence.

"Squawk," said Rosie.

"She can say 'Gear-Ar,' but it'll take another six months to teach her to say 'Delly,'" said a Mrs. Olson, who declined to reveal her connection with Rosie, although they seemed good friends.

"She loves Ghirardelli chocolates, though," said Mrs. Olson, loyally. "Won't eat anything else."

Peevish Nibble

A young lady stopped to pet Rosie and Rosie demonstrated peevishly that she was also fond of human flesh.

"She doesn't mean it," said Mrs. Olson.

A man munched his way up to the Ghirardelli booth.

"Don't eat those," said Lawrence, suddenly, "They're cocoa beans."

The Chronicle got back in the meeting room in time for the questioning of Publicist Druck by the candy men.

"Now, Mother's Day is coming up and we'll be competing with flowers and I was wondering if there was anything we could do without stepping on their toes too much," asked a candy man.

Pretty Crass

"Forgive me for saying this," said

Druck with the air of a father leveling with his child about Santa Claus, "but Father's Day and Mother's Day are pretty crass commercial propositions. Your industry is just going to have to organize if it wants its share of the business."

A man in the audience leaped to his feet. "Even if things were going well, we'd need a public relations campaign," he said stridently. "But we're in an industry in distress. We need this badly and nothing could be plainer."

Everybody applauded this fight talk heartily.

In this mood, the candy men buckled down to the final topics on the agenda—such technical matters as "The Cocoa Bean—A World Product and a Problem" and "Financial Operations of Candy Manufacturers Reveal What?"

In addition to reporting speeches and exhibits and interviewing participants, the reporter often reports something about the program for next day. He also reports the election of officers of an association.

All statewide and nationwide organizations supply assistance to the reporters. Some associations have a professional publicity aide and others rely on certain local members or certain officers to supply reporters with advance copies of speeches, tickets, slates of officers, and other kinds of information. At some conventions the association has a press room with typewriters and telephone facilities.

CHAPTER *11*

Human Interest Stories and Interviews

In addition to reporting events in the conventional news story form, newspapers publish stories that report incidents that are humorous, pathetic, and picturesque. Some stories of this kind are about animals. Newspapers also publish stories about personalities that are either in the form of an interview or in a form that has come to be called a "profile."

HUMAN INTEREST STORIES

We might call the first kind of story a *human interest* story. Such stories are not necessarily newsworthy but are a form of popular literature. Their impact depends mainly on the way they are written; the skillful writer can develop a small incident into a rewarding reading experience for the usual reader.

"I Want Blue Jeans When I Get My Legs"

"When I get some legs," young Richard Matlock once promised his mother, "I'll learn to walk."

Richard, now 4, kept his promise. Yesterday he walked for the first time in his life.

Doctors and therapists at Texas Scottish Rite Hospital for Crippled Children gave Richard what nature tragically withheld. He was born without legs and without a right arm, and he had a deformed left hand.

His mother, Mrs. Windle Matlock of Dallas, works. So far she hasn't watched her son walk. But when she does, she hopes to keep a promise too.

"I want some blue jeans when I get my legs," he had said, and she agreed Richard would have them.

Dolphin Smarter Than Human Mother

If you're a mother whose baby has colic, and you're at wit's end trying to think what to do, it probably won't cheer you up much to hear that mother dolphins are a whole lot smarter than you.

We didn't say that. Dr. John C. Lilly did.

Colic is a serious matter to baby dolphins, Lilly explains, because a gas bubble on the baby's tummy can turn the baby over and cause it to drown.

But Mother simply uses sonar—an echo-sounding ability—to detect the gas bubble. Then she burps the baby by ramming it amidships—right in the belly—with her beak. And that, as you can imagine, would make any baby burp.

Human mothers, says Lilly, in a slyly triumphant tone, can't burp their babies this way, and as for detecting colic by using sonar—well, have you ever tried it?

This example of the dolphin's intellectual capacity is contained in the book, "The Dolphin in History," co-authored by Lilly and Dr. Ashley Montagu and recently published by the University of California.

Lilly, a neuropsychologist with the Communications Research Institute in Miami, Florida, is engaged in further study of dolphin behavior, sound emission and mimicry of human speech.

His part of the book is entitled "Modern Whales, Dolphins and Porpoises as Challenges to Our Intelligence."

THE INTERVIEW

The interview is a news story form which reports a prominent or colorful person's opinion or experiences (e.g., adventures) and includes something about his personality. The most frequent occasion for an interview is when the personality, who lives elsewhere, visits the local community, as when a prominent person comes to town to make a speech or a foreign person comes to town for business or social reasons. When a prominent person is to make a speech in the evening some afternoon newspapers try to report an interview with him in advance of the speech.

Preparation

An interview can be no better than the preparation of the interviewer. This is because the reporter must know what questions to ask and must either know something about the person to be interviewed or about the special field in which the person is engaged. In most instances, when a reporter is assigned to interview a person he tries to find out in advance all he can about the person from the newspaper's morgue and from biographical reference works such as *Who's Who in America*. When the interviewee is a scientist the reporter reads in the public library about the subject's special field. On the basis of what the reporter has learned, he prepares some questions in advance. Some reporters try to make an appointment a few hours in advance of the time set for the interview to permit the interviewee to give some thought to the subject of the interview; this practice usually assists the interviewing process and causes the interview to yield more information.

Conducting the Interview

There are no rules for conducting an interview because each person interviewed is different. The reporter's problem, in most instances, is how to get the interviewee to start to talk. The opening questions, therefore, are important. The reporter should not ask questions that call for only a yes-or-no response. Another problem is how to induce the interviewee to keep on talking. One interviewer has been successful by remaining silent for a while after the interview has begun; this makes the interviewee uncomfortable so that he continues to talk.

Some interviewers take copious notes, others trust their memory and take notes only about exact names, places, amounts, etc. Many interviewees prefer that the interviewer take notes because it assures that opinions and statements will be reported accurately. When the reporter is not certain how the name of a person or place is spelled, he should use the first opportunity to ask. (There was, for example, the interview by a student reporter of a distinguished philosopher who reported the interviewee's references to Jeremy Bentham as "Jeremiah Benjamin.") The reporter not only takes notes on what the interviewee says but about the interviewee's personal appearance and his behavior and mannerisms during the interview.

Some reporters who interview a scientist ask for his telephone number so they can check back with him to insure accuracy. It is often advisable for the reporter to preserve his notes for a while in the event that the interviewee complains that he was misquoted.

The foregoing observations relate to the situation in which one reporter interviews a person by appointment. When some public figures visit a community, however, they are accompanied by a publicity aide and hold a press conference. One reporter cannot develop a good interview under such conditions, especially when radio and TV reporters participate in the mass interview. For the reporter who has made some advance preparation, it is advisable to remain at the scene after the mass interview has concluded and ask his own questions.

Form of the Interview

The structural organization and style of the interview depends upon whether the reporter emphasizes the opinion and statements of the interviewee or his personality. Although the beginning of the story may be an opinion or a statement (usually in indirect discourse), the interview may include a great deal about the interviewee's personality, and vice versa. Here are a few beginnings:

> A French princess voiced admiration in Denver yesterday for the American woman—and the time-saving gadgets she has in her home.

> Tanned from tennis and looking forward to a match today, Associate Justice Hugo L. Black, of the United States Supreme Court, was willing to discuss anything but Supreme Court decisions with reporters here today.

> People who are good at criticizing the American way of life are supposed to be waspish like Henry L. Mencken and Sinclair Lewis.
> Vance Packard has been just as nasty as they were in his best-selling books. But personally he's no wasp.

Here is an interview which emphasizes opinion and which does not emphasize personality or include many direct quotations. It is from the *Buffalo Evening News*.

"American" Different From English — Earl

The myopic machine that is American big business has its funny side.

So thinks a young English nobleman who's teaching this year at the State University of Buffalo.

Greystall Ruthven, the Earl of Gowery, had been here just a few days and was getting settled in his Main street apartment.

His wife, Zandra, called the telephone company to get service at their home, and absent-mindedly told the company to list the phone under the title of Lord Gowery.

The next day a phone company official phoned and said "You can't have that kind of listing. It's free advertising."

Mr. Ruthven says he's "still not quite sure what kind of advertising" the company meant.

Title Can Be a Nuisance

Life in Buffalo has been sort of that way for the 23-year-old earl since he and his wife arrived.

"Titles are an endless cause of fascination to Americans," he said, "and having one can of course become a nuisance."

Americans seem to be neurotic about nobility, Mr. Ruthven said, "for they seem to like or hate those with titles" and nobility in general.

No particular fuss is made over having a title in England, he explains. He makes very little of his own title.

"My grandfather was given the title for his work as governor-general of Australia and, since my father is dead, when my grandfather died it was passed on to me. It's as simple as that."

Worked as Reporter

An Oxford graduate, Mr. Ruthven worked as a reporter on the Times of London before accepting a year's teaching visit in the UB English department.

Mr. Ruthven teaches a freshman English course, aids in the instruction of an upper class Shakespeare course and is a poet in his own right.

"Judging from the freshmen I have, the high school system doesn't seem too good," he said. He says he spends too much time teaching the fundamentals of English grammar "which of course should be taught between the ages of 8 and 12."

"American is definitely a different language from English," he says. "I must correct them without stopping them from writing American. This is a difficult thing to do unless they know the fundamentals of our common language."

But Mr. Ruthven finds little else to worry him about the university. He came here because "he didn't want to pass up the chance" to work at UB, and research in the UB library's fine poetry collection.

Here is an interview—mostly direct quotation—which emphasizes the personality of the interviewee. It is by Art Hoppe of the *San Francisco Chronicle*.

1-Man Foreign Aid Force Returns

"So I walked up to Nehru and said, 'You President Nehru?'"

"And he said, 'Yes.' And I said, 'You're lucky, President. I'm going to interview you.'"

Which is as good a way as any to introduce Aloysius Eugene Francis Patrick Mozier, a 50-year-old sailor, boxer, soldier of fortune and humanitarian with a heart as big as his gift of gab.

Mozier, an engineer for the American President Lines, just got back in town from a trip around the world on the President Polk.

Along the way he handed out 75,000 packets of vegetable seeds and chatted, he says, with Nehru, Mossadegh and Mao Tse-tung, to name a few.

"The President of Indonesia and I got to be pretty good buddies. I couldn't remember his first name, so

I called him 'Butch.' He called me 'Paddy.' They all do. They like it when you're democratic."

He Gives Seeds

Paddy's acceptance in the world's courts stems from the dynamic way in which he administered his one-man Marshall Plan.

"Up to a couple of years ago, my hobby used to be color movies and slides. Then I was in Korea riding around in Admiral Hill's jeep and we saw this little girl stumble and fall down.

"I picked her up and took her to this hospital, but she died right in my arms. The nurse said it was malnutrition. 'Malnutrition!' I said. 'You mean with all this lovely valley you can't grow anything!' And it turned out they didn't have any seeds. So, on my next trip I gave out 75,000 packages, and I figure those have grown into about $1,000,000.

"This last trip I took along another 75,000 plus 8,000 pounds of cucumber seeds. Gave a carton to everybody in the crew to store for me and it didn't cost me anything for freight. Nobody objected. I was in the Navy for 30 years and used to be welterweight champ of the fleet."

Into Red China

Paddy handed out his seeds when the ship touched at Japan and again at Hong Kong. It was from there, on July 20, that he went into Red China, he says.

"I was dressed up in my cowboy outfit playing my guitar up on this stage entertaining people like. And when I was through these four guys came up to me and said, 'Come on out for dinner.'

"It turned out they were Communist officials and they told me 'We don't want to fight. We just have to have an honorable way out.'

"Well, they said I was a second Will Rogers and why didn't I come to Shanghai and make everybody happy. So we got in their car and drove up to the border and took a plane to Shanghai. I took 1,000 packages of seeds along and handed them out to the farmers.

"At the border a couple of guards pointed tommy guns at me and I pretended to whip out my pistols and shouted, 'Boom! Boom!' at them. They about died laughing and I knew they were not going to hurt me.

Meeting with Mao

"I stayed two days in Shanghai and then I went to Peiping and these four guys took me to see Mao Tse-tung.

"He was a pretty smart cookie and spoke some English. He said he didn't want to lose the decision, but would take a draw.

"He told me: 'You come back. You do good work,'" said Paddy, lapsing into pidgin English.

Well, Paddy got back to Hong Kong, took another plane and caught up with his ship in Manila. He then continued his Johnny Appleseed work in Singapore, Ceylon, Pakistan, Egypt, Italy and France.

No Seeds to Indians

Despite his interview with Nehru, he failed to give any seeds to the Indians.

"They wanted to charge me duty on them and that was just too much," said Paddy. "I don't know what's wrong with those people." . . .

When he got back to San Francisco, Paddy opened his accumulated mail.

"Here's one from Manila. They want 1,000 seedlings, mostly elms. And what do you know, they've named a park and a street after me there. Isn't that nice, now."

A reporter can sometimes achieve the effect of unity when he is able to conclude an interview with a "punch" ending, as was done in the foregoing example.

The "Profile"

What used to be called a "personality sketch" is now called a "profile"—probably after the *New Yorker's* name for a sketch that portrays the subject as a human being with foibles as well as with a record of achievement. In preparing a *New Yorker* profile, the writer interviews persons who know the subject, including those who are his rivals, competitors and—sometimes —his enemies. Newspapers and wire services now carry personality sketches they call "profiles" although they include very few unfavorable evaluations.

Interesting subjects for such sketches are available locally. Also visitors to the community are often good subjects. The sketches include more about the unusual achievements of the subject than they do of their personality characteristics. Some examples: a blind auctioneer, a woman who operates an airport, and a woman who is president of a 70 million dollar business. Here is a "profile" of a blind female bowler; it is by Richard Field in the Portland *Oregonian:*

Excels at Game She Never Sees

They call Genny Reeves "Oregon City's Wonder Bowler."

She started bowling two years ago, got a strike in her first lesson; hit 160 after three weeks; and 203 this January.

She has been a Northwest champion twice, won several other tournaments and is now headed for national honors.

It's a remarkable record for any bowler. But for Genny Reeves it is something more. Because she is blind.

"Bowling," she says, "has opened up a wonderful, new world for me. I did not realize people could be so kind.

"Most people classify the blind as people sitting on a street corner with a tin cup selling brooms. This always annoyed me and was one reason why I tried so hard to overcome my own disability."

She Heard an Ad

Genny, 26, trim and attractive, has been blind since she was 4. She was struck in the eye by a pellet from a toy gun.

From that time forward her life was changed. She moved in a world of total darkness.

For nine years she studied at Salem School for the Blind and afterwards at West Linn high school.

In 1953, she married and today is the mother of Terry, 7, and Tammera, 4.

Her bowling career began in May, 1960 when she heard an advertisement offering free bowling lessons at

Tri-City Bowl to blind persons living in Clackamas county.

A few days later she started learning a game she's never seen. Aided by instructor Patti Mann, she paced the length of the lanes, felt their texture and ran her hands over the contour of the gutters.

How She Learned

She changed into overalls and crawled on hands and knees over the pindeck, feeling the shape, weight and location of each pin.

Next, she learned to get her position for delivery. This she does by taking one step sideways from the ball return and one-and-a-half steps forward.

From here, using a smooth, three-step approach, she delivers the ball from an identical spot and sends it speeding down the lanes.

The numbers of the pins left standing are called to her by a colleague, and she then concentrates on picking up the spares.

Genny reckons to play every day of the week. She is a member of two leagues, the Pin Splitters, at Tri-City Bowl, and Freight Lines League at Powell. She also substitutes in four other leagues.

Now Genny has one big ambition remaining. This is to play in the National Blind Bowling tournament being held June 7 through 10 in Philadelphia.

"I guess it would cost an awful lot of money," she said, "but it would mean more to me than anyone could possibly realize."

Exercise: *1*. Write a 450-word interview with Dr. Ralph E. Knutti, director of the National Heart Institute, based on the following questions and answers (reprinted from *U.S. News & World Report,* published at Washington, D.C., Jan. 14, 1963). Do not permit your story to exceed 450 words.

Q. How do members of the medical profession account for sudden, fatal heart attacks at a time when the patient is undergoing treatment?

A. Actually, most deaths from coronary heart disease are sudden and unexpected.

Q. What about drugs that are supposed to remove the danger of a sudden blood clot?

A. There are drugs which inhibit the clotting ability of blood, and which are frequently used following a "heart attack"—coronary thrombosis—or in the hope of preventing an attack when suspicious symptoms appear. Whether or not such drugs prevent an attack is controversial at this time.

Q. What are the suspicious symptoms that might cause a person to expect a heart attack?

A. An important one is angina pectoris—pain, often severe, usually associated with physical exertion.

The pain is located in the middle of the chest, frequently traveling down the left arm.

Q. What should a person do on feeling such pain?

A. See his physician promptly.

Q. Have you found out anything new about the cause of heart attacks?

A. Current evidence indicates that certain people are prone to heart attacks. Factors to be considered in this "proneness" are age, sex—under age 60, heart attacks are chiefly a male disease—high serum cholesterol, high blood pressure, abnormal findings in electrocardiographs, gross obesity, a family history of heart disease.

Q. Is there anything a person prone to heart attacks can do to avoid them?

A. Physicians agree that periodic complete physical examinations at least once a year are helpful in spotting early changes, for which preventive and curative measures may be instituted. The physical examination, then, would be recommendation No. 1.

Middle-aged and older folks can, if they will, adopt certain helpful measures on their own, such as watching their weight, getting adequate exercise and avoiding excesses in general.

Q. What about other kinds of heart disease? Has any progress been made in treating them?

A. There are three types of heart disease in which there have been definite declines in the 1962–61 period.

They are: rheumatic fever and chronic rheumatic heart disease—28 per cent decrease; nonrheumatic endocarditis and other myocardial degeneration—88 per cent decrease; and hypertension—high blood pressure—with or without heart involvement—33 per cent decrease.

Q. What has brought about the decrease in these heart ailments?

A. In the case of rheumatic fever, a disease which occurs largely in children, prompt identification of streptococcus infections and treatment of them, as well as their prevention, by the use of antibiotics are responsible for the decline.

In bacterial infection of the heart valves, which occurs in endocarditis, modern antibiotics have transformed a heretofore invariably fatal disease to a fully curable condition in 75 per cent of the instances. In chronic rheumatic valvular as well as in congenital heart disease, cardiac surgery has made remarkable progress.

Q. Can anything be done about the condition known as "hardening" or "narrowing" of the arteries?

A. One of the most important advances made in the past decade has been in the surgical treatment of atherosclerotic disease in certain arteries. It is now possible to replace with plastic tubes vital arteries such as the aorta or the carotid arteries, or to open them up to remove from them clots which tend to obstruct them.

Q. But the cause of sudden heart attacks and their prevention is still pretty much of a mystery?

A. In specific regard to coronary heart disease, progress has been made in the sense that the disease can be identified more accurately. This is due to improvements in diagnostic methods as well as improvement in the abilities of our individual physicians to make a sound diagnosis of coronary heart disease so that patients with this condition can have prompt treatment.

Q. Any other progress?

A. Our hospitals, and even ambulances, have oxygen available for the treatment of the acutely ill individual. The judicious use of anticoagulants has been a real breakthrough. And for the person having had one heart attack and surviving, recurrences have been diminished by proper preventive measures.

Yes, we have made progress, but we have a long way to go in the ultimate conquest of this serious disease. [Copyright 1963, U.S. News & World Report, Inc.]

2. Retype the following news story supplying the necessary paragraphing and quotation marks:

Serenely the good ferry Golden Shore steamed halfspeed through the fog, San Francisco bound from Sausalito today. Suddenly a wild-eyed man dashed past the Passengers Keep Out sign into the wheel house. Captain, he panted. Captain! My wife is about to become a mother. Congratulations, said Captain Edward Halling calmly. Congratulations be damned! cried breathless George Babcock. I don't want congratulations. I want help! She's going to have the baby here, now. Below on the decks, startled passengers heard the jingle of engine room bells, felt the ferry leap full speed ahead. But the sturdy Golden Shore, tearing recklessly through the fog, was no match for the stork, who swooped down on the boat like a hungry sea gull right smack between Alcatraz Penitentiary and the Hyde street ferry slip. Deckhands dashed through the ship crying: Is there a doctor aboard? Dr. Dorhmann K. Pischel pushed his corn flakes aside in the restaurant. I'm a doctor, he said, gulping the last of his morning coffee. We have a case for you, explained the deckhand. What kind of a case? A—baby . . . That is, a baby any minute. . . . I mean a lady who's going to have one! Heavens! I'm an eye specialist. . . .

CHAPTER 12

The Obituary

Readership studies show that the kind of news story that is highest read —by both men and women—is the obituary. Many readers scan the obituary columns every day to learn who has just died. They expect to learn about the death of somebody they knew or of some personality who is well known, such as an athlete, actor, or former high official. Readers are also interested, in some instances, in the names of survivors, the cause of death, the age of the deceased, and the time and place of the funeral.

Newspapers usually learn about the death of a local person from undertakers who fill out a form supplied by the newspaper. The undertaker talks usually with a member of the deceased's family and learns the date and place of birth, the time and place of death, the names of survivors, and the arrangements for the funeral and burial. The newspaper usually learns the cause of death from the physician who signed the death certificate or from the Department of Health. In some instances, relatives or friends also bring to the newspaper or telephone facts about the deceased's career. Proofs of paid "Death Notices," or "Funeral Notices," are also supplied by the advertising department to the editorial department on some newspapers.

After the undertakers' forms have been delivered to the newspaper, the city desk reads them and decides which are most newsworthy. A rewrite man or reporter is often assigned to telephone relatives or friends to obtain additional information about the deceased's career. Such assignments are regarded by many newspaper men as dull and distasteful. Most obituaries are about people who have had an ordinary and colorless career and there is little of interest that can be said about them. By digging, however, the writer can often turn up a fact that distinguishes the deceased in some way. These are some examples of such identification:

. . . originator of miniature golf.
. . . credited with being the first to propose painting a white center line on highways.
. . . who worked 40 hours a week as a clerk until he was 100 years old.

> . . . who built a modest feed business into a multimillion-dollar banking career.
> . . . considered the dean of local radio broadcasters.
> . . . who became a court reporter at the age of 63 in 1954 after he had lost heavily in the stock market.
> . . . [a judge] who imposed the death sentence on "Red Light Bandit" Caryl Chessman.
> . . . once the toast of the musical comedy stage in Budapest.
> . . . a former president of the Bar Association.

Those newspapers which value obituaries highly as news require the news writers to try to expand the usual obituary facts when the city editor suspects there may be some interesting additional fact about the life of the deceased. Before telephoning a member of the family, the news writer examines clippings in the newspaper's morgue. These may indicate, among other things, something about the early career of the deceased—how he got started in an occupation or business. Some newspapers first telephone one or more neighbors to try to learn something that the family might not remember to mention when the reporter telephones the family.

One newspaper reporter who likes to write obituaries because he believes they are important has some advice about telephoning members of the family:

> . . . Phoning newly bereaved people at ungodly hours is a must. If you really want to do the job, you follow your leads where they lead—even to persons sleeping in shock or under sedatives or after months or even years of watching a loved one die. You'll hate it. It's never easy.
> But until you learn, you'll never know how brave and eloquent and tough people can be. And how enormously grateful to you, if you help them get started on "grief work" . . . "death work."
> *Put yourself in the role of the bereaved.* I'll be the reporter.
> Death is the one thing you never were readied to face. You're overwhelmed with problems, red tape, frustrations, shock, jobs to do. And terrible fatigue. Maybe titanic guilt feelings. You don't know where to start.
> The phone rings. You answer in the dark.
> "Good morning," I say. "This is the News-Call Bulletin."
> (The newspaper. Your problem has meaning. You're not alone.)
> "Luther Meyer speaking."
> (You don't know me. But you hear a person . . . quiet, confident.)
> "Can you help us?" I say.
> (Help someone else? That's a switch. You're the one who needs help.)
> Then I ask for a picture, and for your personal report on the style and meaning of the life of one you loved.
> Maybe 999 times out of 1,000 that breaks the dam. What I want is what

you want. We're helping you to get on swiftly, efficiently with one of the "death work" jobs that bugged you most—telling the world.

But I focus on the life. That's your focus too. I start as far as possible from death, asking, for example:

"Was he a native of San Francisco?"

"Was he the child of pioneers? . . . When did they come west?"

Usually the life story unrolls without a hitch, with increasing vigor of voice. You and the stranger have built a bridge together. And by the time you ask the necessary questions about the death the bereaved talks with candor and courage and clarity. And enormous gratitude. He should be stronger, readier, more confident for the next "grief work" jobs.

There'll be tears. Be glad. Wait. Strength follows. Don't fake schmaltzy sympathy. Be businesslike, direct.

When folks are husked by loss they become eloquent as poets and honest as angels. Like one "widow" who quietly said that hers was a union without benefit of clergy, that a legal wife might be alive somewhere, but "must you print that?" You'll feel honored by the trust, certain that you've seen a marriage stronger than bonds of law could make. . . .[1]

In the following obituary, the news writer has lifted the report of a death out of the ordinary class of obituaries by learning an interesting fact and writing the obituary in an unusual way.

> This morning, for the first time in eight years, the flag pole was bare at 1542 Siesta Drive in Los Altos.
>
> Albert G. Bowers, who had made a practice of instructing groups of neighborhood children in respect for and care of the American flag, was dead of an apparent heart attack.
>
> "He didn't miss raising that flag a single day in all those years," said his son, Adm. John M. Bowers (USN Ret.) of Sunnyvale. "But I don't think I'll put it up today. It was his flag, and I guess the pole will stay bare now."
>
> Mothers in the neighborhood often sent their youngsters to Mr. Bowers for instruction in flag etiquette, and he also worked with groups of Boy Scouts, Cub Scouts and Girl Scouts.
>
> The 77-year-old Bowers, a retired civil engineer, was one of the engineers-in-charge during the construction of Treasure Island in San Francisco Bay for the 1939 World's Fair. . . .
>
> Prior to that, he managed a rubber plantation in South America and then

[1] Luther Meyer (of the San Francisco *News-Call Bulletin*), "How to Write Obituaries—An Expert's Formula," *Scripps-Howard News*, May, 1961, pp. 11–12.

spent the next seven years as the engineer-in-charge of a large breakwater project at Chefoo, China.

Until last year he was an administrative officer with the Marshall Plan in Denmark. . . .

Mr. Bowers was a native of Pennsylvania. . . .

He is also survived by a second son. . . .

Immediately after the death of an eminent public figure, the newspapers and wire services do not have enough time to write an adequate evaluation of his career. For this reason, the large newspapers and the wire services write obituaries in advance and, from time to time pending the death of the person, bring the obituaries up to date. Thus when death comes to an eminent politician, literary figure, or other personage the obituary is one that was written with considerable care. On the death of some prominent persons, newspapers also telephone local people who have known or have been closely associated with the deceased for statements of evaluation, usually tributes to the deceased.

The following obituary, by the Associated Press, is about a noted sports figure:

GALVESTON, Texas—Babe Didrikson Zaharias, the greatest woman athlete the world has known, died today after a stubborn battle with the one competitor she couldn't beat—cancer.

Into her 42 years, she packed athletic triumphs that began with an AAU basketball tournament, including AAU track records, the Olympics and finally the golf courses of the nation.

Early this morning before her death, George Zaharias, her husband, said:

"She's had enough agony, sadness and pain. And so I'm losing my wife, partner and love. God's will be done. I know she'll live forever in the hearts of millions."

A Succession of Operations

Almost from the start she was known affectionately to sports fans as The Babe, a tag hung on her by her family.

She showed versatility early. She could lick any kid in the block, won a marble tournament and a harmonica contest.

Cancer struck in 1953 just after she won the golf tournament named for her—the Babe Zaharias Open in Beaumont, Texas.

After she had undergone surgery this time, she came back to win seven golf tournaments.

But the cancer couldn't be stopped and her life became a succession of operations and of day following day in John Sealy Hospital here. . . .

Took Five First Places

Six times sports writers named her Woman Athlete of the Year in the annual Associated Press poll. On the 1950 ballot, sports writers named her the Woman Athlete of the Half Century.

In 1932 she won the National AAU women's track and field championship singlehanded, taking five first places and tying for another.

The first time out on the golf course she shot a 95. Her caddy was Lloyd Mangrum, later to become a golf great himself.

Within a month she was in the low 80s. Before long she was able to outhit her women rivals 100 to 150 yards off the tee.

She won some 90 tournaments. She won everything offered, climaxed by victory in the British Amateur in 1947.

Then came a fabulous offer of $300,000 for some golf movies and for a tie-in with a sporting goods firm. She turned pro and made a fortune in sports.

She was expert in everything she tried. Once she played the outfield for several innings with the Dallas professional baseball team, getting a hit and making some fine catches. She once toured the country as a billiards player.

Rule 6.3 of the *Associated Press Style Guide* says: "A wife becomes a widow on the death of her husband. It is redundant to say 'widow of the late.'

"John Jones is survived by his *widow* (not 'wife')."

Exercise: *1.* There are two misspellings in this sentence: "Internment will be in Forest Lawn Cemetary." What are they?

2. Here is a news agency story written for publication in a newspaper and below it is the same story as written for the radio wire of the same news agency. What are the characteristic differences in the lead, the sentence structure, the sentence length, the tense of the verbs and the handling of quotations? The newspaper story:

PITTSBURGH—Firms which make nearly half the nation's paints, varnishes and lacquers, and the men who run them were under indictment today—charged with a conspiracy to fix the prices of their products.

A federal grand jury, acting on complaints of the U.S. government, handed down the indictments in the U.S. district court yesterday, naming 14 major paint companies and 20 officials.

These companies, the indictments said, handled more than 45 per cent of the nation's billion dollar yearly paint business.

Attorney General Tom Clark said the cases were a part of the government's antitrust program aimed at "illegal conspiracies" in the housing fields.

He said Commerce Department records "indicate that prices in the paint industry rose more rapidly after the removal of OPA ceilings than in any other industry."

The indictments specifically accused the firms of engaging in "a combination and conspiracy to fix, stabilize, maintain and control the prices, discounts, allowances and terms of sale" of their products.

The firms, the indictment said, agreed "to exchange with each other information about prices charged . . . and other factors affecting prices."

In Cleveland, spokesmen for two of the companies under indictment protested there was no basis for the charges.

Adrian D. Joyce, chairman of the board of Glidden Co., said:

"There's nothing to it. We never met with any other paint concern to discuss prices and costs. Our prices are very much the same as other firms' due to competition."

Luther H. Schroeder, treasurer of

the Sherwin-Williams Co., declared:

"We don't see any basis for it (the charges) whatsoever."

The radio story:

Indictments have been returned against the firms which make nearly half the nation's paints, varnishes and lacquers. These firms and the men who run them have been charged with a conspiracy to fix the prices of their products. But in Cleveland, spokesmen for two of the companies are protesting that there is no basis for the charges.

A federal grand jury handed down the indictments yesterday, naming 14 major paint companies and 20 officials. According to the indictments, these companies handle more than 45 per cent of the nation's billion-dollar yearly paint business.

Attorney General Tom Clark says the cases are a great part of the government's antitrust program aimed at what he calls quote illegal conspiracies unquote in the housing fields.

Clark adds that Commerce Department records quote indicate that prices in the paint industry rose more rapidly after the removal of OPA ceilings than in any other industry unquote.

The indictments charge that the firms agreed quote to exchange with each other information about prices charged and other factors affecting prices unquote.

The chairman of the Glidden Co., Adrian D. Joyce, has replied to it. Quote We never met with any other paint concerns to discuss prices and costs. Our prices are very much the same as other firms' due to competition unquote.

And the treasurer of Sherwin-Williams Co. says: "We don't see any basis for the charges whatsoever."

CHAPTER 13

Science and Technology

Since the end of World War II newspapers have increasingly recognized the interest that many readers have in reports about science, medicine, and technology. A measure of this recognition is the fact that there are about 200 active members of the National Association of Science Writers and more than one thousand members of the Aviation Space Writers Association. The *New York Times* has six full-time science writers in its New York office and two in its Washington bureau.[1] Several other newspapers have one or more science writers, as have the wire services, and several newspapers have a general assignment reporter who specializes in science writing but devotes about one-half of his time to news in that field.

Most science reporters are self-taught, but several have studied one or more sciences to the extent that they know the vocabulary and the basic principles of the sciences and technologies.

Science writers obtain their material at scientific meetings, from scientific journals, from news releases by universities and research laboratories, and from personal contacts with individual scientists. At scientific meetings the participants supply advance copies of the papers they are to present. The science writer selects some of these to report and often interviews the authors, either before or after the paper is read, for the purpose of getting a clearer explanation of certain parts of the paper. The science writer who is near a university has a sort of "beat": he visits scientists to learn about their current research. He also finds out in which journal the research will be published and the approximate time of publication. He then arranges with the scientist to procure a copy of the report when it is submitted to the journal and he writes a news story at that time. The story is not released, however, until it has appeared in the journal. The reporter also does this when the research appears in a book. Some science writers also read certain

[1] Hillier Krieghbaum, "Opportunities in Science News Reporting," an address to the Sigma Delta Chi Region One Convention, June 1, 1963.

journals for newsworthy research reports of which they do not have advance information.

RELATIONS WITH SCIENTISTS

For some years scientists regarded newspaper reporters with suspicion because of the sensational and inaccurate treatment of their research findings in the Sunday newspaper supplements. Now, however, many science writers have developed a trusting relationship with individual scientists that is based on the science writers' satisfactory previous reporting of the scientists' research. In many instances the writer submits his news story to the scientists before publication to insure thorough accuracy; in other instances, the writer reads a part of his news story to the scientists on the telephone.

VOCABULARY

Because of the rapid advance of science in some fields the science writer is having to learn the definitions of new terms. Several recently published up-to-date references are available to him. Some of these are: *Short Glossary of Space Terms* published by the National Aeronautics and Space Administration;[2] John Foster, Jr., *Science Writer's Guide,* which contains 204 pages of science terms and six pages of medical terms;[3] and James F. Holmes, *Communications Dictionary: A Compilation of Terms Used in the Fields of Electronic Communications and Data Processing.*[4]

DEVELOPING A MEDICAL GLOSSARY

The reporter of medical news can develop his own short glossary if he will learn certain stems and affixes. The organs and parts of the body have Latin and Greek names because medical science had its beginning in ancient times. If the reporter will learn some of these names and certain prefixes and suffixes, he will have little difficulty in translating most of the terms he will meet, for he will understand how they are derived.

For example, some of the organs are: *gastro* (stomach), *cardia* (heart), *nephros* (kidney), *hepar* (liver), *enteron* (intestines).

Some of the prefixes and suffixes are: *dys* (ill, painful, difficult), *osis* (a diseased condition), *itis* (inflammation), *endo* and *ento* (within), *ectomy* (to take out), *otomy* (to open), *oscopy* (to look into).

[2] Obtainable from the Superintendent of Documents, Washington 25, D.C., 25¢.
[3] Columbia University Press, 1963.
[4] John F. Ryder Publisher, Inc., New York, 1962.

Thus, *gastritis* is acute or chronic inflammation of the stomach; *hepatosis* is enlargement, degeneration, or inflammation of the liver; *dysentery* is inflammation of the colon, and *dyspepsia* is disturbed digestion; *nephrectomy* is the removal of a kidney; and *cystoscopy* is the procedure of looking into the bladder with an instrument called a "cystoscope."

The reporter of medical news will get considerable help from *Blakiston's Illustrated Pocket Medical Dictionary*[5] and *The Merck Manual of Diagnosis and Therapy*.[6]

WRITING SCIENCE NEWS

Most news is about something that the usual reader can understand because he has learned something about it. But when the reporter writes about science he not only has to translate certain terms but often has to explain a cause and effect relationship. The material is so often complex that no one can develop a single set of rules for writing about science. About the only rule that fits most situations is one that relates to the beginning of the news article, for the writer's first objective is to induce the reader to begin the article and to continue his reading. There are a few ways that this objective can be achieved.

One device is to begin by asking a question. Here is an example by David Perlman of the *San Francisco Chronicle:*

> A Canadian geophysicist proposed an answer yesterday to one of evolution's major mysteries.
> Why is it, the scientists ask, that during certain periods of geologic history life suddenly seems to spurt? At those geological moments hundreds of new living species appear; other long-established species undergo rapid and profound change; all life seems to enter an era of chaotic mutation.
> Dr. Robert J. Uffen, of the University of Western Ontario in Canada, described a theory of earth magnetism and evolution yesterday at a session of the International Union of Geodesy and Geophysics in Berkeley. . . .

A second example of this device is on page 162, in which the writer, who is explaining the expanding universe, asks the question "Why is the world dark at night?"

---

[5] McGraw-Hill Book Company, Inc., New York.
[6] Merck, Sharpe and Dohme Research Laboratories, Rahway, N.J.

Another way to induce the reader to start and go on reading is a beginning that presents something happening. This can usually be done when the writer is describing an instrument or some other scientific object. Here is an example by Stuart H. Loory in *This Week:*[7]

> In a laboratory at Schenectady, N.Y., a group of General Electric engineers recently pointed a basketball-size instrument at a diamond, pulled the trigger and burned a hole right through the diamond in two hundred millionths of a second.
> At Lexington, Mass., a group of scientists from M.I.T. and the Raytheon Co. pointed the same type of device at the darkened moon. The resulting flash illuminated a two-mile circle on the moon's surface as easily as switching on a lamp.
> This new scientific tool has been named the "laser" (rhymes with razor). . . .

The student who aspires to be a science writer will profit from analyzing good models. Here is an excellent model by Bruce Bliven which explains the concept of "the expanding universe" in such a way that almost any reader can understand the concept.

WHY IS THE SKY DARK AT NIGHT?[8]

In the answer to this apparently simple question, raised over 100 years ago, lies a clue to an astounding discovery about the universe

Since the childhood of our race, mankind has accepted the darkness of the nighttime sky as an unquestioned commonplace fact of life on earth. The sun rises each morning, bringing with it daylight. When the sun sets, the one major source of light is gone. Hence the sky can no longer be bright. So have reasoned generation upon generation of men—but their reasoning overlooked something.

The first man who seems to have thought deeply about this phenomenon was a German physician, Heinrich W. M. Olbers, who lived in Bremen and who, in 1826, set out to produce a scientific and mathematical answer to the question: *Why is the world dark at night?*

Dr. Olbers had a lifelong passion for astronomy. Even during the years when he was practicing medicine he spent the greater part of each clear night in his homemade observatory on top of his house, studying the heavens. He located the comet of 1815, which was named for him; he took part in

[7] Nov. 11, 1962, p. 7.
[8] *The Reader's Digest,* July, 1963, pp. 203–6. Reprinted by permission of the author. Copyright, 1963 by The Reader's Digest Association, Inc.

the rediscovery of Ceres and discovered Pallas and Vesta—three tiny planets that circle the sun. But his greatest achievement was to ask this seemingly obvious question.

The sun, Olbers figured, provides only about half the light we on earth should theoretically be receiving; the other half should come from the billions of stars in the heavens. With all that starlight, why is midnight not as bright as day?

Dr. Olbers would have been even more puzzled had he had today's knowledge of the incredible vastness of the universe, the uncounted billions of light-giving stars in the depths of space. Our sun and its planets are only a microscopic part of the Milky Way, an average-size galaxy containing 100 billion stars—which are on the average as bright as our sun. And the Milky Way itself is only one of a seemingly limitless number of galaxies. Radio telescopes can now "hear" several billion light-years out into space; and however far they penetrate, in every direction, the galaxies continue to appear.

The number of the stars is, in fact, far beyond the power of the mind to grasp; yet so great is space that it is sparsely populated.

Though he was aware of only a small part of the stellar universe, the total number of stars known to Dr. Olbers was yet huge indeed. Taking into account their numbers, brightness and distance, making painstaking calculations, he came to an amazing conclusion: with light streaming from so many stars, the sky should *not* be dark at night. The earth even at midnight should be blazing with light and heat. It should, in fact, be frying.

How did he figure this? Suppose, said Dr. Olbers, you think of the universe as a vast hollow ball studded with stars and trillions of miles in diameter, with the earth as its center. Light will reach the earth from a multitude of stars; and while the rays from those far away will be very faint, this will be offset because the farther out you go, the greater the number of stars. In fact, the number of stars increases much faster than the distance (just as the volume of a sphere increases in proportion to its radius). Thus the weakening of the light at greater distances is *more than offset* by the greater number of stars there are when such distances are taken into account. No matter how weak the effect of any one star, therefore, if the number is large enough and the elapsed time long enough, the planet at the center should be ablaze with light and heat.

Why is this not so? Why then *is* the sky dark at night? The good doctor thought that interstellar fog must absorb almost all the starlight. But other astronomers were not satisfied that this was a sufficient explanation, and the question became famous as "Olbers' paradox."

For 100 years astronomers tried to solve the paradox. A clue came only 16 years after Olbers had raised the question, but nobody at the time recognized its relevance.

In 1842, an Austrian professor of mathematics, Christian Doppler, discovered what has ever after been known as the Doppler effect. Stand by a railroad track: as a train comes toward you the pitch of its whistle sounds high, but after it has passed, the whistle sounds lower. Doppler found the clue. As the train approaches, the sound waves it sends toward you seem, to you, shortened or "crowded"—and since short-wave sounds are higher pitched, the whistle sounds higher. Conversely, when the train speeds *away* from you, the sound waves must travel a greater distance; so they seem to you to be farther apart and therefore sound lower.

The Doppler effect applies to light waves, too. Light waves appear to the eye as longer when they come from an object moving away from us; they seem shorter and "crowded" if the object is approaching us.

With light the effect shows up in color. Light waves are longer (and weaker) at the red end of the color spectrum, shorter at the violet end. So light waves from a source that is moving away tend to be shifted down the spectrum toward the red end, a phenomenon called the "Red Shift." Thus astronomers came to realize that a slight redness in the light coming from a celestial body means that it is moving away from the observer.

Among those in this century who pondered Olbers' paradox, knowing there *must* be an answer to it, was Dr. Edwin P. Hubble of California's Mount Wilson Observatory. In 1924, with the superior instruments available, Dr. Hubble found that light from distant sources, from distant galaxies outside the Milky Way, showed the Red Shift. This, he reasoned, could only mean that their light waves were being stretched out—hence these stars, these whole galaxies of stars, must be traveling away from us at tremendous speed.

Could it be? Hubble continued to watch the sky, and the evidence mounted that this was so. He found that the farther out he looked, the redder was the light that his telescope picked up. In fact, he saw the galaxies were escaping from us at speeds that increased in a mathematically precise manner with their distance.

Hubble concluded that the whole universe is expanding—everything in it is moving farther and farther apart from everything else. Other observers confirmed his theory, and "the expanding universe" became the fundamental, though almost unbelievable, discovery of modern astronomy.

With this discovery Dr. Olbers' question at last was answered. *The sky is dark at night because the universe expands!* The galaxies are moving away from us so fast as to weaken the radiation we receive from them. This is what gives us our restful nocturnal darkness, and also saves us from being vaporized in the never-ending shower of hot starlight. Were it not for this fact, life on earth would not be possible.

When the writer is using a scientific term or is describing a phenomenon, he should search his mind for an analogy that the reader will understand. This device was discussed on pages 91–92.

CHAPTER *14*

Some Communication Theory

The preceding chapters have prescribed how news should be written. The discussion could be summarized in a set of prescriptive rules. But what would be the rationale of the rules? Would they be merely the dicta of former editors who have passed them down to present editors? Or would they be based on scientific laws that psychologists have derived from experiments?

The correct answer is that they would be both. Some intelligent editors, from their introspection and observation, have developed rules that match the findings of experimental psychologists. But some other editors operate by mere rules of thumb without making much analysis of why the rules are sound or unsound. You, however, will be more successful if you analyze what you do in terms of theory; that is, ask yourself why you do certain things in a certain way. You may also in the future be more successful in adapting your practices to the technological and social changes that will affect news reading and listening. The purpose of this chapter, therefore, is to discuss a few of the processes of communication that relate to newswriting.

THE COMMUNICATION PROCESS

The process of news communication is analogous to "information theory" which was developed by mathematicians in the field of electrical engineering.[1] The news writer or news broadcaster may be thought of as an *encoder* and the reader or listener as a *decoder,* with the encoder sending a message to the decoder in written or spoken symbols. The encoder should select those symbols which minimize *ambiguity* and should arrange them in the order that demands *the least effort* on the part of the decoder.

[1] See C. E. Shannon and W. Weaver, *The Mathematical Theory of Communication* (Urbana, Ill., 1949); see also G. A. Miller, *Language and Communication* (New York, 1951).

This would be easy to do if all of the decoders who receive the amplified communication had semantic capacities equal to those of the encoder, and if there were no "noise"[2] in the channel of communication. But the encoder is usually a person of education who has a large stock of symbols to choose from whereas many decoders have a more limited vocabulary and a more limited experience world. When a particular news communication does not immediately yield meaning to the reader or listener he shifts his attention to another news story. There should be no discrepancy between the communication codes (language) of the encoder and decoder.

"Noise"

Disturbances in the channel of communication that alter the message in some way after it has left the decoder are termed "noise" by information theory specialists. There is an analogy for "noise" in news communication. "Noise" often interferes with news communication because the reading or listening is done while the decoder is doing something else; for example, eating, riding in an automobile, or ironing. The news reader or listener also makes less of an original commitment than does the reader of a book. This is because the time available for news reading or listening is often controlled by one's living pattern: it must be fitted between other activities which require a serious commitment or which offer a valuable reward. Thus, news reading is done at breakfast, on a train, or before it is time to shop or to listen to an interesting television program.

To compensate for the "noise" he anticipates on the news communication channel, the encoder of a news message selects symbols and arranges them in an order that will facilitate comprehension.

Redundancy

Redundancy in information theory is that part of a message which is unnecessary and therefore repetitive. Information theory specialists have demonstrated mathematically that redundancy increases the probability that a communication will be understood. If parts of a message are lost (because of "noise"), the message can yet be intelligible if the message is sufficiently redundant: the redundant symbols supply enough contextual clues for the decoder to supply the "missing" parts.

An excellent example of how repetition increases the probability that the communication will be understood is a news story by James Marlow, of the Associated Press Washington bureau, about the expected arrival in the United States of 813 displaced persons from Europe. The following facts were pertinent: (1) there were then in Europe 750,000 persons who had been classified as displaced persons; (2) the special law passed by the

[2] This term is explained below.

United States Congress permitted the admission of a total of 250,000 (these being in addition to those who were admitted under the existing law which regulated admission of aliens by annual quotas from various countries); (3) only 40,000 displaced persons had previously been admitted under the existing law; and (4) 22 per cent of all displaced persons are Jews.

The writer repeated Fact 1 four times, Fact 3 five times, Fact 4 twice, and the fact that 813 displaced persons were due to arrive "tomorrow" three times. Why so much repetition? The writer was aware of the possibility that some readers would interpret the statistics to mean, perhaps, that 750,000 displaced persons were arriving, or that 205,000 European Jews were admitted every year under the existing law, and so forth.

Repetition (iteration) is practiced almost universally in public speaking, but some news writers have an exaggerated fear of redundancy. The news writer, however, can use repetition without being offensively monotonous. There is a real difference between wordiness in literary style and a repetition whose purpose is to increase the efficiency of communication. Hence, the problem for the news communicator is how to facilitate immediate comprehension without making the reader feel "as if he's listening to bagpipes with only the drone working."[3] As Fowler has said, "A dozen sentences are spoilt by ill-advised avoidance of repetition for every one that is spoilt by ill-advised repetition."[4]

Reducing the probability of ambiguity is what Herbert Spencer a hundred years ago called "economizing" the reader's "attention" when he wrote in his "Essay on the Philosophy of Style":

> A reader or listener has at each moment but a limited amount of mental power available. To recognize and interpret the symbols presented to him, requires part of this power; to arrange and combine the images suggested requires a further part; and only that part which remains can be used for realizing the thought conveyed. Hence the more time and attention it takes to receive and understand each sentence, the less time and attention can be given to the contained idea; and the less vividly will that idea be conceived. . . .
>
> Carrying out the metaphor that language is the vehicle of thought, there seems reason to think that in all cases the friction and inertia of the vehicle deduct from its efficiency; and that in composition, the chief, if not the sole thing to be done, is to reduce this friction and inertia to the smallest amount.[5]

How We Read

Eye camera photographs show that we perceive words in groups. That is, the eye proceeds from left to right with fixations at certain points in the

---

[3] S. S. Smith, *The Command of Words* (New York, 1949), p. 13.
[4] H. W. Fowler, *A Dictionary of Modern English Usage* (London, 1950), p. 495.
[5] *Essays: Moral, Political and Aesthetic* (New York, 1865), pp. 11–12.

line of type. One span may include several words or, in the case of the slow reader, only a part of one long word. Occasionally there are regressions: the eyes go backward to reread a part of a line or a few long words. The photographs exhibit more regressions by slow readers than by fast readers.[6]

Whatever the speed of the individual reader, his eyes focus on words and groups of words and he stores up in his memory their provisional meaning until he has reached the end of the sentence. This is an active process in which the reader thinks along with the writer—perceiving images and evaluating. Each word or group of words he comprehends in terms of the context that was presented in previous words or sentences.

Context

Verbal context is the parts of a written or spoken discourse that precede or follow a specific expression and are directly related to it. Communication is facilitated when the writer, being aware of how context operates, builds it into his message. Thus, he may use an unfamiliar word if he takes care to supply context. An example:

> The vice president today denounced *filibustering*.
> The Senate must change its rules, he said, to prevent a few senators from talking to death a bill they don't like. A few senators can thwart the will of an overwhelming majority, he added.

The contribution of context to comprehension has been demonstrated by Wilson L. Taylor, who developed a measure of readability that tests the ability of a reader to supply missing (prescinded) words in a passage.[7] A group of subjects is given passages from which every *n*th word has been prescinded, and are asked to supply the missing words. Success in supplying the missing words in a particular passage is a measure of the readability of that passage. Success, of course, is related to the amount of context the writer has included in his writing. The important contribution of context to comprehension was further demonstrated by Taylor when subjects were presented with passages from Gertrude Stein's and James Joyce's writings; Joyce, for example, used words which were not in a dictionary. Subjects scored low comprehension on the Stein and Joyce writings although the same passages had reasonably high readability scores on the Flesch formula,[8]

---

[6] The average reader reads at the rate of about 250 words a minute.

[7] See " 'Cloze Procedure': A New Tool for Measuring Readability," *Journalism Quarterly*, Vol. XXX (1953), pp. 415–33.

[8] See pp. 111–112.

which measures average sentence length and word length. Thus, Taylor's test is a measure of how closely the reader's decoding of a message corresponds to the encoder's way of writing.

Nonverbal context is also a factor in communication. Its importance for newspapers is in attribution,[9] as when a newspaper reports a statement made by a person, the person quoted being the nonverbal context of the statement. Some readers interpret a statement in terms of the person who made it. Asch[10] submitted a statement about capitalism and collective bargaining to two groups of subjects. One group was told that the statement had been made by Eric A. Johnston, president of the Chamber of Commerce of the United States; the second group was told that the source of the statement was Harry Bridges, the radical labor leader. Since the statement was more congruent with the labor leader as the source, one-fifth of the subjects who had been told that Johnston made the statement questioned the authorship. The other four-fifths of that group, however, interpreted the statement so that it would be congruent with the source. That is, *they altered the content of the communication to fit the supposed context.* This fact of social psychology should be kept in mind by news writers.

Because this is an introductory textbook the foregoing discussion of the theory of communication has been limited to the scope of the book. The student who wishes to obtain an overall survey of the field should read *The Process and Effects of Mass Communication* by Wilbur Schramm (Urbana, Ill., 1954).

[9] See pp. 87–90.
[10] S. E. Asch, *Social Psychology* (New York, 1952), pp. 420–26.

Reporting Public Affairs

CHAPTER 15

The Courts

The state provides an apparatus, called a court, so that one person may sue another person to enforce his rights or to redress or prevent a wrong. This same mechanism is also used by the state to punish a person who commits an act that is injurious to society.

An example of the first situation is when William Jones owes Joe Smith $5,000 but refuses to pay him. Smith may employ an attorney to file an action against Jones. Smith, who is called the "plaintiff," must pay a small fee to a court to recompense the state in part for the time spent by the court clerk and process* servers. Smith must also pay fees and travel expenses for any witnesses who testify in his behalf. If he wins the case, he possibly may recover from Jones these costs in addition to the $5,000 debt. But the state pays the salary of the judge, the clerk, and the bailiff and supplies the courtroom. The state does this because it would be disadvantageous to society if private rights could be protected only by private justice, perhaps in the form of violence.

This same mechanism is available to a private party to redress a wrong, as when Henry Brown is injured when he is struck by James White's automobile. It is also available to a private party to prevent a wrong, as when the XYZ Corporation is infringing a patent that was developed by the ABC Corporation and the latter petitions a court to enjoin the XYZ Corporation from further infringement and also to pay damages to the ABC Corporation.

CIVIL AND CRIMINAL LAW DISTINGUISHED

All of the aforementioned actions are *civil* actions. When a court is used to punish an offender for an act deemed injurious to society—not just to another individual—it is enforcing *criminal* law. An example: when James White struck and injured Henry Brown with his automobile he also struck and killed Thomas Green. He was arrested and charged with involuntary manslaughter.

---

* When a term is not defined in the text and is followed by an asterisk, it is defined in the Glossary of Legal Terms (Appendix C).

It is important that you learn at the beginning of this discussion the difference between a criminal and a civil action. A criminal action is the proceeding by which a party is accused of a public offense and brought to trial, being prosecuted in the name of the state. A civil action is prosecuted by one private party against another private party for the declaration, enforcement, or protection of a right, or the redress or prevention of a wrong.

Thus, when Henry Brown demands damages of James White, whose automobile injured him, the case is entitled "Henry Brown, Plaintiff, *vs.* James White, Defendant." The criminal case of the state against James White, however, is entitled "The People of the State of California, Plaintiff, *vs.* James White, Defendant."

The state (and the federal government) may also be a party to a civil action, either as plaintiff or defendant. But these are usually situations in which a private person has a claim against the state or the state asserts a claim against a private person.

When a court allows a judgment for a plaintiff in a civil action, the result is a money award against the defendant or an order of the court directed to the defendant restraining him from doing a certain act or commanding him to do a certain act. The judgment does not necessarily impute criminality to the defendant's act or motive. In a criminal case, however, the judgment of the court results either in a fine or imprisonment or death penalty or a finding of "not guilty"; this is because the defendant has been accused of an offense against the community which is in violation of a law.

In addition to the above mentioned situations, a court is also used for certain special proceedings. Here are two examples:

1. Some of the heirs of the late Thomas Green are dissatisfied with the bequests they received under his will.

2. The UAQ Corporation is insolvent and owes several creditors.

These two situations, and some others, will be discussed in detail in later chapters.[1]

THE BASIS FOR LITIGATION

At any given moment somebody is injuring another either *ex delicto** or *ex contractu**, somebody is going broke, somebody is making a will, and some spouse is considering a divorce. All of these situations are subject to the rules of conduct that we call law. Most of the situations are resolved by conference between the parties' attorneys, but enough of them are resolved by a trial to generate a vast amount of business for our courts. Why there is so much litigation is explained by a distinguished attorney:

[1] See Chaps. 26 and 27.

I have represented defrauded business men who fight their deceivers for fortune and power. I have seen them pour out their venom against their opponents until they suffered heart attacks or were ulcerated. I have witnessed struggles for the protection of copyrighted property, where the pride of authorship, being dearer than life itself, consumed the creative artist. I have seen public figures libeled or accused of wrongs which could wreck their life's work, strike back at their detractors. I have observed men with spotless reputations who were indicted, suffer nervous breakdowns. I have witnessed children sue their fathers to deprive them of their businesses, or brothers engaged in fratricidal contests without quarter. I have seen defendants in antitrust suits beleaguered by plaintiffs seeking treble damages or defending themselves against Government actions aimed to break up their enterprise, painstakingly built over a lifetime. I have participated in will contests in which relatives were at each others' throats for the inheritance.

All these litigations evoke intense feelings of animosity, revenge, and retribution. Some of them may be fought ruthlessly. But none of them, even in their most aggravated form, can equal the sheer, unadulterated venom of a matrimonial contest.[2]

SUBSTANTIVE AND PROCEDURAL LAW DISTINGUISHED

Newspaper reporters examine the court calendars and select to report those proceedings that are of greatest public interest or importance. Of chief interest and importance to the reader is the result of a trial, but in some proceedings the evidence is also of interest or importance. To report the evidence accurately, one must understand the procedures and the legal vocabulary. It is not necessary to know much about substantive law (except a modicum of criminal law), but it is necessary to understand procedural, or adjective, law.

There are numerous subjects of substantive law, such as real property, torts, contracts, and agency. Substantive law is that body of rules which defines, creates, and regulates rights. Procedural, or adjective, law is that body of rules of procedure and practice whereby the substantive law is administered. Several chapters of this book relate mainly to procedural law, for the reporter must understand it.

COURTS AND THEIR JURISDICTION

The constitution or statutes of a state specify the jurisdiction of each type of court that it has established. The constitution of the United States also determines which types of cases shall be heard and determined in a federal court, and federal statutes, as well as the constitution, specify the jurisdiction of the various federal courts. Jurisdiction is the power to hear and determine a specific cause.

[2] Louis Nizer, *My Life in Court*, p. 153. Copyrighted 1961 by Louis Nizer. Reprinted by permission of Doubleday and Company.

Let us look at the cases mentioned on pages 173–174 and note the court that is appropriate for each. First, there are two cases which would be tried in the federal District Court. These are the UAQ Corporation insolvency and the ABC Corporation *vs.* XYZ Corporation patent infringement cases. The insolvency case must be tried in a federal court because the United States constitution reserves the bankruptcy power to the federal government (Art. I, sec. 8). Since the same section of the United States constitution reserves to the federal government the authority to issue patents, the patent infringement case must also be tried in a federal court.

The other cases we have mentioned would be tried in a state court. These are: Jones *vs.* Smith, a suit to collect a debt of $5,000; Brown *vs.* White, a suit for damages for injury by an automobile; the State *vs.* White, a prosecution for involuntary manslaughter; and Estate of Thomas Green, a will contest.

Most civil and criminal actions are in state courts because, under the United States constitution, all powers not specifically *delegated* to the federal government are *reserved* to the state governments.

These cases would be tried in a local court of original jurisdiction, or court of first instance as it is sometimes called.[3] This court is most frequently called the Circuit Court, District Court, or Superior Court. The federal court of original jurisdiction is called the District Court.

There is such a state tribunal in nearly every county (or comparable subdivision of a state). In addition, there are local courts of *limited* jurisdiction which hear and determine minor civil cases and criminal misdemeanors (i.e., offenses which do not amount to felonies). Thus, if the demand in the Jones *vs.* Smith case had been for a much smaller amount than $5,000, the case would probably have been tried in such a court rather than in the usual court of original jurisdiction. Similarly, if White, the driver of the automobile, had struck Brown's automobile without injuring Brown, the state might have prosecuted White in a court of limited jurisdiction on a misdemeanor charge of speeding or reckless driving.

The place (i.e., county) in which a case is tried is called the *venue*. One of the factors that determines the venue of a case is the place in which the injury was done. Venue should not be confused with jurisdiction, which relates to the power of the court to act.

The judgments of the state courts inferior to the courts of original jurisdiction are reviewable by the latter. Likewise, the states and the federal government have established appellate courts to review the judgments of the courts of original jurisdiction.

The most common name of a state appellate court is Supreme Court.

---

[3] In a few situations an appellate court is a court of original jurisdiction. For example, the United States Supreme Court has original jurisdiction in cases affecting ambassadors and consuls and cases in which a state is a party.

Several states, however, have established intermediate appellate courts to relieve the highest appellate court. In such states, the court system is represented by the chart on this page.

COURTS OF LIMITED JURISDICTION

There are about 30,000 Justices' Courts in the United States, most of them in small communities. The magistrate in such a court is usually called *justice of the peace.*

STATE JUDICIAL SYSTEM

STATE SUPREME COURT
Court of final resort. Some states call it Supreme Court, Supreme Court of Errors, Court of Appeals, Supreme Judicial Court, or Supreme Court of Appeals.

INTERMEDIATE APPELLATE COURTS
Only 16 of the 50 states have intermediate appellate courts, an intermediate appellate tribunal between the trial court and the court of final resort. A majority of cases are decided finally by these appellate courts.

SUPERIOR COURT
Highest trial court with general jurisdiction. Some states refer to it as Circuit Court, District Court, Court of Common Pleas, and, in New York, Supreme Court.

PROBATE COURT
Some states call it Surrogate Court or Orphans' Court (Pa.). It is a special court which handles wills, administration of estates, guardianship of minors and incompetents.

MUNICIPAL COURT
In cities it is customary to have less important cases tried by municipal justices or municipal magistrates.

COUNTY COURT
Has limited jurisdiction in both civil and criminal cases.

JUSTICE OF THE PEACE AND POLICE MAGISTRATE
Lowest courts in judiciary hierarchy. Limited in jurisdiction in both civil and criminal cases.

In urban communities there are similar courts with the same or slightly higher civil and criminal jurisdiction, usually called Municipal Courts. Some cities have Police Courts with minor criminal jurisdiction.

In general, such inferior courts have jurisdiction in civil cases involving relatively small amounts of money (often $500 or less) and criminal jurisdiction for misdemeanors. Usually, the magistrates of such courts may hold preliminary examinations of persons accused of felonies with authority to commit them to the action of the grand jury or for trial in a court of original jurisdiction. Such magistrates issue warrants of arrest and determine bail.

In some states the kind of justice administered in these inferior courts is scandalous. The magistrates need not be lawyers. They are not paid a salary but collect fees and fines. They become collection agencies and they split fines with local policemen and constables. They operate speed traps for out-of-town motorists. Since they are compensated by fines and fees, the defendant in their courts in both civil and criminal cases is at a disadvantage. Several states have reformed their inferior court system by requiring the magistrates to be lawyers and by paying them adequate salaries. Such reform is not easy to legislate in some states because the justice of the peace is a member of the local political organization.[4]

There are no inferior courts in the federal jurisdiction, but the United States Commissioner may try certain misdemeanors under specified circumstances, as explained on page 197.

COURTS OF ORIGINAL JURISDICTION

Most civil cases and all felony cases are tried in a court of original jurisdiction. These state courts sit in the county seat. In urban areas, the court has several judges. In thinly populated areas, one judge and one prosecuting attorney are elected to serve a judicial district composed of two or more counties. The court sits in each county by rotation at some time during the term of court. A clerk, however, is elected for each county in the judicial district.

The name of the court of original jurisdiction in each state is listed on page 179.

HOW A BIG COURT IS ORGANIZED

The largest court in the United States is the superior court of Los Angeles county. A brief description of its organization will supply some

[4] For a description of this office as it operates in some states, see Joe Alex Morris, "The 'JP': Should He Be Abolished?" *Saturday Evening Post,* October 11, 1958, pp. 19, 100–106.

Courts of Original Jurisdiction

Alabama	Circuit[1]	Nebraska	District[1]
Alaska	Superior	Nevada	District
Arkansas	Circuit[1,2]	New Hampshire	Superior[1]
California	Superior	New Jersey	Superior[1,2,3]
Colorado	District[1]	New Mexico	District[1]
Connecticut	Superior	New York	Supreme[1,3]
Delaware	Superior[3]	North Carolina	Superior
Dist. of Columbia	Supreme	North Dakota	District
Florida	Circuit	Ohio	Common Pleas[1]
Georgia	Superior[1,3]	Oklahoma	District[1]
Hawaii	Circuit	Oregon	Circuit
Idaho	District[1]	Pennsylvania	Common Pleas[1]
Illinois	Circuit[1,3]	Rhode Island	Superior[1]
Indiana	Circuit	South Carolina	Common Pleas[1]
Iowa	District[3]		General Sessions
Kansas	District	South Dakota	Circuit
Kentucky	Circuit	Tennessee	Circuit[2]
Louisiana	District	Texas	District[3]
Maine	Superior	Utah	District
Maryland	Circuit[1]	Vermont	Superior[2]
Massachusetts	Superior[1]	Virginia	Circuit
Michigan	Circuit[1]	Washington	Circuit
Minnesota	District[1]	West Virginia	Circuit[1]
Mississippi	Circuit[2]	Wisconsin	Circuit
Missouri	Circuit[3]	Wyoming	District
Montana	District		

[1] Has a separate probate court variously called Probate, County, Surrogate, Orphans', or Prerogative court.
[2] Has a separate chancery (equity) court.
[3] Has concurrent jurisdiction with other courts in certain areas of the state. The names of such courts may be found in Martindale-Hubbell, *Law Directory*.

---

understanding of the amount of specialization there is in our courts of original jurisdiction, including many that are smaller than the Los Angeles county court.

About 150,000 cases are filed annually in this court and about 120,000 of them are disposed of in some way (by trial, settlement, or dismissal) within a year. The court has 102 judges. It also has 19 court commissioners who are lawyers, numerous examiners, referees, bailiffs, probation officers, deputy clerks, and clerical workers—a total of about 250 persons.

Fifty-four of the judges serve in the civil division, fourteen in the criminal division, two in the probate division, three in the appellate department (reviewing cases from twenty-three municipal courts), three in the juvenile court division, and one in the psychiatric division. The others are in departments which handle domestic relations and conciliation, pretrial, discovery, adoptions, writs and receivers, and law and motion. In addition are the court commissioners who are qualified to serve as judges *pro tem*.

The judges in this court elect the presiding judge. The presiding judge assigns the other judges to the various departments and divisions. He is responsible for the master calendars (i.e., the trial lists, sometimes called "trial dockets") for both civil and criminal divisions. He is also the administrative officer of the court.

TERMS OF COURT

In some jurisdictions, the calendar year is divided into "terms." In nonpopulous judicial districts which include more than one county, one to three terms of court are held in each county during the calendar year. In populous counties, however, the court sits for virtually the entire year. Technically, the court term has importance with reference to vacating of judgments entered, the rule being that the judgment is final (although subject to appeal) after the term has ended.

THE JUVENILE COURT

To deal with the problems that relate to the delinquency, neglect, and dependency of children, the states have either established special courts or have provided for special proceedings in the existing courts. In general, the system removes child offenders from the regular criminal courts, permits of informal proceedings, and provides for separate and private court records. The law distinguishes criminality from delinquency. In some states, delinquency includes acts for which an adult is not punishable, such as truancy, incorrigibility, and association with immoral or vicious persons.

The procedure usually is as follows: (1) A *complaint* is made; (2) a preliminary inquiry determines whether or not a formal *petition* should be filed (only about one-half of the complaints result in the filing of a petition); (3) a petition is filed by a police officer, social worker, the parents, or some other person—usually the same person who made the complaint; (4) investigation is made by the juvenile court's probation officer into the child's history and environment, and sometimes the child takes a physical or mental examination; (5) an informal hearing is held from which the public is excluded; and (6) the juvenile is either adjudicated a delinquent or his case is dismissed.

When the court determines a child to be delinquent the child may be: placed on probation under certain conditions, such as making restitution of property or paying for damages to property; placed in a foster home; or committed to a state training school or juvenile correctional institution.

When a child above a certain age is charged with commission of a grave crime (such as homicide or armed robbery) the criminal court in some states has concurrent jurisdiction with the juvenile court or, in other states, has exclusive jurisdiction. The juvenile court may also waive jurisdiction so that the case may be heard in a regular court.

In several states, the court of original jurisdiction or an inferior court functions as the juvenile court. In these states, when the court has two or more departments, one or more judges specialize as juvenile court judges; In other instances the judges serve as juvenile judges in rotation.

Independent juvenile courts have been established in several states and in certain cities in other states. Three states—Utah, Connecticut, and Rhode Island—have statewide juvenile courts. (Utah is divided into six juvenile court districts.)

Who is subject to the jurisdiction of the juvenile court? First are "children." The upper age limit in a very few states is 21 years and in a few other states is 16 years; in most states it is 18 years.

Some adults in some jurisdictions are also subject to the juvenile court's jurisdiction, including any person who contributes to the delinquency of a minor. In neglect and dependency cases, the parents or guardians are subject to the court's jurisdiction. A child may be made a "ward" of the court if he has no parents or guardian, if he refuses to obey a parent or guardian, or if his parents are depraved.[5]

Youth Will Go To Clinic in Sex Death Case

Seventeen-year-old Don Jackson will be committed to the Youth Authority for his part in the death of a teen-age girl friend.

Superior Court Judge H. T. Southwood said today he will approve a recommendation to that effect made by the county probation department.

Young Jackson, who admitted giving 17-year-old Mary Wills two capsules containing a poison, reportedly to induce a miscarriage, thus will become a ward of the juvenile court.

[5] The juvenile court jurisdiction for each of the fifty states is described in F. B. Sussmann, *Law of Juvenile Delinquency* (New York, 1959), Appendix I. The problem of juvenile crime is discussed by the head of the juvenile bureau of the Los Angeles County sheriff's office in H. L. Stallings (with D. Dressler), *Juvenile Officer* (New York, 1954).

He will not have to stand trial in superior court. The juvenile court will have jurisdiction over him until he is 21 years old, District Attorney Paul McDonald said.

"Don Gave Me Something"

John Morris, chief probation officer, filed an amended petition today reducing the murder charge to intent to commit an abortion.

"This has been a most difficult case to deal with," Morris said. "The further our investigation and testing progressed the more it became apparent that this lad was filled with many personal conflicts and was very much in need of extended clinical care."

Young Jackson will be sent to the Youth Authority Clinic. From there he may be returned to his own home on parole, sent to a forestry camp, placed in a Youth Authority school, or in a hospital for further observation and treatment, Morris said.

Jackson was picked up for questioning September 28 after Miss Wills, a high school senior, collapsed at the home of a friend and gasped:

"Don gave me something while at school. I think it was a vitamin pill. I'm going to have a baby."

Youths To Be Tried In Superior Court

Two teen-agers who beat a school teacher and left him to die on the streetcar tracks were ordered yesterday to face murder charges in superior court.

Juvenile Court Judge Charles Banta, after a lengthy hearing, ruled that the high school youths were "unfit" to be tried under juvenile law.

On April 29, James Hawkins, 27, of 564 Ethridge street, was robbed and savagely beaten by the two boys and left on the tracks at 10th and Chestnut streets—where he was run over by a streetcar.

The youths, Larry Hall, 16, and Thomas Musto, 17, tried to escape identification by burning the papers in

Hawkins' wallet and throwing the wallet in a lake.

Both had previous police records.

Asks Children Be Wards of Court

Juvenile court officials filed a petition yesterday to have the six abandoned Hale children made wards of the court.

The court's investigators charged the parents, Robert and Betty Hale, with neglect, drinking, and irresponsibility.

The Hales left their six small children in their flat at 239 Merriam street over the week-end. It was only after neighbors heard the youngsters crying Sunday night that they were taken to the Youth Guidance Center.

Juvenile Court Judge Charles Banta issued a detaining order which authorized the Youth Guidance Center to hold the children pending a full-scale hearing by a court referee.

The father of the children told the investigators he was drinking heavily over the week-end and that when he returned home Monday to find the children gone he assumed that his wife had left them with friends.

The mother, who had left the children Sunday, telephoned the police yesterday from Bend, Oregon, where she was stranded without funds after driving there with friends.

Reporting Juvenile Offenses

Newspapers do not report juvenile court proceedings, although in some instances judges permit reporters to attend a proceeding. The theory of the law on juvenile delinquency is that the youth will more likely be rehabilitated if he is not exposed to publicity; or, conversely, that the scorn of his peers, who know about his offense, will have an adverse effect on his personality; also that he might lose future employment opportunities.

When juveniles are arrested, however, their names are usually entered on police records. The newspaper then has to decide whether or not to publish the names. In twelve states the law prohibits or restricts publication of names of juvenile offenders.

Most newspapers do not publish the names of arrested juveniles, although they do report the arrest and the circumstances of the offense. Delinquents are referred to in news stories as "two Hillsborough youths, etc." or "a contractor's 15-year-old son, etc."

Many newspapers, however, use the names when a grave crime is reported, especially when the age of the offender is toward the upper limit of "juvenile" as defined by law. About one-half of all crimes committed in this country are by persons whose age is only slightly above the upper limit adopted by most states; about 15 per cent of all crimes are committed by persons under 18 years of age.

In recent years, a good many editors and some judges have come to question the theory that publicity is bad for the juvenile offender. Some editors argue that, in most types of cases, the juvenile dislikes the publicity more than the payment of a fine. Others argue that publication does not injure the delinquent because his associates and friends learn about his offense anyway. Publication, they assert, makes the parents deservedly ashamed. Some editors differentiate a first offense from a repeated offense when deciding about publication of names. There seems to be little objective evidence to answer the question whether publication protects the juvenile or makes him a "hero" among his peers.

For class discussion: *1*. Which of the arguments appear to be valid in this excerpt from *The AP Log* of February 26–March 4, 1959?

> An impromptu debate has been stirred by the arrest of Roy Campanella's 15-year-old son, David, on charges involving juvenile delinquency. The question: Should the boy's name have been published? An article in the February 28 issue of *Editor & Publisher* told of soul searching in New York editorial rooms before the original publication. The question figured in a week-end conference of editors and judges, called by the National Probation and Parole Association to discuss juvenile court problems. It was raised in correspondence from AP members.
>
> All four New York morning papers, which had first crack at the story in editions of February 24, used the name. A big factor in the decisions, as reported by *Editor & Publisher,* was the prominence of the father, a former big league baseball star and a leader in fighting juvenile crime.
>
> In the view of Luke Carroll, assistant executive editor of the *Herald Tribune,* "Young people engaged in crime or in conduct that may have serious effect on the community become news. . . . Young Campanella, as the son of a famous newsmaker, was news."
>
> Turner Catledge, managing editor spoke for the *New York Times:* "Youth gangs and youth fighting is a gnawing problem. . . . We felt we had an obligation to our readers to publish the facts of this rumble, although, of course, the Campanella name made the story bigger than it would otherwise have been."

This reasoning was criticized at the juvenile court conference by Fendall Yerxa, executive editor of the Wilmington (Del.) *News*. He spoke of the widespread principle of withholding names of juvenile offenders, and said, "We and they (New York papers) violated the principle for only one reason: the prominence of the name."

Two of the judges attending, Luther D. Youngdahl, of the United States District Court, Washington, and Harry W. Lindeman, of the Essex County, N.J., Juvenile and Domestic Relations Court, also spoke against use of the name as "unjust and unfair."

But what would have happened if the name had been withheld and, as inevitably it would, had leaked out later? Frank Starzel, AP general manager, brought up that point: "There would have been a greater hue and cry about favoring the son of a famous man than about using the name." The *Times'* Turner Catledge said, "We have much less to apologize for than . . . if we had withheld the name."

Another angle came out in the views of AP members: Was the story blown up out of proportion? "Young Campanella is just another kid who got into trouble. There are thousands of others like him," wrote an upstate New York editor. A sports editor from the South wanted it known that he is a staunch segregationist, but "derned if I don't think this is one colored boy getting a heckuva bad time through some ill-advised publicity."

Behind the question in point on the Campanella case is the broader one involving the use of the name of any juvenile who gets into trouble. This was a major point of debate at the New York conference, attended by twelve editors and six judges.

Some of the judges argued against the theory that publicity is a deterrent to crime. If that is true, Judge John Warren Hill, of the New York Domestic Relations Court, wanted to know: "Why hasn't it deterred crime in the 18–20-year-old group who are the worst offenders and have the most publicity?"

Judge Francis McCabe, of the Rhode Island Juvenile Court, did not see "how any child's name in the newspaper can help the child." However, Alfred H. Kirchhofer, of the Buffalo *Evening News,* said he had "never seen any statistics that prove that using names does damage. There would have to be more evidence."

Sam Day, of the New York *Journal-American,* argued that "We're not protecting the public if we don't use names. A 12-year-old can kill you as dead as an adult can." Kirchhofer recalled recent cases of "sex offenders who aren't named in the newspapers and are running around loose . . . and mothers are quite worried about their daughters' safety. We think the names of such offenders ought to be printed so that people will know who they are and to be able to protect themselves."

The age deadline beyond which use of names is justified also came in for discussion. Judge Hill endorsed "the philosophy of treating children, particularly those under 16, differently from older ones." But Judge Henry G. Sweney, of the Media, Pa., Court of Common Pleas, said, "It makes no sense that the law should say over 16 you can publish the name; under 16 you can't."

No formal decision came from the conference, and none was expected. In Catledge's words, "trying to arrive at a standard for applying judgment to a very unstandardized situation is impossible." Norman Isaacs, of the *Louisville Times,* who presided, put it another way: "The truth is, none of us know what's right or wrong. Many papers will call up the judge when they are confused—but sometimes he's as confused as we are."

2. A New Hampshire statute prohibits publication of the names of juveniles who have been arrested in connection with a criminal offense. John Smith, a 17-year-old youth, living in New Hampshire, killed his entire family—his parents and two brothers. How would you write this news story if your paper were published in New Hampshire? If you filed a story for a wire service?

OFFICERS OF STATE COURTS

The Judge

The chief officer of a trial court is the judge. All other officers of the court, including the attorneys admitted to practice in the court, are his servants and assistants. The judge is a legal umpire: he decides all questions of law, rules on the admissibility of evidence, instructs the jury as to the law, and directs the entry of a judgment. Ancillary to those functions, he questions veniremen,[6] excuses veniremen, issues bench warrants (of arrest) and subpoenas for witnesses; he sometimes questions witnesses. In a very few jurisdictions he evaluates the evidence for the jury, as is regularly done in British courts.

The judge exercises "inherent power," whether authorized by statute or not, to assure efficient and fair administration of justice. He may, for example, cite and punish for contempt a recalcitrant witness, a disorderly spectator, an attorney who behaves without decorum in the course of a trial, or a newspaper reporter or photographer when the reporter or photographer has interfered with the administration of justice.

In connection with pending actions, the judge issues *orders* (in some circumstances called *rules*). An order is a directive or ruling by a judge other than a judgment. It is made either in writing or orally by the judge and is entered in the court's minutes by the clerk, usually after a hearing on "law and motion day."[7] An order is granted usually on the *motion* of an attorney. A motion is an application by a party for an order in a pending suit. It is made either in writing on notice to the adverse party or orally in open court.

When a court of original jurisdiction has two or more judges, one of them is the *presiding judge.* Which one is determined by election, rotation, or seniority. The presiding judge is the administrative officer of the court.

[6] See p. 191.
[7] See p. 188.

He usually assigns cases to specific judges and is responsible for the calendars. He usually hears the law and motion calendar,[8] which involves ruling on the legal technicalities presented by attorneys in motions that relate to the preliminary pleadings.[9] He is also the judge who handles applications for temporary restraining orders and injunctions. In some jurisdictions he assigns particular judges to the departments. He usually instructs the grand jury.

The term "presiding judge" should not be applied to any trial judge in a court of original jurisdiction unless the particular trial judge happens also to be the presiding judge of the whole court. The term is sometimes used with reference to the "chief judge" when three judges sit, although the term is incorrect when used in this way in the federal jurisdiction.

A party may request disqualification of a judge, alleging prejudice. Statutes of the several states or the rules of appellate courts provide various ways of meeting this situation. In some jurisdictions an attorney may disqualify a judge by merely filing an affidavit of prejudice. In some instances, the presiding judge or the State Judicial Council, on application, assigns a different judge to hear the case. A judge who believes that he might not be considered impartial because of a relationship of some kind to one of the parties may recuse himself.

The Clerk

Next to the judge, the clerk is the most important officer of the court. For each department of the court there is a deputy clerk. The clerk—or his deputies—are the officials with whom the reporter has most frequent and intimate contact. The reporter not only examines the papers filed in the office of the clerk prior to a trial, but during the course of a trial consults the clerk (or deputy clerk) or the clerk's records to obtain information about pending cases. The reporter visits the clerk's office twice or oftener each day to examine papers filed by parties during that day.

The deputy clerk assigned to a particular department attends the trials. He thus: acts as a secretary for the proceedings; assists in the drawing of jurors; administers oaths to witnesses and jurors; reads jury verdicts and polls the jury when requested to do so by one of the parties; issues processes*, such as summonses, subpoenas, and writs of attachment; and enters the judgments and orders made by the judge.

The clerk is the custodian of all papers and trial exhibits and of monies paid into the court. He transmits records to the appellate court. In advance of a trial, it is he who issues a summons to the defendants and subpoenas for the witnesses.

[8] See p. 188.
[9] See Chapter 16.

Court records: When a party begins a civil action against another, he files a *complaint*. The clerk issues a *summons* which requires the defendant to appear or to answer. At the time of the filing, the clerk assigns a serial number to the case. All subsequent papers relating to the case, such as the defendant's *answer* and the written *motions* made by the parties, are kept by the clerk.

The clerk makes an entry for every paper filed in each case in a permanent record book—usually loose-leaf—called the *register*. Each case has a number for the particular year in which it was begun. The register records the names of the parties, the titled description of each paper filed (e.g., "motion to make the complaint more definite and certain"), the date of its filing, the minutes of the judge's ruling on each paper, and the amount of the filing fee collected. If the case goes to trial, the clerk records in the register each of the exhibits of the plaintiff and the defendant, the names of the witnesses for each party, and the names of each juror, including those who are excused.

The clerk also keeps two books, called the *plaintiff's index* and the *defendant's index*. These list alphabetically the names of the parties and the case number. By referring to one of these indexes, the newspaper reporter can locate the case in the register by its number.

All of the papers filed in a civil action, from the plaintiff's complaint to the final judgment, are called the *judgment roll*. When a case is sent to an appellate court for review, the judgment roll is sent up.[10] Some statutes refer to the aggregate of these documents, exclusive of the exhibits, as *papers*.

The clerk also prepares for the presiding judge certain lists called *calendars,* or *dockets*. In some jurisdictions there are separate criminal, law, and equity calendars. From time to time these cases are "called" in the order in which they are listed, and the attorneys respond in some manner. Some civil cases are settled and are removed from the list.

The sequence of cases must be adjusted at certain times to give priority to applications for temporary restraining orders, injunctions, and declaratory relief. Thus, a stockholder, believing he will suffer irreparable injury, petitions the court to enjoin the holding of a stockholders' meeting scheduled for the next day. This application, since it has priority over the usual cases, interrupts the sequence of the calendar.

The clerk also keeps a *motion calendar*. For each case that has not been disposed of, the clerk, in accordance with the papers which were filed by the attorneys in the previous week, schedules the motions they have filed. On "law and motion day"—usually a Monday but sometimes more than one day a week—the judge in charge of the motion calendar calls the case.

[10] See p. 430.

The clerk records the ruling of the judge, usually after the judge has heard argument by the attorneys. Here is a portion of a typical calendar:

PROBATE
9264—Estate of Earl Carpenter. *Probate of will.*
8806—Estate of May H. Bullivant. *Petition for letters.*
6580—Estate of George Corcoran. *Final account. Three demurrers. Four petitions.*
8472—Guardianship of Estate of George Clay, incompetent. *Account.*

CIVIL
32355—Attilo v. Rix. *Order to show cause.*
22307—Sara F. v. Richard Walker. *Motion.*
22319—Rose v. Frank Gillison. *Order.*
32194—Albert F. Wheeler v. City Rwy. *Demurrer.*
32279—Emilio Verna v. Adelia O'Malley. *Trial.*
27178—W. C. Ferrell v. May Raleigh. *Motion for change of venue.*
25138—Cornelius Duke v. Theodore Dubuc. *Motion for new trial.*
23287—Ruth v. Edward King. *Motion to set aside judgment.* 11:00 A.M.
31805—William B. Elkington v. Pearl Wassermann. *Jury trial.* 1:30 P.M.

CRIMINAL
32288—The People v. Louis Figoni. *Time to sentence.*
33350—The People v. Sam Burke. *Time to plead.*
33871—The People v. George Krug. *Arraignment.*
32916—The People v. Benjamin Wilson. *Trial to be set.*
30010—The People v. Joseph Rabinowitz. *Trial.*

After both attorneys in a case have filed a "memorandum to set" or a stipulation, the judge sets a time for the trial and the clerk notifies the attorneys, usually by postcard. This means that preliminary motions have been disposed of and the case is "at issue." Each case thus set goes to the bottom of a list called the *trial calendar,* or *trial docket.* The presiding judge assigns the case to a particular judge.

In accordance with the practice in various jurisdictions, the clerk keeps other records, such as a *minute book,* a *judgment docket,* an *execution docket,* a *motion book,* an *attachment record,* and a *fee book.* Most courts also have an *index of judgments.*

Court Commissioners, Masters, and Referees

In some situations the judges need considerable assistance in carrying on the detailed work of the court. To perform duties that are partly judicial and partly clerical, there are *court commissioners.* These officials take affidavits and depositions, take and approve bond in civil cases (including examination of the sureties), and administer oaths. Some of them also handle the details of probate proceedings. In most jurisdictions, commissioners need not be attorneys.

On more of a judicial level, however, the court appoints attorneys who are called *masters* and *referees*. In some situations "special" masters or referees are appointed for particular cases. In other situations there are "standing" masters who are available for any cases a judge wishes to "refer" to them; and in every federal District Court a *referee in bankruptcy* is appointed for a term of years.[11] Some proceedings involve complicated accounts or require technical evaluations (e.g., water rights). In such instances a referee or master is appointed by the judge either to make a fact-finding report or to try the issues. The master's report is subject to confirmation or rejection by the judge, and the parties may except to the findings. The master's main function is to narrow the factual or legal issues in a case. He usually devotes many days—sometimes as much as a year—to hearing witnesses, examining documents, and reviewing this evidence.

COURT OKAYS BLAST CLAIMS

Portland, Ore.—Federal District Judge Paul Bingham signed an order yesterday approving the reports of two special masters in the Roseburg blast disaster cases.

David Sandeberg and B. H. Goldstein, the special masters, awarded $1,195,000 for death, personal injury and property damage.

The masters held hearings in Portland, Eugene, and Roseburg.

COURT TO REAPPORTION

Madison, Wis.—A federal court yesterday took jurisdiction in the legislative reapportionment stalemate.

The three-judge court appointed a special master to supervise realignment of the state's election districts to conform with the state constitution.

In a separate order, the court directed Emmert Wingert, former state Supreme Court justice, whom it appointed special master, to "consider and try the issues and consider plans of apportionment which may be submitted to them."

To enforce their orders, courts sometimes appoint *monitors*. Monitors, for example, have been appointed to supervise the election of labor union officers after members had sued, charging fraud by the incumbent officers.

The court also appoints *receivers* as temporary managers of a business

---

[11] See p. 409.

pending the determination of an action. Receivers sometimes are appointed to manage a business while a suit is pending.[12]

The Jury Commissioner or Jury Commission

The task of selecting prospective trial (petit) jurors is assigned to a jury commissioner, to the court clerk acting as a jury commissioner, or to a jury commission usually composed of the sheriff and two other citizens appointed by the court of original jurisdiction. The method of selecting prospective jurors varies in the different states, but the method described below is fairly typical.

In January of each year the jury commissioner, after being notified by the presiding judge as to how many prospective jurors will be required for the year, compiles a list of twice as many as will probably be needed. The list comes primarily from the register of voters, but the jury commissioner may also use telephone and city directories and the tax roll. He tries to obtain a cross-section by selecting a proportionate number from each geographical subdivision of the county and for each name which begins with *A, B, C,* etc. Sometimes questionnaires are mailed to ascertain whether or not the selected persons are qualified.

This list is submitted to the presiding judge whose clerk writes the names on slips of paper and places them in a hollow wheel. The wheel is revolved so as to mix the slips, and a required number of slips is drawn. The names are placed on the jury lists. Names are later taken from the lists as they are needed for various trials. This list is called a *panel.* The prospective jurors who are summoned by the sheriff or by mail are called *veniremen* (from the writ, called *venire facias,* served by the sheriff on the prospective jurors). When a panel of jurors has been exhausted and the sheriff is directed to summon additional persons not on the original list, such persons are called *talesmen.*

Prospective grand jurors[13] are selected from a different universe, viz., citizens of high standing in the county. Usually, the presiding judge, with the assistance of the clerk, compiles a list of such persons; in some jurisdictions each judge nominates a specified number of citizens. Then the presiding judge draws about thirty names from the list by lot. These persons are summoned and are examined by the judge and the prosecuting attorney. Finally a certain number are selected to serve for the term of court. Each state by statute specifies the size of the grand jury, the number varying from six in one state to twenty-three in some other states. In some jurisdictions the grand jury has a clerk; in others a member of the grand jury acts as a secretary. It is the practice in some jurisdictions for the presiding judge

---

[12] See pp. 223–224.
[13] The functions and operations of the grand jury are discussed on p. 331 *ff.*

to appoint a foreman; in others the grand jury elects a foreman as well as an alternate foreman and a sergeant-at-arms.

Attorneys

Some attorneys who practice before the courts represent the private parties engaged in litigation; other attorneys are paid by a government to prosecute (and sometimes defend) accused persons. Technically, both types of attorney are officers of the court. In each county or judicial district is a prosecuting attorney to represent the state in criminal cases. His title is usually *district attorney, prosecuting attorney, solicitor,* or, in a few states, *attorney general.* He is usually elected by the voters.[14] The federal government appoints a prosecuting attorney, called the *United States attorney,* in each federal district court. He represents the United States in both criminal and civil cases.[15] Cities and counties usually have an attorney to represent those governments in civil cases; they are called *county attorney, city attorney, solicitor,* or *corporation counsel.*[16] In some states this official represents his government in both civil and criminal actions.

The private attorneys who represent parties in civil actions are remunerated by fees paid by their clients. In liability cases, the attorney often charges the plaintiff a "contingent" fee; that is, one-third to one-half of the award, if he wins the case. This arrangement permits a person who is without funds to sue and collect compensation for injury.

Only attorneys who meet certain requirements established by the state are permitted to practice in the courts of that state, although, in some states, any defendant may act as his own attorney.

Most attorneys are willing to explain legal points to newspaper reporters and to advise them in advance about certain evidence to be presented in the trial or certain colorful persons who will be witnesses. Some attorneys specialize in certain types of case, such as bankruptcy, admiralty, taxation, and anti-trust law.

Other Officers

The *official reporter* is a stenographer appointed by the court to take the testimony of witnesses and to prepare from his shorthand or phonographic notes a transcript of the evidence. The transcript includes, in addition to the testimony, the objections made by the attorneys, the exceptions taken, and, in criminal cases, the arraignments, pleas, and sentences of defendants, the summation of the prosecuting attorney, and all statements, remarks made, and oral instructions of the judge.

---

[14] This office is discussed on pp. 287–288.
[15] This office is discussed on p. 301.
[16] This office is discussed on p. 472 and p. 499.

Although an official of the court who is paid by the county, the official reporter receives compensation also from supplying copies of the transcript, at officially fixed rates, to the parties. Usually a defendant in a criminal case is entitled to a free transcript when he takes an appeal. In important trials, newspapers may buy a part or all of the daily transcript. Usually two or more official reporters, in long trials, work in relays, taking notes and transcribing their notes. They can thus supply a copy of one day's transcript very shortly after the end of each day's session.

The *bailiff,* or *tipstaff,* is the sergeant-at-arms of the court. He is often a deputy sheriff (or deputy United States marshal). He announces the opening of court, calls witnesses to the stand, ushers jurors to and from the jury room, keeps order in the courtroom, and acts as a messenger for the court.

An *interpreter* is sometimes utilized when a witness does not speak the English language. After being sworn, he interprets the questions and answers of the witness. He is permitted to paraphrase the answer to some extent, and counsel are, in certain circumstances, permitted to ask "leading questions"[17] of the witness.

Other officers who perform functions in connection with criminal cases are the *coroner,* the *probation officer,* the *United States commissioner,* and the *United States marshal.* Their functions are discussed in Chapter 19. In a few jurisdictions there is a *public defender;* he is paid a salary to defend indigent defendants in criminal cases.

FEDERAL COURTS

1. Bill Smith, a citizen of Illinois, while driving his automobile on an Illinois road, collided with an automobile driven by George Jones, a citizen of Illinois.

2. Jim Black, a citizen of Illinois, while driving his automobile on an Illinois road, collided with an automobile driven by Dave Hill, a citizen of Wisconsin.

3. Fred Brown, a citizen of Illinois, while driving his automobile on an Illinois road, collided with an army truck driven by Henry White, a soldier.

4. Dick Hart, a citizen of Illinois, while driving his automobile on an Illinois road, collided with an automobile driven by Tom Smith, who had stolen the automobile in Wisconsin.

In the first situation, Bill Smith and George Jones would settle their controversy in an Illinois court because both are citizens of Illinois and the accident happened in Illinois.

[17] See p. 247.

In the second situation, the controversy could be settled in either an Illinois court, since the accident happened in Illinois, or in a federal District Court sitting in Illinois, provided the amount in controversy was as much as $10,000.

In the third situation, if Fred Brown wanted to sue the United States government or if the government wanted to sue Fred Brown, the controversy would be determined in a federal District Court under the Federal Tort Claims Act. For many years a citizen who had a claim against the federal government for an alleged injury to his person or property had to persuade Congress to pass a private bill. This was under the doctrine of "sovereign immunity"—meaning that the government could not be sued by one of its citizens without its consent. In recent years, Congress has enacted some blanket statutes which assent in advance to certain kinds of suits. One of these is the Federal Tort Claims Act, which permits federal agencies to settle claims that involve less than $1,000 and permits the citizen to sue in a federal District Court for a claim in excess of that amount. Another federal statute permits a citizen to sue the United States on a contractual[18] obligation. Most suits of this nature are brought in a special court, the Court of Claims. In certain of these claims, however, the federal District Court has concurrent jurisdiction with the Court of Claims when the claim does not exceed $10,000.

U.S. Pays Widow $150,000 for Death

An award of $150,000—the largest ever agreed to by the government in a suit brought under the Federal Tort Claims Act—was made yesterday to a 54-year-old local widow.

The award, in the form of an out-of-court settlement approved by Federal Judge Allen Barron, was made to Phyllis Torza, of 876 Walker drive. Her husband, Morton, died as the result of an automobile collision two years ago with a car driven by an FBI agent.

Mrs. Torza's attorneys' fees, which were approved by Judge Barron, were $30,000, which amounted to the maximum statutory fee of 20 per cent of the award.

---

[18] See definitions of *ex contractu* and *ex delicto* in Appendix C.

In the fourth situation, the collision could give rise to a civil suit in a federal District Court. Also, in a criminal action, the United States government could prosecute Tom Smith in a federal District Court for violation of the Dyer Act, which prohibits transportation of a stolen automobile across a state line.

Criminal Jurisdiction

Here are some other situations in which the federal District Court would have criminal jurisdiction:
1. A crime is committed on federal property or a federal reservation.
2. A crime is committed by an Indian on an Indian reservation.
3. A federal officer shoots and kills a man in Illinois; he would be prosecuted by Illinois and be defended by the United States.
4. A crime is committed within the maritime jurisdiction of the United States. Thus, a smuggler who was convicted of the murder of a federal officer four miles off the coast of Florida was hanged on the steps of the Miami post office.

Crimes against the United States are discussed on page 314.

A person indicted for a federal offense committed in one state and arrested in another state is permitted to plead guilty before a federal court in the state in which he is found. If he wishes to plead "not guilty," however, he must return for trial to the state in which the federal offense was committed.

Civil Jurisdiction

The civil jurisdiction of the federal courts is limited to those types of cases which are specified in the United States constitution. Most of these are listed in section 2 of Article III, as follows:
1. All cases in law and equity arising under the federal constitution and laws and treaties made by the United States.
2. All cases affecting ambassadors and consuls.
3. All cases of admiralty and maritime jurisdiction.
4. Controversies to which the United States may be a party.
5. Controversies between two or more states.
6. Controversies between a state and the citizens of another state.
7. Controversies between citizens of different states (when the amount in controversy is $10,000 or more).
8. Controversies between citizens of the same state claiming lands under grants of different states.
9. Controversies between a state, or the citizens thereof, and foreign states, citizens, or subjects.

Because the United States constitution delegated certain powers to the federal government, federal courts have jurisdiction over cases, both civil and criminal, that are controlled by those powers. These powers are bankruptcy, patents and copyrights, regulation of foreign and interstate commerce, coinage and currency, the postal power, the taxing power (of the United States government), and the war-making power. In addition to these powers, the federal government has the power (that all governments have) to insure its authority and to protect itself against fraud and theft.

Removal of Cases to Federal Court

When a plaintiff files a civil suit in a state court and the federal court has concurrent jurisdiction (e.g., because of diversity of citizenship of the parties), the defendant may remove the case to the federal court. The defendant petitions the federal District Court for the district and division within which the action is pending. When he files the petition he attaches to it a copy of all the pleadings, processes, and orders which are on file in the state court at that stage of the action. He must also supply a surety bond to indemnify the plaintiff for the costs caused by the removal should it be determined that the case after all was not removable or was improperly removed.

Certain criminal actions are also removable, such as the accusation in a state court of a federal officer charged with a crime against the state. This is sometimes done by the issuance of a *writ of habeas corpus*[19] by the federal court directed to the state authorities. Removal is not the same as "change of venue."[20]

Publisher Denied Venue Change

GRAND RAPIDS, MICH.—Two California pornographic book publishers, indicted here by a federal grand jury, were denied a change of venue to the federal district court in Los Angeles today.

Tod Souchak and Wes Brown were indicted last month on 19 counts charging interstate shipment of obscene books from California to Michigan.

In a 15-page decision, Federal District Court Judge Raymond Starr, of Grand Rapids, denied the motion for transfer of the case.

---

[19] See p. 322 and p. 423.
[20] See p. 214 and p. 346.

The Law Administered in Federal Courts

The law applied in *civil* cases which are determined in federal courts is, in general, the law of the state in which the court sits. That is, the federal court applies the state statutes or follows the decisions of the state's highest court. There are some exceptions, as when the highest state court has not spoken or when the rule of the state court represents a wide departure from well-established principles.

Federal District Courts

The federal court of original jurisdiction is the District Court. At least one District Court sits in each state but some states have as many as four federal judicial districts, these being designated as northern, southern, eastern, western, and middle districts. In the fifty states and Puerto Rico there are 88 districts. Court is held in the principal city of a district and also in a few other localities within the district. In several states the district is divided into "divisions," designated as northern and southern divisions. Some districts have a single judge, but others have more than one; the New York southern district, for example, has twenty-five.

The District Court has separate criminal, civil, admiralty, and bankruptcy dockets.

Federal District Courts have more formality and dignity than do most state courts of first instance.

Certain types of cases (28 U.S. Code 2281, 2284) must be heard by a bench of three judges, one of whom is a circuit judge. Such cases involve the constitutionality of a state or federal statute when an injunction has been applied for.

Officers of the Federal District Court

Each district has a clerk, a United States attorney, a United States marshal, one or more referees in bankruptcy, probation officers, court reporters, United States commissioners, and their assistants.

A federal judicial officer with whom newspaper reporters have frequent contact is the *United States commissioner*. He is a federal justice of the peace in that he holds preliminary examinations in criminal cases, fixes bail, issues warrants, administers oaths, takes depositions, and rules on applications for extradition. Persons arrested for a federal offense appear before him either for examination or for executing bail. Certain designated commissioners are authorized by federal district judges to try petty offenses allegedly committed on federal property or reservations, provided the defendant gives his written consent; the commissioner does not have authority to try any other cases. The United States Commissioner has no functions in connection with civil cases.

$100,000 Bail Set in Embezzlement Case

Arnold Besselink, 40-year-old manufacturer, charged in a federal complaint with conspiring to embezzle national bank funds, was held yesterday in lieu of $100,000 bail.

The high bail was set after federal officials estimated the bank shortage may exceed $3.5 million.

U.S. Commissioner Russell Brewer set the $100,000 bail over the protests of Besselink's attorneys, in an unusual Sunday afternoon hearing in which federal officials had argued that it should be an unprecedented $500,000.

An FBI agent, Fred Thirsk, told the Commissioner that Besselink "owns or has access to" a private airplane.

Federal Appellate Courts

The Supreme Court and the Courts of Appeals are the federal appellate courts. In general, the ten Courts of Appeals (called "circuits") and the District of Columbia circuit review cases that have been decided by the federal District courts and federal independent boards and agencies. The Supreme Court reviews cases decided by the state appellate courts and other federal courts in which the constitutionality of a state or federal statute or a treaty is presented. There are exceptions to the foregoing statement which are too numerous to mention in a book of this scope (see Title 28, Chapter 81 of the *United States Code*).

The ten Courts of Appeals sit in about twenty different cities.[21] The bench is composed of three to nine circuit judges as well as certain District Court judges designated by the circuit judges. A Supreme Court justice is also assigned to each circuit, but in recent years they have not sat. That judge in each circuit who is senior in commission and has not reached his seventieth birthday is the "chief judge."

Special Federal Courts

Four special courts have been established to deal with certain types of cases. The Court of Claims decides certain suits against the United States and determines claims referred to it by Congress and the executive depart-

---

[21] By circuits: (1) Boston, San Juan, P.R.; (2) New York city; (3) Philadelphia; (4) Richmond, Va., Asheville, N.C.; (5) Atlanta, Montgomery, Fort Worth, New Orleans; (6) Covington, Ky.; (7) Chicago; (8) St. Paul, Kansas City, Omaha, St. Louis; (9) San Francisco, Seattle, Portland; (10) Denver, Wichita, Oklahoma City.

FEDERAL JUDICIAL SYSTEM

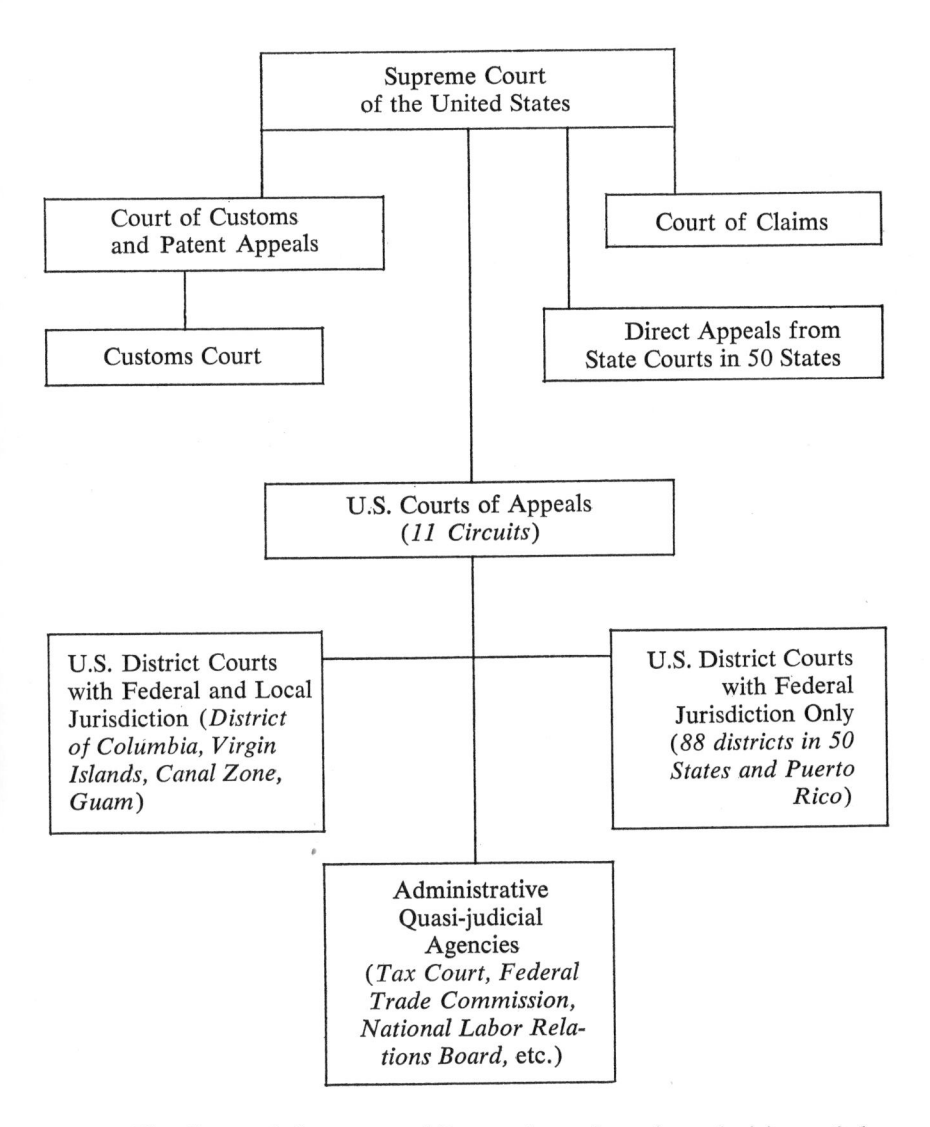

```
                    ┌─────────────────────┐
                    │   Supreme Court     │
                    │ of the United States│
                    └─────────────────────┘
           ┌──────────────┼──────────────────────┐
┌──────────────────┐      │            ┌──────────────────┐
│ Court of Customs │      │            │ Court of Claims  │
│ and Patent Appeals│     │            └──────────────────┘
└──────────────────┘      │            ┌──────────────────────┐
         │                │            │ Direct Appeals from  │
┌──────────────────┐      │            │ State Courts in 50 States│
│  Customs Court   │      │            └──────────────────────┘
└──────────────────┘      │
                    ┌─────────────────────┐
                    │ U.S. Courts of Appeals│
                    │    (11 Circuits)     │
                    └─────────────────────┘
┌──────────────────┐                    ┌──────────────────┐
│ U.S. District Courts│                 │ U.S. District Courts│
│ with Federal and Local│               │ with Federal     │
│ Jurisdiction (District│               │ Jurisdiction Only│
│ of Columbia, Virgin │                 │ (88 districts in 50│
│ Islands, Canal Zone,│                 │ States and Puerto│
│ Guam)            │                    │ Rico)            │
└──────────────────┘                    └──────────────────┘
                    ┌─────────────────────┐
                    │   Administrative    │
                    │   Quasi-judicial    │
                    │     Agencies        │
                    │ (Tax Court, Federal │
                    │ Trade Commission,   │
                    │ National Labor Rela-│
                    │ tions Board, etc.)  │
                    └─────────────────────┘
```

ments. The Court of Customs and Patent Appeals reviews decisions of the Customs Court on classifications and duties upon imported merchandise, decisions of the Patent Office as to patents and trade-marks and legal aspects of the findings of the Tariff Commission. The Customs Court reviews appraisals of imported merchandise and decisions of the collectors of customs as to exclusion of merchandise. The Court of Military Appeals is the final appellate tribunal in court martial convictions.

For class discussion: If, on your civil court beat, nine judges were hearing cases at the same time, what method would you adopt in order to report them as completely as possible?

CHAPTER *16*

Civil Actions: Plaintiff's Pleading

Here is a *complaint* filed in a civil action by a pedestrian who was struck by an automobile owned by an oil company and driven by an employee of the company. The plaintiff is suing both the company and the employee. Read it now because reference will be made to it several times in this and later chapters and an exercise is based on it.

State of Washaska } SS In Superior Court
Dale County

Madison Wilson, Plaintiff
    v.
Universal Oil Company
and Ira Thompson,
    Defendants

No. 0000
COMPLAINT

The plaintiff above named appearing herein by Johnson & Hall, his attorneys, for a cause of action alleges and respectfully shows to the court:

1. That as plaintiff is informed and verily believes, the Universal Oil Company above named now is and was at the times hereinafter mentioned a foreign corporation duly organized and existing under and by virtue of the laws of the State of Indiana; and at the times herein mentioned transacted and now transacts business within the State of Washaska.

2. That as plaintiff is informed and believes, the above named Ira Thompson was at all times hereinafter mentioned an agent, servant, and employee of the said Universal Oil Company, a foreign corporation, and that at all of said times said Ira Thompson was acting as the agent, and employee of said defendant Universal Oil Company, a foreign corporation, in the course of its business and such employment.

3. That the city of Jonesboro, Dale County, Washaska, herein mentioned, is a duly incorporated city organized under and by virtue of the laws of the State of Washaska; that State Street and Cook Street and all streets and highways herein referred to are duly laid out and established public streets and highways located within the corporate limits of said city.

4. That on the sixth day of November, last year, at about ten o'clock in the evening, plaintiff was walking in a westerly direction on the north side of Cook Street in said city of Jonesboro.

5. That as plaintiff reached a point on said street where said Cook Street intersects with State Street at a regular street intersection; that said intersection is one over which many people constantly traveled as said defendant Ira Thompson knew.

6. That at said time and place the said Ira Thompson drove an automobile in an easterly direction along and upon said Cook Street and thence in a northwesterly direction upon said State Street; that as plaintiff is informed and believes, the said automobile belonged to and was the property of the said Universal Oil Company and the said Ira Thompson was then and there operating and driving the same in the course of and as a part of the business and employment of the said Universal Oil Company.

7. That as the said automobile driven by the said Ira Thompson crossed the street intersection over which plaintiff was walking as aforesaid, said Ira Thompson carelessly and negligently drove and operated said automobile at an excessive, unlawful and dangerous rate of speed, and so as to endanger the life and limb of plaintiff and others who might be upon said street and highway; that at said time and place, the said Ira Thompson carelessly and negligently failed to maintain control of the said automobile, or to sound a horn or give any other signal before attempting to cross said intersection or to keep a lookout in the direction in which he was proceeding for pedestrians or to keep the same in a proper place or position upon said highway.

8. That the defendant carelessly and negligently failed to take proper steps or measures to reduce the speed of or to stop said automobile, either as he approached or after said automobile struck and collided with said plaintiff as hereinafter alleged.

9. That by reason of the said negligence and carelessness of the said Ira Thompson as the agent, servant and employee of said Universal Oil Company in the course of its business and employment, the said automobile driven by said Ira Thompson as aforesaid ran into and struck the plaintiff with great force and dragged him along said street and highway a considerable distance.

10. That thereby plaintiff's right shoulder was broken in two places; he sustained numerous other bruises and injuries, internal as well as external; that his right arm, shoulder and hand were seriously injured; he was subjected to a considerable expense for hospital, medical and surgical treatment and for care during his said illness in connection with said injuries; that as a result of said injuries plaintiff has, as he verily believes, been permanently maimed and crippled, has suffered great pain of body and mind, and will continue to suffer pain and to be subjected to expense in connection with said injuries; that he has been and to some extent will continue to be incapacitated from attending to his business; all to his damage in the sum of Ten Thousand Dollars ($10,000.00).

WHEREFORE, plaintiff demands judgment against the said defendants and each of them for the sum of Ten Thousand Dollars ($10,000.00) damages, together with the costs and disbursements of this action.

JOHNSON & HALL
Plaintiff's attorneys

State of Washaska ⎱ SS
Dale County ⎰

Madison Wilson, being first duly sworn upon his oath, deposes and says that he has read the above and foregoing complaint, knows the contents thereof and that the same are true.

MADISON WILSON

REMEDIES

The injured pedestrian, in filing this complaint, is utilizing the means supplied by the state to obtain compensation for an alleged wrong. The law assumes that citizens (including corporations) have both rights and duties. The law also provides a *remedy* for the enforcement of rights and the redress of civil wrongs. In the present case, the law assumes that the pedestrian had a right to use a public street and that the automobile driver had certain duties in connection with his use of the street. On the basis of the uncontroverted facts stated in the complaint, the plaintiff will recover damages from one or both of the defendants. The plaintiff is said to have a *cause of action;* that is, ground on which a civil action may be sustained by the court. The means by which the violation of the plaintiff's rights is compensated is the remedy.

In some circumstances, a plaintiff may have more than one remedy. Let us suppose that your neighbor's swimming pool is so constructed that it drains a great deal of water on to your lawn. You not only have a remedy to compensate you in money damages, but also the remedy of injunction to prevent excessive discharge of water in the future.

The court sometimes decides that a plaintiff does not have a cause of action because the operating facts he alleges are not an adequate ground, i.e., that the plaintiff does not have the rights he asserts or the defendant the duties that the plaintiff asserts that the defendant has. If, for example, a plaintiff sues his physician on the ground that the physician did not cure his ailment, he cannot recover money damages—unless the physician had been negligent—for the usual physician does not give such a warranty.

Judge Kisses Off Her Kissing Suit

A 21-year-old mother of two, Mrs. Bernard Hebert, who claimed a tooth extraction impaired—among other things—her ability to kiss, lost a $30,000 damage suit against her dentist.

Circuit Judge David Holscher yesterday directed the jury to bring in a verdict for Dr. Fred Farlow, the dentist.

Mrs. Hebert charged the extraction of a wisdom tooth last year caused a loss of feeling in her jaw, chin, lips, teeth and gums.

The petition asserted "plaintiff's ability to perform the age-old art of kissing has been impaired and lost."

The defense, in the one-day trial, countered that numbness can occur for a number of reasons.

"I think," said the judge, "that it is a matter of law that the plaintiff has not proved the defendant was guilty of negligence."

Rule × Facts = Judgment

The end result of a civil action is a decision of the trial judge which is called a *judgment*. The judge determines the rights and duties of the parties by applying a rule (i.e., a principle) of law to the facts. Frequently, a jury is used to determine the facts, but the finding of a jury cannot stand if it is in conflict with a principle of law. For example, the law in most states is that a plaintiff cannot recover damages in a tort[1] action, such as the plaintiff being struck by an automobile, if he contributed to the accident by his own negligence. Should a jury award damages in such a case and also find that the plaintiff contributed his negligence, the judge will not render judgment for the plaintiff.[2]

"LAW" AND EQUITY

Here is a statement in a defendant's answer to a plaintiff's complaint: ". . . This answering defendant alleges and says that if the statements in plaintiff's complaint constitute a cause of action of any nature whatsoever against him, that the same is a cause of action *at law* and not *in equity,* and that the court is without power or authority to grant the relief prayed for against him in this case."

What do these terms mean—action "at law" and "in equity"? Why does the defendant say that the court cannot grant the relief prayed for, viz., an order to enjoin the defendant from removing cut timber stored on the defendant's farm?

What the defendant is saying is that the court may have the power to

---

[1] A tort is a civil wrong done to a person independent of contract.
[2] The doctrine of "contributory negligence" is discussed further on p. 230 and p. 263.

award money damages to the plaintiff for not delivering to the plaintiff the timber he allegedly promised to deliver and which the plaintiff had contracted to sell. That is, the plaintiff already has a remedy "at law" and the court, therefore, cannot grant "equitable relief," such as an injunction. When a plaintiff has an adequate remedy at law his complaint for equitable relief should be dismissed.

There developed in England (later transplanted in the United States) two sets of rules. By the thirteenth century there were three "great" courts in England (King's Bench, Common Pleas, and Exchequer). These were called "law" courts because they administered the "common law."

The common law developed in this way. After William I conquered the Saxons in 1066 he wanted to establish "the King's justice." He sent judges (justiciars) to hold court in the shires and hundreds. These judges administered the Saxon law as they found it in the existing courts. Building on this imperfect customary law, the judges improved justice by supplementing the customary law with certain absolute rules which they brought over from Normandy and which derived from the Roman law. They wrote down their decisions so that eventually there was a statement of the law that was common throughout the realm. The law, supplemented by certain legislation, came to be called the "common law."

A defect of this law was that, with one important exception (which will not be discussed), the only remedy a plaintiff had was for money damages. The common law, in other words, would not order a defendant to do anything except to pay money. It would not, for example, enjoin a wealthy neighbor who lived upstream from polluting the water that flowed into your farm. Since the only remedy you had for this violation of your rights was money damages, the wealthy neighbor could actually buy the right to injure you.

Nor did the common law provide any remedy to compel a person to do what he had promised to do. Although the common law recognized certain rights of a plaintiff, it did not enforce them on behalf of an aggrieved party. In the course of time, therefore, some persons who believed they had no adequate remedy at law petitioned the king, who referred the petitions to his chief minister, the chancellor. The chancellor then issued a *writ* directed to the defendant requiring him to do justice to the defendant or to appear before the chancellor to show cause why the petitioner's prayer for relief should not be granted. The defendant (respondent) was required to answer the petition under oath. This procedure amounted to trial of the case by the chancellor (without a jury). The chancellor's judgment was called a *decree,* which is the term used today for a judgment in a suit for equitable relief. Gradually there developed a new set of rules supplementary to the rules administered by the law courts; these rules came to be called *equity.* Also there developed two different court systems—the law courts and the courts of chancery, or equity.

Equitable Remedies

In addition to injunction,[3] equitable remedies refer to contracts and torts.[4]

Specific performance compels a party to carry out the provisions of a contract by doing or omitting the acts he has promised to do or to omit. Specific performance is decreed, generally, when an award of damages for breach of contract is an inadequate remedy.

Equity will also decree that a contract be revised because of mistake or fraud (*reformation*) and that a contract be cancelled when fraud has been proved (*cancellation*) or annulled with restoration of the consideration received or its value (*rescission*).

Dispute Over Home "Extras" To Be Tried

A dispute about "extras" to be provided with a $40,500 house in the Crescent Park section will be tried in superior court.

Charles Hawkins is asking the Cook Construction Company for reformation of contract and for damages.

Hawkins alleges that the construction company agreed to install at the house a sprinkler system, complete landscaping, a sunken garbage can, additional kitchen cabinets, a firewood storage box and an automatic clothes washer and dryer.

Mr. Hawkins alleges he asked to have these particulars included in the written agreement but that the defendants said that would not be necessary because the items were always furnished in this type of property.

Later, the complaint states, the construction company was asked repeatedly to make the installations but did not do so.

---

[3] This remedy is discussed in more detail on pp. 424–428 with reference to nuisance, unfair competition, strikes, and boycotts.

[4] In common law pleading there were *forms* of action. These were classified as (1) action to recover land (chiefly "ejectment" and "entry and detainer"); (2) contract actions ("debt," "covenant," "assumpsit," and "account"); and (3) torts ("trespass and case," "trover," "replevin and detinue," and "deceit").

Forms of action have been abolished in most states, as will be explained below.

Hawkins asks that the purchase agreement oe reformed to incluJe the "extras" and that, in lieu of the installations, the defendant be ordered to pay $1,500 damages plus $750 compensatory damages.

For class discussion: In the news story above, substitute "defendant" for "the Cook Construction Company" and "plaintiff" for "Charles Hawkins" in the third, fourth, and fifth paragraphs. Will the hurried reader's comprehension of the details of this story be facilitated or be retarded by the substitutions?

Equity also has jurisdiction over the foreclosure of *liens,* including *mortgages.* Foreclosure is a proceeding in which a court decrees transfer of property in satisfaction of a debt. In a mortgage foreclosure when the value of the property, which had been pledged, is less than the debt, the creditor is entitled to a *deficiency judgment* for the difference. There are several types of liens. A lien is a claim against property which makes the property security for the performance of an act.

Architect Files Lien on Monorail

SEATTLE—A $28,276 lien against the World's Fair monorail system was filed yesterday by Los Angeles architect Adrian Wilson.

Wilson filed the lien with County Auditor Robert Morris and then filed a superior court action to foreclose the lien against Alweg Rapid Transit System of the State of Washington.

The architect claims the money is due him, in addition to earlier payments, for design work on the monorail system, which runs from downtown Seattle to the fair grounds.

Sixten Holmquist, president of Alweg Rapid Transit, said Wilson had been paid $38,000 for designing the monorail terminal. He said the payment was made on the basis of 6 per cent cost and Wilson is asking 15 per cent.

Other differences: There are two other differences in the two sets of rules—law and equity. In general, the issue of the facts in an action at law is determined by a jury—but in a suit in equity the judge decides the facts as well as the law. The reason for this distinction is that the chancellor had to decide the facts before he could decide whether or not to grant the writ petitioned for. He tried the whole case. In modern equity practice the judge sometimes refers certain issues of fact to a jury, but its verdict is purely advisory.

A second difference between law and equity is that equity has jurisdiction *in personam* and law has jurisdiction *in rem;* that is, equity operates on the party, and law on the subject matter (e.g., the property). The distinction is not as clear as this statement implies but it has significance in connection with service of a summons on a party and enforcement of a judgment.[5]

Modern Practice

The English legal system was transplanted to the American colonies, but it was not until 1848 that the State of New York legislated "code" pleading, which permitted the joinder of actions at law and suits in equity. Most other states, to a greater or less extent, have followed New York. Yet a few states still have separate courts of law and equity, the judge of the latter having the title of "chancellor." In several other states the courts have separate law and equity dockets. The formal distinction between law and equity has been abolished in federal courts. In England, the Judicature Acts of 1873 and 1875 effected a merger of the two systems.

It is not entirely correct to say that, in most jurisdictions, the distinction between law and equity has been wiped out. The substantive principles of the two systems are so different that no legislative act can really extinguish them.

Divorce Cases

Historically in England the legal separation of husband and wife was determined in the ecclesiastical courts (see Cast *v.* Cast, 1 Utah 112). After the Crown assumed this authority, the action was handled procedurally as if it were equity. The judgment in a divorce, separation, or annulment case is a decree, just as it is in an equity suit. A jury is used in such cases only to determine some issue, such as adultery.

DECLARATORY RELIEF

The courts not only enforce a party's rights but, in some situations, will *declare* an interested party's rights and duties before there has been any breach of obligation. A person who is interested under a deed, will, or contract or a person who contemplates some act and does not wish to

[5] See p. 212.

violate another's rights nor to have his own rights violated petitions a court for a *declaratory judgment*. The court, after a hearing, makes a binding declaration.

This type of proceeding is also available to determine the validity and meaning of certain statutes, the legality of bond issues, and the qualifications of a candidate for an elective office.

A declaratory judgment is more than an advisory opinion by a court: an actual, present controversy must exist over a proper subject. Such relief, for example, was denied to a voter who was not a candidate and had no legal interest when he petitioned for a declaration that the Communist party and its candidates were not qualified for places on the ballot. A pregnant wife who had taken drugs which had been the cause of numerous malformed births in other countries petitioned an Arizona court to declare that a proposed abortion would be legal under Arizona statutes, which permit it only when the expectant mother's life is endangered. In denying the petition because no controversy was involved, the judge said: "Those who contemplate committing burglary or a killing cannot ask the court in advance for a declaratory judgment that they would be acting within the law."

IS "FAIR TRADE" LAW VALID?
ALBUQUERQUE, N.M.—The Skaggs Drug Center filed a petition in district court today against General Electric Company, asking for a declaratory judgment on the constitutionality and validity of the New Mexico "fair trade" law, which permits a manufacturer and retailers within a state to establish retail prices of the company's products.

CONVICT LABOR ISSUE
SALEM, ORE.—Through Attorney General Robert Y. Thornton, the State Board of Control asked Marion county circuit court today for a declaratory judgment as to the meaning of statutes which forbid the use of convict labor on state land.

STATUTES AND REPORTED DECISIONS

Where does a lawyer or a judge or a newspaper reporter look up the law? The rules of human conduct which the courts enforce are in statute books and the volumes of reported appellate court decisions. Legislatures enact statutes. The statutes must conform to the organic law contained in the state and United States constitutions. Statutes enacted by state legislatures and the Congress are published in volumes called *session laws*. From time to time these session laws are collected and arranged under appropriate headings and published as *codes*. Thus, the citation "28 U.S.C. 2281" refers to the *United States Code*.

The decision of an appellate court is accompanied by the court's *opinion*, which explains the reasons for the decision. These opinions are published for the information of lawyers and judges. The rules stated by the appellate courts tend to "settle the law" on the particular subject matter, for they are regarded as precedents for determining similar cases when they arise.

Many of the decisions construe a statute. In the absence of a statute relating to the subject matter, however, the judges search the common law to find a basis for their decision; for that part of the common law which has not been abrogated by statutes remains in force in the United States today. Much of the common law has been enacted into statutes, and some of the common law has been modified or repealed by statutes. Some common law rules have been abrogated as vicious or undemocratic. One example is primogeniture (the right of the eldest son to succeed to the estate of his ancestor to the exclusion of the younger sons); another is the fellow-servant doctrine whereby an employer was not liable for an injury suffered by one of his employees through the fault of another employee.

Common law *crimes* are recognized neither in the federal jurisdiction nor, for all practical purposes, in the states because of the large number and variety of statutes on crime.[6]

> Exercise: Look up in the law library the following federal statutes and state the popular name of each: 47 U.S. Stat. at L. 2122; 41 U.S. Stat. at L. 305; 49 U.S. Stat. at L. 1375; U.S. Code of 1934, Title 18, sec. 408a.

PLEADINGS

A plaintiff commences an action by filing with the court clerk a *complaint* and a request to the clerk to issue a *summons* directed to the defendant. The summons and a copy of the complaint are *served* on the defendant by a competent person. Within a specified period (about twenty days), the defendant must submit himself to the jurisdiction of the court by filing an appearance or a responsive defense. If the defendant fails to do either, in most circumstances, the plaintiff is entitled to a default judgment.

Normally, of course, a defendant files a defense or an objection in law.

[6] Statutes and reported decisions are discussed again on pp. 439–440.

An affirmative defense or an objection in law requires, in turn, a response by the plaintiff. These written formal documents constitute the *pleadings*.

Service

The form of a summons follows:

Madison Wilson	In the Circuit Court
v.	State of Washaska
Universal Oil Co.	Dale County
and Ira Thompson	

Case No. 000000
SUMMONS

The State of Washaska, To the said Defendant:

You are hereby summoned to appear within twenty days after service of this summons, exclusive of the day of service, and defend the above entitled action in the court aforesaid; and in case of your failure so to do judgment will be rendered against you according to the demand of the complaint, of which a copy is herewith served upon you.

P.O. Address:
Security Trust Building
City of Jonesboro
County of Dale   JOHNSON & HALL
State of Washaska   *Attorneys for the Plaintiff*

When personal service is required the summons may be served by a deputy sheriff, a deputy marshal (in a federal court action), or other competent person. Service usually consists of delivering a copy to the defendant personally, but in some jurisdictions it may be left at his dwelling house with a responsible person who lives there or may be delivered to his agent. If the process* server is not an officer of the court, he must make an affidavit of proof of service. Personal service is required in most civil actions. It can be served only within the state. It may be served on a nonresident who is voluntarily within the state. For example, a tort action (assault) was once filed in New York against a Chicago American League baseball player, a resident of another state; for some time, in order to evade service, the baseball player did not accompany his team to New York when games were scheduled with the New York Yankees.

Puts Summons On Actress's Stomach

A process server broke up a matinee performance of the Broadway play "Come on Strong" yesterday when he reached across the footlights to serve a summons on leading lady Carol (Baby Doll) Baker by dropping it onto her stomach.

Miss Baker, along with Van Johnson, was lying on the stage floor doing exercises during a scene in the first act.

Co-producer Hillard Elkins said the summons was from Warner Bros. motion picture studios and notified Miss Baker she was being sued for $66,000 for breach of contract.

Reciprocal *substitute* service is authorized in some states when a nonresident is a defendant in an automobile liability case: the statutes in such states designate the motor vehicle director or the secretary of state in which the defendant is a resident as the defendant's agent to accept service when the plaintiff lives in another state which has a similar statute and the accident happened in his state.

Constructive* service is authorized when the state court has jurisdiction *in rem* over property in the state owned by a nonresident (e.g., in a contested probate proceeding) and in divorce cases. This is accomplished by mail, posting in a public place, or publication in a newspaper.

A defendant who believes he has been improperly served may move to *quash* the summons.

Hoffa Libel Suits Have New Setback

DETROIT—A U.S. district court today ruled that the summonses served on Jack Paar and Robert F. Kennedy in Teamster Union President James R. Hoffa's $2.5 million libel suit were null and void.

Judge Theodore Levin held Paar and Kennedy had been improperly served outside the state of Michigan. The court ruled on a question of jurisdiction on a motion to quash the summons.

The practice of most courts is to dismiss a case when proper service is not made within a reasonable length of time.

Hoffa brought the suit a few months ago, alleging libel and defamation of his character on one of Paar's television shows.

In some jurisdictions a plaintiff is permitted to have a summons served on the defendant before the plaintiff files the complaint. Other jurisdictions, however, require that both the summons and a copy of the complaint be served at the same time. In a few jurisdictions a plaintiff must file with the clerk a *praecipe,* which is a demand that a summons be issued and served.

Appearance: A defendant *appears* when he files a defense or an objection in law. This is called a *general appearance,* for he thus submits to the jurisdiction of the court. A defendant, however, may enter a *special appearance* for the purpose of contesting jurisdiction of the court over his person without submitting to the jurisdiction. A defendant may also enter an appearance even though he has not been served.

Some Terms Distinguished

It should be noted that the terms "summons" and "complaint" are used with different meanings in criminal actions. A corporation accused of a criminal offense is brought to bar by a summons instead of a warrant of arrest because a corporation cannot be physically arrested. A "citation" signed by a motorist agreeing to appear in traffic court is also a summons rather than a warrant of arrest. The process served on prospective trial jurors and grand jurors is also called a "summons."

There is also a distinction between "summons" and "subpoena" (sometimes spelled "subpena"). The latter is a process by which a party to a civil or criminal action can compel the attendance of a witness at the trial or compel the witness to give a deposition.[7] Literally, subpoena means "under punishment," for, historically, a baron might refuse to testify voluntarily at the request of a commoner. Subpoenas are often signed in blank by the clerk and served by an attorney. The process server must tender the witness one day's witness fee and travel expenses if they are demanded. The form of a subpoena, omitting the caption, follows:

THE PEOPLE OF CALIFORNIA
To WILLIAM GREEN
    YOU ARE COMMANDED to appear and attend a session of the above entitled court to be held on _____ at _____ _.M., in the courtroom of Department 3 of said court at the courthouse in the city of San Jose, then and there to testify as a witness produced by the plaintiff (defendant) in the above entitled action, now pending in said court.
    Disobedience to this subpoena may be punished as a contempt by the above entitled court, and for such disobedience you will also forfeit to the party aggrieved thereby the sum of one hundred dollars and all damages which such party may sustain by your failure to attend as hereinabove required.
    Dated _____   _____ *Clerk*
                        By _____ *Deputy Clerk*

[7] See pp. 216–220.

Subpoena duces tecum is a process which requires a witness to attend the trial and to bring with him certain documents and records in his possession. A judge sometimes grants a *motion to quash* such a subpoena, as when the material is a trade secret.

The term "complaint" has two meanings in connection with crime: (1) it is the name of the sworn statement of a "complaining witness" who applies for a warrant of arrest of a suspected offender;[8] and (2) it is also used in a literal sense to mean the report by a citizen to police about an offense.[9]

The Complaint

The purpose of the complaint in a civil action is to inform the defendant of the *nature* of the cause which the plaintiff states against him so that he is put on *notice* as to the *issues* of law and fact he must meet at the trial.

The complaint is a factual statement of the plaintiff's claim and a demand for relief. The complaint is not a statement of law and is not argumentative. It assumes that the facts stated will be proved by the evidence to be presented at the trial and that the law, in consequence, entitles the plaintiff to relief.

The parts of the complaint: It will be noted that the complaint on pages 201–203 has the following parts:

1. The *caption,* which includes the statement of venue (i.e., the place), name of the court, and the serial number of the case.

2. The *names of the parties.* When the aggrieved party is an infant or is incompetent the plaintiffs are the parent or guardian. One or more stockholders of a corporation sometimes sue the corporation's officers on behalf of all the stockholders; such suits are termed *derivative.* A plaintiff or defendant is sometimes *substituted* for the original plaintiff or defendant who has died or whose interest has been transferred; some types of action "survive" the death of a party.

Third persons having claims against a plaintiff or defendant in a pending action may be joined as defendants or plaintiffs and required to settle their conflicting claims so as to relieve the plaintiff or defendant from multiple liability. For example, a life insurance company has issued a policy with the policyholder's widow named as beneficiary, and later has issued a duplicate policy with the decedent's sister as the beneficiary, the duplicate having been issued on the representation that the original had been lost. The sister sues the insurance company and the latter moves to require the widow to *interplead.*

A third person who has an interest in a pending litigation or in the

---
[8] See p. 316.
[9] See p. 276.

success of one or both of the parties may join the plaintiff or the defendant voluntarily as an *intervenor;* in some situations leave of the court is required.

In later sections of this chapter the terms "joinder of parties" and "misjoinder of parties" are used. The courts desire to avoid injury to an absent person and to settle several similar controversies in a single action. For these reasons third persons may be compelled to join as plaintiff or defendant. A person who believes he has been made a party to an action unnecessarily or improperly may object.

In some circumstances, several actions relating to the same matter are filed against the same defendant. The court has discretion to *consolidate* them into a single action.

Likewise, under certain circumstances, when several parties are made defendants in an action, some of them, to avoid prejudice or in furtherance of convenience, may move for a *severance*. When this motion is granted each defendant may answer separately and have a separate trial.

When there are no adversary parties but there is a petition to the court for adjudication of some *res,* such as an estate in probate, the action is entitled, for example, "In re Estate of James Johnson" (*in re* means "in the matter of"). In a somewhat similar situation, as when a creditor pleads an interest in a bankruptcy action, the title is "Ex Parte Johnson" (*ex parte* in this context means "on behalf of (only) one party"). In an admiralty case involving a ship, the defendant is the ship, and when the United States sues to confiscate a smuggled or contraband article the title is, for example, "U.S. *vs.* One Diamond Ring." There is also a type of proceeding, discussed on pages 420–423, in which the title is, for example, "State of Wisconsin ex rel. Jones *vs.* Smith"; *ex rel.,* an abbreviation of *ex relatione,* means "on the information of," and Jones is the informer and complainant with the state as the plaintiff.

3. *Statement of jurisdiction.* In some complaints, the plaintiff makes an allegation of jurisdiction. This is required in all civil actions in the federal courts. It is also necessary when the plaintiff or defendant is a foreign (i.e., an out-of-state) corporation licensed to transact business in the state in which the suit is filed; note such a statement in the paragraph numbered 1 of the complaint on pages 201–203. The statement of jurisdiction is not required in all actions in state courts.

4. The *allegations* in which the plaintiff avers the fact that establish his cause of action. These usually recite time, place, and circumstance. When more than one ground of action is alleged, each is considered a *count*. For example, an allegation that a defendant electric power company maintained a nuisance in a public park in the form of a tower supporting noninsulated wires would be one count, and an allegation that the defendant was negligent in failing to insulate the wires would be a second count. Federal rules of

practice require only "a short and plain statement of the claim showing that the pleader is entitled to relief."

5. The *demand* or *prayer* (the *ad damnum* clause, meaning "to the damage") in which the plaintiff states the amount of damages he demands or the equitable relief he prays for. The amount of damages demanded is often exaggerated but sometimes for good reason.[10] The newspaper reporter sometimes evaluates the newsworthiness of a complaint by the amount of damages asked. One newspaper, for example, does not report the filing of a suit when the claim is less than a certain amount unless there are other newsworthy elements in the complaint, such as the names of prominent parties.

Damages are sometimes classified as *general* and *special*. General damages are those which the law presumes to have resulted from the injury; special damages must be proved. Thus, the law presumes a loss of reputation when one is libeled; but when one's property or product is disparaged he must prove the actual amount of damages (e.g., as measured by loss of sales or lowered selling price). *Punitive,* or *exemplary,* damages are awarded for malice and gross misbehavior with a view to punishment of the defendant. *Nominal* damages (e.g., one cent) are sometimes assessed as merely a vindication of the plaintiff's character, as in a libel action. *Liquidated* damages are those which have been stipulated by the parties to a contract or have been ascertained by a judgment. *Unliquidated* damages are those that remain to be determined.

Costs, usually allowed to the prevailing party in an action, include the fees paid to the clerk for filing, to process servers, jurors, and witnesses; costs do not include attorney's fees.

6. The *signature of the plaintiff's attorney.*

7. The *verifying part,* or *verification,* is an affidavit by the plaintiff himself as to the truth of the allegations.

DISCOVERY AND DEPOSITIONS

Let us suppose that you wrote a popular song and that some other person plagiarized it and that you then wished to file a suit for an injunction and for damages. Since you would have to prove that the defendant had heard your composition, you could not sustain your suit unless you had procured *his* evidence. The law in most jurisdictions provides that you can obtain and perpetuate such testimony even before you have filed the suit because some of the evidence necessary to pursuing the action is in the exclusive knowledge or possession of the adverse party. This disclosure by the defendant (and also of other parties having knowledge or relevant documents) is called *discovery.* Because the procedure varies considerably

---

[10] See *Journal of the American Judicature Society,* Dec., 1959, p. 113.

among the different states, we shall describe the federal District Court practice.

Under one such federal rule, an injured party may file a verified* petition which shows that the petitioner expects to be a party to an action but is unable to bring it without discovery. The petition must further state the subject matter and the facts which the petitioner needs to establish and his reasons for obtaining such facts. The petition also states the name of the adverse party (or parties) and lists the names and addresses of the persons to be examined and the substance of the testimony he expects to elicit from each. The petition is for an order which authorizes the petitioner to take *depositions*. A deposition is the testimony in writing of a party or witness taken under oath outside of court.

Notice to the adverse party is served by the petitioner. After a hearing on the petition, the court may make an order designating the persons to be examined, specifying the subject matter, and specifying whether the depositions may be taken upon oral or written interrogatories. The evidence so taken may later be used in a trial or other judicial proceeding that involves the same subject matter.

In a few instances a civil action has been instituted and a discovery examination held for the purpose of conducting a "fishing expedition" that might obtain an admission that could be used in a later criminal prosecution.

Depositions may be taken not only for the purpose of discovery, but also for use as evidence after an action has been commenced. Statutes in most states provide that such depositions may be taken without leave of the court. The procedure usually is for the parties to meet in the office of one of the attorneys. The parties and witnesses are examined and cross-examined before a person who is authorized to administer oaths, such as a notary public, court commissioner, or official stenographer. The evidence is taken stenographically, transcribed, and submitted to the witness for his signature, unless statutes or court rules provide otherwise.

When a party or witness refuses to answer a question, a judge may compel him to answer after a hearing. Refusal may be considered a contempt of court. A judge may also compel the witness to produce certain documents and to permit inspection of disputed objects and copyings of letters and documents.

Electronics Firms Exchange Charges

Ampex Corporation and Mach-Tronics Corporation, fighting over trade secrets, accused each other yesterday of failure to obey a superior court order.

Ampex attorneys asserted Mach-Tronics refused a court-ordered inspection of its MVR-10 compact video recorder. They said Mach-Tronics officers took the position after first inspecting Ampex's rival portable recorder.

But Mach-Tronics attorneys said Ampex did not show the model of the machine in existence last October. Therefore, they said, they refused inspection of their own device.

These charges were made in affidavits presented yesterday to Superior Court Judge Edmond Scott.

Ampex has filed a $2 million lawsuit against the fledgling Mach-Tronics Corporation, asserting that Mach-Tronics pirated trade secrets and personnel in developing the portable video recorder MVR-10.

Inspection Confidential

Mach-Tronics denies the charge. Its president, Kurt R. Machein, says he conceived the idea for the small-sized recorder after leaving the employ of Ampex last October 3.

Both firms were under court order to allow inspection of rival machines at a super-secret conference in superior court Thursday.

The inspection was part of pretrial discovery procedures authorized by law. The court order barred any outsiders and specified that any information obtained by the inspection was to be used only in the court case. Otherwise, it was to remain confidential.

Same Machine?

Denis T. Rice, attorney for Mach-Tronics, asked Judge Scott to order Ampex to show cause why the firm should not be held in contempt of court.

He said the machine demonstrated during the inspection was not the device in existence on October 1, at the time Machein resigned his position with Ampex.

Rather, he said, major revisions had been made in the machine—which Machein presumably wouldn't know about—and could not be accused of pirating.

Rice also charged that Ampex used pre-recorded tapes of broadcast television programs in demonstrating its video recorder. This, said Rice, did not prove that the Ampex machine could record television reception and then play it back.

Depositions are sometimes taken so they may be used in cross-examination at the trial to contradict and impeach the testimony of the witness or party who gave the deposition. They are also taken to perpetuate the testimony of a witness who, for some reason, cannot attend the trial.

When a party wishes to obtain the testimony of a witness in another state, his attorney applies to the court for a *commission* to take a deposition. The attorney then employs another attorney in that state to examine the witness before an authorized person in that state. Or, in other instances, the attorneys of both parties go to that state for the examination. The adverse party then has an opportunity for cross-examination. Since a witness living outside the state is not subject to subpoena issued from a state court in another state he is a voluntary witness. All or a part of certain depositions are later read into the evidence at the trial by the attorney for one of the parties.

Reporting Discovery Examinations

Discovery examinations are often reported by newspapers. Judges have rendered contradictory rulings on the right of a news reporter to attend the examinations. Some judges adopt the view that, since it is a judicial proceeding, reporters have the right to attend. Other judges adopt the view that a party is at a disadvantage and should be protected from publicity at this stage of the action because the "whole story" can be reported only at the trial. In several instances reporters have been excluded from a discovery examination at the request of one of the parties.

Newsmen Barred At Pre-trial Session

Reporters were barred yesterday from pre-trial examination of witnesses in Fairbanks, Morse and Company's suit against Penn-Texas Corporation.

The newsmen were kept out of the session, held at Fairbanks, Morse offices, by Leonard S. Sheriff, a lawyer for the witnesses being questioned.

The witnesses are members of an investing group that bought common stock of Fairbanks, Morse and Company and sold it to Penn-Texas.

The examination was conducted by Fairbanks, Morse attorneys, who are taking depositions in preparation for a trial of a Fairbanks, Morse suit which seeks to prevent Penn-Texas from voting any of its Fairbanks, Morse stock in the proxy contest.

In Chicago, Judge Joseph Sam Perry, who will hear the action, said that "any deposition taken for the purpose of use as evidence in my court should not be taken in secret once they have been filed with me. I've never handled such matters in secret before."

However, he drew a distinction between depositions taken for evidence and those taken "for information only," and said he would take no stand on admitting the press to sessions of the latter type.

A commission to take the deposition of a witness residing in a foreign country is usually directed to a United States consular officer or foreign judge and is called *letters rogatory*.

PROVISIONAL REMEDIES

At the commencement of a suit, a plaintiff has available to him certain provisional (i.e., temporary) remedies pending the determination of the action. When he fears that a debtor may abscond or that a property may be dissipated pending the action or he wishes the court to obtain jurisdiction *quasi in rem** over a nonresident defendant who cannot be personally served, he may apply for the appropriate writ after he has filed the complaint in the main action.

In addition to injunction, the remedies are *attachment, garnishment, arrest and bail, claim and delivery,* and *receivership.*

Attachment

Under some circumstances the plaintiff, at the time he commences the action or at any time before judgment, may either require the defendant to give security for the amount of the judgment sought or may have the defendant's property attached. A *writ of attachment* is issued after the plaintiff makes affidavit that: (1) the contract for payment of money is unsecured by a mortgage, lien, or other pledge; (2) the defendant is a nonresident of the state; (3) the defendant has evaded service of the summons; or (4) the defendant has left the state. Some states also permit attachment when the claim is made that the defendant is about to remove his property from the state. Also, when the federal government is party to an action to collect taxes it can attach the defendant's property.

For the writ to issue, the plaintiff must post bond to indemnify the sheriff who attaches the property.

The defendant, in most states, by giving bond, can dissolve the attachment and thus have his property released.

The writ directs the sheriff to attach and "keep safely" the property seized. Such property may be real estate, growing crops (which the sheriff may cultivate and harvest), chattels*, shares of stock, debts due the defendant, and the defendant's bank accounts.

Where the property or debt is in possession of a third party (as, for example, in the form of bank deposits or wages due the defendant) the third party must be indemnified.

The procedure of serving such a writ on a third party who owes a debt or wages to the defendant is called *garnishment,* and the third party is designated as the *garnishee.*

Millionaire Sues Longtime Friend

Horace Lepre, the eccentric Las Vegas millionaire, filed a writ of attachment yesterday on the home of his longtime friend, Mrs. Holly Holscher.

He also filed a suit yesterday for a $12,800 debt.

The property at 41 East Hampton Avenue was attached this morning by the sheriff's office and the summons was served on Mrs. Holscher.

Mrs. Holscher said today that she had understood the $12,800 check he gave her last year was a gift, not a loan.

Judge Denies Writ To Attach Assets

Judge H. T. Southwood of superior court yesterday denied an application for a writ of attachment against Walter Boros.

He rejected the contention of Barber

& Crowley, a brokerage firm, that the financier had left the country to avoid paying for 11,700 shares of Certified Products Corp. common stock. The brokers made an affidavit that Mr. Boros ordered the shares between May 31 and June 8.

In a counter-affidavit, Mr. Boros said he had not ordered the stock and had kept Barber & Crowley informed of his whereabouts after he left June 9 on a two-week trip to Europe.

In a written opinion, Judge Southwood said that Barber & Crowley's affidavit was "woefully insufficient to indicate that the defendant's departure from the state was with the intent of defrauding creditors or to avoid service of process."

An attorney for Barber & Crowley said denial of the writ had no effect on the firm's suit to collect $310,000 from Mr. Boros.

The firm had petitioned to attach Mr. Boros' assets, such as his nine-room apartment, to insure collection if Barber & Crowley win the suit.

Arrest and Bail

A defendant in a civil action may be arrested when, to defraud his creditors, he is about to depart from the state or when it is believed that he intends to conceal or dispose of his property. The order for arrest is issued on the affidavit of the plaintiff after the plaintiff has supplied indemnity bond. The defendant, after arrest, may be released either by giving bail or after depositing in court the claimed amount.[11]

ARRESTED IN DEBT ACTION

Robert Fleck is in jail because he could not raise $40,940 bail yesterday on a civil order of arrest.

Fleck is being sued for that sum in superior court by Gay Menefee, who charges Fleck "swindled" him out of a lumber mill.

Judge H. T. Southwood signed the order of arrest yesterday after Frank Cupit, Menefee's attorney, presented an affidavit which stated that Fleck might try to leave the jurisdiction and that he had disposed of certain assets.

[11] In some jurisdictions, the court's order served on the defendant is called a *writ of ne exeat.*

Claim and Delivery

When an action is for the recovery of personal property instead of damages, or for recovery and damages for detention, the plaintiff may obtain delivery of the property pending determination of the action. After the plaintiff has made affidavit that he is the owner of the claimed property and that it is wrongfully held by the defendant, the sheriff takes the property and delivers it to the plaintiff. The plaintiff must furnish bond. Sometimes the defendant chooses to retain possession by supplying bond to indemnify the plaintiff. When an action is for specific recovery or damages (i.e., it is not the provisional remedy of claim and delivery), it is called *replevin*.*

HOTEL LOSES FURNITURE

While guests looked on, all of the furniture in the Elizabeth Hotel lobby and dining room was carted away yesterday.

Deputy Sheriff Jerre Martin, supervising the removal, said he would come back tomorrow for the furniture in the 600-odd rooms upstairs.

"Not paid for," was his laconic explanation.

Attorney Hiram Atherton, representing the Hart Hotel Suppliers, Inc., creditors of the hotel, explained that the deputy sheriff was executing a writ of replevin.

Harry Henderson, manager of the Elizabeth, said he would have new furniture carried up on the freight elevators tomorrow as fast as the plaintiff in the suit could have the old furniture removed.

Receivership

In connection with some civil actions, when the plaintiff fears loss, material injury, or removal of property, the court may appoint a receiver to take and keep the properties and to manage certain properties.

Receivership for Company Whose Head Is Missing

The Ellis Oil Company was placed under a receivership yesterday by U.S. District Court Judge Paul Bingham while U.S. deputy marshals were searching for the company's president.

An attorney who filed the application for receivership said he thought J. H. Ellis, Jr. and his wife had fled the country.

Judge Paul Bingham said a receiver had been appointed because "there is imminent danger the property of the defendant may be placed beyond the jurisdiction of the court and beyond the reach of creditors."

The receiver was appointed after the filing of a suit against the firm by the Chandler Oil Refining Company, which claims Ellis owes them $16,976.

The affidavit asserts that Ellis, his wife, and some relatives and employees were transferring funds and assets of the Ellis company.

CHAPTER 17

Civil Actions: Responsive Pleading

The main purpose of pleading at common law was to identify the actual *issues* involved in the case. Intricate rules of pleading developed so that a great amount of formality was required. Each pleading had a specific form and name. The following scheme describes the procedure, which is almost entirely outmoded both in England and the United States.

Plaintiff	Defendant
1. *Declaration:* the first pleading of the plaintiff	1. *Traverse* (general denial) or plea in confession and avoidance (i.e., new matter pleaded by the defendant)
2. *Replication:* plaintiff's response to defendant's plea in confession and avoidance	2. *Rejoinder:* defendant's response to plaintiff's replication
3. *Surrejoinder:* plaintiff's response to defendant's rejoinder	3. *Rebutter:* defendant's response to plaintiff's surrejoinder
4. *Surrebutter:* plaintiff's response to defendant's rebutter	

Under this method of pleading the case could go to trial after the defendant had filed a general denial (*traverse*). But, if he alleged new matter (*plea in confession and avoidance*), the pleading could continue until the issues had been identified.

A new theory of pleading was adopted in New York in 1848 and in England in 1875. It emphasized as the purpose of pleading the identification of the material *facts* rather than the issues, and thereby got rid of most of the specific forms. It is called *code* pleading as distinguished from common law pleading.

A third theory of pleading, called *notice* pleading, was adopted for federal courts after 1934. It requires that pleadings need only state in a general way the claims, counterclaims, and defenses relied upon in the action with notice to the adverse party.

Most states have adopted simplified rules of civil practice based on the identification of fact theory of pleading. A half dozen states, however, still require common law pleading and some of the code pleading states still use many of the old Latin terms for certain motions.

RESPONSIVE PLEADING

Within about twenty days after a defendant has been served with a summons and a complaint he must file a responsive pleading. If he files a pleading called an *answer,* which denies the allegations in the complaint, the issues of fact are joined and, at some time in the future, the case is set for trial. In common law pleading, a general denial, called a traverse, is said to be a "plea in bar" since it challenges the plaintiff's case "on the merits*."

Instead of filing a general denial, however, a defendant may file an objection. If, on law and motion day, the judge sustains the objection without leave for the plaintiff to amend his complaint, the defendant is excused from further pleading and the judge will grant his motion for dismissal of the plaintiff's action. The defendant's objection may, however, be the kind which, although sustained by the judge, entitles the plaintiff to amend his complaint.

The defendant also may file an answer in which he alleges new matter which the plaintiff is required to answer. The plaintiff's answer to the new matter allegations of the defendant is usually called a *reply;* in common law pleading it is called a *replication* and in some code pleading states is called an *amended complaint.*

The Answer

Here is the answer filed by one of the defendants, Universal Oil Company, to the complaint on pages 201–203. Note the paragraph numbered 5.

State of Washaska ⎱ SS   In Superior Court
Dale County ⎰

Madison Wilson, Plaintiff
     v.
Universal Oil Company
and Ira Thompson,
Defendants

No. 0000

ANSWER OF DEFENDANT

The Universal Oil Company, defendant herein, appearing by its attorneys, Melville and Ebon, in answer to the complaint of the plaintiff, admits, denies, and alleges:

1. Admits the incorporation of the Universal Oil Company as alleged in the complaint, and that at the same time mentioned in the complaint, said defendant was and now is engaged in the transaction of business within the state of Washaska.

2. Admits that the defendant Ira Thompson is an employee of this answering defendant, and alleges that he has been employed by the Universal Oil Company for about two years last October past.

3. Admits the incorporation of the city of Jonesboro as alleged in the complaint, and further admits that State Street and Cook Street are public streets and highways within the corporate limits of said city.

4. Admits on information and belief that on the sixth day of November last year at about ten o'clock in the evening at the intersection of said streets, the plaintiff sustained injuries to his person by coming in contact with an automobile owned by Universal Oil Company and then being driven by Ira Thompson.

5. Alleges on information and belief that said car so driven by the defendant Ira Thompson was plainly visible to plaintiff for a distance of fully two hundred feet while approaching the place where the accident occurred; that said automobile was approaching said street intersection from the east on the right hand side of the center of that portion of Cook Street reserved for vehicle traffic; that as said car approached said intersection, the plaintiff carelessly and negligently left the sidewalk, knowing that said car was approaching, and carelessly and negligently walked out on that portion of the street reserved for vehicle traffic to a distance of about five feet from said sidewalk, directly in the path of said approaching car; that said plaintiff upon reaching said portion about five feet from said sidewalk, carelessly and negligently failed to keep a proper lookout for the approaching car, and carelessly and negligently attempted to cross in front of said car without giving the driver thereof any warning of his intention, and thereby came in contact with said car and sustained personal injuries. Further alleges upon information and belief that said car was driven at a lawful rate while approaching said intersection where this accident occurred, and that the injuries complained of were caused by the negligence of the plaintiff.

6. Further answering, this defendant denies each and every material allegation and thing in plaintiff's complaint contained not hereinbefore expressly admitted.

WHEREFORE, the defendant demands judgment that this action be dismissed as against this defendant, and that it have judgment against the plaintiff for its costs and disbursements incurred herein.

MELVILLE AND EBON
Attorneys for the defendant
Universal Oil Company

Defenses and Objections

In common law pleading the defendant, preliminary to a plea in bar, may file a *plea in abatement* or a *demurrer*. A plea in abatement is a "dilatory" plea in that it objects only to the manner of the plaintiff's action and is sometimes made for the purpose of delay. A demurrer is an objection to the legal sufficiency of the plaintiff's action, viz., that the facts stated in the complaint do not, in law, amount to a cause of action.

Many code pleading states have abolished the several pleas in abatement, but permit the same issues to be raised in a demurrer or answer. Federal rules of practice have abolished both the plea in abatement and the demurrer; all such defenses and objections must be asserted in the answer or by motion except that a response to a counterclaim may be made in a *reply.*

The principal dilatory pleas (i.e., pleas in abatement and pleas to the jurisdiction) are: (1) lack of jurisdiction over the subject matter or the person; (2) improper venue; (3) lack of capacity to sue; (4) nonjoinder of necessary parties; (5) misjoinder of parties; (6) misjoinder of causes; (7) another action is pending; (8) the action is brought prematurely; and (9) insufficiency of process or service (motion to quash the summons).

When a party is sued on account and the pleading is general or defective, he may move for a *bill of particulars;* that is, require the adverse party to present, within a short time, an itemized or more specific account.

When one party objects to parts of a pleading because they are superfluous or immaterial, he *moves to strike* such parts.

> . . . Chrysler Corporation asked the court to require Mr. Newberg either to make his complaint in his suit against the company more specific or to allow Chrysler to take "discovery" depositions from him.
>
> Chrysler, in its motion, also asked the court to strike from the complaint a number of charges as "immaterial, irrelevant, impertinent," and "scandalous." These include many of Mr. Newberg's charges that he was made a "scapegoat" by Chrysler management to cover up other corporate abuses.

Demurrer

A demurrer tests the complaint as a matter of law. Until the judge has decided the question of law the defendant is not required to file a formal answer (i.e., denial) to the complaint. When the judge sustains a demurrer he is ruling that the plaintiff has no cause of action. A simple example is the one cited on page 203 in which a plaintiff sues a physician alleging he did not cure his ailment. A more common example is this one: P sues D for libel; the judge sustains D's demurrer on the ground that the words published are not, as a matter of law, libelous.

Here is another example: referring back to the paragraph numbered 3 on the complaint on pages 201–203, you will note that the plaintiff took pains to allege that the city of Jonesboro was an incorporated city and that State and Cook streets were "established public streets and highways." The reason for this allegation is that the driver of an automobile on such streets has certain legal duties and rights and a pedestrian has certain legal duties and rights. If, however, the accident had happened on a logging road in a forest on the private property of a lumber company and a pedestrian had sued a truck driver or the lumber company, or both, for injury, the rights and duties of the parties would not be the same as in the Jonesboro case. The pedestrian injured on the logging road would probably have no cause of action. If he had filed a complaint, the defense would file a demurrer which would assert that the complaint was legally insufficient. The judge would rule on this point of law, probably after a hearing or after the submission by the parties of memoranda of "points and authorities." If the judge sustained the demurrer, the defendant could move for judgment of dismissal. If the judge overruled the demurrer, the defendant would be required either to file a formal answer or to accept judgment against himself.

In some situations the law and the facts are such that the judge sustains a demurrer "with leave to amend." The plaintiff then may file an amended complaint, which the defendant must answer; in such situations the demurrer objects to defects in the complaint that can be corrected, such as uncertainty or misjoinder of parties.

When some cases are dismissed because the judge has sustained a demurrer, the judge's order is "dismissed with prejudice." This means that the plaintiff cannot sue the defendant again on the same allegations.[1] In other situations the order is "dismissed without prejudice."

Demurrer Upheld In Suit for Libel

Superior Judge H. T. Southwood yesterday sustained a demurrer to a $125,000 libel suit filed by a former police inspector against District Attorney Wesley Harlow.

Thomas Jones, the plaintiff, has ten days in which to amend his complaint.

The judge's action was based on the grounds that a letter the district attorney wrote last year to Police Chief Henry Hawkins was a "privileged communication" between law enforcement agencies.

---

[1] Technically, if the plaintiff should sue in another court, on the same charges, the determination of the issue of *res judicata** is for the second court.

> Jones' complaint had alleged that the letter wrongly associated him with a suspected bookmaker and was responsible for his dismissal from the police force.

Another type of defense which is sometimes raised on demurrer is *statute of limitations*. Statutes in all states bar civil suits commenced after a certain number of years. The law does not require a defendant to preserve his accounts beyond a reasonable time and the law recognizes that witnesses to an act or a transaction may die or leave the state after a reasonable time.

Pleading New Matter

A defendant may admit the allegations in the plaintiff's complaint but present an *affirmative* defense to excuse the effect of the allegations. An example is a tort action in which the defendant admits he struck the plaintiff but alleges that he (defendant) is a police officer and had the legal right to strike the plaintiff, who was resisting arrest. When the plaintiff, in response to this new matter, denies he resisted arrest, an issue of fact is joined and the parties go to trial. At the trial the defendant has the burden of proof to show that the plaintiff resisted arrest. The defendant's pleading of new matter is called in common law pleading a *plea in confession and avoidance,* and the plaintiff's response to it is called a *replication;* in some code pleading states and in federal practice the plaintiff's response to the defendant's plea in confession and avoidance is called a *reply* and in other code pleading states is called an *amended complaint*.

A somewhat similar pleading is the defense of *contributory negligence*. Paragraph 5 of the answer on pages 226–227 is such a defense. Here the oil company does *not* admit its employee's negligence, as would be done in a plea in confession and avoidance, but pleads separately that the negligence of the plaintiff was a contributing proximate cause of the injury. At the trial both parties have a burden of proof to prove the negligence of the other.

Counterclaim: New matter is pleaded by the defendant when he asserts a counterclaim in his answer. In such an affirmative defense he does not attack the plaintiff's claim but asserts an independent cause of action, such as a setoff* to the plaintiff's claim.

Cross-complaint: When a defendant is sued he may, if the court permits, file a cross-complaint against the plaintiff or a third party in addition to his answer to the original complaint. The third party must be served and may demur or answer as to the original complaint.

Wife Denies She Was a "Spendthrift"

A woman who admitted she has 100 pairs of shoes has denied in an answer to her multimillionaire husband's divorce suit that she was a "spendthrift."

Mrs. Kate Thirsk, of Palm Beach and New York, yesterday filed an answer to a divorce suit filed last June 23 by Philip Thirsk, New York City broker.

Thirsk, 68, alleged his wife was guilty of extreme cruelty and had a violent and ungovernable temper.

He had averred in his complaint that, "due to Mrs. Thirsk's extravagant tastes and whims," the family expenses amounted to $30,000 a month.

Mrs. Thirsk, in her answer and counterclaim, asked a divorce and also

1. That the court determine the validity and rights of the parties under an agreement creating an irrevocable trust of $300,000 from which, she said, she received $15,000 annually.

2. That the court order her husband to pay as alimony such money as the court deems proper.

Supplier Sued in Radiant Heat Case

Two new parties were brought into a leaky radiant heating system case yesterday when a building contractor filed a cross-complaint against a plumbing contractor and a supplier of tubing.

Walter Knudsen, the building contractor, who had been sued by Cooper Motors, Inc., filed the cross-complaint against Julius Gustin, plumbing contractor who had installed the system, and the Dickinson Pipe Co., who had furnished the tubing.

He asked $20,000 damages to his business reputation and good will.

Cooper Motors, in suing Knudsen, had asked $10,000 damages for a new system and $10,000 for aggravated illness caused by lack of heat.

> In his answer to the auto agency's suit, the building contractor alleged that the plumbing contractor had advised the use of Dickinson Co. tubing, which, he asserted, is defective.

Exercise: After referring to the code of civil practice in your state, prepare a statement which describes responsive pleading. For example, what terms are used to describe the objections and defenses of the defendant and what are the grounds, if any, for a demurrer?

Demurrer to Answer

There are a few grounds on which the plaintiff may demur to the defendant's answer. In one code state these are:

1. The answer does not state facts sufficient to constitute a defense or counterclaim.
2. The answer is ambiguous, unintelligible, or uncertain.
3. The answer has improperly joined several causes of counterclaim or not stated them separately.

The News Story

In metropolitan communities the newspaper reports only those pleadings that are newsworthy because of the names of the parties or the circumstances. The name of the plaintiff or defendant or other person mentioned in the pleadings may make the filing of a suit newsworthy, as when a party is well known in the world of sports, theater, cinema, politics, society, or business. A legal contest that involves a large amount of money or the control of interesting or large assets (e.g., a racing stable or a baseball club) is also considered newsworthy. Readers are also interested in cases with unusual circumstances.

When should the reporter use legal terms that are not understood by many of his readers?

1. In most instances the reporter may use a term if he builds a context that explains the term or supplies an example.[2] The news story on page 229 is an illustration: the term "demurrer" is easily understood by the reader because the second paragraph explains the result of the judge's ruling and the third paragraph states the question of law. In the following sentence the writer supplied an example: "Chancery court appointed Coleman Dorsey, a Wilmington lawyer, as a sequestrator *to take control over shareholdings of the defendants.*"

2. When it is thought important for complete comprehension of the action and when space is not an overriding consideration, the reporter can

[2] See pp. 113–114.

explain the term parenthetically. An example: "The Dann group's action is what is known as a 'derivative' suit to recapture for the corporation any compensation received by the officers that is alleged to belong rightfully to the corporation."

3. In many instances, use of a specific term is not requisite to comprehension of a legal action and need not be used at all.

An investigator asked a randomly selected sample of 105 readers to define forty legal terms.[3] The most familiar terms were these: *jury* (defined by 91 per cent), *defendant* (81 per cent), *plaintiff* (74 per cent), *alleges* (64 per cent), *appealed* (53 per cent), *bound over* (40 per cent), *indictment* (37 per cent), *civil action* (33 per cent), and *felony* (23 per cent). *Mandamus,* however, was defined by only 10 per cent and *demurrer* by only 2 per cent.

> For class discussion: *1.* In reporting the filing of a complaint or answer, which of these verbs is *not* appropriate: *alleged, averred, said, stated, charged, argued, complained?*
> *2.* Which of these words is misspelled: *parties* or *attornies?*
> *3.* What is the plural of *counsel?*

When several names must be used in the news story the reader may be confused as to who are the plaintiffs and defendants, especially when the names of the parties are not known to most readers. An example is the news story on page 231 which refers to four different parties. The device of referring to two of them in the later part of the story as "the building contractor" and "the plumbing contractor"—rather than by actual name or as "defendant" and "cross-defendant"—is calculated to make the story more easily comprehended.

When Is a Pleading Privileged*?

It sometimes happens that the plaintiff, in his complaint, makes untrue statements about the defendant that are injurious to the defendant's reputation. The question then arises as to whether or not publication by a newspaper of the false statements constitutes libel.

The rule is that the newspaper's report of a judicial proceeding is *conditionally* privileged (i.e., the publisher is exempted from liability), the conditions being that the report be fair and accurate and published without malice. The rule is based on the social theory that "it is desirable that the trial of causes should take place under the public eye" (Cowley v. Pulsifer, 137 Mass. 392). But what constitutes a judicial proceeding?

[3] J. R. Barber *et al.,* "Legal Terms in the Montana Press," *Montana Journalism Review,* Spring, 1963, pp. 29–31.

Until a few years ago the universal rule was that the pleading was not privileged until it had reached the attention of a judge—say, on a motion by the defendant. The mere filing of a pleading with the court clerk did not make it privileged. This is still the majority rule. It is also the rule endorsed in *The Restatement of the Law of Torts* (par. 611c). In the federal jurisdiction and in some states, however, the rule now is that "a lawsuit, from beginning to end," is "in the nature of a judicial proceeding" (Campbell *v.* New York Post, Inc., 245 N.Y. 320); that is, the pleading is privileged as soon as it has been received by the clerk.

For class discussion: In a jurisdiction in which a complaint is privileged when it is filed, it is possible for a shyster lawyer and a "gold-digger" to file an untrue and scandalous set of allegations in a "paternity" suit against a wealthy man. Does the fact that a threat to file such a pleading can facilitate blackmail cause you to believe that this is not a good rule?

JUDGMENT WITHOUT TRIAL

There are several situations which allow for rendition of judgment in favor of one of the parties without a trial of the issues of fact.

Judgment by default is rendered on the merits for the plaintiff when the defendant fails to answer. This is not permitted in some kinds of cases.

Judgment by consent, or *judgment by confession,* is entered when a defendant authorizes a verdict against him for a specified amount of money.

In certain equitable proceedings the parties may make an agreement which is called a *consent decree.* Although not a judgment, the agreement that the decree is a just determination of their rights is made under the sanction of the court. Such agreements are often made in civil antitrust proceedings between a business firm and the United States attorney general.

Judgment on the pleadings is entered for the moving party (either plaintiff or defendant) when the judge decides that the adverse party has failed to state a cause of action or defense. The motion is somewhat similar to a general demurrer, which was discussed earlier.

Summary judgment is moved for by one of the parties to compel the adverse party to disclose the kind of proof he intends to present when the moving party suspects that the proof of his opponent is sham. Unlike the motion for judgment on the pleadings, this motion attacks the proof rather than the pleadings. Its purpose is to show there are no genuine issues as to any material fact. The parties submit affidavits, counteraffidavits, and depositions as to facts. The judge then determines whether there are any issues to be tried. Motion for summary judgment is denied when the judge decides that there are genuine issues of fact. In some civil antitrust proceedings begun by the United States government, summary judgment proceedings are almost in the nature of a trial since the judges read and evaluate several long depositions; but there is no oral testimony.

Many suits for money damages are *settled* before the cause goes to trial or during the trial—usually for an amount less than was demanded. Under the sanction of the court, the attorneys stipulate for dismissal. Newspaper reporters first learn of compromises and settlements from the court clerk, then ask the attorneys about the details.

Girl Settles for Loss of Her Legs

The $325,000 damage suit of Jane Becker against Eugene Shere, Milford contractor, has been compromised, attorneys disclosed in court today.

Judge Bronson Cartwright approved settlement of the suit filed on behalf of the 14-year-old girl after an accident on Sterling Lake in which both of her legs were severed by Shere's speedboat.

Attorney Ralph Berg said Jane would receive $95,000 and her father, Wyatt Becker, $20,000 for medical expenses and for her continued care.

Jane's attorneys will receive fees of $41,000 of which $1,750 was allocated for court costs.

PRETRIAL CONFERENCE

A recent procedure to reduce the time spent in trials of civil cases is the pretrial conference. The procedure is mandatory in New Jersey and is increasingly used by the larger courts in some other states.

After a case has reached the "memorandum to set" stage, the attorneys for the parties meet with a judge either in his chambers or in a courtroom. The purpose of the conference is to eliminate uncontroverted questions of law and fact with the view to narrowing the issues for trial. At the end of the conference the judge dictates to a phonographic reporter a "pretrial order" which lists the matters which the parties have agreed upon and have stipulated. This procedure not only reduces the time consumed in the trial that follows but often facilitates settlement of a case without a trial; the judge's order, however, does not refer directly to settlement.

Pretrial conferences are not attended by newspaper reporters. In important cases, however, the reporter sometimes reports the results of the conference, obtaining his information from the judge, clerk, or the attorneys.

Bridges Case
Counsel Can't Agree

Pretrial proceedings in the U.S. government's civil suit aimed at stripping Harry Bridges of his citizenship collapsed yesterday as attorneys for both sides announced they had failed to agree on two vital issues.

The impasse will probably result in adding three to six weeks of actual trial to the case, now scheduled to commence June 20.

The lawyers had been trying to get together on two things: (1) a document containing testimony from experts on Communism, to be introduced to show the nature of that party; and (2) whether Bridges' personal beliefs should be made an issue in the case.

"From discussions I have had," government prosecutor Lynn Gillard told federal Judge Louis E. Goodman, "there is apparently an impossibility of agreement on either of the stipulations."

Defense Attorney Norman Leonard echoed him.

Judge Goodman had suggested the stipulations in hopes of narrowing the issues to be tried.

As a result of the deadlock, proof of the Communist party's aims will have to be established by evidence introduced at the trial. The government will also be free to try to present evidence concerning the longshoreman leader's beliefs.

Bridges, a native of Australia, is accused of having obtained his U.S. citizenship in 1945 by fraud in that he falsely denied membership in the Communist party.

This and the preceding chapter have discussed what happens in civil actions preliminary to a determination of the actions by a judge (and often a jury). The next chapter explains the trial in a court of original jurisdiction of the issues of law and fact.

Exercise: *1.* Write a 350-word news story based on the complaint on pp. 201–203.
2. Write a 100-word news story based on the answer on pp. 226–227.

CHAPTER 18

Civil Actions: The Trial

These steps are taken in the jury trial of a civil action in a typical court of original jurisdiction:

1. The judge or clerk calls the case. The attorneys state that they are ready.
2. The jury is selected and sworn.
3. The plaintiff's attorney makes an *opening statement* outlining the issues and facts he expects to prove by evidence. The statement is factual, not argumentative. It is a statement of what he expects to prove; it is not evidence.
4. The plaintiff's attorney calls the witnesses he has subpoenaed and questions them. This is called *direct examination*. As each witness completes his direct examination the defense attorney, if he wishes, *cross-examines* them. The plaintiff's attorney conducts a *redirect examination* of some of his witnesses after they have been cross-examined. Then he tells the court: "The plaintiff rests."
5. The defense attorney makes his opening statement.
6. The defense attorney examines the defense witnesses he has subpoenaed. These may be cross-examined by the plaintiff's attorney.
7. The plaintiff's attorney calls and examines witnesses to rebut some of the defendant's evidence. In general, this is not additional evidence but *rebuttal* of defense evidence. In some situations, however, the court permits additional evidence.
8. The defense attorney presents his rebuttal evidence.
9. Each attorney makes a *summation,* or *argument,* based on the evidence that the jury has heard.
10. The judge *instructs* the jury on the law of the case.
11. The jury retires and deliberates.
12. The jury returns its verdict.

13. The judge renders a judgment which is entered in the judgment roll or minutes by the clerk.

14. The judgment is "satisfied"—if necessary—by a *writ of execution* directed to the sheriff.

Sometimes, at certain stages of the trial, one or both of the attorneys present motions. As will be explained below, these motions may have the effect, when granted by the judge, of concluding the trial at some stage before the case has been submitted to the jury.

SELECTING THE JURY

Most state constitutions and the United States constitution (seventh amendment) provide that a party has the right to have a jury determine issues of fact in "suits at common law."[1] This means actions at law as distinguished from suits in equity for which a jury is not generally required. In practice, however, both parties often waive trial by jury in actions at law, and a jury is sometimes used in cases in which law and equity are joined to determine the "legal" (i.e., nonequitable) issues.

The jury in a civil action is usually twelve members. Sometimes a smaller number is used in inferior courts.

At the beginning of the trial the judge explains briefly to the prospective jurors the nature of the case. The usual procedure of selection is for the clerk to draw twelve names from the trial jury list, seat the twelve prospective jurors in the jury box, and swear them. Then begins the process of *voir dire* ("to speak the truth"), which is an examination of the prospective jurors as to their qualifications and possible bias. In ten states the *voir dire* is conducted by the judge alone; often his questions are put to the jurors collectively instead of to the individuals. In eleven states the *voir dire* is conducted by the attorneys alone. In the remaining twenty-nine states the questioning is by both the judge and the attorneys.

The purpose of the *voir dire* is to determine whether the prospective jurors stand indifferent to the interests of the parties. Conventionally the questions relate to the prospective juror's kinship or business relationship with one of the parties or attorneys or to his ownership of stock in a company which is a party to the suit. Some questions relate to the specific case; for example, in a suit against a Hearst syndicated columnist, a question was "Are you a regular reader of the Hearst newspapers?" In some cases a question may test bias toward a class of persons (e.g., labor union officers).

After the *voir dire* has concluded, each of the attorneys may *challenge* one or more prospective jurors for *cause*. This means that an attorney be-

[1] But in England today fewer than 3 per cent of common law cases are tried by juries.

lieves the particular prospective juror is or may be biased in favor of the adverse party. When the judge agrees with the challenge he excuses the prospective juror. The judge, however, may decide to retain the prospective juror. There is no limit to the number of challenges for cause. In a San Francisco graft trial (criminal) early in the century 992 veniremen were examined on *voir dire*. For every prospective juror who is excused another takes his place in the jury box and is questioned.

After the challenges for cause have been concluded and the jury box is again provisionally filled, each attorney, alternately, is entitled to a certain number of *peremptory* challenges. A peremptory challenge is one taken without assigning any reason; for example, an attorney may exercise a peremptory challenge on a man or woman of a certain racial extraction because the adverse party is of the same racial extraction. In some instances an attorney has obtained the names of persons on the jury panel and has investigated them in advance of the trial to guide him in the exercise of his party's peremptory challenges. The number of peremptory challenges available to each party is limited by statute. The number varies from three to six for each party. When there are co-defendants the defense is sometimes permitted one or two additional peremptory challenges. In some criminal cases the selection of a jury is a tedious procedure because of so many challenges for cause, but selection of a jury for a civil case is nearly always a shorter and simpler procedure.

EVIDENCE

The judge usually requires the plaintiff's attorney to present the testimony of his witnesses so that the narration of events will proceed chronologically or logically. This practice is followed to assist the jury in comprehending the issues. When there is a valid reason for changing the order of proof, however, it is usually permitted. An example is when an attorney withdraws a witness temporarily and calls another witness to prove relevancy of the first witness's testimony and then recalls the first witness; otherwise, some of the first witness's testimony could not be admitted.

Burden of Proof

Which party has the burden of proof is determined by the pleadings. Normally the plaintiff has the burden of proof when the defendant's answer is a general denial. But when the defendant sets up an affirmative defense the burden of proof "shifts" to him during the trial. For example, when a life insurance company is sued by the beneficiary and the company (defendant) pleads suicide of the insured as a defense, the defendant has the burden of proof on that issue.

What Is Evidence?

Evidence includes the testimony of witnesses, stipulations and admissions of the parties, maps, documents, letters and other writings, and sometimes physical objects, such as X-ray films and clothing. Testimony is the evidence given by a witness in the form of answers to questions put by counsel.

Writings and physical objects are termed *exhibits*. All exhibits are marked or stamped by the clerk for identification. Each exhibit is given a serial number, such as "Plaintiff's 3" or "Defense's 4." This is done so there will be no confusion when reference is made to the exhibits by counsel. Some exhibits are offered and accepted "for identification only," whether or not the judge admits them as evidence. This is done to get them into the record in anticipation of an appeal on the ground that they should have been admitted.

When a physical object, such as a house or a large piece of machinery, cannot be brought into the courtroom, the jury is permitted to "view" the premises or to "inspect" the machinery. When this is done an officer of the court (e.g., the bailiff) conducts the jurors to the location. Controversy sometimes ensues in a trial when one of the parties asserts that the object to be viewed (e.g., a stairway) is not in the same condition as it was at the time of the disputed event (e.g., the accident).

Demonstrations are conducted in some trials. For example, a witness plays music or exhibits the scars which resulted from an injury. Demonstrations which are in the nature of experiments are sometimes permitted to test some of the facts in dispute.

Court Becomes Operating Room

A courtroom yesterday became an operating theater—complete with operating table, anesthetist, instruments, surgeon, attending physician, nurses and patient. Surgeon Douglas Fairman went through the motions of taking out the patient's tonsils.

He didn't really operate, however. It was all part of a court hearing in a suit filed by Mrs. Dorothy Moon, a widow, against the General Hospital and Dr. Fairman. She charged Dr. Fairman with negligence and rough handling during a tonsil operation on her husband three years ago. He died later.

The mock operation was staged to show how a patient's head is handled during a tonsillectomy. The court said it would rule later on the suit.

Magician Performs In Court; Wins Suit

A magician confused a jury so much yesterday it decided to award him $2,275.

The magician, Bob Sharpe, brought his bag of tricks into district court to fight his breach of contract suit against the Ralston Purina Co. of St. Louis.

Sharpe had contended the company hired him to perform before dealer and sales meetings in nine cities and then reneged on the contract.

The company claimed Sharpe's tricks hadn't mystified anyone at a dress rehearsal. Therefore, attorneys said, Sharpe had been fired from a company-sponsored show.

But the jury took only 30 minutes to decide Sharpe's sleight of hand had convinced them.

Sharpe began his court performance by producing four eggs from an empty bag.

His attorney, Alfred Busch, said, "Let the record show that Mr. Sharpe produced four eggs from an empty bag."

"From a purportedly empty bag," a defense attorney said.

Sharpe then put the eggs in a pan and apparently changed them into baby chicks.

Then he caused some cigarettes to rise from a fresh package. . . .

When a writing (e.g., a letter) is not available a witness is sometimes permitted to testify as to its content. This is called "secondary" evidence as distinguished from "the best evidence," which is the original writing. Secondary evidence is never admitted unless the party offering it "lays a foundation" (by testimony of a witness) to explain satisfactorily why the original writing is not available.

Laying a foundation: The attorney must, as a preliminary, lay a foundation for the admissibility of physical evidence; as, for example, showing that a photograph or a diagram is a faithful representation. Presentation of a time card to show the defendant was not at work on the day in question must be preceded by testimony of the payroll clerk as to identity and fidelity of the card.

What evidence is admissible? Evidence must be *relevant, material,* and *competent.* We need to discuss here only the criterion of competency. The competency of evidence demands some explanation of two rules. One of these relates to "hearsay" and the second to "opinion."

Hearsay: This type of evidence generally is inadmissible, although there are several exceptions because of necessity. When a witness testifies not to what he knows personally but to what he has heard said by others, his evidence is hearsay. Such evidence is not admissible because the adverse party does not have the opportunity to cross-examine the person who is not in court and does not, therefore, have the opportunity to refute or explain the conversation. An example: in an action to reinstate a life insurance policy which had been cancelled by the company because of the state of the insured's health, an officer of the insurance company testified that he had employed an investigating agency to make a secret investigation of the insured's health and offered to testify as to the content of the agency's report. This evidence was excluded.

> For class discussion: *1.* In a suit over appropriation of another firm's trade-marked product name, a market research agency employed by the defendant interviewed a national sample of 2,000 users of the plaintiff's product and offered to testify that the plaintiff's trade-mark was considered by most of the users to be a generic name for the product, not just the name of a specific brand. Would this evidence be admissible or would the defendant be required to present the testimony of the individual users who had been interviewed? (In this connection read DuPont Cellophane Co. v. Waxed Products Co., 85 F.2d 75, and Cleo Syrup Corp. v. Coca Cola Co., 139 F.2d 416. See also H. C. Barksdale, *The Use of Survey Research Findings as Legal Evidence* [Pleasantville, N.Y., 1957].)
> 2. What about radar evidence in either a civil or criminal trial to measure rate of speed of an automobile driver accused of speeding? Is it hearsay evidence?

Opinion: With certain exceptions, which are explained below, the testimony of a witness must be statements of fact, not opinion. An attorney may not, under most conditions, ask an "argumentative" question, one which elicits an inference by the witness. An example:

DEFENSE ATTORNEY: Now if the defendant had been trying to conceal the automobile, would she have taken it to a parking lot?
PLAINTIFF'S ATTORNEY: Objected to as argumentative and not proper cross-examination.
THE COURT: Objection sustained.

In testifying as to what he has *perceived,* any witness may give his testimony in terms which include inferences unless the judge finds that, for him to make such inferences, the witness must have a special knowledge, skill, experience, or training which he does not have. Thus an eyewitness may estimate the rate of speed of an automobile and a great variety of other matters of everyday life such as age, size, value, and weight.

About many other matters, however, the court will admit only the opinion of scientists, doctors, chemists, engineers, appraisers, and others who are in business and the professions and who have a special knowledge of their field.

Such experts must "qualify" on *voir dire* examination before being permitted to testify. Thus the experts are asked questions by counsel about their education, experience, and writings. In some instances the judge, after objection, declines to admit their testimony. This happened, for example, in a case in which the defense tried to qualify a carpenter after the plaintiff had presented the expert testimony of a wood technologist.

Privileged* Communications

Some witnesses may not be required to testify about communications between themselves and a person with whom they have a confidential relationship. An attorney may not testify as to matters communicated to him by his client. This is the privilege of the client, not of the attorney; if the client discloses the communication, the attorney need no longer hold it confidential. An attorney is not bound by this rule, however, if the client has told him that he intends to commit a crime or a fraud.

A variety of other confidential relationships are protected by statute in many states although the privilege is regarded as of dubious value by leading scholars on the law of evidence.[2] Only a few of these confidential relationships are protected in England.

A majority of states have statutes which extend privilege to communications between the priest and the confessant, and most states have statutes which apply to the physician-patient relationship. The statutes apply sometimes in civil cases, but more often in criminal cases. All states have statutes that govern testimony about the communications between husband and wife. Although the statutes vary as to the competency of such testimony,

---

[2] See Clinton DeWitt, *Privileged Communications Between Physician and Patient* (Springfield, Illinois, 1958); also 8 Wigmore, *Evidence* (3rd ed., 1940), sec. 2380.

in general, one spouse in a civil action may be compelled to testify for or against the other if the other consents, but in a criminal action one spouse may refuse to testify in spite of the other's consent.[3]

Disclosure of a newsman's source: A dozen states[4] have statutes which protect the newsman (and in some states, also radio, television, and wire service managers and newsgatherers) from compulsory disclosure of his sources of information. In Pennsylvania a document, as well as an oral communication, has been held to be a newsman's source of information. The California statute, which has been amended to include others, besides newspaper men, is typical of eleven of the statutes:

> A publisher, editor, reporter, or other person connected with or employed upon a newspaper cannot be adjudged in contempt by a court, the Legislature, or any administrative body for refusing to disclose the source of any information procured for publication and published in a newspaper. (*Code Ann., Civil Proc.,* sec. 1881[6], 1955.)

The legislatures of an equal number of states have refused to enact such statutes, and some newspapers have opposed their enactment in their own states. A United States Court of Appeals affirmed a ten-day sentence given a New York newspaper reporter (Torre) for refusing in a pretrial discovery proceeding to identify the television network executive who made to her (Torre) certain alleged defamatory remarks printed in the newspaper and on which actress Judy Garland was suing the network. The court held that Torre's refusal to name her source deprived the plaintiff (Garland) of necessary testimony in a civil case.[5]

The theory on which the above-mentioned statutes is based is that newspapers would be less eager to expose corruption in public life without such protection, and that the public, as a consequence, would be deprived of such information. In an effort to reconcile the various interests, a legal writer has proposed a statute along these lines:

> It is hereby declared to be the public policy of this State that no person engaged in the work of gathering or disseminating news shall be required to disclose before any proceeding or by any authority the source of information procured by him in the course of such work unless disclosure be essential to prevent injustice or to protect the public interest. In granting or denying a testimonial privilege under this Act, the court or other authority shall have due regard to the nature of the proceeding, the merits of the claim or defense, the adequacy of the remedy otherwise available, the relevancy of the source, and the possibility of establishing by other means

---

[3] The California statutes are rather typical. See *Civil Code of Procedure,* sec. 1881(1), and *Penal Code,* sec. 1322.
[4] Alabama, Arizona, Arkansas (qualified), California, Indiana, Kentucky, Maryland, Michigan, Montana, New Jersey, Ohio, and Pennsylvania.
[5] Garland v. Torre, 259 F.2d 545.

that which the source is offered as tending to prove. An order compelling disclosure shall be appealable, and subject to stay.[6]

For class discussion: "A newsman is investigating a report that the local bank is in trouble because somebody has lifted some money. So he goes to the bank president who says the cashier stole $10,000 but please don't quote him saying so. Instead of digging further, the newsman writes a story saying that an official of the bank says Joe Johnson, the cashier, stole $10,000; and let's also assume the newspaper is foolish enough to print it as it stands.

"The police grab Joe Johnson and throw him in jail and after a few days of polite questioning, they turn him loose. He hasn't stolen the money at all, it seems. Joe Johnson sues the bank for what happened to him, and the newsman is called as a witness in a civil suit." (From a speech by W. H. Fitzpatrick, *Wall Street Journal*, Feb. 6, 1959.) Should the law protect the newsman or the bank cashier?

Examination

The series of questions put to a witness by an attorney is called examination. When an attorney examines a witness to prove the case for his party the questions are called *direct examination,* or *examination-in-chief.* The same attorney, however, may call and examine the adverse party; such a witness is called an *adverse witness.*

At the conclusion of the direct examination of a witness, the attorney for the adverse party may *cross-examine.* The purpose of cross-examination is to qualify or nullify what was testified to on direct examination. An effective cross-examiner can sometimes convert plausible testimony given on direct examination to an entirely implausible version. To achieve this result, however, the cross-examiner must usually make intense preparation before the discovery examination as well as before the trial.[7]

In general the scope of cross-examination must be confined to matters testified to on direct examination and on matters which are calculated to impeach the credibility of the witness. These two limitations tend to promote order and method in the presentation of a case since they permit each party to present his side of the case without being interrupted by matters that, at the time, could confuse the jury. However, questions on new matter are sometimes permitted on cross-examination when failure to allow

---

[6] Anon., "Compulsory Disclosure of a Newsman's Source: A Compromise Proposal," *Northwestern University Law Review,* 54:243–54 (1959).

[7] For some excellent examples of successful cross-examination, see Louis Nizer, *My Life in Court* (Garden City, N.Y., 1961); also F. L. Wellman, *The Art of Cross-Examination* (New York, 1903, 1937).

it would permit the jury to draw erroneous inferences from the direct examination.

Cross-examination which is calculated to discredit the testimony of a witness is called *impeaching* the witness. A witness may be impeached by showing his lack of knowledge of the matter, his bias or interest, and his ill reputation for truth, honesty, and integrity. This is often done by showing contradiction or inconsistency between his testimony at the trial and his previous testimony at a discovery examination. Generally, in proving contradiction, the adverse attorney is required to lay a foundation by refreshing the witness's memory as to the time and place at which he made the first statement; the reason for this rule is to prevent unfair surprise*.

Normally a party may not impeach its own witness since the theory is that the party calling the witness vouches for his credibility. There are some exceptions to this rule. In some situations when an attorney requires testimony of a witness for whose credibility he cannot vouch, he moves that the witness be called as "the court's witness." This can be done in a civil case only when both parties consent.

A *leading question* is one that is so framed that it suggests the answer desired or assumes a fact that is in controversy. An example:

> Q. In March of last year, as the result of an advertisement you inserted, did you receive a letter?
> MR. WILSON: Objected to as leading.
> THE COURT: Sustained.
> Q: As the result of an advertisement you inserted, did you receive any response?
> A: I did.
> Q: What was received?
> A: I received a letter with a peculiar signature.

A leading question may not be asked on direct examination (i.e., of the party's own witness) except when the witness is hostile to the party calling him, is a child of tender years, or one whose memory is exhausted for some particular such as a proper name, or when the question is merely preliminary. A leading question may be asked on cross-examination.

Redirect examination, or *reexamination,* is the term used when, after cross-examination, the attorney reexamines his witness on matters which had been brought out in cross-examination. The purpose of redirect examination is to explain, rebut, or avoid the effect of testimony given on cross-examination; that is, to "rehabilitate" one's own witness.

Objections and Exceptions

The testimony of a witness is sometimes interrupted by objections from the opposing counsel as to its admissibility. When the judge overrules the objection, the opposing counsel is entitled to an *exception,* that is, a formal objection to the ruling of the judge. "Taking an exception" implies that the moving party intends to cite the refusal on appeal if an appeal is taken. In some jurisdictions, including the federal, it is not required that an exception be taken, but in others the ruling cannot be cited on appeal unless it had been excepted to.

Sometimes a witness answers a supposedly objectionable question before the opposing attorney has had time to object. Then the opposing attorney moves to "strike" the testimony. Such a motion is addressed to the witness's answer, not to the attorney's question.

Any argument before the judge by the attorneys on the admissibility of evidence is made outside the presence or hearing of the jury. Sometimes the attorneys talk to the judge in low tones of voice at his bench; sometimes the jury is excused during prolonged argument; and sometimes the judge hears the argument in his chambers.

A DAY OF TESTIMONY

Here is the testimony in the case of Madison Wilson, plaintiff, *vs.* Universal Oil Company and Ira Thompson, defendants. The pleadings are on pages 203 and 226. The superior court judge is H. T. Southwood. To conserve space, only the answers to questions have been reproduced—except in a few instances. This testimony must be read entirely if the reader is to comprehend the processes involved in a civil action. A written exercise will be based on this testimony.

[The first witness for the plaintiff is STANLEY SANDERS, a civil engineer who had drawn a plat of the intersection of Cook, State, and Clark streets, which is plaintiff's Exhibit 1. He is examined by Walter Hall, the plaintiff's attorney. Sanders explained to the jury the details of the plat. The pleadings had stated that Ira Thompson, a defendant, was driving in a westerly direction on Cook street and turned in a northwesterly direction at the intersection with State street.] *Sanders further testified:*

I took a measurement to ascertain from what distance back on the curb on the north side of Cook street you would have a full view of the crosswalk on Clark street, which shows that at 28 feet you can plainly see the entrance to the door at Tommy James' to the corner, which would render the entire crosswalk on Clark street visible from that point.

I measured the view to ascertain the distance at which you could obtain a full view of that crosswalk from the point ten feet out from the curb of Cook street, and at that distance you have a full view of the crosswalk on Clark street; that is, 53 feet from the corner—from the property corner at the intersecting lines on the easterly line of Clark street and the northerly line on Cook street.

I measured from the property lines in from the edge of the sidewalk.

[*Cross-examination by Theodore Melville, defense attorney*]

By the use of a ruler and the scale of the map, I can determine very closely how far down on State street a person can look from a point opposite to the Stamison corner looking down State street in a westerly direction. Cook street is 42 feet between the curbs and State street at the crosswalk is 49 feet. The sidewalk is 12 feet.

IRA THOMPSON, called as an adverse party, being duly sworn, testified as follows:

[*Examination by Mr. Hall*]

My name is Ira Thompson. I live in Jonesboro. I am 37 years old. I am employed by the Universal Oil Company. I have been employed two years and was in its employ last November 6 as a salesman. I was furnished with an automobile to use in the discharge of my duties. It is a Ford sports car.

I was operating this car in discharge of my duties on last November 6 at the time this collision occurred. [*Answer stricken out on motion as calling for a conclusion from the witness.*]

My duties as salesman were everything in general in my field. I drive to the different service stations in this car. When my driving for the day ended, my duties did not necessarily involve putting the car up for the night. My practice had been to store it in the garage at my home. I was on my way home the night in question.

There were no definite hours set when my day started or when my employment commenced or when it terminated.

On the evening of November 6 I was driving this car. It was an open car. I drove on Cook street. About 10:10 that evening I reached the intersection of Cook street and State street. There was no one in the car with me. Just prior to that I had been down to the Universal Oil Company in the city of Jonesboro. I was returning there after having been there transacting business of the company. [*Before answer completed, objection taken on the ground that the question called for conclusion of the witness, and was incompetent, irrelevant, and immaterial. Overruled. Exception taken.*]

George Baxter was in charge of the local station. Some of my conversation with him at the station that evening related to business of the company. My mission in going there was not exactly to carry out my duties as the company's employee.

I was asked these questions and made the following answers upon my adverse examination [*i.e., discovery examination*]:

"Only thing I did was to go down to the station and visit with the boys, attendants, which we are supposed to do occasionally, call on our station."

That statement is true.

It wasn't specified that I should make a call of that character in the performance of my duties any night, but I called that night. I was supposed to make calls of that character whether it was that night or some other night.

As I approached the intersection of Cook and State streets that evening, I did not see anyone crossing from the Michel corner or starting across toward the Stamison Restaurant.

Of course, I was looking straight ahead. I did not see any one starting to cross there and come to a stop and wait for me to pass, to go by, or crossing on the crosswalk from the Michel Jewelry Store north toward Stamison's Restaurant. There wasn't anybody there.

As I was approaching and as I reached the intersection of Cook and State streets my speed was about 15 miles an hour. I had been proceeding at not much greater speed 30 or 40 feet back. I would judge that my speed down through the block east of Stamison's Restaurant was about 18 miles an hour. I did not maintain that speed up to the intersection of Cook and State streets. I imagine I was about 150 feet east of the east line of State street when I started to slacken my speed. As I went by the Jonesboro Mortgage, Loan and Trust Building I was going about 18 miles an hour. This building is about 60 feet east of the Stamison Restaurant corner. It is the third door east, and at that time I was going 18 miles an hour. As I reached the crosswalk from the Michel Jewelry Store to the Stamison Restaurant I should think I was going about 15 miles an hour.

It was raining. The pavement was wet. I wouldn't say that the pedestrians were holding their heads down to avoid the rain beating in their faces.

When I first saw Mr. Wilson I was about in front of the Rolley Meat Market. He was about at the edge of the sidewalk where the crosswalk goes across. Mr. Wilson had gotten out about four feet on the crosswalk when my car hit him. While my car traveled from over in front of the Rolley Meat Market to the point where I hit him, he moved about four to six feet.

I didn't notice whether he was walking very slowly or rapidly. While Mr. Wilson went that four to six feet my car traveled about 120 feet.

When I first saw him he was about to cross the State street crosswalk. He was standing up on the sidewalk. I couldn't say right on the edge of the curb. He was standing on the sidewalk. When I first saw him, in my estimation, he was about 150 to 200 feet from me. He hesitated after he had progressed out to this point and was about to step off the curb. I imagine I was about 40 to 50 feet from him when he hesitated.

I slowed down to about eight miles an hour at that time. When he hesitated I threw out the clutch. I slowed down to just about eight miles an hour, I figure. For the 40 feet before I hit him I was going about eight miles an hour. I was not about 40 feet distant when he started forward again, just about ten feet from him when he started forward.

I have had experience in stopping that car. You can stop it in six feet by applying your brakes when you are going eight miles an hour. I don't remember that I applied my brakes when I saw him start forward, when I say that he was ten feet from me.

I probably testified on my adverse examination that I did not apply my brakes.

At that time there was nothing to prevent me from applying my brakes and stopping my car after I saw him start forward in time to avoid hitting him. But, instead of applying my brakes, I went right ahead when I saw him start forward. When I saw he halted I did not notice which way his face was turned. He must have seen me or he wouldn't have hesitated. I thought he looked toward me, yes sir. I did not notice him looking at all.

I don't remember sounding my horn. I did not give any other signal.

When my car hit Wilson he was about four feet from the curb on the right hand side of State street. I had ample room to pass or swing out to the west or south. If he had remained standing where I said he was, I would have passed within a few inches of him if he had not moved an inch. I did not figure that he was quite that close, and didn't realize that I was going to come that close to him even though he didn't move at that time. He hadn't moved very far when I hit him.

I couldn't tell whether he was crossing the street approximately between the white lines, the crosswalk. I don't know how close he was to those lines. I testified on my adverse examination that I couldn't say that he was right on the line. He was close to the lines and that was true. I don't know how close.

My car traveled about 15 or 20 feet after I struck Mr. Wilson. It stopped about 15 or 20 feet from the sidewalk line. It was about this side of Robinson's Hardware Store that I stopped, somewhere near the stairway leading up to the Tommy James place and the Robinson Hardware Store.

I pulled up to the curb. I did not apply my brakes. As I went westerly on State street, I turned towards the curb. I traveled at an angle toward the curb to the point where I hit him to the point where I stopped, about a 45-degree angle. I was about three feet from the sidewalk when I stopped. I think I was far enough from the sidewalk so that later on I pushed the car into the curb.

I remember John Lyons coming up there that evening. I don't remember whether it was just when I was engaged in attempting to extricate Mr. Wilson from beneath the car. I don't remember whether before I attempted to get Mr. Wilson from beneath the car I moved the car backwards. I testified on my adverse examination just enough to get the car back off Mr. Wilson, back toward the James store. I moved it back several feet—three or four feet.

I did not stop the car as soon as I could have, as soon as I hit Mr. Wilson. I could have stopped the car almost instantly at the speed I was going.

I did not notice the condition of Mr. Wilson's clothing when I got him out from under the car as to whether it was torn or not.

I was familiar that there was a crosswalk at this point. I didn't know it was a dangerous corner.

I probably testified on my adverse examination that I knew it was a dangerous corner at that time.

I did not see Mr. Wilson while he was crossing the Clark street intersection. I looked to see whether anyone was going over that intersection as I approached the intersection of those three streets. If he had been on that intersection, I would have seen him.

I testified on my adverse examination that there was no statement made by me at that time to the effect that it was Mr. Wilson's fault at that time.

After Mr. Wilson had been removed from beneath my car, I moved the car forward again, that is, sometime after he had been carried into the cigar store. I moved it up far enough so that it would stand up against the curbing after I came back from the cigar store. I moved it between ten and fifteen feet. I suppose I had to go ten feet before I went into the curb at this 45-degree angle, although I had started to turn it towards the curb at a point four feet from it and then traveled up to the time that I first stopped. I judge I was four or five feet when I first stopped the car.

I traveled to the right of the center of Cook street as I approached the intersection.

I knew down at this intersection at this time and at some time prior thereto that at State street there were signs which read "Stop." I also knew that as you approached the intersection from either direction on Cook street there were signs which said "Slow."

I was about ten feet from Mr. Wilson when he stopped, and started forward. He couldn't have stopped very long.

I testified on my adverse examination that I used my foot brake and stopped. That was true. That would bring it to a full stop after I hit him. I knew I struck Mr. Wilson the instant I hit him.

[*Examination by Mr. Melville*]

In stating that I applied the foot brake, I mean I applied my brake some distance along after the accident.

MADISON WILSON, being duly sworn, testified [*on direct examination by Mr. Hall*]:

My name is Madison Wilson. I live at 314 West Cook street. I have lived in Jonesboro 60 years. I will be 61 in February. I am a part owner of the Wilson Bottling Company and, prior to last November 6, was working in the plant of that company. My condition as to being able to work prior to that time was all right. I helped out in the bottling department down below, worked around.

On the evening of November 6 I was up to the Home Theatre. I left the Home Theatre about 10 o'clock. It was raining then. I went down as far as the First National Bank corner from there and crossed over and I went down the other side of McSorley's Cigar Store. As I crossed over from the First National Bank I walked down on McSorley's Cigar Store side of Cook street. I walked in the cigar store. I wanted to dry out until it stopped raining.

I waited about five minutes or so and it didn't stop, and so I went out and started down across Clark street over to Tommy James's. I started in a westerly direction on Cook street toward Tommy James's corner and crossed Clark street.

I stopped at the curb looking right and left and did not hear or see anything. I didn't see or hear any cars. I stopped at the curbing to step off between the lines, right at Tommy James's. On the curbing next to State street I looked to the left and down to the right and in front as you go around. I had a view for quite a ways there. No car was in view and I didn't see no car or hear any. I didn't see any car within the range of my vision. After taking that view I started to walk across between the paint lines.

I started to walk across and all at once there I was hit. I thought a house fell on top of me. I presume it probably was about the middle of the street, maybe around the middle there. I couldn't tell just how far it was when I was hit. There was no horn sounded or warning given by the car.

After I stepped down from the curbing and started to go across the intersection I didn't stop at any time before I was hit. When I was hit I hollered, and I presume he must have heard me hollering.

He got out of the car and he says, "Are you hurt?" I hollered right away when I was hit. The car must have gone quite a distance after I was hit. It must have been down in front of the first entrance to the City Hall. When they got me out from under the car my recollection is that it was in front of the first entrance to the City Hall, where the car was when it stopped. I was laying under the car while the car was passing over the intersection down to the point where it stopped. I was dragged.

I had a top coat. I still have that top coat.
Exhibit 2 is the coat I was wearing at the time I was struck.
That coat was in good condition prior to the time I was struck. It was not ripped. It now has a ripped seam down the center of the back and also at the arm.

[*Exhibit 2 is offered in evidence and received.*]

Exhibit 3 is the shirt that I wore that night. The dark spot there is oil that leaked on it. That spot was not there before I was struck. It was not torn in the back before I was struck. The dark spot down the side was not there before I was struck.

[*Exhibit 3 is offered in evidence and received.*]

When Mr. Thompson came around from the front and asked me whether I was hurt I said, "Yes, for God's sake get me out of here." I says, "Why didn't you blow your horn?" and he says, "Wait, wait just a minute there," and he got around and pushed the car out from over me.

Well, I remember that somebody picked me up after I was gotten out from under the car, and just about that time I see that there was a bunch coming out of the cigar store and everything got black then, and I fainted away about that time. I was in on a couch in the cigar store when I regained consciousness. I know a doctor came to attend me. Dr. Carlson.

I was experiencing pain in the right shoulder. My whole side was kind of paining me. It was a severe pain. I could pretty near bite a spike nail.

After Dr. Carlson came he took me to the hospital and I was cared for there by him. I remained there twelve days. I was confined wholly to my bed about eight days. Doctor took an X-ray picture. He set the shoulder. It pained me during that twelve days. It pained me when I drew my breath. I had to lie on my back. I was unable to lie on my right side. I can't now without it paining me. I couldn't sleep. Opiates were administered to relieve the pain.

My hospital bill was $71. The doctor's bill was $141.50.

I went home after I left the hospital. The bandage remained on my shoulder after I got home for about eight weeks. I was unable to do any work during that time.

It took about three weeks after the eight weeks before the bandage was removed before I could get my arm down. It must have been six or seven months before I could do any work after the injury. I am right-handed. It would pain me every time I would try to use it. These fingers, I couldn't straighten them out. I can't straighten them out now.

QUESTION: Now what is your time worth in the bottling company?

MR. MELVILLE: That is objected to for the reason it is calling for the conclusion of the witness.

THE COURT: Sustained.

[*Exception taken*]

THE COURT: What wages was he getting? Doesn't that tell the story?

MR. HALL: Well, he got a part of the profits; he wasn't paid wages.

THE COURT: Very well.

MADISON WILSON: I was drawing a salary there at the bottling works, $125 a month.

Yes, Mr. Thompson came to the hospital on one occasion. He came there the Sunday evening following. I presume it was his wife; there was a lady that came with him, and my daughter and my wife were in the room.

QUESTION: Did he say anything about this occurrence?
ANSWER: Yes, sir.
MR. MELVILLE: That is objected to as incompetent, irrelevant, and immaterial.
THE COURT: Well, Mr. Thompson being the defendant, the evidence is competent as to him, at any rate. I suppose it will have to be received. It isn't competent as to the defendant oil company, however.
[*Exception taken*]
MADISON WILSON: He said something about how the accident occurred. He said, "I don't think you know me, Mr. Wilson?" I looked at him and I says, "No." "Well," he says, "I am the dirty cur that hit you." He says, "Of course, I knew when I hit you, but I must have dragged you quite a distance."

[*Cross-examination by Mr. Melville*]

After I crossed De Witt street I went on the westerly side of Cook street toward the cigar store. I don't know the exact directions. McSorley's Cigar Store is about in the middle of the block up toward De Witt street. I stayed in there about five minutes and then started down Cook street toward Clark street. I went down Cook street then until I came to Stamison's Restaurant and then crossed Clark street and came to Luke's Cigar Store. That was where I was going to.

I went over to the sidewalk there. It was right at the edge of the curbing where I stepped off, on the curbing nearest the cigar store. Those paint lines were distinct that evening. I looked to the left before I stepped down, toward the direction of Cook street. From the Stamison corner I probably could—well, it would be about the middle of the block that I could see. I could look right up across the street. I could probably see the traffic there 100 feet or so beyond the Stamison corner. I can't say how far I could look from the point I stopped up Cook street. I don't remember seeing anybody up that street when I was there.

I didn't see any automobile on Cook street. I didn't see any lights of a car approaching there.

On my adverse examination I stated that I stayed at McSorley's Cigar Store until it stopped raining a little bit. That statement was true.

I said I waited there until it let up a little and then I started out, and while I was walking down it began raining harder.

I spoke to Ralph Ward as I walked down there. He was standing in the doorway of McSorley's Cigar Store. He is the chief of police of Jonesboro.

As I stepped off the curb in front of the James place, I walked there, walked fast, of course. When it is raining you wouldn't walk like you naturally walk. I didn't run any. I walked a little faster than ordinary. I looked again as I walked across the street to see whether there was any traffic coming down State street or Cook street. I looked when I stepped off the curb.

I think it was about the center of the street that I was hit. I didn't hear anything of an automobile immediately before that.

After I started across I looked straight ahead. The left of my body was struck by the car, the left hand side. When the car hit me it just threw me over onto the pavement and I hit on my shoulder. I am five feet three and one-half inches tall. The front of the car hit me. I don't know whether it was the fender or the front part of the car that hit me.

The car stopped about in front of the first entrance to the City Hall. On my adverse examination I was asked:

QUESTION: "Then you yourself couldn't say now, except from what somebody told you, as to where the car stopped?"

ANSWER: "Stopped around in front of the Robinson Hardware Store, around there." That was true.

QUESTION: "You walked a little faster than you ordinarily would?"

ANSWER: "No, sir, I wouldn't say that I walked any faster than I walk at any time."

I probably made that answer, and as near as I can remember I did make that answer.

QUESTION: "The rain that evening and just that particular moment didn't make any difference at all?"

ANSWER: "No. It would if I was walking a very long ways; I was only going across the street there."

I am one of the partners of the Wilson Products Company. Before the accident I was not working there every day. I was kind of a reserve man, when I was needed, a helper.

My salary wasn't stopped while I was laid up in the hospital.

I didn't tell Ira Thompson at the hospital in substance that I didn't blame anybody on account of the accident.

[*Redirect examination by Mr. Hall*]

Of course, I looked. Yes, I looked all the time. I told you before I stepped off the curbing and I looked up and down, right and left, and in front, and seen nothing, heard nothing; you naturally would have your eyes open.

My object was to get out of the rain as quickly as possible and get over to the cigar store.

JOHN S. LYONS, being duly sworn, testified as follows:

My name is John S. Lyons. I live in Jonesboro. I have lived here for sixteen years. My business is real estate. I am acquainted with Mr. Wilson and Ira Thompson. I am not related to either of the parties. I have no interest in any way in this law suit.

I walked on the south side of Cook street in the block where the Stamison Restaurant is located on November 6, going west. It was about 10 o'clock when I reached the Michel Jewelry Store. I started across the street toward the Stamison Restaurant.

I observed a car going west on Cook street as I was crossing. I was nearly half way across the street when I first saw the car, half way across Cook street, which is right at the east line of the intersection of Cook, State, and Clark streets. The car was about three-quarters way up the block and I was standing there about the center of the crossing. I did not continue across. I waited. It was coming so fast it startled me and I stopped. I did not take any chance of crossing the street.

I have ridden in automobiles and have observed the speed of motor vehicles before this. I am able to estimate approximately the speed of a motor vehicle. This car was going anywhere from twenty-five to thirty miles an hour.

It turned down State street after it passed me. Its speed was not changed. Shortly after it passed me I heard something, an impact.

I kept on going home across Clark street. When I got along by the Tommy

James place I saw this car. It was standing still at the time. It was out or a little below the entrance to the City Hall.

No horn was sounded or warning given by this car at or before the time that I heard this impact.

When they got him up on his feet I asked who it was and they said Madison Wilson, and I asked him who his family doctor was and he said Dr. Carlson, and so I immediately started for the cigar store to have someone call Dr. Carlson.

[*Cross-examination by Mr. Melville*]

On my former examination, I testified I didn't pay much attention to the rate of speed from the point where the car passed to the point where the car pulled up to the curb. I did pay attention after the car passed. What I refer to is that I didn't pay much attention to the speed of the car after the impact came. That is what I meant by that answer.

DR. HENRY CARLSON, being duly sworn, testified as follows:

My name is Henry Carlson. I live in Jonesboro. I am a physician and surgeon and licensed to practice in this state. I have practiced in Jonesboro a little over thirteen years. During that time I have been called on to treat fractures and dislocations of the shoulder and other bones of the body.

I am acquainted with Madison Wilson. I was called to attend him on the night of November 6. I examined him at the cigar store. He was in a sort of stupor and severe shock. At that time I just felt of his clothes and arms and through his clothes, and found that he had a crepitus in the right shoulder. Crepitus means a grating of the bones. We took him to the hospital. We bandaged him up and gave him an opiate for the pain and the next morning we took some X-ray pictures.

I think, as I remember, most of his pain he had down in his shoulder, terrible pain in the shoulder. He also had pain in the right knee.

When an X-ray was taken the following morning it disclosed he had a fracture of what is known as the surgical neck of the humerus. There was a fracture of the surgical neck of that bone just about two inches taken from the upper part of the head, that is, right up near the head of the bone and fastens onto the bone, and there was a transverse jagged fracture, with an apparent splitting of the upper fragment. I have brought the X-ray with me. [*X-ray marked Exhibit 4 and received. Stipulated that the X-ray may be withdrawn from the files and returned to the hospital.*]

During the time he was in the hospital he had a great deal of pain. I had to give heat to his arm and give opiates as necessary. For a man of his age, the big majority of them have pain for the rest of their lives off and on.

I made a recent examination of him the day before yesterday. He has got a retarded motion in this way. He hasn't complete motion in every direction. He can't get his hand back of his back there. For instance, in trying to get on a shirt, coat, or vest he requires help and he has weakness in his right hand. I believe that the weakness to grasp with his right hand is permanent.

[*Cross-examination by Mr. Melville*]

So far as the fracture is concerned, he had a satisfactory recovery.

It is my impression that Mr. Wilson now has pain. You find that out as a result of your manipulations. I would twist the arm a little. I don't think there is any injury to his hand. I think that is probably muscular, in the nerves around the shoulder joint. I think the weakening of the grip is due to the condition of the shoulder. Entirely so, I think. It shouldn't have any connection with the arm having been bandaged up and the hand not having been used at this time, just over a year.

RALPH WARD, being duly sworn, testified as follows:

My name is Ralph Ward. I live in Jonesboro. I am one of the police officers of the city. I was on duty the night of November 6. I remember Mr. Wilson having been struck by an automobile that night. Just prior to the time he was struck I was along the Jonesboro Loan and Trust Company on the north side of Cook street. I saw a Ford sports car pass at that time. I have seen cars driven, have observed their speed. My judgment is the car was going about 20 to 25 miles an hour. Shortly after the car passed I heard something. I heard a kind of impact, something striking. I was still standing in front of the Jonesboro Loan and Trust Company.

I saw Thompson later on that evening. I talked to him concerning the accident. He did not claim at that time it was Mr. Wilson's fault. He didn't say anything to the effect that Mr. Wilson stopped and started up again. I did not see Mr. Wilson at the scene of the accident. I saw him in the cigar store. He appeared kind of dazed. Thompson did not give any reason why he had not stopped the car sooner.

I probably observed the car until it proceeded to the center of the intersection. Its speed continued about the same as when it passed me.

[*Cross-examination by Mr. Melville*]

I watched that car because it is usually a custom for an officer to observe cars when they are going by. There was nothing particular about the speed as it was passing that made me watch it, nothing more than any other. I thought this car was going a little more than ordinary speed. I think that is another reason why I watched it. I thought if it would ever hit a person it would be dangerous.

I made a statement on the next day to Mr. Miles. I stated, "I estimated that the car was going somewhat more than fifteen miles an hour, but not a dangerous speed at that time of the night."

[*Plaintiff rests.*]

MR. MELVILLE: I made my request for a special verdict, didn't I?

THE COURT: Yes, sir, I have the special verdict prepared.

MR. THOMPSON, recalled by Mr. Melville, testified as follows:

I have lived in Jonesboro for about two years and a half. I have been working for two years for the Universal Oil Company. Last November I was living at 314 West Franklin street. That is west of the place where the collision happened—about five and one-half blocks west.

I was looking for a contractor when I left my home that evening. His name is Marquis. I went to look for him different places downtown. I left my car at the station. After I got through going around to these different places I went back to the station. It was raining at the time. The station closed at 10 o'clock. I took Keller home, the man who runs the station. I drove him to his home on East Martin street. I then went back to Cook street and came down Cook street toward the intersection of Cook street with State street.

As I came toward the intersection of Cook and State streets I could look down to a point in front of James' soft drink parlor and saw someone standing there. I could not say just where he was standing, within probably two or three feet from the edge of the sidewalk there. At that point Clark street comes in also from the right.

As I came to about the Stamison Restaurant corner I slowed up. I shut off the gas, I mean I reduced the supply of gas, I closed down the motor entirely.

I drove up to Mr. Wilson, close to him to see whether he would cross the street. I was going about eight miles an hour, and I thought he was going to give me the right of way, and I went on. I figured that I had the right of way because there was no stop sign. By halting and stopping I got the impression that he was giving me the right of way. When he stopped my car was in low gear. After I couldn't see him no more, on account of the side curtains, I felt an impact of him hitting the fender. When he hesitated I went on. I came over a little more. I gave her a little more gas to get the speed of the motor up, to throw it in high as you naturally would. I couldn't watch him all the time. When I saw he halted I looked straight ahead. I couldn't see him all the time because of the side curtains on that side. Between the fender and the lights struck him, the right hand ones.

After I felt the impact I stopped the car as soon as I could. After knowing that I hit somebody, in the excitement, I did not know what to do until I run down aways, I think about fifteen feet. I shut off the gas; that is all. I left my car in about the center of the street on the right hand side of the center, about five feet from the curb, I should judge. I stopped in front of the stairway leading up over the Robinson Hardware Store. It is only about fifteen or twenty feet figuring by the white lines in the middle of the street. You can't stop a car in any more than that unless you apply your brakes, as I told you I didn't do. I did not know at that time that Mr. Wilson had come in contact, that he was being dragged along by the car.

From the time I first saw Mr. Wilson until I hit him I watched him continually. During that time he was starting across State street toward the cigar store that has been referred to. He didn't walk very fast. He did not continue to walk all the way. He stopped about four or five feet from the curb. At that time I was about ten feet from him. After that I gave it more gas. It was not raining hard before the accident, drizzling.

[*Cross-examination by Mr. Hall*]

I didn't put my car in low in front of the Stamison Restaurant; it was about ten or fifteen feet before I hit Mr. Wilson that I put it in low; it serves as a pretty efficient brake. You can't stop a car at eight miles an hour in a foot; five feet would be the most. In low, as I went over the intersection where Mr. Wilson was hit, I could have employed the customary way of stopping it at any time. I did not make any attempt to stop it in that manner. It was raining hard enough so that it obscured my vision.

[Defendant rests.]

SUMMATION

Some civil cases are submitted to the jury without argument. In some instances, argument is restricted to certain issues. The party which has the burden of proof opens and closes in the absence of contrary statutory provisions. In one state the practice is for the plaintiff to commence the argument and also close it, if he wishes. In another state the defendant makes his argument first and is followed by the plaintiff. Where the plaintiff has the right to commence and close, he may, in some instances, waive the right to commence; often this is a matter of trial tactics.

The time allowed for the summations is in the discretion of the judge and depends upon the volume of evidence and the complexity of the issues. When, for example, there have been four days of evidence the time allocated for argument is one day. When more than one attorney for the same party is involved in a case the attorneys often divide the time between them. The number of parties also is a factor in the division of time.

The argument usually recapitulates the testimony of the individual witnesses and emphasizes the salient points with the view to maximizing or minimizing the weight of such testimony. The attorneys sometimes read from the testimony and evaluate it. Prejudicial statements are seldom made in arguments by attorneys in civil cases, but in criminal cases prejudicial statements are sometimes the ground for reversible error.

INSTRUCTION OF THE JURY

You will recall the paragraph on page 204 which was headed "Rule × Facts = Judgment." This paragraph explained that the judge determines the rights and duties of the parties by applying principles of law to the facts presented at the trial. After the attorneys have completed their argument, the judge *instructs,* or *charges,* the jury as to the law of the case. The jury's verdict must be within the context of the law as the judge states it.

Instructions normally include a statement as to which party has the burden of proof and what the law says are the rights and duties of the parties. The latter statement usually requires a definition of some of the words and phrases of the law (e.g., "ordinary care"). In some cases the instructions state the criteria for awarding damages if the jury should find for the plaintiff.

Attorneys in most jurisdictions are required to submit to the judge and to the adverse attorney a typewritten copy of the instructions they request at the beginning of the trial. In federal practice, instructions may be submitted "at the close of evidence or earlier if the court directs." When questions of law are developed in evidence but were not disclosed by the pleadings, additional requested instructions may be given to the judge at a later stage of the trial.

Each attorney drafts instructions which are in accord with his theory of the case and which he deems favorable to his side. He cites authorities to which the judge may refer. The judge may adopt the proposed instructions of one party and reject those of the other or he may amend either set. The record must show which instructions he rejected; for, on appeal, the defeated party may try to show that the jury was improperly instructed. The judge usually informs the attorneys of the instructions he will give before the attorneys begin their summation.

The judge reads his instructions to the jury. In the majority of states, the jury in a civil case may take a copy of the written instructions into the jury room; one state prohibits this practice, and some states have no law on the subject. When the jury is not permitted to have a copy of the instructions, it sometimes returns to the courtroom to ask the judge to read again certain parts of the instructions.

In a few jurisdictions the judge may comment on the evidence, but most judges, when permitted by statute, prefer not to do so.

The judge's instructions in the Madison Wilson *vs.* Universal Oil Company and Ira Thompson case are reproduced below on pages 263–266.

THE VERDICT[8]

After the judge has charged the jury, the jurors go to the jury room. In some jurisdictions the first juror selected is ex officio the *foreman;* in others the foreman is elected by the jurors as their first order of business in the jury room. The foreman is the chairman of the jury during its deliberations. He is also the jury's spokesman in that he signs the verdict, speaks for the jury when communicating with the judge, and announces the verdict when it is returned orally in open court. In most jurisdictions the jury is supplied with a blank printed verdict form.

In more than one-half of the states and in federal courts, the jury in a civil action must return a unanimous verdict; in other states the requirement is a three-fourths or a five-sixths majority. When the jurors, after a considerable time, have not been able to reach a verdict the bailiff escorts them into the courtroom and the foreman so reports. The judge may ask them how they stand *numerically* or how many ballots they have taken. He may then ask them to return to the jury room to try again. Whenever the judge believes that the jurors are deadlocked he discharges them and the case may be set for retrial.

This is not the same as a *mistrial.* A mistrial is a negatived trial which is due to an irregularity in the proceedings, such as misconduct of a juror or of a party at some stage of the proceedings. After a mistrial has been declared the case is set for retrial.

[8] A corruption of *verum dictum,* literally, "truly said."

Mistrial Declared in Lung Cancer Case

A judge declared a mistrial yesterday in a lung cancer case before the jury was selected.

Mrs. Bernard Mayfield is suing the Gilbey Tobacco Co. for $779,000, charging her husband's death resulted from his smoking two packs of cigarettes a day.

After an investigator for the plaintiff informed U.S. District Court Judge Paul Bingham that relatives of prospective jurors had been questioned about the prospective jurors' smoking habits, the judge declared the mistrial.

Judge Bingham said the case could not be tried by the panel because of the atmosphere created by the questioning.

Frank January, attorney for the plaintiff, announced he would request a new trial.

Judge Bingham interrupted proceedings to state that he had received information that a prospective juror had been telephoned by a person claiming to be making a cigarette survey for the state university.

Seven of the 11 prospective jurors in the jury box and 13 others on the panel raised their hands when the judge asked if they had received similar calls.

Later some of the prospective jurors said some of their relatives had been asked on the telephone if they smoked, what brand, and if it was a filter type cigarette.

Mrs. Mayfield's husband died last October after an operation for removal of cancerous vocal cords.

After a verdict has been reached, the jurors return to the courtroom and take their places in the jury box. The foreman hands the verdict to the judge or the clerk and the clerk reads it aloud. The clerk or the judge asks the jury if such is their verdict. On the demand of one of the parties, the jury may be *polled*. The clerk, addressing each of the jurors separately, asks whether the verdict as read correctly expresses his (or her) determination.

In some situations a jury may return a *sealed verdict*. This usually happens when the case is given to the jury late in the day. The jurors, after reaching their verdict, write it out, sign it, place it in an envelope, hand the sealed envelope to the bailiff, and go home. At the opening of court next day the jurors assemble. The envelope is opened and the verdict is read into the record.

In reaching its verdict, the jury in a civil case decides by a *preponderance of the evidence* whether or not the party with the burden of proof has prevailed. There is a different criterion in a criminal action, as will be explained on page 357.

In many civil cases, the jury returns a *general* verdict; that is, it "finds for the plaintiff" or "finds for the defendant." In some situations in certain jurisdictions, the judge may, on request of a party, require the jury to answer certain questions of ultimate fact as well as to return a general verdict. The purpose of requiring the special findings is to test the validity of the general verdict; that is, to ascertain whether or not the general verdict is consistent with the facts. When the general verdict is inconsistent with the facts, the findings of fact control the verdict.

Special Verdict

A *special* verdict is a finding of facts *only*. The jury answers a set of questions but does *not* find for either of the parties. The judge, on the basis of the special verdict, renders judgment for one of the parties. The purpose of a special verdict is to prevent the jury from disregarding the legal rules in the judge's instructions as they could do in reaching a general verdict.

Here are some questions answered unanimously by a jury in a case in which a man sued a tobacco company after he had lost one lung in a cancer operation. Note that the jury decided that cigarette smoking was one of the causes of lung cancer but that there was no breach of warranty by the tobacco company.

1. Was the smoking of Chesterfield cigarettes by the plaintiff the cause or one of the causes of cancer in Pritchard's right lung? *Yes,* 12.

2. Is the defendant chargeable with negligence which is the proximate cause of the plaintiff's injury? *No,* 12.

3. Is the plaintiff chargeable with negligence which contributed in any degree to his injury? *None,* 12.

4. Did the defendant make any express warranty upon which the plaintiff relied and by which he was induced to purchase Chesterfield cigarettes? *No,* 12.

5. If the defendant is liable, what is the total amount of damages? *None,* 12.

We have referred previously to the doctrine of "contributory negligence,"[9] which is that a defendant in certain tort actions may plead as an affirmative defense that the negligence of the plaintiff was a contributing proximate cause of the injury. A jury in a special verdict sometimes finds both that the defendant's want of ordinary care was the proximate cause of an injury and that the plaintiff contributed to produce the injury. The latter finding usually nullifies the former. Only a few states have adopted the doctrine of "comparative negligence," which is a doctrine of admiralty law. This doctrine requires that the blame for an accident may be apportioned. For example, a plaintiff is awarded only that part of the damage that the defendant is responsible for (e.g., 60 per cent).

INSTRUCTIONS IN WILSON vs. UNIVERSAL OIL CO. ET AL.

Here are the judge's instructions in the Madison Wilson *vs.* Universal Oil Company and Ira Thompson case. You will need to comprehend them in preparation for an exercise that is to be assigned.

Ladies and gentlemen of the jury:
As you understand, this case is to be submitted to you on what is called a special verdict. That is, certain questions covering the controversial issues of fact in the case are to be submitted to you for answer.
It is for you, the jury, to determine the facts according to the evidence, and then it will be for me, as the judge, to direct judgment according to the law on the facts that you find.
The questions are so framed that each except that as to damages is to be answered by "Yes" or "No."
The burden is on the party contending for the affirmative of a question to satisfy you of the affirmative to a reasonable certainty by a preponderance of the evidence. That is, answer "Yes" if you are satisfied to a reasonable certainty by a preponderance of the evidence that the fact is as expressed by that answer, and if you are not so satisfied you will answer "No."
I will now read *Question 1:* As he approached the place of collision did Mr. Thompson fail to use ordinary care? (*a*) In respect to speed? (*b*) In respect to keeping a lookout? (*c*) In respect to sounding his horn? (*d*) In respect to controlling his car?
Speaking generally, ordinary care is such care as persons of ordinary care and prudence ordinarily exercise under like circumstances, such care as the great mass of men ordinarily exercise under like circumstances.
The violation of a statute regulating the use of automobiles on the highways constitutes a want of ordinary care.
In respect to part *a* of Question 1, I will instruct you that a statute provides that no person shall drive an automobile on the streets of a city faster than 15 miles an hour, or recklessly or faster than is reasonable and proper having regard to the width, traffic and use of the streets, or so as to endanger the life, limb, or property of any person; that on approaching a street inter-

[9] P. 230.

section or when the view is for any cause obstructed, as by rain, the speed shall be reduced to such a rate as will tend to avoid danger of accident.

And irrespective of statutory regulations, ordinary care requires that such rate of speed shall be maintained that the driver can stop his car within the distance that he can see.

In connection with part *b* of the first question, I will instruct you that one driving on a highway is required to keep such a lookout ahead and at the immediate sides of his line of travel as is reasonably necessary for the protection of persons in or likely to come into his line of travel who are themselves exercising ordinary care.

In connection with part *c* of Question 1, I will instruct you that the statute provides that an automobile shall be equipped with a horn or other signalling device. There is no statute requiring the horn to be sounded on approaching a crossing or a person. But in view of the statute referred to and the manifest purpose of it, it is necessary to use the horn whenever its use is reasonably necessary for the protection of persons in a situation of danger. The object of the horn is that it may be used as a warning; and it should be used as such when the circumstances are such as to make it reasonably apparent that a person is ignorant of the approach of the car and that such use will serve to avert collision or other injury to such person.

In connection with part *d* of Question 1, I will say that the question is put to direct your attention to whether Mr. Thompson used ordinary care in respect to stopping his car or turning it in order to avoid collision with Mr. Wilson. There are no statutory regulations in respect to this matter. The conduct of Mr. Thompson is to be measured by the degree of care ordinarily exercised by the great mass of men in similar circumstances. When one is suddenly confronted with a situation of danger which is not himself at fault in creating, so that he has no time for deliberation but must act on the spur of the moment, he is not held to that course which in retrospect may appear would have avoided or mitigated injury. If in such case he exercises his judgment and acts upon it, he is not chargeable with want of ordinary care, although it appears that had he done differently the injury would have been prevented.

A want of ordinary care on Mr. Thompson's part is not to be inferred from the fact that a collision occurred. The fact in that regard must be determined from the evidence, and the circumstances disclosed by it.

In considering whether the defendant was wanting in ordinary care for not stopping his car or turning it to avoid collision, you will particularly bear in mind whether Mr. Wilson stopped or so slackened speed as to lead Mr. Thompson reasonably to infer that he was yielding the right of way. Mr. Thompson and Mr. Wilson, the one as a pedestrian and the other with an automobile, had equal rights on the public streets and each was bound to respect the rights of the other and to govern his movements accordingly with ordinary care.

Question 2: If to *a, b, c,* and *d* or any one of them you answer "Yes," answer 2. Was the want of ordinary care thus found the proximate cause of the collision?

The proximate cause of an injury is the efficient cause, that which produces the injury as a natural and probable result under circumstances such that a person of ordinary intelligence and prudence ought reasonably to foresee that some injury to another might naturally and probably result.

Question 3: Was there any want of ordinary care on the part of the plaintiff that proximately contributed to produce the collision?

Ordinary care has already been defined. By proximately contributing is meant so contributing that the collision resulted naturally from the want of ordinary care involved operating as a contributing cause, under circumstances such that a person of ordinary intelligence and prudence ought reasonably to foresee that the want of ordinary care involved might naturally and probably contribute to produce some injury. If you find that there was any want of ordinary care, however slight, on Mr. Wilson's part that proximately contributed to produce the collision, you will answer the question "Yes."

Pedestrians may not heedlessly cross streets without taking the least precaution to discover and avoid approaching automobiles. They are not required, as a matter of law, to keep a constant lookout to the left as they approach the middle of the street. Nor having looked once are they absolved, as a matter of law, from looking again.

If a person looks once and no automobile is in sight that would reach him before he reached the center of the street, if it were travelling at a lawful rate of speed, he is not required to look again unless an approaching automobile be called to his attention by his sense of hearing or by observation otherwise.

One may rightly assume that others will use ordinary care in approaching and to rely upon that assumption until the contrary appears or ought to have been known.

Question 4: Was Mr. Thompson acting in the line of his duty as an employee of the defendant oil company at the time of the collision?

You will determine this question from all the evidence in the case respecting the duties, authority and course of conduct of Thompson so far as the latter appears to have been known to the company.

Question 5: In case the court awards plaintiff judgment upon your verdict, at what sum do you assess his damages?

In answer to this question you will fix the sum that will in your judgment fairly and reasonably compensate the plaintiff for all injuries resulting to him from the collision.

The items to consider and allow for are the hospital and physician's bills for the care of his injuries; the pain and suffering that have resulted up to this time, and such, if any, as he will suffer in the future from the injuries at the time received; such inconvenience as has or will be caused by restricted movement, if any you find has resulted from the injury to his shoulder; and such limitations of lines of work, if any you find, as has resulted from the injury to his shoulder.

In fixing damages you will be fair and just and bear in mind that compensation for such injuries as the preponderance of the evidence satisfies you to a reasonable certainty the plaintiff actually has sustained, or actually will sustain in the future, as a result of the collision, is the idea that must control your assessment.

You are the sole judges of the credibility of each and every witness sworn upon the trial as well as of the weight and effect of the evidence as a whole.

It takes only five-sixths of the jury to reach a verdict in a civil case. So as ten or more of you agree you will return your verdict. It is necessary, however, that at least ten and the same ten shall agree to all the answers in order that the answers made shall constitute a verdict.

It follows that when at least ten, and the same ten, have agreed upon all the answers, your foreman will sign the verdict so agreed upon and you will return it into court.

For class discussion: Judge Jerome Frank has written that jurors often do not understand the judge's instructions; that they have to determine facts under conditions which do not permit of clear thinking (e.g., listening to uninteresting witnesses in complex actions about somebody else's quarrel, and sometimes in an emotional atmosphere); and that their minds wander to a consideration of their own affairs so that—no matter how well equipped they are to think about their own affairs—they cannot make valid decisions under courtroom conditions. For these reasons, he concludes that the facts in civil cases should be determined by the judge as is almost the universal practice in England. (*Courts on Trial* [Princeton, N.J., 1949], pp. 142–43.) Do you agree or disagree?

MOTIONS DURING TRIAL

In the course of a trial, one of the parties may contest the sufficiency of the opponent's evidence as a *matter of law*. The law requires that the party with the burden of proof present substantial evidence to make out a *prima facie* cause of action. A prima facie case is one that is strong enough to succeed unless rebutted. When the attorney for the adverse party believes that there is an insufficiency of evidence to establish a prima facie case he requests the judge to render judgment for him.

At common law whenever the defendant wished to make such a motion it was called *demurrer to the evidence*. That term is used today in only a few jurisdictions. It has been succeeded by the motion for *nonsuit* and the motion for a *directed verdict*. It should be noted that such motions attack the sufficiency of evidence, not the pleading; they are, therefore, different from demurrer,[10] which asserts that the plaintiff's allegations in his complaint do not constitute a cause of action. The motions for nonsuit and directed verdict refer to the material variance between the allegations in the pleading and the proof to support them.

Nonsuit

The motion for nonsuit is made by the *defendant* after the plaintiff has rested his case; and in a few instances after the plaintiff's opening state-

[10] Discussed at pp. 228–229.

ment. The defendant concedes the truth of the plaintiff's evidence but denies, as a matter of law, that the evidence supports the plaintiff's case. An example: a plaintiff suing an insurance company to collect on a permanent disability policy fails to establish a prima facie case that the injury has wholly and permanently prevented him from engaging in any employment for wages or profit, as he alleged in his complaint. A second example: a plaintiff suing a physician for malpractice fails to prove by expert witnesses that the physician did not exercise the reasonable care and skill that is usually exercised by physicians and surgeons of good standing.

In some jurisdictions, when the motion for nonsuit is granted it operates as an adjudication on the merits in favor of the defendant, but in other jurisdictions it is not a bar to a new action.

In some jurisdictions the motion is called an "involuntary" nonsuit to distinguish it from a "voluntary" nonsuit which results from the failure of the plaintiff to follow up his suit or from absenting himself from a proceeding at a set time.

Ex-student Is Loser In Suit vs. College

Crescent College was granted a nonsuit yesterday in a $50,000 damage suit against it by a former student.

Henry Crowninshield was suing the college for loss of his left eye. He testified yesterday that on last May 4 some unidentified person discharged a BB gun on the campus and the shot struck him in the eye.

Superior Court Judge Eugene Quillen ruled that Crowninshield had failed to prove any negligence on the part of the board of trustees of the college.

Directed Verdict

The motion for a directed verdict operates in the same way as does a motion for nonsuit. However, it is made at the close of the defendant's evidence and may be made by *either* party.

In some jurisdictions, when the judge grants the motion, he directs the jury to retire to the jury room and sign the verdict for the party he specifies. This is a mere formality. In other jurisdictions the judge simply renders a judgment for the moving party without the formality of a jury verdict.

Attorneys frequently move for nonsuit or a directed verdict perfunctorily with little expectation that the motion will be granted; for the judge grants the motion only when he believes that the opponent's evidence is insufficient to support a verdict in his favor after giving to the opponent's evidence all the value to which it is legally entitled.

MOTIONS AFTER VERDICT

The attorney for the losing party sometimes makes three motions alternatively after the verdict but before entry of judgment. These are: (1) a motion for *judgment notwithstanding the verdict* (*non obstante veredicto*), (2) a motion to *set aside the verdict* and grant a *new trial,* and (3) a motion for *reduction of damages.* Thus, the judge may deny the first motion and grant the second or deny the first two motions and grant the third.

In most jurisdictions the motion for judgment notwithstanding the verdict is granted only after the judge has previously denied a motion for a directed verdict. Thus the judge denies the motion for a directed verdict at the close of the defendant's case and submits the case to the jury subject to his later determination of the questions of law that had been raised on the motion for a directed verdict.

Court Annuls Jury's Verdict

Superior Judge H. T. Southwood filed a memorandum opinion yesterday saying he plans to set aside a $25,000 damage award made to Alphonso Middlecoff May 10.

Judge Southwood said he will grant the motion by the defendant, Dr. W. R. Keller, a physician, for a judgment notwithstanding the verdict of the jury which heard the case.

In the trial Middlecoff contended Dr. Keller's negligence in treating him when he was a patient at St. John's hospital with two broken legs resulted in the amputation of one leg near the knee.

At the time the verdict was returned Judge Southwood scolded the members of the jury before discharging them.

The motion to set aside the verdict is coupled with the *motion for a new trial.* The judge grants the motion on the ground that (1) he had made erroneous rulings or had given erroneous instructions to the jury adverse to the losing party or (2) the verdict or the findings of fact are against the evidence or the weight of the evidence. On the second ground this often means that the jury has disregarded the judge's instructions. In some civil actions an additional ground is the discovery of new evidence favorable to the defeated party. The motion operates as a stay until the judge has had time to consider the arguments of both sides. Other grounds for granting a new trial are irregularity in the proceedings, misconduct of the jury, surprise*, and excessive damages.

Judge Voids Verdict Based On $1 a Reader

A $40,000 libel verdict against the Daily Times was set aside yesterday by Superior Court Judge H. T. Southwood and a new trial ordered.

Judge Southwood ruled that the verdict was so completely inconsistent with the evidence that it "unmistakably indicated" it was intended to punish the newspaper for its stand in the local school situation.

He said he could find no connection between the evidence presented and the verdict reached by the jury.

A jury last week found against the newspaper after deliberating 23 hours. It took them only 20 minutes to reach the $40,000 figure. They awarded Thomas Kroll, former school superintendent, a dollar for each Times reader.

The $40,000 figure was reached by taking the number of papers printed and multiplying it by 3.5, the average number of persons in a family.

Judge Southwood criticized the method of fixing damages. He accepted the defense argument that the jury must take into consideration the damage sustained and the measure of that damage.

The verdict must not be based on chance, lot or mathematical formula, he ruled.

"I think it has been clearly shown that the verdict is so excessive as to unmistakably indicate it was reached as the result of passion and prejudice,"

Judge Southwood said. "This court holds that substantial justice has not been done."

When excessive damages has been a ground for granting a new trial the judge rules alternatively that, if the prevailing party does not consent in writing, to damages of a certain amount, he will grant a new trial. When such consent is given the verdict is not set aside but amended.

Doctor Gets Damages Cut

A $230,000 damage verdict for malpractice against a local physician was reduced to $87,500 yesterday in Superior court.

A jury rendered the original award last month in favor of J. D. Brewer, 2939 14th avenue.

The jurors acted on his suit against Dr. Davis Lester, an orthopedist of 540 Graham street, whom Brewer accused of negligence.

Brewer said he was permanently crippled because the physician had failed to detect his broken hip and prescribe proper treatment.

After the jury verdict Superior Judge H. T. Southwood ruled that he would grant a new trial on the ground of "insufficiency of the evidence to justify the verdict" unless Brewer abandoned his claim to $87,500.

The customary procedure on a motion for a new trial is for the defeated party to file the motion with notice to the adversary. After the filing of affidavits and counteraffidavits, a hearing is held by the judge who had presided at the trial.

Slander Suit to Be Retried, Judge Rules

Retrial of a slander suit against the Second National Bank was granted yesterday by Judge Walton Reed in circuit court.

A jury last week awarded $125,000 damages to Fred James, a former employee of the bank. He charged that bank officials had defamed him after he had been discharged for union activity.

The application for a new trial was based on two grounds. One was that Harry Davis, a juror, had stated that he was not a member of a union and had had no trouble with employers. An affidavit offered by the bank alleged Davis was a member of a union and had been in controversy with the management of Central Utilities, Inc.

The second ground was that the jury had awarded James $65,000 special damages as "prospective earnings." The court ruled yesterday that special damages can only be based on earnings already lost.

Exercise: Write a 450-word news story for a morning newspaper reporting the testimony, verdict, and judgment in the Wilson *vs.* Universal Oil Company and Thompson case. Even though you report the testimony of some witnesses very briefly, do not omit the testimony of any except Stanley Sanders. Make the following assumptions: (1) that the trial was completed, the verdict returned, and judgment rendered on the same day; (2) that the jurors' answers to the questions on the special verdict were as follows:

1*a*. Yes, 12
1*b*. Yes, 12
1*c*. Yes, 12
1*d*. Yes, 12
2. Yes, 12
3. Yes, 12
4. Yes, 12
5. $3,500 plus hospital and the doctor's bills.

(3) that the judge denied the defendant's motion for a directed verdict made before the case went to the jury; (4) that the judge granted the defendant's motion for a judgment notwithstanding the verdict.

For class discussion: In your opinion, should the jury have answered "Yes" to Question 3?

SATISFYING THE JUDGMENT

A money judgment against a defeated party is satisfied by the voluntary payment of the amount to the clerk of the court. Until the judgment has been satisfied the defeated party is a *judgment debtor*. The judgment is customarily enforced by the issuance by the clerk of a *writ of execution*. The writ is directed to the sheriff (or United States marshal) commanding him to levy against the personal property and, if necessary, the real property of the judgment debtor and to sell it to satisfy (or partially satisfy) the amount of the judgment. Supplemental proceedings may be instituted by the judgment creditor to "discover" the assets of the judgment debtor.

Some types of property are exempt from execution. In most states these are: the judgment debtor's homestead up to a certain appraised value (e.g., $12,000 for a head of a family); necessary furniture, wearing apparel, and fuel; and tools with which the judgment debtor earns a living (e.g., farming implements and livestock up to a certain value, artisan's tools, and a fisherman's boat and nets).

"Dream Mansion" Sold for $49,000 At Sheriff's Sale

The $337,000 "dream house" of gambler Mike Pisano was sold at auction today—for $49,000.

The high bidder was Kenneth Burke, industrial relations manager for the Mowo Corporation.

A throng of 250 looked on as Meredith Stamps, who heads the civil department in the sheriff's office, opened the auction at the main entrance to the county courthouse.

In all, there were six bidders and 16 separate offers for the three-year-old mansion at 5150 Mayfield drive.

The proceeds of the sale will go to William Holguin, the contractor who built the house. Holguin's judgment against Pisano was for $110,000.

Technically, the sheriff's deputy said, Pisano has the right to repurchase the house within one year from the date of sale provided he pays the auction price, the taxes, and the balance owing to Holguin. Pisano may also continue to live in the house for one year.

Other proceedings to enforce judgment may be brought against a third party (e.g., garnishment) and against the judgment debtor, such as civil arrest, receivership, and civil contempt (e.g., after an alimony decree).

For class discussion: What is wrong idiomatically with these sentences: (*a*) "At the opening of the trial, attorney Bruce Campbell made a motion for a continuance." (*b*) "The complaint holds that the defendant negotiated a note on the third day of March"?

CHAPTER *19*

Law Enforcement Agents

Since World War II crime has increased four times more than has the population. This fact has caused an expansion of the agencies that enforce the criminal law. Since a great majority of the population lives in urban communities, the main agency is the local police department. However, many states have highway patrol or state police departments, and the federal government stations various types of criminal investigators in certain communities. Counties also have expanded their law enforcement activities in the sheriff's office or the office of county police. The states also have special liquor and narcotics agents.

Most police reporters, as soon as they go on duty, have the task of what is known in some cities as "calling the box." This means that they telephone for information to the district police stations, the sheriff's office, the state highway patrol, the United States Coast Guard, the receiving hospitals, and, in some instances, to the F.B.I., the coroner, and fire stations. Most newspapers have a man on both the day beat and the night beat regardless of which cycle in which the newspaper is published.

LOCAL POLICE ORGANIZATION

A city's police organization is generally responsible to a civilian board variously known as the Board of Public Safety, the Board of Police and Fire Commissioners, or the Police Commission. The responsible uniformed official is usually called the chief of police. Although the organization of no two police departments is quite the same, the following are the typical divisions with which the newspaper reporter is in contact:

>Communications Bureau
>Identification Bureau
>Record Bureau
>Bureau of Missing Persons

Juvenile Aid Bureau
Bureau of Criminology
Vice Bureau
Traffic Bureau
Detective Bureau

The last two bureaus supply the most interesting news, although the others are important to the reporter when he needs certain kinds of information.

The *Traffic Bureau* has a number of policemen assigned to traffic control, to traffic law enforcement, and to accident investigation. Members of the Accident Prevention Detail investigate nearly every accident call sent over the police two-way radio. They try to reach a wreck within a few minutes after receiving the call to investigate the cause and to gather necessary information for possible citations or arrests or for later civil court actions. The reports they turn in usually include statements of the persons who are involved in the accident. They carry in their cars cameras, measuring devices, and first-aid kits. This detail also includes a hit-run squad. The squad hastens to accidents which have been reported as hit-run to gather evidence; sometimes a driver has been arrested and charged with hit-run driving six months after the accident happened.

Fender Skirt Leads To Hit-Run Driver

Tracing of a dislodged fender skirt to Hiram Graves, 1188 Madison street, led to his arrest yesterday on a hit-run charge.

Graves is charged with running into a parked car last Sunday night and critically injuring Ernest James, a pedestrian.

He left a fender skirt from which Officer Francis Donohue identified the make and year of the car. Visiting local auto dealers, Officer Donohue found the fender skirt had been sold to the Olympic Garage. There he found Graves' car being repaired.

The *Detective Bureau* is the source of the most interesting news. In a large city it is usually divided into about a dozen details. Usually these are:

Robbery Detail
Burglary Detail

Homicide Detail
Bunko and Pickpocket Detail
Pawnshop Detail
Auto Theft Detail
Bank and Check Detail
Hotel Detail
Stock and Bond Detail
General Assignment Detail

POLICE RECORDS

The names of police records are not the same in all cities, but they have the same purposes. Records, for example, are made of all *complaints* received and of all arrests made. The complaint sheet records *incidents* reported by radio, call-box, and private telephone by operating units and private citizens. The incidents are mainly burglaries, suicides, and traffic accidents. This sheet has various names, such as *24-hour sheet*.

The *arrest book* (also called "arrest cards," "arrest sheets") records who was arrested, when, where, why, and by whom. It is sometimes called *prison book* or *blotter*.

Bulletins are facts sent by teletype to district stations and to other "points" (i.e., cities, highway patrol stations, etc.) for the information of those who receive them. A teletype in police headquarters also receives similar bulletins. Although these records carry bare details, they indicate the specific officers who can supply additional details.

Other records are identification records and reports about crimes under investigation. The newspaper reporter does not need to refer to the former and is often denied access to the latter.

All of these are central headquarters records. District stations have somewhat similar records (e.g., arrest cards and complaint forms), some of which are transferred to the central headquarters when the prisoner is taken there. All of these are usually open to inspection by the reporter, but some of them, such as the report of a homicide detail detective to his superior about a case he is investigating, are not; reporters seek this kind of information from the chief of detectives or from other detectives, who may or may not tell them every fact they know.

To understand records, reporters must know some of the codes that are used. The two-way radio, for example, reports to the Communications Division such occurrences as "501" (drunk in street), "511" (attempted suicide), "911" (personal injury), or "2000" (prison break). The offenses for which prisoners are booked are frequently designated by a particular section of the penal code, such as "sec. 2180" (burglary).

The matter found in the usual police records is generally privileged, but an interview with a policeman, in most states, is not privileged.

HOW THE POLICE WORK

In investigating crimes by professional criminals the police rely to a great extent on the information supplied by what the underworld calls "stool pigeons." These are ex-convicts who fear being returned to prison, hoodlums who have been double-crossed or who want to eliminate a rival, petty criminals attracted by a reward, and women scorned by a former lover.

The police also have a *modus operandi* file of the criminal history of those who have been arrested. A criminal tends to use the same methods repeatedly in his criminal activities. He employs the same kind of tool for burglary, enters the same type of premises, steals the same kinds of articles, and operates at the same time of day or night. Some known criminals also have idiosyncrasies, such as gum chewing, and peculiarities of speech and manner that identify them. Fingerprint, name-index, and photographic files are also kept.

Tedious investigation is often required for the solution of a crime. When there are no eyewitnesses, detectives sometimes have to interrogate a great many persons, such as taxi drivers, and visit a great many places, such as pawnshops, repair shops, laundries, cleaning establishments, and rooming houses. They also have to examine a great many criminal records and photographs.

They sometimes start with just one or two physical facts, or clues. In the case of the murder of a woman who ran a rooming house there were no eyewitnesses, and the detectives began their investigation with a single fact: a stub was missing from the landlady's receipt book. Upon learning that she could not write, and that a certain roomer always filled in the receipts for her, they telephoned this man, who was in a distant state on a vacation. He mentioned having made out a receipt to a "Bill Stanford." The records of the Identification Division showed that a youth named William Stanford had been convicted of armed robbery and had escaped from the detention home. With a photograph of the youth, the detectives visited numerous rooming houses in the district. They found three places at which he had formerly stayed. They surrounded one of the places and when the youth returned next day they caught him. In his pocket was the missing stub from the receipt book. He confessed to the murder.

The reporting of clues which are connected with the personal relations of the principals—that is to say, clues which point to a motive for committing the crime—requires more skill than mere reporting of physical clues. This, of course, is true not only because such evidence is not objective, but because the reporter cannot publish such information except at the peril of committing libel and of casting suspicion on innocent persons.

Scientific devices are also used. Most large city police departments and all state police departments, as well as the F.B.I., make considerable use of crime laboratories for the analysis of blood stains, firearms, bullets, footprints, handwriting, soil, hair, fibers, and wood.

WORKING WITH THE POLICE

In most large cities both the police and the reporters have learned that it pays to cooperate—that each has his own job to do. The major exceptions are in small cities and in rural sheriffs' offices. The New York city police department distributes to policemen a *Manual of Procedure* which contains a fairly long section on "Public Relations." Three of the numbered paragraphs are as follows:

> 20. The public press performs a service for the public, the importance of which should be clearly understood by police officers. It is the function of the press to keep the public informed on matters of public interest, including the activities of departments, officials, and employees of the city government.
> 21. While police officers must exercise discretion with respect to information of a nature that cannot and should not be divulged it is equally important to promptly release to representatives of the press such information as is permissible.
> 22. Cooperation with accredited representatives of the press and other accredited agencies of publication is extremely important in promoting good public relations. A cooperative attitude, and a courteous explanation when necessary, will usually result in a more desirable presentation of the facts from the police viewpoint.[1]

O. M. Wilson's standard volume *Police Administration*[2] warns policemen against attempting to conceal departmental weaknesses or the derelictions of individual policemen. He also advises that newspaper reporters should have access to the daily bulletins and that they should be assisted in their gathering of facts "rapidly, accurately, completely and promptly" after the facts become known to the police.

To Print or Not to Print?

In the search for criminals, newspapers are frequently useful because they print descriptions of suspects, of material witnesses, of automobiles, and of instruments, and these are seen or read by many persons who afterward identify them and report to the police. On the other hand, newspapers

---

[1] J. K. Pope, *Police-Press Relations* (Fresno, California, 1954), p. 217.
[2] (New York, 1950), pp. 415 ff.

sometimes interfere with crime detection by informing criminals of the plans made to catch them. One newspaper, for example, announced the direction in which the police were searching for a criminal by reporting that policemen were watching a motor launch at a certain pier with the expectation that the criminals would return to get it. The reporter sometimes thoughtlessly assists the criminal by mentioning certain details which the police want to suppress. When a newspaper published that the criminal had dropped his key ring at the scene of a theft it warned the thief that the police would be able to identify him; and when a newspaper published that a burglar, who had killed a woman, stole her wrist watch it warned him not to take the watch to a pawnshop.

In a few instances newspapers themselves try to capture criminals. Considering the great improvement in police methods and personnel which have come about in urban communities in recent years, newspapers are almost never justified in engaging in such activities.

The newspaper reporter is sometimes requested by a police officer or by someone else to suppress a news story—because "the news may kill the boy's father." The correct position for the reporter to take is that his city editor, not he, must decide the question. In a competitive situation one newspaper always runs the risk of being "scooped" by its rival; in a noncompetitive situation as well as in the competitive situation the ethical responsibility is for the city editor.[3]

The police sometimes withhold from the reporter during their investigation of a crime those records which are regarded as interoffice communications. These are usually the reports of detectives to their superior officers. The law regarding the right of access of a newspaper to police records is thin and divergent. The author of the definitive volume on the law of access to public records has this advice: "Sugar, plus judicious admixtures of strength and determination, catches more 'police news' than vinegar."[4] In some communities, however, a newspaper has been successful in suing out a writ of mandamus[5] to obtain access to certain police records.

WRITING THE CRIME STORY

Most crimes are not interesting. They are reported as chronicle and make small demand upon the writer's literary skill. But the unusual crimes —those containing the elements of drama, mystery, or humor—merit the

---

[3] For a narrative of some concrete instances of requests for suppression, see T. Prager, *Police Reporter* (New York, 1957), Chaps. 7 and 8. The author was a police reporter for the New York *Daily News*.

[4] H. L. Cross, *The People's Right to Know* (Morningside Heights, New York, 1953), p. 96.

[5] The writ of mandamus is discussed on pp. 416–418.

literary technique of a skilled news writer. Too frequently, however, crime stories are written by men capable only of using many adjectives and of employing exaggerated imagery. To write exaggerated accounts of crimes, to produce news stories that drip with false sentiment, is a work the self-respecting craftsman will not allow himself to perform. The newspaper man, because his function is to report what is interesting, ought to make use of every legitimate device that will make his story interesting. But he is not required to adjust his style to the lowest level of popular taste.

The news writer, unlike the imaginative writer, works under a disadvantage that tends to minimize that chief characteristic of the literary craftsman; viz., restraint. Unfortunately the necessity of writing a story immediately after witnessing the event and the pressure of the deadline sometimes cause even the competent news writer to write "at the top of his voice." But the news writer should try to be aware of this limitation while he is writing and should even revise his stories after publication so as to rid himself of the fault of employing clichés and exaggerations.

Most crimes that are interesting have at least the semblance of plot. The news writer should be able to recognize such narrative material and to employ narrative technique. The following news story is an example of how a rewrite man with a sense for narrative supplies an atmosphere for a simple set of facts.

Killing Caused By Arithmetic

Carson H. (Hank) Turner had a few bucks in his pocket Saturday night when he met a bum in Tipton. He loaned the guy $2.50 and got an old .32 calibre revolver and a few shells as security.

He took the gun back with him to the labor camp at the De Campos ranch where he lived and showed it to his best friend, Leonard Wells, 47.

They tried the thing out. It worked and made a very satisfactory noise as it fired a bullet through the ceiling of their cabin.

Later, some fellows came around and had a few drinks. Turner and Wells started to argue over arithmetic problems.

Wells was pretty smart at arithmetic. Once Hank Turner was so mad he fired the revolver at the floor between Leonard Wells' feet.

Wells kept outsmarting Turner on the arithmetic problems. Hank got mighty upset. He pulled the gun and shot Leonard Wells twice in the heart.

Wells got up from the table and walked around the old pot-bellied stove with a surprised expression on his face. Then he sat down and died.

Hank Turner was in jail here today. He could not explain.

"I wouldn't have killed Leonard Wells for anything," he said. "Leonard was my best friend."

By attention to detail the writer achieves *vividness*. The following article in *Time* illustrates the considerable amount of reporting (*Time* calls it "research") that was required to obtain the facts.

That morning, burly Barney Doyle went to early Mass, hurried through breakfast and left the house at 8:30— to get a good seat for the double-header between the Giants and the Dodgers. Doyle, 53, a ship's carpenter, was a faithful Giant fan; whenever he could, he went to watch his favorites. He took along a friend's son, freckled Otto Flaig, 13.

From their seats in the upper grandstand of Manhattan's vast Polo Grounds, they faced home plate and, above it, rising over the top of the oval grandstand, a row of dingy apartment houses on Coogan's Bluff. In one of these houses a young Negro, with a .45 pistol he had found in Central Park, was preparing for a celebration all by himself; he had saved his only bullet for July 4.

In the stadium, Doyle, Flaig, and 49,000 others sat watching as the Dodgers, at 20 minutes after noon, walked onto the bright green grass of the field.

Up on Coogan's Bluff, 14-year-old Robert Peebles had climbed onto the roof of his dirty yellow apartment house, raised his .45 pistol and fired it, for the fun of it, into the air.

His bullet looped swiftly over the Polo Grounds, sped toward Seat 3, Row C, Section 42. Just as Barney Doyle, his score card in hand, turned to speak to young Otto Flaig, the bullet smashed into Doyle's left temple, sank into his brain and stayed there. Doyle, suddenly bleeding, slumped forward.

"What's the matter?" asked Otto, and got no answer. Doyle was already dead. After police carried off the body and helped Otto away, standees scrambled to the two vacant seats, and the game began.

Clichés

Here is a list of clichés that are sometimes used in crime stories; most of them should be avoided.

launch an investigation   *innocent bystander*
fusillade of shots   *unshakable alibi*
rushed to a hospital   *heavily armed policeman*
appear on the scene   *grim faced policeman*
explore every avenue   *gained access through*
sickening thud   *vanished into thin air*
took to his heels   *cloak of secrecy*
taken into custody

Explaining Crime

Some newspapers in reporting unusual or bizarre crimes attempt to answer the question "Why did he do it?" Although reporters lack the professional competence that is requisite for analyzing personality structure, they can sometimes report some relevant environmental factors (e.g., the home and family situations) and can sometimes obtain (from the prisoner or the prisoner's relatives or acquaintances) a personality history of the accused person. Most readers are just as interested in those facts as they are in the details about how the crime was committed and what the scene of the crime looked like.[6]

> For class discussion: *1.* When a newspaper reports that John Smith, who has no criminal history, is being sought by the police in connection with a crime, which is the better term to use: "sought as a suspect" or "wanted for questioning"?
>
> *2.* A vacuum cleaner salesman was arrested on a warrant on a charge of obtaining money under false pretenses and was released

[6] For a discussion of this role of the newspaper and for a bibliography of individual newspapers' treatment of crime stories, see S. Kobre, *News Behind the Headlines* (Tallahassee, Florida, 1955) and S. Kobre and J. Parks, *Psychology and the News* (Tallahassee, Florida, 1955).

on his own recognizance. A newspaper reported: "A Johnson City man is being held here on charges of obtaining money under false pretenses from two Erwin residents." Is the expression "being held" justified or is there a more appropriate expression?

3. The prosecuting attorney tells reporters that a man arrested in a homicide case has confessed the crime. Which is the more appropriate expression: "signed a confession" or "signed a statement"?

4. Is there ever a "crime wave"?

THE POLICE COMMISSION

The chief of police has authority to suspend a policeman for misconduct or dereliction of duty, but it is the commission which has the power to discharge or otherwise penalize members of the force. At its regular meetings the commission holds hearings at which the chief of police proffers charges and at which the accused policeman may, if he wishes, be represented by counsel.

Police Officer Fired; Two Are Disciplined

One policeman was booted off the force and two others were disciplined last night by the Police Commission.

The three had been accused by Floyd Byers, a tinsmith, of pistol-whipping him at a night club last Saturday night while the officers were off duty.

The trouble arose when a bottle was hurtled across the floor and struck Byers' foot.

Patrolman Henry Dawson was the officer who was dismissed. Patrolman Robert Scott was suspended for 60 days and Patrolman Chet Rose was reprimanded.

In another case the Commission exonerated Detective Charles Maginn, who was accused of arresting and beating Henry Miles after Miles had reported being robbed in his home by Hobart Brooks.

The detective denied beating Miles and said that Brooks, whom he had arrested, charged Miles with being an accomplice.

"I would do the same thing again

under the same circumstances," he said.
Detectives William Allis and Noble Murray said they were present and that Maginn never struck Miles.

The commission generally passes on promotions recommended by the chief of police. Promotions are usually reported by newspapers.

HOSPITALS

News that emanates from hospitals is usually obtained by the police reporter. At certain intervals he telephones the hospitals for the purpose of making general inquiries. When police records have informed him that the victim of an accident or crime has been taken to a hospital, he sometimes makes a special telephone call.

In some communities newspapers have encountered difficulties in obtaining adequate information from hospitals because of a mutual lack of understanding as to the role and obligation of the physicians, hospital administrators, and the newspapers.[7] Some newsmen are not aware of the doctor's obligation to his patient to protect the patient's privacy and welfare and the medical profession's ethical code as to the publicizing of the individual doctor. Nor are all physicians aware of the obligation of the newspaper to print the news. Some hospitals fail to designate spokesmen to supply information. For these reasons some state and local medical associations and newspapers, after consideration of all of the factors, have adopted "codes of cooperation." The following code, adopted[8] in the state of Iowa, is typical:

CODE OF COOPERATION

To guide the medical profession and hospitals in their relationships with newspapers, radio, and television news broadcasters these considerations must be fundamental:

The primary obligation and responsibility of all doctors and all hospital personnel is the welfare of the patient.

Newspapers and radio news broadcasts exist for the common good, to bring matters of general interest and importance to the public quickly and correctly.

In addition to these general principles, the following rules are suggested for specific instances:

[7] For a discussion of these roles and obligations by doctors and newsmen, see Josiah Macy Foundation, *When Doctors Meet Reporters,* H. Krieghbaum, comp. (New York University Press, 1957).

[8] Approved as a basic working agreement by: Iowa Radio News Association, Iowa Daily Press Association, Iowa Press Association, Iowa State Medical Society, Iowa Hospital Association, Iowa State Nurses' Association.

Doctors-Hospitals

The name of the attending doctor shall be made available to the newsman, if requested, but the doctor's name shall not be used in the news without his consent. He shall give information to the press and radio where it does not endanger the doctor-patient relationship or violate the confidence, privacy or legal rights of the patient.

Each hospital shall designate spokesmen who shall be competent to give authentic information to the press, radio and television in emergency cases at any time of the day or night. Information shall be provided as rapidly as possible without interfering with the health of the patient.

Nothing in this paragraph, however, contemplates the providing of any information which shall jeopardize the hospital-patient relationship or which violates the confidence, privacy or legal rights of the patient.

The designated spokesman for the hospital may frequently be the nurse in charge. If so, it is her obligation to the patient, doctor and hospital to give authentic information within the limits of this code as follows:

Accident or Emergency Cases

The newsman shall be given the following information:
1. Name, age, address, occupation and sex of the injured.
2. Nature of the accident, such as automobile, explosion, shooting, etc.
3. Extent of injuries: their degree of seriousness when ascertained. *In most cases, condition reports limited to such words as good, fair, serious, or critical are sufficient.*
4. Deaths.

Illness of a Personality in Whom the Public Is Rightfully Interested

The nature of the illness, its gravity, and the current condition, with the consent of the patient or next of kin.

Medical Associations

The executive offices of the Iowa State Medical Society and officers of county medical societies shall be available for newsmen to obtain authentic information as promptly as possible on health and professional subjects. If the information desired is not immediately available, it shall be the duty of the executive office either to obtain the information or to locate a competent authority from whom newsmen can obtain it directly.

Officers, committee chairmen or designated spokesmen of the various professional associations may be quoted by name in matters of public interest for purposes of authenticating information given. A list of current spokesmen of the various associations shall be maintained at the headquarters of the county medical societies and shall be kept up to date. This shall not be considered by their colleagues as a breach of the time-honored practice of avoiding personal publicity, since it is done in the best interest of the public and the profession.

Newsmen

Press, radio and television newsmen, recognizing the first obligation of the doctor and hospital is to safeguard the life, health and legal rights of the patient, shall cooperate by refraining from any action or demands that might jeopardize the patient's life or health and rights.

When a doctor or hospital authority authorizes a quotation directly by name, press, radio and television newsmen shall make certain to the best of their ability that the quotation is accurate both in content and context.

Press, radio and television newsmen shall exercise editorial judgment to avoid publishing material designed solely to exploit the patient, doctor or the hospital.

On all matters of general health news, the newsmen shall make all reasonable effort to obtain authentic information from qualified sources indicated above before proceeding to publication or broadcast.

Reporters cannot be too careful in reporting accidents. Nearly every serious accident results in a lawsuit or in the filing of a claim by an injured person. Inaccurate news stories about accidents may affect the judgment of juries or of the public, and thus cause an unfair assessment of damages or a loss of trade to a store. Accidents are difficult to report because reporters must rely on the information furnished by the police and by eyewitnesses, and these accounts frequently differ in many important details. In the matter of automobile accidents, especially, reporters should be careful to report correctly the driver's or owner's name and make every effort not to exaggerate the extent of the injury or the damage. Newspapers, in reporting accidents, frequently protect their reputation for accuracy by quoting the eyewitnesses directly instead of reporting the accident in the manner of the omniscient observer, and by using such expressions as "A car *said to have been driven* by John Doe. . . ."

Few newspapers report the specific poison used in a suicide or attempted suicide on the theory that publication of the information will increase the number of suicides.

Since the reporter at police headquarters reports only the "spot" news that originates in hospitals it is necessary that other reporters obtain feature stories. It is the policy of newspaper editors to keep in touch with hospital superintendents and attendants and with physicians and, from time to time, send reporters on special assignments. Stories about interesting operations and treatments and about remedies developed by the research of physicians on hospital staffs may be obtained—although in many instances the physician's name cannot be used because of the rules of the medical societies.

FIRES

News about fires is also obtained by the police reporter. Fire alarms sound in police headquarters and in some newspaper offices, and patrolmen go to fires in their districts to handle the traffic and to prevent citizens from interfering with the fire fighters. The reporter finds out the identity of the owner and tenants, the approximate amount of damage, amount of insurance, probable cause of the fire, injuries and deaths, and special problems in fighting the fire. His sources of information are police officers, fire captains, the fire chief, the fire marshal,[9] and sometimes a representative of the insurance underwriters.

Fire Does $50,000 Damage to Store

Fire roared through Bailey's Furniture Store this morning, destroying or damaging $50,000 worth of stock and gutting one side of the building.

Fireman Larry Simonini suffered severe burns when blazing tar fell on his unprotected hand.

Stanley E. Bailey, owner of the store, at 200 Hamilton Ave., said the fire started shortly after 9 a.m. in the rug department.

Five pieces of apparatus and 18 men from the fire stations at 440 Bryant St. and 2253 Park Blvd. responded.

"The heat and smoke were terrific," Fire Marshal Herbert Nelson said. "Firemen had to use masks in order to penetrate the dense billows of smoke pouring from broken windows."

Fire Chief Louis F. Ledford and Fire Marshal Herbert Nelson today were continuing an investigation, but at press time had not found any indication of the cause of the fire.

PROSECUTING ATTORNEY[10]

In certain political subdivisions of every state is an officer—usually an elected officer—who represents the state as plaintiff in criminal actions. He is called the *prosecuting attorney, district attorney, state's attorney, commonwealth's attorney,* or *attorney general.* Generally each county has a prosecuting attorney, but thinly populated areas are divided into judicial districts of two or more counties with a prosecuting attorney for the whole district who is assisted by a county attorney or solicitor in each of the component counties.

[9] A fire marshal is an official whose main duties relate to fire prevention rather than fire fighting. He inspects commercial and industrial buildings in which explosives and inflammable materials are stored (e.g., dry cleaning establishments). He investigates fires to determine the cause, especially when there are suspicious circumstances.

[10] See p. 390 for a discussion of the ethical role of the Prosecuting Attorney. Also, see references to County Attorney on p. 472 and to City Attorney on pp. 499–500.

In addition to his duties with respect to crimes, some prosecuting attorneys also serve as legal adviser to the county governing board and defend the county and the county officers in civil suits.

In some states under some circumstances the state attorney general has power to supersede the local prosecuting attorney.

It is the duty of the prosecuting attorney and his staff, when he has assistants, to receive complaints and to investigate alleged crimes with the view to prosecuting offenders. In populous counties the prosecutor often has his own staff of investigators, although he works closely with city policemen, the sheriff, and state highway policemen. He is, therefore, a source of information to newspaper reporters about crimes during the time of investigation.

In metropolitan counties the prosecuting attorney has a large and highly organized staff. In one large city, the office is divided into the following departments: (1) the complaint bureau, (2) the indictment bureau, (3) the homicide division, (4) the bail department, (5) the preliminary hearing department, (6) the appeals bureau, (7) the trial division, and (8) the medical examiner.

. . . In answer to a question as to whether anything had been developed in the bombing of Leon Ellis' home, District Attorney Munson said: "Nothing positive."

"We're working on that and we're also working on the division of the slot machine money," Mr. Munson said. "We have our suspicions as to the persons Ellis had to pay, but we are seeking proof and going over his records.

"I had heard reports that gambling had opened up in the county outside the city so I had an investigation made before the raids of Sunday morning."

He indicated further that he is not taking the word of anyone for granted about conditions in the county when he said:

"Nine out of ten anonymous complaints received at this office prove to be true statements. I send a copy of the complaints to the chief of police with a request for a report."

The prosecutor said his own investigators mail their reports to his home "sometimes in envelopes that look like invitations, and sometimes in plain envelopes so that they are not conspicuous."

CORONER

In most states there is a *coroner* for each county. When informed that some person has been killed, has committed suicide, or has died under circumstances that suggest a crime or criminal negligence or when no physician has signed a death certificate, the coroner investigates. The coroner has the authority to summon a jury to hold an *inquest* and to subpoena witnesses to testify. He may also make or direct to be made a post-mortem examination of a corpse and direct exhumation of a corpse.

The coroner's jury returns a verdict which charges a specific person or persons with a crime, exonerates suspected persons, or admits its inability to determine the cause of death or to fix blame. The latter is called an *open,* or *noncommittal,* verdict; an example: "James Carr came to his death at the hands of police officers, but we are unable to determine whether the killing was justifiable."

When the jury decides that a specific person is responsible for a death or believes that further investigation is necessary, the coroner certifies the verdict to the prosecuting attorney with a transcript of the testimony. In some states the coroner is required to issue a warrant of arrest for a person not already in custody whom the jury has accused. The following is an example of a verdict which accuses a specific person: "Gordon Sparks died from a head injury suffered in a fall as the result of a blow delivered by Paul Anderson who was defending himself." The verdict of a coroner's jury is not an accusation on which a person can be tried for a crime: the grand jury must indict or the prosecuting attorney must file an information (depending upon the law of the state).

The most useful inquests are those that inquire into the causes of mass deaths, as in hotel fires and transportation collisions.

How Were 32 People Trapped? Coroner Inquires

A coroner's jury today is seeking the answer to four questions about yesterday's street car-gasoline truck collision in which 32 persons were killed.

These were:

1. Was the street car too overcrowded, making escape impossible?

2. Did the rear doors jam shut or did they open—even temporarily?

> 3. Did metal bars outside windows of the car prevent escape?
> 4. Did the trolley's motorman miss a switch signal, causing the car to turn left into the switch at too high speed into the path of the oncoming truck?
>
> Conductor Patrick Kelly described the collision.
>
> "The only thing I know I was on the floor," he said. "There were flames in front of the car and people were rushing to the rear. I set the rear doors to open so that people could get out.
>
> "But they couldn't. They piled up. I hollered at them. I pleaded with them to stand back. Then I was swept out with the crowd.
>
> "I was carried out with the crowd through the rear window. I don't know how it was opened."
>
> Other witnesses testified, however, that a woman passenger smashed the glass with her fist.
>
> Joseph Kingston, operating vice president of the railway, testified that the bars on the side windows are standard safety equipment and that a person could get out of the windows if they were opened wide enough. . . .

Many students of government consider the coroner no longer performs any essential function that is not already performed by other officers or which could not be better done by police specialists. They recommend that the office be abolished. Only seven states, for example, require that the coroner be a physician; in many states the coroner is an undertaker. Most large cities now have *medical examiners,* who are expert in the determination of death, trained *toxicologists,* and trained *pathologists.* Many states have similar officials who are made available to rural counties which cannot afford to have them on a full-time basis.

One argument for preserving the coroner's inquest is that it has sometimes provided an opportunity for the press to expose the dereliction of law enforcement officers.

FEDERAL INVESTIGATORS

Nine separate federal agencies station investigators in several communities. These are not mere inspection officials but intelligence agents, some of whom have authority to make arrests. Federal officials not engaged in this type of investigation are discussed in Chapter 33. The United States marshal makes arrests on behalf of some of the agencies; his duties are discussed on pages 301–302.

Eight of the nine agencies are specialists for investigating a certain type of law violation. The ninth agency—the Federal Bureau of Investigation (F.B.I.)—investigates all federal crimes which the other eight agencies are not authorized to investigate.[11]

Postal Inspection Service

These officials not only audit the finances of post offices, but engage in detective work that relates to the mails, including the tracking down of train robbers. They are concerned with depredations upon the mails; use of the mails to promote lotteries and to defraud; mailing of explosives, poisons, firearms, intoxicants, letters of extortion and threat, and obscene and scurrilous matter; forgery of money orders; and complaints of interception or tampering with the mails.

Janitor Stole Mailed Donations, Charge

Postal inspectors today charged a post office janitor with the theft of religious and Christmas charity contributions.

Joseph Hammer, according to Postal Inspector in Charge Melville Tapper, opened letters addressed to the Rev. Donald Hall, who has been appealing for funds from Station KFKA.

Hammer is also accused of opening Christmas seal letters addressed to the County Tuberculosis Association.

Postal inspectors started investigation last month after listeners to the Rev. Mr. Hall's broadcasts reported to him he had not acknowledged their contributions in his regular broadcasts.

When the postal inspector learns that a certain person or firm is using the mails for a fraudulent purpose, he requests the postmaster-general to issue a *fraud order*. If the evidence is satisfactory to the postmaster-general —who often holds a hearing—he instructs the local postmaster to stamp "fraudulent" on all mail addressed to the suspect and to return it to the

[11] An extraordinarily interesting exposition of these nine agencies—and some others—is M. Ottenberg, *The Federal Investigators* (Englewood Cliffs, New Jersey, 1962).

sender; this order also directs the postmaster not to cash money orders drawn to the order of the suspect or his agent.

Many of the postal fraud news stories are of human interest because of the unusual nature of the fraud or the peculiar methods used by the violator. Telling fortunes, selling fake stocks and fake instructions by correspondence, conducting "endless chains," employing women to do "home work" on embroidery; these are some of the fraudulent schemes which reporters have written about in an interesting manner.

"After 37 You Can't Get Rid of Wrinkles"

Not much can be done about wrinkles after the age of 37, Dr. Nicholas Newall, state university medical center dermatologist, said yesterday.

Between the ages of 37 and 40, Dr. Newall said, "senile degeneration" of exposed areas of the skin begins.

He testified at a Post Office Department hearing in the case of Mrs. Grace Le Brun, operator of the Age Wise Cosmetics Co. at 516 Langley St.

Mrs. Le Brun, according to the Post Office, has indulged in false and misleading advertising in her mail order cosmetics business.

Dr. Newall testified before Hearing Officer George Hammond, who came here from Washington, D.C.

Dr. Newall said two products sold by Mrs. Le Brun to persons hoping to stave off wrinkles contain mainly glycerine, sodium chloride and water.

These ingredients would have only a surface effect at best, said the dermatologist. After 37, he added, wrinkles will form regardless of what a person uses.

United States Secret Service

The main function of the Secret Service (Treasury Department) is to suppress counterfeiting of government currency and coin, and forgery of other government obligations and securities. It is not only a crime to counterfeit, forge, or alter currency or coin, but also to utter (i.e., pass) a counterfeit, forged, or altered instrument. The Secret Service maintains fifteen district offices, headed by a *supervising agent,* and several agents located in cities within the districts. The agents also investigate violations of the Federal Farm Loan Act, the Federal Farm Credit Act, the World War Adjusted Compensation Act, the Gold Reserve Act of 1934, the Government Losses in Shipping Act, offenses against the Federal Deposit Insurance Corporation, and counterfeiting of liquor revenue stamps and government transportation requests. This agency also is responsible for the protection of the President.

Bogus Money Ring Trapped by Farmer

CHICAGO—The nation's biggest counterfeiting ring was rounded up today on a tip from a farmer who distrusted "city slickers."

Secret Service agents announced the arrest after a farmer was paid for a Thanksgiving turkey in counterfeit currency.

The farmer's identity was withheld to protect him from the possibility that associates of the ring might seek revenge.

Harry D. Anheier, supervising agent of the Secret Service office here, said the counterfeiters printed $600,000 in bogus money and that agents had followed the trail of the spurious bills from Detroit to Los Angeles.

Those arrested were George Kanakas, 52. . . .

It was Kanakas who bought the turkey from a Des Plaines, Illinois, farmer.

The farmer said Kanakas did not "even watch me when I weighed the bird. I figured there must be something wrong with anybody that trusting."

So he got Kanakas' auto license number and took the $20 bill Kanakas had given him to the bank where the cashier said it was counterfeit.

Customs Agency Service

This is the field force of the Customs Bureau's Division of Investigation and Enforcement. In addition to *customs agents* stationed abroad, some members of the service are stationed in various communities in the United States; there are also several hundred *customs port investigators*. Their investigations mainly relate to the smuggling of diamonds, watches, narcotics, and marijuana.

Clerk Didn't Know $100,000 of Jewels Were in Codfish

Ralph Kirkland, suspect in a $100,000 customs jewelry theft here, admitted yesterday he was "scared to death" and wished he had gone to authorities long ago with his codfish story.

Kirkland told reporters yesterday that the codfish offers the only reasonable explanation of the disappearance of the jewels from a customs warehouse and their reappearance in his home at 1987 W. 35th St.

The jewels in question are the property of Mrs. Eva Lutz who had them brought to this country from England by a niece and stored in the warehouse for two years while she arranged for entrance into the United States.

He Took Fish Home

Loss of the jewels was not discovered until Mrs. Lutz arrived to claim them last July.

The suitcase had not been opened for inspection prior to that date, but bindings and customs seals were found broken.

After almost two years of investigation by customs agents, some of the jewelry was located through a local jeweler and traced to Kirkland, a 53-year-old storekeeper clerk employed by the customs service for the past twenty years.

It was then, under questioning of agents, he told his codfish story.

The men were allowed to and often did take home fish that had been removed from incoming cargoes for inspection.

He Began to Wonder

One day as he was leaving work, a fellow employee (now deceased) handed him a package and said it contained codfish.

He didn't like codfish but his wife did. So he took the package home and turned it over to her.

He thought no more about it until after his wife died last December.

Then, in cleaning up the house, he found the jewels. At first, he said, he thought the jewels were heirlooms his wife had brought here from Denmark.

He sold $2,500 worth, he said, and gave some away.

When loss of the jewels at the customs warehouse was discovered, he said, he began to wonder about the package of codfish.

He Got Some of It Back

He said he recalled a time shortly after bringing the package home when his wife asked him suspiciously where the package had come from. But nothing was said about it containing jewels.

He said he had spent the week-end, after being questioned by customs agents, rounding up some of the jewelry he had given away to turn it over to authorities.

Some of the jewelry already has been recovered from a jeweler who purchased it and has been turned over to Mrs. Lutz.

Collector of Customs William Himstead, who is being sued for $50,000 by Mrs. Lutz for loss of her treasure, said investigation of the case would continue.

Intelligence Division of the I.R.S.

The 1600 *special agents* of the Internal Revenue Service investigate the evasion of payment of income, amusement and (certain) excise taxes, and the nonpayment by employers of payroll withholding deductions for Social Security. They are sometimes called "T" men.

Their investigations sometimes lead to the conviction for tax evasion of corrupt local politicians and labor union leaders and racketeers. The agents, who are trained in accounting and law, are sometimes able to prove that pay-offs have not been reported as income. Gambling czars have sometimes been convicted for evading payment of the excise tax (stamp) on gambling.

T-men Scrutinize Seized Bet Records

Agents of the federal internal revenue intelligence division moved into the newest local betting syndicate investigation yesterday.

The T-men showed up at central

police station and examined records of bank deposits seized by police late Wednesday in a raid on the Film Row Club. The deposits on some days were as high as $31,645.

They were further interested in the fact that seemingly hardly any cash went into the club's account.

Alcohol and Tobacco Tax Division

Special investigators of this division of the Internal Revenue Service investigate violations of the laws relating to the manufacture, warehousing, and distribution of spirituous and fermented liquors, wines, and industrial alcohol, the taxation of tobacco, and the interstate shipment and sale of certain firearms, such as machine guns and sawed-off shotguns. The investigators have authority to arrest illicit distillers, bootleggers, smugglers of cigarettes, and other violators of these laws.

SOLD MACHINE GUNS?

A local gun expert, David Taylor, was arrested yesterday and charged with selling unregistered machine guns to Toby Walls.

Agents of the U.S. Treasury Department's Alcohol and Tobacco Tax Division arrested him.

Walls, a 30-year-old drug store clerk, identified Taylor as the man who had sold him most of the 14 machine guns found at Walls' home.

The discovery of a marijuana cigarette in Walls' possession led to the finding of the guns together with two cases of dynamite, lewd photos and Nazi uniforms.

THE JUSTICE OF IT

"A man is entitled to a good drink of whiskey."

So saying, Federal Judge Paul Bingham fined bartender Manuel Turnesa $1,000 yesterday for watering whiskey at the Park Club, 1535 Park St.

Turnesa was arrested by agents of the U.S. Alcohol and Tobacco Tax Division last month for reducing the proof of several bottles of whiskey by adding soda water.

Bureau of Narcotics

This bureau, which has fifteen district offices in the United States, investigates and prevents violation of the federal narcotic and marijuana laws

(Harrison Act) and the Opium Poppy Control Act. It issues permits to import crude narcotic drugs and to export preparations made from them. It determines the quantities of narcotic drugs to be manufactured in the United States for medicinal purposes. The agency maintains agents in foreign countries. It concentrates its investigations on the important dope traffickers and relies mainly on state and local officials to investigate and arrest local peddlers.

Doctor Is Held on Narcotic Charges

Dr. T. S. Creek, 67, of 450 Williams St., physician and surgeon, was arrested yesterday on charges of issuing prescriptions for morphine to drug addicts in violation of the Harrison anti-narcotics act.

He was arrested by Deputy U.S. Marshal Tom Wertenbaker.

After the arrest, Robert Parton, special agent of the district Bureau of Narcotics office, said "the largest source of morphine in the tricities has been stopped."

Customers of Dr. Creek included several widely known ex-convicts, housebreakers, and small-time crooks, Mr. Parton said.

At his office in the Wilson building Dr. Creek had been watched carefully for the past two months, the special agent said. His operations involved very large sums of money since he charged high rates for prescriptions and had a large number of "patients," he added.

Federal Bureau of Investigation

Field divisions of the F.B.I., headed by a *supervising agent in charge,* are located in forty-eight cities of the continental United States, and *resident agents* are stationed in several other cities. The six thousand special agents investigate all violations of federal laws with the exception of those assigned to the other investigating agencies mentioned in this chapter. There are 170 different types of violation. Many of these laws have been referred to in other sections of this book. Thus, the F.B.I. is the main detective force of the federal government. It also devotes considerable time to investigations that involve the internal security of the United States. Announcement of some arrests is made only by the Washington office. The F.B.I. helps to enforce state laws by beginning an investigation whenever a fugitive crosses a state line. It begins an investigation of a kidnaping twenty-four hours after it happened on the theory that the victim could have been taken out of the state within that period.

FBI Finds "Badman" In Luxury Trailer

JACKSONVILLE, Fla.—FBI agents captured luxury-loving Lee Emory Downs outside his sumptuous house trailer and brought him here today for arraignment as one of the nation's "ten most wanted men."

A dozen federal agents closed in on the 43-year-old burglary fugitive yesterday in a Daytona Beach suburb where he has been living in a television-equipped trailer with his ex-convict wife.

Three Now Held on White Slave Charge

A third alleged member of a tristate white slavery ring was arrested today, the Federal Bureau of Investigation announced.

Special Agent Steven Demming said that Mrs. Charlotte Ferber, 59, was being held in Ft. Collins, Colorado. Mr. and Mrs. Richard Martin were arrested Friday.

The same 14-year-old girl made the complaint against the trio. She said she had been transferred from Omaha to Laramie, Wyoming, for immoral purposes.

Special Agent Demming said Mrs. Ferber had been convicted on the same charge six years ago in Denver.

Immigration and Naturalization Service[12]

The 137 offices of the Immigration Service are headed by a *district director,* a *divisional director,* or an *inspector in charge.* At ports the inspectors

---

[12] See p. 511 for an expanded discussion of this agency.

decide to admit or exclude incoming aliens, sometimes detaining them while investigating whether or not they are "desirable" or are eligible under the quota system established by law. The inspectors also patrol the southern and northern borders of the country to prevent the illegal entry of aliens.

The inspectors in coastal and inland cities also locate and arrest aliens who are subject to deportation. Aliens may be deported because they entered illegally, overstayed the time permitted by their visa, are dangerous to the national security, or on other grounds stated in Title 8, sec. 5 of the *United States Code*. The citizenship of racketeers who had been naturalized has been revoked on the grounds that they made false statements in their applications for naturalization; after the revocation of their citizenship they have been deported.

Aliens are arrested on a *deportation warrant* and are given a hearing by a panel of inspectors whose decision must be approved by the Commissioner of Immigration and Naturalization in Washington. An appeal may be taken to the Board of Immigration Appeals in the office of the attorney general. This board is a quasi-judicial body which has the power to review the orders entered by or under the direction of the Commissioner in cases relating to admission and deportation and in cases of penalties imposed on shipping companies.

Nabbed East Indians Face Deportation

United States Immigration authorities, after a frantic scramble this morning, succeeded in arresting 25 agricultural workers from India.

The raid, led by Chief Immigration Inspector Claude Montonye, was at 5 a.m. at Losse ranch near Sunnyvale. In a bunkhouse the officers found the East Indian workers, who immediately took off in all directions.

After an hour's search, three of the East Indians were pulled out of a chicken house, where they had huddled with a group of frightened hens.

Fourteen of the group were found to have temporary work permits and were released. The others were seamen who had jumped ship in New York harbor two years ago.

Deportation Hearing For Swede Ends

The deportation hearing of Lief Hammer, official of a Swedish seamen's union and a former steamship company official, ended today.

Daniel Shapiro, presiding immigration inspector, said he expected to return his findings to Washington in a few weeks. Then briefs may be submitted.

Mr. Hammer admitted membership in the Swedish Communist party for six years. He testified, however, that during the war, the F.B.I. asked him to ferret out Nazi-inspired activity on the waterfront.

During cross-examination Mr. Hammer admitted that the army had barred him from boarding transports during the war.

Hjalmar Bjornson, Swedish vice consul, testified that Mr. Hammer had performed efficiently at the Scandinavian Shipping office and was regarded as a valuable official.

Coast Guard Intelligence Division[13]

This unit operates as a maritime police force. It investigates violations of laws that relate to smuggling, navigation, immigration, neutrality, quarantine, oil pollution, and the anchorage and movement of vessels within territorial waters. It also investigates crimes committed in navigable waters and on the high seas; the crimes range from murder to hit-and-run collisions of motorboats. A member of the Coast Guard is a *coastguardman;* the plural is coastguardmen.

"Mystery Men" Seized in Gulf

HOUSTON—Federal officials released just enough information yesterday to deepen the mystery surrounding two men taken off a boat by the Coast Guard near Galveston Island.

J. S. Kershner, of the Houston of-

---

[13] See p. 509 for a discussion of the other activities of the Coast Guard.

fice of the Immigration and Naturalization Service, said the two men were Robert Stevens, an American citizen, and Renald Silva, a Cuban.

Kershner said the Cuban was granted political asylum and said he was going to the Miami area.

None of the federal bureaus would say they are investigating how the Cuban and American happened to be arrested on the high seas of the Gulf of Mexico while in a small boat.

The boat contained diving and radio equipment, gun racks and a compass.

Federal Agencies as News Sources

The local investigators of some of these federal agencies must obtain permission from Washington before they announce arrests. Also, when the United States marshal makes an arrest on behalf of an agency which lacks authority to make an arrest he does not have much information about the nature of the alleged offense. The reporter, therefore, sometimes learns of arrests from the United States attorney, although, in most instances, he obtains additional information from the agency involved.

United States Attorney

In each federal judicial district is a United States attorney with a staff of assistants. His office represents the government in nearly all criminal and civil matters within his district. Reporters learn from this office about indictments by the federal grand jury. The reporter learns about arrests quite often from the United States marshal, the United States commissioner, or some federal investigative agency, but he obtains the details of the cases from members of the United States attorney's office as well as from some of the investigative agencies.

The United States attorney is consulted whenever a pardon or parole is sought for a person in federal prison who was prosecuted by him. Applications for pardons and clemency are made to the President who refers them to the Office of the Pardon Attorney in the Department of Justice. In the case of certain local persons of notoriety who have been convicted, pardons and rumors of pardons are newsworthy.

United States Marshal

This official is the federal sheriff. Although appointed by the attorney general for four years, he takes orders not only from the Department of Justice but also from the Administrative Office of the United States Courts and the judges of the federal courts he serves. To assist him he has several deputies, some of whom are designated as field deputies and some as office deputies. Some of the deputies reside in other cities in the federal judicial district than the city in which the marshal's office is located.

The main function of the marshal is to serve as an officer of the federal court—as an "arm of the law." He makes arrests on federal warrants, serves processes relating to private litigation in the federal courts, subpoenas witnesses, summons venires, and seizes property on writs issued by the federal courts; he sometimes auctions some of this property.

The marshal also is a disbursing officer of the monies appropriated for the maintenance, support, and operation of the federal courts. He pays federal judicial officials, disburses fees to witnesses and jurors, and pays the local government for the support of federal prisoners held in local jails.

The marshal is also a federal jailer. Because the federal government maintains a local jail only in New York city, prisoners awaiting trial or commitment are housed in county and city jails. For the safekeeping of prisoners confined for a few hours while waiting to appear for trial or to make bond, there is a small grille lockup in the marshal's office. Whenever prisoners are sentenced to penal confinement they are transported to jail by the marshal. Prisoners sentenced for the term of "a year and a day" are sent to federal penal institutions, but prisoners sentenced for a shorter term are confined in local jails at the expense of the federal government.

Newspaper reporters check the "custody sheet" in the criminal department of the marshal's office in the early forenoon to learn about cases to come before the United States commissioner for a preliminary hearing or for making bail. They check the "disposition sheet" to learn about arrests, releases from custody and prisoners transferred to local jails or to federal penal institutions.

42 TO PENITENTIARY

Aboard a special coach equipped with barred windows, forty-two federal prisoners bound for the United States penitentiary at Leavenworth, Kansas, left here at 4 p.m. yesterday in custody of L. S. Deering, deputy United States marshal. . . .

Another prisoner, Sam Shackelford, is being taken to the federal reformatory at Chillicothe, Ohio, because he is only 20 years old. He is in the custody of John T. Maxwell, deputy marshal.

SHIP SELLS FOR $1

Pacific Far East Lines paid $1 and assumed mortgages of $757,476 in buying a freighter at the U.S. marshal's auction yesterday conducted on the steps of the main post office.

Sale of the 11,000 ton S.S. Lanakila was ordered when the former owner, Dorma, Inc., was unable to pay a $188,000 repair bill owed to Todd Shipyards.

SWEDISH SHIP SEIZED

The Swedish freighter Paramatta was seized today by a U.S. marshal after two lawsuits totaling $800,000 were filed against the ship's owners.

For class discussion: If you heard a rumor late at night that an unknown man had been arrested on a charge of smuggling jewelry, which of the federal officials mentioned in this chapter or in Chapter 33 would you telephone first? If you could not locate that official, which official would you call next?

Probation Officers

The chief federal probation officer operates under the direction of the District Court and of the Department of Justice. He usually has one or more assistants.

CHAPTER 20

Criminal Actions: Crimes

A crime offends everybody. It is committed against all of the people in the state, not just against another person or another person's property. For this reason a criminal action in some states is entitled "The People of New York *vs.* Smith" or "The Commonwealth of Massachusetts *vs.* Smith" or "The State of North Dakota *vs.* Smith" or, in a federal court, "The United States *vs.* Smith." A crime is an act or an omission[1] prohibited by law. The offender may be punished by death, imprisonment, or fine and, in some instances, removal from office or disqualification to hold office.

The same act may be both a crime and a tort (i.e., a civil wrong done independent of a contract). Thus when D's automobile strikes P, D may be prosecuted by the state for reckless driving and also be sued by P in a civil action for damages. D may have to pay both a fine to the state and damages to P (if P files and wins a civil action against him). There is this difference, however: for P to win the civil action he has only to prove his case by a *preponderance of the evidence,* but for the state to win its case it must prove D's criminal guilt *beyond a reasonable doubt.*

KINDS OF CRIMES

Most of the crimes prosecuted in the state courts involve the alleged moral turpitude of the defendant and are classified as crimes *mala in se* ("wrongs in themselves"). But there are other crimes that are not inherently wrong but are merely prohibited by law; thus adulteration of food is a crime even though the manufacturer or processor had no criminal intent and no knowledge of the adulteration.

Crimes are also classified as *felonies* and *misdemeanors.* Felony implies a serious crime, such as larceny or homicide, whereas misdemeanor implies

[1] An omission such as "neglect" or "negligence" as a cause of a death.

a milder crime, such as the violation of a traffic ordinance, indecent exposure, or gaming. In general, a felony is punishable by death or confinement in a state penitentiary and a misdemeanor by fine or imprisonment in a local jail.

Crimes are often described in indictments by their statutory name; as, for example, drunkenness, tampering with a voting machine, operating a game of chance, illegally possessing narcotics, and maintaining a disorderly house. Crimes can be classified better, however, if we use common law names in so far as is possible. One classification of common law crimes differentiates five types: (1) crimes against persons; (2) crimes against the habitation; (3) crimes against property; (4) crimes against good morals and public peace; and (5) crimes against public justice and authority.

CRIMES AGAINST THE PERSON

Several different crimes against the person are distinguishable in law. (1) There is *simple assault,* which is merely threatening another by doubling the fist or by some other gesture to do bodily harm to another coupled with the aggressor's present ability to do physical injury. (2) When the threat is violent enough to cause another to flee it constitutes *aggravated assault,* such as assault with a deadly weapon; when there is intent to kill by administration of poison the statutes usually designate the offense as "assault in the first degree." (3) When the victim has actually been struck by the assailant the attack constitutes *battery;* spitting on another, drenching another with water from a hose, and striking a rider's horse are mild examples of battery. (4) When in the course of an assault and battery the attacker disables or disfigures a member of his victim's body the crime is *maim (mayhem)*; for example, to knock out another's teeth or to injure his eye is maim. (5) When a person forcibly bears another person away against his will the crime is *kidnaping.* (6) When an officer unlawfully restrains the liberty of a citizen by placing him in confinement the offense is *false imprisonment.* (7) When a female is taken away by violence or persuasion for sexual purposes the crime is *abduction.* (8) When a man has unlawful carnal knowledge of a woman without her consent the crime is *rape.* It is the practice of the most ethical newspapers to omit the name or picture of a victim of rape except when there is good reason, such as rape and murder of the same victim.

Homicide

The gravest of the crimes against persons is *homicide;* that is, the killing of a human being by the act or omission of another human being. For the crime of homicide to lie the victim must have died within one year and one day after the fatal injury was inflicted. Homicide has various lay names differentiated by the personal relationship of the slayer and the victim, such as *fratricide* (killing one's brother), *matricide* (killing one's mother), *parricide* (killing one's parent), *filicide* (killing one's child), and *uxoricide* (killing one's wife).

Two kinds of homicide are recognized in law; namely, *justifiable* homicide and *felonious* homicide. Homicide is said to be justified when it has been committed by accident or misfortune, upon sudden and sufficient provocation, by an officer acting in his line of duty, by one who is resisting an attempted murder, or by one in defense of his habitation. Any other form of homicide is felonious.

Felonious homicide is either *murder* or *manslaughter*. Murder is defined as homicide "with malice aforethought"; manslaughter, consequently, is homicide without malice.

Manslaughter is either *voluntary* or *involuntary*. Voluntary manslaughter is homicide committed intentionally in the heat of passion or as the result of extreme provocation; for example, a husband who surprised his wife with an adulterer. Involuntary manslaughter is accidental homicide, such as that resulting from reckless driving, from the discharge of an "unloaded" gun, from poison administered by mistake for medicine, or some other form of criminal negligence.

Murder is generally of two degrees which are differentiated by statute on the ground of malice, expressed or implied. In first degree murder there is an expressed malice and premeditation, such as murder committed by lying in wait or by poison, or murder which accompanies the commission of a felony. In second degree murder there is no premeditation yet an intent to kill at the moment or an attempt to inflict an injury without caring whether or not it causes death. For example, a man was convicted of second degree murder because of his reckless disregard of another's life: utterly drunk, he fired a pistol through a window at a stranger and killed him.

Penalties

A manslaughter verdict implies a sentence for a term of years; some states place the upper limit at twenty years and other states at ten years; the lower limit is always one year. Second degree murder is punished by a longer sentence, the lower limit often being five years and the upper limit being life. First degree murder is generally punishable by either a life term or by death. In some states the only penalty for first degree murder is death; in other states the worst punishment is a life sentence. In those states which permit a choice between a life sentence and the death penalty the jury may recommend a life sentence. Sometimes juries find a defendant guilty of a lesser crime than the crime he is charged with: thus, guilty of manslaughter when tried for murder.

CRIMES AGAINST THE HABITATION

The common law recognized two crimes against the habitation—*burglary* and *arson*. The common law definition of burglary is the "breaking and entering" of the dwelling house of another in the nighttime with intent to commit a crime therein. The statutes, however, have extended the definition to include the breaking and entering of shops, warehouses, railroad cars, and, in some states, tents and inclosed gardens. Statutes generally distinguish burglary as in the first or second degree. In one state, for example, first degree burglary is the entering of a building to commit theft in the nighttime or when armed with a deadly weapon in the daytime, all other forms of burglary being in the second degree. The terms "breaking" and "entering" have a technical meaning; connivance with a servant to gain entry has been interpreted as "breaking," and boring a hole in the floor of a granary to steal grain has been interpreted as "entering."

Arson, at common law, was the malicious burning of the dwelling of another. Most statutes have extended the definition to include barns and outhouses and some have eliminated the reference to "another." Some states differentiate three degrees of arson, making distinction between nighttime and daytime, between a dwelling and an outhouse, and between another's building and one's own building.

CRIMES AGAINST PROPERTY

The law recognizes several different crimes against property, some of which are statutory and some common law crimes.

Larceny, a common law crime, is taking and converting to use the personal property of another with felonious intent. *Grand* larceny and *petty* larceny are differentiated by the value of the goods stolen and by other criteria, such as the nature of the property (automobile, horse, sheep, etc.). In one state for a charge of grand larceny to lie the value of the goods must be seven dollars; in another state the value must be five hundred dollars.

Some states, by statute, have abandoned use of the term "larceny" and have substituted the term "theft," including also in this term obtaining by false pretenses.

Robbery, which is a crime against both the person and against property, is not the same as larceny. The charge of robbery lies whenever the thief exercises violence on the person of the victim or puts him in fear in order to take his personal property. The property may be taken either from the victim's person or in his presence.

Exercise: Look in a dictionary for the meaning of (1) *thug* and (2) *revolver*.

Extortion is the obtaining of real or personal property from another with his consent induced by a wrongful use of force or fear or under color of official right. Examples are threats to accuse another of a crime, to do some unlawful injury to him or to his property, his relatives, or his corporation, or to expose or to impute to him any disgrace. The crime is a felony when it involves force or threat just short of robbery; in other circumstances it is a misdemeanor.

Embezzlement, a statutory crime, is a form of larceny executed by means of a breach of confidence. In embezzlement the property is not taken from another but was already lawfully in his possession through reason of the trust placed in him by the owner of the property; thus a bank cashier, who has the bank's funds lawfully, may not appropriate them to his own use. Embezzlement is often difficult to prove because the accused in many cases can deny that he took the money and can offer the excuse that he made a mistake in using his discretion in expending the funds. Accusations of embezzlement are most often brought against employees, agents, trustees, and public officers.

Obtaining by false pretenses, a statutory crime, is committed by one who designedly, by false pretenses, with intent to defraud another, induces the other to give him title to his property. Actually this is larceny by false pretense. This crime does not apply to a salesman who expresses too high opinions of the goods he is selling to a possible buyer, but to persons who deliberately misrepresent facts, such as a civilian who, by dress and word, personates a soldier or a married man who pretends to be single and promises to marry a woman other than his wife in order to obtain her property.

Receiving stolen goods is a statutory crime. The receiver of stolen goods is guilty whether he receives the goods in order to sell them for a profit or a fee, or whether he intends merely to conceal the goods and the theft. The underworld term for a professional receiver of stolen goods is "fence."

Forgery is altering or falsely making a piece of writing for profit or for the deception of another. A person is guilty of *uttering a forgery* when he offers a forged instrument regardless of whether or not it is accepted by the other party.

Counterfeiting of coin, currency, and similar obligations of the federal government is prosecuted by the United States although some states also have statutes against counterfeiting.

Malicious mischief, a misdemeanor, is an offense against property which ranges from the malicious killing of animals belonging to another to malicious defacing or mutilating of another's property.

CRIMES AGAINST GOOD MORALS AND THE PUBLIC PEACE

The following crimes against decency and good morals are sometimes felonies: *bigamy, abortion, incest,* and *seduction.* There are a variety of sex offenses which, on the first offense, are misdemeanors. Some of these, which require no definition, are adultery, indecent exposure, prostitution, gaming, conducting a lottery, and printing, distributing, or exhibiting obscene matter.[2]

As late as 1964, there were 19 states which prohibited *miscegenation;* that is, the marriage of whites and non-Caucasians.

Statutes also provide punishment for certain offenses against the public peace. *Libel* is the malicious defamation of either the living or the dead, including a class of persons.[3] *Affray* is when two or more persons fight in a public place to the terror of the public. *Riot* is a tumultuous disturbance of the peace by three or more persons assembled of their own authority. *Disturbing the peace* consists of doing a number of acts, such as making loud or unusual noises, quarreling, challenging to fight on a public street or highway, firing a pistol or gun within a city or town, using vulgar or profane language in the presence or hearing of women and children. This offense is often called "disorderly conduct."

When one has *threatened* the person or property of another he can be required to furnish bond to "keep the peace." This proceeding is not a trial, for no crime has actually been committed.

CRIMES AGAINST JUSTICE AND AUTHORITY

Three offenses against public authority require no definition. These are obstructing an officer in a performance of his duty, breaking prison, and rescuing a prisoner.

[2] When is a book or a film "obscene"? This definition has met court tests rather well: "Obscene" means that (1) to the average person, applying contemporary standards, the predominant appeal of the matter, taken as a whole, is to prurient interest, (2) i.e., a shameful or morbid interest in nudity, sex, excretion, which goes substantially beyond customary limits of candor in description or representation of such matters (3) and is matter which is utterly without redeeming social importance. California *Penal Code,* sec. 311 (a). See E. and P. Kronhausen, *Pornography and the Law* (New York, 1959); C. N. Paul and M. L. Schwartz, *Federal Censorship* (Glencoe, Illinois, 1961); and State of New York, *Report of the Joint Legislative Committee to Study the Publication and Dissemination of Offensive and Obscene Material* (Legislative Document, 1962).

[3] A libel is a crime as well as a tort—its publication may tend to disturb the public peace.

Compounding a felony consists in abstaining from prosecution of a felony or concealing or withholding evidence of a crime for a consideration; the most common example is refraining to prosecute one who has stolen your property on his agreement to return the property or to make restitution.

Perjury is giving false testimony under oath in a judicial proceeding or in an affidavit, deposition, or tax return. *Subornation of perjury* is the procuring of another to give false testimony. *Bribery* is receiving or offering undue reward to any person whose business or profession is connected with the administration of justice (including jurors) or to voters or government officials to induce them to act contrary to their duty or dishonestly. *Embracery* is an attempt unlawfully to influence a jury.

Contempt—generally a misdemeanor—is the willful disregard or disobedience of public authority; for example, to refuse to answer questions on the witness stand or in depositions, to make a disturbance in the courtroom, to disobey an order of the court (such as an injunction), or to report unfairly a judicial proceeding.

Contempt of court (or of a lawmaking body) may be punished by fine or imprisonment. When the contempt consists of an omission to perform an act which the respondent has been ordered to perform and which he is capable of performing, he may be imprisoned until he has performed the act. Performance or assent to performance constitutes "purging" of the contempt. Trial of a contempt is "summary"; that is, there is no jury trial.[4] In some instances the judge is the complainant as well as the judge and the jury, although he usually directs the prosecuting attorney to prosecute the contempt. A federal court rule provides that, when the contempt charged involves disrespect to or criticism of a judge, the judge is disqualified from presiding at the trial or hearing except with the defendant's consent, another judge being substituted.

Contempt may be either civil or criminal. A *criminal* contempt is against justice and authority; a *civil* contempt is against a litigant. A civil contempt results from an act of omission; it consists in the failure by a litigant to comply with a court order, such as disobedience of an injunction. Civil contempt is thus a remedy of the aggrieved party.

Union Is Cited For Contempt

HONOLULU—A federal court issued a criminal contempt citation

---

[4] Under the federal Norris-LaGuardia Act, a citation for contempt arising out of a labor dispute must be heard by a jury.

> yesterday against Newton Miyagi, secretary of Local 142, International Longshoremen's and Warehousemen's Union because Miyagi sent $52,000 to international headquarters in San Francisco in disregard of a court order.
> Federal Judge J. Frank McLaughlin also cited the local for civil contempt.
> The Juneau Spruce Co., of Alaska, recently won a million-dollar judgment against both the international on the mainland and the Hawaiian local.
> Judge McLaughlin had forbade Local 142 to remit funds owed to the international.
> Miyagi said he gave George Anderson, San Francisco attorney for the international, $16,000 in a paper bag on January 19. Last Friday, he said, he cabled $36,000 more.

Criminal contempt may be *direct* or *indirect* (*constructive*). Direct contempt is committed in the presence or environs of the court; constructive contempt is that committed outside the court; for example, publication by a newspaper of a grossly inaccurate or unfair report of a trial is construed as contempt.

MISCELLANEOUS OFFENSES

Numerous offenses are defined in the various statutory codes that relate to specific subject matter. Some of these are the motor vehicle code, the election code, the fish and game code, the health and safety code, the insurance code, the revenue and taxation code, the school code, and the business and professional code (which relates to licensing and false advertising). Municipalities also punish violations of city ordinances which relate to health and safety; these are misdemeanors.

ATTEMPTED CRIME

Acts that go farther than mere preparation but fall short of completion of a crime and which are done with the definite intent to commit a crime are punishable as attempted crime. The prosecution, however, must prove an overt act toward commission of the crime; the mere preparation is not an attempt. For example, two men planned a robbery and started out in an automobile, but were arrested before they reached the person they intended to rob; this did not constitute attempted robbery. Two persons, for the purpose of defrauding an insurance company by committing arson, collected a considerable amount of inflammatory materials but, before striking a match, abandoned their plan; this did not constitute attempted arson.

SOLICITATION

To solicit another to commit any crime punishable at common law is solicitation. Some states have adopted this part of the common law, but others have made the solicitation of only certain crimes punishable, especially robbery, murder, grand theft, and numerous crimes against public authority, such as perjury, bribery, and forgery. The procuring of another to give false testimony is *subornation of perjury*.

CONSPIRACY

When two or more persons agree to commit a crime and do an overt act to effect the object of the agreement, the crime is known as conspiracy. In most states conspiracy is a felony. Under federal law conspiracy to violate a federal law is a felony even when the crime which is the object of the agreement is punishable as a misdemeanor. An overt act need not be proved when the object of the conspiracy is to commit burglary or a felonious assault.

> . . . One of the overt acts of the alleged conspiracy charged in the indictment was that Stoner telephoned Carl Jones the morning of the crime. Calvin Jones, his brother, testified that such a call was made.
> Stoner admitted that he telephoned Jones's office but, he said, he did that only to find if Jones were in town. He said he did not want Jones to know that he had left San Diego without completing some business down there.
> McNamara now brought Stoner to the state's allegation that he met Jones in Chinatown and there completed the arrangements to murder Mrs. Jones that night.
> Stoner said he went to Chinatown to meet a girl called Eva Lee and did not see Jones. . . .

Sometimes an indictment accuses certain conspirators as co-defendants but names others only as co-conspirators. The co-conspirators, however, may be indicted as defendants in a subsequent prosecution.

PARTIES TO A CRIME

The common law recognized these parties to a crime: principal in the first degree, principal in the second degree, accessory before the fact, and accessory after the fact.

A *first degree principal* is one who either performs the act or is responsible for it; for example, a physician who with felonious intent prescribes medicine and procures an innocent person to give it to the victim is a first degree principal. The *second degree principal* is one who, though not performing the act, is present and gives aid to the principal; for example, a burglar's "lookout."

An *accessory before the fact* is one who advised or planned the criminal act or otherwise abetted it prior to its commission but who was not present. An *accessory after the fact* is one who, although not present, but with knowledge of the crime, afterwards aided the principal to evade arrest or prosecution. Statutes in most states have abolished degrees of principal and consider an accessory before the fact as a principal.

All persons who are principals or accessories before the fact are termed *accomplices*. In most states an accessory after the fact is not an accomplice because he did not participate in the *identical* offense. This distinction has meaning in connection with the testimony of an accomplice.[5]

At common law a person who had knowledge of the commission of a serious crime and did not report it could be prosecuted for *misprision of felony,* a misdemeanor. An example: a physician who treated a person for gunshot wounds and did not report it. Most states have statutes which punish for such acts of omission.

A class of person who may be arrested and detained without being made a party to a crime is a *material witness*. To insure the testimony of a "material and necessary" witness before the grand jury or at a trial, the state may arrest him and release him only on high bail. This is done when it is believed that the witness may leave the jurisdiction or, if not detained in jail, may be killed by agents of a defendant who fears the witness's testimony.

STATUTE OF LIMITATIONS

Statutes provide that prosecution for most felonies cannot be initiated after the lapse of a certain number of years. For most felonies the limitation is from three to six years, and for misdemeanors one year. There is no limitation on prosecution for murder, and some states have no limitation on the prosecution for embezzlement of public funds or the falsification of

---

[5] Note the difference between an accomplice and a co-conspirator.

public records. Where the defendant is out of the state when the offense was committed the limitation does not generally start to run until after he has returned to the state.

FEDERAL CRIMES

The *United States Criminal Code* classifies offenses as follows: offenses against the existence of the government; neutrality; the election franchise and civil rights; rights of citizens; operation of the government; public justice; currency and coinage; the postal service; foreign and interstate commerce; offenses relating to official duties; the slave trade and peonage; within the admiralty, maritime, and territorial jurisdiction of the United States and piracy.

Many offenses included in the classifications mentioned above are direct violations of some criminal statute which the United States constitution authorizes Congress to enact, such as counterfeiting and frauds against the federal government. But Congress in recent years has enacted statutes to punish offenses in which the offender has made use of a means over which the United States government has regulatory power but are ultimately offenses for which only the states can prosecute. For example, offenses against morals cannot be punished directly by the federal government, but can be reached through statutes which prohibit the use of the mails, as when a person has sent obscene literature or information about lotteries. Similarly the federal government's power to regulate interstate commerce supplies the authority for the Mann Act which prohibits the interstate transportation of a woman for immoral purposes. Under the interstate commerce power Congress has prohibited, among others, the following offenses: theft from freight cars and the interstate transportation of stolen vehicles, securities, prize-fight films, machine guns, kidnaped persons, and strikebreakers. Criminals who have been unsuccessfully prosecuted by a state for such offenses as bribery, extortion, and murder have been convicted in federal courts for income tax evasion and for using the mails in connection with a fraud. There are other federal statutes that punish for violations of the Food, Drug, and Cosmetics Act, the Fair Labor Standards Act, the National Labor Relations Act, the National Bank Act, the Atomic Energy Act, and the Civil Rights Act.

Congress has authority to enact laws under the various powers of the federal government that are specified in the constitution. Some of these are the postal power, the taxing power, the power to regulate foreign and interstate commerce, the war-making power, and the power to regulate bankruptcy. Powers not specified in the constitution are reserved to the states by the Tenth Amendment.

CHAPTER 21

Criminal Actions: Arrest

These are the steps taken in bringing to bar a person suspected of committing a felony or high misdemeanor:

1. A private person or a law enforcement officer files a sworn *complaint* with a magistrate.
2. The magistrate, on the basis of the complaint, issues a *warrant of arrest*.
3. A law enforcement officer makes the arrest.

(*In many situations the sequence of these steps is reversed:* an officer makes an arrest without a warrant and then files the complaint. There is also the situation in which a person is indicted by a grand jury and is then arrested on a *bench warrant*—also called a *capias*—issued by the judge before whom the indictment was returned by the grand jury.)

4. The person arrested is "booked" and is often released on bail.
5. In some situations the suspected offender is given a *preliminary examination* at the conclusion of which a magistrate determines whether the suspected offender shall be discharged or "held to answer."
6. He is formally accused by indictment or information.
7. He is arraigned.
8. He pleads.
9. He is tried.

Usually arrest is by an officer on a warrant of arrest. Actually, persons may be arrested without a warrant by either an officer or a private citizen. An officer may arrest a person without a warrant when a felony or a misdemeanor which amounts to a breach of the peace is committed or attempted in his presence; when the officer (or a private citizen) has a reasonable suspicion that a felony has been committed and that the person is guilty; when the person has committed an offense in court; and when a person has escaped from jail or prison.

A private individual may (and is required to) arrest a person for a felony committed in his presence and may arrest for a breach of the peace; he may also arrest on reasonable suspicion that a felony has been committed, but is liable for false imprisonment and assault and battery if it turns out that a felony was not committed.

In American and English law (unlike the law in continental Europe) the individual officer, not the state, is liable for a false imprisonment. As a consequence, American policemen (or the city on their behalf) buy insurance from indemnity companies.

THE COMPLAINT

A complaint is a sworn application for a warrant of arrest. A complaining witness—also called a *prosecutor*[1]—makes an affidavit, "on information and belief," that a particular offense has been committed and that there is "probable cause" for suspecting a particular person or persons. The complaining witness may be either a private person or a law enforcement officer.

The form of a typical complaint for a misdemeanor follows:

State of Wisconsin ⎱ ss   In Police Court
County of Dane   ⎰   Of City of Madison

    Personally came John Roberts who, on oath, saith that to the best of his knowledge and belief, Edward Eddings did, on the ninth day of March, in the year 19—, in the city of Madison and county aforesaid, commit the offense of assault and battery upon the person of said John Roberts by striking him violently with a stone, contrary to the statutes of Wisconsin as provided, and this deponent makes this affidavit that a warrant issue for his arrest.

    Sworn to and subscribed before me
the ninth day of March, 19—

JOHN ROBERTS   WILLARD EVANS
                                                                                Judge of Police Court

Seeing Is Believing, But Hearing Isn't

Municipal Judge James J. Welsh explained yesterday that, while seeing is believing, hearing is not enough.

With that, he dismissed charges against 17 men and three women arrested in a gambling raid February 29

---

[1] A female complaining witness is called a *prosecutrix*.

at the Yee Ying Tong Association, 35 Spofford Alley.

Officers Robert Kane and Edward Nevin testified they broke into the association's headquarters after hearing "noises of gambling." Then they seized the gambling paraphernalia, arrested one man as keeper and the other 19 persons in the room as visitors.

Judge Welsh said he had to dismiss the charges because the officers did not actually see the law being violated.

THE WARRANT

A warrant is an order of a court directing a law enforcement officer to arrest the person described in the warrant and to bring him before the court for further proceedings. The warrant which was based on the foregoing complaint had this form, including the *return** of the arresting officer:

State of Wisconsin ⎫   In Police Court
County of Dane   ⎭   Of City of Madison

To the Chief of Police, Lieutenants or Patrolmen in the City of Madison and to any Sheriff or his Deputy, Coroner, Constable or Marshal of said State—

Greeting:
John Roberts makes oath before me that on the ninth day of March, in the year 19—, in the City of Madison and county aforesaid, Edward Eddings did commit the offense of assault and battery upon the person of said John Roberts.

YOU ARE HEREBY COMMANDED, To arrest the body of said Edward Eddings and bring him before me, or some other judicial officer of the State, to be dealt with as the law directs.

Witness the Honorable Willard Evans, Police Court Judge
Given under my hand, this ninth day of March, 19—
WILLARD EVANS, *Judge of Police Court*

I HEREBY CERTIFY that I received the within Warrant on the ninth day of March, 19—, and served the said Warrant by arresting the within named defendant, Edward Eddings, and bringing him into court this ninth day of March, 19—.

ARTHUR DEERING
Chief of Police of the City of Madison

Serving the warrant consists in telling the person named in the warrant that the officer has the warrant in his possession and stating the substance of it. The officer is generally required to show the warrant when the suspected person demands to see it. The officer usually confirms the identity of the person arrested by asking his name.

In general the peace officer in one county may not serve a warrant in another county, but most states provide by statute for service of a telegraphic warrant in another county or they send or take the warrant to another county. A federal warrant may be served anywhere in the territorial jurisdiction of the United States.

Many states have enacted the *Uniform Act on Fresh Pursuit* which provides that a law enforcement officer of a state may enter the reciprocating state "in fresh pursuit" of a person accused of a felony and arrest him. He must then take him to a magistrate in the county in which he made the arrest. The magistrate may either discharge the prisoner or hold him in jail or admit him to bail pending extradition proceedings.

The facts stated in a *warrant,* when reported by a newspaper, are privileged; that is, if the facts are untrue, the news story is not libelous. But in several states the facts stated in the *complaint* are not privileged. The main risks taken by the newspaper, however, derive from the publishing of untrue additional facts not mentioned in the complaint and from inaccuracies as to the identity of the accused person.

SEARCH AND SEIZURE

The Fourth Amendment to the United States constitution protects peoples' rights "to be secure in their persons, houses, papers and effects against unreasonable searches and seizures." Evidence obtained by illegal search is, therefore, not admissible in a criminal trial.

Search and seizure are legally justified when they are *incidental to a proper arrest* because they are deemed to be "reasonable" within the meaning of the Fourth and Fourteenth Amendments. It is not reasonable, for example, to conduct a search of a defendant's home without his consent forty-eight hours after he has been arrested at a place distant from his home. Search must also relate reasonably to the offense for which the arrest is justified; for example, searching a cab for heroin after the driver had been arrested for double parking is not related to the traffic violation for which he was arrested.

Search and seizure are justified when a magistrate issues a *search warrant* which is based on *probable cause*. A magistrate cannot legally issue a search warrant that is based on mere affirmation or suspicion. For a search warrant to issue, one or more witnesses must make affidavits which state supporting facts, and the magistrate must be satisfied that there is probable cause for the grounds to exist. The warrant, moreover, must particularly describe the property sought and the place to be searched. The warrant must be served in the daytime unless the magistrate directs otherwise. The officer who serves it must give a receipt to the person from whom the property is taken and must deliver the property to the magistrate together with a detailed inventory of the property. The form of a search warrant used in a federal criminal case follows:

In the District Court of the United States
for the Northern District of California, Northern Division

To any Marshal or Deputy Marshal:
  Affidavit having been made before me by Richard Berlman that he has reason to believe that on the premises known as No. 216 East Dupont Circle, in the City of San Francisco, in the Northern District of California, there is now being concealed certain property, namely, certain dies, hubs, molds, and plates, fitted and intended to be used for the manufacture of counterfeit coins of the United States, and as I am satisfied that there is probable cause to believe that the property so fitted and intended to be used is being concealed on the premise above described,
  YOU ARE HEREBY COMMANDED, to search the place named for the property specified, serving this warrant and making the search in the daytime, and if the property be found there to seize it, prepare a written inventory of the property seized and bring the property before me.
  Dated the second day of April, 19—
                                ZECHARIAH ALBEE
                                *U.S. Commissioner for the Northern
                                District of California*

Can Eager Cops Believe Their Ears?

The state supreme court hinted yesterday that it is doubtful whether the cooing of pigeons would justify police officers in thinking somebody was in distress.

The implication came in a ruling granting Simon Newton a hearing in his appeal from conviction of stealing a radio from a music store last year.

Newton was the prime suspect. So three police officers went to his girl friend's apartment and bent their ears to the keyhole.

They reported they heard "snoring or moaning as of someone in distress."

Pigeons?

Naturally, they said, they got a pass key from the landlord to investigate.

They entered. There was no one in distress. In fact there was no one in the room at all. But there was the **stolen radio.**

Newton was arrested and convicted

in Superior court. He maintained the evidence was obtained illegally.

The officers explained away the sounds they said they heard by declaring, "They must have been pigeons."

The Supreme court decided yesterday that it wants this matter discussed before it rules on whether Newton's conviction was proper.

BAIL

After a person has been arrested he is "booked"; that is, taken to a jail or to a magistrate where his arrest is recorded and where he may apply for admission to bail. He is usually permitted to telephone an attorney, friend, or relative.

To avoid staying in jail pending trial or action of the grand jury (or pending appeal of a decided case) and to guarantee his appearance, the defendant may either deposit a specific sum of money or government bonds for the amount of the bail or pledge his equity in real estate in an amount twice the face of the bail. Or he may have two sureties—other than his attorney—furnish a written undertaking called *bail bond*. Bail is often supplied by a surety company which charges a premium for assuming the risk. Sometimes a hearing is held by a magistrate to determine the value of a surety's equity in real estate, witnesses being called and examined.

The form of an appearance bond in a federal court case follows:

In the United States District Court
for the Northern District of California, Northern Division

We, the undersigned, jointly and severally acknowledge that we and our personal representatives are bound to pay to the United States of America the sum of Ten Thousand Dollars ($10,000).

The condition of this bond is that the defendant, Cornelius van Dyke, is to appear in the United States District Court for the District of California at San Francisco in accordance with all orders and directions of the Commissioner in the case of the United States *v.* Cornelius van Dyke; and if the defendant appears as ordered, then this bond is to be void, but if the defendant fails to perform this condition, payment of the amount of the bond shall be due forthwith. If the bond is forfeited and if the forfeiture is not set aside or remitted, judgment may be entered upon motion in the United States District Court for the Northern District of California against each debtor jointly and severally for the amount above stated together with interest and costs, and execution may be issued or payment secured as provided by the Federal Rules of Criminal Procedure and by other laws of the United States.

[Date and signatures of sureties and signature of U.S. Commissioner follow.]

The usual bail bond provides for summary judgment on forfeiture, and statutes usually make it the duty of the prosecuting attorney to sue out a writ of execution on the sureties' property. In some counties, however, the prosecuting attorney neglects to do this. Another bad practice that occurs in some jurisdictions is the willingness of magistrates and bond recorders to permit some of their political friends to pledge the same parcel of property—often a vacant lot—on several bail bonds simultaneously.

The surety for a defendant, at any time before forfeiture, may surrender him or empower another to surrender him and have the bail bond exonerated, the defendant being recommitted.

In general a defendant is entitled to bail for all offenses except a capital crime (i.e., one for which the penalty is death) and, in the discretion of the magistrate, he may be admitted to bail when accused of a capital crime. The magistrate has the discretion to fix the amount of bail. The amount depends upon the gravity of the crime and the defendant's criminal record. The magistrate usually asks the prosecuting attorney to recommend the amount. The prosecuting attorney and the defendant's attorney sometimes argue about the amount and sometimes the defendant's attorney returns to court at a later date to move for a reduction in bail. In some circumstances, when there is reason to believe that the defendant will flee the jurisdiction, the prosecuting attorney asks the court to raise the amount and have the defendant put in jail until he provides the additional bail. The names of the sureties are sometimes of interest to newspaper readers.

Courts are coming to realize that many arrested persons should be released on their own recognizance (i.e., without bail). Suspects who cannot afford bail often spend up to fifty days in jail awaiting trial. In 1964, a foundation was financing experiments in a few large cities to test the feasibility of releasing indigent misdemeanor suspects without bail. The foundation grants were for the salaries of additional persons to investigate the financial status of arrested suspects.

No Bail Reduction In Death Plot Case

Municipal Judge Marcellus Rowe refused yesterday to let Mrs. Alice Johnston go free on bail of less than $25,000.

So the 69-year-old retired school teacher went back to her prison cell. Mrs. Johnston, accused of trying to hire a man to murder her former son-in-law said she had no hope of raising $25,000.

Shelley Shields, Mrs. Johnston's attorney, said he thought the bail was "punitive" and declared the highest bail ever asked for a woman was $10,000.

District Attorney Jay Fairchild replied that police had sound tapes of Mrs. Johnston's instructions for the murder.

"A person of such a mind to plan a crime like this constitutes an extremely poor bail risk," he argued.

Mrs. Johnston was at liberty for seven hours on Wednesday on bail of $10,000 set by Judge Rowe and she surrendered when the district attorney asked that the sum be increased.

The case is to go before the grand jury Monday night.

BAIL SUPPORT WITHDRAWN
The Rev. Martin Ross, erstwhile pastor of an East End church, went to jail today after he lost part of his bail support.

James Ford, former church trustee and one of the sureties, indicated he had "lost faith" and asked to be released from his obligation in an $8,000 property bond on which Mr. Ross had obtained his freedom.

Mr. Ross has been accused of theft of church funds.

HABEAS CORPUS

The writ of *habeas corpus ad subjiciendum* is a speedy remedy to compel law enforcement officers either to bring a specific charge against a person who has been arrested or to release him from restraint. The term means "have the body" and is used in the sense indicated in the writ below.

State of California
County of Santa Clara } SS   In the Superior Court

The People of the State of California
To: THOMAS ANDERSON, Sheriff of the County of Santa Clara

Greeting:

We command you, that you have the body of Doyle Kelly, by you imprisoned and detained, as it is said, together with the time and cause of such imprisonment and detention, by whatsoever name said Doyle Kelly shall be called, or charged, before the Honorable Fred Thomas, Judge of said Court, in Department 3 thereof, in the Court House of said County, in the City of San Jose, on the seventh of December, 19—, at 10 o'clock in the forenoon of that day, to do and receive what shall then and there be considered concerning to said Doyle Kelly, and that you notify Candler Black, District Attorney of said County.

And have you then and there this writ.

> WITNESS, Hon. FRED THOMAS
> ATTEST my hand and seal of said Court, the day and year last above written.
> RALSTON STONE
> *Clerk*

When no charge has been filed against a person who is detained, his attorney files a *petition* applying for the *writ*. The clerk issues the writ with the approval of a judge unless the circumstances are unusual. The writ is directed to the custodian of the prisoner (i.e., sheriff or jailer) and is served on him. A copy of the petition is also given to the prosecuting attorney who, on behalf of the custodian, files a *return**. The return states facts to controvert the allegations contained in the petition. The judge holds a hearing to determine the issues. The burden of proof is on the petitioner. When the judge decides that the prisoner is detained legally he *vacates* the writ; when he decides otherwise he orders the prisoner to be discharged. The writ is vacated in some cases when the return indicates that the prosecuting attorney had filed a complaint after having been served with the writ, the purpose of the writ having thus been achieved.[2]

Writ Frees Man Held as Suspect

Doyle Kelly, a suspect in the Tim Dalton gangster murder case, walked out of court today, freed on a writ of habeas corpus.

Judge Fred Thomas agreed with Kelly's attorney, Joseph Egan, that the prisoner had been illegally detained because no preliminary examination had been held since his arrest last week.

"The statutes are very clear on the six-day time limit," the judge declared.

Assistant District Attorney Harold

---

[2] In the nineteen-twenties in Chicago when police had great difficulty in convicting gangsters for numerous murders, they adopted the practice of detaining suspects and witnesses secretly in hotel rooms, instead of jails, for several days of questioning. To combat this practice, the organized criminals telephoned every three hours to a girl "on the box" in their attorney's office. When a gangster failed to report, the attorney assumed that he had been arrested and immediately filed a petition for a writ of habeas corpus.

> Burbank argued that the case be taken under advisement. Had Judge Thomas agreed, the police would have had additional time in which to question Kelly, who, they say, was in the company of Dalton a short time before the murder.
>
> Kelly last year completed a term in a federal penitentiary for selling narcotics. . . .

In continental European countries there is no such writ as habeas corpus. But the laws provide that a prisoner may not be detained for longer than a certain number of days without being charged with an offense. However, there are several escapes from the rules so that some persons are held for a considerable time without being charged.

EXTRADITION AND RENDITION

Extradition is the *surrender* by one state or nation of a person accused or convicted of an offense outside of its own territory and within the jurisdiction of the other state, which demands his surrender. *Rendition* is the *return* of the person to the demanding state or nation.

Article IV, section 2 of the United States constitution provides that "a person charged in any State with treason, felony, or other crime, who shall flee from justice, and be found in another State, shall, on demand of the executive authority of the State from which he fled, be delivered up, to be removed to the State having jurisdiction of the crime."

To implement this constitutional provision, Congress in 1793 enacted a statute (18 U.S.C. sec. 3182) which requires proof by the demanding state that the accused person is actually a *fugitive* from justice; that is, that he committed a crime while physically present in the demanding state. Most states in recent years have enacted the *Uniform Criminal Extradition Act* which provides that a person may be extradited for the commission of an act in the asylum state or in a third state which intentionally *results in* a crime in the demanding state.

The extradition procedure operates in this way. A prosecuting attorney in the demanding state applies to the governor of his state for a *requisition of extradition*. The application must be accompanied by a copy of the indictment, information, complaint, judgment, or sentence.

When the governor of the demanding state approves the application he issues a *warrant of extradition* which directs a specific law enforcement officer, as the agent of the demanding state, to go to the asylum state and present the demand for rendition to the governor of the asylum state.

The governor of the asylum state, however, may hold a hearing when requested by the alleged fugitive. There are numerous instances in which a governor has refused to surrender the fugitive.

When the governor of the asylum state approves the extradition he issues a *warrant of rendition* which directs law enforcement officers in his state to arrest the alleged fugitive and to take him before a magistrate. At the arraignment the magistrate informs the alleged fugitive of the demand, the nature of the alleged crime, and his right to counsel.

The alleged fugitive may waive extradition by giving his written consent to return to the demanding state. But he may also attack the governor's warrant of extradition in the courts of the asylum state in habeas corpus proceedings. When the court finds that the warrant was issued without a sufficient showing it discharges the prisoner from custody.

Governor Ponders Was It Murder?

MADISON, WIS.—Whether an alleged murder victim died from natural causes was a question before Governor Hiram G. Schroeder today at an extradition hearing.

The state of Minnesota is trying to extradite Mrs. Harriett Miller, of Belmont, after charging her with complicity in the murder of Barnett Shepard, of Minneapolis.

Two Minnesota assistant attorneys-general argued today that Shepard was drugged and taken to an apartment to prevent his $8,000 law suit from coming to trial, and that he died from the effects of the drug.

Attorneys for Mrs. Miller presented affidavits from a University of Minnesota pathologist and pharmacologist that Shepard died from natural causes. They conducted a post-mortem examination.

The pharmacologist, Dr. Compton Woods, however, admitted in the affidavit that some poisons, including chloroform, morphine, and certain alkaloids, could cause death without leaving any trace.

Attorneys for both parties will seek affidavits from pathologists on the question of whether or not Shepard's death could have been caused by a defective heart.

Court Blocks Attempt To Extradite to Texas

NEW YORK—A criminal court judge today blocked an attempt by Texas authorities to extradite M. G. Wheeler, president of Commercial Solvents Corp., to Texas for trial on anti-trust charges.

A Potter county, Texas (Amarillo) grand jury indicted Mr. Wheeler and Texas business man Billie Sol Estes last summer on charges they conspired illegally to cut prices of anhydrous fertilizer in West Texas.

Justice Sidney A. Fine ruled the Texas indictments, under which Governor Rockefeller signed extradition papers on November 13, were insufficient to warrant extradition under New York state law.

He cited a provision of New York law on requests for extradition of a New York state resident for a crime allegedly committed outside the demanding state.

The state asking extradition must allege that consequences of the crime occurred in its state and would have been a crime if they had occurred in New York state.

In the case of Mr. Wheeler, the Texas indictments allege that Mr. Wheeler and Mr. Estes met in New York, where they agreed to fix prices of fertilizers in Texas.

The indictments, however, do not allege that prices actually were fixed in Texas, Justice Fine held. Thus the indictments do not allege any consequences which might be ruled a crime in New York, he said.

Mr. Wheeler is fighting extradition because, he contends, the Texas indictments are political and without foundation.

Parents and spouses accused of the crime of wilfully failing to provide financial support for dependents in another state may be extradited on pain of compliance with the court's order to render support. Nearly all states have provided for this procedure by enacting the *Uniform Reciprocal Enforcement of Support Act.*

International extradition is governed by bilateral treaties, each nation agreeing as to which crimes are extraditable. The United States does not have extradition treaties with all other nations. When a fugitive flees to a foreign country with which the United States has an extradition treaty, the governor of the demanding state applies for extradition through the United States Department of State.

CHAPTER 22

Criminal Actions: Accusation

The modes of accusation are these:

1. *Complaint,* the state's only pleading in most misdemeanor cases and its initial pleading when a preliminary examination is held.

2. *Indictment* by a grand jury. In some states this is the only mode of accusation in felony cases.

3. *Information* filed by the prosecuting attorney on his oath, a pleading used in several jurisdictions which is the equivalent of indictment. In some states a grand jury is impaneled only under special circumstances, all other accusations being by information. In more than one-half of the states the prosecuting attorney has the option of initiating criminal proceedings either by filing an information or by presenting evidence to the grand jury; in those jurisdictions, however, the grand jury has the authority to return an indictment or a *presentment*[1] on its own initiative. The United States rule is as follows:

> An offense which may be punished by death shall be prosecuted by indictment (Fifth Amendment). An offense which may be punished by imprisonment for a term exceeding one year or at hard labor shall be prosecuted by indictment or, if indictment is waived, it may be prosecuted by information. Any other offense may be prosecuted by indictment or by information.

4. Proceedings for removal from office of a county officer (e.g., prosecuting attorney or sheriff) in some states is initiated by an *accusation* by the grand jury. In this instance the officer is not accused of a crime but of misfeasance, malfeasance, or nonfeasance.

PRELIMINARY EXAMINATION

Unless a defendant has already been indicted by a grand jury he is entitled to a preliminary examination. At this hearing the state's pleading

[1] This term is defined on p. 333.

is a complaint. When the accused person has been arrested without a warrant, the prosecuting attorney must file a written complaint in advance of the hearing. When a complaint is used as a pleading to which the accused pleads guilty, it must contain the same allegations as would an indictment or an information.

A preliminary examination (sometimes called a preliminary hearing) is a hearing given to an accused person by a committing magistrate to determine whether there is *probable cause* to hold the defendant to answer. "The purpose of the preliminary hearing is to weed out groundless or unsupported charges of grave offenses, and to relieve the accused of the degradation and the expense of a criminal trial."[2]

The expressions "held to answer" and "bound over" mean that when the magistrate determines there is probable cause the accused is either held to trial or to the action of the grand jury, depending upon the mode of accusation in the particular jurisdiction. The defendant is required to renew his bail or is held in jail. When the prosecution is to be by information and the magistrate holds the accused to answer, the prosecuting attorney is required to file an information a few days after conclusion of the hearing; otherwise the accused may be released in habeas corpus proceedings.

When an accused person waives preliminary examination he is held to answer in that court which has jurisdiction to try him for the stated offense, i.e., the court of original jurisdiction. The magistrate who presides at the preliminary examination is often the judge of a court of limited jurisdiction and cannot accept a plea of "guilty" in a felony case.

The expression "probable cause" means that the evidence is sufficient for a man of ordinary prudence to believe that the accused may have committed the offense although the evidence at the hearing is not sufficient to justify a verdict of guilty in a court of original jurisdiction.

At the hearing the prosecuting attorney, if he can, presents just enough evidence to establish probable cause; this is a matter of strategy, for he does not want the defendant to know all of his evidence. The accused may cross-examine the state's witnesses and may also offer a defense. In some cases the accused is discharged by the magistrate.

Alleged Matricide Held for Trial

Municipal Judge Marcellus Rowe yesterday held Jouett Nelson to answer in superior court for the strangulation of his mother.

[2] Jaffe v. Stone, 114 P2d 335.

But at the preliminary examination the 42-year-old musician's attorney, Donald O'Connor, compelled the prosecution to present more evidence than it had apparently planned to present.

The only witness presented by Deputy District Attorney Jay Fairfield was Sheriff's Inspector Ernest Lema.

Sheriff's deputies say that Nelson strangled Mrs. Mary Nelson and later gave himself up.

Inspector Lema testified that Nelson admitted killing his mother. Lema was cross-examined by O'Connor. Then the deputy district attorney said he had completed the state's case.

O'Connor jumped to his feet and moved that the defendant be released.

"There is no evidence that this defendant is the man who committed the crime," he said. "There is no evidence that a crime has been committed."

The judge denied the motion but admonished the state's attorney to present more evidence.

"All I know about this case yet is what I have read in the newspapers," the judge said.

Fairfield recalled Lema and questioned him about details of the alleged confession.

Defense Attorney O'Connor cross-examined Lema for 20 minutes and twice during his cross-examination renewed his motion for dismissal of the complaint.

Judge Rowe denied the motions, then ruled there was sufficient evidence to hold Nelson for trial.

Statutes in some states provide for the exclusion of the public from a preliminary examination on motion of the defendant. The rationale of this procedure is that persons who may be impaneled as jurors in the defendant's trial may be influenced to the prejudice of the defendant by hearing or reading the state's uncontradicted evidence that was presented at the preliminary examination.[3]

[3] WINNIPEG, Manitoba—the proprietor of the *Winnipeg Tribune* last week was convicted on two counts under a criminal code provision forbidding publication of an admission or confession given in evidence at a preliminary hearing.

The provision is as follows:

"Everyone who publishes in any newspaper, or broadcasts, a report that any admission or confession was tendered in evidence, unless the accused has been discharged or

INFORMATION

The form of an information filed by a United States attorney in a misdemeanor case follows:

In the District Court of the United States
for the Northern District of California, Northern Division

United States of America
            v.   No. 0000
Ernest Hayes

The United States Attorney charges:
On or about the seventeenth day of October, 19—, in the Northern District of California, Ernest Hayes unlawfully caused to be introduced into interstate commerce, by delivery for shipment from the city of San Francisco, California, to the city of Santa Rosa, California, a consignment of cans containing articles of food which were adulterated in that they consisted in whole or in part of decomposed vegetable substance.

                                                            WENDELL COLLIER
                                                           United States Attorney

As explained on pages 328–329, a prosecuting attorney cannot prosecute a defendant on an information until a magistrate, in a preliminary examination, has determined in open court that there is probable cause for holding the defendant to trial or unless the defendant has waived the preliminary examination.

In jurisdictions in which crimes can be prosecuted by information the prosecuting attorney will initiate criminal proceedings in nearly all cases by information. This is because most of the cases are routine, because the prosecuting attorney has strong evidence, or because the proceeding conserves the time of the grand jury for the most important cases. An information can be amended easily in the courtroom by the prosecuting attorney when it is necessary to do so. The disadvantages of the information as compared with indictment will be discussed on pages 337–338.

THE GRAND JURY

In fourteenth-century England there developed the institution of "le graunde inquest," the members of which were summoned by the sheriff to

---

has been committed for trial, before the trial has ended, is guilty of an offense punishable on summary conviction."

Magistrate Ian Dubienski fined the newspaper $125 and costs on each count.

In the case of Clarence Russell Richardson, accused of the strangulation death of his wife, the newspaper published a constable's testimony that Richardson had told the constable he killed his wife after entering a suicide pact with her. Richardson was convicted of manslaughter and sentenced to ten years in prison. (Adapted from *Editor & Publisher*, Dec. 1, 1962.)

each session of the county court to hear complaints and to return accusations when they believed the evidence merited a trial. This jury of inquiry became known as the "grand jury" because it consisted of twenty-four men, whereas a petit (trial) jury was composed of only twelve men.[4] The number in each of the United States is fixed by statute and varies from six to twenty-three.

Grand jurors do not—ideally—represent a cross-section of the community as do trial jurors, but are men and women who are thought to be above average in intelligence, age, wealth, and social position. A fairly typical procedure for selecting grand jurors is this one: the judges of the court of original jurisdiction in the county make nominations to the presiding judge (or another judge assigned to handle the grand jury). Then they meet to winnow the master list. This screened list of about thirty, called a *venire,* is summoned to appear before the presiding judge, and the individuals are questioned as to their availability and possible conflicts of interest. Newspapers often publish the names of the venire when it is made available by the clerk. Finally, the presiding judge selects nineteen by lot.

The grand jury is assembled and sworn and hears the judge's "charge," or "address." This is an address in which the judge explains the duties of the grand jurors and the requirements placed upon them by the statutes, including the right to present an accusation based upon their own investigation as well as upon the prosecuting attorney's investigation. The judge sometimes calls to their attention rumors of criminal conditions in the community.

The judge in most jurisdictions appoints a foreman, and the jurors often elect a secretary.

The term of the grand jury varies in the states—from one month to one year. A federal grand jury may sit for as long as eighteen months.

In some jurisdictions the jury meets every day for several days and then recesses or is discharged. In other jurisdictions the jury meets all day once a week. In others they meet once a week only in the evening.

The grand jury's investigations are of two kinds. The grand jury considers, first, evidence in cases involving persons already arrested and held in jail or under bail. It considers, secondly, criminal cases in which no arrests have been made or conditions which ought to be remedied by the criminal law; in the latter instance the conditions are often called to their attention by private citizens. In addition, it inquires into the operations of the county government.

When the grand jury considers cases in which arrests have already been made the prosecuting attorney is present. He presents to the grand jury the

[4] The grand jury was abolished in England in 1933.

evidence he has and requests that an indictment be voted in each case. The grand jury, unlike the magistrate at a preliminary examination, does not often hear evidence in defense of the accused. But if the evidence presented by the prosecuting attorney establishes a prima facie case, the grand jury votes an indictment. This is by a majority or some number specified by statute; for example, when the size of the grand jury is nineteen, twelve votes are needed. The foreman then endorses "true bill" on the form which the prosecuting attorney has prepared. Whenever the grand jury votes that the evidence presented by the prosecuting attorney is insufficient to establish a prima facie case the foreman indorses on the form "ignoramus" ("we ignore it").

In the course of its investigations the grand jury subpoenas witnesses. These are interrogated by the prosecuting attorney, the foreman, and the other members of the grand jury. Some witnesses are asked, before testifying, to sign a waiver of their constitutional immunity to self-incrimination. They may refuse to do so.

The grand jury sometimes considers cases upon its own initiative and decides that a crime has been committed and that certain persons should stand trial. Cases of this kind relate to crimes of which the prosecuting attorney has not taken notice but which are of such public concern as to demand investigation. Such cases usually concern vice conditions, election frauds, and derelictions of public officials. Grand juries also delve into certain alleged immoralities, such as the sale by newsdealers of obscene magazines. In most jurisdictions an accusation by the grand jury on its own motion is called a *presentment.* This term is used in some jurisdictions, however, with reference to a resolution or report of the grand jury and is not a formal accusation on which someone can be prosecuted, but an opinion expressed by the grand jury.

In some jurisdictions a grand jury at some time will create a public sensation by an investigation it makes on its own initiative of alleged corruption of certain public officials. Such investigations are sometimes necessary because of the indifference of the prosecuting attorney. In other instances, they result from the initiative of one or two dominating zealots or exhibitionists on the grand jury who attach too much credibility to rumors that some politically motivated citizen has brought to their attention. Such grand juries are called "runaway" grand juries because they fail to accept advice from the judge who is in charge of the grand jury.

The grand jury is not a very efficient investigator because it does not have the funds that are necessary in some situations to employ competent investigators and accountants. In a few instances when it is evident that the prosecuting attorney is politically motivated the grand jury can obtain funds by justifying a special request to the county Board of Supervisors.

Statutes in some states provide that the grand jury may request the state's attorney general to investigate and report to the grand jury.

Another duty of the grand jury is to inspect the county penal and eleemosynary institutions, such as the jail and county hospital, and to inquire into the conduct of county officials—a "watchdog" function.

Grand juries in some states divide into committees; some of these are: audit, welfare and relief, county buildings, education, law enforcement, county offices, county hospitals, and county roads. The grand jury may investigate the records kept by public officials and interrogate the officials. When they wish to investigate the conduct of the prosecuting attorney or members of his staff they have the authority to exclude them from the grand jury room.

When the grand jury investigates public institutions and officials it submits a *report* which lists some of the shortcomings of the county government or of its officials and praises other institutions and officers. For example, grand juries have reported that a new local jail is needed and that a new county charter is needed to replace an archaic form. In a few instances grand juries present *resolutions* about public policies that are not directly related to local affairs, such as a pronouncement in favor of a sales tax and criticism of certain state-adopted textbooks.

List of Gaming Devices Issued By Grand Jury

A complete inventory of every gambling device in the county, together with its location, was included in the grand jury report submitted today.

The grand jury handed Judge Hale McKay two documents. One was the report on gambling and the other was a 23-page report on county fiscal procedure.

The gambling information was obtained by investigators for the attorney general at the request of the grand jury. The report will be given to the district attorney, the sheriff, and local chiefs of police, but otherwise will be suppressed by Judge McKay.

Recommend New Library

The report on fiscal procedures criticizes several departments of government:

> 1. The assessor's office for failure to certify the assessment roll to the controller.
> 2. The tax collector for failure to deposit monies daily with the county treasurer, as required by charter.
> 3. The justice court of Edgerton for lack of proper records of receipts and disbursements.
>
> The grand jury recommended a survey of management of the county hospital. It praised the superintendent of the county poor farm for efficiency and his considerate treatment of the inmates.
>
> New quarters for the county library were also recommended.
>
> "Lack of room and proper facilities are more pronounced here than probably any other place in the control of the county government," the report said in referring to the library.

A judge may suppress a grand jury report, thus making it unavailable to newspapers.

In one state the legislature enacted a law[5] providing for *public* testimony before a grand jury when (1) "the subject matter of the investigation is one affecting the general public welfare, respecting matters involving alleged corruption or misfeasance or malfeasance in office or dereliction of public officials or employees" and (2) a judge so directs. This practice is of doubtful value and the statute has seldom been used.

REPORTING GRAND JURY SESSIONS

After the indictments have been returned, the judge in charge of the grand jury issues *bench warrants* (also called *capiases*) commanding the sheriff to make arrests. (A bench warrant is also issued in other circumstances, as when a witness who has been subpoenaed fails to appear or a convicted defendant fails to pay his fine.) The practice of courts is to permit newspaper reporters to examine the indictments which are returned (except those of persons not yet arrested, and especially those of persons who are likely to flee the jurisdiction). The clerk and sheriff, who have possession of indictments after they have been returned to the judge, exercise some discretion as to when they permit reporters to publish indictments. Details about testimony before the grand jury in each instance of indictment is ascertained from the district attorney or one of his deputies.

[5] California *Penal Code*, sec. 925a.

Grand Jury Indicts Youths in Party Raid

Twelve members of the gang which attacked guests at a Hillsborough house party were indicted yesterday on charges ranging from assault with intent to do great bodily harm to burglary.

Twenty-three witnesses—the gang's victims, the party hostess, police officers, and a member of the gang—testified.

Each of the 12 suspects was charged with at least five felonies. Leonard Lardner, 19-year-old salesman, of 4349 Leighton street, identified as one of the ringleaders of the two attacks on the Hillsborough house party, was charged with nine felonies. . . .

Tavern Owner Escapes Indictment

The grand jury yesterday refused to indict tavern owner Rufus Shafter for a brawl in which he admittedly shot two people.

District Attorney Thornton Willis said the jury believed evidence was too conflicting to warrant an indictment.

Eleven witnesses, including the two who were wounded in the June 20 fracas at Shafter's Red Barn tavern, testified.

They were Robert Weir and Emma Willard.

Shafter had told police he was trying to get Weir and his brother to leave the tavern because they were bothering other patrons.

Wallace Weir, brother of the victim, drew a knife, according to Shafter. Shafter got out his pistol. He hit Weir on the head with it, he said, and the gun went off accidentally.

The single bullet struck Weir, then hit Miss Willard just as she was entering the door.

Reporters, of course, are not admitted to the grand jury room. Testimony before the grand jury is secret for two reasons: (1) to prevent persons who are being investigated from fleeing and (2) to protect accused persons from publication of *ex parte* evidence (the evidence of only one party to an action) which they have no opportunity of refuting. In some circumstances some newspapers, in reporting a grand jury investigation, explain the difference between an investigation and an indictment. Here is an example from the *Wall Street Journal:* "A grand jury's consideration of evidence does not imply guilt of any criminal act. While a grand jury can return a criminal indictment, it also can reject the evidence presented as insufficient to warrant trial."

Grand jurors themselves are forbidden to divulge their proceedings. Witnesses are free to discuss their own testimony, and can be interviewed after they have left the grand jury room. Prosecuting attorneys are sometimes willing to talk. In some instances they supply in advance the names of witnesses who will testify and sometimes, at the conclusion of a grand jury session, issue statements that review the testimony that was heard and reply to reporters' questions.

In some situations, such as those involving political corruption, where it is believed there will be great difficulty in convicting certain politicians, the prosecuting attorney tries the case in the newspapers. This is an instance of the end justifying the means and is of doubtful validity.

Indictments returned by a grand jury are privileged*, but grand jury "reports" which comment upon any person or official who has not been indicted are not privileged in all states, especially when the comments do not relate to the person's fitness for office or his fidelity to a public trust.

INDICTMENT vs. INFORMATION

The chief advantages of prosecuting by information are the time conserved by the grand jury for its important investigations and the fact that an information found defective by the judge can be amended in court by the prosecuting attorney, whereas a defective indictment must be resubmitted to the grand jury.

One advantage of the indictment, aside from the possibility that a prosecuting attorney may be indifferent to conditions that need correction, is that its witnesses testify under oath. The prosecuting attorney who "questions" witnesses in his office or elsewhere during the investigation of a case usually cannot put them under oath. A second advantage of the indictment is that it may be kept secret until the grand jury has completed its investigation, thus preventing accomplices from fleeing the jurisdiction before the investigation has been completed.

OTHER PROCEEDINGS FOR THE DISCOVERY OF CRIME

In some states a judge or a prosecuting attorney is empowered to examine witnesses for the discovery of crime. After a complaint has been filed that there is probable cause that a crime has been committed, the magistrate subpoenas witnesses and examines them. In Wisconsin the proceeding is called a "John Doe" proceeding because the purpose is to discover the offender as well as to establish the commission of an offense; in Michigan, where a judge acts as a "one-man grand jury," the proceeding has been effective in the investigation of corruption in government.[6] Texas law permits "courts of inquiry" to be convened to gather evidence to be used in court cases and by grand juries.

It is doubtful that newspaper accounts of all such proceedings are privileged, for a warrant of arrest is not issued until after the proceeding has ended, if then.

FORM AND PARTICULARITY OF THE ACCUSATION

The form of an information and of a complaint were exhibited on pages 331 and 316 respectively. The form of an indictment (in a federal case) follows:

In the District Court of the United States
for the Northern District of California, Northern Division

United States of America
        v.   No. 10243
Louis Wallace *et al.*

    The grand jury charges:
    1. Prior to the twenty-second day of May, 19—, and continuing to the fourteenth day of August, 19—, the defendants Louis Wallace, John Stiles, and Richard Miles, devised and intended to devise a scheme and artifice to defraud purchasers of stock of Western Prospecting Company, a California corporation, and to obtain money and property by means of the following false and fraudulent pretenses, representations, and promises, well knowing at the time that the pretenses, representations and promises would be false when made: That the Western Prospecting Company owned a mine at or near San Bernardino, California; that gold ore was being obtained at the mine and sold at a profit; that the current earnings of the company would be sufficient to pay dividends on its stock at the rate of six per cent per annum.
    2. On the eleventh day of June, 19—, in the Northern District of California, the defendants, for the purpose of executing the aforesaid scheme and artifice and attempting to do so, caused to be placed in an authorized

[6] Wisconsin: *Statutes,* sec. 361.02; Michigan: *Compiled Laws,* secs. 17217–20.

depository for mail matter a letter addressed to Mrs. Mary Brown, 110 Main Street, Stockton, California, to be sent or delivered by the Post Office Establishment of the United States.

SECOND COUNT

1. The Grand Jury realleges all of the allegations of the first count of this indictment, except those contained in the first paragraph thereof.

2. On the eleventh day of June, 19—, in the Northern District of California, the defendants, for the purpose of executing the aforesaid scheme and artifice and attempting to do so, caused to be placed in an authorized depository for mail matter a letter addressed to Mr. John J. Jones, 220 First Street, Batavia, New York, to be sent or delivered by the Post Office Establishment of the United States.

A True Bill
EDWARD WILBUR
Foreman

WENDELL COLLIER
United States Attorney

Most of the particularity in accusations that was required at common law is now obsolete in modern criminal pleading. An accusation is regarded as sufficient in those states which have adopted modern criminal pleading when the accusation informs the defendant of the charge so that he may prepare a defense.

The statement of the offense cannot be ambiguous for these reasons: (1) the relationship of the offense to the penalty prescribed by statute and (2) the protection of the defendant from prosecution for the same offense after having been convicted or acquitted for the same act or omission. When the accusation uses the exact language of the statute the accusation is regarded as sufficient.

Some states, however, still require a good deal of particularity. For example, the conclusion of the accusation must state that the offense is "contrary to the form of the statute in such case made and provided and against the peace and dignity of the state of ———." The terms, "unlawfully," "wilfully," and "knowingly" are often required, especially the expression, "knowingly," when intent is an essential element of the offense, as in murder by poison. The time and place of the offense must be stated rather precisely in some states. In some states, too, the prosecuting attorney is required to supply the defendant with a *bill of particulars* which states more specific details, as when the defendant, accused of uttering a worthless check and, having at various times uttered several valid checks to the complaining witness, may demand that the prosecuting attorney designate the specific check which is alleged to be worthless.

In most jurisdictions the defendant is entitled to know the identity of his accusers. For that reason the grand jury foreman annexes to the indictment the names of all witnesses who have testified. Some states also supply the defendant with a copy of the testimony taken before the grand jury or during the preliminary examination when one has been held. When this is done less particularity in the accusation is necessary because the transcript of the testimony supplies adequate notice to the defendant of the charges against him.

Count

An accusation frequently contains more than one *count*. An anti-trust indictment of the old Standard Oil Company several years ago contained 1,462 counts. A count is a separate charge which refers to the same act or transaction. Thus, the defendant referred to in the news story below was tried on a single indictment, being charged with two offenses on each of eighteen acts, making a total of thirty-six separate counts.

Whether a defendant may be tried separately on each count depends upon whether or not the counts are connected. For example, a defendant cannot be tried at the same time for the murder of two or more different persons; he can, however, be tried at the same time for rape and for lewd and lascivious conduct where both offenses have allegedly been committed on the same day and with the same victim. A defendant may be convicted on some counts and acquitted on others.

Public Administrator Indicted on 36 Counts

Francis Quarles, public administrator for 16 years, was indicted by the grand jury today on 36 counts of embezzlement involving more than $58,000.

Quarles was arrested on a bench warrant issued by Superior Judge H. T. Southwood. Bail was set at $5,000 cash or $10,000 bond.

The indictment charges 18 separate offenses under two different statutes: (1) misappropriation of public funds for one's own use and (2) misappropriation of funds for a use not authorized by law.

The indictment contained 18 counts under each of the two subsections of a statute, charging misappropriation from 18 decedents' estates under his administration.

The amounts ranged from $1,225 in the estate of Ambrose Phillips to

$6,000 in the estate of Herbert Tree.
Sixteen witnesses testified before the grand jury, being mainly trust officers of banks.

Joinder of defendants: The rule in federal practice is: "Two or more defendants may be charged in the accusation if they are alleged to have participated in the same act or transaction or in the same acts or transactions constituting an offense or offenses. Such defendants may be charged in one or more counts together or separately and all of the defendants need not be charged in one count." This subject is discussed again on page 350.

For class discussion: What are the modes of accusation in your state? Are they as efficient as some other modes discussed in this chapter?

CHAPTER 23

Criminal Actions: Defendant's Pleading

In response to the plaintiff's (i.e., the state's or United States') pleading, a defendant may either answer (i.e., enter a plea in bar) or present objections or defenses that challenge the process or the form of the accusation or the jurisdiction of the court.

Pleas in bar are:
1. Guilty.
2. Not guilty.
3. *Nolo contendere* ("I will not contest it"), sometimes called *non vult contendere*. This plea is not accepted in some jurisdictions and in federal courts in some antitrust criminal actions. It is equivalent to the plea of guilty but avoids a trial. Defendants whose health is precarious have entered the plea. Others have also entered the plea to avoid the record of a trial which later could be used against them in a civil action.

"No Contest" Plea In Dimes Theft

Former Postmaster Scott Sewell pleaded nolo contendere (no contest) in federal district court yesterday to charges he embezzled March of Dimes funds entrusted to his care as treasurer of his county's chapter.

Judge Paul Bingham accepted the plea over objections of Assistant United States Attorney Vincent Watson.

The plea will be treated, for the purpose of judgment, as a plea of guilty.

Sewell's attorney, Fred Babbitt, said Sewell entered the plea because a guilty plea could jeopardize pension rights the postmaster had earned during his 17 years in civil service.

The assistant United States attorney objected vigorously, saying: "Guilt is amply clear. Besides, he held a post of relatively great importance."

4. Former jeopardy, former conviction, or former acquittal. The United States constitution and the constitutions of the states provide that no person shall be twice put in jeopardy for the same offense. A defendant is in jeopardy when he is placed on trial for the same offense on a valid indictment. "Placed on trial" means that, in a jury trial, a jury has been impaneled and sworn; no testimony needs to have been introduced. If at that point, there is reason for the court to declare a mistrial and the defendant does not consent to the ruling, he has been placed in jeopardy and cannot be tried again for the same offense. "The same offense" does not mean a different count in the same indictment. Nor does it mean a trial for the same act which is a crime against another government. Thus, a defendant acquitted in an Illinois court of robbing a bank in Illinois was prosecuted and convicted in a federal court for the same act, the robbery also being a violation of a federal statute. The indictment on which a defendant is tried must be valid. Thus, if a man who has been improperly indicted on a larceny charge is acquitted, he may be indicted and tried on a charge of receiving stolen property. The terms "double jeopardy" and "twice in jeopardy" are synonymous with "former jeopardy."

5. In some jurisdictions in murder cases, the statutes provide for the plea of *not guilty by reason of insanity* in addition to the plea of not guilty. This means that the defendant is tried first on the not guilty plea and, when found guilty, is tried a second time by the same or a different jury on the insanity plea.

ARRAIGNMENT AND PLEADING

The proceeding by which a defendant is brought to bar to plead in response to an accusation is *arraignment*. It consists in reading the accusation to the defendant and delivering a copy of it to him and asking him whether he pleads guilty or not guilty. When he pleads guilty the plea is entered. The proceeding also demands that the defendant be asked if the name by which he is accused is his true name and whether or not he has counsel. If the name by which he is charged is not his true name, his true name is recorded.

In most instances, as will be explained, the defendant does not enter a not guilty plea at his arraignment; instead, the court sets a date called "time to plead" a few days after the arraignment so that the defendant and his counsel will have time to consider what plea he shall enter and to consider offering objections to the accusation before entering a plea. In those instances in which an attack on the accusation is to be made, a longer continuance is granted for preparation of the motions. The court on a set day disposes of all motions before the defendant enters his plea. The following is the record of an arraignment on an information and the defendant's plea:

In the Superior Court of the County of Santa Clara
State of California

At a session of the Superior Court, held at the Court House, in the County of Santa Clara on the sixth day of February, 19—.
Present: Hon. Fred Thomas, Superior Judge
Ralston Stone, Clerk, and Max Birck, Sheriff.

The People of the State of California
                    Plaintiff
        v.
Walter Neiswanger
    Defendant

This being the time fixed for the arraignment of defendant, he is now produced and appears in open court, Monroe Barnes, the District Attorney, moves to have the defendant arraigned, whereupon the information herein is now read to the said defendant and a copy thereof delivered to him by the Clerk.

The defendant, Walter Neiswanger, being now asked if the name by which he is charged in the information is his true name answers that it is his true name; and being further asked by the Court whether he has an attorney answers that he has retained Hanson Croly.

The defendant being then asked by the Court whether he pleads guilty or not guilty to the charge in the information herein, answers that he pleads not guilty; which said plea is duly entered and trial is set for the seventeenth day of February, 19—, at 10 o'clock in the forenoon.

I, Ralston Stone, Clerk of the Superior Court of the County of Santa Clara, do hereby certify that the foregoing is a full, true, and correct copy of the record of arraignment and minutes of the court made in the above entitled action, on the date mentioned in the caption thereof.

In witness whereof, I have hereunto set my hand and the seal of the Superior Court, this sixth day of February, 19—.

RALSTON STONE, *Clerk*
By WILLIAM STANLEY, *Deputy Clerk*

The defendant must appear personally at his arraignment when he is accused of a felony in an indictment or information. When, in some jurisdictions, a defendant is charged with a misdemeanor on a complaint his plea may be entered by his attorney.

One-third of the persons accused in criminal cases cannot afford to employ an attorney. This has meant that many of them have not received the same protection as have more fortunate defendants. Until 1963, five states required court-appointed attorneys only for capital cases, and at least ten other states only for certain felony cases. Few states, moreover, provided for a free transcript of the trial on appeal or for investigators' and experts' expenses prior to a trial. The provisions of federal law were no better protection for indigents than was the law in some of the most backward states.

This situation was remedied in 1963 when the United States Supreme Court held that the states must supply free lawyers for indigents accused of "serious" crimes and free counsel on appeal from a conviction.[1]

In 1964, Congress passed the Criminal Justice Act of 1964 (Title 18, sec. 2 U.S.C. amended; 78 Stat. 552), which provides for compensation of attorneys appointed to defend indigent defendants in the federal courts and for investigators and experts when approved by the court.

Many local bar associations have a panel of members whom the court can call upon to defend indigents. A few counties maintain the office of *public defender* whose staff, including investigators, is paid by the county.

When a defendant pleads guilty either at his arraignment or later, a time is set for sentencing. The plea of guilty must be made in open court by the defendant himself (except that a corporation can enter the plea by counsel). There are some instances in which, after a plea of guilty in a capital crime, the judge hears evidence to assist him in deciding the severity of the sentence; this is done on motion of the defendant in anticipation of mitigation of the sentence.

The court, under some circumstances, permits a defendant to change his plea of guilty to not guilty at some stage of the action.

When a defendant stands mute—i.e., refuses to enter any plea—the court enters a plea of not guilty on his behalf.

The following news story reports an arraignment on a complaint:

Corporal Arraigned In Bathtub Slaying

Army Corporal Charles Gwin, charged with the bathtub murder of his young bride, made his first court appearance yesterday.

The 6-foot 6-inch corporal stood quietly before Municipal Judge Marcellus Rowe for arraignment while his

[1] Gideon v. Wainwright, 372 U.S. 335 (1963). See also A. Lewis, *Gideon's Trumpet* (New York, 1964), a dramatic history of this case by the *New York Times* reporter who covers the Supreme Court. In 1953 (Griffin v. Illinois), the Supreme Court had held that an indigent defendant in a state court was entitled to a free transcript on appeal.

parents watched anxiously from the rear of the courtroom.

"Your true name is Charles Gwin?" the judge asked.

"I am Charles Gwin," he said.

Gray Hoffman, his attorney, asked that February 27 be set as the day for entering Gwin's plea. Judge Rowe agreed.

Outside the courtroom, Homicide Inspector Henry Lawes said he expects to take the evidence before the grand jury next Tuesday night.

A grand jury indictment would take the case directly to Superior Court, making it unnecessary for the prosecution to reveal its principal evidence at a preliminary hearing.

OBJECTIONS TO THE ACCUSATION

At common law certain pleas and motions are made which attack the accusation. These are made and ruled on by the judge before the defendant enters a plea. Although the formal names of most of these motions and pleas are no longer used in modern pleading, they are still used in some states. These names are: (1) plea to the jurisdiction, (2) plea in abatement, (3) motion to quash, and (4) demurrer. The defendant's objectives in some of these are achieved in modern practice by a *motion to set aside* the accusation. In federal practice, the objectives are achieved in a *motion to dismiss*.

A *plea to the jurisdiction* denies that the court has jurisdiction to try the defendant for the particular offense or it asserts that the offense was committed outside the court's territorial jurisdiction. Statutes and court decisions have become so definite that this plea is seldom invoked. For example, the venue of a murder is usually the county in which the victim died rather than in the county in which he was shot. When an offense is committed in proximity to the border of two counties, statutes frequently provide that either county has jurisdiction. Nevertheless some questions of jurisdiction still arise—as when poisoned candy mailed in one state causes a death in another state. In some instances a plea to the jurisdiction results in dismissal of the accusation.

The plea to the jurisdiction should not be confused with the *motion* for *change of venue*. The latter motion does not challenge the authority of the court to try the case but requests removal of the trial to another jurisdiction on the ground that prospective jurors in the other county have not been exposed to as much pretrial publicity that is adverse to the defendant. Proof that the defendant will not receive a fair trial in the county in which he has been accused is submitted in affidavits. The state replies with counteraffidavits, and a hearing is held.

In some circumstances a judge has denied the motion for change of venue but has impaneled a jury from another county. Some statutes provide for change of venue to an adjoining county after jury panels have been exhausted by challenges for cause.

Site of Fraud Charge Trial Is Changed

PECOS, TEXAS—District Judge J. H. Starley upheld a defense argument Wednesday that Billie Sol Estes couldn't get a fair trial in his home town and said he will transfer the case to Tyler, 529 miles east of Pecos.

Attorneys representing Estes unexpectedly asked Monday for immediate trial of the count in the indictment that he bilked farmer Thomas A. Bell of $162,144 in a purchase agreement involving liquid fertilizer tanks.

District Judge Otis T. Dunagan told reporters in Tyler Wednesday night he had talked to Judge Starley and would accept the case. No date will be set until the Pecos judge signs a formal order on July 23.

Plea in abatement, a dilatory motion, charges some defect in the accusation, such as wrong name of the defendant. Since the plea is not to the merits, it only results in delay when upheld by a judge. At common law it means that the state is required to bring a new indictment in an amended form or that the information must be amended. The state, at common law, may demur to this plea.

Motion to quash is an attack on the form or substance of the accusation; for example, that the indictment was returned by a handpicked jury (*challenge to the array*), or that less than a quorum of the grand jurors voted on the indictment. At common law the motion can attack the accusation on the grounds that there is an improper joinder of defendants or of counts, or that the statute of limitations has run on the particular offense.

Demurrer

At common law, a demurrer challenges the legal sufficiency of the accusation on the grounds that the accusation does not charge an offense or that it charges an offense which the defendant is not required to answer;

that is, the facts stated in the accusation do not constitute a crime or they charge a crime for which the defendant is not required to answer.

An example of the first class: a newspaper reporter listened to a tape recording that had been made secretly by law enforcement officers and was indicted for conspiracy to violate an anti-wiretapping law; the judge dismissed the indictment. An example of the second class: defendants were charged under the Municipal Code for violation of an anti-gambling law; the judge dismissed the complaint on the ground that the defendants should have been accused under the State Penal Code.

Charge Dismissed vs. Football Player

Herbert O'Neill, state university football player indicted on a charge of taking a bicycle, was exonerated by Superior Court Judge H. T. Southwood today.

The judge sustained a demurrer to the charge filed by O'Neill's attorney, Delbert Enfield, and dismissed the indictment. The demurrer objected to prosecution of the felony charge under the State Motor Vehicle Code.

Enfield contended a bicycle was not intended for inclusion in that part of the state code relating to theft.

The football player was accused of taking the bicycle of an East High School youth last June 29 without his permission but without attempt to steal. He was indicted October 11.

O'Neill said he had borrowed the bicycle from a friend, not realizing that it did not belong to the friend.

The term "demurrer" is used in some states to include some of the grounds mentioned in the various common law pleas defined in foregoing paragraphs. Thus, in one state grounds for a demurrer include not only those mentioned in this section but also lack of jurisdiction of the offense, defect of form, and joinder of offenses without a separate statement.

When the judge sustains a demurrer the case is dismissed unless the circumstances are such that the information or complaint may be amended. In some cases, on an indictment, the case can be resubmitted to the grand jury to cure the defects.

When the judge overrules a demurrer the defendant must then plead.

DISCOVERY BEFORE TRIAL

Discovery in criminal cases is much more limited in scope than is discovery in civil cases.[2] The state is limited by the constitutional provisions against search and seizure and self-incrimination.[3] The defense is also limited; this is mainly because the state cannot appeal an acquittal verdict—a considerable advantage for the defendant.[4]

The scope of discovery permitted the defendant varies considerably among the states. In most jurisdictions the defendant is entitled to know the names of the witnesses who testified before the grand jury. The defendant also learns about some of the state's evidence when a preliminary examination is held but, as was explained on page 328, the prosecuting attorney can instead take the case before the grand jury in those jurisdictions in which he has that option. In federal practice and in some states the defendant is entitled to copy or photograph documents, papers, and tangible objects which the state or government has obtained from him or from others. Originally at common law the defendant did not have this advantage. In some states the defendant is entitled to have a transcript of the testimony before the grand jury. In some jurisdictions the defendant must be supplied with statements made by state or government witnesses, but only after the witness has testified at the trial. Some states permit a defendant to take a deposition in another state.

In federal practice and in some states, with leave of the court, the defendant may require the state to file a *bill of particulars* before or after arraignment, as was explained on page 339. A bill of particulars is sometimes amended by the prosecution after it has been filed.

U.S. Told to Supply More Facts to D.A.

A federal judge yesterday required the government to present a bill of particulars in its case against District Attorney Edmund Gaines for conspiracy to violate the alcohol revenue laws.

On motion of the defense, Judge Paul Bingham ordered the government to amplify its charges by identifying a distillery named in one count of the in-

---

[2] Discovery in civil cases was discussed on pp. 216–217.
[3] See pp. 318–319. Also, under the Fifth Amendment, a person cannot be compelled to be a witness against himself.
[4] See p. 429.

dictment and by supplying the names of two alcohol tax agents alleged to have been offered a bribe to permit operation of the distillery.

The judge also directed the government to make definite, if possible, the dates on which Gaines is alleged to have demanded $5,000 from Cecil Lewis and William Cady.

Judge Bingham denied the defendant's motion to require the government to show whether or not it had any evidence personally identifying Gaines with the acts of the alleged conspirators.

Nearly all states have a rule or statute which requires a sort of bill of particulars from the *defendant* when one of his defenses is to be *alibi* ("elsewhere").[5] The defendant is required to give to the prosecuting attorney on the day of arraignment a written notice which states particularly the place where he will claim to have been when the offense is alleged to have been committed. In default of this notice, evidence of the alibi will not be received unless the court, for good cause, admits it.

OTHER MOTIONS BEFORE TRIAL

A motion for *severance,* made by one or more of the defendants, accused jointly, is granted when the court is satisfied that one or more of the defendants has a separate defense and would be placed at a disadvantage in a joint trial if his or their defense had to be combined with the defense of the other defendants. It is also granted when one of the defendants is unable to stand trial because of illness.

A motion infrequently made is to *disqualify the judge* before whom a trial is to be held. Statutes and court rules differ considerably. Usually, however, the defendant is required to support by affidavit his challenge of the judge on grounds of interest or bias. Sometimes a case is transferred to another department of the same court and in counties of small population a State Judicial Council has power in some states to assign a judge from a different county to sit.

The prosecuting attorney may ask leave of the court to "nol pros" (*nolle prosequi,* i.e., "do not wish to prosecute") an accusation. He may also move for dismissal of one or more counts or of one or more of the jointly accused defendants. Dismissal of a defendant in this way is not a bar to further prosecution if the motion for dismissal has preceded the trial. The

---

[5] This expression is used colloquially to mean "excuse," but literally means "at another place."

entry is usually, "dismissed without prejudice," which means the prosecutor may later renew the prosecution by the usual methods.

Sometimes the prosecuting attorney amends an information to reduce the charge; thus, from first degree murder to voluntary manslaughter. In some instances, the reduction induces the defendant to plead guilty to the lesser offense; in other instances, the prosecuting attorney anticipates that the jury will convict for the lesser offense but not for the original offense.

A defendant's *motion to suppress* certain evidence obtained illegally is sometimes granted.

CHAPTER 24

Criminal Actions: The Trial

It is not necessary for newspaper reporters to listen to the evidence in all criminal cases. In many cases the only matter of interest is the result of the trial. After a jury has announced a verdict and the judge has pronounced sentence the clerk enters the judgment in the minutes. A typical entry is as follows: "No. 3374, State *v.* Jones, Guilty, Three years. Jury No. 1, as follows [here follow the names of the jurors]." Or the entry may read, "Not Guilty" or "Dismissed Without Prejudice." Some wire services in reporting an acquittal have adopted the practice of reporting the defendant was found "innocent" or was "acquitted" in order to avoid any possibility of the word "not" being dropped out of the expression "not guilty" during transmission.

By consulting with the clerks two or three times a day, the reporter can learn the disposition of the less important criminal cases. He should be familiar, of course, with all of the cases so that he can report the character of the crime charged, and, perhaps some of the details of the case.

THE SETTING OF THE TRIAL

A first-day story of very important trials sometimes includes a description of the setting and of the principals and their relatives and friends who are in attendance. Although courts of justice ought not to be treated as mere stages set for the amusement of spectators and newspaper readers, no harm is done in providing the reader with a picture of the trial scene. The principal harm arises out of the sensational reporting of unsavory cases, not from reporting interesting cases in an interesting manner. The following description of the setting of a trial supplies the reader with a background for understanding the case and with a conception of the forces engaged and the stakes at issue.

Smiling as ever, sharp eyes twinkling behind his gold spectacles, Mr. Van Dusen entered the courtroom to face the charges with every mark of serene confidence. His wife, his son, his son's wife, the battery of expensive counsel followed in his wake.

Mr. Rood, the co-defendant, stooped, thin, gaunt and gray, chewing on an unlighted cigar, came almost shuffling in, his legal battery around him. They nearly filled the well before the bench.

A score of newspaper men formed the next phalanx. Three inadequate rows took care of the few spectators who could get in, including some witnesses, among whom were Henry Louis Dill, the Philadelphia publisher, and United States Senator Wilson, whose investigation had helped to indict the defendants.

After eighteen months of sparring in grand jury rooms and judges' chambers, the trial to determine whether a cabinet officer had accepted a bribe was about to begin.

STAGES OF THE TRIAL

These steps are taken in a criminal jury trial for a felony in the typical court of original jurisdiction:
1. Selection and swearing of the jury.
2. Reading of the accusation and the defendant's plea.
3. Opening statement of the prosecution.
4. Presentation of the prosecution's evidence by direct, cross-, and redirect examination.
5. Opening statement of the defense; this statement is sometimes made after the prosecution's opening statement.
6. Presentation of defendant's evidence.
7. Presentation of rebuttal evidence, if any, by both parties.
8. Summation by both parties.
9. Judge's instructions to the jury.
10. Deliberation by the jury.
11. Return of the verdict.
12. Sentence (when defendant has been convicted).
13. Execution of the judgment.

Some jurisdictions permit a *motion for a directed verdict* or a *motion for judgment of acquittal;* other jurisdictions permit a *motion for advice to acquit,* which is not binding on the jury. Such motions may be made either at the conclusion of the prosecution's case or after conclusion of the defendant's case. These motions are discussed below on pages 376–377.

SELECTION OF JURORS[1]

Attorneys in criminal cases realize the vital importance of selecting jurors. In important cases the attorneys have previously investigated the background of every member of the panel. For one reason or another connected with the personalities of the principals or the issues, one side or the other has already decided not to accept veniremen of a certain kind of background and they sometimes try to select those of a particular background. An example of this strategy was in the 1913 trial of two California men accused of violating the federal statute which prohibits the interstate transportation of a woman for an immoral purpose (Mann Act): the government managed to keep all bachelors off the jury.

The procedure of selection is approximately the same as in a civil case[2] except that usually each side is entitled to a greater number of peremptory challenges—often twenty for each side. When defendants are tried jointly each is entitled to a certain number of additional peremptory challenges and this total may be matched by the prosecution.

A criminal jury more often has alternate jurors—from two to four. In some jurisdictions the alternate jurors sit with the regular jurors but do not deliberate unless they are substituted during the trial for a disqualified juror; in other jurisdictions the judge, at the conclusion of the case, selects by lot twelve of the total to deliberate and discharges the remaining jurors.

After the jury has been impaneled in an important case the reporter should list the jurors' names, sex, address, and occupation.

Selection of Jury In Olmstead Case Continues Today

The prosecution in the Olmstead murder case accepted a jury of eight men and four women yesterday at 5:20 p.m., but the defense exercised a peremptory challenge.

As the result, the tedious process of selection will continue today with

---

[1] Seven states permit waiver of jury trial for any felony, and eight others permit waiver in all except capital cases.

[2] See pp. 239–240.

Judge Dutton Ashurst ready to summon another venire if the present one should be exhausted.

The trial of Fred Olmstead, secretary of Boilermakers' Local No. 10, accused of shooting to death Democratic Assemblyman Leroy McGoldrick, began Wednesday morning.

Since then 27 prospective jurors of a venire of 50 have been examined and 19 have been excused. The state has two more peremptory challenges it can use to disqualify prospective jurors and the defense has four.

Two Held Disqualified

One juror was challenged "for cause" by the state yesterday because he was a member of Olmstead's union. Defense Attorney Albert Bragg objected to the challenge, declaring, "This juror is just one of 4,000 members of the union."

"Yes," Judge Ashurst said, "but the questions are to find out whether he is closer to the defendant than to the other 3,999 members. It seems he has had the closest relationship with the defendant."

The defense challenged "for cause" Mrs. Marie Brown, wife of a branch bank manager, who said under examination, "Most of the strikes called by this union could have been settled without a work stoppage."

Judge Ashurst ruled her off the jury, saying, "Isn't it possible some prejudice might creep into your hearing of the evidence?"

Mrs. Brown said "No."

In his examination of prospective jurors, Defense Attorney Miles Hildebrand asked involved questions with the apparent purpose of indoctrinating the jury with conceptions of the case favorable to the defense. Judge Ashurst sustained the state's objection to that line of questioning.

For class discussion: The publication by newspapers of the names and addresses of jurors should be prohibited by statute, in the opinion of Judge Bernard S. Meyer of the Supreme Court of New York, on the ground that the jurors are sometimes subjected to the weight of public opinion, especially through telephone calls. Do you agree or disagree? Why?

OPENING STATEMENT

After the jury has been sworn the prosecuting attorney makes an opening statement in which he outlines for the jury the nature of the evidence he will present and tells his version of the facts. Whether the defendant's attorney follows immediately with his opening statement or reserves it until he is ready to present the defendant's evidence is a question of strategy. In some instances he risks revealing to the prosecution his line of defense and presents an opportunity for the prosecution to controvert it while presenting its own case.

The opening statement cannot be argumentative or emotional, although this prohibition is liberally construed by some judges. The opening statement, technically, must refer only to evidence that will be presented by the party making the opening statement.

> . . . Morris Weston, the chief defense counsel and noted as a spellbinder, was halted in the midst of his recital of the romance of the meeting of the "redhaired Irish boy and the black-haired Kentucky boy in the desert 41 years ago."
>
> "I don't think this will be a part of the evidence," Judge Garret said sternly after Prosecutor Duffy had objected.
>
> Another time Mr. Weston was stopped in the middle of an oratorical flight attributing the prosecution to the "outstretched talons of senatorial politics," which the court held was "argumentative" and "unfair."

EVIDENCE

Some of the rules and procedures for presenting evidence in civil actions were discussed on pages 241–244. This section will discuss only those particulars in which there are differences between a civil and a criminal action.

Witnesses

The clerk of the court is required to issue as many blank subpoenas as the defendant's attorney needs and they are served without cost to the defendant. In some states the defendant—but not the prosecution—may take the deposition of material witnesses who reside outside of the state. Both parties, in those states which have enacted the Uniform Act to Secure the Attendance of Witnesses from Without the State in Criminal Cases, may require a witness residing outside of the state to attend and testify.

Character witnesses sometimes testify on behalf of the defendant as to his good character and general reputation. The prosecution is not permitted to present witnesses to testify as to the defendant's bad character, but when the defendant makes his character an issue by presenting witnesses in his behalf the prosecution may present rebuttal witnesses to testify as to the defendant's bad character.

Witnesses in criminal trials are more often sequestered ("put under the rule") than in civil cases. Sequestration consists in putting the witnesses in a waiting room until they are called to testify; thus when they testify they are unaware of the previous testimony.

BURDEN OF PROOF

Because the law presumes innocence the prosecution has the burden of proving the main issue, viz., guilt. Guilt must be proved beyond *reasonable doubt*. Judges have had a lot of trouble in defining this term. One state finally solved(?) the problem by enacting a definition of reasonable doubt derived from the definition of a Massachusetts judge in 1850 and requiring that it be read as a part of the judge's instructions:

> It is not a mere possible doubt; because everything relating to human affairs, and depending on moral evidence, is open to some possible or imaginary doubt. It is that state of the case, which, after the entire comparison and consideration of all the evidence, leaves the minds of jurors in that condition that they cannot say they feel an abiding conviction to a moral certainty of the truth of the charge.[3]

There are, however, a few special issues on which the defendant has the burden of proof in overcoming certain legal presumptions. That is to say, the "burden of going forward with the evidence" is shifted to the defendant. For example, since the law presumes that everybody is sane the defendant must prove his insanity by a preponderance of the evidence.

ORDER OF PROOF

The prosecution usually begins its case by establishing the fact of the crime, called the *corpus delicti*. This includes proof of (1) the essential elements of the crime and (2) the commission of the act by a criminal agency. In a larceny case these would be (1) taking and (2) carrying away (3) the personal property of another (4) with criminal intent. In a murder case the corpus delicti is the death due to a criminal agency. Usually

[3] Calif. *Penal Code:* sec. 1096, quoting Justice Shaw (5 Cush. 295), 1850. There is some reason to believe, although no objective evidence is available, that criminal case juries often determine guilt by a preponderance of the evidence. For a criticism of the jury system, see J. Frank, *Courts on Trial* (Princeton, N.J., 1949), Chaps. 8 and 9.

the first witnesses for the prosecution in a murder case are those who testify to the corpus delicti, viz., a coroner or a coroner's physician or other physicians and detectives and policemen.

The corpus delicti in a murder case is usually proved by direct evidence, but it may be proved by circumstantial evidence; that is, evidence which accounts for the death when the body of the victim is missing. A man was convicted of killing a girl and throwing her body into the ocean although the body was never found. The corpus delicti consisted of a pistol which belonged to the defendant, a bloody seat cover of the defendant's automobile, and school books and clothing belonging to the victim. Thus it is possible to prove the corpus delicti by circumstantial evidence—although proof of the defendant's guilt must be beyond reasonable doubt.

Although a defendant cannot be convicted unless the corpus delicti has been proved, it is not always necessary to prove it in the first stage of the trial. It is prejudicial to the defendant, however, to present first a considerable amount of circumstantial evidence not related to the corpus delicti but calculated to establish in the minds of the jurors a bias toward the defendant and thus to make the jurors more likely to believe the evidence about the corpus delicti when it is presented later.

The corpus delicti cannot generally be established by the defendant's own confession unless it is made in open court, nor may an extrajudicial confession of guilt by the defendant (i.e., one made to police officers before the trial) be admitted until the corpus delicti has been proved.

Prove Fact of Crime First, Judge Rules

The prosecutor must prove a crime has been committed before he can continue the chronological presentation of his case against a prominent physician accused of trying to poison his wife.

Superior Court Judge H. T. Southwood made that ruling late yesterday in the trial of Dr. Marcus Nash.

Dr. Nash, 42, is charged with attempting to kill his wife, Helen, by injecting poison in her arm in the guise of taking a blood sample when she was ill last fall.

After Judge Southwood's ruling, District Attorney Nathan North said he would call Dr. Ernest Dewey to the stand when the trial resumes Monday. Dr. Dewey attended Mrs. Nash when she was in the hospital last September.

The prosecutor told the jury the state would show the physician carried on a romance with Virginia Nash, a nurse who formerly was married to Dr. Nash's brother.

Judge Southwood ruled out earlier testimony of a long distance operator. The judge said interception of a telephone message in detail would be illegal.

Sure You Weren't Murdered? No, Witness Testifies

The man who claims he is Ted Knight went on the witness stand here this morning and testified that he is the same person whom three men now on trial are charged with torturing and burning to death.

The witness said his real name was Newton Knight Hollister but in recent years he had gone under the name of Ted Knight.

He said he was an inmate of the state hospital for nervous diseases for a few months and escaped.

He described his arrival in the Berea community last January, staying the first night at the home of H. S. Halsey, father of Herman Halsey, one of the defendants.

Started to Get Married

His first job as a farm hand, he said, was with Tom Hancock, another defendant. Next he worked for Herman Halsey.

Then he began relating the story of his movements on the day Knight was reported to have been killed.

He and Herman Halsey and Eric Hoffman, a third defendant, started to Sunnyvale to get a marriage license for him and Joan Jackson, he said. They all got drunk, he added, and he fell off a mule.

He said he regained consciousness two or three hours later and went first to the Jackson home and then to Herman Halsey's home.

Judge Lets Trial Go On

"The next morning," he said, "Joan told me she wanted to put off the wedding until fall."

He continued to trace his movements from that time until he was found at Pendleton ten days ago.

In conducting the direct examination, the defense counsel asked:

"You weren't beaten to death and burned last March, were you?"

"Well, I don't look like it and don't feel like it," he replied amid laughter.

At the conclusion of the state's direct testimony, the defense moved for an instructed verdict of acquittal on the ground that the state had failed to establish the corpus delicti. Judge Harold Devoer overruled the motion.

The evidence to establish the corpus delicti was an odd assortment of charred bones which the state contends are the remains of Knight.

ADMISSIBILITY OF EVIDENCE

For a defendant's *confession* to be admitted a foundation must be laid; that is, the confession must be preceded by proof that it was made voluntarily, not by being extorted by threats or prolonged and continuous questioning ("third degree"). A confession is a declaration by a defendant made voluntarily that he is guilty of the offense with which he is charged.

An *admission,* however, is admissible. An admission is acknowledgement of a fact tending to prove guilt.

> When there is conflicting testimony [in most state courts] as to the circumstances under which a confession was obtained, voluntariness is generally left to be determined by juries. When a jury feels satisfied that a confession is truthful, it is not often disposed to discard it simply because the defendant's recollection of facts was prodded by psychological pressure in a police station. A jury is unlikely to rule out a confession unless members of the jury think it was extorted by outright physical brutality. And when the defendant seems to the jury to be a "hardened criminal" or a person of poor repute and criminal associations, it is unlikely to accept his charge that he was beaten if the police officers involved deny it.[4]

[4] A. Barth, *The Price of Liberty* (New York, 1961), p. 51. This book supplies an excellent analysis of the law relating to the rights of defendants and the practices of law enforcement officers. In 1964, some state courts reversed the convictions of defendants who had been questioned by police without the presence of their lawyers and who had not been informed of their constitutional rights, after the United States Supreme Court (Escobedo *v.* Illinois) had held that admissions obtained under such circumstances could not be admitted as evidence at a trial.

Testimony as to extrajudicial statements or acts of an alleged co-conspirator said or done outside the presence of the defendant is not admissible against a defendant until independent evidence has been presented to prove a conspiracy and the defendant's connection with it.

The judge sometimes admits evidence of the kind mentioned in the foregoing paragraph, as well as certain other types of evidence, subject to its being connected to the defendant by later proof. When the later proof is not submitted or the prosecution fails to connect the evidence to the defendant, the defense may *move to strike* the evidence that was improperly admitted.

Any physical evidence presented must have a connection with the issues being tried. For example, a defendant admitted that, in the deceased's automobile, he struck the deceased in self-defense, knocking him to the pavement and causing a skull fracture. The prosecution, however, introduced an automobile crank, wrench, and tire iron as possible weapons. This was held reversible error because the automobile did not belong to the defendant and no blood stains or fingerprints were found on the objects to connect them with the defendant.

Tape recordings may now be admitted as evidence in several jurisdictions after a proper foundation has been laid to prove their validity.

CROSS-EXAMINATION

Frequently a criminal case is won or lost because of the cross-examination. If the reporter is to perceive the significance of certain portions of cross-examination, he must have noted carefully what had previously been testified to. The following story is an example of effective cross-examination.

Blast, Not Bludgeon, May Have Caused Death, Doctor Says

A state pathologist—who earlier had testified that Mrs. Marie Thompson was bludgeoned to death—admitted today under cross-examination that her wounds might have been caused by something else.

An explosive blast in the galley of her yacht might have shattered the back of her skull, Dr. Harry Humphrey, a state's witness admitted. His testimony on direct examination had been damaging to the defendant, Melvin Williams.

Defense Attorney Homer Wills showed him a picture of the side of Mrs. Thompson's head, then asked:

"Wouldn't it have been possible for that injury to be caused by a foreign object being hurled through the air by the force of an explosion?"

"It could have been caused that way," the physician replied.

Asked Second Autopsy

Later he admitted that a four-inch screwdriver, found in the woman's matted hair, might have been the instrument that caused such a wound.

The doctor spent his third day under cross-examination, mopping his brow frequently. He stirred restlessly in the witness chair as Wills, at one point, asserted that his admittedly erroneous testimony before a grand jury was at least partially responsible for the murder indictment.

The doctor yesterday acknowledged that he had mistakenly told the grand jury he had examined the organs of the deceased at a post-mortem when in fact he had not.

REPORTING THE EVIDENCE

Because some criminal trials contain the elements of drama, they are among the best news stories and there is consequently a present danger that homicide and divorce cases will be too frequently presented as shows to entertain that section of the public which enjoys morbid sensations. Sharing the blame for the evils inherent in the practice of "super-reporting" certain murder and divorce trials are the sensational newspapers, prosecuting attorneys, defense attorneys and weak judges; all seem to forget their responsibility for the calm administration of justice.

We are concerned here only with the dramatic and other literary elements that pertain to the reporting of criminal trials. The plight of the person accused of a crime or the plight of his victim is frequently as interesting to a reader as is the well-conceived plot of the imaginative writer. The creative writers borrow many of their plots from real life and only enhance them by the invention of new characters and situations. The principals and witnesses in criminal trials are sometimes like those one encounters in novels and dramas. The conflict theme and the devices of suspense and climax are also elements in criminal trials, though seldom as apparent as in fiction, in which the writer's imagination has free rein.

Dramatis Personae

To the spectator in the court room and the newspaper reader, each principal and witness is a *dramatis persona*. Some of them even resemble heroes and villains, but to portray them deliberately as heroes and villains is not justifiable. If, by self-revelation, a defendant, witness, or attorney makes himself a hero or villain, the reporter, of course, should be grateful for the opportunity to make his story interesting; but the reporter ought never to treat the characters as anything but what they reveal themselves or each other to be. Yet the reporter should understand that to his reader every person in a trial is, after all, a character. For that reason he ought to describe them—describe their persons and manners, if necessary. Some examples follow:

> Then came Mr. Rinehart, a thick-set, balding man wearing a suit, and a brown shirt with an open collar. He spoke at a measured pace, his voice deep and containing a trace of Austrian accent.

> Mr. Hambly, the witness, was a scowling man who kept his massive head cocked to one side, as if it were too heavy for his muscular neck. Beetling brows, broad and high cheek bones and a jutting chin dominated his rugged face.
> He talked in a deep, sure voice, and when he groped for an answer, grimaced and seemed trying to swallow his lower lip.
> At such times he untwined the fingers which he customarily kept locked together in his lap, and when the answer came he emphasized it with little chopping motions of his hands.

> Mr. Harrison was nervous. His eyes were never still. His tongue wet his lips again and again. He spoke with the sharp, crisp enunciation of the well-educated Englishman.
> Twice his face reddened and he snapped back at his questioner with obvious anger.

Although identification and description of a witness is usually necessary, the reporter should avoid attaching "labels" to characters. The constant reference to a principal in a homicide trial as the "thrill-slayer," "the Fox," or "the Romeo of the rubbing table" (when the witness was an osteopath) usually presents a false image of the person and may prejudice the readers against him. Seldom does any label fit a character; to label a character is not only untrue characterization but proof of a lack of literary skill. If a writer cannot present a picture of a character through self-revelation, by the testimony of other characters, and by a simple description of manner, dress, and gesture, he is too incompetent as a literary craftsman to be entrusted with character delineation.

Situations

The most difficult kind of evidence to report is that which reveals situations and episodes connected with the commission of the crime or the events leading up to it. When the reporter is allowed ample space in which to describe the situations, the most effective and fairest method is to quote the verbatim testimony, deleting some of the irrelevancies. But the reporter is usually compelled, because of lack of space, to condense the testimony, sometimes making use of direct quotations but for the most part translating testimony into indirect quotation. A certain skill, therefore, is required to make a selection of details that will present an effective picture and represent the actual testimony of the witness.

It is the selection of precise details that makes the story interesting. The exact distance between the slayer and the victim, the exact interval between shots, the exact words which were spoken, the gestures and postures of the principals, the actual setting of the scene, the exact hour of the incident— these are the materials of a news story which, if handled imperfectly by a reporter, not only render his account untrue or half true but detract from the interest in the story. Note in the following story how the writer alternately uses direct and indirect quotation.

Dr. Condon Met Hauptmann in Bronx Cemeteries

Two rendezvous with the Lindbergh kidnaper in Bronx cemeteries were described in Hunterdon County Court today by the go-between, Dr. John F. (Jafsie) Condon.

On the second occasion, he testified, he gave $50,000 ransom money to a man calling himself "John." This man, he identified today as Bruno Richard

Hauptmann, who is charged with the murder of the Lindbergh child.

The 74-year-old retired teacher of physical education related how he had inserted a classified advertisement addressed to the kidnaper and, in response, received two notes. These he showed to Colonel Lindbergh.

The second note, he said, told him to go to a frankfurter stand 100 feet beyond the last station on the Jerome Avenue subway line. He was driven there by Alfred Reich, a friend. The time was about 8:30 p.m.

Under a stone on the porch he found a note. Following directions in the note, he was driven to Woodlawn Cemetery, stopping about 60 feet from the gates.

Identifies Hauptmann

He saw a man from inside the gates wave a handkerchief, and he crossed over.

Q.—Who was the man you spoke to between the gates?

A.—John, as given to me by himself.

Q.—And who is John?

A.—John is Bruno Richard Hauptmann.

Q.—Now what did Mr. Hauptmann say to you?

A.—He said, "Did you got it the money?"

Q.—And what did you say, sir?

A.—I said, "No, I couldn't bring the money until I saw the package."

Dr. Condon said there was a rustle in the leaves and the man said, "There is a cop!"

Condon Chases Kidnaper

The defendant, Dr. Condon said, grasped the steel bars of the gate and climbed "turner" fashion to the top—nine feet. Then he jumped down on the witness's side.

Q.—And then what happened?

A.—He said, "Did you sended the cops?" I said, "No, I gave you my word. I wouldn't do that, and I kept my word." He then said, "It is too dangerous" and started to run in a northerly direction.

The witness then related how he chased him to 223rd street and persuaded him to come back and sit on a bench.

Dr. Condon testified that he said, "Don't ever do that again. I am square with you, and the truth to a kidnaper is the same as the truth to a ———."

"The man said, to me," he continued, " 'It is too dangerous. Might be twenty years or burn. Would I burn if the baby is dead?' "

Dr. Condon said he reassured him and then asked, "How am I to know that I am talking to the right man?" The man said, according to the witness, "The baby was held in the crib with safety pins."

During the conversation Dr. Condon said, the man had drawn the lapels of his coat up to his chin. . . .

Interpretation

The reporter can assist the understanding of the reader by making certain interpretations of the testimony. He should try to divine the main issues during the early part of the trial in order to make them clear to the reader after the testimony has revealed them. For example, the innocence or guilt of the defendant sometimes turns upon identification of the person who actually committed the crime; it is incumbent upon the reporter to report carefully the evidence of identification and the defense or alibi. Or the issue turns upon some circumstance, such as proof and denial that the fatal bullet was fired from the defendant's gun. Or the issue turns upon motive, making it necessary for the reporter to identify clearly the persons who testify as to the actions and conversations of the defendant and his connections with the victim or the victim's wife or sweetheart or husband or brother. The following is an example of interpretation:

> . . . This testimony (that the defendant wanted to get rid of his wife) **accorded with the theory** advanced by the prosecution.
>
> Thereafter when the state's witness came under cross-examination, Attorney Lawrence questioned her diligently **to find support for the defense theory** that Williams was an alcoholic who seldom knew what he was up to.
>
> The lawyer sought to plant in the jurors' minds the portrait of a youth who, if he killed, did so while his mind was blank for a time.

Because the time element is often important in a criminal trial the reporter can help the reader understand its meaning, as the following paragraphs indicate:

> . . . Mr. Fulton's testimony was important because it knocked six hours off of the time gap fixing Williams' whereabouts on the day and night of the fatal shooting.
> Until today testimony had placed Williams at his home at 2:30 p.m. but had been blank until he stumbled into a tavern at 8:30 p.m., saying his wife had been shot.

The reporter should beware, however, of stating very strongly the effect of certain testimony on the jury. He is in no position to estimate effect; in too many cases the effect of testimony on the reporter has been at variance with its effect on the jury. In the following instance, for example, the jury found the defendant guilty:

> . . . The state's case against Wilton Johnson **took a severe shaking** today when a conscience-stricken witness made a dramatic confession that he had lied under oath during his first appearance on the stand.

Certain expressions which do not constitute "editorializing" can legitimately be used to convey to the reader the sincerity of a witness. For example, "He emphatically denied that . . ." and "For two and one-half hours he resisted a cross-examination effort to break down his story."

Anticipating Developments

Where the reporter in advance of the trial has made himself familiar with its issues, he is able, as the trial proceeds, to understand the significance of the evidence and of the attorneys' questions. He is, therefore, not wholly unprepared when certain startling disclosures are made and he knows what emphasis to give them. By consulting with attorneys during recess he can learn some facts which are worth advance notice or worth remembering during the course of the trial. Whether or not the defendant will testify, whether or not a "surprise" witness may be introduced, what instructions to the jury each side will ask, whether or not certain attorneys will withdraw —these are a few of the things to be reported that are not revealed in the testimony. The following news story, although it does not quote any source, was based on conversations with attorneys on both sides:

Local Prejudice Plea Overruled in Glab Murder Trial

The life of Edward Glab will be gambled against legal technicalities with the defendant preferring death to a finding that he is insane. This was indicated at the end of the second day of his trial.

Glab is accused of persuading Mrs. Dorothy Greenwald to come to Northboro to marry him, and then killing her.

Defense Attorney Bernard Dimmick permitted the state to introduce all evidence that concerned the discovery of Mrs. Greenwald's body in the drainage ditch behind the Glab garage.

It was learned today that, should the jury find Glab guilty, the defense hopes to win on appeal. The reversible error hoped for would be the failure of the state to connect the crime with Glab and to show prejudice in the community.

This was the apparent meaning of the defense motion for a change of venue, which Judge Clarke Bourne denied yesterday.

Her Clothes in Glab Garage

The state today introduced testimony to show that Mrs. Greenwald's body was found garrotted. The court received in evidence the clothing she wore when she left her home in Delaware to "make her home in the West" with "Ernest Spitzer," the alias allegedly used by Glab in his matrimonial campaign by mail.

This clothing, the state showed, was found in the Glab garage after the discovery of the body.

Tomorrow the state will introduce evidence to show that Glab had constructed in his home a trap door and an improvised gallows.

The general expectation is that the case will be concluded within a week. The state has offered thus far only witnesses to the corpus delicti (that is, the fact that a crime was committed).

Glab intends to offer two witnesses

—never yet located by the police—
who, he asserts, did away with the
woman. . . .

Form of the Trial Story

Indirect quotation is the form in which testimony is most frequently reported because it represents a condensation of a great number of questions and answers, many of which are relatively unimportant. Some testimony, however, is so important or is given in such a dramatic manner, that it needs to be quoted directly. When verbatim testimony is to be quoted at length it is better for the reporter to arrange with the official reporter to provide him with a portion of the transcript; for it is a more natural representation of the witness's words than is indirect quotation. In some criminal trials the issues are so involved that a mere reporting of testimony does not permit of its being easily understood. In such cases the reporter should condense the testimony into "points." The following is an example:

> . . . The testimony of the state's witnesses today purported to show:
> 1. Dr. Abrahams was told the girl was married and that her husband could not afford to have a child, although agreeing to pay the surgeon $175 to avoid having one.
> 2. That after performing the abortion, Dr. Abrahams, through neglect, allowed the girl to develop a fever which ultimately caused her death.
> 3. That a nurse suggested to Dr. Abrahams that he try another operation which might save the girl's life, but that Dr. Abrahams said: "No, she has no money."
> 4. That the surgeon had refused to allow a priest to attend the girl in her dying moments, fearing discovery of the criminal operation.

Readers are sometimes confused as to who is testifying when the reporter presents the direct quotation of one witness after the direct quotation of another. A good rule is to *begin the sentence with the name of the next person who is being quoted* after having just concluded the directly quoted testimony of the prior witness.

In the news story examples in this chapter, note the appropriate use of these verbs in the reporting of testimony: *testified, said, asserted, continued, added, recited, described, related, stated, admitted, replied,* and *acknowledged.*

For class discussion: Is "took the stand" a cliché?

MOTIONS DURING TRIAL

A motion for a *mistrial* by either party is granted in some circumstances, as when a key witness becomes too ill to testify. The motion is granted on the defendant's motion when some incident happens that is prejudicial to the defendant. Some examples: the prosecution arrests one of its witnesses for perjury in the courtroom in the presence of other prospective witnesses; the prosecuting attorney makes a statement which is not evidence and is prejudicial to the defendant; and a newspaper during the trial publishes a dramatic prejudicial statement about something the prosecution says it expects to prove. Granting of the motion aborts the trial and a retrial is held.

In some jurisdictions a *motion for a directed verdict of acquittal* is permitted. No jurisdiction permits a motion for a directed verdict of conviction. The motion to direct the jury to acquit may be made by the defendant after either party has concluded its case. The ground for the motion is that the prosecution's evidence is insufficient to convict. This is a question of law for the judge to decide. An example: in a conspiracy case requiring corroboration, the state was able to produce only one witness.

When the motion is made and after the attorneys have argued, the judge grants or denies it. When the motion is granted the judge directs the jury as in civil cases.[5]

In some of the jurisdictions which do not permit the motion for a directed verdict of acquittal, there is permitted the *motion for advice to acquit*. When it is granted the judge advises the jury to acquit but the jury is not bound by his advice.

Directed Verdict Acquits Sheriff

Judge Z. L. Moody today directed a verdict of not guilty in the case of Sheriff Walter Dinwiddie who was tried on the charge of attempting to bribe Senator Arthur Cline.

Defense Attorney Craig Butts moved for a directed verdict at the close of the state's case. Judge Moody then told the jury he was taking the case away from them because the state had failed to prove the bribery in the legal meaning of the term.

---
[5] See pp. 266–269.

Summations[6]

Unless argument is waived the prosecution opens and has the right to close. The reason for this rule is that the prosecution has the burden of proof on the issue of guilt.

The argument must relate only to the evidence. It has been held prejudicial when a prosecuting attorney has discussed verdicts in similar cases, has stated that he would not have prosecuted the case unless he knew the accused was guilty, and has told the jurors they should be afraid to meet their fellowmen if they did not convict.

Prosecuting attorneys in some cases have exceeded the bounds of fairness, decency, and good taste by these emotional statements about the defendant: "He is an animal"; "He would cut out your heart with a razor, wipe it on his sleeve, and go upstairs to dinner"; and "He is public enemy number one of all the world."

Since a defendant cannot be compelled to testify against himself it is prejudicial in some jurisdictions for the prosecution to infer guilt from the defendant's failure to testify. In some jurisdictions, however, the prosecution may comment on the defendant's failure to explain or deny some of the prosecution's evidence.

Portions of the attorneys' summations are sometimes worth including in a news story. The *New York Times* devoted forty-two columns to the prosecution's summation in the Hauptmann case in 1935. The reporter, to be fair, should divide the space nearly equally between the two sides.

INSTRUCTING THE JURY[7]

The judge explains to the jury the law relating to the offense; for example, the difference between murder and manslaughter. He instructs that proof of guilt must be "beyond reasonable doubt" and includes the defendant's theory of defense. His instructions also include certain admonitions as to the jury's conduct during their deliberations.

When the instructions are worthy of being reported, they should be reported accurately so that the reader will not be confused when the verdict is returned. When newspapers in Boston some years ago failed to report the judge's instructions adequately readers were puzzled as to how two men could be found guilty of the first degree murder of another man whom they had never seen. Three men had engaged in a burglary and two had gotten away and were waiting in an automobile for the third who, meeting the watchman, shot and killed him. The Massachusetts law is that a murder

---

[6] Cf. the discussion of summations in civil cases at pp. 258–259.
[7] Cf. the discussion of instructions to the jury in a civil case, pp. 259 *ff* and 263 *ff*.

committed during the commission of a felony is first degree murder. The defense argued for instructions that would hold that the crime of burglary had been completed at the time of the shooting. The judge, however, ruled as to the two men in the automobile that the crime of burglary was still in process.

Judge Allows One Of Six Verdicts

The jury in the case of Reid Deering, who shot and killed Patrolman Vernon Hauck, can return one of six verdicts.

Judge H. T. Southwood instructed the jury today that, in addition to "not guilty" and "not guilty because of insanity," any one of the following verdicts can be returned:

Guilty of first degree murder.
Guilty of second degree murder.
Guilty of voluntary manslaughter.
Guilty of involuntary manslaughter.

A first degree murder verdict carries with it a mandatory life sentence.

The judge, in commenting on the testimony of Walter Pierce, an ex-convict, told the jury:

"You should consider the fact that one of the witnesses had been convicted of felony and determine whether or not his credibility has been affected thereby. . . ."

THE VERDICT

The jury in a criminal case is required to reach a unanimous verdict—except in Louisiana, and in that state unanimity is required when the accusation is for a capital crime.[8]

Some juries find they cannot reach a unanimous verdict according to the judge's instructions and, consequently, return to the courtroom to request the judge to clarify the instructions. Juries when apparently at uncompromising disagreement return to the courtroom and report that they are unable to reach an agreement; in that event the judge either sends them back to make another effort or he discharges them. Ordinarily when there is a hung jury a second or even a third trial is held.

[8] In a few states a conviction for a misdemeanor may be had on the concurrence of two-thirds or three-fourths of the jurors.

Although in most jurisdictions the jury may return an oral verdict in open court, it is usually supplied with two short forms—"guilty" and "not guilty"—one of which is signed by the foreman.

The form of a guilty verdict is usually: "We, the jury, in the above entitled cause, find the defendant, ———, guilty *as charged* in the indictment (information)." The form varies, however, when the jury convicts on one or more counts and acquits on the others. The jurors ballot on the counts separately. The form also varies when the jurors must determine the degree of the crime and when the law provides that the jury fix the penalty. In some instances the accusation charges first degree murder, but the jury finds the defendant guilty of a lesser degree and so states on the form.

It is important sometimes for the reporter to tell his readers how long a time was required for the jury to reach a verdict.

The reporter should be present when the verdict is returned in an important case not only to learn about the verdict but to describe the effect of the verdict upon the principals and, if circumstances require it, to obtain statements from the principals and the attorneys.

Court Drama Unfolds As Abbott Hears Fate

Bailiff J. H. Fitzpatrick was just starting down from the jury room on a routine errand when he heard the knock.

The big, tired man who had guarded Burton Abbott's jury for seven days stopped, whirled about and went back upstairs.

"Tell the judge we have a verdict," foreman Harry A. Whitehead said.

And when the bailiff walked back down to the courtroom, buttoning his dark blue jacket, one look at his face was all that was necessary.

Suspense

Everyone there knew that this was it. That after all the long, interminable days and nights of waiting, the dazed belief that perhaps there would be no verdict at all, it had finally come.

What is it like to see a man doomed to death?

Quiet, in the jammed courtroom, only a little rustling among the spectators. A heaviness in the air, a grim portent of what was to come.

The bailiff looked at the clock. It was 4:20 p.m.

The suspense in a happening of this sort is hard to bear, even for those who are there on business and have work to do—the newspaper reporters and photographers, court attachés and attorneys.

It is agonizing for some: Elsie Abbott, the mother, escorted into the room at 4:31 p.m., biting her lips, her face deathly pale. Georgia Abbott, the red-haired wife, white and shaking, sitting in an attitude of prayer.

Courtroom Drama

Officers in plain clothes take up strategic positions.

The mother sits with a vacant half-smile on her face. Georgia still prays.

Short, stocky and fatherly Judge Charles Wade Snook comes from his chambers and addresses the suddenly hushed crowd:

"I want to say to the spectators and everybody else, the jury is about to come in with a verdict. Which way the verdict has gone, nobody knows except the jury.

"If there is any demonstration of any type by any person in the court room, I will order them taken into custody by the sheriff."

It is 4:43 p.m.

The jury is still upstairs. Abbott is still in the jail, changing into the dark blue suit he wears to court.

Prisoner Enters

Four minutes later his light step is heard on the stairway and the man whose life is now in the balance walks quickly into the room.

He seems to be smiling faintly. His face is a mask which cannot be read.

All eyes are on him: Is this man about to be found guilty of a dreadful crime? Is he to die in the San Quentin gas chamber? Will the jury set him free?

A bright light is on his thin face. Everyone stares.

4:50 p.m.—This thundering symphony of nervousness and suspense rises to the crescendo. The jurors walk in.

And they give the time-honored sign of convicting juries. Not one looks at the defendant. Their heads are actually averted from him.

They look very weary and they look sad.

And then the words that are so commonly known that they seem ordinary and casual:

"Ladies and gentlemen, have you agreed upon your verdict?"

The foreman's voice booms out sturdy and firm:

"We have, Your Honor."

The agony of suspense will not end. Bailiff Fitzpatrick accepts the two fateful slips of paper from foreman Whitehead's hand, walks deliberately to the judge's bench and gives them to him.

Double Death

And then the judge hands the two verdicts to young Robert Snyder, his clerk. It is Snyder's task to let Abbott—and all the people here—know what has been done.

It is now 4:52 p.m.

His low voice is barely heard:

The kidnaping count: Guilty. Death.

The murder count: Guilty. Death.

Abbott's head drops and he clenches his teeth like a person stricken with a sudden pain.

His mother rears up, then bows her head against the spectator's railing.

Georgia Abbott sits with her hands clasped so tightly that the knuckles are white. She says nothing.

Stricken Mother

Elsie stands, stricken, dazed: "It isn't justice!" Her voice is a low, vague murmur. The syllables are slurred. Her eyes are vacant.

There is some cold legal business to be done now—the polling of the jury: "Is this your verdict?" "It is, Your Honor"; setting of the date for sentence: February 3.

When it is done Abbott stands, turns briskly and strides lightly into the stairwell and up the stairs. He never looks at his wife and mother.

He came down the stairs a man still "cloaked in the presumption of innocence."

He goes back up, a man guilty of kidnaping and murder and sentenced to die.

On the first landing, in the shallow

sand-tray on the floor lies what remains of the cigaret he dropped there as he came down from jail to hear himself condemned. (Jane Eshleman Conant in San Francisco *Call-Bulletin*.)

MOTIONS AFTER THE VERDICT

After the jury has returned a guilty verdict, a defendant may enter a *motion for arrest of judgment* or a *motion for a new trial*. The first motion is made in connection with a *motion to set aside the verdict* on some of the grounds that were mentioned with reference to the motion to quash and demurrer.[9] That is, the motion attacks the accusation. When granted, its effect is to place the defendant in the same position he was in before the accusation was filed: usually this means he is discharged. The motion is directed to a question of law; this may also include the averment that the verdict is not supported by the evidence.

Jury Reversed In Passport Case

Federal Judge Paul Bingham ruled yesterday that a jury which convicted Cary Barnum of conspiring to obtain fraudulent passports had "based its verdict on inference."

The judge thereupon set aside the verdict and ordered Barnum released. He cannot be tried again on the same charge.

"Suspicion, however strong, cannot be allowed to take the place of substantial evidence," Judge Bingham explained.

"The government failed to carry the burden of proof that Barnum had exclusive control of the typewriter (on which false birth certificates were made out to obtain passports).

"In order to reach their verdict, the jurors had to base inference upon inference."

Barnum, an attorney, was indicted for conspiring with Choy Kum to obtain the fraudulent passports for Chinese by forging birth certificates.

[9] Pp. 346–348.

Barnum went to trial September 2. He was defended by Albert Whalley, who made the motion to set aside the verdict when Barnum appeared before Judge Bingham yesterday.

The government had presented in evidence a typewriter on which a number of forged birth certificates allegedly had been written.

The defense contested the introduction of the typewriter on the ground that it could not be proved that Barnum had been in exclusive possession of it.

In his closing argument for the defense, Whalley declared that Choy Kum might have used the typewriter without Barnum's knowledge. He accused the government of using "guilt-by-association" tactics.

A motion for a new trial attacks some procedure during the trial or states that there is newly discovered evidence. Unlike the motions discussed in the foregoing paragraphs, the motion for a new trial does not attack the accusation. This means that, when the motion is granted, the defendant is not released but is permitted to have a reexamination of the issue of guilt in the same court before another jury. The grounds for the motion are such irregularities as improper conduct of the jury, improper instructions of the judge, and newly discovered evidence.

The motion is usually made orally prior to the sentence. Often, however, the judge sets a date for a hearing so that the defendant may prepare affidavits in support of the motion. Attorneys frequently make perfunctory motions for a new trial with only slight expectation that the motion will be granted.

Cox Jury Failed To Deliberate, Charge

Motion for a new trial for Dr. J. B. Cox, convicted of the murder of Helen Davis, his co-ed lover, was filed today in circuit court.

Judge Walton Reed will hear the application next Monday.

The motion charges, in effect, that the jury which convicted the physician "elected a foreman, substituted a prayer for the usual deliberation on the merits of the case, and immediately returned a verdict of guilty."

The verdict was returned Wednesday only twenty-eight minutes after the jury retired.

The motion criticizes the "procedure of the court" and assails Prosecutor Thomas Moser's "brutal tactics" before the jury.

The motion also charged "passion and prejudice" on the part of the trial judge.

In situations in which a defendant has pleaded guilty and has been sentenced and later alleges the plea was entered because of fraud or mistake, the defendant applies for a *writ of coram nobis* when he has no other remedy; for example, an allegation that the defendant pleaded guilty to a murder charge on the promise by a police officer that the death penalty would not be imposed. The defendant's objective is to have the plea changed to "not guilty" on the ground that a fact existed which would have resulted in a different verdict if it had been known and had been presented at the trial. The writ lies to correct errors of fact, not law, and is rarely applied for.

JUDGMENT AND SENTENCE

Technically, the verdict of a jury is a finding of fact and is not equivalent to a judgment, although in some jurisdictions the jury, instead of the judge, determines the penalty. The judge, in the light of the jury's finding, makes the judgment. The judgment when made is entered in the minutes of the court. Judgment and sentence are synonymous, sentence being the formal pronouncement of the judgment.

Sentence is pronounced soon after the conclusion of the trial but is delayed long enough for the judge to receive and evaluate the probation report. The defendant is accompanied to the bar by his counsel, who sometimes offers one of the motions discussed above, pleads mitigation (such as financial condition of the defendant's family), or requests bail pending an appeal. The prosecuting attorney also sometimes opposes the requests of the defense counsel. Here is the form of a judgment:

In the Superior Court of the County of Santa Clara
State of California

At a session of the Superior Court, held at the Court House, in the County of Santa Clara, on the 26th day of June, 19—.

Present: Hon. H. T. Southwood, Judge; Henry A. Pfister, Clerk, and George W. Lyle, Sheriff.

The People of the State of California, Plaintiff
against
Leonard Firsten, Defendant

Department 4

Defendant is duly informed by the court of the information presented against him on the 3rd day of May, 19—, for the crime of burglary, and of his arraignment and plea of Not Guilty, of his trial and the verdict of the jury, on the 25th day of June, 19—, of Guilty.

Defendant is then asked if he has any legal cause to show why judgment should not be pronounced against him, to which he replies None.

And no such cause appearing the Court, it is now Ordered, Adjudged and Decreed that the said Leonard Firsten be imprisoned in the State Prison of the State of California, and that he be taken by the Sheriff to the Warden of the State Prison at San Quentin.

The defendant is remanded to the custody of the Sheriff of the County of Santa Clara.

When a death sentence is given it is the trial judge who fixes the date of the execution.

For class discussion: Which is executed—the guilty defendant or the sentence of the court?

Exercise: What is the derivation of the word "electrocution"?

Financier Gets 5-Year Sentence

Rudolf Ripley, a financier who once headed three companies listed on the New York Stock Exchange, was sentenced yesterday to five years in prison and given a maximum fine of $160,000 by Federal District Judge Paul Bingham.

Mr. Ripley was described by Judge Bingham as a "freebooter who raided the seas of a free economy."

The financier was convicted January 27 on charges of conspiracy and wilfully failing to file required financial reports with the Securities and Exchange Commission when he was president of Kent Corporation, Inc.

Judge Bingham characterized Mr. Ripley as a "freebooter" after the financier had described himself as a "mariner befogged in a sea of government regulations."

Mr. Ripley contended: "I did not loot the Kent Corporation. I did not bilk its assets."

If there was a shrinkage of assets, he said, it was because of "writedowns" of company asset values.

"I have no money," he told the court before he was sentenced. "I lost my entire fortune in the Kent Corporation."

Judge Bingham, in denying bail, said the evidence at the trial showed the "investing public was looted of hundreds of thousands of dollars" by the financier's manipulation of the market in Kent Corporation stocks and by the "siphoning off" of the company's assets.

Arguing for committing Mr. Ripley, U.S. Attorney David Forbes commented it would be an "affront to justice to see a photo of Mr. Ripley playing gin rummy in Brazil."

"He has used other names before and could melt so no one could find him," he asserted.

Mr. Ripley's attorney, Morgan Sargni, contended "there never was any question of flight or disappearance."

PROBATION

After the verdict, in most jurisdictions, a probation officer investigates the background of the convicted defendant to assist the judge in determining the severity of the sentence. The probation officer checks on a possible previous criminal record and talks to friends, relatives, former teachers, or former employers of the defendant about his family background, his job situation, and how amenable he might be to rehabilitation. The officer then writes a report, which sometimes includes letters from interested persons, and makes a recommendation to the judge.

The judge then decides whether or not to admit the defendant to probation and, when he does, what conditions to impose. The conditions always require the defendant to behave well and sometimes to reimburse injured parties. In some cases a judge grants probation by not imposing judgment and in other cases by imposing judgment but suspending its execution. In some cases the judge imposes a part of the penalty and suspends the other part; thus a defendant is sentenced to thirty days in jail and five additional months on probation. The defendant on probation is often required to report regularly to a probation officer.

Probation Allowed For Young Mother

Mrs. Irma Waters, 21, a slender slip of a girl, was placed on probation today by Judge George Harris, having pleaded guilty last week to passing $1,000 in bad checks.

Chief Probation Officer Roger James reported she is the mother of a five-year-old child, has promised to make good all of the checks, and has a good record.

Bilks His Friends; Denied Probation

Louis Pfeffer, 52, accused of bilking friends and business associates of $250,000 in an export scheme, was sentenced yesterday to one to ten years in state prison.

He was denied probation by Judge R. S. Dallas.

Probation Officer Walter Powers reported that he "not only took advantage of those who had confidence in him because of his established business reputation, but permitted his victims to bring in their friends who were in turn victimized."

At the end of the term of probation, or sometimes before the end of the term, the defendant appears and moves for a termination of his probation.

A defendant placed on probation, whose subsequent conduct is considered bad, may be rearrested and have his probation revoked.

Contractor Ends Probation Period

Joseph Rhoton, who was involved in a street contract bribery fraud, yesterday was granted a termination of his five-year probation period.

Judge Oscar Loomis restored Rhoton's civil rights and cancelled his $40,000 surety bond. Rhoton had served four months of a six-month county jail sentence.

Raid Causes Court To Revoke Probation

Mrs. Luigi Rocco, who gained probation on a grand theft charge, yesterday stood before Judge Stanley Swanson and heard her probation revoked.

The action followed a raid Wednesday night on an alleged abortion mill at 4828 Pinto Street in which Mrs. Rocco and Peggy Ford, a practical nurse, were arrested.

After revoking her probation, Judge Swanson ordered Mrs. Rocco into custody of the sheriff, denied her plea for bail, and set February 15 for sentencing on the theft charge to which she had pleaded guilty last July.

Today she will be arraigned on charges of abortion resulting from the Wednesday night raid.

At the hearing on Mrs. Rocco's probation Leslie Morris, adult probation officer, informed the court of her arrest at the alleged abortion mill.

INDETERMINATE SENTENCE

Statutes in some states fix definite terms of imprisonment for specific offenses. In other states the statutes fix minimum and maximum terms but permit the exact term to be determined by a state parole board (called by various names in the different states); such sentences are called *indeterminate* sentences. They are not fixed until after the prisoner has served long enough for the board to observe his behavior in prison.

Abortionist Given Three-Year Term

The state prison board yesterday fixed the sentence of Mrs. Luigi Rocco, convicted of conspiracy to commit abortion, at three years.

Her conviction, under the statute, had provided for an indeterminate sentence of two to five years.

The sentence fixed yesterday is subject to a nine-month reduction for good behavior. She will be eligible for parole next March after having served for one year.

When a defendant has been found guilty on several counts of an indictment or for more than one crime or is convicted of an offense when he is already under conviction for a previous offense, and the court orders that he shall begin serving one sentence at the expiration of another, the sentences are referred to as *cumulative* sentences and are said to run *consecutively*. In most cases, however, when a defendant has been found guilty on more than one count in an accusation the court orders the sentences to run *concurrently*.

Judge Gets Tough In Torture Case

Three youths, convicted last week of the torture-robbery of James Cameron last January 31, were sentenced today to state prison.

Eugene Quillen, 19, alleged leader of the trio, and Leslie Fay, 17, were sentenced to serve consecutive terms for first degree burglary and assault with a deadly weapon.

Generally, when a defendant has been convicted of two or more offenses the terms for each offense run concurrently. But Quillen and Fay will start serving a second term after they have completed the first.

Steven Wisner, 21, was sentenced to serve concurrent terms on the first two counts.

The youths face a possible sentence by the parole board of from five years to life imprisonment on each of the burglary and robbery counts.

Quillen and Fay are faced with an additional sentence of from one to ten years on the assault count. Their applications for probation were denied.

MITTIMUS

After sentence has been pronounced, the clerk of the court gives to the sheriff (or United States marshal) a *mittimus,* which authorizes and directs the sheriff to transport the prisoner to jail or to prison, and authorizes the prison warden to accept the prisoner. Newspapers sometimes report the fact that certain prisoners have entered a state or federal prison. The form of a mittimus (omitting the caption) is as follows:

> The People of the State of California to the Sheriff of the County of Santa Clara, Greeting:
>
> In accordance with the judgment a certified copy of which is endorsed herein and hereby referred to and made a part hereof:
> You, the said Sheriff of the County of Santa Clara are hereby commanded to take and deliver the therein named defendant Henry Ragland to the Warden of the State Prison at San Quentin.
> And these presents shall be your authority for the same
> AND HEREIN FAIL NOT.
> Witness, the Hon. Mark Winston, Judge of said Superior Court at the Court House etc., etc.

STATE AND FEDERAL PRISONS

Progressive states and the United States segregate types of prisoners in different classes of penal institutions. In California, for example, the state provides: one institution for male offenders thought by the prison board to be capable of "moral rehabilitation and restoration to good citizenship"; one institution for females convicted of felonies; one institution for male first offenders; and a fourth institution for male prisoners who have previously served a term of imprisonment in any state or federal penitentiary. Work camps for prisoners are also provided.

The United States maintains seven *penitentiaries,* five *reformatories,* eight *correctional institutions,* five *juvenile and youth institutions,* six *camps,* and one *medical center.* In New York city the federal government maintains its own jail, called *detention headquarters.*

FINE

A defendant who is fined may, in some circumstances, pay the fine to the clerk of the court in installments. When the defendant is unable to pay a fine he is required instead to go to jail where his imprisonment counts as a credit of one dollar to five dollars a day (depending on the jurisdiction) toward payment of the fine.

PAROLE AND PARDON

After a prisoner has served a part of his sentence he is eligible to *parole.* The chief exceptions are ex-convicts, prisoners with cumulative sentences, and those who have tried to escape. After his release on parole, he may not leave the state without the consent of the board of parole. Technically he is still a prisoner. Violation of his parole causes his reimprisonment.

Playboy Promoter Leaves Prison

Clinton Dale, 38-year-old playboy promoter who was sent to prison for a socialite apartment house swindle, was paroled from San Quentin prison yesterday.

He had served two and one-half years of a one-to-ten-year sentence for grand theft. He must still serve three and one-half years on parole.

The Adult Authority said Dale will take a job in television.

The power of *pardon* is usually granted to the governor of the state, although several states have established certain procedures, such as the provision for an advisory board and the requirement of notice to the prosecuting attorney; these have the effect of compelling the governor to act judicially rather than capriciously. The prisoner who applies for a pardon tries to support his application with letters from the judge, prosecuting attorney, and the jurors by whom he was tried.

A person convicted of a felony is usually deprived of his civil rights, including his right to vote, his right to hold public office, and his right to act as a trustee. A pardon restores some or all of these rights, depending upon the statute of the particular state. In some states a convicted person placed on probation without a sentence being imposed does not lose his voting rights.

Hard Luck Perjurer May Get Pardon

A full pardon for Franz Werfel, 51, former assemblyman sent to prison six years ago for perjury in a liquor license bribery case, was recommended to Governor Wiley Smith yesterday by the Adult Authority.

Werfel's 23-year-old wife died of bulbar polio shortly before the legislator went to prison.

While he was behind bars, his daughters, now 10 and 8 years old, contracted rheumatic fever and have been under long treatment.

His mother went blind of glaucoma and is bedridden. Werfel has been car-

> ing for her since he was paroled four years ago.
>
> A merger last summer cost Werfel his job as office manager of a business firm.
>
> Because of his prison record Werfel is unable to get a license for real estate work in which he now has a chance for a job.
>
> Members of the Adult Authority agree that Werfel had rehabilitated himself in his four years out of prison and was also entitled to pardon on the grounds of undue hardship.

The governor also has the power to *commute* a sentence; that is, to reduce it, as when a death sentence is commuted to life imprisonment. The governor may also *reprieve* a person sentenced to death; that is, stay the execution pending an application for judicial review.

CHAPTER 25

Fair Trial vs. Free Press

From time to time the criticism is heard that certain newspapers have deprived a defendant in a criminal case of his right to a fair trial by the publication of inadmissible evidence either before or during the trial. As we shall see, the newspapers sometimes share the blame with those who conduct and participate in the trial.

RIGHT TO ATTEND AND REPORT[1]

The United States constitution and the constitutions and statutes of nearly all of the states require that a criminal trial shall be public (except when the defendant requests the exclusion of the public). The Sixth Amendment, for example, provides: "In all criminal prosecutions the accused shall enjoy the right to a speedy and public trial by an impartial jury." This is primarily a right of the defendant, but several courts have held it is also a right of the public since it is desirable that the people know whether or not justice is being administered fairly. Some appellate courts have also held that the presence of the public is a potent influence toward fairness on the judge, jury, and counsel.

Some states have passed statutes permitting the exclusion of the public in certain types of criminal cases. The statutes are of doubtful constitutionality.[2]

Statutes establishing juvenile courts usually provide for secret sessions and have been upheld on the theory that the child is not being tried for a crime.[3] Some statutes extend the juvenile court's jurisdiction over adults in

[1] The most complete discussion of this subject up to 1953 is in H. L. Cross, *The People's Right to Know* (New York, 1953).

[2] "A judge . . . has no right . . . to restrain or dictate what portion of court proceedings shall be made available for reading by the public."—People v. Jelke, 284 App. Div. 211, 130 N.Y.S. 2d 662 (1954). In a separate action connected with this case (United Press International v. Valente, 308 N.Y. 71), the New York Court of Appeals denied the right of a newspaper to require an open trial and asserted its rights in this respect to be no greater and no less than those of the general public.

[3] See the discussion of juvenile courts on pp. 180–181.

child neglect cases, but in some of the states having such statutes, the statutes providing for secrecy have been held invalid as to adults.

The foregoing discussion relates to the right of newspapers to attend and report criminal trials. Some state constitutions and statutes require that civil as well as criminal trials shall be public and they provide for no exceptions. The theory is that, in deciding a case between private persons, a court is also deciding, in effect, the rights and duties of many persons who are not parties to the action. Some statutes that require public civil trials provide for exceptions in divorce cases and sex cases—on the ground that publicity is injurious to morals. The constitutionality of these statutes has not been adequately tested.[4]

PRETRIAL REPORTING

By quoting prosecuting attorneys or policemen prior to a trial, newspapers sometimes report facts that are inadmissible as evidence, such as (1) confessions and admissions and (2) the defendant's criminal record.[5] Theoretically, prospective jurors who read the facts may develop a bias against the defendant.

Some years ago a man with a previous conviction was arrested in London on charges of theft and issuing a forged check. He had published an autobiography. In reporting his arrest, a London newspaper referred to the defendant's previous conviction, quoting from the autobiography. The editor was fined one thousand pounds for contempt of court. In pronouncing judgment, the Lord Chief Justice said:

> It was clear that after the arrest of the unfortunate man and before his trial statements, very manifestly to his detriment, were printed about him which certainly could not have been given in evidence at the trial unless he gave them in evidence himself. . . . Indeed, it might be said . . . that if a man had a bad character even greater care should be taken not to prejudice the case against him.[6]

In the United States there has been a great amount of pretrial reporting of inadmissible evidence. One book by a *Chicago Tribune* reporter describes a notorious case.[7] The authors of *Convicting the Innocent,* state that evi-

---

[4] English law requires that divorce trials be public but also prohibits the publication of testimony; only the names of the parties, the nature of the case, and the result of the action may be published.

[5] For a discussion of inadmissible evidence, see pp. 360–361.

[6] F. J. Mansfield, *Sub-editing* (London, 1932), pp. 182–83. In 1949 the editor of the London *Daily Mirror* was sentenced to three months in prison and fined 10,000 pounds for the newspaper's pretrial report of inadmissible evidence in connection with an arrest in a murder case.

[7] Paul Holmes, *The Sheppard Murder Case* (New York, 1961). In 1964, the convicted defendant in this case, who had served ten years of a life term in an Ohio

dence about prior conviction was a factor in twenty-two of the wrongful convictions they investigated.[8] The *Chicago Tribune* found the situation so intolerable some years ago that it was moved to publish an editorial which is quoted in part:

> Criminal justice in America is now a Roman holiday. The courts are in the Colosseum. The state's attorney's office often is an open torture room of human souls. Exposure of the process of justice, originally a public safeguard, has been exploited as a field for popular amusement. . . .
>
> The injury to justice is in publicity before the trial. Newspaper trials before the case is called have become an abomination. The dangerous initiative that newspapers have taken in judging and convicting out of court is journalistic lynch law. It is mob murder or mob acquittal in all but the overt act. It is mob appeal. Prosecuting attorneys now hasten to the papers with their theories and confessions. Defense attorneys do the same. Neither dare do otherwise. Half-wit juries or prejudiced juries are the inevitable result.
>
> The *Tribune* has its share of blame in this. No newspaper can escape it. They have met demand, and in meeting it have stimulated public appetite for more. . . .
>
> There is one remedy. Drastic restriction of publicity before the trial must be imposed by law. England by custom and by law imposes such restrictions. English papers print only the briefest and coolest statement of the facts before the trial. Three papers there were fined heavily not long ago for news reports that to us were mild. Publicity before the trial should be restricted, it may be, to official statements by police or state's attorney. If that be unfair to the defense, some other rule should be worked out. It is a problem suitable for the American Bar Association to take up. In conjunction with representatives of the press a fair but stringent law could be devised. . . .
>
> It will in no way threaten the freedom of the press. It is only a delay. It is enforced waiting so that the official instruments of justice may have a chance to operate. . . .
>
> The case against preliminary publication of crime news is irrefutable. The problem must be met by law.
>
> This must be balanced by full publicity for the trial itself. The hard won principle of public justice cannot be denied. No matter what the sacrifice, the administration of justice in principle must be public.[9]

Much of the blame for pretrial publication of inadmissible evidence attaches to prosecuting attorneys, according to Judge Samuel M. Leibowitz,

---

penitentiary, was released by a United States district court in a habeas corpus proceeding. One of the grounds was the inability of the trial court in 1954 to obtain impartial jurors because of the publication in Cleveland newspapers of inadmissible evidence. See also Irvin *v.* Dowd, 366 U.S. 717 (1961) and Marshall *v.* U.S., 360 U.S. 310 (1959).

[8] E. M. Borchard and E. R. Lutz, *Convicting the Innocent* (Yale University Press, 1932), pp. xv–xvi. Cited by J. Lofton, "Justice and the Press," *Saint Louis University Law Journal,* 6:448, 464 (1961).

[9] July 23, 1924.

of the Kings County (New York) Court, for many years before appointment to the bench the outstanding criminal lawyer in New York city.[10]

Two remedies for controlling the prosecutors have been suggested: (1) enforcement by local judges and bar associations of Canon 20 of the American Bar Association's Canons of Professional Ethics, and (2) establishment of the prosecuting attorney's office as a career service. Canon 20 is as follows:

> Newspaper publications by a lawyer as to pending or anticipated litigation may interfere with a fair trial in the courts and otherwise prejudice the due administration of justice. Generally they are to be condemned. If the extreme circumstances of a particular case justify a statement to the public, it is unprofessional to make it anonymously. An ex parte reference to the facts should not go beyond quotation from the records and papers on file in the court; but even in extreme cases it is better to avoid any ex parte statement.

Since a prosecuting attorney is a member of the bar, his local bar association could cite him for contempt before a judge. But bar associations are often far removed from criminal practice because most of their members—especially their leading members—are engaged only in civil practice.

The late Judge Robert P. Patterson suggested: that the local prosecuting attorney should be removed from politics through appointment by the governor from a list of qualified attorneys submitted by the local bar association; that assistant prosecuting attorneys be career personnel appointed for long terms at good salaries; and that each state establish a department of justice to which the prosecuting attorneys would be responsible. In addition, he recommended that schools for prosecuting attorneys be established similar to the F.B.I. and police schools.[11]

The English system—also operating in Canada and other Commonwealth countries—is not applicable in this country. English judges are former barristers appointed for life terms by the Lord Chancellor. In the United States, with few exceptions, judges of state courts are elected for short terms and probably will always be elected.[12] "The truth is," wrote a distinguished Michigan editor-publisher, "that the courts and the lawyers don't like to

---

[10] Q. Reynolds, *Courtroom: The Story of Samuel M. Leibowitz* (New York, 1950), pp. 129–30. See also E. R. Griswold, "When Newsmen Become Newsmakers," *Saturday Review*, Oct. 24, 1964, pp. 21–23, and M. R. Wessel, "Controlling Prejudicial Publicity in Criminal Trials," *Journal of the American Judicature Society*, Oct., 1964, pp. 105–9.

[11] "Scandal of Our District Attorneys," *This Week*, Jan. 13, 1952, p. 12.

[12] States provided in their constitutions for election of judges after the unfair behavior of several of the federal judges appointed in the administrations of Presidents Washington and John Adams. See A. Beveridge, *The Life of John Marshall* (Boston, 1929), Vol. III, Chaps. 1 and 2.

proceed against newspapers. They are too powerful. . . . Everyone is afraid to act."[13]

Increasingly judges are declaring mistrials and the United States Supreme Court is reversing convictions in cases in which inadmissible evidence has been published in newspapers. But reversal of a conviction is an inadequate remedy for an indigent defendant because of the expense of appeal and of a second trial and because of his deprivation of liberty when he is kept in jail. A second trial is not always an adequate remedy when defense witnesses have died or moved from the locality during the time required for appeal. Change of venue, too, is an extra expense for the state and an inconvenience to witnesses.

Voluntary restraint by newspapers has increased in recent years, and this solution may be preferable to adoption of the English system; for it is an important function of the press to keep the public informed about police action in a criminal case. In some areas, representatives of the bar, newspapers, and broadcasters have agreed on a statement of principles. An example is the statement agreed to in 1962 in the state of Oregon:

STATEMENT OF PRINCIPLES
ON THE
COVERAGE OF NEWS OF CRIMINAL PROSECUTIONS

Oregon's Bill of Rights provides both for fair trials and for freedom of the press. These rights are basic and unqualified. They are not ends in themselves but are necessary guarantors of freedom for the individual and the public's right to be informed. The necessity of preserving both the right to a fair trial and the freedom to disseminate the news is of concern to responsible members of the legal and journalistic professions and is of equal concern to the public. At times these two rights appear to be in conflict with each other.

In an effort to mitigate this conflict, the Oregon State Bar, the Oregon Newspaper Publishers Association and the Oregon Association of Broadcasters have adopted the following statement of principles to keep the public fully informed without violating the right of any individual.

I. The news media have the right and the responsibility to print and to broadcast the truth.

II. However, the demands of accuracy and objectivity in news reporting should be balanced with the demands of fair play. The public has a right to be informed. The accused has the right to be judged in an atmosphere free from undue prejudice.

III. Good taste should prevail in the selection, printing and broadcasting of the news. Morbid or sensational details of criminal behavior should not be exploited.

---

[13] Stuart Perry, "Trial by Newspapers," 30 *Mich. Law Rev.*, 228, 238 (1931). Cited by F. Thayer, *Legal Control of the Press* (4th ed.; Brooklyn, 1962), p. 591. See also F. E. Inbau (ed.), *Free Press—Free Trial: A Report of the Proceedings of a Conference on Prejudicial News Reporting in Criminal Cases* (Evanston, Ill., 1964).

IV. The decision concerning the publication of the news rests with the editor or news director. In the exercise of judgment he should consider that:
   (*a*) an accused person is presumed innocent until proved guilty;
   (*b*) readers and listeners are potential jurors;
   (*c*) no person's reputation should be injured needlessly.

V. The public is entitled to know how justice is being administered. However, it is unprofessional for any lawyer to exploit any medium of public information to enhance his side of a pending case. It follows that the public prosecutor should avoid taking unfair advantage of his position as an important source of news; this shall not be construed to limit his obligation to make available information to which the public is entitled.

In recognition of these principles, the undersigned hereby testify to their continuing desire to achieve the best possible accommodation of the rights of the individual and the rights of the public when these two fundamental precepts appear to be in conflict in the administration of justice.

For class discussion: Some editors have said there is no case on record which proves that a defendant has ever been convicted because of the publication of inadmissible evidence. How would you reply to that assertion?

DURING THE TRIAL

Sometimes jurors and the bailiff are housed in a hotel for the duration of a trial and are not permitted to read news stories or hear broadcasts that report the trial. Often, however, jurors return to their individual homes overnight, having been admonished by the court not to read or listen to reports of the trial. In the latter situation some jurors disobey the court's admonition. When, therefore, there is published or broadcast evidence which the judge had refused to admit or evidence which the parties had not yet presented, one or other of the parties is prejudiced. Here is an example that was prejudicial to the state:

The defendant was charged with rape (i.e., having carnal knowledge of a woman by force and against her consent). A physician who had examined the prosecutrix after the alleged rape was asked by the defendant's counsel if, in his opinion, any force or violence had been used. The prosecution objected and the objection was sustained. The defendant then demanded that the physician's response and the defendant's exception to the judge's ruling be admitted to the record so the appellate court could later decide whether or not the response should have been excluded. Out of the presence of the jury the physician then answered that, in his opinion, no force or violence whatever had been used. The local newspaper reported the incident including the physician's answer. The court the next day granted the state's motion for a mistrial, for by then the situation was what it would have been if the judge had overruled the state's objection. The jury had not been locked up. Since this was the third trial of the defendant on this charge (the first trial was declared a mistrial and judgment of conviction in the second was reversed by the appellate court), the state was now put to the expense of a fourth trial.[14]

In a murder trial the defendant's brother was asked by the prosecution why the defendant had purchased the rifle which he had used to shoot his sister-in-law. He was not permitted to answer. The local newspaper the next day published this paragraph in a report of the trial:

> . . . Prosecutors said that Virgil [the brother] was prepared to testify that Paul had bought the deer rifle for the purpose of shooting a city detective, Walter Hart, who had arrested him for carrying weapons. The court sustained an objection to his answering a question about the gun purchase.

On the following day the local newspaper published this paragraph:

> . . . Judge Hoy refused to let Virgil answer why Paul had bought the deer rifle. Virgil said in the corridor later that Paul bought the gun to shoot Detective Walter Hart who once had arrested Paul on a weapons charge. Defense counsel contended publication of this statement had been prejudicial.

For class discussion: What is your opinion about the propriety of the following news story?

"Whose Shorts?" Is Trial Mystery

> The mystery of the yellow shorts with the black fern-leaf design was left hanging before the jury hearing Dr. James Brumback's gem-fencing trial yesterday in superior court Judge Orla St. Clair's decorous courtroom.
>
> The shorts, or underpants, or drawers, were flourished by the dignified young prosecutor, Chief Assistant District Attorney Norman Elkington, as Inspector George Hoover of the

---

[14] *Publisher's Auxiliary*, Aug. 27, 1955.

Police Robbery Detail ascended to the witness chair....

"Will you tell us," enquired Elkington, "the circumstances under which you saw these shorts on the afternoon of . . ."

He was interrupted by objections of Emmett Hagerty, attorney for Frank Mendes, who is one of Brumback's co-defendants in this trial. Mendes will be tried later on robbery charges with two Oak Street roommates and another current co-defendant, Adolph (Ed) Bigarani.

No Search Warrant

"Those shorts are not binding on the defendant Mendes," Hagerty argued, or sentiments somewhat to that effect.

Morris Grupp, representing Bigarani, and Leo Friedman, defending Dr. Brumback, indicated that the shorts shouldn't bind their clients either.

Besides, Hagerty argued, the shorts were taken without a search warrant. He was allowed to examine Hoover on this point.

"The article was taken offa the person that was wearing them," explained Inspector Hoover, who is a large, powerful detective, capable of frisking anybody of anything, and who explained in a grave, forbidding voice.

For Identification

This fascinating disclosure did not seem to satisfy Judge St. Clair's understanding of precedents set in the celebrated case of "People vs. Cahan." So he ruled that the shorts were at present binding on no one present.

The shorts were marked "for identification," and remained in tantalizing view of the jurors, who cannot by law learn more about them. Therefore, any jurors reading this article are enjoined not to peek at the explanation of the puzzle printed in bold face type at the conclusion of this article. . . .

Elkington confided to the press that the shorts were stripped from Steve Sorrentino, a robbery suspect, and they carry the same laundry mark found on a handkerchief that was intermixed with recovered loot from the robbery.

Is stricken testimony privileged? Although there are no cases on record, Thayer says "it would seem that" such testimony is not privileged since the same information obtained out of court is not privileged.[15]

Reporting Testimony in Advance

Several instances are on record of newspaper reporters, during a trial, interviewing jurors' families, predicting the trial result on the basis of evidence not yet admitted, of paying witnesses for advance stories, and reporting the attorneys' versions of evidence they say they expect to present.

"Surprises" Due In Dr. Sam Trial

CLEVELAND—Both sides seized upon the sixth week-end recess of Dr. Samuel H. Sheppard's wife murder trial today to prepare "more surprises."

Asst. Prosecutor John Mahon said the state expects to complete its case next week with these witnesses:

Dr. E. Richard Hexter, who will dispute Dr. Sam's claim he was seriously injured in fierce struggles with the "real killer" of his pregnant wife, Marilyn. Dr. Hexter examined Dr. Sam on the July 4 murder morning and says he found no indications of serious hurts.

Mary Cowan, chief medical technician for the coroner's office, who will testify that part of the "trail of blood" through the Sheppard home in Bay Village is definitely human.

Temper Tantrum

Thomas Reese, father of the murdered Marilyn, who will describe his tense discussions of his only daughter's death with his son-in-law.

Thomas Weigle, Marilyn's cousin, who has made a sworn statement to police that he saw Dr. Sam display a savage temper when he got angry with his son Sam, and that Marilyn told him such displays were not unusual in the Sheppard home.

Susan Hayes, the former suburban Rocky River model and Bay View Hospital technician, who will be asked

---

[15] Thayer, *op. cit.*, p. 428, n. 12.

to help provide what Mahon calls "the motive for Marilyn Sheppard's murder."

Chief Defense Counsel William Corrigan said he would "definitely" use Dr. Sam as a defense witness unless his motions to dismiss the case for "lack of evidence" are granted after the state rests.

An Example of Press Responsibility

After the trial of fourteen defendants in a narcotics case had begun in 1962, the United States attorney wrote to the ten daily newspapers in the New York city area requesting them not to refer to the criminal records of any of the defendants and pointing out the possibility of a mistrial if they did so. Two of the defendants were members of a Mafia gang, as the newspapers knew. All of the editors complied with the prosecutor's request. The defendants were convicted. After the trial the prosecutor wrote a letter of appreciation to the editors.[16]

For class discussion: (a) "The National Association of Broadcasters has protested a recent *Saturday Evening Post* editorial opposing television coverage of the Billie Sol Estes trial in Tyler, Texas. . . .

"The magazine had contended in its Oct. 20 issue in an editorial entitled 'No Place for Television' that the object of court trials is justice, not publicity, and that every effort should be made to maintain a calm and judicious atmosphere. Mr. Bell [a representative of the broadcasters' association] said in his reply:

" 'Wherever people have a right to go in person they have the right to hear and see—through the facilities of broadcasting, just as through the newspaper reporter's pen and pencil.

" 'Because of the enormous size of the nation today, it is possible for only a small number of the people to attend trials in person. This is all the more reason to have broadcast coverage.

" 'Of course, broadcast journalists—or anyone else—should not be allowed to distort or interfere with the purpose of a trial. But to deny all broadcast coverage because of the existence of broadcasting equipment is to overlook the fact that technically it is possible to cover a trial with radio and television without anyone being aware that a microphone and a camera are in the courtroom.' "
(*Editor & Publisher*, Dec. 1, 1962, p. 52.)

---

[16] *Editor & Publisher*, Aug. 11, 1962, p. 14. Also, for a report of newspaper cooperation with the Secret Service, see *Editor & Publisher*, March 29, 1959, p. 111.

(*b*) Canon 35 of the American Bar Association's Canons of Judicial Ethics, as amended in 1963, is as follows:

"Proceedings in court should be conducted with fitting dignity and decorum. The taking of photographs in the courtroom, during sessions of the court or recesses between sessions, and the broadcasting or televising of court proceedings detract from the essential dignity of the proceedings, distract participants and witnesses in giving testimony, and create misconceptions with respect thereto in the mind of the public and should not be permitted."

A second paragraph excepts certain portions of naturalization proceedings.

(*c*) United States Supreme Court Justice William O. Douglas has written:

"The courtroom by our tradition is a quiet place where the search for truth by earnest, dedicated men goes on in a dignified atmosphere. . . .

"The concept of the public trial is not that every member of the community should be able to see or hear it. A public trial means one that is open rather than closed. The public exists because of the aversion which liberty-loving people had toward secret trials and proceedings. . . . That is the reason our courts are open to the public, not because the Framers wanted to provide the public with recreation or with instruction in the ways of government.

". . . I feel that a trial on radio or television is quite a different affair from a trial before the few people who can find seats in the conventional courtroom. The already great tensions on the witnesses are increased when they know that millions of people watch their every expression, follow each word. The trial is as much of a spectacle as if it were held in the Yankee Stadium or the Roman Colosseum. . . .

"Photographing a trial with ordinary cameras does not entail those evils. But it spawns evil of its own. . . . A man on trial for his life or liberty needs protection from the mob. Mobs are not interested in the administration of justice. . . . Even still pictures may distort a trial, inflame a proceeding by depicting an unimportant miniscule of the whole, or lower the judicial process in public eyes by portraying only the sensational moments. . . .

"As one trial lawyer recently said: 'It is the fact of photography, the fact that the intrusion is present, the fact that all the principals to the trial—judge, witness, lawyer, jury—are "on stage" which is inescapably distracting from the task at hand. It is the fact these participants are made actors which is dangerous and disturbing. If unwilling actors, then their essential dignity as human beings is being violated. If willing actors, then they may be far more dangerous to the life, liberty and property of the litigants because their principal concern will not be compliance with their oath, but with the question of their effectiveness as actors.'" ("The Public Trial and the Free Press," 46 *American Bar Association Journal* 840, 841, 842 (1960); quoted by Thayer, *op. cit.*)

Having read these three arguments, do you agree or disagree with Canon 35 with respect to (*a*) radio, (*b*) television, and (*c*) still pictures?

CHAPTER *26*

Probate

The state has laws to regulate the disposition of a decedent's property. These laws recognize the right of persons to devise and bequeath[1] their property and the right of persons and institutions to take such property.

In every state there is a court which construes wills and supervises the administration of decedents' estates. Since much of the work is administrative the judges are assisted by court commissioners and clerks. In one-fourth of the states probate matters are handled by judges of the court of original jurisdiction. In the other states there are special courts which are called Probate Court, County Court, Orphan's Court, Surrogate Court, Prerogative Court, and Courts of Ordinary.

When a person makes a will and dies he is said to have died *testate;* when he dies and leaves no will he is said to have died *intestate*. The person who makes a will usually nominates in the will one or two persons or a trust company to be executor[2] of his estate. To such persons the court issues *letters testamentary,* which authorize him to carry out the provisions of the will. When a person with property has left no will, some relative—often a spouse or son—usually applies to the appropriate court for *letters of administration,* which authorize that person—the *administrator*—to settle the estate. Some states have *public administrators* in each county to perform this function when no relative or other person has applied. When a nominated executor renounces his appointment or fails to apply for letters testamentary or when the sole executor dies, the court appoints an *administrator with the will annexed*. The administrator performs the same functions as the executor.

PROVING THE WILL

The first step in probate proceedings is the filing of a petition by some person (a nominated executor, a devisee or legatee, or some other person with a pecuniary interest) to prove the will, that is, to "probate" it. The

[1] Real property is "devised" and personal property is "bequeathed."
[2] A female executor is called *executrix*.

court is said to "admit the will to probate." The petition usually contains the names and addresses of all of the known heirs, the character and estimated value of the estate, and the name of the person or persons to whom letters testamentary should be given.

After the filing of the petition, the clerk of the court sets a date for hearing and gives notice by publication; notice is also served personally or by mail on the heirs and on any executors named in the will who did not join in the petition.

Proving the will consists of taking the evidence of one of the subscribing witnesses or, if none is available, of proving the handwriting of the testator and of one of the witnesses. Generally a will must have been attested by two witnesses. A *holographic* will (i.e., one in the testator's own handwriting) does not need to be attested by a witness. Courts sometimes admit to probate a *nuncupative* will; that is, an oral will made by a person in military service or by a person in expectation of immediate death from an injury received the same day. Such a will can, however, usually dispose only of personal property of a reasonably small amount.

Some wills have a *codicil;* that is, an alteration made after the execution of the will which changes the terms of the will.

Any person with a pecuniary interest may contest the petition for probate. This is done by filing a notice called a *caveat* ("let him beware") which informs the judge that the will may not be valid. The judge, often with the assistance of a jury, determines the issue either by denying the petition to probate or by signing an order admitting the will to probate.

No Witness, No Will; Widow Can't Become Sole Heir

A technicality of law will prevent a Lexington woman from becoming the sole heir to the estate of her late husband.

Probate Judge James Dilkes today denied admission to probate of a Canadian army legal form signed in 1945 which left to Mrs. Evangeline Muir the estate which was estimated to be "more than $10,000."

The judge based his refusal on the state law that at least one of the witnesses must appear.

Mrs. Muir said she did not know the present whereabouts of either of the two witnesses. They were members of the same battalion.

The case must now be considered as if Mr. Muir had died without making a will. This means that both of the sons, as well as the widow, will share in the estate.

Judge Dilkes, however, did admit to probate a hand-written codicil (addition) to the will which was on the back of the document. The handwriting was proved.

This holographic (that is, hand written) addition named his son, Campbell, of Seattle, as the sole heir if Mrs. Muir should have died before her husband. A second son, Wilson, of Spokane, Washington, was not mentioned in the codicil.

After a will has been admitted to probate the judge issues letters testamentary or letters of administration, as the case may be, authorizing the executor (or administrator) to do those things that are necessary to the settlement of the estate.

A will is usually "recorded" after probate; that is, copied for perpetual memory and deposited in a county records office.

THE NEWS STORY

The newspaper reader is extremely interested in the wills of decedents, as has been shown by newspaper readership studies. In small towns a person with considerable property is scarcely dead before his acquaintances begin to gossip about the amount of his estate and the probable division of it. In most community newspapers all wills are published at length. In both small and large cities there is great interest in the wills of wealthy or prominent persons. Most wills probated in large cities are not worth a news story; most of them are usually published in very brief form in the column devoted to "Court Briefs." But whenever a newspaper reporter discovers an important or interesting will he copies the provisions and writes a complete news story.

Frequently the point of interest in the news story is the *amount of the estate*. The probable amount may be usually obtained from the petition of the executor, who is sometimes (but not always) required to furnish penalty bond of approximately twice the estimated value of the estate; also the appraiser files an inventory in which the value of each item is set down. In some wills the interesting fact is that the estate is extraordinarily large—

as in the case of a priest who bequeathed one million dollars—and sometimes—as in the will of the Supreme Court Justice who left an estate of only fifteen thousand dollars—that the estate is surprisingly small.

In some wills the chief point of interest is the *heirs* or other legatees; for example, a rich eccentric willed his estate to "Miss Florida." In some wills prominent millionaires have disinherited their children or, as in one instance, bequeathed a divorced wife "thirty pieces of silver." There are many newspaper readers who have loyalties to certain educational, religious, and eleemosynary institutions and are, therefore, eager to know whether or not certain philanthropists have left bequests to "their" college, church, or hospital. Many persons too are eager to know "what will become of" a great newspaper or circus or other private business of an institutional character, over which its owner exercised a peculiar personal management.

Quite often the interesting feature in a will is the *character of the estate*. Sometimes the least eccentric person owns the queerest kind of personal property, and it is interesting to know about it and to know to whom it is bequeathed. Some readers also want to read the list of stocks which shrewd, wealthy men owned. Again certain claims against the estate that are listed in the inventory filed by the executor frequently reveal that the estate of a person thought to be wealthy is almost entirely encumbered. Oftentimes, too, there are queer provisions in the will as to the manner in which the bequests shall be put to use by the legatees.

Inventory Shows Banker Died in Debt

Reed Sanger, who was president of the First National Bank when he died last November, had more debts than assets, an inventory filed in Probate Court revealed yesterday.

His estate was appraised yesterday at $25,515. But already on file were claims totalling $43,082.

The estate's principal asset was one common share of First National Bank stock valued at $23,000.

The largest claim against the estate was $32,604, filed by the Security Trust Co. Of that sum, $17,604 was for overdrafts on a commercial account and $15,000 for an unpaid loan.

Other claims were for unpaid taxes and department store bills due as far back as three years ago.

ADMINISTRATION OF THE ESTATE

After a will has been admitted to probate, one or more appraisers is appointed by the judge. Usually one of the appraisers is an official inheritance tax appraiser. Some appraisements, when filed in court, are newsworthy for the reasons mentioned above.

The executor takes possession of all real and personal property; pays claims against the estate and accrued and inheritance taxes; collects debts due the estate and receives rents and profits. He sometimes manages a going business for a period and may be authorized by the court to borrow money when this is necessary toward conserving the estate. He may also institute actions for the recovery of property or to determine any adverse claim; and he may defend a suit against the estate.

The executor gradually liquidates the property that is not partitioned* and from time to time makes an accounting with the court. A newspaper report of confirmation of sale of real property is sometimes interesting, as when a well-known hotel is sold. At some time the executor petitions the court for a decree of partial distribution of the estate.

Eventually the executor makes a final accounting and the court issues a decree of discharge. In connection with the final accounting the executor renders a bill for his own services and submits the bills of his attorneys. The amounts of the bills for "extraordinary services" are sometimes contested by the heirs.

$100,000,000 Estate Now Less than 0

The tangled estate of R. Will Gilbert, valued during the war at $100,000,000, was closed in probate court yesterday, showing an insolvency of $1,805,000.

After Lindsay Holt, executor, had rendered his third and final accounting, Probate Judge Stanford Guilford entered a decree of discharge.

After all claims had been settled not only was nothing left for the miller's widow and Mrs. Charles Kane, his daughter, but their own unsettled claims against the estate totaled $1,805,000.

The widow previously had obtained $750,000 on a $1,055,000 claim and the daughter $500,000 on a $2,000,000 claim.

Cox Heirs Protest Administrator Fees

A $100,000 Cox blowup over the estate of Henry (Pinky) Cox, Wade county politician, was building in probate court today.

A petition asking that amount for services was filed yesterday by the Southern Trust Co., the executor, and its attorneys, Regan, Rankin & Dubois.

Protests against the amount were made by attorneys representing seven nieces and nephews who will inherit most of the $1,000,000 estate.

One of these, Charles Trowbridge, termed the fees "exorbitant." He said some of the work charged for has already been done by the Willis Trust Co. and payment made for it.

The Southern Trust Co. asks $35,000 and the law firm $65,000.

Services charged for include locating heirs and determining a "multitude of questions of law and fact."

CONTESTED WILLS

A will that has been probated may be contested within a limited time after probate by any person with a pecuniary interest who was not a party to a contest before probate or who had no notice of such a contest. A contest is begun by the filing of a petition for revocation of probate and with notice to the heirs. The court determines the issue by the rules of procedure in civil cases and applies the laws of the particular state that relate to the estates of decedents. In some situations a jury is used.

The grounds for contesting wills are numerous. Some petitioners allege mental incompetency of the testator, duress, fraud, or undue influence. Sometimes a will is alleged to contravene public policy, as when a father bequeaths to a daughter provided she divorces her husband. Sometimes the legitimacy of birth of an heir is questioned. Sometimes the issue turns on the order of death of the members of a family killed in an accident or a catastrophe. In instances in which the decedent has died intestate, the contest relates to the distributive shares to which each claimant is entitled. Some wills are drawn in such an ambiguous manner that the actual intentions of the testator require interpretation; the construction of a phrase, or even of a punctuation mark, may mean the difference of many thousands of dollars to some of the contestants. The *proponent* has the burden of proving the due execution of the will and the testator's testamentary capacity, but the burden is on the *contestant* to prove undue influence. So frequently are the situations in will cases mysterious or of human interest that they qualify as the basis for excellent news stories.

Ex-convict Faked Claim as Heir; Witness is Held

Probate Judge James Trueblood yesterday denied both claims of Ernest Murphy, ex-convict, to the estate of the late Barton W. Burns, multimillionaire recluse.

The court ruled there was no evidence to support Murphy's assertion that he was Burns' son by a secret marriage.

The judge also found against Murphy's contention that a lost or stolen will named him sole legatee of the estate.

The decision gives the fortune to two second cousins of Burns—Mrs. Boyce D. Wilson, Erie, Penna., and Mrs. Edward B. Burns, Chicago.

Was There a Jennie Mallott?

A dramatic climax to the week's trial was presented yesterday when Attorney Martin B. Doak, representing the cousins, brought a tombstone into court.

He said the tombstone came from what was said to be the grave of Murphy's mother, Jennie Mallott. The inscription read, "Jennie M. Burns, Mar. 12, 1919—Aug. 2, 1936."

Alexander Costigan, cemetery sexton, testified he explored below the stone last week and found no grave.

He added that the marker was put in the cemetery last spring and that he saw Murphy taking pictures of it. The rear of the stone showed it had once marked the grave of one "Rowena Johnson."

Attorney Doak, contending that Murphy had invented his claims to the Burns estate while an inmate of the Missouri penitentiary, presented witnesses whose testimony indicated that a Jennie Mallott may never have existed.

Witness Is Arrested

The Rev. O. M. Cox, pastor of the Baptist Church, produced church records showing that the woman Murphy named as his maternal grandmother had given birth to a child two months before the date Murphy gave for the birth of his mother.

Murphy's story was that his mother died while giving birth to a child when she was 14 years old. He said her relative, Mrs. Orville Murphy, reared him as her own son in order to hush scandal.

John Edelmann, star witness for Murphy, was arrested last night on orders of Judge Trueblood and must show cause Saturday why he should not be sentenced for contempt of court.

Judge Trueblood said he found that the letters introduced in the trial by Edelmann were signed with a rubber stamp of Murphy's signature. He added that post office cancellation marks on the envelope had been drawn with pen and ink.

GUARDIANSHIP

The same courts which supervise the estates of decedents usually supervise the estates of orphan children. A *guardian* in such an instance corresponds to the executor of a decedent's estate, although a guardian may take care of the minor as well as manage his property. Guardians are sometimes appointed by a testator in his will because a minor is not permitted to take property under a will. A minor over 14 years of age may usually elect his guardian. The court sometimes appoints a guardian, usually a relative or friend, after receiving a petition. The guardianship terminates when the minor (i.e., the *ward*) reaches his "majority."

A court sometimes appoints a *guardian ad litem* ("pending the suit") to prosecute or defend a suit for a minor (also called an "infant").

A guardian is also appointed by a court for an incompetent adult. Some states provide for the appointment of a *conservator* to manage the estates of aged people.

Guardianship Sought for Rich Widow

A petition for guardianship of Mrs. Helen Eddy, 74, wealthy widow, yesterday disclosed a wrangle between her grandson and her business manager.

The grandson, Otis Nash, 21, charged that Mrs. Eddy is "mentally incompetent" and "would be likely to be deceived or imposed upon by designing persons."

Earlier this week, Nash filed a petition for a writ of habeas corpus charging that Mrs. Eddy was being illegally hidden away by her business manager, Milton Owen.

Owen responded that Mrs. Eddy was in Livermore Sanitarium of her own volition. Nash reported he and his attorney subsequently went to Livermore and found that Mrs. Eddy had been moved to Monterey.

Nash thereupon filed the guardianship suit asking that he be made Mrs. Eddy's guardian and that the Bank of Commerce be made the guardian of her estate.

Owen, who manages the Newcomb Hotel for Mrs. Eddy, told reporters: "Mrs. Eddy has been sick for a couple of years and Nash hasn't gone near her. Now he is getting anxious."

Owen produced a power of attorney giving him the right to act for Mrs. Eddy in her business affairs.

The guardianship and attendant matters will be heard in Superior Court next Thursday.

CHAPTER 27

Bankruptcy Proceedings

When individuals or business firms acquire an oppressive debt, federal law provides procedures which are of assistance to both the creditors and the debtor. The United States constitution delegated to Congress the power to "establish uniform laws on the subject of bankruptcies throughout the United States" (Art. I, sec. 8).

Under the Bankruptcy Act an *individual* may voluntarily or involuntarily surrender his assets to his creditors and be discharged with respect to his debts.[1] He can then make a fresh start and not be hounded by creditors. The law also provides for a proportionate distribution of the bankrupt's assets, if any, to creditors, thus preventing some creditors from becoming preferred to other creditors.

When a *business firm* is insolvent the law provides for a similar liquidation and distribution of its assets. In addition, when the firm is solvent but is not able to pay its debts as they mature, the law provides for the rehabilitation of the firm and its continuance in business by effecting an *arrangement* with its creditors. This procedure provides for a *composition* of the firm's debt; that is, the creditors agree to accept (say) twenty-five cents on the dollar as full payment of the debt. Or it provides for an extension of the debt maturities. The procedure (Chapter XI of the Bankruptcy Act) applies mainly to small firms.

A similar arrangement, under Chapter XIII of the act, is available to the wage earner. This provides for the wage earner to consolidate his debts and to pay them on a monthly installment *plan* which the court approves. The debtor thus avoids the stigma of bankruptcy.

For *large corporations,* the law considers the interest of the stockholders as well as of the creditors and provides for a *reorganization* of the capital structure of the corporation (Chapter X).

In summary, the bankruptcy law provides for *liquidation and distribu-*

---

[1] There are a few classes of debts not affected by discharge (sec. 17). Also, **certain assets are exempted from surrender or seizure.**

tion of a debtor's assets, for *rehabilitation* of a business firm, and for capital *reorganization* of a corporation.

From 75 to 90 per cent of all bankruptcy proceedings are of wage earners who have become hopelessly indebted for installment plan purchases or to personal loan companies. In many such instances the debtor's liabilities exceed his assets and he is insolvent, but the law also provides for a composition or extension (Chapter XIII).

Many of the business firms involved in bankruptcy proceedings are not necessarily insolvent but are overextended. Without some type of relief, however, they would later become insolvent. Their problem is usually due to overexpansion or to some catastrophic business misfortune such as cancellation of a government contract. They exhaust their working capital and cannot borrow enough money to restore the working capital to normal requirements.

The problem of large corporations often traces to the fact of their undercapitalization; that is, they are top-heavy with long-term debt in relation to their equity capital.[2]

Railroads in financial difficulty are a special case which we shall not discuss.

The law is not only of help to a debtor in the ways that have been mentioned, but the creditors are protected in these ways when the debtor is insolvent: (1) there is an automatic receivership for conservation of the debtor's assets and (2) there is a pro rata distribution of the assets to the creditors, thus preventing some creditors from receiving preference.

COURTS OF BANKRUPTCY

The Bankruptcy Act establishes the federal district courts as "courts of bankruptcy." So much administration is involved that the judges are assisted by one or more *referees in bankruptcy* whom the judges appoint for a term of years. Each referee is assisted by a clerk. The referee is not only an administrator, but an assistant judge. Although his rulings must be approved by a judge, the referee makes most of the decisions that the proceedings require.

THE STAGES OF THE PROCEEDING

These steps are taken although *not exactly in this order* and do not apply in all bankruptcies: (1) the filing of a petition for a bankruptcy adjudication, (2) notification of creditors, (3) receivership, (4) adjudication, (5) the first meeting of creditors at which the creditors have the right

[2] For an explanation of capitalization, see Chap. 30.

to elect a trustee and to examine the bankrupt about his assets, (6) discharge of the debtor, and (7) administration of the estate, which includes distributions to creditors.

All of these steps are taken when the debtor is adjudicated a bankrupt. In other situations, as will be explained, a *plan* is developed and *confirmed* by the judge so that a firm continues in business or the capital structure of a corporation is reorganized. We shall first describe the procedures when the debtor is insolvent.

THE PETITION

A petition in bankruptcy is *voluntary* or *involuntary,* depending upon whether it is filed by the debtor himself or by the debtor's creditors. A debtor who wishes to surrender his assets to his creditors employs an attorney to prepare and file a voluntary petition. Attached to the petition is a verified schedule of all of the debtor's assets and liabilities.

An involuntary petition is filed by at least three creditors with the view to taking the debtor's assets before they are further dissipated, or to prevent him from treating some of his creditors as preferred creditors to the disadvantage of other creditors. Creditors may try to force into bankruptcy corporations (except municipal, railroad, insurance, and banking corporations and savings and loan associations),[3] partnerships, and all individuals with debts of one thousand dollars or more except wage earners and farmers.

In response to an involuntary petition, the debtor may deny that he is insolvent and that he has committed an *act of bankruptcy*. Upon one or both of these issues a trial of the issue is held. If the debtor is found to be insolvent or to have committed an act of bankruptcy, he is adjudicated a bankrupt. An act of bankruptcy has occurred when the debtor has:

1. Conveyed, transferred, concealed, or removed any part of his property with intent to hinder, delay, or defraud his creditors.

2. Transferred, while insolvent, any portion of his property to one or more of his creditors with intent to prefer such creditors over the others.

3. Permitted, while insolvent, any creditor to obtain a lien upon any of his property through legal proceedings.

4. Made a general assignment for the benefit of his creditors.

5. While insolvent, permitted voluntarily or involuntarily the appointment of a receiver or trustee to take charge of his property.

6. Admitted in writing his inability to pay his debts and his willingness to be adjudged a bankrupt.

[3] Nor may any of the corporations mentioned above in the parentheses file a voluntary petition.

REPORTING THE PETITION

The reporter prepares news stories about petitions in bankruptcy in about the same manner that he reports pleadings filed in civil actions. The petitions are filed with the same federal district court clerk except that in large cities the office of the clerk has a separate "bankruptcy department." Most petitions in bankruptcy are worth only a routine story and are frequently published in the column devoted to "Court Briefs." Some details, however, are often of more than ordinary interest. Sometimes the fact that a certain person or a long-established firm is the petitioner in a voluntary petition or is the respondent in an involuntary petition is of interest. Sometimes the surprisingly small or large amount of assets or liabilities is a point of interest. Sometimes the unusual character of some of the assets is of human interest, as when certain securities held by the debtor are listed as valueless, or the insolvent person is forced to surrender a fine mansion, stable of horses, yacht, or other proud possession.

In addition, when the reporter lists the creditors there is interest in the fact that certain persons or firms or banks stand to lose heavily; in a few cases the bankruptcy of one firm has led to the bankruptcy of one or more of its creditors. The mere identification of the creditors is also sometimes of human interest, as in the insolvency of a hygienic laboratory when the majority of the creditors were country physicians who had paid deposits for laboratory work, or in the insolvency of a lecture bureau when the creditors were season ticket holders for a series of lectures.

In preparing news stories from petitions in bankruptcy, reporters must be careful when copying the names and amounts listed. To refer to a voluntary petition as an involuntary petition, or to confuse the name of a solvent firm or person with an insolvent firm or person is libelous. An example: confusing the Atlas Building and Supply Company with the Atlas Brush and Supply Company. To refer to the respondent in an involuntary petition or a petitioner under Chapter XI as a "bankrupt" is probably libelous since a debtor is never bankrupt until he has been adjudicated so in a bankruptcy court.[4]

Marine Supply Firm Files in Bankruptcy

Delbert Tuttle, who has been doing business as The Tuttle Supply Company with offices at 1820 Union Avenue, filed a voluntary petition in bankruptcy in federal court yesterday.

---

[4] However, see sec. 1(4) of the Bankruptcy Act.

He listed his liabilities as $131,355 in unsecured claims and $10,850 rent owing in Honolulu. His assets were given as stock in trade (marine supplies) worth $36,485.

Creditors Claim Bakery Insolvent

Three creditors today filed an involuntary bankruptcy petition against the French Baking Company, 525 Division Street.

Thomas Lockridge, former advertising agent for the bakery, listed a claim of $101,000; Allingham and Gilbert, an outdoor advertising firm, listed a claim of $1,468; and the First National Bank listed a note of $4,850.

ADJUDICATION

On the filing of a voluntary petition (other than one filed in behalf of a partnership by fewer than all of the partners) the judge or a referee makes the adjudication or dismisses the petition. In the case of an involuntary petition, a debtor may contest the petition, denying insolvency or denying having committed any "act of bankruptcy." A trial is held to determine the issue. It is heard by a judge or, if he directs, by a referee. The debtor is entitled to a jury trial of the issue of his insolvency.

Ex-candy Maker Is Adjudged Bankrupt

Federal Judge Duncan Holmes yesterday adjudged Harrison Dinerman, former president of the Wayne Advertising Agency, a bankrupt.

He signed the order after a jury had found that Mr. Dinerman had committed an "act of bankruptcy."

The act consisted in giving an $18,000 mortgage on his home at 2432 McKinley Boulevard to Winston Tufts.

This action gave Mr. Tufts a preference over other creditors at a time when Mr. Dinerman was knowingly insolvent, the jury found.

Other main creditors are the First National Bank and the Willis Trust Company, which held notes of Mr. Dinerman totalling $50,000.

FIRST MEETING OF CREDITORS

After adjudication, the referee calls a meeting of all creditors. With the referee presiding, claims of creditors are presented and are allowed or disallowed. The unsecured creditors then proceed (when there are assets) to elect a *trustee*. In some situations there is a contest among the creditors in the election of the trustee. The judge must approve the trustee. When creditors fail to appoint a trustee the judge may do so. When the assets are small the referee usually appoints a trustee. In some instances three trustees are appointed. The trustee is empowered to take possession of the bankrupt's assets, to liquidate them, and to pay the cash to creditors in the form of *dividends*. He is authorized to employ an attorney to advise him and to bring and defend suits on behalf of or against the bankruptcy estate.

Examination of the Bankrupt

Either at the first meeting of creditors or at an adjourned meeting the creditors may examine the bankrupt as to his assets. The bankrupt is required to testify under oath as to the transfer or concealment of any assets. This hearing is sometimes a "fishing expedition."

Broker, Wife Deny Transfer of Assets

The wife of a partner in an insolvent brokerage firm denied today that her husband had transferred several hundred thousand dollars to her before the firm closed its doors.

She was Mrs. George Stanley, wife of one of the partners in Stanley Brothers, which is involved in bankruptcy proceedings

Mrs. Stanley admitted to Referee in Bankruptcy James Hudson, however, that practically all of her husband's property was in her name.

The George Stanleys' two homes, she said, were in her name, and one month ago her husband gave her $10,000 to pay bills.

She also admitted her husband built a $40,000 home last year for their married daughter.

George Stanley denied transferring any of the firm's assets and declared that, to his knowledge, none of his partner brothers had done so.

ARRANGEMENTS UNDER CHAPTER XI

A debtor may file a petition under this chapter either voluntarily or after creditors have brought a proceeding; in the latter situation the debtor may file either before or after adjudication. The petition states either that the debtor is insolvent or is solvent but unable to pay its debts as they mature. The petition may include an application for the court to stay suits by the creditors. The court may permit the debtor to continue to operate the business or it may appoint a receiver to operate it.

At the first meeting of creditors the debtor presents an *arrangement* proposing an extension of time for payments or a reduction of payments, or both. An example is the proposal of a debt-ridden but solvent firm to repay all of its debt over an eleven-year period after selling an issue of debentures to acquire additional working capital.

Creditors vote whether to reject or accept the arrangement, which must be approved by the judge. When the plan is not deemed adequate for a rehabilitation of the company, the firm is either forced into liquidation or is required to reorganize its capital structure under the provisions of Chapter X, depending upon the degree of solvency, or on the firm's capital structure, or on both.

Actually, Chapter XI was enacted to fit the problems of small businesses, and a frequent result of a petition is a composition of a firm's debts. This is because creditors often would rather accept early payment of a part of their claims than to wait longer for a larger recovery.

In some instances large firms with low working capital have tried to apply Chapter XI to their problems—mainly to avoid losing control of the business to a reorganized company. In several such cases, however, the Securities and Exchange Commission has intervened with the result that the companies have had to withdraw their Chapter XI petition and apply under Chapter X. This is because Chapter X, which was enacted to fit the problems of large corporations, provides more safeguards for the corporation's stockholders and bondholders than does Chapter XI.

Court Orders Yuba To Reorganize

Federal District Judge George B. Harris yesterday ordered a reorganization of Yuba Consolidated Industries,

Inc. under the provisions of Chapter 10 of the federal bankruptcy act.

Last fall Yuba filed a voluntary petition under Chapter 11. This chapter permits the court to stay creditors' rights while the company works out a plan of payment.

On February 8, however, the Securities and Exchange Commission asked the court to order the company to operate under Chapter 10.

The SEC motion said: "It is the commission's position that the procedures under Chapter 11 are inadequate for the accomplishment of a thoroughgoing reorganization of Yuba, and do not provide the safeguards for public investors which are provided under Chapter 10."

Chapter 10 provides for corporate reorganization, recapitalization, and protection of investors.

The SEC also said Chapter 10 provides for thorough investigation to determine whether there have been any "irregularities and misconduct of officers."

A committee of Yuba's unsecured creditors had opposed the SEC motion. They asked that Yuba either be ruled bankrupt and the creditors paid from the liquidation or that the company be permitted to continue to operate under Chapter 11.

The SEC had described Yuba as a "corporate cripple" and called its present financial condition "chaotic."

REORGANIZATION UNDER CHAPTER X

A corporation has liabilities to both creditors and stockholders. In addition to such creditors as suppliers and holders of short-term notes, a corporation may have long-term debt in the form of bonds or debentures. It may also have preferred stockholders as well as common stockholders. In a reorganization these classes of creditors and stockholders have diverse interests. Chapter X provides for the development of one or more *plans* by the trustee, the debtor, or the various interests (or all of these) and the approval by the court of one plan. A detailed discussion of the proceedings under Chapter X is deferred until the more complete explanation of the various types of securities in Chapter 30 of this book.

CHAPTER 28

Extraordinary Remedies

In addition to the legal and equitable remedies discussed in earlier chapters there are extraordinary remedies. Most of these were called *prerogative writs* because they did not issue as a matter of the litigants' right but as a prerogative of the crown. They have these names: *mandamus, prohibition, certiorari* (pronounced "ser-shi-o-ra-ri"), *quo warranto,* and *habeas corpus. Injunction,* an equitable remedy, is also regarded as one of the extraordinary remedies.

These writs are used in public law; that is, they are commands to an administrative officer, a board, or a judge. Some of them are also available in private litigation when the petitioner has no other adequate remedy.

Some of them may be applied for in a court of original jurisdiction, but some must be applied for originally in an appellate court.

MANDAMUS

Mandamus ("we command") is a writ that compels action. It is issued on application of a party who has a personal interest or of a party acting in the public interest. In some situations the petitioner must show a direct, personal, and pecuniary interest aside from a mere citizen's or taxpayer's interest. Mandamus is most frequently addressed to administrative officials who perform ministerial acts, but may also issue against a board, commission, inferior court, or corporation. A ministerial act is one which does not require discretion (i.e., a judgment). The writ commands the performance of a duty which the law requires to be performed because of the board's or officer's office or trust. The writ has been issued, for example, to compel a Board of Health to grant a license to a chiropractor; to compel a water company to fix water rates; to compel a secretary of state to issue a certificate of election to one entitled to it and to place the name of a candidate on election ballots; to compel a city council to issue a license for the exhibition of a motion picture film; to compel a commission and a court to take jurisdiction in a proceeding; to compel a court to restore the name of an attorney to its rolls; to compel a railroad to resume and continue operation; and to compel a corporation to open its books to inspection by a stockholder. It does not lie, however, against a governor or against the President of the United States.

Applications for the writ are sometimes denied because the petitioners are ignorant of the restrictions placed upon issuance of the writ. Some of the restrictions are these: (1) The writ may compel a public officer or board to act, but it cannot affect the discretion of the officer or the board; for example, it can compel a city council to levy taxes but it cannot fix the tax rate. (2) The writ will not issue when there is any other adequate remedy. (3) The writ may not compel the performance of a duty arising out of contract; for example, the writ lies against a school board to compel the reinstatement of a suspended pupil but it does not lie against a teacher because a teacher is only an employee under contract to the board.

The usual procedure is to apply first for an *alternative* writ which orders the respondent either to perform a certain act or to show cause why it should not be performed. A *peremptory* writ may be issued after a hearing on the merits at the time the respondent makes a return to the alternative writ. In some states the petitioner must be the state, represented by the attorney general or county attorney, with the complaining party being the "relator,"[1] but in other states the action is in the name of a private party. In the former case, however, the writ generally issues as a matter of course without the intervention of an official. When the petitioner's interest is private (and in some states when it is public) he must show he stands to lose some substantial right or interest.

When an interested party, in contrast, desires to *restrain* an official from performance of a ministerial act, his remedy is injunction.

Entitle Petition: Court Tells Attorney General

The supreme court today directed the attorney general to prepare a title for the initiative which would ban political assessments by labor unions.

Attorney General Marvin Stearns had refused to entitle the measure, challenging the good faith of its sponsors. He said he had earlier entitled a

[1] For an explanation of this term, see p. 421.

similar measure which had been allowed to lapse with no effort being made to get voters' signatures on it.

Mr. Stearns argued today that he had a "limited discretion" to pass upon initiative petitions and to require good faith from their sponsors.

The court, in issuing the writ of mandamus, held that the attorney general's function is "purely ministerial."

Negro Can't Compel Firm to Sell House

A Negro who had sued to force a real estate firm to sell him a house in East Willows today lost his case.

Thomas Owens last week sued the firm of Rapp and Noble, asking a writ of mandamus. Circuit Judge Lester Davis today sustained the firm's demurrer to Owens' action.

This type of action, Judge Davis ruled, can be brought only against public officers, not against private individuals or corporations.

PROHIBITION

The writ of prohibition is a judicial order from a superior court to an inferior court or other tribunal which exercises judicial functions to prevent the tribunal from exceeding its jurisdiction. In general, the writ arrests the proceedings before judgment. It is not corrective of any errors except the question of jurisdiction. It is addressed to the inferior court, not to litigants; the proper writ addressed to litigants is injunction.

The writ has been issued: to prohibit a lower court from enforcing a judgment; to nullify a restraining order issued by a lower court; to prevent a disqualified judge from acting in a certain case (although it does not act to disqualify him); and to prevent a justice of the peace from punishing for contempt of the district court.

Tax Body Asks Writ To Halt Refund Case

The supreme court tomorrow will hear arguments on a petition for a writ of prohibition against Judge Dudley Dahl of Vernon county circuit court.

The petition, filed by the state tax commission, asserts that Judge Dahl is exceeding his jurisdiction in reopening an income tax refund case in which the plaintiff is the Norman Construction Co.

Last year the Vernon county circuit court awarded the company a refund of $10,011 and the state paid it. Recently the company sued for an additional refund and Judge Dahl granted the motion to reopen the case.

Court Lifts Ban on Dunn County Board

The supreme court today issued a writ of prohibition to stop the Dunn county circuit court from interfering with the election of a chairman of the Dunn county board of supervisors.

The effect of the writ is to vacate Circuit Court Judge W. B. Quinlan's temporary restraining order against members of the board. His order has prevented the board members from holding a meeting to elect a chairman.

CERTIORARI

A writ of prohibition only prevents an inferior tribunal from exceeding its jurisdiction; it does not quash proceedings after judgment. The writ of certiorari ("to be made certain in regard to"), however, permits this by commanding the lower court to send up the record for a review.[2] The reviewing court then does not, generally, correct errors of the inferior tribunal but merely examines the record to ascertain whether or not the tribunal exceeded its jurisdiction; the effect of this review, therefore, is to quash the proceedings (as when the reviewing court annuls a contempt conviction) or to affirm the proceedings.

There are certain exceptions to this general statement. One is the tendency for some courts to correct errors of law when reviewing orders of state quasi-judicial commissions. Another is the practice of the United States Supreme Court in using certiorari to permit it to select for review certain cases from the highest state courts, the Court of Appeals and the Court of Claims. The Supreme Court generally grants the writ when it

[2] In some circumstances the writ may also issue before judgment, but seldom does.

believes a substantial federal question is involved. It denies more than four out of five applications for the writ. The form of the writ follows:

> To Lewis Malin, Esquire, Judge of the Thirteenth Circuit Court, County of Rowan,
> Greetings:
> Whereas, upon the petition of the plaintiff, herein verified by the certificate of Arthur Fleming, Esquire, an attorney of this court, it manifestly appears that you, exercising judicial functions in a certain action, have made a certain order [described] to the injury of a substantial right of the plaintiff and that *there is no appeal* or other plain, speedy and adequate remedy, and being therefore willing to be certified of the said proceedings:
> We, therefore, command you that you certify and send to the Supreme Court on the 13th day of June, 19—, annexed to this writ, a transcript of the record of the proceedings aforesaid with all things touching the same as fully and as entirely as it remains before you by whatsoever names the parties may be called therein that the same may be reviewed by our said court, and that our said court may further cause to be done thereupon what it may appear of right ought to be done, and in the meantime, we command and require the said Lewis Malin, to desist from further proceedings in the matter to be reviewed.

Issuance of the writ by an appellate court does not necessarily mean that the court will decide in favor of the petitioner. When the court consents to review a case by this means it merely consents to review it. When the appellate court, on the other hand, refuses to issue the writ in a particular case it does not express an opinion about the case; it merely states "Writ denied." Some reporters who do not understand this practice have presumed that when the court refuses to issue a writ of certiorari it has thereby decided in favor of the respondent. The denial of the writ, of course, does have the effect of upholding the status quo.[3] After the court has granted the writ, it reviews the case to the extent already mentioned and hands down an opinion.

When a reviewing court decides that a case has been improperly removed to it by writ of certiorari, it sends a *writ of procedendo* to the trial court with instructions to proceed with it there.

QUO WARRANTO PROCEEDINGS

Although the writ of quo warranto ("by what right") is obsolete, the proceedings to try a person's title to office are in the nature of quo war-

[3] When the United States Supreme Court denies an application for a writ of certiorari (and expresses no opinion on it) the wire news services in Washington have often reported that the court "upheld" a certain state law. This is because the petitioner had wanted the Supreme Court to review the decision of the highest state court, which had upheld the law, and to find the statute unconstitutional. Actually the Supreme Court had not examined the law any further than to determine that no "substantial federal question" was involved.

ranto. Such proceedings have been used to oust officials, to prevent foreign (i.e., out-of-state) corporations from doing business within a state, to enforce forfeiture of a corporate franchise, to contest the validity of a municipal charter and amendments thereto, and to exclude a person from practicing a profession without a license or certificate.

The proceeding is not a civil proceeding in the sense that any private person can use it against another. Nor is it criminal, although the attorney general or prosecuting attorney institutes it in the name of the state. Generally the proceeding is brought by the prosecuting official filing an *information in the nature of quo warranto* with a private person as *relator* (i.e., informer). The case is ordinarily styled "The State *ex rel.* John Doe *v.* Richard Roe." When an individual has a private right distinct from the right of the public (such as a right himself in the office) the statutes sometimes authorize him to institute the proceeding independently when the attorney general or prosecuting attorney has refused to act.

Generally there is no absolute right to institute the proceeding, the permission of the court being required. The petition is usually considered by the court on ex parte allegations, but in some jurisdictions a rule to show cause is issued and the respondent makes a return. In any event, after the court has permitted the institution of the proceeding a trial ensues.

When a private party desires to start the proceeding he must first prove to the court his interest in the action. For example, in one state the petition of a defeated candidate in a three-cornered election was denied on the ground that, regardless of whether or not his successful opponent was eligible, the petitioner himself did not receive enough votes to be elected even though the votes of the successful candidate were not counted. In most jurisdictions, however, it is held, in suits to oust municipal officers, that any citizen has sufficient interest to entitle him to bring an action.

Will Absences of Councilman Put Him Out of Office?

Did the Shorewood City Council grant Councilman Morton Steelhammer permission to absent himself at any time during the period of March 25 to July 8?

On the court's answer to this question depends the title of office of Mr. Steelhammer or of Thomas Atterbridge.

Superior Court Judge Harlan

Powers heard final arguments today in a proceeding in the nature of quo warranto. Attorneys have five days in which to file briefs, after which Judge Powers will consider the case.

The Council voted last month that Mr. Steelhammer had forfeited his title to office and appointed Mr. Atterbridge for the unexpired term.

Mr. Atterbridge's attorney, Allen Walsh, at the hearing yesterday, introduced the minutes of the meetings for the dates in question. These showed that Mr. Steelhammer was not present at any of the meetings. Nor do they show that he was granted permission to absent himself.

Mr. Steelhammer testified that, because of illness, he was excused from the March 25 meeting and that he was under doctor's orders to remain at home.

Councilman John Olds and Wallace Rice testified, in behalf of Mr. Steelhammer, that they had given their permission for his absence and that Mayor Chester Smith, in a conversation with them, agreed to the councilman being absent.

City attorneys for Southgate, Chesterfield and North Bend received permission from Judge Powers to file amicus curiae (friend of the court) briefs.

Reply Due Soon in Power Dam Case

SALEM, Ore.—The Portland General Electric Co. said today it will file an answer before the deadline next Thursday in the Pelton Dam case.

Attorney General Robert Y. Thornton last week filed in Supreme Court a petition for quo warranto challenging the right of the electric company to construct the Pelton Dam on the Deschutes river without obtaining a permit from the state.

The electric company reportedly has expended more than $2,000,000 in construction operations up to this time.

The company contends it is complying with a ruling of the Federal Power Commission and does not need a permit either from the state engineer or the state Hydroelectric Commision.

When a private citizen wishes to bring an action against an officeholder or a corporation he must first sue out the writ; that is, bring an action to prove to the court that he is entitled to prosecute the action in the name of and on behalf of the state. If he is successful, the writ issues. Then a second action follows in which it must be shown that the incumbent officeholder is not entitled to his office or the corporation is not entitled to its franchise.

While a proceeding in the nature of quo warranto is used to oust someone holding an office by usurpation, removal from office of one entitled to hold it is accomplished by other means.[4] In some states, too, members of boards and certain officers may be removed by a *recall* election.

When a corporation performs an act not authorized by its charter the act is said to be *ultra vires* ("beyond the powers").

HABEAS CORPUS

This writ was discussed on pages 322–323 in connection with the detention of a person against whom no formal accusation had been filed. The writ may also be used to free a convicted person, after other remedies have been exhausted, by challenging the jurisdiction of the trial court or the validity of the legal process. For this purpose the convicted person applies for the writ in an appellate court and a hearing is held.

Indian Slayer Wins Habeas Corpus Writ

Rayna Tom Carmen, 43, Mono Indian, won another chance yesterday to overturn his four-year-old conviction of murder.

The Supreme Court granted his petition for a writ of habeas corpus and set a hearing on the case for Dec. 8.

Carmen was sentenced to death for the fatal shooting of another Indian, Wilbur Dan McSwain, at North Fork, Madera county.

At issue in the case is the question whether the state courts had juris-

---

[4] See p. 328.

diction to try Carmen for the crime which occurred on an Indian homestead belonging to the federal government.

Carmen is now in a "death cell" at San Quentin penitentiary.

The writ is also used in some jurisdictions to test the constitutionality of a law, to obtain custody of an infant, and to obtain the testimony of a witness at a trial when the witness is in prison or in jail.

Bridge a Game of Skill, Not Chance, High Court Holds

Bridge was defined as a game of skill and not chance in a 5 to 2 decision of the state Supreme Court yesterday.

The court granted a writ of habeas corpus to Betty Loeb Allen, 58, proprietor of the Los Angeles Bridge Club, West Hollywood, who had been arrested by Los Angeles vice squad officers last February 9 for violating a city antigambling ordinance.

She asked the writ on the grounds that bridge is a game of skill and not gambling and that the city ordinance was invalid because state gambling laws preëmpted legislation in that field.

The Supreme Court's majority decision, written by Chief Justice Phil S. Gibson, said that, since bridge is not a game of chance, there was no need for the court to consider the validity of the Los Angeles ordinance.

When the writ issues to a warden to remove a prisoner for trial for an offense allegedly committed in the jurisdiction in which he has been accused, it is called *habeas corpus prosequendum*.

INJUNCTION[5]

Injunction is an order directing the performance or the restraint of an act. It is granted when there is no adequate remedy at law. The chief use

[5] Injunction as an equitable remedy was discussed briefly on pp. 205–206.

of the injunction in private litigation is to conserve property and property rights; for example: to enjoin nuisance, waste, trespass, and injury to a unique chattel; to protect the owner of a patent, copyright, or trade name; to prevent unfair competition in trade; to prevent unlawful strikes, picketing, and boycotts; to delay or prevent the payment of dividends and the holding of a stockholders' meeting; and to prevent a multiplicity of suits. Its use in public matters has been extensive; for example, it has been used to enjoin officials from spending certain moneys in the public treasury and a state public utility commission from enforcing a certain schedule of electric rates.

An injunction will not issue in any of the following instances: to stay a judicial proceeding except to prevent a multiplicity of suits; to prevent the execution of a statute by officers when the statute is for public benefit; to prevent a breach of contract except for certain kinds of personal services; or to prevent the exercise of a public or private office lawfully held.

Ordinarily the writ is negative in that it preserves the status quo. In some instances, however, it is mandatory; for example, a *mandatory injunction* may require a corporation to pay preferred dividends which its directors had declared. It is also available in public law, instead of mandamus, when it seeks to compel an act where the time to act has not yet come; for example, to compel a secretary of state to recognize the nominees of one of two rival Republican conventions of the state which had been recognized by the national party organization.

The form of a permanent injunction (omitting the caption):

> The above-named plaintiff having filed his complaint in our Superior Court against the above-named defendant, praying for an injunction against said defendant, requiring him to refrain from certain acts in said complaint and hereinafter more particularly mentioned; on reading the said complaint in this action, duly verified by said plaintiff, and it satisfactorily appearing to the judge of said court therefrom that it is a proper case for an injunction, and that sufficient grounds exist therefor, and the necessary and proper undertaking having been given:
>
> We, therefore, in consideration thereof, and of the particular matters on the said complaint set forth, do strictly command that you, the said Oscar Warren and all your servants, counselors, attorneys, solicitors and agents, and all others acting in aid or assistance of you, and each and every one of you, until the further order of said court, do absolutely desist and refrain from cutting down any fruit or shade trees located on the premises of the plaintiff, Don Davenport, on Lot Number ten (10) of the tract of land known as the Addison Tract in the City of Jefferson, Lincoln County, or razing any building located on the said premises.
>
> Witness the Honorable Terrell Walker, judge of the said Superior Court, at the courthouse in the county of Lincoln, and the seal of the said court, this nineteenth day of May, 19—.
>
> (Seal)   EDGAR BONNELL, *Clerk*

Injunctions are *permanent* (also called *perpetual*) and *temporary* (also called *provisional* and *interlocutory*). A permanent injunction is applied for to enjoin a respondent from dumping mining debris in a creek above the plaintiff's land. A temporary injunction is applied for when the plaintiff's purpose is to preserve the status quo *pendente lite* (i.e., while the suit for a permanent injunction or the main action is pending). At the time the temporary injunction is applied for the plaintiff also applies for a permanent injunction or an accounting or for some other type of relief or compensation; it is ancillary to the main action. After the rights of the parties have been determined, the temporary injunction is either discharged or made permanent.

The procedure in applying for a temporary or permanent injunction or for both is for the plaintiff to submit affidavits with his application and to give notice to the adverse party. In some jurisdictions the plaintiff must give an undertaking to indemnify the respondent; when a government is party an undertaking is not required. The respondent usually submits counter-affidavits and, on a date set by the court, the application is heard. After the writ issues it is served on the respondent; disobedience constitutes contempt. The writ is not effective, of course, until it has been served.

After an injunction has been granted it may be *vacated* (or *dissolved*) on the motion of the respondent. For example, after a court had enjoined the Benrus Watch Company, Inc., from voting its shares of Hamilton Watch Company (to prevent Benrus' controlling its competitor), Benrus sold all of its shares and the court vacated the injunction.

An injunction may also be modified in its terms.

STRIKE BAN EASED
A sweeping antipicketing injunction against AFL teamsters striking the John L. Inglis frozen food plant was modified yesterday.
As originally issued by Superior Judge James L. Atterridge, the injunction banned all picketing. The order now permits peaceful picketing on public streets.

Temporary and permanent injunctions are granted only after notice to the respondent and a hearing. In most states and in federal practice, however, a *temporary restraining order* may be granted ex parte. It may be of only short duration (usually ten days) and only after the plaintiff has made affidavit that great or irreparable injury will result before the dispute can be heard on notice. An order to show cause why a temporary injunction should not be issued is also usually served with the temporary restraining order. In one action involving alleged fraudulent stock manipulation, the

Securities and Exchange Commission applied for a temporary restraining order, a temporary injunction, and a permanent injunction. In some jurisdictions the judge will not issue a temporary restraining order unless bond has been posted; in one labor dispute during World War II, a large corporation which had been granted a temporary restraining order was later required to pay $327,000 damages to the labor union's weekly newspaper.

PROXY BAN ISSUED

An injunction barring Detroit attorney Sol A. Dann from soliciting proxies against Chrysler Corp. management was granted by the United States District Court yesterday.

The injunction sought by the Securities and Exchange Commission replaces a temporary restraining order granted a week earlier.

A temporary restraining order is sometimes *extended* when the rights of the parties have not been determined at the expiration of the order.

Judge Extends UAL Anti-strike Order

CHICAGO—A U.S. district court judge today issued a stern warning against any plans to stage a wildcat ground crew strike against United Air Lines Friday.

Judge Joseph Sam Perry extended a temporary restraining order banning any walkout after he was told strike notices were already being distributed at Chicago's O'Hare international airport.

"If there is defiance of a court order, these men are headed for being discharged from their jobs," the judge said.

Mechanics and ground crewmen belonging to the International Association of Machinists (IAM) went on strike Aug. 21 against United at airports from New York to Portland, Ore.

The strike was stopped when U.S. district court Judge Bernard Decker issued a restraining order effective until Friday. At that time a federal court was to hear arguments on

United's request for a preliminary injunction.

The union came into court early today asking that the order be vacated, and United's attorney Stuart Bernstein retorted with a charge that strike notices were being distributed at that moment.

Judge Perry then extended the restraining order banning any walkout until 6 p.m. Sept. 5.

Exercise: Here are the words most often misspelled in news stories of the courts. Tomorrow ask a friend to pronounce them while you try to write the correct spelling.

admissible	corpus delicti	judgment
affidavit	counsel	marshal (U.S.)
alleged	defendant	plead (past tense of)
appellate	demurrer	supersedeas (p. 431)
co-respondent	habeas corpus	warrant

CHAPTER 29

Appellate Procedure

When a party is dissatisfied with the judgment in his case in a court of original jurisdiction he may ask an appellate court to review the judgment. Depending upon the circumstances, the dissatisfied party, when successful on appeal, will obtain a retrial under more favorable conditions or have judgment entered for him. In some situations both parties are dissatisfied and appeal.

In every state is established a court which has the power to review cases which have been determined in the courts of original jurisdiction. In forty states the reviewing court is called the *Supreme Court*. In the other states it is called the *Court of Appeals,* the *Court of Errors and Appeals,* the *Supreme Court of Appeals,* the *Supreme Court of Errors,* and the *Supreme Judicial Court.* In order to relieve the docket of the highest appellate court, sixteen states have established *intermediate* appellate courts, called by various names, to review certain types of cases.

Although the appellate courts are nearly always located in the state capital, the cases they review originate in a local court. The local newspaper, therefore, has a continuing interest in reporting some of the decisions of the reviewing court, as when the court reinstates an indictment which had been set aside by the local trial court. Some decisions are of statewide interest to citizens; for example, an appellate court may rule that a certain tax is unconstitutional or it may uphold the constitutionality of an alcoholic liquor control law.

TAKING AN APPEAL

Most civil cases in state courts may be appealed without leave of the trial court. In a criminal case the prosecution cannot appeal from an acquittal although it can usually appeal from an order of the court which sets aside the accusation, from a ruling for the defendant on a demurrer to the accusation, or from an order which grants a new trial.

Statutes specify which types of cases may be appealed. In those instances in civil actions for which review is not automatically provided the defeated party may apply to an appellate court for a *writ of certiorari;* this writ was discussed in Chapter 28 together with certain other methods of review.

A defeated party must appeal his case within a reasonable time after the trial—about sixty days after entry of judgment. The limit, which is fixed by statute, is usually sixty to ninety days after entry of the judgment, decree, or order.

Notice of appeal in a criminal case can usually be given by an announcement in open court or by filing a notice with the clerk a few days subsequent to the conviction. In a civil case appeal is taken by the filing of a written notice with the clerk. The party who appeals must give bond for the cost of the appeal; when he loses the responding party recovers his costs.

PERFECTING THE APPEAL

The manner of perfecting an appeal varies in the different states. A typical procedure in a civil case is as follows. The defeated party, after filing notice of appeal, directs the court clerk to make a copy of the judgment roll—that is, the pleadings, motions, and orders[1]—and to attach the transcribed record of the case including the testimony, exhibits, the judge's instructions, and the requested instructions which the judge had denied. The record in most states is called the "case." Some states require a *bill of exceptions;* that is, a specification of the errors (e.g., the judge's instructions, rulings) which the appellant wants the appellate court to rule upon. In most states provision is also made for submitting the case on a short statement of the record.

The copy of the record of the case is submitted to the trial court judge for certification. The adverse party may at this time request the inclusion in the record of certain omitted documents or papers. The parties, by stipulation, may also omit parts of the record. By signing a certificate that the record is correct, the judge is said to have "settled," or "allowed," the appeal. This record is then sent by the clerk of the trial court to the clerk of the appellate court. In many instances the parties print the record and supply about twenty copies to the appellate court.

The most frequently used term for the party which takes the appeal is "appellant." In some jurisdictions, however, he is also called "plaintiff in error." The respondent is sometimes called the "appellee" and the "defendant in error" and, in equity in some states, "respondent." Some states preserve the same title for an appealed case as it bore in the trial court; thus, the plaintiff in the trial court is still called the plaintiff in the appellate court although the party taking the appeal was the defendant in the trial court.

[1] See p. 188.

Whenever both parties are dissatisfied with the judgment in the trial court they may both appeal, each appeal being called a *cross-appeal*.

STAY OF PROCEEDINGS

The perfecting of the appeal, in most civil cases, automatically stays execution of the judgment of the trial court. But the appeal from the granting of a prohibitory injunction is not stayed, and the appellant must sue out a *writ of supersedeas* in the reviewing court; that is, a certificate to the sheriff or marshal directing him to defer execution of the decree. Granting of this writ is discretionary with the court. The appellant is required to post bond.

Transit Strikers Return to Work

Seattle's week-old transit strike is over by court order. The transit system will resume operations this morning.

Superior Court Judge James W. Hodson issued an injunction against the strike which has tied up Seattle Transit System operations since Nov. 23.

The striking union, Local 586, Street Car Men's Union, asked the Washington state supreme court for a writ of supersedeas that would hold in abeyance the injunction until the higher court heard an appeal of the entire case.

The Supreme Court, meeting in special session yesterday, denied the union's request.

August Antonino, union business representative, said, "We will instruct our members to return to work in their regular shifts."

When a death sentence has been imposed execution in most states is automatically stayed pending an appeal although the convicted person is placed in a "death cell." A sentence of imprisonment is stayed when an appeal is taken in a federal court. In several states, however, granting of a stay is within the discretion of the trial court. Staying of payment of a fine in most jurisdictions is granted when the defendant deposits the amount of the fine or gives bond. Granting of bail pending review of a criminal case in which the sentence of death has not been imposed is usually discretionary with the trial court. When a defendant has been imprisoned during the appeal proceedings and loses his appeal he is sometimes granted credit by the trial judge or parole board for the time served.

SCOPE OF REVIEW

In general, the appellate court reviews only questions of law; for example, did the trial judge make the right ruling when he denied a motion for a new trial or were his instructions to the jury proper? In some circumstances, however, the sufficiency of the evidence is a question of law, although there are few instances of reversal on this ground. Statutes prescribe the scope of review when decisions of quasi-judicial state regulatory agencies are contested, as in electric rate cases.

Appeal and Error

Formerly, an action at law was reviewed by *writ of error* and a suit in equity by *appeal*. On a review by writ of error the correctness of the rulings of the judge were considered; for example, his ruling in sustaining or overruling objections to evidence, in charging the jury, and in various other matters which are purely questions of law. The decision of the jury on the facts was not reviewed. On an appeal, however, the appellate court reviewed not only the law but the facts. The fundamental reason for this distinction was that there was no jury in a suit in equity and the judges of the appellate court, therefore, had the right to reexamine the facts as found by the judge of the trial court.

In most states and in federal practice today there is no distinction between review by writ of error and by appeal. Even in such states, however, the review of the cases tried before a jury tends to approximate in its scope the review that was formerly had on a writ of error, and the review of cases in which no jury was required tends to approximate in its scope the review by appeal.

The distinction between review by writ of error and by appeal, where it still exists, is more than a mere matter of form. The main distinction is in the scope of the review; that is, whether the appellate court reviews a judgment that was based upon the verdict of a jury or reviews a decree that was entered in a case tried before a judge alone. In this chapter the term "appeal" is used generically to denote both methods of review irrespective of the form of review.

What Is Appealable?

Statutes determine what is appealable. In civil cases the appeal is usually from the judgment of the trial court. But some orders in civil cases may be appealed when an order is equivalent to (that is, leads to) a judgment; for example, when the court sustains the defendant's demurrer and enters a judgment of dismissal.

In criminal cases a convicted defendant may appeal from a judgment of conviction or from an order denying a new trial. The prosecution may not appeal a judgment of acquittal. But in most jurisdictions the prosecution may appeal an order which sets aside an accusation, grants a new trial, or reduces the degree of the offense. When a trial court sets aside an accusation the appellate court may order its reinstatement.

THE BRIEFS

In addition to the record the parties file briefs. Except for briefs filed by an *amicus curiae*,[2] the briefs must be printed and several copies supplied. The briefs are arguments, under headings, that also contain citations of previous decisions of appellate courts.

The appellant files an opening brief, the appellee a reply brief, and the appellant (sometimes) a closing brief. There is also sometimes a cross-appellant's reply brief. The briefs set forth, under headings, the points of the law that the parties rely on with accompanying argument and citations of authorities for each point. Some jurisdictions require that each of the headings of the appellant's brief be stated as an *assignment of error;* that is, a specification of the error the appellant will rely on.

Authorities are rulings made by the review court (or sometimes other courts) in similar cases and constitute precedents. Courts tend to follow the doctrine of *stare decisis* ("to stand by decided cases") because it is desirable that the law have stability and certainty so that individuals and corporations, in making decisions and agreements, can rely on the law. Courts are generally bound by precedents, but when novel cases arise they sometimes believe it is necessary to overrule a prior decision.

Newspaper reporters can always obtain a copy of the parties' briefs from their attorneys and from the clerk of the appellate court. The bureaus of the wire news agencies, located in cities in which appellate courts sit, often prepare in advance each month, from the briefs and records filed with the court, short digests of the important cases that are likely to be decided in the near future. They mail the digests to client newspapers, identifying each digest with a serial number. Afterward, when the appellate court decides any one of the cases the news agency includes the number in its teleprinter

[2] Literally, "friend of the court." When an individual, a government, or an association has an interest in an appealed case to which it is not a party and it desires to influence the reviewing court, it asks leave to file a brief as *amicus curiae*. An appellate court, on its initiative, may also request some expert individual to file a brief in a particular case so that the court may have the benefit of his specialized knowledge of the law.

report with information as to the court's decision. Sometimes the information consists only of the words "affirmed" or "reversed." In such instances the local newspaper writes the appropriate lead and appends to it the digest of the case.

THE HEARING

The procedure in the various state appellate courts differs to such an extent that only the procedure in one state will be described. The briefs and the record in the case are filed with the clerk of the appellate court who prepares a printed *calendar*. (Most appellate courts have a fall and a winter calendar in which from two hundred to three hundred cases are listed.) The clerk takes about forty cases from the calendar and places them in order on an "assignment." He then notifies the attorneys as to when their cases will be called for argument. In some instances, attorneys do not find it necessary to appear to supplement their briefs with oral argument. While hearing oral argument the justices—usually about seven—sit together. They have read the briefs in advance of the hearing. Some of the justices make notes during the argument and some ask questions of the attorneys. The questions are sometimes indicative of how certain judges will decide the case. About five days is required to hear the argument in all of the assigned cases. After the court has concluded the hearings on the assignment it adjourns for about three weeks to consider those cases. Only the hearings on the most important cases in state courts are reported by the press.

Quarles Appeal Argued in Court

Francis Quarles, former coroner and public administrator, argued yesterday for reversal of his embezzlement conviction.

His attorney, Walter Lane, told the Supreme Court that Quarles had been found guilty of a crime "in a vacuum"—like disturbing the peace in a soundproof room.

In February of last year a jury convicted the official of appropriating to his own use $58,282 over a six-year period. The alleged misappropriations were from estate funds entrusted to the public administrator's office.

Attorney Lane said yesterday that all the estate affairs were wound up on time and that "no person lost a cent by reason of Quarles' actions."

Only Careless

In reply, Deputy Attorney General Arnold Bailey hit at the crime-in-a-vacuum theory. He said Quarles had used the public money "to build a funeral parlor."

The official had made up charges in one account by transfers from others and "when the pressure was on" had to borrow money privately to make up losses, Bailey told the court.

Lane maintained the Quarles indictment was invalid because it dealt only with funds from private estates.

Lane also denied that any of the money went into a funeral parlor. He conceded only that Quarles had been guilty of "carelessness of bookkeeping."

Quarles, sentenced to serve one to ten years in prison, is free on bail.

The case was taken under advisement.

CONSIDERING THE CASE

The justices retire to their separate chambers and devote independent consideration to the cases, each reaching a conclusion as to the appropriate decision which should be made in each case. Next they go into consultation, taking up each case in order and, if possible, agreeing upon a decision in each case. Whenever they disagree a ballot is taken and the majority vote determines the decision. When the vote is equally divided (due to the non-participation of one or more justices), the effect is to affirm the judgment of the trial court.

The decision is embodied in an *opinion;* that is, the reasoning of the court in arriving at the decision. In addition to the *majority* opinion, one or more *dissenting* opinions are prepared by justices who disagree with the majority decision. Although ordinarily one justice writes an opinion for the whole bench, any justice may prepare a *concurring* opinion in which he reaches the same decision as the other justices but arrives at it by a different line of reasoning. Each justice who prepares an opinion concerning a decision in which there is unanimous agreement furnishes a copy to each of the other justices who read it prior to a second consultation. At the second consultation the justices go over the various opinions and make necessary corrections and changes. About one month elapses from the time the justices hear the argument on the assignment of about forty cases until they are ready to render their decisions.

Sometimes an appellate court prepares a *per curiam* ("by the court") opinion. It is the opinion of the whole court but does not indicate which justice wrote it; usually the chief justice writes such opinions.

THE DECISION

On a regularly assigned day—usually a certain day of the month, such as the first Monday—the decisions are announced and the opinions are made public. Each justice on that day reads the opinions which he has written. Secrecy surrounds all the conduct of the justices prior to the announcement of the decisions; there are almost no instances of "leaks" in appellate courts.

The legal result of an appeal is an order from the appellate court to the trial court to proceed in a certain way. When, for example, the reviewing court agrees with the trial judge who had sustained the defendant's demurrer before trial, the judge's ruling having been appealed by the plaintiff, the reviewing court is said to have *affirmed* the trial court, and the trial court is directed to *dismiss* the case without holding a trial.

When a case has been appealed by the losing party on the ground that the trial judge improperly instructed the jury or refused to admit certain evidence offered by the losing party, and the reviewing court agrees with the appellant, the case is said to have been *reversed*. The effect of the appellate court's decision, therefore, is to vacate the judgment. This usually means that the reviewing court *remands* the case for a new trial in which it is presumed that the trial court next time will not err in the same respects; that is, the trial judge will adopt the losing party's instructions or will admit the evidence that had been excluded.

In a few instances, the reviewing court reverses the lower court only in part and sometimes the decision is a reversal with directions to modify the judgment.

REPORTING THE DECISION

To write a news story from an opinion in a short time is a difficult task unless the reporter has previously acquainted himself with the issues involved in the case. By reading briefs in advance, the reporter can learn enough about the case to write a news story from the opinion after it has been handed down. Some opinions are very long and the steps in reasoning are difficult for a reporter to follow when he is pressed for time. Some cases are so important that they must be digested quickly and published immediately. Since some decisions are the biggest news of the day, affecting the stock market or public affairs to an extraordinary extent, the news stories must be prepared both speedily and accurately. A wire news service once sent out a "flash" on one of the most important cases ever to come before the United States Supreme Court which represented the exact contrary of the court's decision; this was because the reporter, misinterpreting the earlier part of the opinion, rushed to file the "flash" without waiting to hear the justice finish reading the opinion.

A few decisions, unimportant in their effect, are yet sufficiently interesting to warrant quotation because of the justice's style or manner of comment. For example, in a more or less important opinion, a justice may include an interesting *obiter dictum* ("said in passing"); that is, a part of the opinion which is incidental or collateral and which does not bear directly upon a point necessarily involved in the particular case. The following quotation, for example, was in an opinion in which the appellate court, having found corruption in an election for mayor and city councilmen, declared the election void, and commented on the large amounts spent by the candidates to hire "watchers" at the polls: ". . . It is a sad commentary upon present day politics that candidates and political parties must pay for almost every character of service rendered in elections. Political and patriotic impulses seem no longer sufficiently potent to impel many voters to discharge their duties as citizens."

Court Releases Big Tax Surplus For Buildings

Effect

Millions of dollars for new state and educational buildings were made available yesterday by the state supreme court's decision in the income tax surplus case.

The decision

In a 4 to 3 decision, the court held that the surplus, estimated at $40,000,000, may be placed in the general fund and then be appropriated by the legislature.

The court upheld the Greene county superior court in a "friendly" suit by Arthur Denison against the state tax commission.

History

The tax commission had ruled that the surplus in the income tax fund could not be transferred to the general fund—that it could only be used to reduce property taxes.

The majority opinion, written by Justice Morris, holds that:

438   REPORTING PUBLIC AFFAIRS

Majority
    1. Surplus income tax funds are a part of the state general fund.
    2. Income tax collections are not a special trust fund.
    3. The state tax commission is not required to submit a state property tax levy to the voters at the November election.

Reasoning
    The opinion said, "We can find nothing in the title of the 1959 income tax bill suggesting creation of anything akin to a trust fund applicable to the surplus collection from the income tax."

Dissent
    The dissenting opinion, written by Justice Duncan, held that income tax funds could be used only for offsetting property taxes.

Reasoning
    Such taxes are not to be regarded as additional taxes but are paid in lieu of property taxes, Justice Duncan held.

Obiter dictum
    The majority opinion, Justice Duncan declared, "marks the end of a wholesome tax relief program. It also marks the dawn of a new tax spending day."

THE MANDATE

The order from the reviewing court to the trial court directing how the trial court is to proceed is called the *mandate,* or *remittitur.* The clerk of the appellate court mails it, along with a copy of the opinion, to the clerk of the trial court who attaches the order to the judgment roll and enters a minute of the appellate court judgment on the docket.

The mandate is not sent to the trial court until about twenty-five days after the decision so that the party which loses in the appellate court will have an opportunity to petition for a rehearing. In the meantime the decision has no effect on the parties. The situation sometimes has a local meaning.

Court Process Delays Marriage

    Charles Wharton, a Negro, and his white fiancee, Evelyn Gonzales, will not immediately apply for a marriage license, he said today after being told the state supreme court yesterday had upheld their right to the license.

> His attorney advised him to wait about 25 days until the appellate court's mandate had come down to the Northrup county circuit court, he explained.
>
> The circuit court last year issued a writ of mandamus directing the county clerk to issue the license, but the court's decree was appealed by the clerk as being contrary to the statutes.

Under some circumstances, the appellate court directs a certain disposition of the case but at the same time retains jurisdiction to assure that its decision will be obeyed by one of the parties. For example, when a three-judge federal court in 1945 required the Associated Press to alter its by-laws so that its service would be available to certain nonmember newspapers, the United States Supreme Court, which upheld the three-judge court, retained jurisdiction so that it could act in the future if the decree was not obeyed in the way the court thought it should be.

THE LEGAL REPORTING SYSTEM

The decisions and opinions of appellate courts are reported in a series of volumes for the convenience of judges and attorneys. Because newspaper reporters sometimes have need to refer to such decisions they should understand the system of law "reporting." The bound volumes which contain the decisions and opinions of the state appellate courts are referred to by the name of the state; for example, the *Wisconsin Reports*.[3] In a few states the reports of the intermediate appellate courts are also reported.

Since the ordinary attorney cannot afford to own a set of reports for every state, the decisions of several states are combined in a single volume. There are eight of these unofficial "reporters," known as *Northwestern Reporter, Southern Reporter, Atlantic Reporter, Pacific Reporter, Southeastern Reporter, Southwestern Reporter, Northern Reporter,* and *Eastern Reporter*. Only a few states report the decisions and opinions of their courts of original jurisdiction, notably New York.

Decisions of the United States Supreme Court are officially reported in a series called the *United States Reports;* one series of unofficial reports is called the *Supreme Court Reporter*. Recent decisions of the federal Courts of Appeals (formerly the Circuit Courts of Appeal) are reported in the *Federal Reporter, Second Series;* and decisions of the federal District Courts

---

[3] The earlier reports in some states bear the name, not of the state, but of the editor or compiler who reported them; for example, the first volumes of the Massachusetts reports are known as *Metcalf* and the first volumes of the United States Supreme Court are cited as *Cranch*.

in the *Federal Supplement.* Earlier decisions of both of these courts are reported in the *Federal Reporter.*

Whenever a case is cited by a judge or an attorney the title of the case is given, then the number of the volume, then the abbreviated name of the report, and finally the page number. For example:

Park *v.* Detroit Free Press, 72 Mich. 560, 40 N.W. 731.
U.S. *v.* One Book Entitled Ulysses by James Joyce, 72 F(2d) 705.
A.L.A. Schechter Poultry Corp. et al. *v.* U.S., 295 US 495, 55 Sup. Ct. 837.
Elmore Development Co. *v.* Binder, 97 N.J. Eq 126, 127 Atl. 693.

CHAPTER *30*

Corporate Finance

Jim Baker, of the *Gazette,* had been reporting the federal District Court for only two months when a large corporation filed a petition for reorganization under Chapter X of the Bankruptcy Act.[1] Several lawyers were involved in the case, each representing a different set of clients. It became apparent early in the case that there were five different types of diverse interest. In addition to the common and preferred stockholders, there were owners of three different kinds of bonds.

At first, Jim was very frustrated by his inability to understand these diverse interests, for he hardly knew the difference between a common stock and a bond. After a while, however, he decided he should become better informed because business was such an important sphere of American life, so many of his readers owned securities of one kind or another, and so many court actions were about corporate business. He looked into some books both at the public library and in an investment broker's office. While at the broker's office, he became more interested in the securities business, with the result that he bought a few shares of common stock in two different companies. As time went on he received quarterly and annual reports from these companies and he studied their balance sheets and income statements. Before a year had passed, he considered himself fairly knowledgeable.

One evening while reading a book on investments Jim suddenly realized that much of the privately held property in the United States was not tangible; that much of it consisted of the ownership of pieces of paper, and that, in most instances, each of the pieces of paper was representative merely of the owner's expectation. Owners of most corporate bonds did own a deferred right in the tangible properties of the corporation (such as its plant), but owners of all other pieces of corporate paper merely held an unsecured obligation or an expectation of future earnings of the corporation. (Federal, state, and municipal bonds and notes, of course, are backed by the credit of the respective governments.)

[1] See pp. 408 and 415.

Jim also came to realize that the market value of the individual types of securities was related, not only to the earnings history and outlook of the corporations, but to the fine print on the pieces of paper they had issued. This fine print told the security owner that some debt securities and some preferred stocks were subordinate to other debt and other preferred stock issues of the same company; and also that some of the debt securities and preferred stocks included the right to convert them into common stock at a specific price.

Later Jim classified these pieces of paper as will be explained below.

TYPES OF SECURITIES

Bond

A bond is an evidence of debt to the bondholder repayable at a specific time and with a specified rate of interest. For example, the market quotation "US Steel 4½s86" means that this bond's yield to maturity, or its "coupon," is 4½ per cent and that it will mature in 1986. The bondholder is a creditor of the corporation, not a shareholder. Bonds are usually issued in $1,000 denominations although quoted on the basis of $100 (e.g., 110½ or 96¼).

A *general mortgage* bond is secured by a blanket mortgage on the company's properties. In some instances, these bonds are issued in a series and are denominated, for example, as "First mortgage bonds, 4½ series" and "First mortgage bonds Series B," thus making one series subordinate to another series for the owners' claims against the company's properties.

A *collateral trust* bond is secured by stocks or bonds deposited with a trustee and pledged by the borrowing company; these are often the stocks or bonds of other companies.

A *convertible* bond includes the right to exchange the bond for the company's common stock at a specified price or ratio during specified periods of time. The purchaser of such a bond anticipates that the price of the company's common stock (and also of the bond) will rise because of increased earnings. For a certain period, therefore, he is receiving a yield on the bond which is higher than he would receive on the same sum invested in the common stock of that company.

From the point of view of the company, a convertible bond issue is equivalent to selling additional common stock at 10 to 20 per cent above the current market price of the outstanding common stock. Because the conversion is gradual the company's common stock equity is diluted gradually. The company's taxes are less when it pays interest on bonds whereas it would not have this advantage if it sold additional common stock and had to pay dividends on it. As the company increases the rate of its dividend on its outstanding common stock, holders of the bonds are induced to convert. The conversion gradually reduces the company's debt and thus improves the quality of the common stock.

The market price of a convertible bond fluctuates with the price of the common stock as well as with the current interest rate.

An *income* bond obliges the issuing corporation to pay interest and repay principal only to the extent of the company's earnings. Such bonds are usually issued in connection with the reorganization of a failing company to the existing holders of the company's unrewarding senior securities.[2] They are subordinate to higher grade securities also issued in connection with the reorganization.

A *debenture* is similar to a bond in that the owner is a creditor of the company. But it is not secured by a mortgage or lien on the company's property, merely its credit. Debentures may also be issued in series.

Most bonds are *bearer-coupon* bonds. This means that a coupon is attached to each bond for each interest date (usually semiannually) and is clipped by the bondholder and presented for interest payment. Unlike a *registered* bond, it is not registered with the issuing company in the bondholder's name and does not require an endorsement by the owner when he sells it. When one sells a bond he is entitled, in addition to the quoted price, to the accumulated interest as of the date of the sale. Income bonds and other bonds that are in default of interest are traded "flat," without interest.

When bonds are issued they are *rated* by such services as Moody's and Standard & Poor's. One set of ratings is Aaa, Aa, A, Baa, Ba, B, C, etc.; another set is rated AAA, AA, A, BBB, etc. (called "prime," "high grade," "sound," "medium grade," etc.).

Gas Co. Bonds Sell at 4.55% Cost

NEW YORK—Halsey, Stuart & Co. and associates topped two other groups in winning Milwaukee Gas Light Co.'s $15 million of first mortgage bonds, due 1987.

The successful bid of 101.06 for a 4⅝% coupon gave the Milwaukee utility an annual net interest cost of approximately 4.55%.

Halsey, Stuart and associates planned to release the issue for general

---

[2] Bonds and debentures are called "senior" securities.

distribution at 101.864, to yield 4.50%.

The 4⅝s are rated A by Standard & Poor's and Baa by Moody's. They will be optionally redeemable by the utility at prices from 106.489 down to par.

Preferred stock

The owner of a preferred stock certificate is entitled to receive a specified dividend, if earned, before payment of dividends to common stockholders. His claim on the assets of the company, in case of liquidation, is usually prior to the claim of the common stockholder. In some instances, after the company has omitted preferred dividends over a specified period (say, for three out of four quarters) the preferred stock is automatically converted into common with voting rights. A few preferred share issues include the right to vote whether or not the dividend has been omitted. Preferred stock may also be issued in series; one series which takes precedence over the other preferred issues is sometimes called a *prior* preferred.

A *cumulative* preferred stock provides that, whenever dividend payments are omitted, the total of such arrears must be paid before dividends may be paid on the common stock.

A *participating* preferred stock entitles the owner to receive not only the specified dividend but an additional dividend when the common stock dividend has increased to a specified amount.

Some bonds, debentures, and preferred stocks are *noncallable*. But most provide that the issuing company, after a specified time, may retire the securities by paying a specified premium over par value. In some instances, the indenture[3] provides for the establishment of a *sinking fund;* that is, the company regularly sets aside funds for redemption of the securities.

The market price of preferred stocks fluctuates with the current interest rate on bonds. A convertible preferred stock, however, fluctuates also with the price of the common stock.

Bowser Arrearage Plan Approved

CHICAGO—Bowser, Inc. holders of common and preferred stock approved yesterday a plan for satisfying a $3 million arrearage on the company's preferred shares.

The plan includes a cash payment

---

[3] A written agreement which states interest rate, maturity date(s), call terms (if any), and the securities that underlie the issue.

to preferred shareholders, change of par value of the stock, issuance of a new class of common stock to preferred holders, and establishment of a sinking fund for retirement of the preferred stock.

Arrearage on the preferred stock was $2,794,493, or $14.40 a share, on June 1, the company said last month. There are 194,062 preferred shares outstanding.

Common Stock

The owner of common stock is a part-owner of the company. Thus, the holder of 1,000 shares in a company which has 5,000,000 shares outstanding[4] owns $\frac{1}{5000}$ of the company's common stock equity. He is an owner, not a creditor. He has voting rights, usually in connection with the election of directors, determination of the number of directors, the issuance of additional shares of common stock, election of the auditor, and the adoption of stock option plans for company officers.[5] He assumes a greater risk than does a preferred stockholder or a bondholder, but he is more highly rewarded when the company is successful.

Dividends on common stock are *declared* by the directors, usually four times a year. The directors may, at any meeting, increase, decrease, or omit the common dividend. Some companies have a policy of declaring and paying a *regular* dividend; that is, the same dividend each quarter during a particular year. Some companies pay an *extra* dividend, in some particular quarter paying more than the usual regular dividend—without committing the company in the next year to paying more than the regular dividend. In addition to cash dividends, some companies pay a *stock* dividend[6] at certain times, although few companies pay them regularly.

Directors almost always vote to retain and reinvest in the business a part of the earnings, if any, rather than pay out all of the earnings in cash dividends. Dividends also are sometimes paid from accumulated earnings even though the company has not earned the amount of the dividend in the particular year.

---

[4] The number of shares issued is not necessarily the same as the number of shares outstanding. The latter term means the number actually held by shareholders or in the company's treasury. Thus, the number of shares authorized (by the articles of incorporation or by later action of the stockholders) may be 5,000,000 but the number outstanding only 4,652,311. *Treasury stock* is stock issued by the company but later reacquired by the corporation. Treasury stock receives no dividends and has no vote while held by the company.

[5] Legally, the common stockholder has a contract with the corporation (a legal fiction). His rights are stated in the company's articles of incorporation and its by-laws and in state statutes.

[6] See p. 453 for an explanation.

In a few instances a company may have two "classes" of common stock —often designated as "A" and "B." Sometimes the "B" stock is entitled to the same dividend as the "A" stock but carries no voting rights. Or, in some instances, "B" stock is entitled to no dividends over a period of years but carries voting rights. Such a policy often has as its objective the control of the company by the holders of one class of stock.

Stock warrant: A few companies have issued stock *warrants;* that is, a certificate which gives the holder the right to purchase a specified number of shares of the company's common stock at a specified price for a limited time. (Another meaning of the term is the certificate which evidences the preëmptive right of a stockholder to subscribe to additional common stock in his company at a specified price. These rights are sometimes traded prior to the issuance of the additional stock.)

REDUCES DIVIDEND

SuCrest Corp. yesterday cut the quarterly dividend to 20 cents from 26¼ cents, payable Jan. 10 to stock of record Dec. 30. The sugar and molasses firm said, "It is anticipated that the loss for the first six months of the fiscal year . . . will be less than that reported at the end of the first quarter."

INCREASES DIVIDEND

Malone & Hyde, Inc. raised its quarterly dividend to 12½ cents a share, payable Jan. 15 to stock of record Jan. 2. The grocers' wholesale firm previously paid 10 cents a share.

DECLARES EXTRA DIVIDEND

Western Tablet & Stationery Co. declared an extra of 10 cents a share with its regular 10-cent quarterly dividend on common stock, payable Jan. 15 to stock of record Dec. 26.

OMITS STOCK DIVIDEND

Pacific Coast Properties, Inc. omitted action on a usual semiannual stock dividend of 2.5%, normally due for payment in February. The company explained: "Indications are that earnings will not be sufficient this year to fully capitalize further stock dividends."

DECLARES INITIAL DIVIDEND
U.S. Finance Co. declared an initial dividend of 5 cents a share, payable in January to stock of record Dec. 31. The company said it intends to declare and pay dividends quarterly.

Par Value

Most preferred stocks have a par value—$100, $50, or $25—and are carried on the company's balance sheet at such a value. Common stocks also have either a par value or a "stated" ("no par") value of $25 or less, which is reflected on the balance sheet at that value. This is simply the value stated in the company's charter.

This value of the common stock plus the retained earnings and the premium[7] (if any) on the common stock constitute the common stockholder's *equity* (usually called *common equity*) in the corporation. This fact will have significance when we discuss later the meaning of stock splits and the issuance and sale of additional common shares to the public. Par value has no relationship to market value.

TYPES OF INVESTORS

Jim Baker asked himself why so many different kinds of securities were issued. Eventually he concluded that various investors required various kinds of "packages." He found that, although many different types of individuals were investors, there were also different types of institutions which were investors. Thus, because trustees of estates and employee pension funds and insurance companies were primarily interested in security of principal and adequate income, they often bought bonds, debentures, and preferred stocks. Insurance companies also bought preferred stocks (as compared with bonds and debentures) because of a tax advantage. Such investors owned most of the senior types of securities with long maturities because their own obligations were long-time. But most investment companies ("mutual funds") which, because of the tax laws, had to pay out to their shareholders 90 per cent of their earnings each year, required bonds with short maturities and common stocks.

Jim also found that the requirements of individuals vary considerably. Thus, retired persons mainly require relatively high income and security of principal, whereas younger persons can afford to invest in "growth type" common stocks which are calculated to yield capital gains rather than immediate high income. Wealthy persons, primarily for tax reasons, require capital gains on stocks and tax exempt interest on municipal bonds.

[7] Defined on p. 451.

THE BALANCE SHEET

As Jim Baker continued his studies of securities he noted there was a considerable difference among companies as to their capital accounts. The capital account is a part of the balance sheet.[8] The balance sheet has two columns, so to speak. One column exhibits the assets of a company; the other exhibits *liabilities and stockholders' equity* to balance the assets. The second column shows (*a*) what the company owes to its creditors and (*b*) the equity of the common and preferred stockholders (when there are preferred stockholders).

Here is a skeletonized balance sheet of the XYZ Corporation; it omits the components of the assets side so that we can emphasize the components of the second column.

ASSETS		LIABILITIES AND STOCK-HOLDERS' EQUITY	
		Liabilities to creditors:	
		Current liabilities	$12,000,000
		Long-term debt (callable bonds)	10,000,000
		Total liabilities	22,000,000
		Stockholders' equity:	
		Preferred stock (100,000 shares; par = $100)	10,000,000
		Common equity:	
		Common stock (1,000,000 shares, par = $10)	10,000,000
		Retained earnings	30,000,000
		Capital surplus	2,000,000
			52,000,000
Total	$74,000,000	Total	$74,000,000

Capitalization and Capital Account

Combining certain components of the second column yields certain accounting concepts for which there are special terms. Thus, when we combine "long-term debt,"[9] "preferred stock," and "common stock" the total is called *capitalization;* that is, capitalization is the sum of all the securities the company has issued ($30,000,000); it is the capital structure of the company. Some companies have a simple capitalization—nothing but common stock. Others have a complex capitalization.

By combining the aforementioned components of capitalization in the XYZ Corporation balance sheet with two other components—"retained earning" and "capital surplus"—we have a concept for which the term is

---

[8] In recent years, some accountants have substituted the term "statement of financial position" for the term "balance sheet."

[9] That is, debt maturing after more than one year.

capital account.[10] We shall explain "retained earnings" and "capital surplus" later.

Net Worth

The difference between the grand total in the second column ($74,000,-000) and the liabilities to creditors (long-term debt plus current liabilities) is called *net worth*. The components of net worth, therefore, are the stated value of the common and the preferred stock, the retained earnings and the capital surplus. The net worth of the XYZ Corporation, you will observe, is $52,000,000. It is the same as the subtotal under "stockholders' equity."

A holder of common shares in the XYZ Corporation would want to know what is the theoretical value of the *common equity*. It is the net worth minus the stated value of the preferred stock; that is, $42,000,000.

Leverage: When a corporation's capital structure includes a considerable proportion of long-term debt (and preferred stock) on which it must earn enough to pay interest and dividends, it is said to be highly leveraged. Leverage is the effect of the capital structure on the earnings of the common shares. Thus, in a period of high earnings, the common stock benefits from the increased earnings; but in a period of low earnings it does not benefit as much because interest and preferred dividends are first charges on earnings. The capital accounts of most natural gas pipeline companies are highly leveraged because their earnings fluctuate less than do the earnings of most industrial companies. Many stocks, of course, have no leverage.

Current Liabilities

A company's obligations which have accrued and are payable in less than one year are called current liabilities. This is an important item to analyze when evaluating a company other than a public utility or railroad. It should be compared with the company's current assets. Generally the ratio of current assets to current liabilities should be 2:1 or higher. The amount remaining after the current liabilities are subtracted from the current assets is called *working capital*.

When total current liabilities are compared with the company's cash and its equivalent (e.g., government securities), we have a measure of the company's *liquidity*. The liquidity ratio is usually expressed as a percentage, such as 41 per cent; this means that "cash and equivalent" is 41 per cent

---

[10] In some financial circles the term "capitalization" is synonymous with "capital account," as we have just used the term; that is, "capitalization" includes the "retained earnings" and "capital surplus" accounts as well as the total of all securities issued by the company. The New York Stock Exchange, for example, has published two pamphlets. One defines "capitalization" as the total of all securities issued and the second pamphlet defines the term as also including the "retained earnings" and "capital surplus" accounts.

of current liabilities. A persistent decline in this ratio usually means that the company will need to raise additional working capital. Cash and its equivalent are sometimes called *quick assets*.

You will note on the complete balance sheet on page 452 that the component items of the current liabilities are these:

> Current installments of long-term debt
> Accounts payable
> Provision for federal income and other taxes
> Dividends declared and payable
> Accrued liabilities

The Retained Earnings Account

Companies report annually to their common stockholders on their "retained earnings" and their "capital surplus" accounts. The following is a statement of the retained earnings account of a particular company. Some accountants call this the "earnings surplus" account and some call it the "earnings retained and invested in the business" account.

Balance at beginning of the year	$27,131,531
Net income for the year	3,449,228
	$30,580,759
Deductions:	
Cash dividends paid ($1.60 a share)	1,612,056
Balance at end of the year	$28,968,703

Two facts are apparent from reading this statement. (1) The company increased its retained earnings account during the past year by $1,837,172 ($28,968,703 − $27,131,531); and (2) the amount paid out in cash dividends to common stockholders was 46.7 per cent of its net income after taxes and the amount retained in the business was 53.3 per cent.

Companies which are fairly static in their earnings, such as many government-regulated public utility companies, pay out in cash dividends a considerably larger percentage of their earnings than the percentage reported above—in some cases up to 90 per cent. Stockholders of "growth" companies, such as International Business Machines Corporation, are better off, however, when the percentage retained and invested in the business is large; for the invested earnings will earn more for the stockholders than they probably would if the stockholder himself had invested them.

When a company has a *nonrecurring* profit or loss in a particular year, it often chooses to credit it to the retained earnings account rather than to operating income. This is because the nonrecurring profit or loss is really not a true operating profit or loss. A coal mining company, for example, sold one of its mines for $4,400,000 cash. Since the mine had been carried on its books at $11,000,000, it had a paper loss of $6,600,000. Because of this *loss,* it recovered $3,100,000 in taxes, making its net loss $3,500,000. This sum it subtracted from its retained earnings account. If the mine had been carried on its book at an amount which would have shown a *profit,* this sum probably would have been added to the retained earnings account. In some instances, however, a company may choose to credit a nonrecurring loss in one year as an operating loss and, in a few instances credit a nonrecurring profit as an operating profit.

Capital Surplus Account

This could be called "capital-in-excess-of-par-value-of-common-stock" account. When a company issues and sells additional shares of common stock—to officers on stock option agreements, to its employees, to the public, or to its own stockholders—it makes two entries on its balance sheet. One entry adds to the total stated value of its common stock the product of the number of new shares sold and the stated value of each additional share (e.g., 100,000 additional shares × $10 par value increases the stated value of the common stock by $1,000,000).

The second entry is an addition to the capital surplus account. This sum is the difference between the total amount received for the stock and the total amount represented by par value (e.g., 100,000 shares sold at $48 a share minus 100,000 shares at $10 par value, or $3,800,000). This difference is called the *premium* on the additional stock and it increases the capital surplus account by $3,800,000. Thus, the statement would read as follows:

CAPITAL SURPLUS ACCOUNT

Balance at the beginning of year	$ 6,500,000
Amount received in excess of par value on 100,000 shares	3,800,000
Balance at end of year	$10,300,000

It should be noted that, when a company issues additional common stock, the proportion of ownership of the individual shareholder is "diluted" (unless the stockholder himself buys a proportionate amount of additional stock). When, for example, the common equity of a company is $60,000,000 and the number of outstanding common shares is 6,000,000, each share, before the sale of additional shares, represents $10 of ownership. After there are 6,100,000 common shares, however, each share represents only about $9.83. Usually, however, when a company issues additional stock it expects to improve its earnings considerably. When this happens the original shareholder will either receive larger cash dividends at a later time or own a proportion of the increased retained earnings or both.

BALANCE SHEET*

Assets	MILLIONS
Current assets:	
Cash	$ 9.0
U.S. government securities	1.0
Accounts and notes receivable	11.4
Inventories	27.0
Total current assets	48.4
Other assets:	
Surrender value of insurance	.2
Investments in subsidiaries	4.7
Prepaid insurance	.6
Total other assets	5.5
Fixed assets:	
Buildings, machinery, equipment at cost	104.3
Less accumulated depreciation	27.6
	76.7
Land	.9
Total fixed assets	77.6
Total assets	$131.5

LIABILITIES AND STOCKHOLDERS' EQUITY	
Current liabilities:	
Accounts payable	$ 6.1
Accrued liabilities	3.6
Current maturity of long-term debt	1.0
Federal income and other taxes	9.6
Dividends payable	1.3
Total current liabilities	21.6
Reserves	3.6
Long term debt:	
5% Sinking Fund Debentures, due July 31, 1976	26.0
Stockholders' Equity:	
5% Cum. preferred stock ($100 par)	6.0
Common stock ($10 par)	18.3
Capital surplus	9.6
Earned surplus	46.4
Total stockholders' equity	80.3
Total liabilities and stockholders' equity	$131.5

* Adapted from *How to Understand Financial Statements* (undated publication of the New York Stock Exchange).

Stock Dividends

One of the common stocks that Jim Baker had bought was that of a paper manufacturing company. Some months after Jim's purchase of the stock, the company's directors declared a 4 per cent stock dividend in addition to the regular cash dividend. Jim had bought 25 shares at $40 a share, paying $1,000 (plus the broker's commission). After he had received a certificate for one additional share (4 per cent of 25 shares), he owned 26 shares instead of 25 shares and his cost per share then was only $38.46 a share ($1,000 ÷ 26). A little later Jim began to receive cash dividends on 26 shares instead of 25 shares.

The reason the company, which had increased its earnings, paid a stock dividend instead of increasing its cash dividend, was to conserve cash for plant expansion and modernization. On the assumption that these additional retained earnings were profitably invested, the original common stockholders, in the long run, were better off to have received a stock dividend.[11]

> Exercise: Before payment of the 4 per cent dividend the company mentioned above had 5,000,000 common shares outstanding (par value of $5), and the balance in the capital surplus account was $100,000,000. On the day the additional stock was issued, the closing market price of the outstanding stock was $45 a share, which was the value the company assigned to the additional stock it gave to its shareholders. Set up a capital surplus account which will reflect the payment of the stock dividend.

The stock dividend mentioned in the foregoing exercise, it should be noted, is a capitalization of retained earnings. That is, the sum of $9,000,000 (200,000 shares × $45) is transferred from the retained earnings account to the common stockholders' equity and the capital surplus accounts. Thus, after this transfer, the retained earnings account would read as follows:

RETAINED EARNINGS ACCOUNT

Balance at beginning of year	$200,000,000
Net income	20,000,000
	220,000,000
Deduct cash dividends	15,000,000
	205,000,000
Deduct stock dividend	9,000,000
Balance	$196,000,000

[11] Jim was also better off from the tax viewpoint. The stock dividend was not taxable as income. Eventually, however, if he sold all of his shares at a profit, he would pay a capital gains tax (which is one-half of the income tax) on a slightly lower cost basis.

Stock Splits

A corporation sometimes finds it advantageous to split its stock—usually 2 for 1, 2½ for 1, 3 for 2 or 3 for 1. Let us say that a company with one million common shares outstanding splits 2 for 1 so that it then has two million shares. If the par value originally was (say) $10, it then becomes $5. But this means that each of the original shares owned by a stockholder is worth only one-half as much, on the company's books, as it was before the split. (In some instances, a company issues new stock to the shareholders—say, 2 to 1—but does not reduce the par value.)

A split is usually made after a company's stock has advanced considerably in market price so that it has become expensive for such investors as Jim Baker to purchase. The main advantage to the company is that the split makes more shares available at a much lower price and thereby attracts new shareholders. Most companies find it advantageous, for purposes of public relations and the marketing of their products, to increase the number of shareholders. The number of General Motors Corporation shareholders, for example, is more than one million and of American Telephone and Telegraph Company more than two million. Splitting the stock also facilitates greater participation by employees in stock purchase plans.

Since most stock splits are made when a company is in a position to increase its cash dividend, some investors and speculators buy the stock on the assumption that the market price will rise, as it sometimes does, especially *before* the split when a split has been rumored. When, however, an increase in the cash dividend is discounted, a stock that has been selling at around 90 is likely to continue selling for some time after the split at around 45, when the split has been 2 for 1.

Although directors have the authority to declare stock dividends, stockholders must usually approve a stock split.

Xerox Holders OK Stock "Split"

Stockholders of Xerox Corp. approved at a special meeting yesterday a 5-for-1 split of the common shares, effective today.

Approval of the split involved increasing Xerox's authorized common to 30 million shares of $1 par value stock from 6 million shares of $1.25 par value stock.

In announcing the stockholders' approval, Xerox avoided the word, "split," terming the action a "change of shares." This was because the new shares will have a par value of $1 instead of the so-called split value of one-fifth of the $1.25 par value of the present shares.

Reverse stock split: In some instances, a corporation has increased the par value of its common shares and reduced the number of shares outstanding. Thus, when a company had 750,000 shares outstanding with a par value of $1, it increased the par value to $5 and reduced the number of shares to 150,000. The company did this by exchanging a new certificate on a 1-for-5 basis. This has usually happened after a company, over a period of years, has experienced losses or low profits, and the stock is selling at a very low price (sometimes for less than $1 a share). The stock, therefore, is not valued highly as collateral. The company believes it will improve its corporate image by increasing the par value of each share by means of a reverse split. A reverse split has also been used to pave the way for the merger of two successful companies when the market price of both stocks was low and they had a large number of shares.

Reverse Split of Stock Approved

Stockholders of Highway Trailer Industries, Inc. approved yesterday a 1-for-5 reverse split of the company's common stock at the annual meeting.

The reverse split will reduce the outstanding common to about 714,000 shares from about 3,570,000 shares.

In the proxy statement for the meeting, the board said it was seeking the recapitalization in part because that, by "decreasing the number of shares outstanding and increasing the market price per share," the shares would be more marketable and more acceptable to stockholders in connection with a rights offering.

Assets

The kinds of assets listed in the complete balance sheet on page 452 are representative of most manufacturing companies.

Book value rests on the assumption that, in the event of liquidation of the company, the assets would actually be worth the value stated on the balance sheet. Book value is discussed below.

Exercise: *1.* Compute the current ratio reflected in the balance sheet on page 452.

2. Compute the liquidity ratio.

Book Value

When Jim Baker was reporting a federal court case that involved the merger of two companies he was puzzled by the frequent references of the attorneys to the book value of the companies' common stock. For he knew that more than one-half of the common stocks listed on the New York Stock Exchange were selling at prices considerably above their book value. After investigation, however, he learned that book value is important in most merger situations or in liquidations, although it may have little relationship to the earning power of a company.

The book value of a share of common stock is obtained by dividing the number of common shares into the common equity. Thus, for the XYZ Corporation (see p. 448), 1,000,000 shares divided into the common equity of $42,000,000 yields a book value of $42 a common share. The book value of a share of preferred stock in the same corporation would be computed by dividing the number of preferred shares (100,000) into the stockholders' equity ($52,000,000). It would be $520.

A bank stock tends to sell at approximately its book value and most railroad stocks sell for considerably less than their book value. The stocks of many companies in growth industries, however, sell at prices much higher than their book value.

STATEMENT OF INCOME

The audited annual "statement of income" of a corporation is sometimes called the "profit and loss" statement. Many companies also supply their stockholders each quarter with abbreviated unaudited statements of income.

The statement of income on page 457 is rather typical. It omits, however, some expense and income items that are reported by railroads and certain types of industrial companies. Some aspects of this statement have considerable significance for the stockholder, and are discussed below.

Operating Profit

The income from operations divided by sales ($22.6 ÷ 115.8 "last year") shows the percentage earned on sales. This was about 19.5 per cent as compared with about 18.5 per cent in the preceding year. This percentage is sometimes called the "pretax profit" after such expenses as interest have been deducted from the operating profit (thus: $21.3 ÷ $115.8).

STATEMENT OF INCOME*

	Year ended Dec. 31	
	Last Year	Prior Year
	(Millions)	
Sales	$115.8	$110.0
LESS:		
Cost and expenses:		
Cost of goods sold	74.8	73.2
Selling, general, administrative expenses	14.2	13.0
Depreciation and depletion	4.2	3.5
	93.2	89.7
Operating profit	22.6	20.3
Interest charges	1.3	1.0
Earnings before federal income taxes	21.3	19.3
Provision for federal income taxes	11.4	9.8
Net income	9.9	9.5
Dividend on preferred stock	.3	.3
Balance of net income available for common stock	$ 9.6	$ 9.2

* Adapted from *How to Understand Financial Statements* (undated publication of the New York Stock Exchange). This statement does not reflect the reduction in the corporate income tax rate enacted in 1964.

Net Income

The amount earned after federal taxes is usually about one-half of the earnings before federal taxes because the "effective" corporate income tax rate for most companies is about 48 per cent of such income. When a corporation has lost money in one year it can "carry forward" such losses in the following years up to five years. State, local, and sometimes foreign taxes are often included in the "costs and expenses" item.

In evaluating a common stock, analysts examine the "net income to net worth" ratio. This may be a more significant ratio than the operating profit margin. Grocery chains, for example, have a very small operating profit percentage, but may earn much more on the corporation's net worth than a corporation in another type of business with a high operating profit percentage. When the net income (i.e., before taxes) is 10 per cent or higher of net worth, analysts assume that a company has satisfactory earnings; the average percentage for all manufacturing companies, however, is less than 10 per cent.

Earnings Per Share

Assuming that the company whose statement of income is exhibited on this page had 4,000,000 common shares outstanding on December 31, the common stock would have earned $2.40 per share last year and $2.30 a share in the prior year ($9.6 ÷ 4.0 and $9.2 ÷ 4.0).

Since the number of shares during a year may vary because of officers' exercising options to purchase shares or because the corporation sold additional shares, some companies—especially in their quarterly reports—report on the *average* number of shares during the period covered by the report instead of the number of shares at the end of the fiscal year.

When additional shares have been issued in one year, the earnings per share are usually adjusted for the prior year to reflect this change. Thus, if 100,000 new shares had been issued last year, earnings for the prior year would have been "restated" as $2.24 a share ($9.2 ÷ 4.1 shares) instead of $2.30 a share.

Canning Corp. Has Top Earnings Record

Reporting a record-breaking quarterly net income equal to $1.50 a share on its common stock, the Canning Corporation set an all-time high record on a yearly basis, the income statement, released yesterday, disclosed.

The efficiency of the company's plants has been considerably improved by the new equipment which went into operation last fall.

The June quarter report shows net profit of $4,321,854 after depreciation, interest and taxes, equivalent, after dividend requirements on preferred stock, to $1.50 a share on 2,868,513 shares of common stock.

This compares with $2,320,816, or 80 cents a share, on 2,868,477 common shares in the preceding quarter.

For the six months ended June 30, net income was $6,642,770, equal to $2.30 a share on 2,868,513 common shares, comparing with $2,305,064, or $1.02 a share on 2,192,284 common shares for the six months ended June 30, last year.

Cash Flow

In some industries, a company's depreciation and depletion are important considerations. Depreciation is the decline in value of a tangible asset due to age and to normal wear and tear. A company must set aside each year a percentage of the historical cost of its plant so that the plant may be replaced in the future. This deduction is taken on the income statement before operating profit has been computed. Depletion of a wasting asset (e.g., petroleum and coal) is also to be subtracted from operating earnings.

The sum of the depreciation (and depletion in the extracting industries) and the retained earnings in a particular year is called cash flow. Thus, if the company whose "statement of income" is on page 457 paid out in dividends one-half of its income available for common stock, its retained earnings ($4,800,000) plus its depreciation ($4,200,000) would produce a cash flow of $9,000,000. On the assumed 4,000,000 common shares this would be $2.25 per share of cash flow.

Cash flow is sometimes significant because it indicates the ability of a company to expand and modernize its plant without having to borrow. And, in a situation in which little expansion or modernization is required for the immediate future, it indicates the ability of a company either to reduce its long-term debt or to increase its cash dividend.

For some companies, the cash flow item may indicate that its reported earnings have really been understated. For other companies, however, it may indicate that reported earnings have been overstated; this is because depreciation is taken on the basis of historical cost of the plant whereas replacement costs have been increased by inflation of prices.

SOURCE AND APPLICATION OF FUNDS

Some corporations have adopted the practice of reporting annually on the source and application of their funds. Thus, the stockholder is told not only how much money the corporation received during the year but also the source of such funds and how the funds were appropriated or spent. The following statements are illustrative:

Source of Funds

Consolidated net profits	$ 5,476,822
Minority interest*	634,562
Net profits before minority interests	$ 6,111,384
Depreciation, amortization, depletion	4,542,084
Additions to long-term liabilities	13,060,000
Working capital	163,499
Miscellaneous	908,692
	$24,785,659

* The reason for this line in the statement is that, when the company acquired another company's stock, it did not acquire all of it—let's say, only 98 per cent. One or more stockholders in the subsidiary company, thus, retained their stock in the old company. Their interests are not consolidated on the books of the parent company but are treated separately. It is a tax advantage for a parent company, in a stock merger, to acquire 80 per cent of the shares in the company which becomes a subsidiary. When it acquires less than 80 per cent, the other company is considered an *affiliate*, not a subsidiary.

Application of Funds

Retirement of long-term liabilities	$ 5,126,085
Capital expenditures	5,960,369
Logging roads and timberlands purchased	1,088,002
Acquisition of subsidiaries	8,160,192
Investment in and advances to affiliates	422,644
Miscellaneous	2,244,201
Dividends	1,784,166
	$24,785,659

SOME RATIOS OF EVALUATION

When reading investment literature, Jim Baker found that he needed to know the meaning of certain terms that are applied in the evaluation of securities. Some of these are explained below, but only to the extent that a reporter needs to know what they mean. An expanded discussion would be needed by the investment analyst.

Interest Coverage

When a corporation has considerable outstanding long-term debt, the investor needs to relate the interest expense to the company's earnings before taxes. This is particularly important for railroads and has considerable relevance in those other industries with high fixed assets, such as steel, paper, and chemical companies. A satisfactory ratio for industrial companies is 5 times interest requirements; for utilities it is 2½ to 3 times.

Pretax Profit Margins

This percentage is obtained by dividing the operating profit (before interest and taxes) by sales, usually without including depreciation as an expense. The type of business determines whether the profit margin is high or low. What is important to the investor is the change upward or downward, from year to year, of the specific company being analyzed. Additional sales should normally increase the ratio and higher costs (e.g., wages and salaries) should decrease it. For all manufacturing companies in the United States an average profit margin of 10 per cent is considered satisfactory. Some analysts compute the profit margin as a ratio of *after* tax earnings to sales. On that basis, a satisfactory average profit margin for all manufacturing companies, over a period of years, is about 5 per cent. But this statement has no meaning unless the type of business is taken into account.

Net Income to Net Worth

Most investors want to know how much a company is earning on its stockholders' investment. This ratio is obtained by dividing net income by net worth (the total of preferred stock, common stock, earnings retained in the business, and capital surplus). When this ratio for all manufacturing companies is 10 per cent it is regarded as a very satisfactory average.

Price Times Earnings

Every investor wants to know, at least once a year, the ratio of annual per share earnings to the market price of his common stock. This is expressed as a multiple; for example, 12.4 times earnings per share.

Such a ratio varies widely both over time and between companies. In an optimistic market climate, some investors have paid more than 100 times earnings for a few stocks which appeared to have dynamic earnings potential. But during the same period this multiple was as low as 5 times earnings for certain depressed stocks. Below are the high and low multiples in selected years for those industrial stocks that compose the Standard & Poor's index of 500 stocks, based on closing prices.

	High	Low
1929	19.45	10.87
1931	30.28	12.96
1941	9.57	7.64
1949	6.88	5.51
1958	19.99	14.64

Yield

The percentage return of the cash dividend based on the market price of a stock is called the yield. Thus, the yield from a $1.60 per share dividend on a stock quoted at 40 is 4 per cent ($1.60 ÷ 40 = .04).

The yield on a stock of a company in a fairly stable industry (e.g., shoes) is usually high as compared with the yield of a dynamic company in the growing electronics industry. Different types of investors like to own different types of stock; some prefer to receive income and others prefer the opportunity for capital gain even with low income.

> For class discussion: What incorrect terminology was used in these news stories?
> . . . Samuel I. Newhouse, head of a newspaper empire, made the bid Tuesday. He offered $150 a share for shares whose highest yield has never been more than $135.
> . . . When the players were informed of the $150,000 bonus paid to the young pitcher, many refused to believe it was all in cash. Some guessed that securities or common stocks may have been involved.
> . . . Mr. Blough had a rough time at the annual stockholders'

meeting. After nearly four hours of often acrimonious exchange with 1,300 coupon clippers. . . .

WHO CONTROLS A CORPORATION

Conventionally, the common stockholders of a corporation, at the annual meeting, elect a certain number of directors. This board normally elects a chairman and other officers including a president. Either the chairman or the president is designated as the chief executive officer of the corporation, and sometimes the same person is both chairman and president.

Some large corporations have committees of directors to determine policy. An executive committee acts between meetings of the full board. The finance committee allocates funds for specific purposes and to subsidiaries; it also recommends policies relating to capital formation, such as issuing bonds.

Operating officials, often headed by an executive vice president, are responsible to the directors for the actual operation of the company and its separate divisions, or both.

Normally, each share of common stock is entitled to one vote. Thus, the holder of 1,000 shares has 1,000 votes. In electing directors such shares may be voted for a list of directors or—if the state statute and the corporation's charter permit—may be *cumulated*. That is, the stockholder may multiply his number of shares by the number of directors to be elected instead of dividing them among the number to be elected. If, for example, fifteen directors are to be chosen, the holder of 1,000 shares could cast 15,000 votes for one candidate or 7,500 for two candidates instead of casting 1,000 for each of the fifteen candidates.

The articles of incorporation of some companies provide for the annual election of all directors to serve until the next annual meeting. In other instances, only a certain proportion of the directors (say, one-fourth) is elected each year for a term of years. As a result of this staggered method, a group of dissident stockholders cannot obtain control of a corporation all at once.

Some corporations are closely held by a family or a very few stockholders. Some are controlled by a self-perpetuating management; every director of Standard Oil Company of New Jersey, for example, is an officer-employee. Most corporations, however, although dominated by management, have "outside" directors who are congenial to management. Annually management solicits *proxies* from stockholders and votes the proxies at the annual meeting.

When the company is losing ground to competitors or has a persistent unsatisfactory earnings record, some stockholders succeed in substituting new directors and new top management officers. This is often done by proxy solicitation by the dissident stockholders in advance of the annual meeting.

In advance of the annual meeting, management circulates to stockholders a ballot listing the matters that are to be voted on, such as the election of directors, approval of an independent auditor nominated by management, and amendments to the certificate of incorporation. The authorization for certain members of the board or for others to cast a stockholder's ballot is called a proxy.

When management solicits proxies it is required by federal statute to supply stockholders in advance of the annual meeting with a proxy statement which sets forth, with respect to directors and principal officers, the amount of their annual compensation (salaries, bonuses, and directors' fees), annual retirement benefits, stock options, and number of shares owned.

Dissident stockholders, as well as management, may circulate proxies and proxy statements that have been approved by the Securities and Exchange Commission.

Dissidents Win Va.-Carolina Control

RICHMOND, Va.—A group of insurgent stockholders won control of Virginia-Carolina Chemical Corp. from the present management and ousted President Joseph A. Howell.

The independent stockholders' committee, headed by Rupert T. Zicki, New York investor, at a special meeting last Wednesday polled 399,613 shares to the management's 211,874, it was announced today.

The group replaced six incumbent directors and removed Mr. Howell as president. It named six of its nominees to the board, including former Virginia Governor John S. Battle.

Mr. Battle said a directors' meeting would be called soon to name a temporary president.

The insurgents and management waged a bitter three-month proxy fight for control of the 61-year-old chemical and fertilizer manufacturing company. The insurgents charged the management was slack and said the company's earnings continued to drop despite a rise in sales.

Mr. Howell denied the group's

charges and declared the drop in profits was due to declining farm prices that had curtailed farmers' buying of the company's products.

REORGANIZATION UNDER THE BANKRUPTCY ACT

As explained on pages 408, 414, a debt-ridden corporation which is a party to a Chapter X bankruptcy proceeding, a trustee in the bankruptcy proceeding, a creditor, or a stockholder of the corporation may file a *plan* for capital reorganization. At the beginning of such a proceeding the judge divides creditors and stockholders into classes according to the nature of their claim and stock ownership. Eventually the judge approves a plan which alters or modifies their existing rights provided that two-thirds of each class has approved the plan.[12] The plan is usually effected through the issuance of new securities.

Here is the plan of one reorganization in which four classes were represented in addition to unsecured creditors who received some payment in cash. The classes are listed in the two tables below as A, B, C, and D.

BEFORE REORGANIZATION

Class	Amount
A. Mortgage bonds, 6%, with accrued interest	$2,280,555
B. Subordinated mortgage bonds, 6%, with accrued interest	$1,360,715
C. Pfd. stock, $25 par, $1.75 div., 285,947 shares	$7,148,675
D. Common, 397,455 shares	?

The next table shows how each class shared in the allotment of the three *new* issues of securities—income bonds, preferred stock, and common stock.

AFTER REORGANIZATION

Class	Income Bonds, 5%	Preferred, $50 Par, 5%	New Common, $2 Par
A.	$398,500	$938,500 (18,770 shares)	0
B.	568,500	$568,500 (11,370 shares)	0
C.	0	0	$571,894 (285,947 shares)
D.	0	0	0

[12] When, in the later stages of the proceeding, two-thirds of any class of creditors or stockholders does not accept a plan that the other classes consider equitable and fair, the law provides for an appraisement of their claim or ownership and payment in cash.

It will be noted that, in this reorganization, the original common stockholders were wiped out—"put through the wringer," is the expression. In other instances than the one just mentioned the common stockholders, in lieu of new common stock, are allotted warrants to buy the new common at a specified price; when the reorganized corporation prospers the warrants eventually have a value. In some instances, however, the original common stockholders are allotted a certain proportion of the new common.

Reorganization of El-Tronics Confirmed

PHILADELPHIA—U.S. District Court Judge John W. Lord, Jr. yesterday confirmed a reorganization plan for El-Tronics, Inc. under Chapter 10 of the bankruptcy act.

He fixed July 26 for a court hearing to pass on the qualifications of nominees for the reorganized company's board of directors.

Under terms of the reorganization approved previously by the court and El-Tronics stockholders, control of the company will pass to Stuart J. Myers, of Warren, Pa., and associates. This group will have the right to nominate five of the seven members of the reorganized board.

El-Tronics will acquire the fixed assets of several Myers companies, paying for them with an issue of $2.5 million of 5%, 12-year subordinated convertible debentures. The Myers group has agreed under the reorganization plan to purchase $500,000 of these debentures for cash. The other $2 million will go to pay for the assets of the Myers companies.

The Myers group also has agreed to buy 1.3 million shares of new no-par common El-Tronics stock for $1.7 million.

The reorganized company will retain the name El-Tronics, Inc., a spokesman said.

Exercise: *1.* Prepare a balance sheet based on the following data (It is necessary that the totals balance; they are $37,637,711):

Receivables	$ 8,323,017
Reserve for federal taxes	592,131
Inventories	9,895,539
Cash	2,641,019
Capital stock	9,411,200
Investments in municipal bonds	111,095
Patents and trade-marks	1
Capital surplus	13,733,577
Earned surplus	13,154,879
Accounts payable	745,924
Plant and property	16,313,908
Miscellaneous investments	353,132

2. List those items above that are (*a*) current assets; and (*b*) current liabilities.

3. What is the net worth of this company?

4. After calculating the pretax earnings per common share for each year (disregarding fractions of one cent a share), write a news story based on the following profit and loss statement of the Pacific Packing Corporation, issued today as of December 31. The company has 3,144 shares of 6 per cent preferred stock of $100 par value and 22,803⅔ shares of common (par value $15). The company had no tax accruals in either year because of losses in prior years.

	This Year	Last Year
Sales	$403,457.64	$298,146.06
Operating expenses*	258,750.43	222,582.76
Operating profit	144,707.21	75,563.30
Nonoperating charges	13,975.53	11,144.51
Net profit from operations	130,731.68	64,418.79
Recovery of processing taxes		165,946.84
Loss from flood damages	108,497.52	
Net Income	$ 22,234.16	$230,365.63

* Includes depreciation and interest charges.

Manuals

Data on corporation earnings and capital structure may be found in such well-known manuals as *Moody's* and *Standard & Poor's*. Several weekly financial journals are published in addition to the daily *Wall Street Journal* and *Journal of Commerce* (New York).

CHAPTER *31*

The County Building

It is characteristic of the American polity that much government is at the local level. More than 150,000 local governmental units perform certain functions and have the taxing power to support their activities. There are more than 3,000 counties and about 17,000 municipalities. There are also nearly 20,000 towns or townships, more than 100,000 school districts and nearly 10,000 special districts (park, sanitary, fire protection, flood prevention, etc.).

The fifty states with only few exceptions, are divided into counties. All of the six New England states and sixteen other states also have towns and townships. These subdivisions of the state perform certain functions of local government, but the county is also an administrative unit of the state and performs certain functions on behalf of the state. In recent times, however, the state has come to perform certain functions that formerly were performed only by the county; thus, we have state police as well as the county sheriff.

The municipality is a corporation chartered by the state to perform those functions of government which are a necessity for urban life, for example, sewage disposal and street lighting.

A new form of local government called *metropolitan* has developed in a few areas. It includes a large city, the county, and the smaller municipalities in the county that surround the city. In the case of Dade county, Florida (Miami) only some of the functions of local government were surrendered by the constituent units. But in the Nashville-Davidson metropolitan government (the city of Nashville and Davidson county) virtually all functions of the various units are now performed by a metropolitan government which is a consolidation of the units.

THE COUNTY GOVERNING BOARD

Every county has a board with certain legislative powers and which is responsible for those administrative functions not performed by elected officers, such as the sheriff. This board levies county taxes, borrows, makes appropriations, and awards contracts for county highway construction and other public works. It also enacts ordinances to regulate a few types of businesses, such as dance halls.

The most common names for such boards are Board of Supervisors or Board of Commissioners, although some boards are called Fiscal Court or County Court. The typical size of the board is five to seven members, although some boards have more members. The members are elected in some states from the county at large and in other states from districts within the county.

In recent times, some counties have adopted charters which provide for a *county manager,* or *county executive,* who is given the power to hire, suspend, or discharge most administrative officials and employees.

The County Clerk

A county official in about one-half of the states is the *county clerk,* who acts as a secretary for the county board. He prepares the agenda for board meetings and keeps the minutes of the meetings. In a few states he is also the clerk of the county court. In some states he also performs some of the functions of the officials whose duties are discussed below, including the issuance of marriage licenses.

FUNCTIONS OF COUNTY ADMINISTRATION

The functions of the usual county administration are these: (1) to assess and collect taxes; (2) to enforce the state laws and county ordinances; (3) to record important documents; (4) to construct and maintain county highways; (5) to administer social welfare; (6) to administer the rural schools; (7) to protect the public health; (8) to engage in county planning and regulate zoning.

TAXATION

Once a year a county official, usually called the *assessor* or *tax commissioner,* places a valuation upon all real and personal property within the county. In some states, the citizens voluntarily appear before the assessor or mail a schedule of their property. In other states, the assessor makes a personal visit to the taxpayer to obtain his schedule; in any event, an assessor at some time or other inspects the property and lists it on the tax roll.

Assessment Procedures

In some states, real property is assessed at its full appraised value, and in other states at some percentage of full value, ranging from 25 to 90 per cent.

Assessment procedures have become quite scientific as state tax commissions have established research departments to study comparative values in different counties of the state and to enforce on county assessing officials the criteria that real estate brokers, fire insurance companies, and appraisal companies have devised.

Assessment procedure calls for the development of a tax map which provides for certain basic land values related especially to the use or potential use of the land. In towns and cities, several other factors, especially the location, contribute to the determination of the value of land. In assessing a particular parcel of land in a town or city, the size of the lot is a criterion as is also whether or not it is on a corner. Improvements on such land are appraised on the basis of square feet and the kind of construction material (e.g., brick, stone, frame). Further differentiations are made with respect to such factors as the number of tiled bathrooms in the home, finished or unfinished basement, kind of foundation, kind of floors, type of heating, and several other factors.

The State Tax Commission usually assesses the county's portion of statewide utilities in each county (e.g., railroads and electric light companies) and certifies the valuation to the county governing body.

After the annual assessment has been completed, the assessor releases the data to newspapers.

Assessed Valuation Rises $4,830,200

A record-breaking property assessment roll of $84,076,500 for the next tax year was reported yesterday by Assessor Bernard Overstreet.

The figure represents an increase of $4,830,200.

This could make a slight decrease in the tax rate if county expenses are not increased. Howard Hazard, chairman of the board of supervisors, however, said, it will be another month before the county knows exactly the total of the allocation of gasoline revenue the county will receive from the state.

The details of the assessment roll are as follows:

Land	$36,041,000
Improvements	39,412,500
Personal property	3,391,500
Utilities assessed by the state	5,231,500
	$84,076,500

After the county board has set the tax rate on general property (i.e., real estate and personal property), the *tax collector* prepares a bill for each piece of real property and mails it to the owner.

County Tax Rate Trimmed by 4¢

The board of supervisors cut the general tax rate 4 cents today.

The board adopted a resolution trimming the new rate to $1.84 per $100 assessed valuation. Taxpayers throughout the county will pay that basic rate with their city and special district taxes on top of that.

Under this rate, the owner of a $20,000 home, assessed at $5,000, will pay $92.

Controller Ira A. Boynton presented the following breakdown of the general tax rate:

General fund	$1.40
Social welfare	.25
Land acquisition	.01
Building fund	.138
Reserves	.03
School service fund	.012

County Property Taxes Due Nov. 1

County tax bills were put in the mail yesterday by Tax Collector Joseph Bogue.

The first installment of 50 per cent of the bill is due November 1 and becomes delinquent December 5. The second installment is due January 20 and becomes delinquent April 20.

After completion of the assessment and after taxpayers have been notified, a board—usually called a Board of Review or a Board of Equalization—sits in the county building for a few weeks to hear complaints and, accordingly, make adjustments in the valuation of individual assessments; in some states the county governing body sits as the board of review.

Dodgers Lose Tax Rise Appeal

The Los Angeles Dodgers lost their "tax series" today with Los Angeles county.

The board of supervisors, sitting as a board of review, upheld the county tax collector's assessment, which will mean a tax hike of nearly $250,000 for the baseball club.

The baseball club asserted that the true market value of its stadium and some 300 adjoining acres was about $19,500,000.

The club argued that the assessed valuation should be less than $5,500,000, leaving taxes again at about $450,000.

The county assessor and his appraisers told the board that $32,000,000 was a realistic market value. They, therefore, placed the assessment at $8,260,000.

It is the function of the county tax collector (or sheriff, in some states) to sell at public auction parcels of property on which the taxes are delinquent. When such sales are made the deed to the purchaser is subject to the condition that the delinquent taxpayer may redeem the property before the end of a specified period by paying the accrued taxes, penalties, and interest. When he does not do so, however, the purchaser is granted a clear title and the parcel goes back on the tax roll.

76 Parcels of Land Sold for Taxes

Tax Collector Edward F. Bryant yesterday sold 76 parcels of tax delinquent property for $9519.63.

The sale was attended by one of the largest groups of potential buyers in the local history of such sales and was marked by spirited bidding.

The prices paid for the property ranged from $7.76 to $336.

The *county treasurer* receives monies from the county tax collector and subventions from the state and is the custodian of them. He disburses the money on requisition. He also administers the county bond funds.

LAW AND LAW ENFORCEMENT

The *county attorney,* or *county counsel,* advises the county board and administrative officers on questions of law, drafts contracts, and evaluates claims against the county.

Some states maintain a system of state police or a highway patrol, but the principal burden of law enforcement remains upon certain county officials, such as the sheriff, the prosecuting attorney, the coroner, and the jailer. Some counties employ crime investigators who have received training in schools conducted by the Federal Bureau of Investigation. County dance-hall inspectors have also been added to the force in some states. The mode of operation of these officials was described in previous chapters. The sheriff, in addition to his law enforcement duties, is also the officer of the court who serves the papers filed in civil actions; these duties were discussed in Chapter 16.

RECORDATION

The state, as a guardian of the rights of property, has in modern times provided a system for recording for perpetual memory and testimony the ownership of title to real property. In every county building, therefore, is a fireproof office in which written instruments are recorded and preserved for all time. Any person who desires to make himself secure in his title to property acquired by purchase or inheritance takes the written instrument that certifies his ownership to this office where, upon payment of a fee, it is copied into a book (or photographed), indexed, and filed. The instruments most frequently recorded are warranty* and quitclaim deeds* to real property, wills admitted to probate, mortgages, releases of mortgages, trust deeds, transcripts of judgments, mechanics' liens and liens on real estate, marriage contracts, official bonds, and military discharges. The official who has charge of the recording office is most often the *county clerk* or *recorder;* in some states he is called the *register of deeds,* and in some states there are two recording officers.

The recorder's office is an important source of news. Business men are especially interested in transfers of property. Reporters on small newspapers usually visit this office twice a day. Newspapers in large cities ordinarily employ some subordinate clerk in the county building to furnish them daily with a summary of all routine statistics of this office, and require their own reporters or real estate editors to obtain only important information, such as the news about a large or unusual transfer of property. This kind of reporting demands accuracy. The reporter can determine the approximate amount of the transaction, when it is not mentioned, by noting the amount of the revenue stamps which are affixed to the original document and noted in the margin of the copied document.

Records of the kind mentioned above are, by law, open to public inspection, as are most financial and administrative records. A newspaper, refused permission to inspect such records, can obtain inspection by mandamus. A few types of records are not open to inspection; these are some of the vital statistics kept by the department of health that relate to adoptions and illegitimate births.

The right of the newspaper to access to public records is discussed in H. L. Cross, *The People's Right to Know* (New York, 1953).

Tremont Theater Is Sold to Group

A deed filed today in the county recorder's office indicates that ownership of the Tremont theater, 456 Tremont Ave., is changing hands.

Revenue stamps on the deed indicate that the sales price was $230,000.

Conveyance of the title is being made by the Tremont Theater Corp. to Southwest Theaters, Inc., of Kansas City.

37-Year-Old Deed Is Finally Recorded

A real estate sale made thirty-seven years ago but which was not recorded then was made a public record for the first time today.

Attorneys for the Daniel Murray, Sr. estate filed a warranty deed with the county register of deeds.

The deed transfers Lot 18, Block 31, which is the property at 554 West 19th street, from Charles H. and Mary Murray to Daniel Murray, Sr.

All parties to the deed are dead, but Daniel Murray, Jr., now resides at the home which his father erected on the lot. Daniel Murray, Sr. died two years ago, and the tardy deed was filed by attorneys who are settling the estate.

Attorneys and members of the Murray family are unable to explain why the deed was not recorded at the time of the sale.

HIGHWAYS

The major highways are maintained by the state highway authorities, but many other highways in a county are the responsibility of the county government. The determination of highway policy, including the matters of financing, routing, and resurfacing of county highways, is a function of the governing body, but the administration of highway funds and the technical supervision of construction and repair are in the hands of an official usually called the *road engineer* or *highway commissioner* who is appointed by the governing board. From him the reporter learns about the progress made in constructing or repairing certain roads, about plans made to close temporarily certain roads with the necessary information about detours, and the condition of certain roads following heavy snowstorms and severe rainstorms.

NOMINATIONS AND ELECTIONS[1]

The administration of state and county elections in most states is vested by statute in an Election Commission which ordinarily is composed of two commissioners, one representing each of the major parties, and a third ex officio member, usually the sheriff, county judge, or county clerk. Prior to each primary or general election, the commission or the county governing board appoints elections officers for each precinct (often called *judge, clerk,* or *inspector*) and arranges for polling places. After the ballots have been cast they are counted and tabulated by the precinct officials and returned to the Election Commission, which officially counts the precinct tally sheets. The commission then awards certificates of election to the successful candidates for county offices and, in the case of candidates for state offices, certifies the official vote to the secretary of state.

The official who is responsible for administering the election machinery is the county clerk, although some counties have another official who is usually called the *registrar of voters*. In this office, candidates file their nomination papers; the law provides a deadline for the filing and withdrawing of candidacies. This office registers those citizens who are eligible to vote and checks the genuineness of the names signed to petitions for referenda and the names of persons who sponsor a candidate. This office supervises the printing of ballots and the repair of voting machines, announces the location of polling places, and administers the process of absentee voting.

[1] A further discussion of this subject is in Chap. 34.

Woman Denies Her Name on Referendum Petition Is Genuine

Mrs. Minnie West, of 1324 West 14th street, a woman truck driver, created a stir Wednesday when she denied she had signed a petition bearing her name as protesting the sale of Courthouse Square.

She was one of a dozen persons who testified at a hearing by the Election Commission in connection with a petition asking a referendum on the sale of the square. The Commission was investigating charges that the petition is not valid.

"It's not my signature," she said. "Except for the firemen's raise, I never sign things like that. Until recently I was driving a truck from 7 a.m. until after dark and no one could have found me home."

Denials that signatures were valid were running about one to five.

Witnesses appeared in response to 1,442 postcards, mailed to persons whose names appeared on the petition.

Signers whose signatures are challenged will have their names stricken from the petition if they fail to appear at the hearing.

Roy Saunders, attorney for the persons protesting the petition, asked names be stricken when women used no first names or used their husbands' names or initials. He said his contention that such names were not acceptable had been upheld by a supreme court decision.

Preston Dorn, attorney for the circulators of the petition, asked each witness if she was known in her neighborhood by the name she signed.

He asked that some of the post cards be put into the record, contending that successful delivery of the cards by the postman proved the persons to whom they were addressed were known by the names on the cards.

Order of Names on Ballot Challenged

County Clerk Charles Culbertson denied today that he permitted two other candidates to file nomination papers for coroner prior to A. H. Lutz, although Mr. Lutz was first in line at the county clerk's office.

Mr. Lutz declared yesterday in an interview that he would contest the right of the other two candidates to first and second place on the ballot. The other candidates are Karl Cady and E. J. Mason.

The charges by Mr. Lutz are the first of their kind to be made in Willis county since the new election laws were passed. Previously, all candidates for an office gathered in the county clerk's office on the appointed day and drew lots for places on the ballot.

SCHOOLS

Each school district in a county elects a Board of Education which employs administrative officials and teachers. The rural schools, however, are subject to some overall administration by the state department of education and a *county superintendent of schools*. The county superintendent, who is often an elected official, has an office in the county building. Reporters obtain from him at various times during the year news concerning the appointment of teachers, the construction of school buildings, the examination of candidates for the teachers' certificate, proposed bond issues to be submitted to voters in the independent school districts, various statistical information relating to the county school system, and information regarding the all-county school enterprises, such as fairs, contests, and athletic associations.

HEALTH

The guarding of public health in the county is usually entrusted to a Board of Health which is made up almost entirely of physicians. The administration is entrusted to an official usually called the *county health officer,* who is always a physician. Progressive communities employ, in addition to the health officer, a *county nurse* and sometimes a *sanitary inspector;* these employees are often provided with office and laboratory space in the county building. Their work is chiefly of a preventive nature. The board has power to quarantine persons infected with contagious diseases and to close schools when epidemics are existent. In well-organized public health work the staff gives physical examinations to school children, issues publicity of an educational nature, provides free treatment for persons infected with the social diseases, and maintains a "pest house" for the confinement of persons infected with certain contagious diseases. The public health service is a source of news at all times, but most often when epidemics are prevalent or are threatened. In some states, the county department of health keeps vital statistics, such as deaths, births, adoptions, and incidence of contagious diseases.

Bedford Is Told To Boil Its Water

Residents of the Bedford neighborhood are warned that they ought to boil all drinking water during the period of the next few days in an announcement made yesterday by Dr. K. J. Knox, county health officer.

Seven cases of typhoid fever have been reported by physicians in Bedford during the past ten days, Dr. Knox said.

The diphtheria epidemic has run its course in this county and parents need have no fear in returning their children to school, a second announcement declared. Altogether, fewer than a score of diphtheria cases were reported in April and only one school was required to close, Dr. Knox said.

SOCIAL WELFARE

Care of needy aged and indigent persons is universally one of the functions of county government. In some states, the care of the insane and the feeble-minded is also regarded as a function of county government, but the state usually assumes the care of such defectives because of the necessity for scientific treatment; the county in such instances often pays the state on a per capita basis for the defectives it sends to the state institution. Many counties have a *director of social welfare* who administers old-age assistance, aid to needy children, aid to the needy blind, and aid to indigents. Most states provide a subvention to counties for social welfare which is a supplement to county funds. The county often provides a home for indigent aged persons.

PLANNING AND ZONING

Some counties have established planning commissions which function as do planning commissions in municipalities (as discussed in Chapter 32). The commission is chiefly concerned with the use of land along public highways and with recreation areas within the county.

SUNDRY OFFICIALS

Many counties have various full-time and part-time officials whose functions are less important than those listed in foregoing sections. The *county surveyor* assists the court to determine the boundaries of real property in litigation. The *humane officer* acts to prevent cruel treatment of children and dumb animals. A *county agricultural agent,* whose salary is paid by the county and the federal government, is employed in many counties. He is a source of information about agricultural activities in the county. His chief duty is to give counsel to farmers regarding the production and marketing of crops and the care and feeding of livestock.

Danger in Use of 2,4-D Is Explained

County Agent Lewis Christie today issued a warning to farmers planning to use 2,4-D weed-killing compound.

He warns that the compound is very powerful and should be used only with certain precautions. The compound, however, is very effective, he said.

Some of the precautions he advised are these: . . .

IMPROVEMENT OF COUNTY GOVERNMENT

The least efficient government is on the county level. In some states, the statutes permit the citizens of a county to frame a charter to establish a more efficient form of government than the traditional form which provides for the election of so many administrative officials. Some counties have adopted a county executive type of government which operates like the council-manager type of city government.

CHAPTER 32

The City Hall

The congregation of large numbers of persons living or doing regular business in an urban community gives rise to certain problems of city housekeeping. The residents must have streets and boulevards, street lighting, ways of transportation, ways of disposing of sewage and garbage, parks, protection against fire, and regulation of traffic. The state, therefore, permits city people to organize as a corporation (municipality) in order to supply themselves with these and other services. Such a government, unlike the state government, does not regulate fundamentally the conduct of persons, but has the narrower function of engaging in urban housekeeping. The central problem of municipal government, therefore, is how to provide the necessary and desirable services at the lowest cost.

PLANS OF CITY GOVERNMENT

The state either grants a municipality a *charter* which permits it to engage in certain functions or it approves a charter which the citizens of a specific municipality have adopted by popular referendum. The powers of the municipality are limited by this charter.

The traditional organization of city government is the *mayor-council* type. Generally, this means that the elected councilmen enact certain rules, determine the amount of taxes to be collected, and appoint officers and boards to administer the affairs of city government. This plan is either a *weak-mayor* or a *strong-mayor* type. The main difference is that, under the strong-mayor plan the mayor has the power to appoint and remove most administrative officials, whereas under the weak-mayor plan administrative officials are largely responsible to council-appointed boards and commissions.

The *council-manager* plan provides for the appointment by the Council of a professional chief administrator who is permitted to appoint and remove administrative officials and employees. This plan usually provides for an elected mayor whose main functions are to keep in touch with the citizenry as to its desires and to present and explain to the citizenry the chief policies and plans of the council; that is, he serves as a leader on the policy level and leaves administration to the professional administrator.

The *commission plan* usually provides for the election of five commissioners. They serve as members of the City Council, and each of them also accepts responsibility for a particular part of the administration. This plan is subject to the criticism that it does not separate policy and administrative functions of government. Few cities, therefore, have adopted it.

In most cities, *boards* or *commissions* composed of lay citizens, are appointed either to serve in an advisory capacity or to accept responsibility for certain parts of the administration. The most common of these are: Public Works, Public Safety, Parks, Library, City Planning and Zoning, and Civil Service. In some instances, these boards or commissions may appoint, promote, and remove the administrative officials and employees who are concerned, such as park superintendent, librarian, and planning engineer. These bodies hold regular meetings and report to the City Council.

THE CITY COUNCIL

Organization

The elected City Council, which holds regular and special meetings, has several *standing committees*. Nearly all councils have the following committees: Finance, Public Safety, Public Works, Recreation and Parks, and Public Health and Welfare. Some councils have other committees, such as Commercial and Industrial Development, Judiciary, Education, Civil Service, Transportation, Public Buildings, City Planning, and Audits and Accounts.

Powers

The usual powers of the City Council are these:

1. Adoption of the annual budget, including the fixing of the property tax rate and of employees' salaries.

2. Authorization of public improvements.

3. Hearing of appeals on the granting of permits and of variances from the zoning ordinances.

4. Adoption by ordinance of basic codes relating to building, zoning, and sanitation.

5. Regulation, under the police power of the state, of certain types of conduct that affect the public health, safety, and welfare; these include traffic regulation, the keeping of animals, the erection of billboards, the location of cemeteries, and the conduct of pool halls.

6. Submission to the electorate of bond issues for public improvements and the sale and redemption of such bonds.

7. Authorization of the annexation of new territory.
8. Appointment and removal of officers.

Ordinances and Resolutions

The actions taken by the City Council are in the form of either *ordinances* or *resolutions*. A resolution expresses the intent, permission, or opinion of the council. A few types of resolution are these: intent to abandon a portion of a street (this is made so that protests can be heard at the next meeting of the council); authority to a city official to sell at auction a piece of city-owned real property at a specific minimum amount; request to the mayor to appropriate from his contingent fund a certain sum for a traffic survey.

Most actions taken by the council are in the form of an ordinance. The preamble to an ordinance usually reads: "The Council of the City of ———— do ordain as follows." The ordinance must be signed by the mayor and attested by the city clerk. Under some city charters, the mayor has power to veto an ordinance which then must be readopted by a two-thirds vote. An ordinance generally goes into effect thirty days after the mayor has signed it. Ordinances which relate to fixing the tax rate, calling an election, and a few other matters become effective immediately. An *emergency ordinance* becomes effective immediately when it is designated as such and is adopted by a two-thirds vote.

Order of Business

The city clerk prepares in advance of the meeting the agenda. He lists the items of the agenda in the regular "order of business." This is usually as follows:
1. Roll call.
2. Approval of the minutes (journal).
3. Petitions and communications.
4. Reports of boards and officers.
5. Reports of council committees.
6. Introduction or presentation by council members of resolutions, bills (i.e., proposed ordinances), and communications. All of this is "new business."

As the clerk, after approval or correction of the minutes, reads each petition and communication, the council adopts a motion that it be "filed" or be referred to an appropriate board, officer, or council committee. These are usually letters of thanks, complaint, invitation, resignation, and suggestion, and petitions for or against certain matters. In connection with petitions, the council often hears citizens who address the council from the floor.

Quiet Little Business Grows Noisy, Charge

A welding shop which started in a garage has grown into a heavy industry and should be forbidden, the City Council heard last night.

Ten letters of protest were read, and George Alpen, 1524 Montgomery street, appeared in person.

Antonio Bruzzone, proprietor of the shop at 742 Dallas street, will be asked to attend the next Council meeting to show cause why his shop should not be abated as a nuisance, the Council decided.

Mr. Alpen told the Council the shop is located in a garage on a lot that is zoned as "residential." The neighbors, he said, are driven to distraction by the noise of air hammers and presses as well as the noise of heavy trucks and tractors driven to the shop for repairs. . . .

The reports of boards and officers, which are required periodically, are usually, on motion, "accepted." The reports sometimes contain "recommendations" and these are referred for consideration to an appropriate committee of the council. Sometimes the boards or officers report findings on matters requested by the council at a previous meeting.

When the council is ready to hear reports from its own committees, the question is often on the "adoption" of their recommendation—usually in the form of an ordinance. Such reports relate to business referred to the committees at a previous meeting.

After this "unfinished business" has been concluded, the clerk calls the roll of councilmen who introduce "new business." When the councilman's proposal is in the form of a "bill," it is referred to a committee for study. This reference is called giving "first reading" to the bill. Usually only the title of the bill is read. This procedure implies that the committee will report its recommendation at a subsequent meeting, either in the form in which it was introduced or in an amended form; a committee may also recommend against adoption. The bill is not debatable at the stage of "first reading."

Procedure of Adoption

All deliberative bodies require that a proposed legislative measure be examined by one of its committees before the whole body takes a vote. This means deferment of action for a period of ten days or longer. An exception is made, under some rules, when a proposed ordinance is declared an emergency ordinance, but a two-thirds vote is required for adoption.

A proposal which is recommended for passage by the committee which considered it is debated by the council. During the course of the debate the measure may be amended. It may also be referred again to the committee. At the conclusion of the debate the presiding officer puts the question of passage on "second reading." When the vote is to give the bill "second reading," the bill must then come up at a subsequent meeting for "adoption" (i.e., final passage).

In several cities, however, councils have adopted the rule of considering passage on "second reading" as being equivalent to "adoption," thus eliminating the third stage of enactment.

Since many readers do not know the meaning of "first reading" and "second reading," the reporter should try to make understandable the precise action of the council. He does not need to use the terms "passed first reading" or "was given first reading." Since this means that the bill was referred to a committee he can simply write, "The proposed ordinance was referred to the Public Works Committee."

Since, however, he cannot avoid using the expression "given second reading," he can indicate to the reader that the bill is still under consideration by adding, "The proposal will come up for adoption in two weeks," or a similar explanation. Under those rules which consider "second reading" as the equivalent of "adoption," he does not have to use the former term at all.

Use of Parliamentary Idiom

The beginning reporter usually has considerable difficulty in reporting a council meeting in a precise and terse way. This is because he is not adequately acquainted with parliamentary idiom. He can make his report more understandable if he will (1) use the appropriate verbal expression for the action taken, and (2) use as sparingly as possible the passive voice. The key verbal expressions that describe precisely the actions taken by a City Council are these:

. . . *enacted* (*adopted, passed*) an ordinance to . . .

. . . *gave second reading to* (*approved on second reading*) an ordinance to . . .

. . . *adopted* a resolution to . . .

. . . *referred* to the Committee on Finance a proposed ordinance to . . .

. . . *defeated* (*refused to adopt, refused passage to*) a proposed ordinance to . . .

. . . *amended* the ordinance to . . .

. . . *denied* the request of . . .

... *appropriated* $7,200 to the Library Board for ...
... *refused to appropriate* $5,000 for ...
... *deferred* (*postponed, decided to postpone*) action on the proposal to ...
... *authorized* the sale of $3,000,000 of improvement bonds ...
... *awarded* a contract to the Allis Chalmers company for ...
... *accepted* the bid of the Freeman Construction company for ...
... *directed* (*instructed*) the city attorney to ...
... *requested* the City Planning Commission to ...
... *granted* more time to the Committee on Public Works to study the question of ...
... *gave permission* to the city engineer to advertise for bids for widening Ninth Street ...
... *heard* a group of citizens protest ...
... *received* a petition from ...
... *received* the recommendation of the Board of Public Safety for ...
... *voted to file* the claim for damages of ...
... *accepted* deeds from Mr. and Mrs. F. G. Clark to property for the extension of ...
... *rejected* all bids for the construction of ...

Because the passive voice indicates that the subject is being acted upon and since the council acts, the reporter should use the active voice whenever possible. The passive voice can be used, of course, to avoid repetition. It can also be used for sentence emphasis. The following sentence, for example, was used for both of those reasons: "An ordinance to forbid double parking was also passed."

Reporting Details

Newspapers should report council proceedings as fully as space will permit. Many readers, of course, are not interested in technical details, and these can usually be omitted. The newspaper should try to report all but the routine actions and should especially report proposals to which a section of the community is likely to object. The debate within the council should also be reported, when space permits, so that readers will know more about the attitudes and abilities of the persons they have elected as councilmen.

It is usually a poor practice to report all of the council's proceedings in a single news story. Instead, the following procedure is recommended, especially for newspapers in small cities:

1. Write a separate news story for each matter on the agenda that is of major or secondary interest—perhaps five or six stories. If necessary, run some of the stories on inside pages.

2. Put the main story on the first page.

3. At the top of the main story, carry a box or precede in bold face which lists in 1-2-3 manner and in one sentence each of the actions which is reported in the separate stories. Although you need not cite the particular page on which each news story appears, the listing will serve as an adequate index for interested readers. Thus:

> The City Council last night took the following actions:
> 1. Enacted an ordinance to forbid the operation of self-service gasoline stations.
> 2. Appropriated $5,000 for preliminary plans for a new sewage disposal plant.
> 3. Deferred action on a proposal to regulate taxicab stands.
> 4. Amended the zoning ordinance to forbid private schools in "first residential" districts.
> 5. Voted second reading to a proposed ordinance to regulate the business of fumigating buildings.

4. Group in one story the minor matters, separating each of them with a 3-em dash or a slug.

Reporting Debate

A reason for reporting debate in a council meeting, in addition to the reasons mentioned above, is that debate brings out considerations which otherwise might not be apparent to the reader. The following news story is illustrative:

Council Delays Action On Cab Stand Bill

The small taxicab companies persuaded the City Council yesterday to defer consideration of the proposed ordinance to regulate taxicab stands.

The bill was introduced by Councilman Dan McMurray and was up for second reading yesterday on recommendation of the Committee on Public Safety.

It would require consent of the owner or first floor tenant of a building for the establishment of a taxicab stand in front of his building.

Councilman McMurray said he fa-

> vored the bill because it would minimize confusion and reduce noise at certain places, especially at hotels where people are sleeping.
> "You mean the Chancellor Hotel, don't you?" Councilman James Lewis inquired. "Doesn't sixty per cent of the cab business originate there?"
> After Mr. McMurray said nothing, Mr. Lewis asserted the purpose of the bill was to throw most of the business to the Ranier Cab company through Harley Hunter, manager of the Chancellor Hotel and (said Mr. Lewis) a stockholder in the cab company.
> Councilman McMurray responded, "That just isn't so!"
> Councilman A. A. Ferguson said he opposed the bill because it meant a delegation of police power to private individuals.
> "It's discriminatory and unconstitutional," he added. . . .

It is the practice of some newspapers to report debate only because it is controversial. When such debate is mere name-calling and does not add to the reader's understanding of the measure or does not assist the reader in making a judgment about a councilman's ability or public attitude, it is usually not worth reporting.

Secrecy

In some cities, the City Council, Zoning Commission, and Board of Education hold "executive sessions" from which the public and the press are excluded. They justify this procedure on the ground that they are acting in the best interest of the taxpayers when they are discussing a lawsuit against the city or board or are considering the purchase of a certain tract of land. In some cities, also, it is the practice of the body to hold an informal meeting (sometimes called a "caucus") in advance of the regular meeting. The real deliberation of the body is in the informal session, voting at the regular session being a mere formality. Informal meetings are also sometimes held at the home of a member of the body or in a private dining room of a club or restaurant.

This secrecy of deliberation has been so offensive that about half of the states now have statutes that forbid secret meetings of local governing bodies. The statutes make an exception to permit secret deliberation on personnel matters, as when the body is evaluating candidates for an appointment or is discussing complaints against an official or employee. These exceptions are to protect the reputation of the individuals concerned.

Below are some of the provisions of a pioneer statute, the Brown Act, which was enacted in California in 1953 and later amended.[1]

> 54953. All meetings of the legislative body of a local agency shall be open and public, and all persons shall be permitted to attend any meeting of the legislative body of a local agency, except as otherwise provided in this chapter. . . .
>
> 54956. A special meeting may be called at any time by the presiding officer of the legislative body of a local agency, or by a majority of the members of the legislative body, by delivering personally or by mail written notice to each member of the legislative body and to each local newspaper of general circulation, radio or television station requesting notice in writing. Such notice must be delivered personally or by mail at least 24 hours before the time of such meetings as specified in the notice. The call and notice shall specify the time and place of the special meeting and the business to be transacted. No other business shall be considered at such meetings by the legislative body. Such written notice may be dispensed with as to any member who at or prior to the time the meeting convenes files with the clerk or secretary of the legislative body a written waiver of notice. Such waiver may be given by telegram. Such written notice may also be dispensed with as to any member who is actually present at the meeting at the time it convenes. . . .
>
> 54957. Nothing contained in this chapter shall be construed to prevent the legislative body of a local agency from holding executive sessions during a regular or special meeting to consider the appointment, employment or dismissal of a public officer or employee or to hear complaints or charges brought against such officer or employee by another public officer, person or employee unless such officer or employee requests a public hearing. The legislative body also may exclude from any such public or private meeting, during the examination of a witness, any or all other witnesses in the matter being investigated by the legislative body. . . .
>
> 54959. Each member of a legislative body who attends a meeting of such legislative body where action is taken in violation of any provision of this chapter, with knowledge of the fact that the meeting is in violation thereof, is guilty of a misdemeanor [punishable by fine and up to six months imprisonment].
>
> 54960. Any interested person may commence an action either by mandamus or injunction for the purpose of stopping or preventing violations or threatened violations of this chapter by members of the legislative body of a local agency.

One fact that has influenced local bodies to hold secret sessions has been the inaccurate or irresponsible newspaper reporting of meetings. Reporters have sometimes emphasized the acerbity of the debate in a way that presents a disproportionate report of the actual deliberations. Reporters also have failed to understand adequately the matters under consideration.

A second form of secrecy in municipal government is practiced on the administrative side of government. It happens when the city manager adopts

[1] *California Government Code*, secs. 54950–54959.

a rule that all news must clear through his office, thus blocking the newspaper's access to the department heads.

Adopting the Budget

Several weeks prior to the end of the fiscal year,[2] the departments of city government prepare estimates of their anticipated expenditures for the next fiscal year. Under the council-manager form of government, these are submitted to the city manager, who amends them as he sees fit. Under other forms of government, with some exceptions, the estimates go to the City Council, which refers them to a committee usually called the Finance Committee.[3] The members of this committee hold meetings with department heads and require them to justify their estimates, especially increased estimates. Shortly before the end of the fiscal year, this committee reports to the council. The council holds a public hearing and eventually adopts a budget. The budget balances approximately the anticipated expenditures and revenue.

Sources of Revenue

Of all taxes collected in the United States in a normal peace-time year, more than 70 per cent are for the federal government and about 15 per cent for the fifty state governments. This leaves about 14 per cent for city, county, and other local governments. Since the higher levels of government preëmpt the main sources of revenue, local governments have to rely heavily on taxes on real and personal property, which is owned by individual homeowners, landlords, and businesses.[4] To prevent taxes on this kind of property from becoming too high, local governments have had to resort to other sources of revenue. The most common sources for cities are these:

1. Real and personal property.
2. The local portion of property of statewide utilities, such as railroads and electric power companies.
3. Occupation and business license taxes.
4. Permit fees.
5. Inspection fees.
6. Fines.
7. Parking meter receipts.
8. Dog and bicycle licenses.
9. Sewer connection and sewer use fees.

[2] The fiscal year for most cities ends on June 30.

[3] Other common names are Ways and Means Committee and Finance, Revenue, and Taxation Committee.

[4] Several states no longer tax personal property in the form of stocks and bonds, bank deposits, household furniture, and inventories held by businesses, but substitute an income tax as a better measure of ability to pay.

10. Admission taxes.
11. Sales taxes (a few cities).
12. Hotel room occupancy.
13. Income taxes (a few cities).

In most states, the cities also receive an allocation of certain state-collected taxes, such as taxes on gasoline and alcoholic beverages and general sales taxes. These grants are spent for streets, schools, and social welfare.

Fixing the tax rate: After the City Council has estimated the receipts from all sources other than from real and personal property and has determined the total amount which will be spent, it fixes the tax rate on real and personal property high enough to yield the required revenues. This means that it divides the amount of revenue to be derived from real and personal property taxation by the assessed valuation of all real and personal property. Thus, if the amount of revenue to be derived from real and personal property taxation is $625,000 and the assessed valuation of all such property in the city is $25,000,000, the tax rate will be 25 mills ($625,000 ÷ $25,000,000 = $0.025) on each dollar of assessed valuation. This is often expressed as $2.50 on each $100 of assessed valuation. Thus, the owner of property assessed at $10,000 would pay a tax of $250.

A specimen budget: On page 490 is the budget of a small city (which operates its own electric, gas, and water utilities with some profit to the city and, therefore, with some tax saving for property owners).

> Exercise: What percentage of its receipts does this city receive from state subventions and grants?

Reporting the Budget Formulation

Newspapers sometimes report the hearings of the Finance Committee when heads of departments appear to defend their requests.

City Budget Body Listens to Protests

The Finance Committee of the City Council last night heard strong protests as they sought to keep intact their announced reduction of $522,750 in next year's budget.

This cut amounts to 5 mills in the tax rate.

Health Director E. J. Bauer, protesting the cut of $12,232, asserted that the duty of his department was to

SPECIMEN CITY BUDGET

Receipts

Balance on hand, July 1, last year	$ 139,635.38
Taxes:	
Real and personal property	828,796.82
Delinquent taxes	13,981.90
City utilities and properties	420,011.14
Solvent credits and payments in lieu	2,061.66
Licenses and permits	21,391.52
Fines and penalties	135,251.50
Rental and sale of property	62,953.93
Interest on current deposits	148,618.13
State subventions and grants	970,842.14
Libraries	16,434.69
Recreation and golf course	210,292.38
Public works and engineering	82,061.62
Service charges	124,924.95
Other receipts not classified	20,427.94
Utilities net gain to General Fund	685,674.56
Other transfers	1,314,170.72
Total receipts and balance	$5,197,530.98

Disbursements

General city	$ 457,392.85
Sundry	251,875.81
Retirement	114,512.34
Street lighting	136,768.73
Hospitalization of citizens	37,378.68
Police department	409,439.85
Fire department	407,426.37
Animal shelter	26,514.28
Library	227,290.63
Recreation and golf course	357,367.55
Public works and engineering	126,539.87
Streets	1,211,996.62
Parks	607,589.96
Lot cleaning and outside services	51,631.65
Bay lands and harbor	141,453.30
Building inspector	56,162.70
Transfers to reserves	519,000.00
Balance on hand, June 30, this year	57,190.39
Total disbursements and balance	$5,197,530.98

save lives, not money. He told the members they were assuming a grave responsibility.

Dr. Bauer declared that although he spent six months studying the budget requests of his department, the Finance Committee had slashed it in a few minutes.

"It's all right to talk economy," he declared, "but you can't budget disease."

President J. W. Torgeson, of the Police Commission, said the Police Department would try to get along with ten of the thirty-nine extra officers requested, but asserted the department would be handicapped.

The Committee stood firm, however. D. E. Coleman, chairman, voiced the sentiments of the economy bloc when he declared, "We have followed a consistent policy of cutting out non-essentials."

He added, "These budget cuts are not going to paralyze any department. We must keep the tax rate down."

He smiled when he commented on Mayor Johnson's reported remark that "Any nitwit can cut a budget."

"Well, he's a new mayor," he said.

Only two other departments—parks and public works—are scheduled to appear before the Committee.

When the City Council adopts the budget it fixes the tax rate on real and personal property.

Tax Rate Rises Only 2 Cents; Rate Is $1.74

The City Council last night adopted a $2,651,817 budget for the next fiscal year and fixed the tax rate at $1.74 for each $100 of assessed valuation.

The budget is $31,971 higher than for the current year, and the tax rate is two cents higher.

The increase represents an additional service on bonds voted during this year. The general fund rate will remain at $1.62, but the rate allocated to the bond fund will be twelve cents instead of ten cents.

Since the county and school tax rates will total $3.45, the total general property tax rate to be paid in equal installments next November and next April will be $5.19.

For typical valuations of local homes the tax to be paid will be as follows:

$ 5,000 valuation ... $ 259.50
  8,000 valuation ...   415.20
 10,000 valuation ...   519.00
 20,000 valuation ... 1038.00

A detailed summary of the budget appears on page 7.

Borrowing

The charter of a city or a state statute sets a limit on the city's capacity to borrow. This is always some percentage of the city's assessed valuation—usually 5 to 10 per cent.

When a city needs short-term funds—as when, near the end of the fiscal year its funds are low and next year's taxes have not as yet been collected—it issues *tax anticipation warrants*. These are short-term notes which the city sells to a bank and which are secured by taxes yet to be collected.

For public improvements, a city either issues bonds or adopts a "pay-as-you-go" plan. The latter system consists of the citizens' voting an extra and special tax for a limited term of years and the city's spending these receipts as they are received. A more usual practice is to issue *serial* bonds; that is, to retire a portion of the bond issue annually, as when each year $10,000 of a twenty-year bond issue of $200,000 matures.[5]

The term for which bonds are issued is related to the longevity of the improvement for which their proceeds are spent. Thus, street repair bonds should be of a shorter term than bonds issued for the construction of a hospital.

The procedure connected with the issuance of bonds is as follows. First, the City Council passes a *resolution of intent* to call an election to submit the question to the voters. If, in the referendum, the voters authorize the bond issue,[6] the council may (but is not required to) have bonds printed to sell to the highest bidder. The bonds, when issued, are purchased by security firms which sell them to the public at a slight profit. In some instances, the bidder fixes the rate of interest and offers a certain price. In other instances, the city fixes the rate of interest and the bidders offer a certain "premium" above par.

---

[5] A less common practice is to issue *sinking fund* bonds. This means that the city deposits a certain amount annually in a sinking fund which earns interest so that all of the bonds can be retired at the end of the term for which they were issued.

[6] The size of the majority required in such elections varies in the different states.

Street Bonds Sold For $401 Premium

A premium of $401 will be paid the city for $230,000 of street improvement bonds as the result of bidding yesterday.

The Union Trust Company was the successful bidder on the 2½ per cent fifteen-year bonds.

Five bidders made offers to the city bond committee but three quickly dropped out. Mayor Thomas Grumm announced at the opening of the meeting that no bid would be accepted of less than par and accrued interest [i.e., for interest between the date of issue and the date of delivery, about eighteen days].

Schloss & Duborg began the bidding with an offer of $225,400. The bids rose then until all but the Union Trust Company had dropped out.

The bidding indicated a less favorable bond market than last spring when $800,000 of 2½ per cent bonds were sold for a premium of $11,400.

The bond committee—composed of Mayor Grumm, City Treasurer Morris Edelstein and Councilman Fred Dickey, chairman of the Council's finance committee—will recommend acceptance of the successful bid when the Council meets tonight.

Bonds of a city are usually "general obligation" bonds. This means the security behind them is the taxing power of the city: in a suit by the owner of a defaulted bond, the courts can require the city to levy special taxes to pay the bondholder. In a few instances, cities can issue "revenue bonds," as when the city owns a water works and issues bonds for the extension of plant and mains with the only security being a lien on the earnings. Such bonds bear a higher interest rate than general obligation bonds.

A few cities have avoided holding bond issue elections by having a private citizen or corporation construct an improvement (e.g., a building) and lease it to the city. This is more expensive than a bond issue because the lessor, who borrows money to construct the improvement, has to pay a much higher interest rate than does the city.

As serial bonds fall due, the council authorizes payment to the holders, and the surrendered bonds are burned. This is called "bond redemption."

Special Assessment Bonds

For the construction of streets and sidewalks and for some other purposes, the adjacent property owner must pay—because the improvement adds value to his property. The city, however, takes responsibility for the construction. The charges levied on the property are called *special assessments*. Special assessment districts are also established for the construction of parking lots, boulevards, and ornamental street lighting, the assessments being levied on property in the area which will benefit from the improvements.

The City Council gives notice of intent to construct the improvement and holds a hearing for the property owners concerned. If the council decides to proceed, it issues special assessment bonds—usually of ten-year maturity—and pays them to the contractor. The contractor sells them to a bond dealer at a discount, receiving cash. The city then bills the property owner annually until the bonds have been retired. The statutes vary as to whether special assessment bonds are obligations of the city (i.e., of all the taxpayers) or only of the property owners benefited.

Henning Road Job Will Cost $54,117

The low bid of $54,117 by the Workman Construction Company for installation of improvements on Henning Road was accepted last night by the City Council.

Improvements to be installed include street paving, curbing, gutters, sidewalks, and a storm drain.

Before awarding the contract, the Council heard several protests from Henning Road property owners who asserted the cost of the improvements was excessive.

The main complaint was that at the time the property owners signed the petition requesting the improvements they were told the costs would not exceed $7.20 a running front foot. Later they were told their assessment would be $10.26 a front foot.

City Engineer Dunlop Bristol explained that the $7.20 figure had been the price quoted in preliminary estimates. The storm sewer, he said, had been added to the improvement later and was responsible for the increase in cost.

He said that since the storm sewer would have to be installed eventually it would be cheaper to do it now before the paving has been laid.

Between Sessions Reporting

Although the Council meets only once a week—in small cities often only once a month—the newspaper reporter devotes much of his time to inquiring and writing about matters that are either before the council or that may come before it for consideration. The various committees of the council meet between sessions, and the reporter talks with the chairman or members at various times. When a committee conducts a hearing, the reporter attends it. Since the various boards and commissions are also concerned with some of the business that will come before the council, the newspaper reports their business in the same way that it does the committees of the council.

Proposed Cardroom Ordinance Defeated

An attempt to revive the proposed ordinance to legalize cardrooms here was killed quickly yesterday.

The City Council Police Committee voted 2 to 1 to table the measure indefinitely.

The two were Max Groth and Alfred Hayes. The dissenting vote was cast by Bennett Heath, committee chairman.

Heath had reintroduced the ordinance, which had lain pigeon-holed in the committee since last August.

A number of tenderloin figures—former cardroom employees and habitués—attended the hearing. Luigi Mancuso, president of the bartenders' union, spoke in favor of the ordinance.

District Attorney Louis Briggs appeared to state that his office is opposed to "any modification of our present laws". . . .

In writing about municipal legislation the reporter will find that many news stories continue over a period of several weeks. In connection with some very important matters which involve policy, such as the renewal of public utility franchises or the local transportation problem, the story may run for a year or for several years. The reporter, of course, should become thoroughly familiar with all the questions at issue and should dig beneath the surface to learn what influences are at work on each side of an important question of policy. He not only should be thoroughly acquainted with the different interest groups in the city and with the motives of the leaders, but should also study a question from an academic viewpoint. He should obtain copies of the particular draft ordinances and of statistics bearing upon the particular projects. He should be familiar with many of the details of the current budget and of past budgets and of the periodic reports issued by the departments and boards.

The city hall reporter who becomes an expert in his field is one of the most important men on the newspaper's staff. Since he knows more than any one else about the realities of city government, he can influence policy either in his own articles or by the advice he supplies to his editors. On some newspapers the city hall reporter writes some of the editorials that relate to city government.

MUNICIPAL ADMINISTRATION

The administration of city government is assigned to ten or fewer departments on a functional basis. The most common functions are these: public safety, finance, public works, public health and sanitation, law, planning and zoning, public utilities, and education.

Public Safety

Responsibility for public safety is usually assigned to a commission called the Board of Public Safety, the Board of Police and Fire Commissioners, or a similar name. The activities of this board were described in Chapter 19.

Finance

The trend in city government is to appoint a chief financial officer, usually called a *controller,* and to make various fiscal officials responsible to him. In some cities, however, the various fiscal officials are independent of each other, and a few are elected. In such situations, the controller is little more than an auditor.

In those cities in which the controller is the chief financial officer, he allows or disallows every requisition issued by a spending department or officer. This means that he may disallow any intended expenditure for which funds were not specifically appropriated in the budget, and should allow those intended expenditures for which funds have been specifically appropriated as items in the budget. When a department needs funds for which the budget has not provided, it must request supplementary funds from the mayor's contingent fund or from the council's unassigned fund.

The *city treasurer* disburses city funds, usually on the approval of the controller. He is the custodian of the city's monies, including the retirement funds for employees. He also attends to the details that relate to bonds, including their sale, servicing, and redemption.

The *tax collector* takes the assessment roll from the assessor and "extends" it. That is, after the council has fixed the general property tax, the tax collector multiplies the rate (or aggregate of rates when he also collects school and special district taxes) by the valuation of each parcel of property and sends a bill to the taxpayer. He later makes a settlement with the council, including a statement of the taxes that are delinquent at the time of the settlement.

The *assessor* is often an elected official. The procedures that relate to assessment were described in Chapter 31.

Public Works

The administration of public works is assigned to several different officials, chief of whom are the *city engineer* and the *street superintendent*. Others are the *building inspector* and the *electrical inspector*. This department draws plans for and arranges for the construction and repair of streets, bridges, viaducts, wharves, and such major improvements as sewage disposal plants. The announcement of plans or contracts for widening, repaving, and constructing streets, for the laying of sewers, the installation of traffic signals, and the erection of street signs are usually worth reporting.

Main Street Repaving Contracts to Be Let

Next Tuesday the city will open bids and let contracts for the repaving of Main street from Fifth to Ninth streets, Harry C. Morris, director of public works, said today.

The contract will include a bonus clause to speed the work in the downtown district as much as possible. He said the work would start in two weeks and require nine weeks.

A contract will also be awarded this week in the two-year program of replacing street signs, Mr. Morris said. This contract will be for signs to be installed in the area bounded by Madison, Jefferson, Twentieth, and Thirty-first streets.

Of interest to many readers are the daily announcement of building permits issued and of monthly reports on local building.

New Medical Clinic Will Cost $150,000

A building permit for the erection of a $150,000 medical clinic building at 680 Northfield avenue was issued by the building inspector yesterday.

The permit was issued to Dr. M. L. Brown, Dr. Herbert Carter, and Dr. Simpson Glass.

The builder will be Orland and Hartford.

The structure will be of modern type architecture and will provide twenty-five rooms.

Other permits issued yesterday. . . .

July Building Was Over $1,000,000

July was a big month for local building.

The building inspector's office issued 206 permits for a total indicated value of $1,089,200.

Of that total, 59 permits were for new residences having a total contract valuation of $672,250.

Five business building permits were taken out for a value of $148,000. Five permits for alterations and repairs were issued, the contract cost being $43,365.

Other permits were for:

11	Garages	$ 15,200
14	Business alterations	100,000
2	Apartment houses	96,000
3	School alterations	950
61	Miscellaneous	11,470

Health and Sanitation

The city *health officer* heads a department of inspectors, nurses, bacteriologists, and chemists. They inspect milk, meats at local slaughterhouses, restaurants, and plumbing. They may recommend the condemnation of unsanitary dwellings and certain other structures. They supervise the operation of the city hospital in those communities that exclusively operate their own hospital. They conduct health centers, and supply visiting nurses in certain indigent cases. The department records vital statistics, including the incidence of contagious diseases, and has the authority to quarantine certain premises. The department also conducts health education services. The office is a source of interesting news during an epidemic. From time to time the department issues vital statistics reports. Seasonally, it issues precautions and directions that are in the nature of health advice. Some cities do not have departments of health but depend upon the county department.

23 Bitten by Dogs Here Last Month

The local epidemic of rabies, the worst on record as shown by January statistics, has reached a new danger point, Health Officer F. S. Malloy said yesterday.

The war on stray dogs, he added, will be relentlessly waged for probably a month longer.

During the month ending yesterday, twenty-three persons were bitten, eleven of whom are now receiving the Pasteur treatment.

Of thirty-two dogs killed and sent to the state health laboratory for examination, twenty-eight were found to be infected. Approximately one hundred dogs which were captured and taken to the city dog pound have been killed.

Do's and Don'ts For Swimmers

Precautions for bathers to prevent the passing of certain diseases were suggested yesterday by Dr. Henry Kendrick, city health officer.

With the swimming season approaching its peak, Dr. Kendrick points out that bathers who overdo this recreation may lower their resistance against disease. He warned especially against staying too long in the water.

His do's and don'ts for the protection of swimmers are as follows. . . .

Law

The chief legal officer of a city is the *city attorney* (sometimes called the *corporation counsel* or *city solicitor*). He advises the City Council and city officials; drafts ordinances, leases, and contracts; issues opinions at the request of officials as to their rights and duties; and represents the city in all civil legal actions, such as personal injury suits, eminent domain suits, and the abatement of nuisances. He sits with the council in its meetings to advise the members on legal points and precedents. He is often, therefore, a source of information to reporters about the details of certain proposed ordinances. In some cities, the city attorney also prosecutes misdemeanor violations of city ordinances.

City Considers Fight On Rate Increase

City Attorney Reuben Greenwood said today he was waiting for certain reports before recommending that the city contest the rate increase requested by the telephone company.

He has asked the office of the city rate engineer to prepare a list of essential rate studies along with a cost budget for them.

Twenty years ago the city spent $120,000 in contesting a rate increase the telephone company had requested of the state Public Utilities Commission.

The increase now asked would cost local telephone subscribers $2,000,000 annually.

Planning and Zoning

Many cities have adopted a *master plan* to control the use of land within their boundaries. The plan is made by an appointed *Planning Commission* assisted by a *director of planning*. Members of the commission are usually business and professional men, architects, real estate brokers, and clubwomen. The commission, first, decides the objectives of the plan; this often means deciding whether industrial, commercial, or residential objectives are to be emphasized, depending upon the economic base of the community. In accordance with the objectives, the commission develops an official map which specifies the location of existing and future parks, thoroughfares, public buildings, transportation routes, and the areas for residential, commercial, and industrial buildings. The plan sometimes provides for slum clearance and urban renewal of certain areas.

Zoning is the division of the city into areas for which a certain land use is specified, together with regulations as to building height, setback, and parking space. Within certain areas, for example, only single-family dwelling units may be constructed and in others multifamily units are permitted. In some areas neighborhood business is permitted and in other areas commercial, light industrial, and heavy industrial uses are permitted. Some cities have adopted zoning ordinances without having, first, adopted a master plan; generally, this is undesirable.

After a zoning ordinance has been adopted, some persons want permission for a *variance* from the ordinance; for example, to construct a neighborhood business in a residential area in which it is forbidden or to construct a high-rise apartment building without adequate provision for setback and parking facilities. Such an applicant must, first, apply to the *building inspector* for a building permit. When the permit is denied, the applicant may appeal. Some cities have a Board of Zoning Appeals or a Zoning Commission which has authority to grant variances; in other cities the City Council sits as an appeals board. Citizens who oppose a variance often attend and participate in the hearing held by the appeals board.

Duplex Rezoning Debate Is on Again

The Planning and Zoning Commission yesterday permitted Holland Hamilton to withdraw "without prejudice" his application for rezoning of a section of the Shorewood high income district in which he wishes to build seven duplex houses. Hamilton's application has been denied by the Commission four times. Under the law, he could not present it for another year, if it were rejected this time.

His attorney, Willard Creighton, asked to withdraw the petition "without prejudice" because of a technical error.

Attorneys for the residents of the district, where only single family dwellings are now permitted, argued yesterday that the application should be allowed to be only withdrawn "with prejudice," thus stalling Hamilton for another year.

The decision yesterday, however, means the Commission will have to hold another public hearing.

At previous meetings, residents have asserted they bought property in this neighborhood on the assumption it could be devoted only to expensive single family dwellings. The construction of duplexes, they said, would depress their property values.

A zoning change to permit the First Christian church to build on the northwest corner of Main and College streets was approved.

The Commission also approved a waiver of setback lines on Gaines street for the new Masonic Temple.

Urban renewal: Since the passage of Title I of the Housing Act of 1949 the federal government's Urban Renewal Administration has supplied financial support and technical advice to cities for urban renewal. Urban renewal calls for the elimination of slums and blighted areas and their replacement with new buildings, wider streets, and other improvements. A city establishes an urban renewal or redevelopment agency and applies to the Urban Renewal Administration for a grant to pay for the preparation of a renewal plan. After the plan has been approved, the Urban Renewal Administration lends funds to the city to pay for the acquisition of land, the demolition of buildings, and the cost, if any, of relocating the residents of the area. The city acquires the property by purchase or by condemnation proceedings. The city uses its own funds to pay for any necessary streets, sewers, or other improvements. The city then sells the cleared land to a private developer for a reuse that is deemed appropriate. Generally the difference between the sales price of the land to the private developer and the acquisition and other costs paid by the city creates a deficit. The federal agency absorbs up to two-thirds (up to three-fourths in cities of less than 50,000 population) of the deficit, and the city absorbs the remainder.[7]

Renewal Plan Is Sent to U.S.

A huge new Western Addition slum clearance project was forwarded to the federal Urban Renewal Administration yesterday.

The proposal would turn Turk street into a six-lane expressway and widen Fulton street to accommodate four lanes of traffic in each direction.

The government would be expected

[7] See T. F. Johnson, *et al., Renewing America's Cities* (Institute for Social Science Research, Washington, D.C., 1962). For a criticism of some aspects of urban renewal, see M. Anderson, *The Federal Bulldozer: A Critical Analysis of Urban Renewal, 1949–62* (Cambridge, Mass., 1964).

to make a cash grant of $25 million and a loan of $67 million. The city's share of $13.7 million would be met by construction of streets and other public works. . . .

Renewal Job Let By San Francisco

A New York realty development concern yesterday was awarded the construction contract for the major part of an urban renewal program.

The company, Dworman Associates, will erect six apartment buildings on a 12-acre site in a renewal area that has been designated as the "Western Addition" by the San Francisco Redevelopment Agency. The building site is at Post and Geary streets near Market street.

Slum-Clearance Suits Are Filed

The Oakland Redevelopment Agency last week filed 50 eminent domain suits against owners of properties in an 11-block area south of Eighth street and west of Brush street.

The suits, filed in superior court, were the first of 140 such suits to be filed in the next two weeks for the slum clearance project.

Half of the area now is residential, 30 per cent of it industrial and the remainder commercial properties.

Public Utilities

Many cities operate a water works and some cities operate transportation, electric, or gas utilities. A commission is usually responsible for their operation. The commission, called by various names, usually appoints a chief administrative official, such as the *superintendent of water works,* and his office is the main news source except for news about changes of rates.

Education

In some cities, education is an independent activity not directly related to the municipal government. In these instances, the Board of Education, usually elected, has power, under the statutes, to fix its own tax rate and to certify it to the city for tax collection. In other cities, the members of the Board of Education are appointed by the mayor.

The matters reported by newspapers relate to the budget and the tax rate, new buildings, new site purchases, appointment of teachers and administrators, and curriculum changes. Some newspapers have an education editor who writes about teaching methods, educational objectives, and other matters of interest to parents.

The Mayor

Because the mayor has responsibility on the policy level and because he usually has considerable power of appointment to boards and commissions, he is the most important single news source at the city hall. Mayors of large cities have regular press conferences and their office issues frequent press releases. The comment of the mayor on the actions and pronouncements of other officials is often requested by reporters.

The mayor appoints various temporary advisory bodies of lay citizens in connection with certain problems, and their meetings are as frequently worth reporting as are those of the regular official bodies.

Mayor Vetoes Move To Transfer Funds

Mayor Scott Orwell yesterday vetoed a resolution passed by the City Council to transfer water department "surplus" funds to the general operating fund and thus reduce the property tax rate.

The Council had acted on an estimate by the Controller that $774,665 in surplus would accrue at the end of the fiscal year. Members of the water works commission, however, have stated that the so-called surplus would be spent for additions and improvements in the water system.

In his veto message, the mayor said there is no one more sincerely desirous than himself of limiting the tax rate.

"But I cannot approve," he added, "any hasty and ill-considered device in an attempt to extract funds from the water department which do not form, in reality, a surplus."

Mayor Lauds Negro College Fund Drive

Mayor Scott Orwell yesterday proclaimed July 7 as United Negro College Fund Day in Sylvania.

The day observance will be the highlight of the national campaign to raise funds for the support of thirty-two private Negro colleges throughout the country.

"These private colleges provide the only higher educational facilities for Negroes in many states," the mayor said.

Aiding the Citizen

Government in large cities is so complex that the inarticulate citizen with a complaint does not know where to go for relief or service. To assist these persons, several newspapers have undertaken to present their complaints to the appropriate city official. Scripps-Howard and other newspapers appoint a staff member—often the city hall reporter—and call him "Mr. Fix-It," "Trouble-shooter," or "Lemme Doit." In this way, newspapers present to the appropriate city official complaints about garbage removal, street repairs, street lighting, loose manhole covers, flat wheels on street cars, smoking chimneys, fire hazards, wrong street names, and abusive policemen. Newspapers also answer numerous inquiries, such as the date that certain taxes are due and what city regulations are with respect to this and that.

Exercise: *1.* Obtain a copy of the annual printed report of your city government and note the differences between the organization of that government and the organization described in this textbook.
2. What is the limit of bonded indebtedness that your city is permitted to incur in percentage of assessed valuation? How near is the city now to this limit?
3. Obtain from a local newspaper or from the city clerk a copy of the current budget and note the sources of revenue. What percentage of revenue is derived from general property taxation? What is the per capita amount spent on the public library?
4. Which is better from the point of view of the city: a bond issue or a pay-as-you-go plan?
5. Improve the following sentence: Councilman Jones made a motion to refer the petition to the committee on public works.

CHAPTER 33

The Federal Building[1]

In every important city the federal government has constructed one or more buildings to provide local federal officials with offices and the federal court with courtrooms. In the smaller cities where the activities of the national government are not many, the citizens frequently refer to this building as the Post Office Building; in some of the cities on the coasts and in inland cities that are ports of entry, the building is popularly known as the Customs House. Ordinarily, however, it is known as the Federal Building. So many and so varied are the activities of the federal government that in the larger cities one building is not sufficient to house all of the local federal administrative offices, and the national government has had to rent various office buildings and warehouses.

In explaining the chief news sources in the Federal Building, this chapter lists the activities and duties of the various officials and illustrates some of them with appropriate news stories. The officials are grouped according to the departments of government at Washington in which they belong. From time to time, however, Congress shifts some of the units from department to department, and it is not always correct to assume that a particular unit has a permanent classification. Those emergency agencies which are deemed of a temporary nature are not described here. The reader who wishes to know about them should consult the current *United States Government Organization Manual*.

POST OFFICE DEPARTMENT[2]

The Postmaster

The head of the postal service in each city is the *postmaster*. He is always a local citizen. Announcements of innovations in service, new postal regu-

[1] The functions of the federal law enforcement agencies which investigate major crimes were discussed in Chap. 19.
[2] Functions of postal inspectors were discussed in Chap. 19.

lations, new postal routes, auctions of unclaimed parcel post merchandise, and monthly reports of postal receipts are furnished by the postmaster. Some of these announcements come from Washington but are released for local publication by the local postal officials. These announcements concern everything from a new commemorative stamp to a notice that mail formerly addressed to Stalino in the Ukraine should now be addressed to Donetsk.

Most of the announcements regarding local mail service come from the *superintendent of mails* or the postmaster. This official announces changes in carriers' routes, times of delivery, extra-delivery zones, and extension of delivery.

New Postal Routes To Serve South Side

Twice daily foot delivery service on two postal routes south of Tenth st. and east of Union ave., which are now served once daily as mounted routes, will be started when the new post office station on Union ave. near Seventh st. opens early next month.

Postmaster Jerry Shields said the two new routes to be converted to foot delivery are located within the area bounded by Union ave., Tenth st., Brundage Lane and Lakeview ave.

In some large cities the division and district *superintendents of railway mail service* and the *superintendents of air postal transport* are sources of news under some circumstances, as in a train robbery or a strike or threatened strike of railway or air line employees.

DEPARTMENT OF THE TREASURY[3]

Bureau of Customs

For the collection of import duties, the prevention of smuggling, and other duties, the Bureau of Customs maintains forty-six district offices in the continental United States, each headed by a *collector of customs*. Goods may be imported from foreign countries only at "ports of entry." Some of these are in inland cities. The collector supervises a corps of appraisers and inspectors who are civil service employees. Goods from foreign countries

[3] Activities of the Secret Service, the Customs Agency Service, the Intelligence Division of the Internal Revenue Service, the Alcohol and Tobacco Tax Division of the Internal Revenue Service, the Bureau of Narcotics, and the Coast Guard Intelligence Division were discussed in Chap. 19.

destined for inland cities are shipped "under bond" by express, mail, freight, or on baggage checks and released after inspection at the port of entry. For the convenience of the public there are also established in some of the smaller cities "ports of delivery" superintended by *deputy collectors* or *surveyors.* In Wisconsin, for example, Milwaukee is a port of entry, and ports of delivery are established at Kenosha, Racine, Sheboygan, and LaCrosse. Some of the goods received at the ports are of such unusual nature or are so rare that their mere description merits a news story. Frequently the collector confiscates contraband goods. On certain dates he sells confiscated and unclaimed goods and goods on which the import duty has not been paid. At times he causes the arrest of persons suspected of violating the customs regulations. The official source for this kind of news is usually the *appraiser,* who is a subordinate official in the collector's office.

This bureau also handles the registry, enrollment, and licensing of vessels and the entrance and clearance of vessels and aircraft. It regulates vessels in the coasting and fishing trades and foreign vessels in territorial waters and investigates compliance with navigation laws.

Customs Fails to Sell Wine Shipment

Collector of Customs William Himstead will try again to sell the 1,161 gallons of Portuguese wine which failed to sell yesterday, he said today.

The collector has held the wine for four years because of $10,545 of unpaid taxes.

No bids were received at the public sale yesterday because the law prohibits sale for less than the tax and requires that the wine be sold in one 484-case lot.

If no bids are received at the next sale, the wine will be poured into the sewers.

Internal Revenue Service

Federal taxes levied within the United States, as distinct from taxes levied upon merchandise imported into the country, are collected by the Internal Revenue Service. Within the United States are about sixty districts. The chief official of the district is the *district collector of internal revenue,* who is assisted by various deputy collectors and clerks. He collects income, estate, gift, excise, and employment taxes. Monthly reports of tax collections in certain classes, such as taxes on tobacco, are released by this office to newspapers and are of interest because they indicate the trend of business in certain industries.

The *Income Tax Unit* of the collector's office is a source of news, especially in the period from January 1 to April 15, when returns are being filed. Newspapers perform a meritorious public service by explaining the complex process of filling out income tax returns. Statistics as to the number of returns filed and the amount of taxes collected are released by this unit.

The Internal Revenue Service frequently files tax liens on the assets of certain individual and corporate taxpayers to assure collection of the judgment it anticipates winning in suits against these taxpayers. These are called "jeopardy assessments." The seized assets are sometimes sold at an advertised public sale. The Internal Revenue Service welcomes publicity about these actions which they regard as warnings to all taxpayers.

U.S. Seizes Assets Of Baseball Club

RICHMOND, Va.—The federal Internal Revenue Service today seized the assets of the Richmond Virginians baseball club of the International League.

The club's assets will be sold to satisfy a $79,218 tax claim. They include the franchise, 18 player contracts and miscellaneous equipment, such as uniforms, bats, balls, and catcher's masks.

Back taxes owed are admissions taxes and social security withholding taxes.

United States Coast Guard

In time of peace the Coast Guard operates under the Department of the Treasury, but becomes a branch of the military service in time of war. It maintains several stations on the coasts, lakes, and rivers of the United States and operates several cutters and airplanes. Its main functions are (1) to operate as a federal maritime police force, (2) to save life and property by rescue and assistance on the high seas and in territorial waters, (3) to guard the safety and efficiency of the merchant marine, and (4) to maintain navigation aids. Its functions as a law enforcement agency were discussed on pages 300–301.

As a rescue and assistance agency it: renders assistance to vessels and aircraft in distress and rescues persons; engages in flood relief work; and removes or destroys derelicts and wrecks.

As an agency to maintain the safety and efficiency of the merchant marine, it: investigates marine disasters; regulates the transportation of explosives on vessels; licenses officers, pilots, seamen, and motorboat operators; inspects and licenses hulls, boilers, and safety equipment of vessels; and enforces laws that relate to the protection and welfare of merchant seamen and to lights, signals, speed, movement, and anchorage of vessels in harbors.

As an agency to aid navigation on the sea and in the air, it maintains lighthouses, lightships, buoys, radio beacons, and radio-direction finder stations.

U.S. Coast Guard Rescues Woman

LOUISVILLE—A woman who identified herself as Mrs. Earl Medford, 42, of 1478 South Third st., was rescued from the Ohio river at 7:45 o'clock Tuesday evening by Captain Walter Farrell, in charge of the Coast Guard station, and Surfman Harry LeFever.

They plunged into the water after she had been carried some 60 feet from the shore. . . .

Both Skippers Say They Watched Radar

SAN FRANCISCO—The freighters Hawaiian Pilot and Jacob Luckenbach tracked each other by radar almost up to the moment they collided off the Golden Gate early Tuesday—and neither skipper expected the collision.

That was their testimony yesterday as the Coast Guard began its Maritime Board of Investigation hearing on the crash, which sank the Luckenbach but took no lives.

Quiet, graying Captain Walter J. Norberg of the Pilot told the board he had changed course but maintained normal 17-knot speed until he saw the Luckenbach's green starboard light crossing his bow, possibly a half-mile ahead. . . .

DEPARTMENT OF JUSTICE[4]

Naturalization

The *Immigration and Naturalization Service* administers the laws relating to the admission, exclusion, and deportation of aliens, and the naturalization of aliens lawfully resident in the United States. It also registers and fingerprints aliens as is required by law. Except for naturalization, these activities were discussed on pages 298–299.

Aliens apply for citizenship to clerks of any court of record—either state or federal. Certain staff members of the Immigration and Naturalization Service conduct an investigation of the background of the petitioner, and one of them acts as examiner in a preliminary hearing on the petition. Aliens who satisfy the requirements of the examiner are certified to the court of naturalization. The court usually sets aside certain days in each term as naturalization days. On the day appointed the alien appears in court and may be further examined by the judge. When accepted he takes an oath in which he renounces allegiance to his former sovereign and pledges allegiance to the United States. Sometimes the chief interest in such sessions is the character of some of the aliens: a prominent alien who had not been naturalized, such as a well-known actor, athlete, or member of the nobility. Sometimes the news interest is in the fact that an applicant is denied naturalization on account of his political philosophy or criminal record; the service makes field investigations of all applicants for citizenship. Frequently the interest is in the character of the questions asked and the answers received.

This Alien Had the Correct Answer

BRUNSWICK, Ga.—Nick Zissis yesterday failed his test on the United States constitution in naturalization proceedings when he was questioned by the examiner for the Immigration and Naturalization Service.

Federal Judge Frank M. Scarlett, however, said: "Let me examine him. I've known Nick for 35 years."

"Who do you think was the greatest of all Americans?" Judge Scarlett asked.

---

[4] The activities of the United States attorney, United States marshal, the Federal Bureau of Investigation, and (in part) the Immigration and Naturalization Service were discussed in Chap. 19.

"General Robert E. Lee," Zissis replied.

"I'm convinced this man is qualified to become a citizen," the Judge ruled.

DEPARTMENT OF COMMERCE

The Weather Bureau maintains more than three hundred local offices at cities and airports in the continental United States. All of these distribute weather information. From thirteen district forecast centers state forecasts are issued, and from about seventy-five of the local offices forecasts for smaller areas are issued. A thirty-six-hour forecast is issued each day at 10 a.m. and is revised about three times during the succeeding twenty-four hours. In addition, thirty offices issue a daily weather map and a daily bulletin which reports weather data from other cities, such as temperatures. Special warnings of storms and cold waves are issued when they are expected to occur. At noon on Tuesdays and Thursdays a general weather forecast is issued for the ensuing five days.

The Weather Bureau supplies the newspaper with statistics on rainfall, temperature, wind velocity, and flood stage. Newspaper readers have an intense interest in weather phenomena and farmers and many business men desire accurate information regarding the influence of weather conditions on crops. Records of the temperature for every hour of the day, of rainfall every day, and other information have been kept by the local stations since 1880.

Writing the Weather Story

Some important newspapers carry nearly a column of weather data every day, and at least eight or nine times a year a weather story is of enough importance and interest to justify a banner headline on most newspapers.

In a news story about a cold spell, the probable duration is a necessary element. The Weather Bureau, in so far as it can, will furnish such information. The reader also wants a comparison with other spells. Another desirable element is a table of hourly temperatures which the reporter can adapt to narrative form if he wishes; the following news story is an example:

> Christmas dawned Friday with the temperature falling. By 10 a.m. the temperature was 4 below zero. It mounted a few degrees during the afternoon, touching a maximum of 8 degrees at 3 p.m., when it started to fall again and continued downward

throughout the night, reaching zero at midnight.

The lowest temperature, 7 below zero, was reached at 7:45 a.m., about the time those who had to work Saturday were en route to offices and shops.

The "cause" of the cold wave, storm, or hot spell is often worth reporting. The reporter who writes the weather story can learn the elements of meteorology from one of several popularly-written books and pamphlets[5] and from conversation with the local meteorologists. Although he will not usually have the space to define such terms as "low pressure area" and "cold front," the reporter can usually write the story in such a way that the uninformed reader will understand the explanation from the context. The following excerpts are examples of how the reporter explains a cold wave and a hot spell.

Warmer Weather Is Not Due Until Monday

L. F. Jones, local meteorologist, said the high pressure area was so extensive Saturday and its center was so far northwest that there is little likelihood of warmer weather for this city until sometime Monday.

The cold air of the high pressure area poured into the city all morning, as shown by the ten-mile wind from the northwest.

Weather Man Tells Cause of Hot Spell

The Bay Area's hot spell of the last 36 hours rode in on a warm, gusty wind off the inland mountains, E. L. Felton, chief of the Weather Bureau office, explained yesterday.

Winds from the inland deserts sweep down the mountain slopes, are

---

[5] For example: G. Kimble and R. Bush, *The Weather* (Penguin Books, Inc., New York). The *New York Times* has published a 34-page pamphlet, *The Weather: How and Why*, prepared by A. S. Kussman. The Superintendent of Public Documents, Washington, 25, D.C., will also supply a 20-page pamphlet, *The Weather Bureau*.

> compressed and heated as they pass through valleys and spill hot weather along the coast, he said.
> In addition, it was explained, this northeast wind—created by the clockwise pattern of a high pressure system over the Pacific Northwest—blocked northern California's traditional sea breeze.

The reporter should also tell what the weather does to people and property. Did the spell of weather cause any deaths or prostrations; did it affect epidemics of diseases; did it "cause" furnaces to overheat and start fires; did it damage crops; did it interfere with communication or travel? Information about such matters may be obtained from public utilities, hospitals, police and fire stations, and county farm agents.

> . . . Some tomato crops which were ready for harvesting were injured by the rain, N. M. Norton, county farm adviser, said. Because the crop this year has been slow, the damage should not be great, he added.
> He warned, however, that if the rains continue, considerable damage will be done to hay and grain crops.

The reporter should be careful to use the appropriate terms to describe certain weather phenomena. The Weather Bureau will supply him with the correct definition of such terms as "sleet," "chinook wind," "cloudburst," "tornado," and "squall." Since confusion arises from the use of terms to describe the various kinds of winds, the reporter is advised to use the Beaufort wind-scale, which, in part, is as follows:

> *Calm* is a wind up to one-half of a mile an hour, and smoke rises vertically.
> A *strong breeze* is 25 to 31 miles an hour, and whistles in telephone wires.
> A *moderate gale* is 32 to 38 miles an hour, and sways whole trees.
> A *fresh gale* is 39 to 46 miles an hour, and impedes walking.
> A *strong gale* is 47 to 54 miles an hour, and breaks signs.
> A *whole gale* is 55 to 63 miles an hour, and uproots trees.
> A *storm* is 64 to 75 miles an hour, and does widespread damage.
> A *hurricane* is 75 miles an hour and upward, and causes excessive damage.

Other Department of Commerce Offices

Releases of statistical data which are of interest to business men, shippers, fishermen, and the general public are supplied by these field offices: *Coast and Geodetic Survey* (tide tables, time of rise and setting of sun and moon, and seismological information about earthquakes); *Bureau of the Census* (information about special population censuses conducted at the request of local governments between the decennial censuses); and *Bureau of Public Roads* (information about federally aided highway construction in local areas).

DEPARTMENT OF AGRICULTURE

Forest Service

This service administers 154 national forests in the United States. It has nine regional offices and numerous Forest and Range Experiment Stations. The forester and his assistants are sources of news about accidents (especially to persons on vacation), forest fires, the opening of timber reserves for sale to lumbermen and vacationists, and projects for reforestation. Feature stories are obtainable from forest rangers who patrol the forests.

Lightning Kills Coach and Wife

> Ray Hamilton, football coach of Eureka University, and his wife, Doris, were killed by lightning in the Sequoia National Forest yesterday.
> Dispatcher Lee Skillicorn, of the U.S. Forest Service's North Fork fire station, said the Hamiltons were struck during a pack trip at a place 40 miles north of Huntington Lake.
> The electric storm also caused spot fires. More than 4,000 acres were burned.

The *county agriculture agent,* a representative of the Extension Service, is a source of news about crop conditions. Some newspapers publish a good deal of advisory material for farmers, some of which is supplied by the county extension agent.

DEPARTMENT OF THE INTERIOR

Fish and Wildlife Service

The function of this service is to insure the conservation of wild birds, mammals, and fish for their recreational and economic values. The service issues regulations for hunting and fishing, and federal game wardens, called *game management agents,* enforce them in cooperation with similar state authorities.

Film Director Has Too Many Birds

BODEGA BAY, Calif.—The federals swooped into this lonely, bayside hamlet yesterday to begin a feud with Alfred Hitchcock and his men who are making a movie called "The Birds" near here.

The feuding was over birds—119 live ones and 40 dead ones.

The federals claimed Hitchcock's men had caught way over the limit. Fish and Wildlife Service Agent Marshall Dillon said there were 54 live gulls in the moviemakers' cages, 24 more than agreed upon, and 40 stuffed gulls, 20 more than the agreed total of dead ones.

The birds were confiscated.

Other Department of the Interior Offices

In all of the western states the *Bureau of Reclamation* is a source of news about the planning and construction of dams and reclaimed acreage.

In seventeen states in which the federal government owns lands the *Bureau of Land Management* administers the Homestead Act, the Taylor Grazing Act, and the Minerals Leasing Act. News from this office relates to grazing permits, claims to lands, disposal of unappropriated federal lands, and mineral leases. Fraud is sometimes an element in the claiming of lands.

DEPARTMENT OF LABOR

Bureau of Labor Statistics

This office collects data on wage rates in 77 cities and on wholesale and retail prices in about 50 cities. The data relating to prices of food, clothing, rent, home furnishings, and other items in the "standard family budget" are used to construct a national consumer price index, which is a measure of the cost of living. The data for certain individual cities are released by the regional offices.

Living Costs Rise In Four Coast Cities

SAN FRANCISCO—It cost more in August to live in Seattle, Portland, Los Angeles and San Francisco.

The Bureau of Labor Statistics reported today the rise in the consumers' price index here and in Portland was due primarily to higher food prices.

At Los Angeles and Seattle the boost was due principally to higher rents and house furnishings.

Independent federal agencies which are concerned with labor and which yield news are discussed in Chapter 35.

The *Bureau of Labor Management Reports* has several field offices which investigate financial abuses by labor unions; these also are discussed in Chapter 35.

DEPARTMENT OF THE ARMY

Corps of Engineers

Stationed in many cities are army engineers who are concerned with the dredging, repairing, and construction of harbors and the repairing and construction of dams, locks, bridges, and levees. They make preliminary plans and surveys, prepare specifications, and supervise construction. The planning, construction, and, in some instances, the operation of these public works are very important in a civic sense; news about them is thoroughly reported by the press. The *resident engineer* is often a source of information about floods.

20,000 Homeless in Northwest Floods

PORTLAND, Ore.—Pacific Northwest flood water edged higher today under the impact of warm rains that melted mountain-top snows and sent them plunging into swollen rivers of the Columbia system.

Damage to date is estimated at $20,000,000 and 20,000 persons have been made homeless.

Colonel O. E. Walsh, district army engineer, estimated damage might go higher if turbulent streams in Washington, British Columbia and in other parts of the Northwest continue their rise. He said the Northwest was being dealt one of the heaviest economic blows in its history.

DEPARTMENT OF HEALTH, EDUCATION, AND WELFARE

Food and Drug Administration

This office enforces those federal laws that relate to food, drugs, and cosmetics. It has sixteen district offices and thirty-nine inspection stations that contain laboratories for testing. The inspectors inspect sanitary conditions in factories, raw materials used, and the controls exercised in compounding, processing, packaging, and labeling products destined for interstate shipment. When violations are found the facts are reported to the Department of Justice with a recommendation for seizure, criminal prosecution, or an injunction action in a federal court. News of these actions usually comes from the office of the United States attorney. When the government wishes to seize any article which has been adulterated, the United States attorney files a "libel of information" against the product and, if the court sustains the libel, the article is condemned.

All Thalidomide Samples Located

All samples of the birth-defect-causing drug, thalidomide, issued to 72 doctors in this state on an experimental basis, have been collected or destroyed, it was announced today by McKay McKinnon, Jr., director of the federal Food and Drug Administration.

McKinnon said his organization, working with the state Department of Health, began a physician-to-physician canvass last Friday.

The drug had been sent to 1,200 selected doctors by the manufacturer.

CIVIL AERONAUTICS BOARD

This independent agency is concerned with the safety of air carrier operations, and it grants or denies certificates to airlines to fly specific routes. It yields some important news on the local level because it investigates all aerial accidents and tries to determine their probable cause. Its *Bureau of Safety* has ten field offices and numerous suboffices. After an important accident, an examiner for the bureau holds a hearing.

An examiner, who corresponds to a master in judicial proceedings, presides over a hearing, takes evidence, and makes a recommendation to the agency or commission. His recommendation may be either approved or rejected.

Bomb Caused Jetliner Crash

CENTERVILLE, Iowa—Federal investigators yesterday pieced together new evidence indicating that a dynamite-type bomb placed in a washroom ripped apart a Continental Airlines jetliner 39,000 feet above the earth.

Experts from the Civil Aeronautics Board gave newsmen their first close-up look at a reconstruction of the rear section of the Boeing 707 jet which crashed into Missouri farmland Tuesday night killing all 45 persons aboard.

CAB Holds Hearing On Feeder Routes

Paso Robles City Attorney James A. Madden yesterday told a Civil Aeronautics Board examiner that Paso Robles—not the city of San Luis Obispo—is the more desirable terminal for air service to San Luis Obispo county.

Madden's statement came during the second day of a three-day hearing on Southwest Airlines' application for renewal of its certificate to serve 28 cities between Los Angeles and Medford, Oregon. United and Bonanza Air Lines have asked to take over the routes. . . .

FEDERAL AVIATION AGENCY

One of the primary functions of this unit is to enforce the safety regulations prescribed by the Civil Aeronautics Board; however, it can only recommend to the CAB revocation of a pilot's certificate.

FAA Grounds Pilot Who Landed in Street

The pilot of a plane that crash-landed Saturday on a Los Angeles boulevard, killing singer Willie Hoffman and injuring the other five occupants, was grounded and charged with "careless and reckless" flying by the Federal Aviation Agency today.

He is Marvin Sibley, who took a charter flight party from Burbank to Palo Alto for the Michigan-Stanford game and return.

J. S. Marriott, regional administrator of the FAA, filed the complaint with the Civil Aeronautics Board today.

FEDERAL COMMUNICATIONS COMMISSION

This commission regulates interstate communication by wire and radio. It is chiefly concerned with radio and television, but also regulates interstate rates of telephone and telegraph companies. It holds local hearings in connection with applications for station licenses and—sometimes—for renewal of licenses and for the assignment of frequencies for various types of radio and television broadcasting. It has the authority to revoke or modify licenses and to cite violators of FCC rules for prosecution in the federal District Court. The agency maintains about thirty district offices; these are chiefly for monitoring and inspecting.

Withdraws Bid for Channel 3 License

SALEM, Ore.—A Federal Communications Commission hearing into an application for Salem's television Channel 3 came to an abrupt halt Monday when the applicant withdrew his application.

W. Gordon Allen, president of Willametteland Television, Inc., told FCC examiner Charles Frederick that harassment by the FCC's broadcast bureau had so complicated the proceedings that he was going to withdraw his application and file it anew. . . .

Allen's attorney, Samuel Miller, told the hearing that Allen's decision to withdraw and reapply was based on indications that further time and money-consuming effort would be required to prosecute the current application.

This was compounded, Miller said, by Allen's discovery that his proposed transmitter site was no longer available. This would require amending the application.

FEDERAL TRADE COMMISSION

This commission, which has ten regional offices, acts to prevent: unfair methods of competition (e.g., price-fixing agreements, boycotts, and combinations in restraint of trade); deceptive advertisements of foods, drugs, cosmetics, and devices; false labeling of wool products; deceptive or immoral trade-marks; and price discrimination forbidden by the Robinson-Patman Act. It enforces these laws by issuing cease-and-desist orders which are either agreed to by the offenders through stipulation or appealed to the United States Courts of Appeals. Before issuing such orders the Commission holds hearings, oftentimes in a local community.

Oilman Lent "Times" Money, FTC Is Told

The Harrodsville Daily Times received $117,400 in loans from Myron Hudson, wealthy Texas oilman, it was disclosed yesterday in testimony at a Federal Trade Commission hearing.

The hearing was one of a series involving charges of unfair competition made against the Times by Lowell Daly, publisher of the Harrodsville Gazette.

Vernon Ellis, publisher of the Times, admitted he had not contributed financially to the newspaper and added he had not known until it had been brought out at the hearing that the Texas oilman had lent the paper money. . . .

At the original hearing in Harrodsville last August, Kirk Spangler, the commission's examiner, ruled out testimony about the financing of the Times. The commission, however, ordered a new hearing and the admission of such testimony.

INTERSTATE COMMERCE COMMISSION

The Interstate Commerce Commission regulates railroads, motor carriers, water carriers, and freight forwarders. Regulation includes the approval or disapproval of proposed rate schedules and compliance with safety standards prescribed by the commission.

SP LOSES LUMBER BUSINESS

The number of railroad cars carrying lumber from Oregon to California and Arizona declined 58 per cent in seven years, according to E. J. Larson, freight traffic manager for the Southern Pacific.

Larson testified yesterday at the opening of an Interstate Commerce Commission hearing into SP's proposed schedule of reduced lumber freight rates.

RAIL HEARING ENDS

The Interstate Commerce Commission yesterday ended an eight-day hearing here on an application by the Southern Pacific Company to discontinue six of its California trains.

H. J. Bond, the ICC examiner, said the Commission is not apt to hand down its decision for six months.

At the final session, W. D. Lamprecht, general manager of the railroad, testified that, if the trains are dropped, 45 crewmen's jobs will be eliminated.

SECURITIES AND EXCHANGE COMMISSION

This commission, which maintains nine regional offices, administers the Securities Act, the Securities Exchange Act, the Investment Company Act, the Investment Advisers Act, and the Trust Indenture Act. A staff of investigators receives complaints and investigates them. In some instances the commission sends an examiner to hold a hearing in a local community.

SEC Scans Books Of Investment Co.

RENO, Nev.—The federal Securities and Exchange Commission today checked the affairs of the Pioneer

Trading Co. to determine whether any of the 3,500 investors scattered over many states had been defrauded of the million dollars they gave the concern to deal in the grain markets.

Its ramifications may be revealed at a formal hearing scheduled for today.

CUSTOMS COURT

The Customs Court has jurisdiction over actions arising under the tariff laws to construe the laws as to the dutiable value of imported merchandise and the rates of duty. The court, composed of nine judges, has its headquarters in New York city but frequently holds sessions at the various ports of entry.

Customs Court Hears Obscene Literature Charge

MILWAUKEE—Fifty-four cases were on the docket when the United States Customs Court convened in the federal building today.

Three of the cases involved the importation of obscene literature in violation of the tariff act.

The court heard fifteen cases of which seven were dismissed. Two were transferred to Duluth, where the court will be in session Friday and Saturday.

One of the obscene literature cases involved Henry Whitehurst, of Hartford, from whom four volumes of "The Sorceress" by Jules Milet had been seized.

The court took the question under advisement.

TAX COURT OF THE UNITED STATES

When the Internal Revenue Service demands more tax from a citizen than he believes is due he has the option of appealing to the Tax Court of the United States to uphold his original return or of paying the extra tax and suing for a refund in the Court of Claims or a federal district court. The Tax Court is composed of sixteen judges. The court holds hearings at various places.

Refugee From Nazis Fights Tax Claim

Werner Grossman, a 70-year-old refugee from Germany, maintained in the U.S. Tax Court here yesterday that he should not have to pay $2,737 income taxes on the $10,000 yearly pension he now receives from the German department store chain he once headed.

The Nazis robbed him of millions of marks, according to Attorney Elmer Harwood, and the pension payments should be considered a restitution of lost property.

CHAPTER 34

Political Party Organizations

Since the scope of this book is limited to the consideration of reporting in the local community, the discussion in this chapter does not touch on national elections and politics; and it relates to the party organization on the state level only to the extent that the operation of the party in the local community can be made understandable.

REGISTRATION

A citizen is not permitted to vote at a primary or general election unless his name appears on a list which was compiled prior to the election.[1] The purpose of such registration is to prevent fraud. The registration affidavit the voter makes often includes his full name, address, and a personal description including height, weight, and color of hair and eyes. To be eligible to vote, the citizen in most states must be 21 years old and must have lived within the state for one year, the county for two to six months, and the precinct for thirty days.

Some states have a *periodic* type of registration, but most large states have a *permanent* type. The periodic type provides for a renewal of registration at certain intervals—from one year to ten years. Permanent registration provides for a registration that is not cancelled until the voter moves, dies, or loses his citizenship; some states also purge the list at certain times of those citizens who have not voted at any election for a period of years—commonly two years.

Exercise: Look up in the dictionary the definitions of *plurality* and *majority*.

[1] There are exceptions in a few states and in the rural parts of some states.

NOMINATION[2]

A citizen who wishes to be a candidate in a primary election is required to file a petition for his name to be placed on the ballot. In most states for certain offices the petition must be supported by the signatures of a certain number of voters. The number is often equal to a specified percentage of the votes cast in a recent election. The petition must usually be filed with the county clerk (and the secretary of state for state offices) a certain number of days in advance of the election and be accompanied by a filing fee (often a certain percentage of the annual salary for the office).[3]

EXPENDITURES

The federal government and most of the states have statutes that regulate the amount of expenditures and contributions. These statutes require that a statement of such expenditures and contributions be filed with the county clerk or the secretary of state, or both, a specified number of days after the primary or general election.[4] Newspapers in the local community and the wire services in the state capital obtain and report these statements.

PARTY ORGANIZATIONS

Political parties have a legal status. The various state legislatures pass laws regarding nominations and elections that require the parties to choose candidates and present nominations in accordance with certain regulations. For example, the statutes provide that the candidate of a party must receive a certain number of votes in order that his party in a subsequent election may be entitled to place the name of a candidate on the ballot, and statutes in some states declare whether nominations shall be made by a direct primary election or by a convention.

Political parties also have a code which they themselves establish independently of the legislature. They adopt rules which bind the party to conduct its business in a particular way. For example, a state convention may adopt the so-called unit rule which requires the county delegates to the state convention to cast the entire vote of the delegation for the candidate or for the proposal that is favored by the majority of the delegates, instead

---

[2] See also the discussion of these procedures on p. 474.

[3] For a complete analysis of all state and federal laws that apply to the nomination and election of a United States senator, see *Election Law Guidebook, 1964*, compiled by the Subcommittee on Privileges and Elections of the Committee on Rules and Administration of the United States Senate, 87th Congress, 2d Session. In each state about the same regulations apply to state officers as to United States senators.

[4] See *Election Law Guidebook* for provisions in each state.

of permitting the individual delegates to cast their votes for their particular choice; and a party may also make rules as to whether a candidate nominated in a convention shall be chosen by a mere majority of the delegates' votes or by a two-thirds majority. Each party in each state makes rules concerning the size and character of certain governing committees and the methods by which the committee members are chosen; in some states, however, the legislature makes such rules.

Party Committees

Party control is of both temporary and permanent character. The temporary control is that which is vested in the convention, and is, theoretically, the higher control. The permanent control, which is frequently the real control, is vested in various committees. Locally, the party is governed by a hierarchy of permanent committees. At the very bottom are the precinct committeemen. Pyramided upon them are the ward committees (in a city), the county committees, and the State Central Committee. In some states there are township and town committees. District committees, made up of members within a congressional, judicial, or legislative district, exist in some states, but the duties of such committees usually devolve upon the county committees, which are bodies of real authority in the party organization.

The committees are usually elected every two or four years and, in most instances, in a year that a state election is to be held. In most states the interested adherents of a party assemble in a caucus by precincts, at the call of the county chairman, to elect a precinct committeeman. The precinct committeemen make up the county committee, except that in some states in which there are large cities, the ward is the smallest unit of party government, and the ward committeemen make up the county committee; in some cities the ward committeemen appoint the precinct committeemen, the ward committeemen themselves being elected. In some instances, county committeemen are elected at a primary election.

The State Central Committee

At the head of the party organization in the state is the powerful State Central Committee. (In a few states there are two state committees, one called the State Central Committee and the other the State Executive Committee.) In most states the State Central Committee is composed of representatives from either the congressional districts or the counties. The committee ranges in size from eleven in Iowa to nearly one thousand in California, the average being thirty to forty members. The members are sometimes elected in the district or county conventions prior to a state convention, sometimes during a state convention by a caucus of delegates, and sometimes in a primary election by a direct vote of the party adherents. Their term of office is usually four years.

The State Central Committee exercises a great deal of power. It selects a campaign committee, fixes the ratio of representation in the state convention, chooses the convention city and makes arrangements for holding the convention, determines the time for the convention and issues the call, appoints or recommends election officials, and sometimes nominates a candidate for high office following the death or disqualification of the regular nominee. The State Central Committee also is the permanent party executive that "nurtures the party's strength" between elections. The newspaper reporter assigned to cover politics ought to be acquainted with the leading members of the State Central Committee of both major parties, and he ought to be especially well acquainted with the member representing his own district so that he may obtain authentic information about party affairs during the intervals between election campaigns.

Conventions

Temporary control of a party is exercised in the party conventions of delegates assembled in a precinct, a ward, a county, a district, or a state. Prior to the adoption of direct primary laws in most states, candidates were nominated solely by conventions, and the practice still survives in some states, especially in those in which the law of the state permits a party the option of nominating by either a primary election or by a convention. In most states, however, the state convention is chiefly a *platform* convention; that is, a convention in which the party determines the issues upon which it will contest an election. The precinct, ward, county, and district conventions meet for the main purpose of choosing the delegates to the state convention, electing members of the State Central Committee, and indorsing the candidacies of certain persons who are seeking the party nominations. The functions of the state convention, described on pages 529–530, vary according to the laws in the various states.[5]

The Local Convention

Nearly all local conventions, such as the county convention, are cut-and-dried affairs. Their business is transacted quickly and, in many instances, before some of the delegates know what is actually happening. The main purpose of the convention is to name delegates to the state convention, the delegates usually being persons whom the party managers can rely

[5] There is no uniformity in party government in the United States, and the statements in this section are about as general as it is possible to make them. Examine carefully the party organizations in your own state and compare them with the general statements made here.

upon to support their favorite candidates or proposals in the state convention. Immediately after the county chairman has called the convention to order, various men or women, who have been appointed beforehand, rise at their cue and make certain motions. Usually, the entire program of business has been typed on sheets of paper and copies have been handed to selected men or women so they will know what to do at the proper moment.

Sometimes, however, local conventions result in contests. When there are two factions or divisions in the party two sets of officers and delegates are nominated and balloted upon. In some local caucuses everybody who attends is entitled to vote, and one side or the other may try to pack the convention. Under some circumstances, the defeated faction carries an appeal to the credentials committee of the state convention.

GOP Convention Names 9 Delegates

Darwin county Republicans yesterday named nine delegates to the state convention to be held next Friday.

The delegates were instructed on the following issues:

1. To urge quick action in constructing a breakwater at Pine Point.

2. To oppose the housing referendum initiative which will be on the November ballot.

3. To revive the state crime commission.

The local convention endorsed State Sen. Horace Rose for vice chairman of the State Central Committee and all of the Republican candidates nominated in the June primary.

The delegates from Darwin county are: . . .

Functions of the State Convention

The functions of the state convention vary according to the law in force in the various states and, also, according to the particular year in which the conventions are held. Generally, the functions of a state convention are:

1. To instruct delegates and alternates to a national convention (in the years in which a President is elected).

2. To nominate candidates for the state elective offices (where there is no requirement for a primary election).

3. To adopt a party platform.

4. To choose members of the State Central Committee.

It is not the convention but a caucus of delegates assembled at the state convention which usually chooses the State Central Committee. The state convention does sometimes elect a certain number of members at large.

The following news story indicates rather adequately what happens at a state convention in a year when a President is not to be elected:

Douglas Henry Cast In "Peacemaker" Role

The Democratic party's new state chairman—Douglas Henry—was offered at the post-primary convention here yesterday as a "peacemaker."

The Swain forces were in complete control as they boosted Mr. Henry into the state chairmanship which they lost two years ago when Thomas Fitzpatrick, Fremont attorney, squeezed into the office.

One of Mr. Henry's biggest jobs likely will be to try to heal the breach between the Old Guard, headed by James C. Swain, of Mosbyville, and an opposition element composed of many younger party members and others opposed to the Swain ring.

The convention's platform said agriculture under Democratic administrations has enjoyed unprecedented prosperity. It urged "a continuing farm program consistent with the needs of our economy."

The platform pledged the Democrats to work for a long-range road construction program with regular progress reports to the people of the state.

The platform condemned the Republican administration of the Highway Department "for its waste of road funds, its useless surveys, unneeded rights of way, and extravagant buildings."

Conferences and Caucuses

Of much greater importance in practical politics than conventions and committee meetings are the conferences and caucuses of party leaders held for the purpose of choosing candidates and for determining campaign issues. Often the conventions and committee meetings merely ratify the decisions made in conferences, and—in communities in which a party is divided into factions—the conferences of the separate factions are, in effect, miniature conventions. Although newspaper reporters are seldom admitted to these conferences, they can obtain a great deal of information by interviewing the leaders. Newspaper reporters who are thoroughly familiar with the records, ambitions, and associations of the politicians have little difficulty in explaining to their readers the motives that determine the make-up of a slate or the choice of campaign issues. They must be able, however, to absorb a great deal of political gossip.

Making Up the Slate

The slate of a faction or of a party is, in most cases, made up by the leaders who actually control an organization or a portion of an organization. Each of the leaders brings to the convention an individual strength based upon the number of votes he controls and this, usually, determines the extent to which he influences the make-up of the slate.

The composition of a slate is determined by two principal factors: (1) the necessity for satisfying the individual leaders, and (2) the necessity for pleasing the voters in the regular election. So far as is possible, the individual leaders agree upon candidates who represent their respective interests, but they must frequently select a high type of candidate, even though the candidate is not an organization man, in order to obtain success for the ticket at the regular election. Moreover, a slate must usually be balanced; that is, must appeal to the various sections of the electorate as well as to the whole electorate. With this purpose in mind, the slate-makers select candidates who will draw voters from particular racial, religious, and sectional elements. Candidates are also named who are likely to attract the votes of women, of former servicemen, of church members, of substantial businessmen, and of particular fraternal orders. Yet a balanced slate, although extremely important to party success, is of little consequence if the head of the ticket is unable to attract voters. The ordinary person is often influenced to vote for a party ticket merely because he desires to support the head of the ticket. The result is that frequently incompetent and dishonest men are elected to responsible positions in government service merely because of the popularity of the gubernatorial or mayoral candidate.

Newspapers ought to report thoroughly the slate-making process of a party or faction, publish the records of the individual candidates prior to the election, and, where it is possible, report the various trades and deals made by the factions of the party leaders.

SOME ASPECTS OF POLITICS

Politics is an enterprise to which a limited professional class—the politicians—devote attention. The usual politician is motivated by the desire to obtain, by election or appointment, a position in the government, together with the power, prestige, or emoluments that accompany the office. Some politicians, however, are motivated by the desire to obtain additional monetary rewards by either the legitimate or the illegitimate appropriation of the public funds. Politicians, generally, are as honest as the ordinary businessman; but because success in politics usually requires the application of a shrewdness that is unfamiliar to the ordinary citizen and because of the adherence of the politician to certain party obligations and his occasional support of certain dishonest candidates of his party, he is often thought to be dishonest.

The Organization

The personal success of a politician is dependent upon his cooperation with other politicians in a group or a party. The organization of the group or party is hierarchical, and is sometimes called a "machine." So great is the necessity for cooperating with the organization that the ordinary politician subordinates the conventional ethical criteria to the obligation that the organization puts upon him.

Modern governments do not usually function except by means of party organizations—either loosely or tightly organized.[6] Ordinarily, a government depends upon the existence of two organizations—the organization which is in control of the offices and the opposing organization, which is desirous of obtaining control of the offices. The opposition organization is sometimes of a rather permanent character, but is frequently of a temporary character, as for example, the casual organization of politicians and private citizens who are mobilized during a municipal campaign for the purpose of obtaining a "reform" administration.

The members of the usual organization are of two kinds: the professional politician and the private citizen who is obligated to the organization or to some member of it.

The Profits of Politics

The professional officeholders and other politicians in the organization are of two classes: namely, the holders of small offices who work for the organization in order to obtain appointment or nomination, and the so-called bosses who direct and control the organization so as to profit by holding offices of prestige or by obtaining lucrative favors from the govern-

---

[6] There are many exceptions.

ment. The latter class, however, is frequently made up of professional politicians who do not hold office but nevertheless control the organization or a part of it in order to obtain favors from the government.

The big profits in politics accrue to the leaders of the dishonest "machine" in the following forms: contracts awarded by the government for materials, supplies, and the construction and repair of public works and public buildings; lucrative fees paid by the government for services rendered, such as special attorneys', receivers', and experts' fees, and fees paid for furnishing official bond for the officeholders; money paid by law violators for protection from arrest or prosecution—usually protection of vice and gambling; money paid for granting permits and licenses to those not entitled to receive them; and money paid for obtaining reductions in the valuation of property for purposes of taxation.

The acceptance of money by politicians as payment for services rendered—the so-called graft—is, however, not a universal phenomenon in politics. Of more frequent occurrence is the acceptance from privileged persons and interests of campaign contributions; this practice is not regarded by politicians as a downright dishonest one, but it is nearly as subversive of political morality as is the acceptance of money directly. Campaign funds are contributed to some candidates because they are agreeable to an "open town"; that is, they will tolerate the operation of slot machines and perhaps other forms of gambling and will enforce the liquor regulations lightly. Campaign funds are contributed to another candidate by wealthy property owners because the candidate intends to hold down taxes rather than promote additional public improvements and social welfare and increase city employees' salaries.

Fortunately, all organizations do not profit by flagrant methods of dishonesty. Most organizations exist by virtue of the control of patronage and the practice of petty graft. Some organizations exist solely through the control of patronage. The attitude of many politicians toward the state, however, is one of exploitation: they conceive the state as an institution they can turn to their own advantage. Private citizens, therefore, must be eternally vigilant.

How Organizations Work

Although the nucleus of a party organization consists of the professional politicians, many private citizens are enlisted to work for the organization. The private citizen who gives his allegiance to an organization is usually under obligation either to the organization or to a member of it. Politicians place private citizens under obligation to themselves by the following means, among others: providing them with special police protection, or by assuring them of the ordinary protection to which they are entitled but have not been receiving; intervening in their behalf with magistrates; keeping them from being dispossessed of their homes when they cannot pay the rent; getting jobs for them or members of their family; aiding them in their relations with the government, as for example, obtaining exemption from jury duty, helping in the filing of tax returns, obtaining licenses, and obtaining garbage removal or street repairs; supplying them coal; and inviting them to free picnics and outings. The private citizen who is most often under obligation to the politician is the poor resident of the large city who is inarticulate as a citizen and baffled and confused by the complexities of government. Cities which have a considerable number of such persons are most likely to have "machine" politics.

The Role of Gratitude

The precinct and ward leaders in urban communities which have highly organized "machines" devote almost all of their free time to doing favors for people who live in their precinct or ward. The more favors a politician does for voters the more voters he has obligated to him on election day. As a President of the United States, who has been a practical politician for all of his adult life, has said, "There's more satisfaction in doing things for people than in anything else, and that's what politics is all about."[7] The late "Boss" Pendergast, of Kansas City, explained exactly how he obligated voters to his organization:

> "Well, I'll tell you how I do it," he said with a look of pride on his face. "It's a very simple thing when you come down to it. There's people that need things, lots of 'em. I see to it that they get 'em. I go to my office on South Main Street in Kansas City at seven o'clock in the morning and I stay there when I'm in town till about six at night and during that time I see maybe two hundred maybe three hundred people. One needs a half a ton of coal. Another woman's gotta get a job for her boy. I see to it that they get those things. That's all there is to it."[8]

Those voters who have put themselves under obligation but who do not like the politician's candidate are faced by a moral dilemma: whether, in the interest of good government, to vote for the better candidate but be regarded as an ingrate, or to do the "honorable" thing although it means worse government.

The city politician is more often regarded by such private citizens as a personal friend than as a public enemy, with the result that gratitude and obligation are frequently more potent factors in determining the conditions of government than are the important issues and the character of the candidates. The only remedy for this situation is to convince the voters, through education in the public schools and elsewhere, that gratitude in politics is a

---

[7] "Alsop Interviews L.B.J.," *Saturday Evening Post,* Dec. 14, 1963, p. 80.
[8] Marquis Childs, *I Write From Washington* (New York, 1942), p. 112.

"vice, not a virtue," and that "every man and every collection of men ought to be treated by us in a manner founded upon their intrinsic qualities and capacities and not according to a rule which has existence only in relation to ourselves."[9] Gratitude as a factor in local politics will decline as the number of citizens who do not feel insecure increases.

Carrying the Precinct

In the hierarchical organization of the well-organized machine the lowest leader is the precinct committeeman. Each precinct committeeman has the responsibility for carrying his own precinct in the primary election. The method by which this is accomplished in one city, which is to some extent typical of the method in vogue in all cities where there are strongly organized machines, has been explained by Frank R. Kent in realistic terms.[10]

The ordinary urban election precinct contains about 600 voters, Mr. Kent explains. If the strength is evenly divided between the two major parties, with a few voters in the minor parties, about 250 voters are entitled to vote in each party primary. Of this total, 65 votes are sufficient to nominate the machine candidate. In the first place, not more than one-third or one-half of the eligible voters will participate in the primary—at the most 125. If the precinct committeeman can control half of this number—65 votes—he will have carried the precinct. How does he control them?

The precinct committeeman's family has at least five votes. The two judges and the clerk of the election, whom the precinct committeeman gets appointed and who receive ten to twenty dollars a day from the state, each control about five votes. Two or three "watchers," or "runners," who are paid out of the party's campaign fund are employed, and each of these is worth about five votes. The man from whom the polling place is rented contributes about five votes. In addition, there are a few city employees in each precinct—street cleaners, clerks, firemen, and the like—who were appointed at the instance of the precinct committeeman; each controls the vote of his own family. The total is easily 65 votes, enough to carry the precinct against a rival candidate who lacks an efficient organization. Add to this number of machine adherents the voters in the precinct for whom the committeeman has done a favor, and the total is overwhelming against the unorganized dissenters within the party.

[9] William Godwin, *Political Justice* (New York, 1926), Bk. II, p. 199. Cf. also Jane Addams, *Democracy and Social Ethics* (New York, 1915), Chap. 7.
[10] *The Great Game of Politics* (Garden City, N.Y., 1923), Chaps. 1 and 4. In scores of cities there is only the semblance of a political machine. See also W. D. Miller, *Mr. Crump of Memphis* (Baton Rouge, La., 1964).

Interest-groups

The success of the organization, however, is not always contingent solely upon gratitude and personal obligation. Two other factors that are sometimes much more powerful intervene: the pressure of interest-groups and the appeal of ideas.

The independence of the politician, especially of the politician who ranks high in the organization, is limited by the pressure that interest-groups bring to bear upon him; some politicians, in fact, are veritable parasites clinging to the body of private business or of labor unions. Politics, being essentially a process in which groups and individuals attempt to make use of the state to their own ends, involves a constant competition, conflict, and accommodation of various material interests, personal ambitions, and ideas. There is, in politics, a continual push and resistance between groups with a constantly shifting resultant balance. The pressure of groups upon the government is transmitted through the politician and turns upon such phenomena as taxes, special privileges, morals, race, party loyalty, personalities, and sectionalism within the community.

Taxes, special privileges, and morals already have been mentioned. That race and nationality are of underlying importance in some communities is recognized in the representation of various races and nationalities on the slate of candidates. Party loyalty means little in those communities in which local elections are now considered to be nonpartisan; in some communities, however, local elections are on a partisan basis and in some others the leaders of one or the other of the two major parties resist the trend toward the nonpartisan basis of local politics. Personalities are to be considered in politics on every level. Sectionalism is a factor in nearly every community to the extent that some people believe their part of town is being or will be neglected by the officeholder.

In addition to interest-groups, nearly every community has a certain number of persons who are interested solely in good government. For want of a satisfactory name, this class can be denominated the "better element." It is the only group to which a wholly intellectual appeal is successfully addressed. Since it includes many of the business and professional leaders of the community and the most thoughtful women, it is the group to which editorial arguments are chiefly addressed by the intelligent newspapers; for, although itself small in numbers, its influence tends to radiate and filter downward until it affects in large degree the opinions of other voters who are without private interest in politics. The future success of democracy depends almost entirely upon the growth of this group in numbers and influence. This class, naturally, is not organized, and in no two successive elections does it contain all of the same individuals. For the candidates and issues are usually determined by the various interest-groups, and the independent voters are usually compelled to support one side or the other without definitely aligning themselves with the interest-groups.

Personal leadership, however, is one of the most important factors in politics, and the newspaper reporter cannot afford to ignore it. Personality alone may elect a popular politician; it is only when powerful issues or the pressures of interest-groups intervene that the personal element in politics is subordinate. Not all of the leaders in a political campaign, however, are politicians. Clergymen, labor leaders, businessmen with a self-interest or a class interest, professional propagandists, newspapers, and some independent citizens exert influence. Such leaders, however, are usually more interested in measures than in candidates, and they endorse and support the candidates who agree to support the measures they favor.

The Role of the Newspaper

The newspaper, as an agency of communication, can better serve the public interest by educating its readers in political values than by acting as a mere propagandist. It is better that the newspaper perform as a teacher in the school of democracy than as a spellbinder on the stump. For, although it is easier for the newspaper, by adopting the technique of the demagogue or charlatan, to win a single campaign, it must again fight the battle of civic righteousness without bringing the voters any nearer to a real understanding of political values. The role of teacher does not prohibit the newspaper from using catchwords or the language of the man in the street, but it does forbid the creation of false issues and the practice of directing nonrational appeals to the mere self-interest and prejudice of the voter. The newspaper should regard the voter as a citizen rather than as a pawn in the game of politics. The newspaper should teach the citizen to act in the public interest instead of as a self-seeker, a Protestant, a Catholic, a Pole, or a farmer.

CHAPTER 35

Labor

News about labor is ordinarily news about labor unions. Except in the event of strikes and lockouts, the activities of unorganized labor are seldom in a state that can be reported in the newspapers. The activities of union labor, however, can be reported rather thoroughly because labor unions pass resolutions, elect officers, strike, picket, negotiate, and perform other acts concerning which verifiable facts are known. These acts are usually the acts of an organized body, and they are performed during the course of a meeting, a conference, or a union election. The first task of the newspaper reporter, therefore, is to become acquainted with the structure of the labor organization in his community.

STRUCTURE OF LABOR ORGANIZATION

The chief national ("international") labor organization is the American Federation of Labor—Congress of Industrial Organizations. It is a merger of the A.F.L. and the C.I.O., the latter organization being the "Industrial Union Department" of A.F.L.-C.I.O. The A.F.L., the older organization, has many craft unions as members whereas the C.I.O. membership is composed mainly of industrial unions,[1] such as the auto workers, steel workers, and rubber workers. (The American Newspaper Guild is also a member of the C.I.O. "department.") Some of the large unions not affiliated with A.F.L.-C.I.O. are the United Mine Workers, the International Brotherhood of Teamsters, and the various railroad brotherhoods.

From time to time during the recent history of organized labor, various local unions were created and afterward attached to national and international bodies; on the other hand, however, there are still organizations of workers in some trades and industries that have no national organization except their affiliation with the "departments" of the A.F.L. Generally, however, workers in a particular craft or industry in a community have formed local unions and obtained charters from a national or international body, and have afterward joined with other unions in their community or region as members of a city, state, or district federation, or "central."

[1] "Craft" and "industrial" are distinguished on p. 539.

The Local

The unit of organization is the local. Locals are differentiated as *craft* locals and *industrial* locals. A typical craft local is the Cigarmakers' Union of Chicago; a typical industrial local is the Brewery Workers' Union of Chicago. The distinction between craft and industrial locals is that in the former body only the workers of a particular craft or trade are members, whereas in the latter body all the brewery workers—including technical experts, teamsters, and janitors—are members. Many of the unions in the C.I.O. are industrial, but only a few of the A.F.L. unions are industrial.

The Council

In most cities the various locals in some of the trades cooperate in the formation of a council. It is composed of delegates appointed to represent the members of the locals whose members are engaged in allied trades, as for example, the unions of plumbers, carpenters, bricklayers, lathers, plasterers, steamfitters, and electrical workers who compose the City Building Trades Council, and the unions of workers in the printing and metals trades who have their councils. The delegates who compose the council are often the officers of the locals. The functions of the council in a city are to discipline member unions for violation of wage agreements and union regulations, to act for the locals in making agreements with employers as to wages and working conditions, and to have the member unions act together in calling strikes and boycotts or in threatening so-called sympathetic strikes.

The City Central, or Federation

Locals in a city, also, form a second type of federation, usually called the city central, or the city federation. It is a body composed of delegates from all of the locals in a city that are affiliated with the A.F.L. The functions of the city central are chiefly political and social. The body acts to defeat or procure adoption of legislative measures, and engages in mediation between workers and employers and promotion of the boycott. In some cities, it is agreed that no constituent body of the federation may strike in that city without the consent of the federation. The city and state federations frequently have different names in different localities, such as the Trades Union Assembly, the Local Trades Union Council, etc.

THE NATIONAL LABOR RELATIONS ACT

In 1935 Congress enacted the National Labor Relations Act (29 U.S.C. 151–166, with amendments in 1947, 1951, and 1959) to guarantee to employees "the right to self-organization, to form, join or assist labor organizations, to bargain collectively through representatives of their own choosing, and to engage in concerted activities for the purpose of collective bargaining or other mutual aid or protection."

The act defines "unfair labor practices" and establishes the National Labor Relations Board with powers to carry out the provisions of the act. "Unfair labor practices" are defined as follows: for an *employer* to:

1. Interfere with, restrain, or coerce employees in the exercise of their rights guaranteed by the Act.

2. Dominate or interfere with the formation or administration of any labor organization or contribute financial or other support to it (this refers to so-called company unions).

3. Discriminate in regard to hire or tenure of employment or condition of employment for the purpose of encouraging or discouraging membership in any labor organization.

4. Discharge or otherwise discriminate against an employee because he has filed charges with or given testimony before the National Labor Relations Board.

5. Refuse to bargain collectively with representatives of his employees.

The board is given power to determine which unit is the more appropriate unit for bargaining in each instance—whether craft unit, plant unit, employer unit, or subdivision thereof. In order to determine who shall be the bargaining representative of the employees, the board may hold hearings and conduct secret elections.

THE TAFT-HARTLEY ACT

A revision of the National Labor Relations Act, enacted in 1947, is popularly known as the Taft-Hartley Act (Labor Management Relations Act, 29 U.S.C. Sup. 151–167). It outlaws the closed shop, forbids secondary boycotts, establishes the Federal Mediation and Conciliation Service, requires a "cooling-off period" in advance of a strike, authorizes injunctions to delay strikes affecting the national health and safety, and makes the general counsel of the NLRB a prosecutor—of employees as well as of employers. This act, in sum, forbids a *labor organization or its agents* to:

1. Restrain or coerce (*a*) employees in the exercise of their rights to organize and bargain collectively or to refrain from any or all such activities, (*b*) an employer in the choice of his bargaining representatives.

2. Cause or attempt to cause an employer to discriminate against an employee because of his membership or lack of membership in a labor organization except under a duly authorized union shop agreement in conformance to provisions of the Act.

3. Refuse to bargain collectively with an employer if it is the representative of his employees.

4. Engage in, or induce or encourage the employees of any employer to engage in, a strike or concerted refusal in the course of employment to handle any goods or perform any services with an object of: (*a*) forcing an employer or self-employed person to join any labor or employer organization, or to cease doing business with any other person; (*b*) forcing any other employer to recognize or bargain with a labor organization which has not been certified by the board as the representative of his employees; (*c*) forcing any employer to recognize or bargain with a labor organization when another has been certified by the board as the representative of his employees; (*d*) forcing any employer to assign particular work to employees in a particular labor organization, trade, craft, or class.

5. Require employees covered by a duly authorized union shop agreement to pay initiation fees which the board finds excessive or discriminatory under all the circumstances.

6. Cause or attempt to cause any employer to pay money or other thing of value, in the nature of an exaction, for services not performed or not to be performed.

PROCEDURE IN LABOR DISPUTES

On a complaint by any person or labor organization that an employer or a labor organization has engaged in or is engaging in an unfair labor practice or on a petition for certification of a bargaining representative, the general counsel of the NLRB directs a regional director to conduct an investigation and, in many cases, to hold a hearing. The hearing is presided over by a trial examiner. His findings are issued as an "intermediate report" and submitted to the board. His decision on representation cases may be appealed to the board; his decisions in an unfair labor practice case may be appealed to the general counsel. The board and the general counsel can enforce their orders by a petition to a United States Court of Appeals. A dissident employee, under the Taft-Hartley Act, may sue in a United States District Court. The regional hearings are often reported by the local newspapers as are the recommendations and finding of facts which the examiner transmits to the NLRB.

DECERTIFICATION HEARINGS
SAN FRANCISCO—The National Labor Relations Board will begin hearings next week on two petitions asking removal of the International Union of Mine, Mill and Smelter Workers as a bargaining agent for employees of

the Bunker Hill Co. in Kellogg, Idaho.

The petitions were filed by the recently-formed Northwest Metal Workers Union of Kellogg, branded a "company union" by Mine-Mill Local 18 officers.

One petition seeks an employee vote on keeping Mine-Mill as their bargaining agent; the second asks a vote to verify the Metal Workers Union as Mine-Mill's replacement.

VOTE TO OUST MINE-MILL UNION

SAN FRANCISCO—Workers of Bunker Hill Co. voted last week to decertify the International Union of Mine, Mill and Smelter Workers as their bargaining agent in a special election at Kellogg, Idaho.

They also voted in the local, independent Northwest Metal Workers Union to represent them in dealings with the company.

The election was administered by the National Labor Relations Board. The vote was 872 to 621 in favor of the local union. Eight workers voted against any union representation.

NLRB CERTIFIES INDEPENDENT

SAN FRANCISCO—The National Labor Relations Board has overruled objections of the International Union of Mine, Mill and Smelter Workers and certified an independent, local union as bargaining agent for employees of Bunker Hill Co. in Kellogg, Idaho.

The local union, the Northwest Metal Workers, ousted Mine-Mill in a special representation election Dec. 10. The older union protested, contending the Northwest group was company-sponsored, and that some Bunker Hill workers were not given a chance to cast absentee ballots.

Thomas P. Graham, Jr., regional director of the NLRB, ruled, after an investigation, that the Mine-Mill protests were not valid, and certified the Northwest Metal Workers as the properly elected bargaining agent for Bunker Hill workers.

When a union or an employer charges an "unfair labor practice," the NLRB makes an investigation and usually issues a complaint and holds a hearing. The trial examiner transmits a finding of fact and a ruling to the NLRB. If one party appeals the examiner's ruling, the NLRB makes a finding and an order. The NLRB may enforce its order by petition to a United States Court of Appeals.

U.S. Cites Pabco —"No Bargaining"

The National Labor Relations Board stepped into the month-old strike at the Pabco plant yesterday with a charge that management refused to bargain with the union.

A management spokesman said the matter is a jurisdictional dispute.

Regional officers of the National Labor Relations Board, however, rejected the management contention and issued a complaint against Pabco. A hearing will be set soon.

The Machinists' union struck Pabco July 31 after the company ended its contract covering 53 maintenance workers. An outside firm was hired to do the work.

NLRB Challenges Shinglers' Quotas

The National Labor Relations Board, at a hearing yesterday, challenged the right of an Oakland shinglers' union to decide how fast its members should work—and then fine eager roofers who slammed too many nails in a day.

There was no question that Local 478, Oakland unit of the International Brotherhood of Carpenters, did both.

Victor Van Bourg, union attorney, said that between October and December last year 14 overly ambitious shinglers were fined between $8 and $49 each.

C. R. Bartalini, secretary of the Bay Counties District Council of Carpenters, said the homebuilders were to blame.

Some employers, he said, made shinglers work so hard "that 70 per cent of our members couldn't compete. Since the industry didn't do anything about it we did," he said. . . .

Steven Dolin, manager of a Hayward roofing firm, testified the union's imposed work quotas were slowing work, raising the cost of homes and could even put some firms out of business.

NLRB attorney Walter Kinz charged that the quota-fine system constituted interference with the rights of shinglers under the Taft-Hartley Act.

And all sides agreed that the case might set an important precedent. There has not been another like it in the building construction industry.

Amendments to the National Labor Relations Act, passed in 1959, forbid: (*a*) a union to "threaten, coerce, or restrain" a secondary employer (*secondary boycott*) to achieve some of the objectives prohibited in the National Labor Relations Act; (*b*) a union to *picket* or threaten to picket where the object is to gain recognition or promote organization of employees under certain circumstances; and (*c*) a union or an employer from entering into an agreement pursuant to which the employer ceases or agrees to cease doing business with another person (*hot cargo*). The hot cargo provision, however, does not apply to an employer in the clothing and apparel business or to the construction industry relating to work to be done at the construction site.

NLRB Charges Illegal Picketing

A National Labor Relations Board hearing was held yesterday on a complaint charging two unions with illegally picketing the local Lane Bryant apparel store.

If unfair labor practices listed in the complaint are upheld, Department Store Employees Local 1100 and Retail Shoe and Textile Salesmen's Local 140 will be ordered to stop the picketing.

The NLRB complaint accuses the unions of picketing the store for the purpose of securing recognition. In addition, the complaint charges, the unions have attempted to bring about a consumer boycott of Lane Bryant merchandise.

Clerks at the store voted 52 to 3 last September 16 against representation by the unions in an election ordered by the NLRB and opposed by the unions.

Outside the hearing, Roland C. Davis, attorney for the unions, said they contend the picketing is not for recognition but only to advise the public that Lane Bryant is a nonunion store.

NLRB Trial Examiner David F. Doyle delayed his ruling pending submission of briefs.

NLRB Asks Ban On Union Boycott

The National Labor Relations Board yesterday asked the federal district court to stop a boycott being waged by the Radio and Television Technicians union.

The Board charged that the union's boycott against Packard-Bell products violated the federal labor law.

The union struck factory service branches of the Packard-Bell Electronics Corp. here on November 1.

Early in December members of the union began handing out leaflets at major department stores urging customers not to buy Packard-Bell products.

Gerald Brown, regional director of the NLRB, said the union's dispute is with the company's service branches, not its manufacturing plant. The law allows a boycott only if it involves a "primary dispute." Despite this, the union urged a boycott of products of the plant.

REPORTING AND DISCLOSURE

In 1959, Congress passed the Labor-Management Reporting and Disclosure Act (Landrum-Griffith Act). The purpose of the act is to protect labor union members against corruption and coercion practices of their officers. Title I establishes a members' "bill of rights." These rights relate to the nomination and election of officers, freedom of speech and assembly in and out of union meetings, dues and initiation fees, court actions by members against officers, and a full and fair hearing when a member has been penalized for his act (other than nonpayment of dues).

Other titles relate to reporting by officers, disclosure of "conflict of interest" by officers, election procedures, bonding of officers, loans by the union to its officers, trusteeships of a local union by the national union and extortionate picketing. The act authorized the Secretary of Labor to administer the aforementioned provisions. Enforcement of the provisions may be had in a federal district court in a civil action.

Court Hears Union Election "Framed"

A rank and file union member testified yesterday he overheard two union officials state that the 1958 election of officers in Local 701, Hoisting and Portable Engineers Union, was going to be "framed."

His testimony was the first taken before U.S. District Judge James W. Crawford, who is hearing a civil action brought by six rank and file union members who are seeking to have the local placed in the hands of a receiver and the officers discharged.

The plaintiffs in the case are seeking to prove there has been an improper handling of union funds and a lack of democratic procedures in the union. . . .

FEDERAL MEDIATION AND CONCILIATION SERVICE

This service exists to assist employers and unions to settle their disputes. Employers and unions are required to file with the service a notice of every dispute affecting commerce that is not settled within thirty days after prior notice to terminate or modify an existing labor contract. The service proffers its conciliation and mediation services either on its own motion or at the request of one or both of the parties. During these conferences the service's negotiators are one of the best sources of news. The staffs of mediators-conciliators are located in seven regional offices and in other major industrial centers.

The service also assists labor and management in the selection of *arbitrators* when an arbitration clause is included in a collective bargaining agreement. The service maintains a roster of experienced and competent persons from which it makes nominations to the parties for their selection.

A separate service—the National Mediation Service—assists in the settlement of disputes in the railroad industry.

Mediator Meets Both Sides in News Strike

PORTLAND, Ore.—Federal Mediator Elmer Williams arranged for separate meetings with union and employer negotiators yesterday in an attempt to end the three-day-old strike against Oregon's two largest newspapers.

Negotiators for Local 48 of the International Stereotypers & Electrotypers Union met with the mediator in the early afternoon and a later meeting was scheduled with the Oregonian Publishing Co. and Journal Publishing Co.

"Both sides are pretty firm. It doesn't look very good at this stage," Mr. Williams said in announcing the first meetings since the strike by about 60 stereotypers began Tuesday morning.

"I felt we would meet separately first in an attempt to find some basis for getting together," he said.

SOME DEFINITIONS

The following brief glossary of labor terms will help you understand some of the concepts underlying labor disputes.

Agency shop: A plant or department in which a nonmember of a union does not have to join the union but has to pay a fee equal to union dues in consideration of his tacit representation by the union; he is not subject to the discipline of the union.

Arbitration: The method of deciding a controversy under which the parties have agreed in advance to accept the award of a third party.

Check-off: The procedure whereby the employer deducts union dues from paychecks and turns them over to the union.

Closed shop: A plant or department which requires labor union membership as a condition of employment. (Outlawed by the Taft-Hartley Act.)

Conciliation: see "Mediation."

Company union: An organization of employees of a single plant or company. It is distinguished from a labor union, which covers a wider field.

In many instances company unions are encouraged by employers to avoid having to bargain with a labor union.

Goon: One employed to use violence in a labor dispute, usually against members of a rival union or against fellow workers to intimidate them to join the union.

Jurisdictional dispute: A situation (often a strike) caused by a dispute between two unions as to whose members have the right to perform certain work.

Mediation: The procedure adopted in a labor dispute when a third party offers his good offices to assist in settling the dispute; approximates *conciliation*. Not the same as *arbitration*.

Open shop: A plant or department which does not require labor union membership as a condition of employment, and which usually refuses to deal with unions.

Preferential bargaining: Policy by which the management gives preferential status to a single bargaining group. It may agree not to negotiate with another group on a given subject first and not to grant another group better terms.

Preferential shop: A plant or department in which the employer agrees to give preference to a labor union's members in hiring new employees.

Right to work law: Generally, a law in about 20 states which permits an employee to work without having to join a union; some of these laws also forbid the "agency shop."

Scab: A strikebreaker or employee who continues to work during the course of a strike in his plant or department.

Secondary boycott: Refusal to deal with or to buy goods from a concern which is the customer or supplier of an employer with whom the boycotters have a dispute.

Shop steward: Employee designated by the union to discuss with the supervisor the grievances of fellow employees.

Union shop: An arrangement between an employer and a union by which the employer may hire any employee—union or nonunion—that he pleases but with the understanding that such employee must join the union within a specified time.

Wildcat strike: A strike by some or all of the employees in a plant which was not authorized by the union.

Yellow-dog contract: A contract offered by the management to individual workers pledging the workers not to join a labor union; presumably outlawed by the National Labor Relations Act.

REPORTING LOCAL INDUSTRIAL DISPUTES

One of the most difficult kinds of news to report is that which involves labor-management disputes. Neither side appears to see much advantage in publicity until some overt act has occurred, such as a strike or a strike vote taken by a union. The result often is that newspapers report the fact of the strike but fail to answer for several days many of the questions that arise in the mind of the reader. From the public's point of view, it is desirable that the major facts be stated as early as possible.

Here is a list of questions about a city-wide strike of building constructors that probably ought to be answered for readers.

How many workers are on strike?

At what places?

What is the effect of the strike on major construction projects (such as a big steel plant and a big hospital)?

What is the effect on home building?

What are the principal demands of the strikers? (A 25 cents an hour increase.)

What was the last offer of the employers? (A 12½ cents an hour increase.)

What are the present contract wage rates for each type of construction labor?

What is the basis for each side's position? (Employers: "We think a 5 to 7 per cent increase is in line with the increase in the cost of living." Workers: "Last year we did not ask an increase because we wanted to create prosperity in the building industry; however, workers in all of the surrounding areas did receive an increase so that this year we are entitled to an adequate raise.")

What are the "fringe" benefits demanded by the union, and do they appear to be essential or were they presented only for bargaining purposes?

What offers and counteroffers were made during the negotiations immediately preceding the calling of the strike?

How large was the majority for a strike when the strike vote was taken in the council meeting?

Has the United States Mediation and Conciliation Service or the state mediation board offered its good offices?

Has either side offered to submit the issues to arbitration?

Were picket lines set up at the start of the strike?

Has any violence resulted since the start of the strike?

What is the daily cost of the strike to workers in terms of wages lost? (20,000 workers earning an average of $18 a day equals $360,000.)

Has the strike caused the shutdown of any industries which supply materials for the projects being struck?

If so, what is the daily wage loss to workers in those plants?

What is the source of that information?

Studying Labor Problems

Such treatment of labor problems as has been possible within the scope of this chapter is barely introductory to the study of labor history, labor economics, and labor law. This discussion is not a substitute for a series of college courses in this field. The reporter who wishes to specialize in labor reporting should read the best and most recent books that explain labor-management relations and should make some continuing study of the court and NLRB decisions that interpret the state and federal acts. His newspaper should subscribe to one of the loose-leaf reporting services that report and analyze labor law.

Appendices

APPENDIX *A*

Style Guide

CAPITALIZATION

Capitalize:
1. All months and days of the week: April, Tuesday.
2. Titles of books, plays, songs, etc.: "The Man Who Came to Dinner."
3. Titles denoting rank, official position, or occupation when they precede the name: Major Edward Williams, Gov. Murray Wilson, Judge Thomas Martin (but Thomas Martin, judge of the Superior Court).
4. Names of associations, companies, leagues, courts, and other organizations: American Medical Association, American League, Boy Scouts of America, Circuit Court, University of California, Motor Sales Company.
5. Geographical names: the Missouri River, Lake Michigan, Gulf of Mexico.
6. Streets, avenues, buildings, theaters, hotels, etc.: Twenty-first Street, the Blackstone Hotel.
7. Names of religious denominations and words denoting the Deity.
8. Names of political parties.
9. Sections of the country, but not the points of the compass: the West, west.
10. Abbreviations of college degrees: M.A., Ph.D.
11. Names of holidays: Fourth of July, Thanksgiving.
12. Names of races: Negro.

Do Not Capitalize:
13. Abbreviations of time of day: a.m., p.m., but 12M.
14. Seasons of the year: spring.
15. Names of college classes: sophomore.
16. Points of the compass: west.
17. College degrees when spelled out: bachelor of arts.
18. Titles when they follow the name: Thomas Martin, judge of the Superior Court.
19. Names of offices in a list of officers: Samuel Starr, president.

ABBREVIATION

Abbreviate:
20. The following titles: Mr., Mrs., Dr., Sen., Rev., Dep. Dist. Atty., Supt., Gov., Lt. Gov., Gen., Adm., 1st Lt., Prof. (only before a full name).
21. Names of states when they follow names of cities: Milwaukee, Wis. (but not "United States").
22. St.: St. Louis.
23. Names of widely-known organizations and agencies of the government (without periods or spaces): YMCA, DAR, FCC, NLRB.

Do Not Abbreviate:
24. Christian names, such as William, Charles.
25. Christmas (not Xmas).
26. Per cent.
27. Names of streets and avenues.

FIGURES

28. Spell out figures under 10 except in a street number (2342 Market Street) or when the figures are in a series of related expressions (the inventory showed 26 rakes, 2 shovels, 32 spades, and 1 hoe).
29. Avoid unnecessary ciphers: 11 p.m., $9.
30. Spell out numbers when they begin a sentence: Twelve years ago, etc. (When the figure is a large one, use "exactly" or a similar term before the figures: Exactly 12,765 persons voted, etc.).
31. Do not use *st, nd, rd, th* in dates: February 4.
32. Spell out fractions used alone (one-third), but use figures when the fraction is part of a number: $8\frac{1}{16}$.

THE DATE LINE

33. Capitalize and punctuate the date line this way:
PORTLAND, Ore., Feb. 11—Two men were killed, etc.

PUNCTUATION

34. Numbers of more than four figures should be pointed off with commas: 23,176.
35. Use a colon after a statement introducing a direct quotation of one or more paragraphs and begin a new paragraph for the quotation; also use a colon after "as follows."
36. Omit a period after "per cent" (except when "per cent" is the last word in the sentence).
37. Omit the commas between a man's name and "Jr." and "Sr."
38. Punctuate the score of a game this way: Yale 10, Harvard 7.
39. Do not use a comma in "4 feet 6 inches tall" and similar expressions.

TITLES

40. When a name is used in a story for the first time, give the full name (or initials) with the title. Thereafter do not repeat the full name (or initials) but precede it with a title or "Mr."
41. Use the actual name or titles: School of Law (not Law School), Southern Pacific Lines (not Southern Pacific Railroad).
42. Write the Rev. Milton Mowrer the first time the name is used; thereafter write it Mr. Mowrer.
43. For a clergyman with the D.D. degree, write the Rev. Dr. Milton Mowrer the first time the name is used; thereafter Dr. Mowrer.
44. When the clergyman is a Catholic, write the Rev. Edward Dunne the first time the name is used; thereafter write it Father Dunne.
45. For archbishops of the Catholic clergy, write The Most Rev. Michael Shaughnessy the first time the name is used; thereafter, Archbishop Shaughnessy.

46. Give the title professor only to faculty members who have a professorial rank.
47. Avoid long titles, such as Superintendent of Public Works Mason Brown. Write it: Mason Brown, superintendent of public works.

ADDRESSES

48. In the news story write an address: Miles Nash, 765 Prewitt Street; George Stanwick, Portland, Me.
49. Omit "of" and "at" before an address.

PREPARATION OF COPY

50. Put an end mark (#) at the end of a complete story.
51. Double-space your copy and write on only one side of the sheet.

APPENDIX B

Glossary of Newspaper Terms[1]

Advance: A news story about a future event.
Banner: A headline that extends across the whole page; also called "streamer" and "line."
Boil: To condense news copy.
Box: A short news story inclosed in rules.
Bulletin: One kind of urgent wire news.
By-line: The writer's name at the top of a news story; sometimes called "signer."
Caption: The descriptive text that accompanies a piece of art.
Chase: A metal frame in which a page of type is assembled and secured by sliding wedges called "quoins"; the quoins "lock up" the page.
Copy cutter: The employee in the composing room who receives editorial copy and apportions it to the individual printers (line-casting machine operators).
Credit line: A line that designates the source of a picture.
Cut: A printing plate that reproduces a photograph or drawing.
Date line: Placed at the beginning of the story, it indicates the place at which an event happened (or from which the story was filed) and sometimes the date the story was filed.
Dummy: A printed form filled in to indicate the placing of individual advertisements, editorial matter, and art.
Dupe: Carbon copy of a news story.
Ears: The upper corners of the front page.
Edition: Newspapers printed during one press run and containing the same matter.
Feature: *Noun.* (1) Generally a news story of human interest that is not spot news; (2) any non-news matter, such as columns and comic strips; (3) the chief aspect of importance or interest in a news story. *Verb.* To give prominence to a news story or to a specific element within the news story.
Filler: Standing matter used to fill space when needed.

[1] Almost none of radio's terminology refers to the news.

GLOSSARY OF NEWSPAPER TERMS 557

Flag: The title (i.e., name) of the newspaper at the top of the front page; it is usually a logotype.

Flush left head: Each line of a headline begins at the left-hand margin. Contra: "step head."

Folio: The number of each page.

Fudge box: A morticed space on the front page in which type is inserted after the page has been stereotyped.

Galley: A metal tray used to contain type after it has been set.

Halftone: A printing plate made from photographic copy and consisting of minute dots.

Handout: A publicity release.

HTK or HTC: Means "head to come," the copy having been sent to the composing room before the head was written.

Jump: That part of a front page story continued to an inside page.

Kill: Direction to the printer on a proofsheet to eliminate the matter indicated.

Lead (pronounced *led*): A thin strip of blank metal, usually two points in thickness. To "lead out" means to put these spaces between lines of type that have been set "solid."

Make over: To change the arrangement of type and cuts in a page of type and to cast a new stereotype plate of the page.

Masthead: The standing heading on the editorial page that contains certain information about the newspaper, such as the name of the publisher, the subscription rate, and so forth.

Overhead: A story sent by telegraph instead of by the leased wires.

Overset: Type that has been set for a specific issue of the newspaper in excess of the space available for it.

Pick up: Direction to the printer to add to the relevant story certain matter that is already in type.

Precede: Short or fairly short matter that is put above a news story and below the headline.

Release: The time stated by the news source for publication of an advance item; for example, "For release Tuesday, Sept. 1 at 6:00 p.m." (For both radio and newspaper.)

Replate: To make over a page and stereotype it.

Revise: *Noun.* A second proofsheet taken to check whether matter corrected on the original proofsheet was corrected as directed.

Rim: The outside edge of a horseshoe-shaped copy desk at which the copyreaders sit. (See "Slot.")

Rule: A type-high strip of metal for printing a continuous line.

Sidebar: A news story relating to a main news story that is an elaboration of the main story.

Slot: The inside space of a horseshoe-shaped copy desk at which the "dealer" or head copyreader sits.

Slug: (1) Any line of type cast by a typecasting machine. (2) The label put on a news story by a copyreader. (3) A blank spacing strip thicker than a lead.

Stet: *"Let it stand."* Direction to the printer in the margin of a piece of copy to set the matter even though it has been marked out. In a proofsheet, it means not to eliminate matter that has been marked out.

Stick: About two inches of type; the amount held in the composing stick.

Stringer: A part-time correspondent for a newspaper or news agency who is paid according to the amount of copy he supplies.

Subhead: A descriptive line in the body of the story to break up the solid-appearing type mass.

Take: The portion of a piece of copy to be set by the individual printer and later assembled with "takes" that other printers have set.

Time copy: Non-urgent news copy set in advance to run in early editions or as filler.

Turn rule: A direction to the printer, in connection with an insertion or add, to place at the bottom of the copy a rule that has been turned upside down so that its base (instead of its fine edge) will be visible to the printer when he assembles the parts of the story.

Typo: A typographical error.

APPENDIX C

Glossary of Legal Terms[1]

Admiralty: A tribunal that has jurisdiction over all maritime causes.
Affiant: One who makes an affidavit.
Affidavit: A written statement of facts subscribed to before a notary public or other officer who has authority to administer an oath.
Alias: From the Latin, "at another time"; a fictitious name assumed by a person.
Ancillary action: An action that grows out of or is auxiliary to another action, as a suit to enforce a judgment.
Assignment: The act by which a person transfers his property rights to another; as when a debtor assigns his property in trust for the benefit of his creditors.
Bailment: A delivery (to a bailee) of goods in trust upon a contract to deliver (to the bailor) after the trust has been executed (by the bailee).
Caveat: Literally, "let him beware." A formal written notice, in the nature of a warning, given to a judge for the purpose of arresting a decree or other judicial order.
Chattel: A type of property that is movable (as distinguished from a freehold or fee in land), such as machinery, stocks, bonds, growing crops.
Cognovit actionem, cognovit note: A written confession by a defendant on a debt which implies a judgment against him so that the plaintiff needs only to issue an execution. A cognovit note is such a confession.
Collusion: A secret, deceitful arrangement between two or more persons to make a deceitful use of the courts in order to defraud a third person or to deceive the court; esp., in divorce proceedings.
Community property: In community property states, as distinguished from common law states, a husband and wife share alike all the property they earn after marriage; the property each had before marriage and inheritance and gifts received after marriage is the "separate" property of each spouse.
Constructive service: A service in a civil action which is not personal but is construed as being so.
Deponent: One who testifies to interrogatory under oath in writing.

[1] That is, of terms not defined in the text.

Devisee: One to whom real property is devised in a will.

Domiciliary: Pertaining to one's domicile, i.e., his permanent habitation.

Easement: A privilege or right which an owner of land has acquired to use or enjoy the land of another, as when one owner has the right to pass through the land of another. A public easement is one which is acquired by condemnation, as when an electric power company has the right to construct its lines on privately-owned land. See also "Servitude."

Eminent domain: The right of a government to take private property for public use.

Entry and detainer: See "Forcible entry and detainer."

Escheat: The reversion of property to the state because there is no heir.

Estoppel: A special plea that prevents a party setting up allegations inconsistent with his previous allegations, i.e., he is estopped to deny the truth of his previous allegation.

Ex contractu, ex delicto: The common law divides rights and obligations (and causes of action) into these two classes. Thus, a civil action arises either out of a contract or out of a tort or similar wrong.

Forcible entry and detainer: A proceeding to recover possession of real property which is forcibly or unlawfully detained; the action does not relate to title, but is to restore possession to the plaintiff and to oust the defendant.

Incorporeal property: Literally, "without body." Property that is in the form of a right, such as copyright or right to purchase common stock.

Infringement: An invasion of the rights secured by patents, copyrights, and trade-marks.

Lien: A charge imposed upon specific property, which is security for a debt or for a duty to perform an act.

Malfeasance: The wrongful doing of an act which the doer has no right to do. "The court held that Josselyn, as agent for his wife, was liable to malfeasance in negligently admitting water into pipes in the second floor of the building without first examining them."

Merits: The substance of the case as distinguished from the technical and collateral aspects.

Misfeasance: Performing a lawful act improperly. "The sheriff was found guilty of misfeasance of office because of his action in executing a writ of attachment on Van Zandt's property which the sheriff believed to belong to George Fanton."

Mortgage: The pledge of a specific property for the payment of a debt.

Nonfeasance: Failure to do an act which an official is required to do by reason of his office.

Oratrix: Used in chancery courts to designate a female petitioner or plaintiff.

Oyer and terminer: From the French, "to hear and determine." The name of a court of original jurisdiction in New Jersey.

Partition: A division of property held by co-owners.

Per curiam: From the Latin, "by the court." Refers to a judicial opinion concurred in by the whole bench of justices composing an appellate court, and, usually, when the opinion is written by the Chief Justice.

Power of attorney: A written instrument which authorizes another to act as one's agent.

Prayer: The request for relief in a bill of equity.

Privilege: A special exemption, advantage, or benefit.

Process: The writ of summons or other writ which compels the defendant to appear; also includes the writ of execution.

Quash: To annul.

Quasi in rem: Literally, "as if." Concerning jurisdiction, a suit about property (*res*) in which the plaintiff cannot obtain jurisdiction *in personam,* but has "as if" jurisdiction.

Quiet title action: An action in which a plaintiff, to remove a "cloud" from his title to a property, sues an adverse claimant for the purpose of having their interests determined.

Quitclaim deed: A deed in which the grantor passes title to the grantee, but which does not guarantee the validity of the title. See "Warranty deed."

Recognizance: A recorded obligation to appear at court on a certain date.

Recrimination: A countercharge by the defendant; esp., in divorce proceedings.

Remand: (1) To send a prisoner back to custody after a hearing which has not resulted in a final judgment. (2) The action of an appellate court in sending a case back to the court of original jurisdiction from which it came, to be finally disposed of there.

Replevin: An action to recover possession of goods; a redelivery.

Res gestae: Literally, "the things done." The essential circumstances surrounding the main fact.

Res judicata: A matter which has been settled by a judgment.

Residuary legatee: The person who receives all of the testator's estate which was not otherwise bequeathed in his will. *Residuary estate:* The remaining part of a testator's estate, after the payment of debts and legacies, that has not been particularly bequeathed.

Return: (1) The report to the court by a sheriff or other officer in connection with a paper he was directed to serve. (2) The answer of the respondent to an alternative writ of mandamus or prohibition. (3) The reporting of a trial jury's verdict. (4) The reporting of indictments by a grand jury.

Scire facias: Literally, "to make known the thing done." In various forms, a writ to annul or revive a judgment.

Sequestrator: A receiver.

Servitude: The burden of restrictive conditions on land which is due to another's easement. See also "Easement."

Setoff: A demand of the defendant to counterbalance, in whole or in part, the plaintiff's claim.

Statute of Frauds: An English statute of 1677, adopted in most of the United States, providing that certain kinds of agreements may not be enforced unless they are in writing and duly signed.

Subrogation: A remedy when a defendant owes a debt to a creditor and a third person, who is obliged to the debtor, discharges the debt; as when an insurance company sues on your behalf for collision damage done to your automobile.

Surprise: The situation when testimony is presented at a trial which could not have been anticipated by the adverse counsel, who moves for a continuance.

Tortfeasor: One who commits a tort.

Trespass: Narrowly, entry on and unlawful injury to another's property.

Trust: An equitable obligation resting upon a person (trustee) to hold property and to administer it for the benefit of another.

Verify: To substantiate; referring to that part of a declaration (complaint) in which the deponent (usually the plaintiff) confirms under oath his belief that the facts alleged in the pleading by his attorney are true.

Warranty deed: A deed in which the grantor of title to land includes a covenant guaranteeing the validity of the title. See "Quitclaim deed."

APPENDIX D

Glossary of Business-Financial Terms

Acceptance: A time draft that has been honored ("accepted") by the party on whom it is drawn, thus becoming legally a promissory note. It may be discounted by the drawer (seller) at a bank, he becoming the endorser.

Amortization: The gradual paying off of a long-term funded debt.

Arbitrage: A method of taking advantages of differences in price. Thus, buying a specific stock in New York at $20 and simultaneously selling it in London at $20.75. The same may be done in connection with preëmptive rights to buy a stock at a certain price, when the stockholder both sells rights and exercises his rights.

At the market: A term used when a customer authorizes his broker to buy or sell a security at the prevailing price at the moment of execution of the order.

Bank reserve: The law requires that banks keep on deposit a certain proportion of their resources with the district Federal Reserve Bank or other specified banks.

Bear: An investor or speculator who thinks the market will decline.

Bid and asked price: The usual prices quoted in "over the counter" markets do not necessarily represent sales, but prices asked by prospective sellers and prices bid by prospective buyers. See "Spread."

Brokers' loans: Collateral loans made by banks to brokers. The amount of such loans is an approximate measure of the speculative activity on the markets at a certain time.

Bull: An investor or speculator who thinks the market will rise.

Call loan: A collateral loan which is due one day after demand; such loans are made in connection with speculation on the exchanges.

C.I.F.: Quotation on an article which includes its cost plus insurance and freight charges to point of delivery.

Equipment trust bonds: Certificates by means of which railroads borrow money for the purchase of rolling stock, the new equipment being mortgaged under a trust.

Escrow: Literally, a "writing." When one party to an agreement deposits with a third party (usually a bank) a grant which is to be surrendered to the party of the second part on performance of a condition, the instrument is said to be delivered "in escrow."

Excess reserves: See "Bank reserve." The amount of a bank's reserves with a depository in excess of the amount required by law. The total of such excess reserves for all banks in the country has importance by reason of its relation to the potentiality for expansion of bank credit.

Ex-dividend: When a stock is sold with the seller reserving to himself the accrued dividend, the stock is said to be sold "ex-dividend." In such a sale, the price is usually the price of the previous day less the approximate amount of the dividend.

Ex-rights: When a company has issued preëmptive rights to its stockholders, the rights may be traded prior to the date on which the rights must be exercised. The buyer of such shares of stock is not entitled to the rights when they are sold ex-rights. See "Ex-dividend" and "Rights."

Floating debt: As distinguished from funded debt, all forms of debt, such as short-term notes.

Funding: The process of converting floating debt into long-term debt by the sale of bonds.

Hedge: The effort to offset a trading position in the present by buying or selling in the future. In general, one transaction to protect against loss in another transaction. See "Selling against the box."

Investment trust: A company whose income is derived exclusively from the holding of securities of other corporations, its portfolio being diversified, although some investment companies specialize in the holding of specific types of securities or stocks in specific industries. There are two classes of investment companies. The *closed-end* company has a fixed number of shares which are transferable, and the shares of some such companies are traded on the New York Stock Exchange. The *open-end* company ("mutual fund") does not have a fixed number of shares, but issues and sells new shares to investors and stands ready to redeem (at the current value of the shares) all shares offered by the holders. Under the Investment Company Act, the open-end company must pay out to its holders 90 per cent of its dividends and a bank (not the company) is the custodian of all shares.

Limit order: An order to a broker to buy or sell a stock at a specified price (or better).

Margin: The amount paid by an investor or speculator to a broker when he buys a security on credit, the broker advancing the remaining amount. Regulation T of the Federal Reserve Board sets the margin, which it changes from time to time.

Mutual fund: See "Investment trust."

Odd lot: Less than the usual unit of trading; on the New York Stock Exchange this is less than 100 shares except in the case of very high-priced stocks when the unit is 10.

Over the counter: Refers to securities sold in a market other than the established exchanges; the dealer, instead of charging a commission, sells at a net price adequate to cover his profits.

Point: With reference to a stock, a point is $1; with reference to a bond, it is $10. A point in the Dow-Jones averages, however, is not $1.

Put: An option to sell to the maker of an option a specified amount of stock or commodity at a specified price during the time of the contract.

Put and call: An option to buy or sell within a certain time limit for the purpose of protecting against loss.

Refunding: The issuing of a new security as a substitute for an existing one in order either to avoid default or to reduce interest charges.

Rights: Privileges granted to stockholders to buy new stock at a concession below the prevailing market price. Rights are traded on exchanges. See "Ex-rights."

Round lot: The unit of trading on an exchange. See "Odd lot."

Secondary offering: The sale, off the exchange, of a very large block of stock at a fixed price close to the prevailing market price.

Selling against the box: A method of hedging to protect a paper profit, which consists of selling an equivalent amount of the stock. See "Short sale."

Short covering: The buying of securities necessary to make delivery on a short sale.

Short sale: When an investor believes a stock will decline and, although he does not own it, orders the broker to sell it at a certain price. The broker borrows the stock from an owner (to deliver to the buyer of the investor's sale) and deposits the amount with the owner. To accomplish his objective, the investor will at some time have to replace the stock even if the price rises. His profit or loss depends upon whether the stock declines or rises.

Sinking fund: A fund into which a company pays a necessary amount periodically for the purpose of redeeming a bond issue. When bonds are issued serially, no sinking fund is required.

Specialist: A stock exchange member who executes for other brokers buy and sell orders in specific stocks, buying and selling with his own money, when necessary, to narrow price fluctuations that could upset an orderly market.

Spread: The difference between the bid and asked price.

Stop order: Instructions to a broker to buy or sell a security when the price reaches a certain point. The customer's objective is different than when he places a "limit" order in that he wishes to limit a potential loss or protect a paper profit by a stop order, whereas a "limit" order merely specifies the price at which the investor is willing to buy or sell.

Syndicate: A group of investment bankers formed to underwrite and distribute a new issue of securities.

Voting trust: An agreement whereby stockholders deposit their shares with a trustee, giving him voting rights on the stock for a specified time but retaining all other rights.

Wash sale: A pretended sale of securities.

APPENDIX E

Suggested Readings

WRITING THE NEWS

Asch, S. E. *Social Psychology.* New York, 1952.
Botter, D. *News Reporters and What They Do.* New York, 1959.
Brucker, H. *Journalist: Eyewitness.* New York, 1962.
Buswell, G. T. "How Adults Read," *Supplementary Education Monographs, The School Review and Elementary School Journal,* No. 45 (Aug., 1937).
Evans, B. and C. *A Dictionary of Contemporary American Usage.* New York, 1957.
Flesch, R. *How to Be Brief.* New York and Evanston, Ill., 1962.
———. *Marks of Readable Style: a Study in Adult Education.* ("Contribution to Education," No. 897.) New York: Teacher's College, Columbia University, 1944.
Fowler, H. W. *A Dictionary of Modern English Usage.* London, 1950.
Fries, C. C. *The Structure of English.* New York, 1952.
Gowers, Sir Ernest. *Plain Words.* London, 1948.
Hayakawa, S. S. *Language in Thought and Action.* New York, 1949.
Horwill, H. W. *A Dictionary of Modern American Usage* (2d ed.). London, 1944.
Klapper, J. T. *The Effects of Mass Communication.* Glencoe, Ill., 1960.
Krech, D. and Crutchfield, R. S. *Theory and Problems of Social Psychology.* New York, 1948.
Lazarsfeld, P. F. *Radio and the Printed Page.* New York, 1940.
Mencken, H. L. *The American Language* (4th ed. and two supplements abridged). New York, 1963.
Miller, G. A. *Language and Communication.* New York, 1951.
National Broadcasting Company. *Handbook of Pronunciation* (3d ed.). New York, 1964.
Osgood, C. E., Tannenbaum, P. H., and Susci, G. J. *The Measurement of Meaning.* Urbana, Ill., 1957.
Partridge, E. *A Dictionary of Cliches* (4th ed.). London, 1950, New York, 1963.
Quirk, R. *The Use of English.* London, 1952.
Schramm, W. *The Process and Effects of Mass Communication.* Urbana, Ill., 1954.
———. *Mass Communications* (2d ed.). Urbana, Ill., 1960.
Shannon, C. E. and Weaver, W. *A Mathematical Theory of Communication.* Urbana, Ill., 1949.
Thorndike, E. L. and Lorge, I. *Teacher's Wordbook of 30,000 Words.* New York, 1949.

REPORTING PUBLIC AFFAIRS

Barksdale, H. C. *The Use of Survey Research Findings as Legal Evidence.* Pleasantville, N.Y., 1957.
Barron, W. W. *Federal Practice and Procedure with Forms* (Rules ed.). 5 vols. St. Paul, Minn. and Brooklyn, N.Y., 1950.
Barth, A. *The Price of Liberty.* New York, 1961.
Borchard, E. M. and Lutz, E. R. *Convicting the Innocent.* New Haven, Conn., 1932.
Bromage, A. W. *Introduction to Municipal Government and Administration.* New York, 1950.
Clark, C. E. *Handbook of the Law of Code Pleading* (2d ed.). St. Paul, Minn., 1947.
Clark, G. L. *Principles of Equity.* Cincinnati and New York, 1937.
———. *Common Law Pleading.* Cincinnati, 1931.
Cosulich, G. *Adult Probation Laws of the United States.* New York, 1940.
Cross, H. L. *The People's Right to Know.* New York, 1953.
DeWitt, C. *Privileged Communications Between Physician and Patient* (3d ed.). Springfield, Ill., 1940.
Ferris, F. G. *The Law of Extraordinary Legal Remedies.* St. Louis, 1926.
Finney, H. A. *Principles of Accounting* (3d ed.). New York, 1948.
Fisher, W. E. *The Taft-Hartley Act As Amended in 1959: a Management Guide* (rev. ed.). Pasadena, Calif., 1960.
Graham, B. *The Intelligent Investor* (2d ed.). New York, 1954.
Graham, B. and Meredith, S. B. *The Interpretation of Financial Statements.* New York, 1950.
Greenstein, F. I., *The American Party System and the American People.* New York, 1963.
Gregory, C. O. *Labor and the Law* (2d rev. ed.). New York, 1958.
Groves, H. M. *Financing Government* (3d ed.). New York, 1950.
Hart, J. *An Introduction to Administrative Law.* New York, 1947.
Holmes, P. *The Sheppard Murder Case.* New York, 1961.
Housel, T. W. *Defending and Prosecuting Federal Criminal Cases* (2d ed.). Buffalo, N.Y., 1946.
Institute for Training in Municipal Administration. *The Technique of Municipal Administration* (3d ed.). Chicago, 1947.
Josiah Macy Foundation. *When Doctors Meet Reporters.* New York, 1957.
Kronhausen, E. and P. *Pornography and the Law.* New York, 1957.
Kunstler, W. M. *The Minister and the Choir Singer: the Hall-Mills Murder Case.* New York, 1964.
Laube, H. D. (ed.). *Cases and Materials on the Law of Decedents' Estates.* Chicago, 1946.
Lewis, A. *Gideon's Trumpet.* New York, 1964.
McCart, S. W. *Trial by Jury.* Philadelphia, 1964.
McCorkle, S. A. *Municipal Administration.* New York, 1942.
Morey, L. and Diehl, O. W. *Municipal Accounting: Principles and Procedures.* New York, 1942.
Morgan, E. M. and Maguire, J. M. *Cases and Materials on Evidence* (2d ed.). Chicago, 1942.
National Archives Establishment. *United States Government Organization Manual.* Washington, D.C., issued annually.

Orfield, L. B. *Criminal Procedure from Arrest to Appeal.* New York, 1947.
———. *Criminal Appeals in America.* Boston, 1939.
Ottenberg, M. *The Federal Investigators.* Englewood Cliffs, N.J., 1962.
Penniman, H. R. *Sait's American Parties and Elections* (4th ed.). New York, 1948.
Pope, J. K. *Police-Press Relations.* Fresno, Calif., 1954.
Pound, R. *Appellate Procedure in Civil Cases.* Boston, 1941.
Ragland, G. *Discovery Before Trial.* Chicago, 1932.
Reynolds, Q. *Courtroom: the Story of Samuel M. Liebowitz.* New York, 1950.
Salter, J. T. *Boss Rule.* New York, 1933.
Selverstone, A. W. *Bankruptcy and Reorganization.* Brooklyn, N.Y., 1940.
Snider, C. F. *American State and Local Government.* New York, 1950.
Snyder, L. *Homicide Investigation.* Springfield, Ill., 1944.
Stallings, H. L. (with D. Dressler). *Juvenile Officer.* New York, 1954.
Straley, J. A. *What About Mutual Funds?* New York, 1954.
Sussman, F. B. *Law of Juvenile Delinquency.* New York, 1959.
Weidner, E. W. *The American County—Patchwork of Boards.* New York, 1946.
Wigmore, J. H. *A Student's Textbook of the Law of Evidence.* Chicago, 1935.
Wilson, O. W. *Police Administration.* New York, 1950.

Index

ABDUCTION, 305
Abstract words, 113
Abstruse words, 113
Accessory, 313
Accomplice, 313
"According to," 89
Accuracy, 87
Adjective law, 175
Adjectives, 86, 126
Administrator, of wills, 399
    public, 399
Admiralty docket, 197
Admission, defined, 360
Adverbs, 86, 126
Affidavit, of prejudice, 187
Affray, 309
Age, 86
Alcohol and Tobacco Tax Division, 296
Alibi, 350
Allegations, 215
American Institute of Public Opinion, quoted, 42
Amicus curiae brief, 433
Answer, 266 *ff.*
Appearance, 213
Arbitrator, labor, 546
Argot, 116
Army Corps of Engineers, 517
Arraignment, 343 *ff.*
Arrest and bail, 222
    book, 276
Arson, 307
Asch, Solomon, quoted, 169
Assault, 305
Assessment procedures, 468 *ff.*
    special, 494
Assets, 455 *ff.*
Assignment of error, 433
AP Log, quoted, 20 *ff.*, 184
Associated Press, 23, 43, 155, 166
Associated Press Style Guide, 156
Attachment, 220

Attorney, 192
    city, 192, 499
    county, 192, 472
    district, 192
    for indigents, 344 *ff.*
    United States, 197, 301
Attribution, 87 *ff.*
    excess, 89
Audience, 31, 33

BACKGROUNDING, 90
Bagdikian, Ben, quoted, 14
Bail, 320 *ff.*
Bailiff, 193
Balance sheet, 448 *ff.*
Bankruptcy, act of, defined, 410
Barber, J. R., quoted, 233
Barth, Alan, quoted, 360
Battery, 305
Bernstein, Theodore M., quoted, 107 *ff.*
Bill of exceptions, 430
    of particulars, 228, 338 *ff.*, 349
Bliven, Bruce, quoted, 131, 162
Board,
    city, 480
    of Equalization, 470
    of Zoning Appeals, 501
Bond,
    appeal, 430
    bail, 320
    defined, 442
    revenue, 493
    special assessment, 494
    serial, 492
Book value, 456
Borchard, E. M., quoted, 388 *ff.*
Borrowing, by cities, 492
Bribery (*see* Embracery)
Budget, city, 488 *ff.*
Buffalo Evening News, quoted, 143 *ff.*
Burden of proof, 240, 357
Bureau of Labor Statistics, 516

Burglary, 307
Bush, C. R., quoted, 36, 85

CALENDAR,
   appellate court, 434
   court, 188 ff.
Cancellation (see Equity)
Canon 20 of American Bar Association, 390
   35 of American Bar Association, 397
Cant, 116
Capias, 315
Capital
   account, 448
   surplus account, 451
Capitalization, 448
Carter, Richard F., quoted, 72 ff.
Cash flow, 458
Catledge, Turner, quoted, 33
Caucus, political, 530 ff.
Cause of action, defined, 203
Caveat, 400
Certiorari (see Writ)
Challenge of jurors, 239
   to the array, 347
   for cause, 239 ff.
   peremptory, 240
Chancellor, 205
Chicago Tribune, quoted, 389
Childs, Marquis, quoted, 534
Christiansen, Arthur, quoted, 54
Chronicle, 37 ff.
Citation, 213
City,
   building inspector, 497
   Central (labor), 539
   controller, 496
   engineer, 497
   health officer, 498
   solicitor, 499
   tax collector, 497
   treasurer, 496
Civil Aeronautics Board, 518
Claim and delivery, 223
Clerk,
   county, 472
   court, 187 ff.
Clichés, 282
Coast Guard, United States, 509
   Intelligence Division of, 300
Code
   of co-operation (crime), 391
      (medical), 284 ff.
   pleading, 208, 225
   United States, 210
   United States Criminal, 314

Commission,
   jury, 191
   police, 283
   to take deposition, 219
Commissioner,
   court, 189 ff.
   jury, 191
   United States, 193, 197
Common law,
   defined, 204 ff., 210
   pleading, 225
Common stock, 445
Complaining witness, 316
Complaint, 180, 201, 212, 214 ff., 316
   amended, 226, 230
Comprehension of issues, 72 ff.
Commute, 386
Confession
   and avoidance, plea in, 225, 230
   defined, 360
   judgment by, 234
Conservator, of estate, 406
Consolidation of actions, 215
Conspiracy, 312
Contempt, 310
Context, 168
Contributory negligence, 204, 230, 263
Control Desk System, 17 ff.
Conventions, reporting, 136 ff.
Copy flow, 16 ff.
Coram nobis (see Writ)
Coroner, 289
Corpus delicti, 357 ff.
Costs, defined, 216
Council Bluffs (Iowa) *Nonpareil,* 38
Counsel (see Attorney)
   corporation, 499
Count, 215, 340
Counterclaim, 230
Counterfeiting, 292 ff., 308
County
   agricultural extension agent, 478
   attorney, 472
   clerk, 468, 472
   director of social welfare, 477
   governing board, 467
   health officer, 476
   manager, 468
   recorder, 472
   register of deeds, 472
   superintendent of schools, 476
Court
   of Appeals (federal), 198
   of bankruptcy, 409
   of Claims, 194, 198

Court (cont.)
　　Customs, 199, 523
　　　　and Patent Appeals, 199
　　district (federal), 197
　　juvenile, 180 ff.
　　Military Appeals, 200
　　probate, 399
　　Tax, of the United States, 199
Craft union, 539
Crime,
　　attempted, 311
　　parties to a, 313
　　solicitation to commit, 312
　　threat to commit, 309
Crimes against the United States, 314
Criminal Justice Act of 1964, 345
Cross, H. L., quoted, 279, 473
Cross
　　-appeal, 431
　　-complaint, 230
　　-examination, 246, 361
Current liabilities, 499
　　ratio, 449
Customs Agency Service, 293
Customs Court (see Court)

DAMAGES, 216
　　reduction of, 268
Debenture, 443
Declaration, 225
Declaratory relief, 208 ff.
Decree, 205, 208
Demurrer, 227, 228, 347 ff.
　　to answer, 232
　　to the evidence, 266
Depositions, 216 ff.
　　in criminal cases, 349
Derivative suit, 214
Diebold, John, quoted, 18
Disclosure of newsman's source, 245
Discovery, 216 ff., 349
Dividend,
　　(in bankruptcy), 413
　　cash, 445
　　stock, 453
Divorce, 208
Docket, 188
Douglas, Justice William O., quoted, 397

EDITOR & PUBLISHER, QUOTED, 396
Election officers, 474
Embargo, 91
Embezzlement, 308
Embracery, 310

Equity, 204 ff.
　　cancellation, 206
Eshleman, Jane Conant, quoted, 373 ff.
Evidence,
　　admissibility of, 242, 360
　　best, 242
　　defined, 240 ff.
　　hearsay, 243
　　opinion as, 243
　　preponderance of the, 262, 304
　　secondary, 242
Examination
　　of the bankrupt, 413
　　defined, 246 ff.
　　preliminary, 328 ff.
Examiner,
　　CAB, 519
　　naturalization, 511
　　SEC, 522
Exceptions, 247 ff.
　　bill of, 430
Execution (see Writ)
Executor of will, 399
Exhibits, 241
Ex parte,
　　defined, 215
　　evidence, 337
Explanation, 91 ff.
Ex relatione, 215, 421
Extortion, 308
Extradition and rendition, 324
Eye-movements in reading, 167 ff.

FALSE IMPRISONMENT, 305
Federal
　　Aviation Agency, 519
　　Bureau of Investigation, 297
　　Communications Commission, 520
　　Mediation and Conciliation Service, 546
　　Tort Claims Act, 194
　　Trade Commission, 521
Felony,
　　compounding a, 310
　　defined, 304
　　misprison of, 313
Field, Richard, quoted, 148
Fine, 383
Fire
　　marshal, 287
　　reporting, 286 ff.
Fish and Wildlife Service, 515
Flesch, Rudolf, quoted, 111 ff.
Food and Drug Administration, 518
Foreclosure, 207
Forest Service, 515

Forgery, 308
Foundation, laying a, 242 ff., 360
Fowler, H. W., quoted, 167
Fraction of selection, 5
Frank, Jerome, quoted, 266
Fraud order, 291

GARLAND V. TORRE, 245
Garnishment, 221
Gideon v. Wainwright, 345n
Godwin, William, quoted, 535
Grand jurors, selection of, 191
Grand jury, 331 ff.
Gratitude, role of, in politics, 535
Griffin v. Illinois, 345n
Guardianship, 406

HABEAS CORPUS, 196, 322, 423
    prosequendum, 424
Holmes, James F., 160
Holographic will, 400
Homicide, 305 ff.
Hoppe, Arthur, quoted, 119, 136, 145
Hospitals, 284 ff.

IDENTIFICATION, 35, 84
Immigration and Naturalization Service, 298 ff., 511
Indenture, 444n
Indictment (see Grand Jury)
Industrial union, 539
Information, 331, 337
Injunction, 205, 206, 424 ff.
    mandatory, 425
    temporary, 426
In re, defined, 215
Inspector,
    building, 497
    food and drug, 518
    postal, 291
Interest-groups in politics, 536
Internal Revenue Service, 508
    Intelligence Division of, 295
Interplead, 214
Interpreter, court, 193
Interpretive reporting, 93
Interstate Commerce Commission, 522
Intervenor, 215

JARGON, 116
Jeopardy, double, 343
John Doe proceedings, 338
Joinder
    of actions, 208
    of defendants, 341
    of parties, 214

Judge,
    disqualification of, 187, 350
    duties and authority of, 186
    elections, 474
Judgment, 204, 378
    by confession, 234
    by consent, 234
    declaratory, 208 ff.
    by default, 234
    deficiency, 207
    execution of, 272
    notwithstanding the verdict, 268
    on the pleadings, 234
    roll, 188
    satisfying the, 272
    summary, 234
    without trial, 234
Jurisdiction,
    civil, 195
    courts of original, 178
    defined, 175
    of federal courts, 193, 195
    in rem, 208, 212
    in personam, 208
    plea to the, 228, 346
Jurors,
    alternate, 354
    challenge of, 239 ff.
    potential bias of, 388 ff.
Jury,
    instruction of, 259 ff., 371
    panel, 191
    selection of, 239, 354
    size of, 239
Justice of the peace, 177 ff.
Juvenile court, 180, 387

KENT, FRANK R., QUOTED, 535
Kidnaping, 305
Krieghbaum, Hillier, quoted, 159
Kristol, Irving, quoted, 41

LABOR COUNCIL, 539
Labor Management Reporting and Disclosure Act (Landrum-Griffith), 545
Larceny, 307
Law and motion calendar, 186, 188 ff.
Lead,
    purposes of, 45
    quote, 52
    summary, 7, 43 ff.
    syntax of, 60, 102
Leading question, 247
Leibowitz, Judge Samuel M., quoted, 389

Letters
   of administration, 399
   testamentary, 399
Leverage, 449
Libel, 309
Lien, 207
Lippmann, Walter, quoted, 38
Liquidity, 449
Loory, Stuart H., quoted, 162
Los Angeles county superior court, 178 ff.

MAIM (MAYHEM), 305
Malicious mischief, 309
Mandamus (see Writ)
Mandate, 438
Manslaughter, 306
Marlow, James, quoted, 166
Marshal, United States, 193, 196, 301 ff.
Massey, Charles F., quoted, 14
Master (see Referee)
Mayor, 504
Mediation and Conciliation Service (see Federal)
Medical glossary, 160
Mencken, H. L., quoted, 117
Mental set, 41
Metropolitan government, 467
Meyer, Luther, quoted, 153
Miller, G. A., quoted, 102, 112
Ministerial act, defined, 416
Misdemeanor, 176, 304 ff.
Misjoinder
   of causes, 228
   of parties, 228
Mistrial, 260 ff., 370
Mittimus, 383
Modifiers, position of, 104
Monitor, 190
Mortgage, defined, 207
Motion, 186, 188
   for advice to acquit, 370
   after verdict, 268
   for arrest of judgment, 376
   for change of venue, 346
   for demurrer, 346 ff., 376
   for directed verdict, 267, 370
   to dismiss, 346
   to disqualify judge, 350
   during trial, 266
   for mistrial, 370
   for new trial, 268, 376 ff.
   to quash, 376, 214
      summons, 212, 228, 346 ff.
   to set aside
      accusation, 346
      verdict, 268 ff.

Motion (cont.)
   for severance, 346, 350 (see also Severance)
   to strike, 248
   to suppress evidence, 351
Mott, F. L., quoted, 43
Murder, 306
Mutual fund, 447

NARCOTICS, BUREAU OF, 296 ff.
National Aeronautics and Space Administration, 160
   Labor Relations Act, 539 ff.
Naturalization (see Immigration and and Naturalization Service)
Ne exeat (see Writ)
Net
   income, 457
   worth, 449
Neuharth, A., quoted, 17 ff.
New Matter, pleading, 230
New trial (see Motion)
New York Times, 16, 94, 100, 107, 125, 371
New York Times Style Book, 10
New York World-Telegram and Sun, quoted, 99
News
   background, 38
   kinds of, 37 ff.
   nature of, 27 ff.
   values, 6
Newshole, 13 ff.
Newsprint Information Committee, quoted, 41 ff.
Nizer, Louis, quoted, 175
Noise, 166
Nolle prosequi, 350
Nolo contendere, 342
Nomination of candidates, 474
Nonsuit, 266 ff.
Normal sentence order, 60, 104
Nuncupative will, 400

OBITER DICTUM, 437
Objectiveness, 98 ff.
Obtaining by false pretenses, 308
Opening statement, 238, 356
Operating profit, 456
Opinion
   of court, 436 ff.
   of witness, 243 ff.
Order,
   defined, 186
   temporary restraining, 426 (see also Injunction)

Ordinance, 481
Owen, Russell, quoted, 125 ff.

PANEL (SEE JURY)
Paragraph, 74
Parallelism, 105
Pardon, 384 ff.
Parliamentary idiom, city council, 483
Parole, 384
Par value, 447
Patterson, Judge Robert P., quoted, 390
People v. Jelke, 387n
Per curiam, 436
Perjury, 310
  subornation of, 310
Perlman, David, quoted, 161
Perry, Stuart, quoted, 391
Pitt, Lee, quoted, 83
Planning and zoning, 500
Plea
  in abatement, 227, 347
  in bar, 226
  in confession and avoidance, 225, 230
  to the jurisdiction, 346, 228 (see also Jurisdiction)
Pleading, 201 ff., 210, 225 ff.
Pope, J. K., quoted, 278
Port
  of delivery, 508
  of entry, 508
Portland Oregonian, quoted, 148
Postal Inspection Service, 291
Postmaster, 506
Potpourri type of news story, 68
Praecipe, 213
Prayer, 216
Precinct, carrying the, 535
Preferred stock, 444
Presentment, 328, 333
Presiding judge, 186, 191
Pretrial conference, 235
Price-earnings ratio, 461
Prima facie, defined, 266
Principal (crime), 313
Prisons, 384
Privilege, conditional, 233 ff.
Privileged
  communication, 244
  testimony, 395
Probable cause, 318, 329
Probation, 380
  officer, 193
Procedendo (see Writ)
Profile, 147

Profit and loss statement (see Statement of Income)
Prohibition (see Writ)
Prosecutor, prosecutrix, 316
Prosecuting attorney, 287
Provisional remedies, 220
Proximity, 35
Proxy, 463
Public defender, 193, 345
Publisher's Auxiliary, quoted, 393
Punctuation, 109 ff.

QUASH (SEE MOTION TO QUASH)
Question and answer device, 95
Quo warranto proceedings, 420 ff.

RADIO, 24
Rape, 305
Readability formula, 111
Reader's Digest, quoted, 162
Reasonable doubt, 357, 371
Rebutter, 225
Receiver, 190 ff.
Receivership, 223, 409
Receiving stolen goods, 308
Recordation, 472
Redundancy, 109, 166
Referee, 190
  in bankruptcy, 190, 409
Reformation (equity), 206
Registration to vote, 525
Reiff, Jean, quoted, 20
Rejoinder, 225
Relator, 421
Release date, 91
Remedy, defined, 203
Remittitur, 438
Reorganization of corporation, 408, 415, 464
Replevin, 223
Replication, 225, 226
Reply, 226, 230
Reporter,
  official, 192
  series, 439
Reprieve, 386
Res, 215
Rescission (equity), 206
Retained earnings account, 450
Return, 323
Riot, 309
Robbery, 307
Role, reading in a, 32 ff.
Rule, 186, 204
  "put under the," 357
Russell, William Howard, quoted, 120 ff.

INDEX

SAMUELSON, MERRILL, QUOTED, 31 ff.
San Francisco Chronicle, quoted, 77 ff., 79 ff., 136 ff., 145 ff., 161
Schramm, Wilbur, quoted, 5, 27, 169
Search and seizure, 318
Second-day story, 80 ff.
Secrecy in city government, 486
Secret Service, United States, 292
Securities and Exchange Commission, 522
Sentence,
    commutation of (crime), 386
    cumulative (crime), 383
    elements within the, 104
    emphasis, 104
    indeterminate (crime), 382
    lead (*see* Lead)
    pronouncement of (crime), 378
    rhythm, 104, 125
Sequestration of witnesses, 357
Service, 211
    substitute, 212
Session laws, 210
Severance, 215, 350 (*see* Motion)
Shabad, Theodore, quoted, 94
Sibilants, 117
Simpson, Kirke L., quoted, 122
Slang, 117
Slate of candidates, 531
Smith, S. S., quoted, 167
Source and application of funds, 459
Specific performance (equity), 206
Spencer, Herbert, quoted, 167
Stare decisis, 433
State Central Committee, 527
Statement of income, 456 ff.
Statute of limitations, 230, 313
Statutes, 209 ff.
Stay of proceedings, 431
Stock
    split, 454
    reverse split, 455
Stone, Melville E., 43
Strikes, reporting, 548
Style, typographical, 8 ff.
Subpoena, 213
    duces tecum, 214
Substantive law, 175
Summation, 258 ff., 371
Summons, 188, 210 ff.
Supersedeas (*see* Writ)
Surrebutter, 225
Surrejoinder, 225
Symposia, reporting, 136

TAFT-HARTLEY ACT, 540
Talesman, 191
Tax
    Court of the United States, 523
    rate (city), 489
Taylor, Wilson L., quoted, 168
Tebbel, John, quoted, 43
Technical words, 113
Television, 24
Temporary restraining order, 426 (*see also* Injunction)
Tense, 107 ff.
Term, court, 180
Terminology, 92
Testimony,
    defined, 241
    a day of, 248 ff.
Thayer, F. M., quoted, 395
Tieback, 80 ff.
Time, quoted, 121, 281
Tipstaff, 193
Tort, defined, 204n
Transcript, 192
Transition, 74 ff.
Traverse, 225, 226
Treasury stock, 445n
Trustee (in bankruptcy), 410, 413

ULTRA VIRES, 423
Uniform
    Act on Fresh Pursuit, 318
        to Secure the Attendance of Witnesses, 356
    Reciprocal Enforcement of Support Act, 326
United Press International, 23
    v. Valente, 387n
UP Reporter, quoted, 94 ff.
United States attorney (*see* Attorney)
    marshal, 31 ff.
Unity of news story, 77
Urban renewal, 502
Usage, levels of, 502, 116 ff.

VENIREMEN, 191
Venue,
    defined, 176
    change of, 196, 346
Verbosity (*see* Wordiness)
Verbs, 126, 369
Verdict, 260, 372 (*see also* Motion)
    of coroner's jury, 289
    sealed, 262
    special, 262
Verifying part of pleading, 217
Voir dire, 239, 244

WALL STREET JOURNAL, QUOTED, 337
Warburg, Jeremy, quoted, 116
Warrant
 of arrest, 315, 317
 bench, 315
 of extradition, 324
 of rendition, 325
 search, 318
 stock, 446
 tax anticipation, 492
Washington Post, quoted, 20 *ff.*
Weather Bureau, 512
White, E. B., quoted, 104
Williams, Nick B., quoted, 14
Wilson, O. M., quoted, 278
Wire service (*see* Associated Press and United Press International)
Witness,
 character, 357

Witness (cont.)
 expert, 243 *ff.*
 impeachment of, 247
 material, 313
Wordiness, 109
Working capital, 449
Writ, 205
 of certiorari, 419, 430
 of *coram nobis,* 378
 of execution, 272
 of mandamus, 416
 of *ne exeat,* 222n
 of *procedendo,* 420
 of prohibition, 418
 of supersedeas, 431

YIELD, 461

ZONING COMMISSION (*SEE* PLANNING AND ZONING)